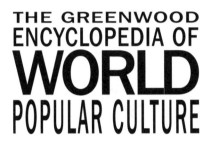

THE GREENWOOD
ENCYCLOPEDIA OF
WORLD
POPULAR CULTURE

The Greenwood Encyclopedia of World Popular Culture

General Editor

GARY HOPPENSTAND

Volume Editors

MICHAEL K. SCHOENECKE, North America

JOHN F. BRATZEL, Latin America

GERD BAYER, Europe

LYNN BARTHOLOME, North Africa and the Middle East

DENNIS HICKEY, Sub-Saharan Africa

GARY XU and VINAY DHARWADKER, Asia and Pacific Oceania

THE GREENWOOD ENCYCLOPEDIA OF WORLD POPULAR CULTURE

NORTH AMERICA

Gary Hoppenstand
General Editor

Michael K. Schoenecke
Volume Editor

GREENWOOD PRESS
Westport, Connecticut • London

Library of Congress Cataloging-in-Publication Data

The Greenwood encyclopedia of world popular culture / Gary Hoppenstand, general editor ; volume editors, John F. Bratzel ... [et al.].
    p. cm.
  Includes bibliographical references and index.
  ISBN-13: 978-0-313-33255-5 (set : alk. paper)
  ISBN-13: 978-0-313-33316-3 (North America : alk. paper)
  ISBN-13: 978-0-313-33256-2 (Latin America : alk. paper)
  ISBN-13: 978-0-313-33509-9 (Europe : alk. paper)
  ISBN-13: 978-0-313-33274-6 (North Africa and the Middle East : alk. paper)
  ISBN-13: 978-0-313-33505-1 (Sub-Saharan Africa : alk. paper)
  ISBN-13: 978-0-313-33956-1 (Asia and Pacific Oceania : alk. paper)
  1. Popular culture—Encyclopedias. 2. Civilization, Modern—Encyclopedias. 3. Culture—Encyclopedias. I. Hoppenstand, Gary. II. Bratzel, John F. III. Title: Encyclopedia of world popular culture. IV. Title: World popular culture.
  HM621.G74   2007
  306.03—dc22   2007010684

British Library Cataloguing in Publication Data is available.

Library of Congress Catalog Card Number: 2007010684
ISBN-13: 978-0-313-33255-5 (Set)
ISBN-10: 0-313-33255-X

ISBN-13: 978-0-313-33316-3 (North America)
ISBN-10: 0-313-33316-5

ISBN-13: 978-0-313-33256-2 (Latin America)
ISBN-10: 0-313-33256-8

ISBN-13: 978-0-313-33509-9 (Europe)
ISBN-10: 0-313-33509-5

ISBN-13: 978-0-313-33274-6 (North Africa and the Middle East)
ISBN-10: 0-313-33274-6

ISBN-13: 978-0-313-33505-1 (Sub-Saharan Africa)
ISBN-10: 0-313-33505-2

ISBN-13: 978-0-313-33956-1 (Asia and Pacific Oceania)
ISBN-10: 0-313-33956-2

First published in 2007

Greenwood Press, 88 Post Road West, Westport, CT 06881
An imprint of Greenwood Publishing Group, Inc.
www.greenwood.com

Printed in the United States of America

The paper used in this book complies with the Permanent Paper Standard issued by the National Information Standards Organization (Z39.48–1984).

10 9 8 7 6 5 4 3 2 1

CONTENTS

CONTENTS

FOREWORD

POPULAR CULTURE AND THE WORLD

GARY HOPPENSTAND

Popular culture is easy to recognize, but often difficult to define. We can say with authority that the current hit television show *House* is popular culture, but can we say that how medical personnel work in hospitals is popular culture as well? We can readily admit that the recent blockbuster movie *Pirates of the Caribbean* is popular culture, but can we also admit that what the real-life historical Caribbean pirates ate and what clothes they wore are components of popular culture? We can easily recognize that a best-selling romance novel by Danielle Steel is popular culture, but can we also recognize that human love, as ritualistic behavior, is popular culture? Can popular culture include architecture, or furniture, or automobiles, or many of the other things that we make, as well as the behaviors that we engage in, and the general attitudes that we hold in our day-to-day lives? Does popular culture exist outside of our own immediate society? There can be so much to study about popular culture that it can seem overwhelming, and ultimately inaccessible.

Because popular culture is so pervasive—not only in the United States, but in all cultures around the world—it can be difficult to study. Basically, however, there are two main approaches to defining popular culture. The first advocates the notion that popular culture is tied to that period in Western societies known as the Industrial Revolution. It is subsequently linked to such concepts as "mass-produced culture" and "mass-consumed culture." In other words, there must be present a set of conditions related to industrial capitalism before popular culture can exist. Included among these conditions are the need for large urban centers, or cities, which can sustain financially the distribution and consumption of popular culture, and the related requirement that there be an educated working-class or middle-class population that has both the leisure time and the expendable income to support the production of popular culture. Certainly, this approach can encompass that which is most commonly regarded as popular culture: motion pictures, television, popular fiction, computers and video games, even contemporary fast foods and popular fashion. In addition, this approach can generate discussions about the relationship between popular culture and political ideology. Can popular culture be political in nature, or politically subversive?

Can it intentionally or unintentionally support the status quo? Can it be oppressive or express harmful ideas? Needless to say, such definitions limit the critical examination of popular culture by both geography and time, insisting that popular culture existed (or only exists) historically in industrial and postindustrial societies (primarily in Western Europe and North America) over the past 200 years. However, many students and critics of popular culture insist that industrial production and Western cultural influences are not essential in either defining or understanding popular culture.

Indeed, a second approach sees popular culture as existing since the beginning of human civilization. It is not circumscribed by certain historic periods, or by national or regional boundaries. This approach sees popular culture as extending well beyond the realm of industrial production, in terms of both its creation and its existence. Popular culture, these critics claim, can be seen in ancient China, or in medieval Japan, or in pre-colonial Africa, as well as in modern-day Western Europe and North America (or in all contemporary global cultures and nations for that matter). It need not be limited to mass-produced objects or electronic media, though it certainly does include these, but it can include the many facets of people's lifestyles, the way people think and behave, and the way people define themselves as individuals and as societies.

This six-volume *Encyclopedia of World Popular Culture*, then, encompasses something of both approaches. In each of the global regions of the world covered—North America, South America, Europe, the Middle East, Sub-Saharan Africa, and Asia—the major industrial and postindustrial expressions of popular culture are covered, including, in most cases, film; games, toys, and pastimes; literature (popular fiction and nonfiction); music; periodicals; and radio/television. Also examined are the lifestyle dimensions of popular culture, including architecture; dance; fashion and appearance; food and foodways; love, sex, and marriage; sports; theater and performance; and transportation and travel. What is revealed in each chapter of each volume of *The Greenwood Encyclopedia of World Popular Culture* is the rich complexity and diversity of the human experience within the framework of a popular culture context.

Yet rooted within this framework of rich complexity and diversity is a central idea that holds the construct of world popular culture together, an idea that sees in popular culture both the means and the methods of widespread, everyday, human expression. Simply put, the commonality of national, transnational, and global popular cultures is the notion that, through their popular culture, people construct narratives, or stories, about themselves and their communities. The many and varied processes involved in creating popular culture (and subsequently living with it) are concerned, at the deepest and most fundamental levels, with the need for people to express their lifestyle in ways that significantly define their relationships to others.

The food we eat, the movies we see, the games we play, the way we construct our buildings, and the means of our travel all tell stories about what we think and what we like at a consciously intended level, as well as at an unintended subliminal level. These narratives tell others about our interests and desires, as well as our fundamental beliefs about life itself. Thus, though the types of popular dance might be quite different in the various regions of the world, the recognition that dance fulfills a basic and powerful need for human communication is amazingly similar. The fact that different forms of popular sports are played and watched in different countries does not deny the related fact that sports globally define the kindred beliefs in the benefits of hard work, determination, and the overarching desire for the achievement of success.

These are all life stories, and popular culture involves the relating of life's most common forms of expression. This *Encyclopedia of World Popular Culture* offers many narratives about many people and their popular culture, stories that not only inform us about others and how they live, but that also inform us, by comparison, about how we live.

INTRODUCTION

POPULAR CULTURE IN NORTH AMERICA

MICHAEL K. SCHOENECKE

In the Declaration of Independence, Thomas Jefferson wrote about the "pursuit of happiness." Although this vague phrase has been interpreted in numerous ways, it certainly captures North Americans' willingness and desire to fill their lives with joy, hope, and promise. Of course, multiple ways to fulfill these needs exist. Some turn to drama, music, television, clothing, sports, automobiles, or their home. Popular culture studies provide one way to gain an understanding of how the culture of everyday people informs and gives meaning to their lives.

North America—made up of Canada and the United States—is a diverse continent. Although Canada's and the United States' histories are intertwined with one another, these countries remain close allies, neighbors, and, in some ways, cultural mirrors of one another. Whereas the United States' larger population centers are coastal areas, Canada's major populations are geographically close to the U.S. border. The countries' proximity and their political similarities encourage a mixing of identities and mainstream cultures. As a result, "the melting pot" phrase captures not only their openness to immigrants but also a sharing between the two nations of all forms of popular culture, while maintaining in some instances their own identities, such as in radio, music, and sports.

Both countries are culturally diverse and for the most part welcome multicultural expression and communities. To celebrate and maintain their connections with their religious, political, and ethnic roots, cultural groups promulgated their values, beliefs, ideas, and identity via popular culture. Their songs, dances, clothing, sports, literature, and other forms of expression identified them and blended with other subcultures and the dominant culture. This volume explores the primary means by which popular culture contributes to and embraces different cultural forms and melds them together to create North American culture.

THE CHAPTERS IN THIS BOOK

The following essays present a mosaic of North American popular culture. Readers will notice similar themes and motifs throughout the chapters. For example, mass production and technology have created some forms of popular culture while improving, expanding, or standardizing other forms. Without a doubt, printing, radio, tapes/CDs, television, and film, in particular, made all forms of popular culture more easily accessible to North Americans as well as to people on other continents. Likewise, importing others' cultures has altered, enlivened, and advanced North American culture.

Although they are separate countries, a cultural border between Canada and the United States is not strong, despite some real differences and the Canadian government's intent to promote Canadian culture. The majority of Canada's 30 million citizens live within 200 miles of the U.S. border, however, and citizens of both countries continue to drive, fly, or sail between countries with few limitations.

Within each country exist diverse regions, states, and provinces. In parts of Canada, for example, French is the primary language, whereas those in Western provinces speak English. In the United States, California culture differs significantly from the cultures of Georgia, Alabama, and South Carolina. Texas culture differs from the cultures of Michigan and Vermont, and so forth. What we purchase, wear, eat, drink, celebrate, watch, and listen to reveals a lot about each individual as well as the country we inhabit. Our mores and folkways speak volumes about what gives meaning to our lives.

Architecture, as Carroll Van West points out, is rooted to the democratization of North America. Roadside restaurants, gas stations, hotels and motels, grocery stores, and other businesses related to travel and food were creatively, craftily, and conveniently located and identified with logos to appeal to the public. As cities—dependent on manufacturers and transportation systems such as railways, waterways, and highways—began to attract business and employees, an emphasis was placed on standardized packaging. To accommodate and to facilitate such placement, popular residential patterns as well as cities like Las Vegas began to emerge; today homeowners can visit Lowe's, Home Depot, or various other home stores to discover ways to improve their residences, a popular North American pastime. Popular architecture across North America is intentionally designed to achieve a specific effect on visitors and/or owners. Architectural styles might be the most significant expressions of North America's cultures.

Joy Sperling's chapter on **Art** explores the "arranged marriage between technology and art for profit." How many of us decorate our homes and offices with posters, mass-produced pictures, sculptures, and/or décor such as vases, ornaments, and other bric-a-brac? Rings, bracelets, earrings, and necklaces are generally purchased at stores that sell mass-produced jewelry. Some artists such as Norman Rockwell, Currier & Ives, and Andy Warhol secured their place in art history by celebrating popular art and by placing their work in museums or popular magazines. As a result, popular art is created and sold to the general public rather than to an ever-diminishing elite.

Dance, Libby Smigel writes, is actually made up of a variety of cultures in Canada and the United States that are diverse and unique, although they may be similar in terms of entertainment. Whereas ballet and burlesque dancing appeal to a smaller, but not less enthusiastic, audience, more well known dances such as the tango, swing, and various forms of youth dances attract a culturally diverse segment of society. Many popular dance forms gained inspiration from musical forms such as the tango and francophone culture in Canada. North American culture invites and encourages dance as a means of personal expression and identity. Television, dance tapes, film, and other forms of mass media have encouraged the elderly and the young to seek dance as a means of exercise.

As Patricia A. Cunningham points out in **Fashion and Appearance**, North Americans are eclectic and contradictory regarding fashion, health, and self-image. Film and television often determine what women and men will wear each year; in other words, the entertainment industry establishes what "looks good" and "how to dress." As a result, trends change yearly. In some instances, North Americans seem to follow the absurd dictum of the old *Saturday Night Live* skit involving Ricardo Montalban (Billy Crystal), who would say, "It is better to look good than to feel good." North Americans' intense aspiration to purchase shoes and clothing that deliberately appeal to the majority of individuals rather than to each individual, however, cannot be denied.

North American **Film**, particularly that of the United States, writes Scott L. Baugh, dominates and dictates cinema worldwide, though film from other cultures is influential both in North America and around the world. Since the 1890s, film has been a means to express national identity as the United States moved from a rural to an industrial nation, as a means to energize Americans to fight during World Wars I and II (as well as Korea and Vietnam), and as a means to express Jeffersonian democratic tradition. Film also presents images of masculinity and femininity; it has explored the contradictory horrors of life as well as the heroic efforts of idealized heroes and heroines. Nevertheless, film, North America's most popular art form, has been forced to adapt. Today, with DVDs and downloading films off the Internet, the industry has been forced to find new ways to address its changing identity as well as that of all people. It seeks to embrace women and minorities, though few so far have achieved artistic success. Film continues to present an ecstatic experience, which filmgoers love.

Beverly Taylor's and Edmund Reiss's chapter on **Food and Foodways** suggests that North Americans are what they eat. However, what do they eat? Recently, fast-food chains such as McDonald's have begun to provide nutritional guides for their patrons in an effort, in some instances, to avoid lawsuits about high-fat, high-calorie foods. North Americans are eating even more convenience foods (both fast foods and frozen or prepared foods) and eating out more as working parents and multiple activities take time away from home cooking. At the same time, however, there is increasing or continuing interest in organic foods, all sorts of ethnic foods, and food preparation equipment. Although the U.S. government provides regulations regarding food preparation, our food preparation and eating habits—often a reflection of ethnic and family backgrounds—help define who we are.

Sharon Scott's and Mary Carothers's chapter on **Games, Toys, and Pastimes** explains how North Americans' pastime activities have not only changed but also "reflect the personality of an entire continent." Like immigrants, some leisure activities have arrived on our shores from other countries. Barbie dolls, for example, based on a German doll from the 1950s, have become a North American icon since their introduction in 1959. As such, the Barbie doll is recognized worldwide and has become a symbol of physical perfection and lifestyle for many girls. According to Gretchen Morgenson, "over 1 billion Barbies have been sold," and in 1997 Barbie accounted for 40 percent of Mattel's total revenue. Without a doubt, collecting, too, has become extremely popular, though such activities demand time and energy as well as money. What we play, collect, and pursue in our spare time reveal our values, images of escape, and fantasies.

"North Americans are readers," as Patricia Bostian indicates in the chapter on **Literature** in popular culture. Although such a statement might surprise educators and politicians, the fact is that North Americans purchase and borrow large volumes of fiction, nonfiction, poetry, and drama. To no one's surprise, Oprah Winfrey's Book Club has encouraged millions to read classic authors as well as more popular forms of fiction. Romance, mystery, horror, futuristic, and inspirational literature are among the most popular genres. What's revealed by these facts? What about the children and adults buying J. K. Rowling's *Harry Potter* series? Perhaps readers are looking for "a good read" and for an opportunity to visit an imagined land filled with adventure. Nevertheless, reading literature enhances and develops the minds of young and old alike.

In the **Love, Sex, and Marriage** chapter, Victor C. de Munck notes that the North American cultural and demographic landscape has changed dramatically. As of October 2006, 300 million people live in the United States; in other words, the population has almost doubled since 1951, with Hispanic families showing the greatest increase. Whereas the number of married couples is higher, the divorce rate is as well perhaps because of the changes in divorce law. To help single individuals find a mate, dating services can now be found on the Internet as well as in local communities. New issues facing North American couples include having potential partners tested for sexually transmitted diseases (STDs). Likewise, interracial marriage has increased, as have gay and lesbian long-term commitments, which have challenged long-standing cultural and social mores.

Canadian and U.S. **Music** share many elements. In the recording industry, both are designed to be financially successful ventures for recording artists and others in the music business. In the 1800s, North Americans' folk music replaced European music. As a result, various new musical genres emerged and appealed to people of all ages and races. To accommodate the diverse listening public, radio stations, records, tapes, and discs, as well as live performances, have dominated the musical landscape. Although as early as 1956, teenagers became the target audience for the recording industry, as Don Cusic notes, music sales appeal to all political, religious, and racial listening interests. Because of radio, television, film, and other forms of mass media, music crosses borders and influences cultures beyond North America, with reciprocal influences coming from other parts of the world to the United States and Canada.

Garyn G. Roberts's **Periodicals** chapter points out that magazines published on a daily, weekly, biweekly, monthly, and quarterly timetable began as early as the 1800s. North Americans continue to subscribe to and read these works, which address a multitude of topics. North American periodicals have included not only works on fantasy, science fiction, horror, war, adventure, and comics, but also the news, business, cooking, decorating, beauty, sports, and more. Many are now being published online as well as in print. Newspapers are trying to reinvent themselves in a world of instant Internet and TV news through their own Web sites and cooperative ventures with other media.

Jennifer DeFore's **Radio and Television** chapter explores the continuous relationship between North American society and two media responsible for changing contemporary life. Although early television was hailed as a means to educate the public, over the past four decades critics have assailed networks for the "dumbing of America." Radio, likewise, has been criticized for numbing North Americans with controversial programming such as Howard Stern's sexist and sexually explicit work and Rush Limbaugh's outspoken politically conservative broadcasts. Controversy, of course, can be good, but one key area that liberals and conservatives alike attack is censorship. To escape FCC regulations, satellite radio has made tremendous gains.

North America is addicted and fascinated to **Sports and Recreation**. As Michael K. Schoenecke's chapter describes, both Canada and the United States have nurtured and created sports that celebrate heroic behavior as well as provide glory to the legends of individual sports and their history. The Super Bowl, for example, which the media covers for better than a week prior to the event, exemplifies the commercialization of sport and the promotion of football as a product; viewers' identities and fantasies are created through a vicarious identification. However, the North American landscape is dotted with sports courts—gyms, ski resorts, swimming pools, parks, and other venues—to encourage people of all ages to exercise and to play on the tennis courts, baseball fields, basketball courts, golf courses, and other facilities.

Theater and Performance, according to Thomas A. Greenfield and Monica Moschetta, is one of the most intimate artist-audience connections in popular culture. However, theater has experienced difficulty connecting with its modern audience. New York City remains the most popular site to see professional plays, but regional theaters have continued to prosper, even though they have limited financial support. To attract audiences and maintain connections with their patrons, theater, particularly local theater, must often rely on revivals of popular older shows rather than mount experimental productions.

Mark D. Howell's chapter on **Transportation and Travel** argues that North Americans have continuously sought to explore means of travel across the United States and Canada and beyond. Whether we use horses, automobiles, boats or ships, trains, or airplanes or whether the providers have been private or public enterprises, North Americans, like the early pioneers, crave transportation systems that will get them to their destination safely and quickly. In particular, the automobile remains a symbol of freedom, strength, and independence: as long ago as 1923, for example, an advertisement in the *Saturday Evening Post* for the Jordan Playboy automobile promoted a car for adventurous, presumably single women, likening the potential driver of a Jordan Playboy to "a bronco-busting, steer-roping girl" who longs for the wide-open spaces of the West. The ability to travel freely, as well as the type of car driven, symbolizes many North Americans' dreams and goals.

ARCHITECTURE

CARROLL VAN WEST

Twentieth-century mass culture—from print to film to television to the consumer revolution—has indelibly shaped the built environment of North America. Despite the profound differences in climate and geography from the northern reaches of Canada to the Gulf coasts of the United States, landmarks of familiarity, be they the standardization of the suburban experience, the three-dimensional billboards masquerading as fast-food restaurants and gas stations along the highways, or movie sets come to life as fantasies of identity and memory, are literally everywhere. They reflect not only a regional aesthetic sensibility but also the particular corporate-driven consumer economy of the United States and Canada as well as the region's long-standing perception of nature and environment as something to be conquered and tamed.

POPULAR ARCHITECTURE IN THE NINETEENTH CENTURY

The story of how popular culture has influenced twentieth-century North American architecture has several worthy beginning places that date back to the previous century: the invention of balloon-frame construction in the timber-starved Chicago area of the 1830s; the drive to grab resources for a region-wide industrial revolution and how those plentiful resources fueled the first great wave of suburban expansion; and the later need, by the close of the nineteenth century, for the great transcontinental railroads, whether the Canadian Pacific or the Union Pacific, to imprint the perceived vacant landscape of the West with their engineered landscapes of steel, platted towns, communication networks, grain elevator sentinels, and standardized plan depots.

The best place to start is the print revolution of the mid-nineteenth century and the immense popularity and influence of architectural "pattern books" in the late nineteenth and early twentieth centuries. The print revolution of the late nineteenth century impacted the choices North Americans had for the design, furnishings, and comfort of their home, bringing before their very eyes affordable architectural elements and new household technology that could be delivered to their doorsteps.

1

At the time of the creation of the United States in 1789, which followed the American Revolution and the great wars between England, Spain, and France over the control of North America, acquiring and owning printed books was an expensive proposition for most of the region's residents. The gentry classes distinguished themselves and their dwellings, in part, by their lavish libraries of books, most often printed overseas or perhaps at the more minor North American publishing centers, like Boston, Philadelphia, Montreal, and New York City, of the East Coast.

Pattern Books and Mass Marketing of Residential Architecture

For most everyone else newspapers and pamphlets were the most common sources of printed discourses. Certainly these publications at times carried images and discussions about building farm homes or other utilitarian structures, as the research of historian Sally McMurry has shown for the midwestern United States. By the mid-nineteenth century, mass-market books designed to propagate both architectural design and a middle-class philosophy of life and comfort were gaining in popularity. Orson Fowler's *A Home for All* (1848), Andrew Jackson Downing's *The Architecture of Country Houses* (1850), and Lewis Allen's *Rural Architecture* (1852) all had their adherents in the States and Canada. But none contained the detailed architectural renderings that encouraged carpenters and builders to follow their recommended designs that closely. Few should be considered as mass-produced standardized designs since, as McMurry has noted, the builders approached the design process creatively, "in which they combined vernacular forms, pattern-books designs, and their own ideas, providing a significant source of innovation."[1]

As this first generation of pattern books were exercising their indirect influence on the North American landscape, a revolutionary period in the technology of printing took place. In 1840 Richard March Hoe, an American inventor, developed a revolving perfecting press; six years later, he developed his first version of a rotary press. These new machines, combined with the new technology of making paper from wood pulp, allowed publishers to print books cheaper and faster. Economies of scale, best expressed in print by the popularity of the dime novel, meant that architectural design ideas could be more easily distributed to a mass audience. Once publishers combined the increased speed and efficiency in printing with the detail capable through photolithography (1859) and zincography (1872), the new technology allowed for the printing of architectural pattern books of a wholly new sort, not self-help guidebooks but detailed volumes of building specifications and architectural designs reproduced in large format that could be easily viewed and adopted by even lesser-skilled carpenters and builders.

Tens of thousands of these new books were printed and distributed across North America from the late nineteenth well into the twentieth century. Popular titles included William Comstock's *Modern Architectural Designs and Details* (1881), *Palliser's American Cottage Homes* (1878), *Shoppell's Modern Houses* (1890), and A. J. Bicknell's *Bicknell's Village Builder* (1878). Most architectural pattern books came from the United States, and recent studies of domestic architecture in Canada admit that the American books were very influential north of the border in both established towns and newer cities. The spread of patterns books were aided by another late-nineteenth- and early-twentieth-century phenomenon, the establishment of free public libraries, where carpenters and builders, who otherwise might not have wanted to buy the books, could look, learn, and then adapt the books' designs to their own building projects.

The popularity of architectural pattern books by the end of the nineteenth century was closely associated with the growing interest in the prefabricated. Mass culture could hardly exist without the technological shift from the handmade to the industrial-forged and from the individual design to the standardized plan. Mass-produced housing, builders and consumers both learned, could be moved from industrial centers to anywhere in the United States and Canada due to the interlocking system of railroads established by the late 1800s.

George F. Barber (1854–1917) was one American builder who put the entire package together. Born in the American Midwest, Barber first established a building firm, Barber and Boardman, in DeKalb, Illinois, in 1884. Four years later, he moved to the American South, at the booming railroad center of Knoxville, Tennessee, where he established an architectural firm with Martin E. Parmelee that specialized in suburban house designs. By 1889 Barber was offering probably the first houses "totally prefabricated in every way," typically in Queen Anne style, that could be shipped by rail from Knoxville to any building site in North America.[2] Barber was to a degree ahead of his time for the success of prefabricated housing. His immediate success came with the production of pattern books, such as *Modern Artistic Cottage or The Cottage Souvenir Designed to Meet the Wants of Mechanics and Home Builders* (1891) and *New Model Dwellings and How Best to Build Them* (1894). His design books proved so popular that Barber established his own publishing company and produced a very popular monthly magazine titled *American Homes*. Contractors raised Barber designs throughout the nation; their blend of classical revival details and Victorian forms and millwork remains fascinating. Other contractors merely erected the Barber house package; one scholar has estimated that North America and Japan had as many as 10,000 "Barber" dwellings. Either type of Barber house was popular because they allowed for "personalized expression realized through mass produced design elements, such as fish scale shingles, turned spindles, latticework, and other adornments."[3]

THE TWENTIETH CENTURY

The Craftsman Influence

What Barber brought to the suburban house exterior, another even more influential early-twentieth-century designer and publisher brought to the suburban lifestyle. Gustav Stickley (1857–1942), a native of Wisconsin, was introduced to furniture making by a Pennsylvania uncle. By the 1880s Stickley and his brothers, Charles and Albert, tried their hand at the furniture business in New York State. In the next decade, some of the Stickley brothers established their own firm in Grand Rapids, Michigan, then a burgeoning center of the Arts and Crafts Movement in the Upper Midwest. Gustav Stickley, by the mid-1890s, had become enamored of the new architectural trends of England, France, and Germany and had fallen under the influence of the Arts and Crafts philosophy expressed by the English writers and critics John Ruskin and William Morris. In 1900, in New York State, Stickley established his own design firm, Craftsman Workshop, and the following year he established his own magazine, *The Craftsman*.

This magazine was among the first popular publications to successfully merge marketing, political philosophy, interior design, and architecture in a single bold package. It contained house plans and designs, with interior sketches of how the house should look furnished by Stickley pieces. It also had stories about living the proper Craftsman life and how to build Craftsman furniture in your leisure time. Stickley was "a pragmatic businessman who mass-produced his Arts and Crafts furniture with the latest machine technology" and who turned his magazine into "a forum not only for architecture but also for garden suburbs and urban planning."[4]

A HOUSE FROM SEARS

From 1908 to 1940 Sears, Roebuck and Company, the largest catalog retailer in North America, sold an estimated 100,000 houses, reflecting some 450 designs developed by the company. The Sears dwellings "consciously reflected popular American taste of the period; designs were selected for their broad appeal and acceptance," not their design innovation.[5] Sears sold homes in the United States and Canada, as did their primary competitors, Montgomery Ward and Aladdin Homes. Many designs were for English Colonial Revival houses; the Tudor Revival cottage was another popular style. Bungalows of all sorts of materials and sizes were the most popular prefabricated house. For instance, the Sears house listed as "The Westly" was a two-story frame bungalow with four large first-floor rooms that was sold from 1913 to 1929 across the United States, from Massachusetts to South Dakota. Other bungalows were smaller and sold for as little as $595.

Like the works by Downing three generations earlier, *The Craftsman* magazine advocated a consistent image of how life should be lived and how good taste could be reflected not only in the house design but also in the furniture and household items one surrounded oneself with. Comfort was paramount: "The right kind of a home does not drag out all that there is in a man to keep it going, nor is the care of it too heavy a burden upon a woman."[6] But unlike the Victorian pattern books, the plain, heavy oak nature of Craftsman style suggested that its environment was one for those fit and hardy. Canadian architectural historian Alan Gowans notes that the magazine "was, as its name suggests, predominantly addressed to a clientele that still thought in sexual stereotypes" and "brings to modern minds an image of the 1910s and 1920s paralleled in comic strip couples, where the Man of the House is so often pictured in shirt sleeves and vest, the Wife in a housedress; the one prone to spend evenings in his basement on some suitably masculine project like Stickley chairs—planing boards, boring decorative holes—while above, something suitably dainty is going on."[7]

Standardized Plans for Houses across North America

Selling a lifestyle became easier as the homes themselves became easier to acquire. Standardized plans, be it through *American Homes*, *The Craftsman*, or *Ladies' Home Journal*, were for sale. Prominent American architect Frank Lloyd Wright (1867–1959) even designed model dwellings for the *Ladies' Home Journal* in the early twentieth century; for a nominal fee the magazine would send consumers Wright's plans. For the North American middle class, the message was clear: buy plans, hire a contractor, and build your dream house, with whatever local adaptations you required. Some consumers preferred to have everything mass-produced and delivered to the building site, where a complete home could be erected in a matter of days. Hundreds of thousands of families bought their house as they might a piece of furniture—from the mail-order catalog that relied on Rural Free Delivery in the United States to deliver the homes and their stuff on time and in good shape.

To entice property owners to embrace their prefabricated designs, Montgomery Ward, Sears, and a plethora of retailers and manufacturers bombarded the new homeowners with images and advertisements of the absolutely necessary items and technology for their furnishings. Architectural historian Kenneth L. Ames points out that such innovations as the radio, movies, and central heating "both triggered and accompanied shifts in the furnishing, use, and, ultimately, the meaning of homes."[8] Cultural historian Karal Ann Marling agrees: "Mass culture is the hallmark of the forty years before the Great Depression."[9] Homes in the twentieth century were rarely places of production—few people were in the basements making furniture or in the parlors knitting or making music. Houses were places of consumption and as the twentieth century unfolded, increasingly sophisticated forms of mass advertising and technology shaped the homes, and built environment, of North America.

Consumer Goods and Ornamentation

The suburban explosion and its accompanied demand for new consumer goods opened doors for women architects, especially in domestic design, where women were assumed to have a "natural" affinity. For example, architects Lois Lilley Howe, Eleanor Manning, and Mary Almy practiced in the first third of the twentieth century, producing over 400 commissions in New England. The suburban sprawl of the century, in other words, also created opportunities for women architects that were rarely available in other fields of architecture or engineering.

Industrial design, in fact, remained a largely male domain well into the twentieth century. The engineer influenced North American culture as an important contributor to how popular culture impacted the built environment. The consumer revolution created a demand for things, gadgets really, that had rarely been viewed as valuable before, but now in the twentieth century they—an electric can opener, for example—became viewed as necessities. As items proliferated, their initial cost kept cheap through ever evolving emphases on standardization and mass production, industrial designers and engineers took center stage in North American architecture. The sleekness and newness of industrial design often appealed to the eye; certainly it appealed to the pocketbook since industrial designs, by their very nature and intent, could be produced in mass quantities for very affordable prices. Contemporary critic John A. Kouwenhoven, however, discovered a more cultural reason when he read the 1951 annual report of the Society of Industrial Designers. The designers, he explained, understood that architecture in the age of mass culture was more often than not "merely a technique of creating or enclosing a functional machine, and in each case the machine must be made efficient and attractive by exactly the same methods employed to make a manufactured product successful on the market."[10] The worship of the functional, of course, could be traced back to the rhetoric of the International Movement in architecture of the 1920s and 1930s. Functionalism became dogma for many North American designers. In 1932 Henry-Russell Hitchcock and Philip Johnson explained, "Design is a commodity like ornament. If the client insists, they still try to provide it in addition to the more tangible commodities which they believe rightly should come first. But they find one sort of design little better than another and usually as ready to provide zigzag trimmings as rhythmical fenestration. For ornament can be added after the work is done and comes into no direct relation with the handling of function and structure."[11]

The Influence of Automobiles and Railroads on Popular Architecture

Was there any place better to see the impact of industrial design—functionalism varnished and unvarnished—than on roadways? Next to the home, the best evidence of how popular culture impacted architecture and design is the power of the automobile to reshape towns, cities, and landscapes through its relationship with the modern engineered landscape. Alan Gowans observes: "Fast-food stands and shopping malls, big signs on poles and little signs shaped like busboys and bowling balls, parking lots and discount stores, and, as their weekend ads always said, 'much, much else,' all jostling and weaving, competing, and complementing—this is the approach to almost any city or town or village" in North America.[12]

As historian John Stilgoe reminds us in his book *Metropolitan Corridor*, the automobile was not the first new technology to reorder the built environment. The railroad from 1880 to 1940 defined a new and different landscape across the country. Indeed, across the North American plains in the early twentieth century, the Great Northern Railroad (United States) and the Soo Line (Canada), among others, built model standardized combination depots that marked hundreds of towns in both nations. These functional buildings served as corporate markers on the otherwise undifferentiated prairie landscape.

Like the railroad, the automobile created its own type of landscape, what scholars for some time have called roadside architecture. Cars were everywhere in the movies; they suggested independence, speed, and more than a bit of excitement. Advertisements for automobiles and associated products dominated the airways—only the tobacco industry held a larger profile, and typically Big Tobacco aligned its image with cars and fantasy. The automobile represented modern mobility and thus pushed the earlier streetcar suburbs into a new era of rapid expansion and development, most of which we decry as mindless sprawl today. The demands of the roadside—and an ever-present demand for comfort and convenience—also meant that entirely new buildings to address needed functions of automobile travel soon littered the landscape.

Gas Station Design

Foremost was the gas station because without fuel, the automobile was just a large and expensive hunk of metal and rubber. Gas stations began as low-tech pumps added to existing transportation buildings, mostly livery stables where people left their horses and buggies when they visited town. Automobiles and horses, however, did not mix, and soon enterprising businessmen were creating separate structures devoted to serving the automobile customer.

First came squarish or rectangular boxes covered with advertising signs typically situated with a driveway just off busy streets. The function of the tiny building was to provide an office for the gas station attendant. Otherwise the place was just a fueling stop. Once companies began to build their own stations, they initially turned to architectural styles popular in the cities and suburbs of the time. The 1910s introduced more architectural embellishment to the concept of the gas station. The Atlantic Refining Company in Philadelphia opened a domed Greek temple station in 1916. That same year in Louisville, Kentucky, Standard Oil Company built a Classical Revival drive-through station. By 1917 embellishments became more exotic when the Wadhams Oil Company, a small Upper Midwest firm, opened a station that looked like a Japanese teahouse, complete with pagoda, in Milwaukee, Wisconsin. Craftsman-style stations, typically distinguished by clay tile-roofed porte cocheres, appeared everywhere in North America during the early 1920s.

Company engineers, designers, and marketers next joined forces to conceive new gas station designs that by their standardized appearance served as corporate three-dimensional billboards directed at the increasing number of drivers speeding down state and federal roads. Phillips Petroleum built standardized English Cottage–style gas stations, the first in Wichita, Kansas, in the late 1920s, followed by 6,749 more in twelve states. Pure Oil also developed an English Cottage style for its stations. Gulf Oil decided to build multiple standardized designs, some in the Spanish Mission style, others in the Colonial Revival style, to better fit into their surroundings. Standard Oil in the United States and Canada adopted more of a Streamlined Moderne look. Esso took the high road, commissioning noted

6

Bauhaus architect Mies Van Der Rohe to design a company station in Montreal. Mies's design, however, proved too expensive for the company to consider as a prototype.

Walter Teague (1883–1960), an American industrial designer who had earlier worked with Eastman Kodak, broke the mold of the revival-style gas stations with his new, sleek porcelain-paneled design for Texaco in 1937. It was among the first of the "oblong box" gas stations. This standardized design, influenced by International and Streamlined Moderne architectural styles, became a roadside landmark as its design conveyed to customers the modernity and speed of the automobile age.

Teague's new Texaco building gave the company a distinctive profile along the American roadway and was part of Texaco's corporate response to the hard times of the 1930s. His design was functionality at its best. Located within a single flat-roofed, rectangular building was an office defined by a large plate glass window where products could be highlighted, one or two service bays (usually distinguished by the title of "Washing" or "Marfak Lubrication"), and women's and men's restrooms on the side. Where Teague differed from others is how he sheathed the entire building with white porcelain tile and then added Art Deco–like streamlining touches and the company's red stars to the upper fourth of the building's facade cornice while bold red letters spelling TEXACO were centered over the office window. By combining the gleaming red and white building with Texaco's distinctive banjo-shaped sign, Teague created a corporate image that distinguished Texaco from the multitude of businesses crying for attention along the North American roadside.

Texaco used the Teague design as a backdrop in many of its print ads and later television commercials through the 1960s. The corporation followed its new design with three other bold moves in the late 1930s: the introduction of Sky Chief gas, a high-octane product served from a silver-painted pump; the establishment of its Registered Rest Room program, where company inspectors traveled the roadways to ensure clean restrooms for travelers (again, Texaco understood the paramount need to provide comfort and convenience); and its 1940 sponsorship of regular Saturday broadcasts of the Metropolitan Opera, so that consumers understood that Texaco also was a classy product for the highbrow and not just middle-class travelers.

Teague's streamlined touch was just one of many similar industrial designs that anticipated the aesthetics of the 1939 World's Fair in New York City. This mega cultural event attracted millions of visitors who were bombarded with images of modernity, especially spectacles where the automobile and the roadside combined with various prototype homes of tomorrow to project a futuristic fantasy of what American life would be in the later decades of the twentieth century. Much attention has been directed to the visionary house designs of Buckminster Fuller and other futurists. But once the focus on the house broadens out to the new suburban-urban landscape, the second most prized consumer item for American families—their car—took center stage. The automobile culture and its landscape were presented as both the present and the future; there was little debate otherwise.

Other Automobile Culture Designs

The success of the oblong box and standardized design in the petroleum industry carried over to other businesses associated with automobile culture. Canadian Tire began in 1922, when brothers John W. and Alfred J. Billes established a tire and parts dealership in Toronto, Ontario. Five years later, they established Canadian Tire, Ltd., and soon began to build a series of stores, all easily recognizable by the huge Canadian Tire logo and their catchy roadside designs.

Automobile culture, the roadside landscape, and suburban sprawl were also closely associated—an association perhaps best captured by documentary photographer Bill Owens's series on California suburbs during the 1960s or the numerous television programs set in suburbs, such as ABC's *Bewitched*. Mass production and standardized designs had ruled in suburbs since the spectacular success of Levittown in New Jersey in the late 1940s and 1950s. Cookie-cutter suburban designs, however, were accepted by millions of homeowners; such designs guaranteed bank financing and future resale value. Lenders and real estate brokers both frowned on the innovative in mid-twentieth-century domestic design.

Another type of automobile-associated dwelling, the mobile home, has received considerably less attention. Today the preferred term is "manufactured housing," with the designation referring to the assembly-line methods of designing and building the mobile home before it is transported to its initial destination. "The mobile home is composed almost entirely of materials that make allusions to other materials," remarks historian Allan D. Wallis, but these illusions "are necessary for the acceptance of the object as a whole. Imitative ready-mades brought together to form an essentially new object is characteristic of many of the most original artifacts of the American environment."[13] The popular taste that drives the mobile home industry produced a very modern dwelling in its materials and reliance on technology, one that "may well be the single most significant and unique housing innovation in twentieth-century America."[14]

The standardized corporate designs that are closely associated with the roadways were not limited to automobile culture. International Harvester, a farm implement company, turned to Raymond Loewy, one of the most noted industrial designers, for a new post–World War II look for its dealerships, be they in Tennessee or Alberta. His 1948 standardized design—flat-roof, rectangular buildings heavily dependent on plate glass walls and gleaming metal supports for its styling—was produced in 386 stores by 1948. Before the company jettisoned the design, some 1,800 similar International Harvester buildings were constructed in North America and across the world.

Fast-Food Restaurants and Motels

Two other key components of the roadside were fast-food restaurants and motels, and both are excellent examples of the intersection between mass culture and design in twentieth-century North America. The first fast-food restaurant company to introduce a standardized design to its operations was White Castle, which began in Wichita, Kansas, in 1921. This hamburger chain featured small, square burgers prepared on a large grill and sold through small white-painted and later white-enameled buildings that featured castle-like turrets and battlements to convey the corporate identity. By the 1950s the company had approximately 230 stores in operation.

White Castles, however, often operated in downtown settings, much like the popular diners of those same decades. The real roadside innovator was Howard Johnson, who in 1925 introduced a high-butterfat ice cream in multiple flavors at a Quincy, Massachusetts, soda fountain and began to build a restaurant empire. During the 1930s Johnson developed a standardized restaurant design—a long rectangular facade faced the road (much like a diner) but then a bright orange roof with a Colonial Revival–style cupola graced the building and made it visible from blocks away. By 1940 about 100 HoJo's stood along the East Coast.

The prototypes of automobile roadside design with the greatest cultural impact, however, came after World War II, with the most influential being the McDonald's restaurant design of the 1950s. Maurice and Richard McDonald established their first restaurant in San Bernardino, California, but in 1948 they decided to jettison their popular business for a wholly new design and management approach. The new store did not use carhops—waiters and waitresses who came to the car to take an order—but relied on self-service, with customers placing their orders at the restaurant's large plate glass entrance. Their restaurants also had a limited menu and did not accept special orders, but they offered extremely low prices.

The McDonald brothers worried, for a while, whether they had sacrificed too much comfort and convenience in exchange for a low price and consistent quality. After a slow start, business started booming—families believed that the price itself offered the convenience of giving Mom a break from cooking—and the brothers looked at creating franchises. They contracted an architect, Stanley Meston, to devise a standardized model, and then they brought in a designer, George Dexter of the Dexter Sign Company, who added golden arches—yellow-painted beams with bright lights—on either side of the restaurant building. The first franchise with the new architecture opened in Phoenix, Arizona, in 1953.

Businessman Ray Kroc became the company's second director of franchises, and Kroc emphasized a standardized approach to food production, location, and the design of

THE STANDARDIZED COMFORT OF HOLIDAY INN

One last example of Place-Product-Packaging from the roadside, again multiplied across the continent, was the standardized design and services associated with the Holiday Inn motel chain from the 1950s through the 1970s. Kemmons Wilson, a Memphis, Tennessee, businessman, opened the first Holiday Inn in his hometown in 1952, and by 1954 he and partner Wallace E. Johnson had started replicating the prototype across the region.

On the surface, nothing was spectacular about his design, with its U-shaped courtyard, office, restaurant, and swimming pool, introduced by an ultrabright highway sign visible from hundreds of yards away. But Wilson produced a quality, consistent product that was basically the same no matter if located in the American South, the Midwest, or the Canadian plains. Comfort was never more a commodity than at Holiday Inn—travelers knew what to expect, from the double beds to the guaranteed clean bathrooms to the bland yet soothing mass-produced artwork. Within a generation of its founding, the company became the first roadside concern to achieve a billion dollars in revenues.

McDonald's. Once he bought out the McDonald brothers in the 1960s, Kroc's persistent vision drove the corporation for a generation and turned the restaurant into one of the best-known brand names in the world. During the 1970s Kroc jettisoned the golden arches built into the building in favor of using the arches as a corporate symbol. The buildings gained mansard roofs and became more family oriented, an image reinforced with a steady dose of Ronald McDonald on television and in print ads. By 1982, in fact, McDonald's was the world's largest private owner of real estate. Its restaurants covered most towns not only in North America but in a good part of the world as well.

McDonald's, and the many other brands of fast-food restaurants that followed its lead, reflects the power of the marketing concept of Place-Product-Packaging on the modern North American landscape. Popular commercial architecture in particular reflected a general assumption that brands guaranteed customer loyalty and that standardized designs for company buildings reinforced brand recognition. This interlocking business/design strategy gained effectiveness with the widespread adoption of television and the development of slick televised advertisement campaigns during the 1950s.

At the time of Kemmons Wilson's retirement from creating the successful chain of road-side Holiday Inn motels in 1979, the North American roadside had become a distinctive place and experience. Canadian geographer Edward Relph admitted that "the most recent commercial strips consist of a series of well landscaped, carefully designed, standardized buildings to meet the major consumer needs of servicing the body and the automobile. It is all very trim," Relph pointed out, but "also lacking in vitality and individuality. Like corporate residential suburbs this is all packaged, but instead of the corporate presence retreating into the background here each corporation has its own distinctive heraldry of a sign or logo, plus company colours and built-forms."[15]

Architect Robert Venturi had earlier worried about the same loss of individuality and design distinctiveness in his influential treatise *Learning from Las Vegas* (1972). He admired the "decorated sheds" of the earlier roadside, when chains such as A&W Root Beer placed their business in a large concrete replica of a wooden beer keg. The conformity of the modern landscape appealed to few architects or designers, but its mass popularity could not be denied. The strip and its three-dimensional corporate signposts remain defining elements of the twenty-first-century North American built environment.

Venturi and other critics were not the only ones to understand that the modern suburbs and commercial strips of North America reflected a corporate ethos that meant far too many were surrounded with environments like the workplace, whether at home or on the road between home and work. Many North Americans searched for escape at two different environments—the cultivated outdoors and the designed fantasylands of amusement parks.

The Cultivated Outdoors

In the first half of the century, first by rail and more popularly by automobile, the majestic landscapes of the Rocky Mountains called out to Americans and Canadians alike. The railroads joined with the federal governments to build massive public parks at Banff and Lake Louise in Canada and at Glacier and Yellowstone in the United States. Canadian developers interpreted their alpine environments in familiar terms—the chalet style of Germany and Switzerland, which even appeared in The Empress, the railroad-sponsored luxury hotel at Victoria, British Columbia. The Canadian Pacific–designed resorts of the Rocky Mountains had a decided continental flair, and counterparts at Montana's Glacier National Park came in the chalet-style Many Glacier Hotel, built by the Great Northern Railroad.

Yellowstone National Park's influential unified style took shape in the early twentieth century. Its initial grand hotel of the late nineteenth century, the Lake Hotel, stood on the banks of Yellowstone Lake, and its classical portico and long horizontal facade reminded visitors of the earlier summer resorts of the Upper Peninsula country of Michigan and Ontario. Then, at the turn of the twentieth century, the Northern Pacific Railway engaged Seattle, Washington, architect Robert Reamer to design a new grand resort at Yellowstone's single most famous attraction, the Old Faithful geyser. Reamer's Old Faithful Lodge is one of the century's true architectural landmarks. He took an existing naturalistic approach to resort architecture, the Rustic style associated with the Arts and Crafts revival in the northeast Adirondack Mountains, and blew it out to meet the massive proportions, and expectations, of the Yellowstone landscape. The building materials and the oversized nature of the hotel also helped to root it in the monumental natural landscape of the park itself, achieving a sense of harmony between the man-made intrusions into the natural world of the parks.

Reamer utilized locally available materials to build an environment that reflected the stuff of nature but then denied that same environment through its bold statement that humans could build a structure just as massive and imposing as what God made at Yellowstone. Its immense lobby, its shifting shadows, the thick log beams, and its enormous overhang defining the entrance are imposing enough. As a human safe haven amid the dangers of the wild, the lodge is an example of a building that defines a place and an era.

The man-made monuments of the northern Rockies mirrored their surroundings. In turn these designs defined an aesthetic that soon multiplied across the landscape, adapted, stripped down, and simplified for what is now commonly called "parkitecture." Exposed wood beams, overhanging shingle roofs, prominent shed dormers, and river rock foundations are design elements that can be found in downtown urban oases or more isolated rural parks. In the last two decades of the twentieth century, the designs of parkitecture began to appear in all sorts of retail and restaurant buildings to suggest that the business was in step with nature or at least offered a menu that reflected the rugged outdoors. Thus, a new design type—the log-veneer restaurant or bar—joined the cluttered streetscapes of suburbia.

Resorts

The other road traveled by resort developers at the turn of the twentieth century was escapism through fantasy and luxury. In a rustic resort, experience trumped comfort; in the great luxury resorts of the gulf coast, comfort through luxury crushed experience. The great luxury resorts of turn-of-the-twentieth-century Florida, then another wilderness being transformed into a playland first for the rich and then for the middle class, were wholly different. Two northern capitalists, Henry Flagler and Henry Plant, created "exotic fantasy" palaces, using design and technology to transform "a sparsely inhabited, scraggily beautiful near-wilderness into what they promoted as the 'American Riviera.'"[16] Flagler and Plant relied on the railroad, the tropical climate, and the Florida beach environment to attract both the wealthy and the middle class. Their properties prospered briefly and then struggled. Resorts remained as contributing elements to Florida's coastal culture until they were surpassed at the end of the century by a new, more popular way of thinking about Florida, desired environments, and the world of popular fantasy.

Amusement and Theme Parks

That new idea first took shape thousands of miles to the west, near the mass media motherland of Hollywood. Disneyland in Anaheim, California, was Walt Disney's way of making his movies and his weekly network television show come alive for visitors. Amusement parks were nothing new, but Disneyland was markedly different, a paean to "imagineering, the imagine engineering of deception," according to Edward Relph. This park, Relph thought, differed from the Kennywoods and the Cedar Points of the past because its "basis lies not in shared social experiences, but in technical knowledge."[17] And it was technology on a grand scale, experienced through its visual, physical, and aural terms, which made the fantasy of Disneyland seem realistic. Here comfort and fantasy trampled on experience—the sense of adventure given over to a carefully contrived and controlled experience where individual choice was minimized.

Disneyland welcomed visitors through its Main Street entrance, where fanciful Victorian facades covered what amount to large souvenir stands and other visitor services, giving the respectability of the past to what amounts to a garish hawking of overpriced trinkets. Disney's image of a clean, perfectly proportioned Victorian townscape had little to do with the actual reality of the Gilded Age, but it did restore popular interest in the often maligned

Victorian styles of architecture. With its imaginary Main Street, Disney struck a deep vein in the popular consciousness—a generation later, historic preservationists joined a "Main Street" project of the National Trust for Historic Preservation that brought a generation of restored and newly re-created historic facades to town squares across the nation. Too many of these restorations were little more than the facadism practiced so well at Disneyland. Disney's Main Street was fake design; too many towns in the United States kept their historic town squares viable, but the layers of history found behind the facades of any historic building were stripped away and replaced with what could have been, or more often what should have been, there 100 years ago.

From its Main Street opening, the Disneyland landscape opened into various fantasy realms where family-friendly rides, most reinforcing popular cartoon figures or popular Disney movies, were available. Over time, the company added new technologically advanced rides with involved storyboards, sets, and action from life-size animations—mini-movies themselves—that became very popular and were copied by other amusement parks across the continent. In time, the most successful rides, such as Pirates of the Caribbean and The Haunted House, became movie franchises for new generations, linking the cinema to the "reality" of the theme park.

Disneyland's success spawned a generation of theme parks, from the Six Flags Over series at multiple suburban locations to Dollywood in the Tennessee Appalachia. But the most successful spin-off came from Walt Disney himself, with the creation of Disney World in central Florida from the early 1970s to the end of the century. Disney always disliked the constraints to his vision that the Anaheim park presented—not enough land, and ironically enough, too much commercial strip development, not part of the Disney vision of a unified, controlled environment surrounding the park.

The tens of thousands of acres acquired in central Florida, near what was then the medium-sized railroad town of Orlando, took care of the space—and gave Disney enough buffer that unattractive strip development would not detract from the visitor experience (although within a generation, Disney World's unprecedented success led to the entire Orlando-Kissimmee area becoming nothing more than a gigantic sprawl).

After its opening in 1972, the Disney World complex expanded over the next generation to embrace such disparate elements as a stock-car racing track, multiple golf courses, a wide range of lodging choices, and new amusement parks based on the themes of movies (Disney MGM), zoos (Animal Kingdom), and the future (EPCOT). The merging of many cultures into one world culture of consumerism is a fascinating theme at EPCOT. In a park dominated by a massive geodesic globe, reminiscent of Buckminster Fuller at his most grandiose, visitors may tour various sections representing different nations, which may be experienced through performances, exhibits, rides, and consumption—food, souvenirs, and crafts.

Another useful barometer of how the corporation embraced images of popular culture and appropriated previous resort experiences to the designed landscape of Disney World is in the evolution of lodging. For several years, the primary company-controlled lodging was the Contemporary Hotel, a modernist vision of a luxury motel complete with the monorail passing through the middle of the facility. By the 1980s and 1990s around the manmade lake of Disney World stood various hotels of fantasy, from the theme of a Polynesian village to the Victorian resorts of the Upper Peninsula and, the most bizarre of all, to the great rustic resorts of the Northern Rockies, aptly named the "Wilderness Lodge." This massive structure stands starkly on flat central Florida landscape, looming over the nearby forests rather than blending into the natural landscape as at Yellowstone National Park. Disney's version of nature in the Northern Rockies also is more predictable—its "geyser" erupts on the hour every hour. No waiting as at Yellowstone!

The Shopping Mall

The enclosed environments of Disney World, be they the miniature world in harmony at EPCOT or the thrill of a fake safari in Animal Kingdom, were undoubtedly popular. And the millions who visited there found this same approach for controlled experience through controlled environments replicated back home in the increasingly growing commercial push for enclosed shopping malls from the 1970s through the 1980s. By 1990 few North American towns with more than 40,000 residents lacked one. Far too many were as mundane as the most nondescript shopping center of the 1950s, and the monotony was doubled by the fact that nationwide chains dominated the shopping experience rather than the more local businesses that had populated the strip centers of a generation earlier. The enclosed shopping malls also spawned exburbs—a new zone between urban centers and the surrounding suburbs—which meant that the enclosed mall was surrounded by circles of other chain restaurants and "big box" retailers while the access roads to the malls became lined with the latest in roadside architecture. Malls became attractions, and chain motels located in the areas between the interstate and the consumer beehives.

One of the grandest mall attractions, combining shopping on an unprecedented scale with theme park–like attractions (golf course, wave pool and beach, ice rink), was the West Edmonton Mall, which was developed in four phases between 1981 and 1998 outside of Edmonton, Alberta. In 1983, after its first two phases, the mall had over 450 stores, an indoor skating rink, and an amusement park. New additions between 1985 and 1998, however, turned what was a huge mall into a major tourist destination. You could visit the West Edmonton Mall and stroll down Bourbon Street and "experience" a taste of New Orleans, try out Chinatown and see the Chinese pagoda and vases, or experience the high style of Paris and other continental venues by shopping along Europa Boulevard. There were more than roller coasters and carousels too. You could experience the tropics at the wave pool and beach, or enjoy a simulation of sky and clouds from the sky ceiling. It is even possible to grab a bit of history, through a display of a replica of the British Crown Jewels.

An Outlandish Confluence of Design, Taste, and Popular Culture: Las Vegas

Consumer palaces, such as the West Edmonton Mall or the Mall of America at Minneapolis, Minnesota, mix the real and the fake into a blended experience of design and environment. Their achievements, however, pale in comparison to North America's most outlandish confluence of design, taste, and popular culture, Las Vegas. Disparaging comments about the design and taste of Las Vegas are constant themes in popular magazines; the bright lights attract, but few really want to admit that they enjoyed being there. After all, this is the city that celebrates the miles-long area called The Strip as the most dominant, significant element in its built environment whereas the somewhat older, largely post–World War II part of town along Freemont Street—still garish but on a more human scale—is known as the historic district. Popular textbook versions of American architectural history, such as those from Alan Gowans's *Styles and Types of North American Architecture* (1992), Dell Upton's *Architecture in the United States* (1998), and David Handlin's *American Architecture*, 2nd edition (2004), just ignore Las Vegas—their books contain no index references to the city.

An essay looking at popular culture and North American architecture, however, cannot avoid the topic of Las Vegas, a rapidly growing city of over 1 million people centered on the activities of some of the best pleasure-zone popular architecture in the world. Ranging from the classicism of Caesar's Palace and the Bellagio to the more cartoonish, mass media–inspired visions of Circus, Circus and Treasure Island, Las Vegas serves up a smorgasbord of images, all real but few based in actuality, from premier destinations across the globe. Knights of the Round Table dominate imagery at Excalibur; the mysteries of ancient Egypt hold forth at Luxor. Wealth and continental sophistication oozes from The Venetian while caged tigers wait to pounce at MGM Grand. There is no need to travel: New York, complete with the Statue of Liberty, Paris with its Eiffel Tower, and Venice's gondolas and canals await travelers. The best in clubs and restaurants, such as Commander's Palace from New Orleans' Garden District, are crammed into whatever emptiness a casino might possess.

At first glance, choice and experience seem to be in abundance at Las Vegas. The impact of popular culture, however, means otherwise—the emphasis is to move toward the most convenient and comfortable experience possible: *standardized* and *mass-produced* after all are mantras for popular culture. The Las Vegas environment is all about control, not choice. Control comes first in the environment itself; a city and industry that sucks this much electricity should not be located in a desert where temperatures are among the highest on the continent. But the great enclosed and interconnected casinos allow visitors to walk a large part of The Strip in the worst heat of the summer by negotiating the endless corridors and skywalks, staying energized and comfortable as they move from one experience to the next. The environment is shunned and ignored, and people build, live, and work in an enclosed environment where outside elements are experienced only when one leaves the air-conditioned car to enter the actual place of work.

Inside the casinos, experiences are controlled and monitored through one-way mirrors, state-of-the-art security cameras, and a maze of slot machines and gaming tables. Enter one building and it is often difficult to find a way to exit. Hordes of businesses and restaurants operate to ensure that there is no need to leave the enclosed casino world, as long as your credit holds up. Privacy exists in only small doses.

Las Vegas is bigger than life. Where else can you share a moment in Paris and cross an avenue to find yourself in Venice? The city's advertisements emphasize that here in your air-conditioned fantasyland environment once-in-a-lifetime events may take place. Mass culture becomes all about consuming in a manufactured environment and precious little about experience and distinctiveness.

In 1972 architects Robert Venturi, Denise Scott Brown, and Steven Izenour looked at the maze of lights, angles, building styles, and apparent disorder of North America's largest gambling center and found, instead, a certain type of logical order. The vitality of Las Vegas and similar roadside imagery, to their minds, underscored "the deadness that results from too great a preoccupation with tastefulness and total design" as it also emphasized "the value of symbolism and allusion in an architecture of vast space and speed and proves that people, even architects, have fun with architecture that reminds them of something else."[18] These words rang true to several significant North American architects in the late twentieth century, and their search to have fun, and convey meaning, became popularly known as postmodern architecture. Alan Gowans argues that postmodernists strove to create an architecture that was "no longer a self-referential art whose critics addressed only each other, whose practitioners spoke only in oracles, and whose public existed . . . only to render homage to the Great Artist."[19]

STYLES IN CONTEMPORARY POPULAR ARCHITECTURE

American architect Philip Johnson, who worked in partnership with architect John Burgee throughout the 1980s, epitomized this search for fun and public acclaim by crafting popularly identified architectural motifs into what were otherwise standard-fare urban modernism. When the *New Yorker* magazine parodied Johnson's "Chippendale" classical cornice on the AT&T skyscraper by dropping a telephone into the opening of the broken pediment, modern architecture suddenly seemed fun.

Postmodern aesthetics mostly took hold in commercial buildings, especially those of suburban sprawl, throughout North America, almost to the point of becoming another monotonous cliché. In domestic architecture, postmodernism was most often expressed through the New Urbanism fad of the 1990s. New Urbanism typically stood the lessons of historic preservation on their head. Most developments are better classified as New Suburbanism, with scaled-down replicas of historic facades, or easily identified architectural elements, grafted into modern condos or standardized designed dwellings. Postmodernism reflected the impact of three generations of popular design on the architectural mainstream in North America. Its bright colors, the sharp angles, and the historic design references suggested to popular audiences that elements of the past could coexist with the demands of the future.

But as the twentieth century closed, the architectural mainstream remained cold to a lasting embrace with pop architecture, and vice versa. Canadian architect Frank Gehry, with his major museum designs from Spain to New York City to Minneapolis, was lionized as the best of the new breed. Gehry's shiny titanium skins and oddly angled "organic" designs, however, have yet to find their replication in the standardized, mass-produced designs of North American popular architecture. Even Gehry's very popular design for the Disney Concert Hall in Los Angeles has gained no imitators in the wider popular architecture of the California roadside. The worlds of popular architecture and academic architecture may today be closer in the materials they use but remain far apart in how they view the function and the role of buildings in modern society.

For supporting evidence, we need only to turn, once again, to the domestic landscape of North America. Many suburban homes by the end of the twentieth century relied on new technology and building materials unimagined at mid-century. New metal alloys, polymers of all sorts, and manufactured wood products either arrived all in one piece ready to be put up or could be glued and stapled together in just a matter of hours. The result, however, was seldom modern in exterior appearance—no matter what architects produced on their computer screens or promoted through slick magazines such as *Architectural Digest*. Revival styles such as colonial, classical, mission, and Tudor remained far more popular; adopting "modern styles" rarely went further than variations on the bungalows or the Prairie styles of the early twentieth century.

Most suburban homes at the beginning of the twenty-first century thus epitomize the impact of popular culture. The movies might highlight the sleek lines of modernism, but the vast majority of North American residents want their homes to look like the homes of the Bundys, the Jeffersons, or the Huxtables, the model middle-class residences of television. Domestic architecture embraces conservatism in architectural detail—but not in overall appearance. The most distinguishing feature of most middle-class suburban homes in the United States or Canada is the garage, which now graces the dwelling's facade to the point of dominating the entire look of the house. Builders have adapted the home—once a bastion against the forces of industrial society, in the words of Andrew Jackson Downing—to accommodate industry's most influential product: the automobile. The placement and size of the garage not only dominate many suburban designs; they also relegate the "front yard" to virtual obscurity (thus explaining in large part the popularity of the "deck" in the late twentieth century).

This revolution in residential design has passed with little comment. Is it because North Americans are so wedded to their automobiles? When cars became commonplace in the 1920s, new homes often had detached garages to the rear of the home; by the 1950s and 1960s the garage was attached, but the great bay door was at the rear of the house. At the turn of the twenty-first century, some suburban designs seem to serve the cars and the overall roadside culture they connect to more so than the family who resides there. The welcoming porch and the hallway entrance are either ignored or missing altogether, as residents typically enter and exit the house via the garage. These new designs suggest that home is not a refuge, a haven, from the demanding outside world; home instead becomes a way station, a rest stop, where you sleep a few hours before jumping back into the car and engaging with the surrounding world. For many North Americans today, the car, not the home, is where the heart is.

RESOURCE GUIDE

PRINT SOURCES

Gowans, Alan. *Styles and Types of North American Architecture: Social Function and Cultural Expression.* New York: HarperCollins, 1992.
Jakle, John A., et al. *The Gas Station in America.* Baltimore: Johns Hopkins University Press, 1994.
———. *The Motel in America.* Baltimore: Johns Hopkins University Press, 1996.
Kouwenhoven, John A. *The Beer Can by the Highway.* Baltimore: Johns Hopkins University Press, 1988 [1991].
Relph, Edward. *The Modern Urban Landscape.* Baltimore: Johns Hopkins University Press, 1987.
Rochon, Lisa. *Up North: Where Canada's Architecture Meets the Land.* Toronto: KeyPorter, 2005.
Wallis, Allan D. *Wheel Estate: The Rise and Decline of Mobile Homes.* New York: Oxford University Press, 1991.

WEBSITES

Architecture of Canada. Accessed May 25, 2006. http://canada.archiseek.com.
Canadian Architecture Collection, Digital Collections at McGill University. Accessed May 22, 2006. http://cac.mcgill.ca/home/digit2.htm.
Levittown: Documents of an Ideal American Suburb. Accessed May 25, 2006. http://www.uic.edu/~pbhales/Levittown.html. A useful collection of photographs, documents, and discussion.
Roadside Architecture in Minnesota. Accessed May 25, 2006. http://www.mnhs.org/places/other/roadside. An excellent state-focused Website on various roadside property types located in Minnesota and photographed by David W. Nystuen.
Society of Commercial Archaeology. Accessed May 25, 2006. http://www.sca-roadside.org. Dating to 1977, the Society of Commercial Archaeology is the leading American professional group that specializes in the study of the roadside.
Wisconsin History Explorer. Accessed May 22, 2006. http://www.wisconsinhistory.org/archstories. The Wisconsin History Explorer has excellent Web pages on the design of suburbs as well as several key components of the roadside landscape, including gas stations, fast-food restaurants, and motels.

VIDEOS/FILMS

History Channel's Modern Marvels: Disney World (United States, 2006). A&E DVD Archives.
History Channel's Modern Marvels: Las Vegas (United States, 2005). A&E DVD Archives.
History Channel's Modern Marvels: Las Vegas Hotels (United States, 2000). A&E VHS Movie.

MUSEUMS

America on the Move Exhibit, National Museum of American History, Behring Center, 14th Street and Constitution Ave., NW, Washington, DC 20013. 1–202–357–2700. http://americanhistory.si.edu/onthemove/exhibition.

McCord Museum of Canadian History, 690 Sherbrooke Street West, Montreal, Quebec H3A 1E9. 1–514–398–7100. http://www.mccord-museum.qc.ca.

The McDonald's #1 Store Museum, 400 N. Lee Street, Des Plaines, IL 60016. 1–847–297–5922, http://www.mcdonalds.com/corp/about/museum_info.html.

The Motor Vehicle in Canada exhibit, Canada Science and Technology Museum, 1867 St. Laurent Blvd., Ottawa, Ontario K1G 5A3. 1–866–442–4416. http://www.sciencetech.technomuses.ca.

Roadside America Exhibit, The Henry Ford Museum 20900 Oakwood Boulevard, Dearborn, MI. 1–800–835–5237. http://www.hfmgv.org.

NOTES

1. Sally McMurry, *Families and Farmhouses in Nineteenth-Century America: Vernacular Design and Social Change* (Knoxville: University of Tennessee Press, 1997 [1988]), p. 47.
2. Gowans (in Resource Guide), p. 172.
3. Jeri Hasselbring, "George F. Barber," in *A History of the Arts of Tennessee*, edited by Carroll Van West and Margaret D. Binnicker (Knoxville: University of Tennessee Press, 2004).
4. Elizabeth Cumming and Wendy Kaplan, *The Arts and Crafts Movement* (London: Thames and Hudson, 1991), pp. 141–142.
5. Katherine C. Stevenson and H. Ward Jandl, Houses by Mail: A Guide to Houses from Sears, Roebuck and Company (Washington, DC: Preservation Press, 1986), p. 19.
6. *Craftsman Homes* (New York: Craftsman Publishing Co., 1909), p. 131.
7. Gowans, p. 263.
8. Jessica H. Foy and Karal Ann Marling, eds., *The Arts and the American Home, 1890–1930* (Knoxville: University of Tennessee Press, 1994), p. xvii.
9. Ibid., p. 2.
10. John A. Kouwenhoven, *The Beer Can by the Highway* (Baltimore: Johns Hopkins Press, 1988 [1961]), p. 109.
11. Henry-Russell Hitchcock and Philip Johnson, *The International Style* (New York: W.W. Norton, 1932), p. 37.
12. Gowans, p. 319.
13. Allan D. Wallis, *Wheel Estate: The Rise and Decline of Mobile Homes* (New York: Oxford University Press, 1991), pp. 164–165.
14. Ibid., p. v.
15. Edward Relph, *The Modern Urban Landscape* (Baltimore: Johns Hopkins University Press, 1987), p. 183.
16. Susan R. Braden, *The Architecture of Leisure: The Florida Resort Hotels of Henry Flager and Henry Plant* (Gainesville: University Press of Florida, 2002), p. 1.
17. Ibid., p. 130.
18. Robert Venturi et al., *Learning from Las Vegas, 2nd ed.* (Cambridge: MIT Press, 1986), p. 53.
19. Gowans, p. 361.

ART

JOY SPERLING

Popular artists in North America have almost always pursued commercial success. The patrons of these artists have likewise considered commercial success a sign of quality. Over the course of U.S. and Canadian history, popular artists have explored, exploited, and developed any and every technology available to market their art and reduce its cost through technical innovations. Popular art in North America has represented the perfect confluence of art and technology for profit. North American artists have actively sought to promote access to art for the greatest number of people and to offer art at the lowest cost that would yield the highest returns for the artist-entrepreneur. The art market in North America has reflected the interdependence of the market economy and the innovations in the communications and industrial sectors of the economy. The intellectual discourse on taste has merged and diverged with these external forces, but public preferences, often relatively autonomous, determine the favored art of the day.

Historically, the development of popular art in North America has been driven by the convergence of several significant forces. First, popular art needs to be popular with the general public rather than with a small, cultivated artistic elite. People must want to see or possess the work of art for any number of reasons, ranging from its attributed "fame" to the prospect that its market value will rise over time. Second, a work of art will become a part of the popular culture if multiples or reproductions are made for sale. These multiples or reproductions may be a print of a famous painting or a cast of a well-known sculpture. Third, the popular impact of any piece of art will likely increase if the work can be duplicated rather than badly imitated; the reproduction and sale of a famous photograph, the possession of a poster in an original edition, or mass-produced pottery are examples where an individual can claim to own an "authentic" work of art. Fourth, the popular diffusion of art will also be facilitated in those cases where the object is quickly and easily (re)produced, cheap to make and purchase, and easily disseminated. Popular art also depends on the existence of a middle class with the disposable income, appetite to consume, and desire to be persuaded that art is something that they should collect and display in their homes as markers of class or good taste. Finally, the existence of popular art is contingent on the existence of a literate, well-connected, mobile community with adequate leisure time for tourism, reading, and the pursuit of happiness.

UNITED STATES

Popular Painting

Nineteenth Century

Portrait and landscape painting predominated in the nineteenth century in the United States. The American Art Union (AAU) contributed to the institutionalization and commercialization of art patronage. The AAU had a significant impact on the U.S. art market and taste in the 1840s. In 1850 roughly 17,000 members paid $5 each to receive its annual engraving and to participate in its annual art lottery. In 1850 the AAU purchased 464 paintings, including 283 landscapes, 125 genre, 25 history, and 25 still lifes. In its 9 years of operation, the AAU claimed to have patronized 221 artists. It changed the face of U.S. popular art by encouraging thousands of Americans to hangs prints on their walls and hundreds of average artists to seek national renown, or at least commercial viability. Emanuel Leutze (1818–68), for instance, painted two versions of *Washington Crossing the Delaware* (1848 and 1851) in Düsseldorf. News of it swept the nation before it even arrived in New York. The AAU hoped to win the print distribution rights, but they went instead to the Cosmopolitan Art Association. By the 1850s American art exhibitions were increasingly open to the public, but they were not always polite or restrained affairs. While the fine art museum cultivated a smaller cultural elite, other museums, like that of P. T. Barnum, were designed as places of excitement, wonder, and entertainment. Barnum's specialty was the "humbug," something known to be fake, but nonetheless enjoyed by the paying public.

Genre Painting. Genre paintings reflected the everyday concerns and interests of the rising middle classes. William Sidney Mount (1807–68) trained on Long Island as a sign-painter. He painted *Bargaining for a Horse* (1835) as a commentary on the Yankee farmer and the city horse dealer as well as on trading for votes. Edward L. Carey engraved the painting (1839) for publication in *The Gift*. The AAU engraved *Farmer's Nooning* (1836) for distribution in 1843. George Caleb Bingham (1811–79) executed genre paintings in Missouri in the 1840s. As an artist and Whig politician, Bingham lobbied for federal funds to clear the passageways of the Missouri and Mississippi rivers for commercial traffic. He painted several versions of the *Jolly Flatboatmen*, one of which he sold to the AAU for engraving and distribution to its membership in 1849. Lilly Martin Spencer (1822–1902) established her reputation by selling paintings to the AAU from Cincinnati but moved to New York in 1848. Most of her income came from the translation of her genre and still life paintings into widely distributed prints (after 1851 to the Cosmopolitan Art Association). Spencer painted women in domestic interiors such as *Kiss Me and You'll Kiss the 'Lasses* (1856) and *The Fruit of Temptation* (1857), an illustration of the "servant problem." Winslow Homer (1836–1910) worked as an illustrator for *Harper's Weekly* and then exhibited *Prisoners from the Front* (1866) to establish his painting reputation. In the 1870s he mostly sold nostalgic scenes such as *Snap the Whip* (1872) and hunting scenes for engraving. Thomas Nast (1840–1902), on the other hand, was one of *Harper's Weekly*'s most famous illustrators. He painted a cycle of thirty-three paintings called the *Grand Caricaturam* (8 × 11′ each) in 1867 as a political commentary on Johnson's failure to support Reconstruction, which he presented on tour with music and a lecture.

Western Paintings. George Catlin (1796–1872) spent 6 years in the 1830s making 600 watercolor paintings and drawings of Native Americans. Catlin's *Indian Gallery* toured America and Europe from 1837 to 1845 accompanied by an *Indian Show* and several books. Buffalo Bill Cody's Wild West show turned the West into theater, while dime novels and railway advertising helped to cultivate the myth in the popular imagination. Yale-educated Frederic Remington (1861–1909) expressed an eastern sensibility in his paintings for an eager *Harper's Weekly* audience. Paintings like the *Last Stand* or *Fight for the Water Hole* were wholly fictionalized. Charlie Russell (1864–1926) actually went to Montana. He prided himself on his detailed knowledge of the Blackfoot people, but his overarching narrative was just as fictional as that of any other cowboy artist. Russell illustrated the *Virginian* and served as a consultant and set designer to several early western movies. Western art has become a multimillion-dollar market since the 1920s. It is no longer the sole preserve of the cowboy artist; Native American artists have appropriated it as their own, using the styles, imagery, and narratives that were once used against them to secure a substantial market share for themselves.

Still Life Painting.   William Michael Harnett (1848–92) was famous for his painted deceptions that were usually hung in bars, saloons, men's private clubs, and hotel lobbies and that sold in department stores, not in galleries. As men's art, the subjects included smoking utensils, books, guns, playing cards, newspaper cuttings, and even paper money "deceptions." Harnett's *After the Hunt* (1885), which shows the accoutrements of male friendship—a gun, a bugle, a hat, and dead game—hung in Theodore Stewart's saloon on Warren Street, New York City. There were other artists whose work was more explicitly commercial but whose images have become ubiquitous nonetheless. The advertising firm of Brown and Bigelow (St. Paul, Minnesota) commissioned Cassius Marcellus Coolidge (1844–1903) to create sixteen paintings of dogs in various human poses (1903). His *Dogs Playing Poker*, two of which sold in 2005 for $590,400, inspired the popular *Dogs Playing Pool* by Arthur Sarnoff (1912–2000).

Twentieth Century

In 1913 the International Exhibition of Modern Art (known as the Armory Show) at the 69th Regiment Armory featured about thirteen hundred works of art, three-quarters of which were by Americans artists. Despite bad press, or perhaps because of it, more than 250,000 visited the exhibition in New York, Chicago, and Boston. Thus, although much of the art exhibited was modern, the message was clear—the American public would visit art museums if invited. Thus since the 1920s the Art Institute of Chicago has tried to engage the public actively. When they purchased *American Gothic* from Grant Wood (1892–1942) in 1931, he was an unknown regional artist, but they promoted *American Gothic* so aggressively that the picture became part of the nation's common visual consciousness. The Art Institute also promoted acquisitions such as Edward Hopper's *Nighthawks* (1942) and Seurat's *La Grande Jatte* (1886), and it pioneered the blockbuster exhibition.

In 1933 President Roosevelt established the first of a series of Federal Art Projects (FAP) under the rubric of the Works Progress Administration (WPA). Artists in the painting division were paid a weekly wage either to produce a required number of paintings (distributed by the government to local communities) or to work on a preapproved mural. Guidelines specified that the imagery should be accessible, recognizable, and suited to its purpose. Most murals were in public buildings or post offices across the country. The Index of America Design, directed by Holger Cahill, employed several hundred artists between 1935 and 1941. They produced 22,000 illustrations of the popular and folk arts of America.

Grandma Moses (Anna Mary Robertson Moses) (1860–1961) had made traditional crafts until her husband died in 1927, when she began painting charming pictures of her past based loosely on Currier and Ives prints. Grandma Moses was discovered by a New York art dealer in 1938 and promoted as a "primitive" artist. In 1947 Moses, actually a very clever businesswoman, contracted with Hallmark Cards, licensing the reproduction of her paintings on paper products, plates, and even fabric. She was the subject of a television movie and several specials and was featured in popular magazines.

In 1947, as the Cold War settled in and the McCarthy hearings started, American artists grew remote, fearing their own political witch hunt. Jackson Pollock (1912–56) rocked the art world by placing his canvases on the floor and dripping paint on them. The success with *Autumn Rhythm* (1950) brought Pollock critical fame, but the photographs of him in illustrated magazines such as *Life* and *Time* captured the public's imagination. He was represented as "Jack the Dripper," an all-American rebel photographed wearing a T-shirt and Levi jeans, smoking cigarettes, and swaggering with a twist of urbane disaffection that substantiated the stories of his upbringing in Cody, Wyoming, his wild streak, his fast cars, his drinking, and his unchecked womanizing. His paintings were featured in magazines nationwide, including a fashion shoot for *Vogue*. Ironically, as Pollock's popular appeal waxed, his artistic reputation waned: Clement Greenberg dismissed him as a has-been in 1952.

The culture of the 1960s shepherded in a time of mass advertising and unprecedented consumerism produced both for and by television. Andy Warhol's (1928–87) pop art addressed both. Instead of imagining his own subjects, Warhol exploited already existing (and superbly designed) advertising images such as the *Campbell's Soup Can* or the *Coca-Cola Bottle*. Not only did he exploit public fame in his persona; he made it the subject of his art in works such as *Marilyn* (1962). He exploded the fine line between advertising and art, high and popular art, and artist and personality, while he moved seamlessly between the worlds of art and commerce. He sold his art for outrageously high sums, and his *Interview Magazine* redefined the nature of fame in America. Warhol said (famously) that in the future everyone would be famous for 15 minutes. His fame has lasted almost 50 years thus far.

A number of artists have had broad popular appeal during the twentieth century without having critical purchase. Their choice of subject matter ranges from the pinup to the bucolic. Howard Chandler Christy (1873–1952) lived and worked in the Hotel des Artistes, New York, where he painted the restaurant walls with somewhat titillating nude girls. In 1932 he painted Amelia Earhart's portrait, an image that was so popular that *Town and Country* featured it on their February 1, 1933, cover. It, like its eponymous subject, however, disappeared soon thereafter. Alberto Vargas (b. 1896–1982), a Peruvian-born immigrant from Switzerland, was hired by *Esquire* in the 1940s to imitate the pinup art of George Petty. His images became synonymous with the pinup girl of World War II. In the 1960s and 1970s he worked regularly for Hugh Hefner's *Playboy Magazine* and defined the eroticized woman for generations of men and boys. LeRoy Neiman (b. 1927) began making sporting illustrations for *Playboy Magazine* in 1954. By 1958 his work was so successful that he was given his own feature, "Man at His Leisure," which ran for 15 years. Between 1960 and 1970 Neiman painted more than 100 sports paintings and murals for eighteen Playboy Clubs, several paintings for the Indianapolis 500, a number of hotel murals, and many celebrity portraits. Margaret Keane (b. 1927) has also garnered popular acclaim for her paintings of children and animals with big eyes. For 50 years, she has sold both the oil painting and prints of each work of art. Her paintings sell for as much as $25,000 each, a sum that explains her lawsuit against her husband (which she won) arising from a dispute over who actually painted (and owned) the pictures. George Rodrigue (b. 1944) began his *Blue Dog* paintings in 1984. He produces paintings, prints, books, and advertisements using the Blue Dog image. His gallery in New Orleans' French Quarter offers works of art that will accommodate almost anyone's budget. In 1999 he produced three Neiman Marcus *Rodrigue Cows* for the Chicago Cow Parade and, in 2000, advertisements for Xerox Color Inkjet Printers. In 1989 Samuel J.

Butcher opened the Precious Moments Chapel and Theme Park in Carthage, Missouri, with murals based on the Sistine Chapel. The gift shop sells the twenty-one original Precious Moments figurines and the 551 new ones, plus a range of merchandise from a baby to a wedding line. Finally, Thomas Kinkade, the trademarked "Painter of Light," paints scenes of pretty cottages glowing in a lush landscape at dusk. Canvas and paper reproductions of Kinkade paintings can be purchased with light boxes in the windows of cottages to keep a light burning at home. Kinkade has fifty licensed partners who produce several hundred licensed products ranging from Hallmark greeting cards and ornaments to Spode and Lenox dinnerware to Messenger Corporation/Renaissance funeral supplies.

Popular Printmaking

The print is perhaps the most significant influence on and form of popular art, particularly when images are produced in multiples and widely disseminated.

THE WONDERFUL WORLD OF DISNEY: A CHILDHOOD FAVORITE

The Disney Corporation has probably been the single most important source of visual imagery for the American child since the 1950s. Walt Disney took so many major children's stories and transformed them into film, print media, and merchandise of so many forms that it is impossible to catalog the range. The Disney Corporation markets directly to children, selling two-dimensional, three-dimensional, and video or DVD versions of their product lines. They sell big toys and small, old stories and new versions, limited editions and limited releases, and they have special memberships, stores in every city in America, and a very popular theme park.

Nineteenth Century

Louis Prang and Company and Currier and Ives published sentimental chromolithographs. Louis Prang, who commissioned Winslow Homer in 1863 to draw sets of sketches for lithographic reproduction, attracted a better-quality customer. Some images, like Eastman Johnson's *The Barefoot Boy* (1867), were praised as morally edifying by good housekeeping guide authors such as Catherine and Harriet Beecher Stowe. Currier and Ives, on the other hand, set the standard for the cheap popular print market after 1875. Most Currier and Ives prints were unsigned. One exception was Frances Bond Palmer's best-selling *Across the Continent: Westward the Course of Empire Takes Its Way* (1868). Currier and Ives prints were mostly about peace and prosperity, the status quo, nostalgia for a placid life, and the changing rural seasons—the antithesis of the life of the average Currier and Ives customer, which was probably filled with the stresses of city life and affected by the social and political issues that attend a nation in flux: work, factory, labor, poverty, and immigration problems. The Currier and Ives store in New York had prints stacked on tables for purchase with sale bins outside. Peddlers roamed the city with prints for sale, and distributing agents mailed prints anywhere in the United States.

The illustrated journals, such as *Harper's Weekly* and *Frank Leslie's Illustrated Weekly*, experienced phenomenal circulation increases during the Civil War, enjoying a joint readership of more than 600,000 by the war's end. Winslow Homer, a staff illustrator covering U.S. life for *Harper's Weekly*, also worked freelance illustrating the Army of the Potomac. Thomas Nast, who produced centerfold illustrations in holiday issues and acerbic political cartoons, is still known for Santa Claus illustrations he drew for several journals (1860s–1890).

Charles Dana Gibson (1867–1944) created the Gibson Girl in 1887, a highly successful mixture of conventional prettiness, coy behavior, and independent pluck. She appeared variously in *Harper's Weekly*, *Scribner's*, *Collier's*, and *Century* but became so popular that she was soon appearing on covers and centerfolds. By 1900 (with the Gibson Man) she was marketed throughout the United States and Europe on prints, calendars, playing cards, fans, china, jewelry boxes, umbrellas, and even wallpaper. Harrison Fisher's (1875–1934) somewhat similar Fisher Girl was first published in *Puck* in 1898 but graced the covers of *Cosmopolitan* between 1910 and the 1920s. Likewise, Howard Chandler Christy's (1873–1952) Christy Girl appeared on so many magazine covers that by the 1920s Christy was asked to produce an illustrated version of *The Last of the Mohicans* with her in the female lead. On the other hand, J. C. Leyendecker, who created the Arrow Collar Shirt man for the Cluett Peabody Company in the 1920s, received hundreds of proposals for marriage weekly—for his Arrow Collar man.

The debate over the publication of religious images in America was played out in popular illustration. The American Tract Society made widespread use of pamphlets to promote millennialism, while *Harper's* sold seventy-five thousand copies of its *Illuminated Bible* in fifty-four installments (25 cents each) between 1844 and 1846. Nathaniel Currier produced 247 lithographs of great works of Christian art, including Leonardo's *Last Supper*. Prints were listed separately as either "Catholic" or "Religious" art until 1856. In the late nineteenth century a debate over the true likeness of Christ was taken very seriously. In the end, a consensus emerged, among some religious groups at least, that Christ probably looked like an Anglo-Saxon amalgam of the Christs represented in Leonardo's *Last Supper* (1495–98) and Michelangelo's *Pieta* (1498–99).

The widespread dissemination of prints in the United States continued to accelerate. As the speed of producing lithographs increased, their production costs dropped and the number of prints in a run increased to many thousands. In addition, the low cost of mailing prints spurred their use in advertising across the nation. In urban centers such as New York, posters advertising Barnum's American Museum filled his 3000-seat theater, just as those advertising Jenny Lind's American debut pushed the price of auctioned seats to $225. Meanwhile, the arms manufacturers Colt and Remington relied on posters to compete and to advertise new products, while new companies such as Kodak Cameras and Columbia Bicycles used posters with girls in control to make their products look easy to use. The major advertising poster companies of the 1890s were the Strobridge Lithographic Company, Cincinnati; The Forbes Company, Boston; and the Courier Lithographic Company, Buffalo. Until the 1890s most advertising posters were anonymous. In 1889, however, *Harper's Magazine* commissioned Eugene Grasset (1841–1917) to design a special cover, and *Harper's Bazaar* hired him to design two holiday posters. In 1893 Edward Penfield (1866–1925) was commissioned by *Harper's Magazine* to create a publicity campaign using monthly posters. In 1894 *Lippincott's* hired Will Carqueville (1871–1946) to do the same. The major magazines that commissioned posters were *Harper's Weekly*, *The Century*, *Scribner's Monthly*, *Lippincott's*, and the *Atlantic*. Within 3 years major artists such as Maxfield Parrish (1870–1966), Will H. Bradley (1868–1962), Louis Rhead (1857–1926), and Ethel Reed (1876–1910) were competing in poster competitions to promote bicycles, sewing machines, soap, and even soda.

The power of the visual image to advertise and to sway public opinion was exploited brilliantly by American railroads. The railway poster dates back to the 1830s but did not figure prominently in advertising until the number of lines and companies proliferated in the 1870s, forcing railroads to compete for business. Ironically, even though freight yielded the largest profits, advertising from the 1880s to the 1940s was directed almost exclusively to leisure and tourism, providing the first example of indirect advertising. Early railroad advertisers also provide examples of product disambiguation using logos, branding, and marketing devices such as connecting specific railway lines to specific luxury hotels.

Other promotions included the Santa Fe Railway's distribution of Thomas Moran's *Grand Canyon* chromolithograph (1892) to teachers and *Los Angeles Times* subscribers, and by 1906 the giveaway of an annual promotional calendar distributed nationally by mail. The famous Santa Fe Calendar pictures, produced over several years, were prints from paintings. But after 1900 the railway also reprinted photographs as publicity postcards and magic lantern slides. By the 1920s only the Santa Fe and the Southern Pacific railways were still producing posters in large quantities. The Santa Fe held fast to the Southwest theme that made it famous. In 1937 it introduced the *Super Chief* train, the exterior painted with a war bonnet and the interior decorated with imitation Hopi and Navajo designs. Santa Fe's posters for "Hopiland" lasted until almost 1950.

Posters were easy to collect. Many were not even displayed but were traded unopened in magazines sold for their posters. Back-issue *Chapbook* posters from the 1890s reportedly sold for between 25 and 50 cents at a time when the magazine itself sold for 5 cents. In 1896 two poster collector magazines started publications (the *Poster* and *Poster Lore*), and although neither lasted into 1897, *Poster Lore* claimed that in 1896 there were 6,000 collectors in the United States, 1,000 in Canada, and twenty companies printing posters.

Twentieth Century

The federal government eventually embraced prints and posters to achieve its political goals, a trend that began with the onset of World War I and continued through the Depression and World War II. In 1916 President Woodrow Wilson created the Division of Pictorial Publicity (DPP) to sustain public support for the war effort. It produced more than 700 posters to encourage enlistment and the purchase of war bonds. The images run the gamut from coarse propaganda based on fear and ignorance (such as the fictional bombing of New York Harbor by the "Hun") to the shameful manipulation of masculine insecurity (such as "Daddy, what did YOU do in the Great War?" or "Gee! I Wish I Were a Man, I'd Join the Navy") to direct pleas to "Buy War Bonds." In April 1916 Charles Dana Gibson offered his services to the DPP. He organized artists and helped to produce some 1438 designs, including an image of the Statue of Liberty with the plea "You Buy Bonds, Lest I Perish." Five million copies of James Montgomery Flagg's (1877–1960) "I Want You for U.S. Army" were printed during World War I and World War II combined. Two million copies of Joseph Pennell's (1857–1926) "That Liberty Shall Not Perish" were printed during World War I.

During World War I the American Red Cross mounted one of the most successful poster campaigns in modern history. The campaign raised $400 million for relief and recruited almost 24,000 nurses. Moreover, one-third of the American population contributed. Red Cross posters were hung in streets, buses, trains, shops, factories, and anywhere else people moved or worked. The Red Cross used heavy-handed Christian symbolism and sentimentality in its posters. The nurses routinely appeared as "The Greatest Mother in the World" alongside statements such as "Let the little Children Come to Me." Some posters asked for donations with questions such as "How much to save these Little Lives?" Other posters portrayed ethereally beautiful nurses surrounded by halos of light, who tended to equally idealized young soldiers lying wounded in their arms. The posters explicitly asked girls to volunteer as nurses and subliminally lured boys to volunteer as soldiers.

The WPA Federal Art Project (FAP) was begun in 1931 and ended in 1939. The FAP produced an estimated 35,000 poster designs, but only about 2,000 designs survive. An estimated 2 million posters were distributed during the 8-year program. In 1938 the FAP operated nationwide, but one-third of the operation was concentrated in the New York office, which sponsored roughly thirty-five designers and twenty printers to produce posters, mostly in screen print (renamed serigraph by Carl Zigrosser), for the U.S. Travel Bureau, education, health, and several other federal programs. The images were expertly designed but lacked persuasive power.

In 1942 the poster division was transferred to the War Department's Service Division, and artists produced posters for training purposes, airport plans, rifle charts, and patriotic posters. The aim of the Office of War Information (OWI) was to unite the nation in a common cause. The OWI placed posters in unexpected places to lend a sense of urgency to the message conveyed. The messages were distilled into a few basic thoughts: "You Buy 'em, We'll Fly 'em," "Time is short so don't waste it," "Loose Lips might Sink Ships," and "United We Stand." One of the most famous posters, designed by J. Howard Miller for Westinghouse, read "We Can Do it" and showed a woman rolling up her sleeves to work. Women were targeted as potential factory workers. Many posters represented women workers as young, pretty, white, married, and middle-class, so that their participation in the workforce would be read subliminally as temporary. In fact, most wartime women factory workers were working-class, single or widowed, and disinclined to leave their jobs after 1945.

Advertising imagery attained a national reach between the wars. McClelland Barclay created a pinup advertisement featuring Miss America for Lucky Strike cigarettes in 1932 that was one of the most widely recognized images of that year. Hadden H. Sundblom (1899–1966) created many of Coca-Cola's most important images in the 1930s, including some of the later Santa Claus series. Gil Elvgren (1914–80) created so-called mayonnaise (smooth, creamy, and white) pinup pictures for 40 years and was the only competition for Alberto Vargas at *Esquire Magazine*. Elvgren, who also worked for Coca-Cola for 25 years, was a staff artist at Brown and Bigelow and had his Elvgren girls printed in booklets sent to almost every GI during World War II, on calendars, on jigsaw puzzles, on nude playing cards, and even on a saucy nude letter-opener. He created the face of at least sixteen different products including Ovaltine, Sealy Mattress, Napa Auto Parts, and GE Appliances.

The most famous nonadvertising print images since the 1920s were Norman Rockwell's (1894–1978) illustrations for the *Saturday Evening Post*. Rockwell executed almost 300 paintings for the *Post* between 1919 and 1963. His most famous wartime images were *Rosie the Riveter* (1943) and the *Four Freedoms* (1943). These latter four images were so popular that the OWI printed 2.5 million for distribution. In 1964 Rockwell took on civil rights for *Look* with his *The Problem We All Live With*, which illustrates a tiny Ruby Bridges going to school, an image that Ruby Bridges said was her personal favorite.

Despite the success of posters in the 1930s and early 1940s, the paper advertising poster could not compete with commercial radio and television by 1950. Although posters are still used for movies, they are rarely a primary form of advertising today. From the 1930s to the present day, movie posters such as *Marilyn Monroe and "Niagara"* (1953) and Saul Bass's *Vertigo* (1958) or *The Man with the Golden Arm* (1955) have called audiences into movie theaters. Likewise, the posters advertising and the covers of rock music albums since the 1960s constitute a space somewhere between advertising and art. These include Stanley Mouse's *Grateful Dead, Oxford Circle* (1966), Wes Wilson's *Bill Graham Presents: Jefferson Airplane* (1966), Bob Fried's *Charlatans: The Youngbloods and the Other Half* (1967), and Victor Moscoso's *Sopwith Camel* (1967). Since the 1960s, political posters have also become increasingly hard-hitting, including Peter Max's *From the Moon* (1969), R. L. Haeberle and

Peter Brandt's *Q: And babies? A: And babies.* (1970), the Committee to Defend the Panthers' *Power to the People* (1970), Georgia O'Keeffe's *Save Our Planet, Save Our Air* (1971), J. Gokey's *This Is How the White Man's Law Fits the Indian* (1972), Xavier Viramonte's *Boycott Grapes: Support the United Farm Workers Union* (1973), Lisa Emmons's *And Then There Was Nothing* (1974), David Lance Goines's *AIDS Prevention* (1985), and the Guerrilla Girls' *Do Women Have to Be Naked to Get into the Met. Museum?* (1989). Modern digital technology has made the personally designed image accessible on an individual basis.

Popular Sculpture

The most popular sculptures produced in the United States during the nineteenth century were genre sculptures by John Rogers (1829–1904). In 1859 Rogers sold *Checker Players* at a Chicago bazaar for $75. Rogers copyrighted the piece and took his second sculpture, *The Slave Auction* (1859), to New York. After learning how to make plaster casts, he made several replicas for sale curbside. In 1860 Rogers created a second version of *Checker Players* and *The Deserted Village*. When exhibited at the academy, the three groups garnered widespread public attention. Between 1860 and 1890 Rogers dominated the tabletop sculpture market. His plaster sculptures usually sold for $6 and were between 8 and 13 inches in height. By 1870 Rogers needed twenty employees to keep up with production. The New York galleries of Goupil and of Williams and Stevens represented Rogers along the eastern seaboard and throughout the Midwest. Rogers designed twenty-three sculptures in the 1860s alone. His most popular sculpture was *Coming to the Parson*, which sold 8,000 copies (at $15 each) in 1870 because it was a favorite among newlyweds, although his all-time best seller was *Checkers Up at the Farm* (1877), which sold 5000 copies a year for 15 years. Between 1860 and 1892 Rogers sold an estimated 80,000 sculptures, employed up to sixty assistants, and faced no competition. His success was a direct result of design skills, production methods, low overhead, and his uncanny ability to read the market. As soon as he retired and sold the business, it collapsed.

Around 1900 Frederic Remington (1861–1909) made a series of tabletop multiple sculptures in bronze, but his work depicted the mythic "West," targeted a wealthier segment of society and commanded much higher prices. Remington continues to exert a pull on the popular imagination. President Ronald Reagan installed *Coming through the Rye* (1902), a sculpture of four drunken cowboys (poor Robert Burns!), in the White House. Today, corporations such as Hallmark Ornaments employ staff artists to design small sculptures series to collect and display in various formats. The sculptures are specific to seasons, holidays, and well-known characters in popular culture. Hallmark Tree Ornaments, for instance, are small enough (at about 3 inches) to encourage large collections, are inexpensive, and offer a wide enough choice to attract a broad range of collectors; they are familiar enough to be attractive but each year offer new variations that make collectors crave more. The quality of design and manufacture of each sculpture is promoted by Hallmark; individual artists are featured in the annual catalog.

High art of the twentieth century has also shaped popular culture. Alexander Calder (1898–1976) turned sculpture on its head around 1930 with the *Mobile*, an abstract construction that hangs from the ceiling and moves with the slightest air current, denying the mass, weight, and stability of traditional monumental sculpture. By the 1950s Calder's *Mobiles* were ubiquitous. Today, everyone recognizes the mobile as a crib toy, but few are aware that it was Calder's invention. John Seward Johnson Jr. (b. 1930), a much less original artist, is known for his life-size trompe l'oeil sculptural groups created at the Johnson Atelier Technical Institute of Sculpture. His work is installed in ordinary settings, mostly in North America. His *Grounds for Sculpture* garden features Johnson's life-size three-dimensional re-creations of famous paintings, providing, the artist claims, "an intimacy . . . that the paintings don't allow themselves."

Washington, D.C., experienced two waves of monument building in the nineteenth and twentieth centuries. The first included the Washington Monument (dedicated 1885), designed by Robert Mills. Henry Bacon Daniel's Lincoln Memorial (1866–1924) followed. It houses Chester French's *Abraham Lincoln* (1922); the memorial still draws more tourists than any other in Washington, D.C. John Russell Pope's Jefferson Memorial (1935–37), which houses Rudolph Evans's *Thomas Jefferson* (1938–43), was built during the interwar period but garners much less attention. In 1911 the Daughters of the American Revolution's national committee established the Old Trails Road as a National Memorial Highway and between 1928 and 1929 commissioned twelve copies of August Leimbach's (1882–1965) *Madonna of the Trail* to be placed in each of the twelve states through which the road passed. The first is sited in Bethesda, Maryland, and the last in Upland, California.

By 1886 a need for gigantism seemed to take hold in U.S. popular sculpture. The Statue of Liberty, designed by the French sculptor Frédéric-Auguste Bartholdi (1834–1904), was ostensibly a gift to the United States from the French nation. Yet the base, which cost much more than the sculpture, had to be paid for by public subscription in the United States. When wealthy New Yorkers could not raise the funds, Joseph Pulitzer raised the needed money from his working-class readers by marketing the statue as a symbol of U.S. freedom. The Statue of Liberty, severed irrevocably of its French connection, still stands sentry before New York Harbor and is perhaps *the* visual icon symbolizing American liberty.

In 1923 Doane Robinson conceived of the idea to have a gigantic monument carved in South Dakota to shore up its failing economy by creating a must-see tourist attraction. After protracted debate, Gutzon Borglum (1867–1941) received federal funding to carve the portraits of four presidents on the face of Mount Rushmore. President Calvin Coolidge demanded that Borglum include, in addition to George Washington, two Republicans and one Democrat. The sculptures, *Presidential Portraits, Mount Rushmore* (1930–41), were unfinished at Borglum's death in March 1941; his son tried to continue, but funds ran out a few months later. The original plan called for waist-length portraits. Still, the incomplete sculptures of Washington, Thomas Jefferson, Abraham Lincoln, and Theodore Roosevelt are 60 feet tall and took 400 workers 11 years to carve. The noses are currently disproportionately large to accommodate for weathering; in 25,000 years they will be perfectly proportioned. Two million people visit Mount Rushmore annually.

Two other very large sculptures are the *Praying Hands* (1980), taken from an Albrecht Dürer drawing (1508–09), and the re-created statue of *Athena*, the goddess of the Parthenon. *Praying Hands* entered the popular imagination in the form of mass-produced small plaster casts, screen savers, and religious artifacts. In 1980 the television evangelist Oral Roberts commissioned a 60-foot bronze sculpture for his City of Faith Medical Center, but it now resides at the entrance to his namesake university in Tulsa, Oklahoma. Nashville's *Parthenon* (1897) was built for Tennessee's Centennial Exposition, complete with plaster replicas of the Parthenon Marbles. In 1982 Alan LeQuire won the competition to re-create a statue of *Athena* (1982–2002) for its interior. This sculpture stands 41′ 10″ tall, is fully gilded, and was funded by the Athena Fund, a community-based organization.

In 2005, Christo and Jean-Claude Christo (both b. 1935) created *The Gates*, a fantasyland of flags in Central Park. The Christos more than matched Borglum's sense of gigantism and outsized ego. It was boasted that *The Gates* was the largest sculpture created since the Sphinx. The media frenzy that the Christos generated brought millions of tourists and their tourist dollars to New York City. As public artists, the Christos are masters of self-promotion, believing that they bring great art to the little people, when in fact they merely offer great "art-utainment."

Postwar Memorials

Felix de Weldon (1907–2003) designed the Marine Corps War Memorial (Iwo Jima Memorial) in 1954 based on Joe Rosenthal's famous *Life* magazine photograph. Memorials commemorating World War II and other postwar conflicts were absent until the 1980s, when Vietnam veteran Jan Scruggs convinced the nation to contribute money to memorialize Vietnam only 6 years after the U.S. withdrawal. In 1981 Maya Ying Lin (b. 1959), a 21-year-old Asian American, won an open competition to design the Vietnam Veterans Memorial (1982) in Washington, D.C. The controversy over her abstract design cut into the earth, its black granite, and its chronological listing of the dead was the topic of much public debate. The Vietnam Veterans Memorial, which cost $4.2 million, was intended to symbolize the sacrifices of both those who gave their lives (whose names are carved on the memorial) and the veterans who came back (who saw themselves

THE NAMES PROJECT: A MEMORIAL

Memorials to the now millions of AIDS casualties represent a completely different kind of remembrance. In 1982 Cleve Jones and Mike Smith began making quilt panels in memory of friends who had died from AIDS in the tradition of nineteenth-century mourning quilts. Originally housed in a San Francisco storefront, Jones and Smith invited the friends and family of others who had died from the disease to create similar quilts. These quilts, when rolled for storage, took up the space of an emaciated human body. Over the years, the *Names Project: AIDS Quilt* has become a significant and enormous memorial to the dead. It was last shown complete in 1993 but is shown in parts in several towns across the United States.

reflected in the polished granite). In the intervening years, the Vietnam Veterans Memorial has come to signify the collective grief of a nation and has transformed public mourning in the United States. Lin's design was not left unmolested. In response to heated, if not widespread, criticism, Frederick Hart (1943–99), who failed to win the competition, "added" a figurative sculpture of *Three Servicemen* (1984) to the side of Lin's memorial; and Glenna Goodacre's (b. 1939) Vietnam Women's Memorial (1993) was placed nearby. The Korean War Veterans Memorial, designed by Frank Gaylord and dedicated in 1995, consists of nineteen stainless steel, fiber-optically lit figures. And on May 29, 2004, the National World War II Memorial was finally dedicated. Strangely, World War II was the only war not commemorated by a monument in Washington; when the memorial was built, it was not simply placed on the Mall but on a central axis between the Washington and Lincoln memorials, signaling its significance in the American imagination.

On September 11, 2001, terrorists flew airplanes into the Pentagon and both towers of the World Trade Center in New York. Americans suffered the kind of collective trauma that demanded some kind of memorial. At the Pentagon and in Pennsylvania, where United Flight 93 was brought down by its passengers, the sites have been marked by simple, restrained, and elegant memorials. In New York, however, the site has become a highly contested space. Construction will not begin before 2009, and its estimated cost is $1 billion. By comparison, the National World War II Memorial cost $182 million, $15 million under estimate.

Popular Photography

Photography as an agent in a changing cultural identity in the United States in the nineteenth century reflected the migration of populations, the transitory nature of city life, and the commercial exchange of ideas and money. Photography helped to fix visually a personal identity in a time in which the visual marker quickly replaced traditional class markers.

Photographs also recorded the United States' growing possessions, its national events, and its industry and scientific achievements. Photography was seamlessly interwoven into the very fabric of U.S. popular visual life by 1855.

Nineteenth Century

Some daguerreotypes were made to document scientific innovations (such as Dr. W. T. G. Morton's use of ether in surgery), national crises (such as some fifty photographs of the Mexican-American War, 1846–48), or significant events (such as a fire at the Oswego Granary Mills in 1853). The most popular kinds of photographs were *academies*, photographs of nude or seminude figures, mostly women, made ostensibly for artists. These soft-core pornographic images comprised the first true mass market in photography.

In 1851 Frederick Scott Archer's (1813–57) collodion process (wet-plate process) and Louis-Désiré Blanquart-Évrard's (1802–72) light-sensitive paper coated with whey and albumen allowed the negative-positive process to flourish, brought about reduced exposure times and printing papers that could be prepared in advance, and commercialized production. This resulted in more natural portraiture, more natural landscapes (using combination printing), and the development of truly popular photography.

The stereograph was the first mass-marketed photographic technology. The stereograph consisted of two photographs of the same object taken in the same camera about 3 inches apart that, when viewed in a stereoscope, looked three-dimensional. Stereographs were mass-produced using wet-plate multiple-print technology, which made photographs quick, easy, and cheap to produce and reproduce as well as profitable to sell. The stereograph was probably the most popular visual parlor entertainment of the nineteenth century; millions of cards were sold in the United States alone. Probably the most successful stereograph publisher was E. and H. T. Anthony and Company (New York), which boasted that their catalog contained over 50,000 different subjects. In the 1880s the publishers Underwood and Underwood published 25,000 stereographs per day. Stereographs provided images ranging from the scientific to tourist sites, to moral tales, to salacious images of spousal infidelities. The more public version of this kind of entertainment was the magic lantern show. Magic lantern slides were images photographed onto glass slides that could be projected by a magic lantern onto a screen. The show might have been part of a panoramic display (Daguerre's panorama had painted slides), or slides might have been used in a public lecture. Some are still found in art history classrooms today.

A particularly U.S. tradition in nineteenth-century portraiture was postmortem photography, particularly of a deceased child. Southworth and Hawes advertised their particular abilities in postmortem photography. James Van der Zee (1886–1983) created a *Book of the Dead* in Harlem in the 1920s. Spirit photography was much more popular. Isaac Rehn (1815–83) and William Mumler (1832–84) were among the best-known spirit photographers, producing photographs of spirits appearing as ghostly shadows or ectoplasm, including the inexplicable movement of furniture. Although these photographs were and are taken seriously by many, they did not go unchallenged and continue to engender controversy.

Another popular form of photography at mid-century was the carte de visite or card photograph. Patented in 1854 by André-Adolphe-Eugène Disdéri (1819–89), the card camera, like the stereograph camera, had several independent lenses that could take up to eight photographs on one photographic plate in one sitting. The photographs were small and fuzzy. The sitter was thus able to exude the appearance of wealth from a distance without the scrutiny of detail. Card photography, like stereography, was driven by the passion to collect. Cards of celebrities sold for a premium. Within the 10 years, millions were sold in the United States—a craze that continues today with cards portraying athletes or cartoon characters.

During the Civil War, personal photographs became important in reminding loved ones of family members. The scrapbook merged the family and the national narrative as cards of Abraham Lincoln, particularly those by Brady, or military leaders were placed alongside those of family members. The war also spurred a boom in itinerant photography and a range of inexpensive portrait photographic techniques. According to the *New York Tribune*, the portable photographic business of three brothers from Pennsylvania made 160 portraits in one day in 1862 at Fredericksburg for $1 each (with a 95-cent profit per photograph). The photograph of choice in the field was the wallet-sized tintype (actually a thin sheet of iron) because it was quick, cheap, lightweight, and durable, if not of great quality.

Commercial photographers dominated the production of documentary Civil War photographs. Only Andrew Russell (1830–1902) was in the employ of the U.S. government. All others, including E. and H. T. Anthony, Mathew Brady, and Alexander Gardner, had to depend on a commercial market for sales. E. and H. T. Anthony issued at least 1000 photographs per day—some celebrity portraits, some troop photographs, camp studies, and a few battle scenes. The photographs ranged from stereographs to large-scale photographs. Almost 1400 photographers supplied houses such as Anthony with photographs, including the most famous Civil War photographer, Mathew Brady. Mathew Brady (1823–96) opened a photographic studio in New York in 1844 as a daguerreotype photographer. He made portraits for Marmaduke Sampson's *Rationale of Crime* and for Francis D'Avignon's *The Gallery of Illustrious Americans* (1850). By 1861 Brady claimed to have collected 10,000 celebrity photographs. His photographs of Abraham Lincoln were among Lincoln's favorites. During the war, Brady amassed a huge collection of photographs but took few himself. Alexander Gardner (1831–82) started in photography as Brady's studio manager in Washington, D.C., but later established his own studio, along with Timothy O'Sullivan (1840–82), another erstwhile Brady employee. They took some of the most memorable (and best-selling) photographs of the aftermaths of the battles of Antietam and Gettysburg. *Gardner's Photographic Sketchbook of the Civil War* (1865–66) sold moderately well, although his photographs were ultimately destroyed. Brady finally sold his war collection to Congress, as did E. and H. T. Anthony and Company.

In the second half of the nineteenth century, the United States and Canada used military engineers and photographers to survey their territory. Surveys of the shared border between Canada and the United States by U.S. (1857) and Canadian (1861) survey teams included photographers. The official *Pacific Railroad Reports* of a survey to map the best routes for the transcontinental railroad was liberally documented with photographs, but Gardner, the eastern team's chief photographer, got considerably more traction from his own commercially published smaller and more exciting version: *Across the Continent on the Kansas Pacific Railway* (1869). Carleton E. Watkins (1829–1916) photographed the "commercial sublime" of the Mariposa Estate close to Yosemite Valley in 1859 on express orders to entice foreign investors to explore the estate's mining potential, while he, O'Sullivan, and Eadweard Muybridge (1830–1904) portrayed Yosemite of the 1860s as a tourist paradise. William Henry Jackson's (1843–1942) photographs of the Yellowstone area were distributed in Washington, D.C., and contributed to its eventual designation as a national park.

In the nineteenth century the British and American tradition of writing, illustrating, publishing, and consuming all kinds of travel and tourist books created a market ripe for exploitation by the burgeoning photographic trade. A generation of fearless photographers traveled worldwide, taking a wide range of photographs to sell either singly or bound in books. It was not until the 1960s, however, when advancements in color print photography made inexpensive, high-quality, color-photographically illustrated books possible, that the "coffee-table book" came into its own and the true "armchair" tourist was born.

In the 1880s three major technological innovations expanded access to and the market for photography: the development of dry plate negatives, the development of celluloid and paper film, and the invention of the halftone reproductive process. Dry plates could be manufactured in advance and stored for use; celluloid film could be rolled in the back of a camera, obviating the need for fragile glass plates and paving the way for handheld cameras; and the halftone process opened the door to mass-produced photographically illustrated books and magazines. Moreover, the light sensitivity of film had increased to 1/5000 of 1 second with a full range of color by 1900.

In 1888 George Eastman (1879–1973) transformed photography by placing the camera directly in the hands of the middle class. The first Kodak cameras were introduced with a simple fixed-focus lens and a roll of film containing 100 exposures. Once the film was shot, the camera was returned to Rochester by mail for film processing and reloading. The Brownie camera was an even cheaper camera (marketed to children) introduced in 1900, and the Kodak Girl camera (marketed to women) appeared in 1901. The snapshot established a new informality in photography, and photo albums were marketed especially for their collection and exchange. Around 1900, custom-made photographs mounted on postcards, just like commercial picture postcards, became freely and inexpensively available. They could be pasted into photo albums or mailed to family and friends. The picture postcard craze between 1900 and 1910 rivaled that of the stereograph. The Detroit Publishing Company produced about 7 million cards per year around 1900, while the U.S. Post Office claimed that about 667 million cards were mailed in 1908 alone.

The 1892 World's Columbian Exposition in Chicago was photographed extensively as an exemplar of U.S. industrial, economic, and cultural ascendancy. Its nighttime lighting by electricity, the amazing engineering of the first Ferris wheel, the industrial, ethnographic, and artistic exhibitions, and the Midway itself, a mixture of living ethnography and gleaming white U.S. architecture, were all photographed for dozens of souvenir books and pamphlets. In California, and later in Philadelphia, Muybridge created 100,000 photographs of human and animal locomotion using cameras tripped by wire. The result was eleven volumes of quasi-scientific photographs entitled *Animal Locomotion* (1887). Muybridge experimented with zoetropes, praxinoscopes, and phenakistoscopes. He eventually invented the "zoopraxiscope" (1879), a gadget that combined the zoetrope's ability to mimic movement with the magic lantern's ability to project an image. Thomas Edison's (1847–1931) kinetoscope (1894), also called a peep show, simply added a length of flexible film to Muybridge's device to signal the beginnings of motion pictures. The x-ray, discovered in 1895, was initially exploited for its popular appeal. It was usually set up in amusement parks and department stores, enticing audiences with its magical but slightly sinister, slightly erotic ability to see through flesh. One department store even advertised x-ray-proof underwear.

At the same time, amateur camera clubs and photographic magazines formed all over the United States. A few were dominated by photographers with aspirations to fine art, such as the Camera Club of New York, but most, like Clarence White's (1871–1925) original Camera Club of Newark (Ohio), held their local meetings and shows with little regard for New York's "fuzzygraphic" styles. And even "art" photographers had to take commercial work to pay the bills. Edward Steichen (1879–1973), for example, was Condé Nast's chief advertising photographer after 1923, established the Department of Aerial Photography in World War I, and served as a naval photographer in World War II.

Twentieth Century

By 1900 improvements in halftone processes made it possible to publish large numbers of photographic documents. In 1901 Eugene S. Talbot published *Degeneracy: Its Causes, Signs, and Results*, which was liberally illustrated with photographs, and around 1900 both the mug shot and the fingerprint came into use. Between 1907 and 1930 Edward S. Curtis (1868–1952) published twenty volumes of *The North American Indian* containing 1,500 photogravures. Jacob Riis (1849–1914) published *How the Other Half Lives*, a book on immigrant life in New York illustrated with his photographs. He also published the same photographs variously in newspapers and magazines and lectured from them as magic lantern slides. Lewis Hine's (1874–1940) photographs on behalf of the National Child Labor Committee helped enact labor laws that have stood for almost a century. The Spanish-American War was described as the first "living-room" war because of the widespread photographic coverage.

By the late 1920s photo-transmission by wire was nationally available but expensive. Prices were cut dramatically in 1935, however, when the Associated Press established its Wire-Photo Division. Photomechanical illustration became so commonplace that every mass-circulation newspaper could afford to be photographically illustrated and hire its own photojournalists. At the same time, *Life* magazine developed the narrative "photo-essay." Margaret Bourke-White's (1904–71) photo-essay, a series of photographs documenting the Fort Peck Dam in Montana, was commissioned for the first issue of *Life* in 1936. Bourke-White, W. Eugene Smith, and others contributed numerous photo-essays (both text and photographs) for *Life* over several years, including reports during World War II. Many of the latter fell afoul of censors; only images of valor or victory such as Joe Rosenthal's (1911–2006) "Marines Raising the Flag at Iwo Jima" made it past them.

The New Deal's federal funding and distribution of hundreds of thousands of photographs created a generation of documentary photographers in America. The primary New Deal program was the 1937 Farm Security Administration's "Historic Section—Photographic" (FSA) headed by Roy Stryker. Stryker controlled shooting locations, images for distribution, and distribution outlets. He placed more than 1,400 photographs per month in outlets that ran the gamut from *Time* magazine to *Junior Scholastic*. None of the photographs were copyrighted; consequently, they are still available from the Library of Congress. FSA photographers included Walker Evans (1903–75), James Agee (1909–55), Arthur Rothstein (1915–85), Gordon Parks (1912–2006), and Dorothea Lange (1895–1965), whose "Migrant Mother" (1936) is one of the most widely reproduced Depression-era photographs.

Postwar Period

In 1955 Edward Steichen organized the *Family of Man* exhibition for the Museum of Modern Art, New York, to counter a growing public malaise engendered by images of the devastation wrought by nuclear bombs, David Douglas Duncan's despairing photographs of American troops in Korea, the vitriol of the McCarthy hearings, and the descending chill of the Cold War. Steichen's exhibition took 500 photographs by photographers from sixty-eight countries and robbed them of their original titles, content, and cultural contexts; it rephotographed them, blew them all up to a standard poster size, homogenized them for color, tone, and form, and reorganized them around Steichen's feel-good themes of love, motherhood, or work. The concluding images of a mushroom cloud, the United Nations General Assembly, or playing children tell a clear story. The public response to the show was overwhelmingly positive, and despite its clearly western (even U.S.) narrative, the exhibition traveled to thirty-eight countries—including Japan and Russia—between 1955 and 1962, drawing 9 million visitors. The book from the exhibition was used in school classrooms across the United States, staying in print for decades.

The Polaroid camera, which took instant monochrome photographs, was developed in 1947. Kodachrome color film was introduced in the 1960s, and by 1970 Polaroid introduced the color Polaroid camera. After the commercially produced video camera came on the market in 1974, the digital camera—the next major innovation in photography—was introduced in the 1990s.

Life magazine folded in 1972, a victim of color photography and television. *Life*'s last years were marked by images of the civil rights movement and the Vietnam War, most notably the June 27, 1969, issue presented in a yearbook form "The Faces of the American Dead in Vietnam." Photographs that became part of the common visual currency of the time included the following: Eddie Adams's "General Loan Executing a Vietcong Suspect, February 1, 1968," John Paul Filo's image of a young woman kneeling over the body of a Kent State student shot by the Ohio National Guard, "Nick" Ut's "Children Fleeing a Napalm Strike," and Ron Haeberle and Peter Brandt's untitled photograph, first published in the Cleveland *Plain Dealer* but soon used in a dramatic antiwar poster accompanied by the text "Q. And babies? A. And babies."

Advertising photography became very slick and effective in the 1960s, making full use of the new color technologies as they appeared. Some photographers, who considered themselves more artists than advertisers, however, avoided color. This group included a few fashion photographers who would later move into "art photography" full-time, including Diane Arbus (1960s) and Richard Avedon (1970s and 1980s). Andy Warhol's *Interview* magazine became full color in the 1980s. Designer Calvin Klein, photographer Davide Sorrenti, and models Kate Moss and Jamie King made black-and-white Heroin Chic photography popular until Sorrenti's drug-related death in 1997. In the twenty-first century Sienna Miller and Kate Moss have made Boho-Chic more fashionable. In the 1990s Annie Leibovitz redefined celebrity photography with fully saturated color images in *Vanity Fair* and in several books. Around 1996 Anne Geddes produced a line of photographs of newborn babies dressed as flowers, insects, and baby animals. The images have reached cult status on two continents. Geddes's Website advertises Geddes baby products, designer checks, office equipment, tote bags, watches, wallpaper, and even 17″ amazingly lifelike newborn baby dolls dressed like the babies in her photographs.

Current popular forms of photography include class photographs taken in schools, graduation and prom photographs taken by "professional" photographers, and wedding photographs presented in albums. Some photographic studios offer special deals for holiday pictures, especially for children, and offer a variety of backdrops, not unlike their nineteenth-century counterparts. These photographs, which are usually very expensive but considered mandatory on certain occasions, follow strictly determined social norms governing pose, dress, format, and number. They come in a variety of sizes from the original full-plate (8 × 10″) size to the original card (wallet) size. They are usually admired if they are stiff and formal in opposition to the snapshot aesthetic, which has ironically now come to signify amateurism among popular audiences.

Since 2000, photochemical photography has moved almost exclusively into the art world. Social documentary photography is considered increasingly suspect. Editors, not photographers, choose images for both print and television today. New social documentary photographers constantly challenge the myth of the neutral image as they eschew victim-based photography. This trend, while important, is also paradoxical at a time when as a society we are saturated with standardized photographs for passports, driver's licenses, medical tests, mug shots, and fingerprints and when some of the most popular prime-time television shows are based on crime scene photography.

The debate over the capacity for digital photography to deceive, ironically, did not originate in the art world but from the first magnificent public use of digital manipulation in the movie *Star Wars* (1977). The ability for photographs to trick the eye is embedded in photography's very origins. No one really believed early demonic stereographs or P. T. Barnum's humbugs or spirit photographs, and no one today really believes the covers of grocery store tabloids. The pleasure is in the humbug. Digital photography has allowed an old parlor game to resurface with a new magic. We enjoy asking ourselves, how do they do that? It is the skillful manipulation of the image that makes the visual humbug so much more delectable because we can't see the seam. Digital photography, the Internet, and ready access to computers allow us to customize our news, our global visual information, or our local visual information. We can take photographs, discard those we dislike on the spot, print our own, share those we want to share by email, fix them, and make ourselves prettier, thinner, and younger, and while we are at it we can even design our children by digitally combining our features with those of another person. And yet, we still look at a photograph with the knowledge that the subject looks out at us with the wistful expectation of immortality.

Jewelry

When Charles Lewis Tiffany (1812–1902) opened his shop for business in 1837, selling stationery and fancy goods on a nonnegotiable price basis, he signaled the beginning of retailing as we know it today, making headlines in the newspapers and bringing in sales of $4.98 on the first day of business. Tiffany branded his store the same year by sending his customers home with goods wrapped up in his now signature Tiffany-blue box. In 1853, when the business changed its name to Tiffany and Company, he also marked every piece of silver with "T. and Co." So, it is not surprising that in 1878, when Tiffany decided to enter the jewelry business in earnest, he publicized it by buying one of the world's largest yellow diamonds, now called the Tiffany Diamond, which can still be seen in Tiffany's 5th Avenue store, and hired the famous gemologist Frederick Kunz (the first hired by a retailer) to supervise cutting the stone.

Tiffany and Company sets the standard for jewelry marketing worldwide. At Tiffany's, the very best has always been available and rather gloriously evident. Audrey Hepburn, for instance, was allowed to wear the Tiffany Diamond briefly to advertise the movie *Breakfast at Tiffany's* (1961). In 1886 Tiffany introduced the "Tiffany Setting," a six-pronged solitaire diamond cut that raises the diamond from the ring band to maximize its refractive qualities and make it sparkle. In 1887 he acquired some of the French crown jewels, gaining him the moniker "the King of Diamonds." On the other hand, Tiffany knew that small sales added up. Thus, in 1902, the "Tiffany Art Jewelry" department was established to create well-designed but not necessarily expensive jewelry. Since then, Tiffany's success is directly attributable to its philosophy that no customer is too rich or too poor. The simplest silver ring is designed, produced, and fitted with the same care as the most expensive diamond ring. The designers have also kept the company alive: Jean Schlumberger (1907–87) joined the company in 1956, Elsa Peretti (b. 1940) in 1974, Paloma Picasso (b. 1949) in 1980, and Frank Gehry (b. 1929) in 2006. Tiffany designs are imitated around the world.

Costume jewelry has a short half-life, but two designers stand out. Hattie Carnegie (1889–1956) designed lavish costume jewelry for well-known clients such as Joan Crawford and the Duchess of Windsor that is still highly sought after. Kenneth Jay Lane (b. 1930) created flashy "baubles" for the rich and famous of the 1970s, including Jackie Onassis, Elizabeth Taylor, Diana Vreeland, and Audrey Hepburn. He may be most famous for a three-strand string of fake pearls that Barbara Bush wore to George Bush's inaugural ball. His jewelry was so popular that when

Saks Fifth Avenue carried it, they sold the entire inventory in one day. Vintage pieces sell at Christie's and Sotheby's; new pieces sell on QVC. He wrote a tell-all book, *Faking It*, in 1996.

Rhinestone or diamanté jewelry was a favorite of Elvis Presley, Liberace, and country music singers in the 1950s, because rhinestones could emulate very large diamonds at a fraction of the cost. The rhinestone-studded suit, a variant of the matador costume, was first created by Nudie Cohn (1902–84) in the 1940s (hence "Nudie Suit"). The rhinestone (named after the river Rhine) is simply crystal with lead oxide added to improve the sparkle, cut on a machine invented by Daniel Swarovski in 1892.

Queen Victoria started a fashion for charm bracelets to which small lockets, glass beads, and tokens were attached. The fashion was revived in the 1940s by returning soldiers who attached souvenir trinkets to chain bracelets. By the 1950s the charm bracelet was a necessary accessory for girls, who collected charms for every milestone in life. They disappeared in the 1960s but have enjoyed a revival since the late 1990s. In 2001 a new Italian charm bracelet, in which charms snapped onto a flat band, was briefly popular, while any number of charm bracelets in gold, silver, or platinum, with or without diamonds, can still be found in the Tiffany and Company catalog.

Ceramics

Potters were among the first skilled craftspeople in the American colonies. The clay found in New Jersey, the Carolinas, and Ohio was fine enough to produce thin-bodied creamware (or queensware). The clay in Pennsylvania could be cast to produce basic yellowware kitchen utensils. Redware could be produced in small shops almost anywhere, although it ceased to be used widely as tableware in the 1860s because of its porousness. In the nineteenth century stoneware manufacture spread throughout the Midwest along the canal and railway systems as well as throughout the South. Around 1900, factory-produced stoneware in New Jersey and Ohio tended to be very cheaply made, and by the 1920s it was used only for whiskey jugs. Rockingham, a glazed yellowware produced in Vermont, Ohio, and Maryland, was cast in molds in Gothic and rococo revival styles with elaborate decorations. It was popularly known as Bennington ware, after its Vermont manufacturing location. White earthenware was first produced around 1865 in Trenton, Syracuse, Brooklyn, and East Liverpool (Ohio). Known as "hotel" china, it is still produced today. In 1863 Ott and Brewer of Trenton began manufacturing American Belleek (porcelain) and Parian sculptures. Walter Scott Lenox, who trained at Ott and Brewer, later established his own company in Trenton, which eventually became Lenox Incorporated (1906), the china of choice for the White House. Although it was not made in America, blue and white Canton ware, sometimes called willowware or "ballast ware," has always been highly prized in the United States. It is the china that Grant Wood has the three ladies drink from in his painting of the DAR. It was still popular in the 1960s in very inexpensive versions.

In 1895 the Heisey Glass factory was established in Newark, Ohio. It produced green-, rose-, and gold-colored glass in molded forms until 1957. Widely known as "Depression" glass, it was a staple tableware for a time, fell out of fashion, and is now enjoying a revival, thanks mostly to the fact that Martha Stewart collects it. In 1871 the Homer Laughlin China Company was founded in Liverpool, Ohio. In 1907 it moved to Newell, West Virginia. Between 1936 and 1973 Frederick Hurton Rhead's Fiestaware, an art deco line originally in bright red, yellow, and green colors, was so successful that the company reintroduced it in 1986. The company is the nation's largest domestic ware producer, capable of 30,000 pieces per day.

Between 1880 and 1920, in response to mass-produced pottery, several small "art potteries" were established including the Rockwood Pottery (Cincinnati), the Rhead Pottery

(Santa Barbara), the Ohr Pottery (Biloxi), and the Binns Pottery (Alfred). The most famous pottery belonged to Louis Comfort Tiffany (1848–1933), eldest son of the founder of the Tiffany and Company silver and jewelry store, who designed a series of Favrile (handcrafted) stained glass lamps and vases in the 1880s. The bold colors, opalescent sheens, and textured surfaces created a new aesthetic in decorative glass design. Each lamp and vase was different, individually numbered, and thus attractive to clients at the Tiffany store. Their profusion of detail and brilliant color was unfashionable by the 1920s, but Tiffany glass objects are now highly prized. In 1998 two lamps sold for $2 million each. Since the establishment of Alfred College (1948), the first college in the United States devoted exclusively to the study of ceramics, the U.S. pottery world has divided into art potters and useful-object potters. In 1950 the English potter Bernard Leach (1887–1979) visited the United States with *A Potter's Book* (1940). He stirred the debate by advocating making useful objects that were also beautiful. Leach's aesthetic pervades the best American pottery today, for example, in the work of Clary Illian (b. 1940) (*A Potter's Workbook*, 1999).

CANADA

Canadian Popular Painting

In 1841 Cornelius Krieghoff (1815–72) painted a series of scenes depicting the course of the St. Lawrence River. Peter Rindisbacher documented the lives of local "Indians" around Fort Garry. Paul Kane (1810–71), inspired by George Catlin's "Indian Gallery," decided that he could do the same for Canada and created 100 canvases based on an 1846–48 trip with fur traders from Ontario to Fort Vancouver. Kane's published account inspired Frederick Verner (1836–1928) to make similar illustrations in 1872.

William Notman (1826–91), a photographer in Montreal in the 1860s, opened his studio to artists also interested in publicizing the landscape. John Fraser (1838–98) and Henry Sandham (1842–1910) joined him, later opening a second Notman studio in Saint John with Allan Edson (1846–88) and Otto Jacobi (1812–1901). Notman artists and photographers were intimately connected with railway expansion. Painters had traveled from Montreal by

NATIVE AMERICAN CERAMICS: ART VS. TOURISM

The Santa Fe Railway was so successful in attracting tourists to the Southwest in the 1920s that Fred Harvey built the La Fonda Hotel in Santa Fe at the end of the line and established his famous "Indian Detour." Harvey also sold "Indian objects" from his custom-built "Indian Building" in Albuquerque and from the "Hopi House" at the Grand Canyon. He sold only the products of Native American artists and craftspeople but made sure that the objects met the expectations of tourists. He sold the pottery of Nampeyo (1860–1942), who was actually a very shrewd Hopi businesswoman at the "Hopi House." Her work was especially prized. She built a family empire by participating in Harvey's tourist myth to generate sales, although she also made elegant works of art that were not "traditional." Other Southwest potters include Maria and Julian Martinez, who made San Ildefonso black-on-black pottery for tourists. Maria signed her work after 1925 and considered herself an independent artist, but market forces demanded that she return to more traditional forms and images to meet tourist expectations. Louisa Keyser, known as Dat So La Lee (d. 1925), was best known for her Washoe baskets. She acquiesced to adopting her "Indian" name while giving displays of basketmaking at the St. Louis Exposition (1919). The tension between meeting market expectations and the desire to experiment with the new continues today.

train to sketch throughout the Matapedia Valley, but in the 1870s they took the transcontinental Canadian Pacific across the prairies and the Rockies. The president of the railway, an avid art collector, provided free passes to artists in exchange for promotional pictures. Fraser and Notman's artists dominated many art exhibitions until 1900. In 1880 the governor-general founded the Royal Canadian Academy of Arts. Lucius O'Brien, its first president, traveled west as the railway reached the Pacific to paint the mountains and Vancouver area.

Canadian painting changed completely in 1920 with the establishment in Toronto of the Group of Seven: Tom Thomson (1877–1917), Frank Carmichael (1890–1945), Lawren Harris (1885–1970), A. Y. Jackson (1882–1974), Franz Johnston (1888–1949), Arthur Lismer (1885–1969), J. E. H. MacDonald (1873–1932), and F. H. Varley (1881–1969). Their style was strongly colored and Postimpressionist; although their paintings aroused criticism, they also stirred patriotic pride and dominated the high and popular art market for 30 years. Abstraction really only emerged in Canada in the 1950s. In 1953 Kenneth Lochhead (b. 1926) established the Regina Workshop and then in 1955 the Emma Lake Artists Workshops, to which he invited Clement Greenberg in 1962. Greenberg's several tours of the prairies and his article "The Art of Prairie Canada" in *Canadian Art* did much to popularize Canadian abstract art.

Landscape painting remains the predominant Canadian popular art genre. Calgary developed a lively art scene because of the Alberta College of Art, its summer school, its proximity to Banff's glorious mountain scenery and ski resorts, the Calgary rodeo, and a healthy winter and summer tourist trade. Likewise in Edmonton, a number of artists have produced popular landscapes of parkland subjects in a photo-realist style.

In Saskatoon, partly because of the modernist tradition at Emma Lake, the number of landscape painters currently selling in local galleries rivals that in Calgary. Prominent among these artists are Ernest Lindner (1897–1988), who paints northern forest interiors and rotting stumps, and Dorothy Knowles (b. 1927), one of the best-known Canadian landscape painters since the 1960s.

Canadian art has expanded rapidly since 1945, in both numbers of artists, centers of activity, and public interest. The Canada Council, the provincial arts councils, and the growth of college and university art departments have all been instrumental in this development. John Lyman (1886–1967), Alfred Pellan (1906–88), and Paul-Émile Borduas (1905–60) established Montreal as a center for radical art in the 1940s, while in Toronto art was and remains more pluralistic. Artists of the 1940s, such as the Painters Eleven (abstract), the Group of Seven (realist), and the Canadian Group of Painters (realist), all produced reasonably accessible art in Toronto. In 1952 and 1953 Simpson's department store even sold the work of several major Canadian painters in a department listed as "Abstracts at Home."

Alex Colville (b. 1920) established a center for realist painting in Atlantic Canada at Mount Allison, while the Nova Scotia College of Art and Design fed the local taste for Atlantic landscapes. In western Canada, the city of Vancouver has the longest tradition in popular art making. Landscape paintings and portraits of boats and ships have provided a steady trade for local artists since the 1940s. Another important category of popular painting in Canada is First Nations art. Based on traditional motifs and images, some of the art seeks to reclaim the narratives of dispossessed cultures and peoples, whereas some engages in the western narrative to sell tourist images.

Canadian Popular Printmaking

A print illustrating Jacques Cartier's (1535) journey to what is now Montreal, published by Giovanni Ramusio in Venice (1556), is probably the first printed image of Canada. The next significant prints were probably Father Louis Hennepin's (1698) first European visual record of Niagara Falls. Neither the presses nor a market existed for widespread printing in Canada until the British spread into the Maritimes and Upper Canada after 1760. After that time, there was a steady migration of artists, engravers, printers, publishers, and readers. Prints by J. W. DesBarres (1770s–80s) and Joseph Bouchette (1830) are typical. The illustrated published reports of voyages or expeditions helped secure funding for future trips. John Webber (1751–93) illustrated James Cook's voyage, while George Back (1796–1878) and Robert Hood's (ca. 1797–1821) watercolors of the boreal latitudes were reproduced in Sir John Franklin's 1823 and 1828 narratives. Back's work was further published (engraved by Edward Finden) in his own *Narrative of the Arctic Land Expedition* (1836). Ironically, the public taste for exploration books only increased after John Franklin's expedition disappeared in 1845, and held through the exploration of the North Pole, the Northwest Passage, and the Antarctic, well into the 1930s. A vast body of popular literature by private surveyors, entrepreneurs, fur traders, naturalists, settlers, and tourists complemented exploration narratives. These were illustrated with engravings, wood engravings, and lithographs. Examples include George Heriot's *Travels through the Canadas* (1807), Coke Smyth's *Sketches in the Canadas* (1842), and N. P. Willis's *Canadian Scenery from Drawings by W. H. Bartlett* (1842).

In 1792 Samuel (d. 1837) and John (1776–1848) Neilson made the first attempt at professional printing in Canada. They printed views of Quebec and Montmorency Falls, as well as a portrait, in their *Quebec Magazine*. Quebec remained Canada's printing center until Montreal's ascendancy in the 1850s and Toronto's in the 1870s. Quebec print publishers included David Smillie and Sons, Adolphus Bourne, and Thomas Cary and Sons, which published James P. Cockburn's *Quebec and Its Environs* (1831). In Montreal, Bosworth Newton published *Hochelaga Depicta* (1839), illustrated by James D. Duncan (1806–81), and in Toronto, Frederick C. Lowe illustrated the *British American Cultivator* (1842).

Lithography and chromolithography were slow to come to Canada. Paul Kane had to publish *Wanderings of an Artist* (1859) in London for want of a Canadian chromolithographer. Catherine Parr Traill's *Canadian Wild Flowers* (1868) was not published in true chromolithographic form until 1885. Yet, when the Toronto Lithographing Company did get going in the 1890s, it was one of North America's largest and most advanced firms, employing some of the best-known artist-illustrators, among them W. D. Blatchly, William Bengough (1851–1923), J. D. Kelly, C. W. Jeffries (1869–1951), and J. E. H. MacDonald. Lithographic houses were established in Hamilton, Montreal, and Ottawa.

John Allanson (1813–53) established wood engraving in Toronto in 1849. He launched the *Anglo-American Magazine* and *Canadian Journal* in 1852, both illustrated with views of Hamilton, Kingston, and Toronto. In the 1880s, under the new name of Brigden's Limited, Allanson's son introduced several photomechanical processes. Both the Toronto and Winnipeg branches attracted well-known artists such as Charles Comfort (1900–1994), H. E. Bergman, and Fritz Brandtner (1896–1969). In Montreal, William A. Leggo (1830–1915) invented a halftone process (Leggotype) in 1869 that was used by the *Canadian Illustrated News* until 1871, when it returned to line engravings for technical reasons. The largest nineteenth-century illustrated publication was *Picturesque Canada*. It was published and sold in serial form between 1882 and 1884, with a text by George Monro Grant. The project was widely admired by the public but caused much ill will among artists, because, although the Canadian illustrators included L. R. O'Brien, Henry Sandham, John A. Fraser, O. R. Jacobi, the Marquess of Lorne, William Raphael, F. M. Bell-Smith, and Robert Harris, they were greatly outnumbered by U.S. artists.

The serial economic depressions of the 1870s and 1880s led a number of Canadian artists to migrate. While expatriates distinguished themselves in England and the United

States, the Toronto Art Students' League (established 1886) fostered popular painting by promoting annual souvenir calendars of Canadian themes between 1893 and 1904 with contributions from C. W. Jeffries, C. M. Manly, Robert Holmes, F. H. Brigden, A. H. Howard, D. F. Thomson, J. D. Kelly, T. G. Greene, A. A. Martin, Norman Price, and J. E. H. MacDonald.

During World War I, Canadian artists contributed to propaganda campaigns organized by both the government and industry. Several contributed images for war posters, including Arthur Keillor. After 1945 a brief resurgence in magazine illustrations provided work for a few Canadian artists such as Franklin Arbuckle (1909–2001), William Winter (1909–96), J. S. Hallam (1898–1953), Jack Bush (1909–77), Oscar Cahén (1916–56), and Harold Town (1924–90). The popular print trade in Canada, however, has become increasingly restricted to children's books in the last 30 years. Barbara Reid (b. 1957), Michael Martchenko (b. 1942), and Suzanne Dansereau are known internationally. Ken Steacy writes and illustrates the *Star Wars* books. Todd MacFarlane self-published the first issues of *Spawn* (which sold over 1 million copies). He now owns MacFarlane Toys, North America's largest action figure manufacturer. John Kricfalusi created *Ren and Stimpy* for the Nickelodeon channel; Marv Newland and Danny Antonucci created the *Grunt Brothers*.

Canadian Popular Sculpture

The earliest popular sculptures in Canada were ship figureheads. These include Denis Mallet's (d. 1704) carving of a figurehead of a lion (1700), a Saint Michael for the *Joybert* (1704), commissioned by the naval captain Louis Prat, and Noël Levasseur's (1680–1740) carved decorations for the *Raudot* (1715), Prat's new ship. The establishment of a French royal shipyard in Canada guaranteed a healthy business in the ship decoration business for the Levasseur family of carvers. The frigate *Castor* includes a beaver figurehead and shield with the arms of France, and the supply ship *Caribou* has a beaver bas-relief sculpture.

After the change in administration in 1760, the Canadian economic situation stabilized, populations grew steady, and church carving supplemented ship carving. The Baillairgé family became sculptors to the king's shipyards in Kingston. Plans for the decoration of two military ships, the *Royal Edward* and the *Earl of Moira*, still exist. The family also carved the mace for Canada's lower assembly and signs for several Quebec merchants. Canadian shipyards worked at full capacity to restock England's merchant navy, which suffered heavy losses during the Napoleonic Wars. Between 1762 and 1879, 2,112 ships were built in Quebec City. Of those, 1,651 had carved figureheads. Other Canadian shipyards were established in Yarmouth, Lunenburg, and Halifax; there were various shipyards along the Saint John Valley, on the Miramichi, in Bath, and in Niagara-on-the-Lake.

It is estimated that 10,000 figureheads were carved in Canada during the nineteenth century and that almost every Canadian sculptor carved at least one. The most famous carvers included Louis-Xavier Leprohon, Louis-Thomas Berlinguet, André Giroux, and Jean-Baptiste Côté. Figureheads on the bow of a ship were usually carved in honor of historical figures, local figures, or family members of the shipowner. There might also be generalized female figures, a variety of animals (including bear, caribou, and beaver), or architectural features. The stern of a ship might be decorated with carvings, but these were usually coats of arms or merely decorative. Carvers who specialized in ship ornamentation exclusively did not sign their work. They also made hand-decorated furniture, particularly chair backs, and were commissioned to make shop signs, navigational instruments, and advertising objects for tobacconists and tavern keepers. By the mid-nineteenth century, steam engines and metal-plated ships replaced the wooden sailing ship, and the advent of small-scale, multiple-cast plaster statuary in the second half of the nineteenth century all but eliminated the traditional wood-sculptor's market. As mass production took hold, the wood-carver became obsolete. Even the best, such as Jean-Baptiste Côté, could not survive.

One genre of popular sculpture that did persist into the twentieth century was ephemeral sculpture. This was very popular in the nineteenth century in the form of triumphal arches and allegorical chariots for parades as well as for theatrical sets. Some major artists include Louis Dulongpré (1754–1853), Joseph Légaré (1795–1855), and Alfred Pellan. Louis Jobin (1845–1928) worked on allegorical floats for the St-Jean-Baptiste parade (1880), including the agriculture float that is preserved in the Musée du Québec. Jobin was also one of the original ice carvers at the early Quebec winter carnivals. His death in 1928 is widely regarded as the end of traditional wood carving. A tourist form of wood carving thrives today, particularly in the town of St-Jean-Port-Joli, although the very modest recent carvings have little in common with the grand wooden sculptures that once decorated ships and churches.

In the 1980s many cities and provinces in Canada instituted public art programs and continue to develop them today. In many jurisdictions, adopted legislation requires that 1 percent of the cost of any public project be allocated for art. The purpose is to place art in the everyday environment. Many provincial governments also administer public art funds raised from private developers. Public art is then commissioned for schools, hospitals, and other public places. Cities that encourage private developers to contribute to public art include Halifax, Vancouver, Toronto, Calgary, and Edmonton.

Canadian Popular Photography

The earliest recorded Canadian photographer was daguerreotypist Joly de Lotbinière, who photographed the Egyptian pyramids in 1841–42, although two Americans, Halsey and Sadd, are recorded as having studios in Montreal and Quebec in 1840, as is a Mrs. Fletcher who owned one in Montreal in 1841. The first successful Canadian photographer was Thomas Coffin Doane (1814–96) in Montreal around 1843. He photographed Newfoundland and exhibited these photographs with portraits of celebrities (such as Lord Elgin) at the Paris Exhibition of 1855. Eli J. Palmer (Toronto) produced daguerreotypes and cards from 1847 to 1870.

The 1851 there were eleven daguerreotypists active in Canada. By 1865 there were 360 photographers. The most famous was William Notman, who had photographic and painting studios in Halifax, Saint John, Montreal, Ottawa, and Toronto and worked in the United States. He photographed the Victoria Bridge in Montreal and the Prince of Wales's inauguration of it (1860). He was appointed photographer to the queen. By the 1870s Notman's staff produced 14,000 photographs annually, mostly views of western landscapes. One of his specialties was composite printing, the most famous of which is the *Skating Carnival* (1869), created from 300 different photographs. In Quebec City, Ellison and Company made distinctive portraits, known for their dramatic simplicity and power, and celebrity cards.

In 1861 Samuel McLaughlin (1826–1914) was named official government photographer and commissioned to photograph the construction of the Parliament Buildings. He made twenty-four prints on mammoth glass plates (27 × 36 inches). Alexander Henderson

(1831–1913) published a series of photograph albums including *Canadian Views and Studies, Photographed from Nature* in the 1860s. Photographers accompanied several government surveys and private explorations in efforts to protect the border from U.S. expansion, to exploit trade and commerce, and to search for gold. H. L. Hime (1833–1903) accompanied an 1858 government survey expedition to Red River country for settlement and exploration. His photographs of prairie landscapes were published in the *London Illustrated News*. In 1871 Notman photographer Benjamin Baltzly accompanied a Geological Survey to determine a transcontinental railway route. In 1864 Charles Gentile photographed the Leech River gold rush. Frederick Dally (1838–1914) photographed the Cariboo goldfields and the Barkerville boomtown. George Robinson Fardon made a panoramic set of views of Victoria that he exhibited at the London International Exhibition in 1862.

Spirit photography thrived in Canada. The Fox Sisters, two young Belleville girls of the 1830s, were the first well-known "spirit-rappers" (two knocks for yes, one for no). The most famous medium of the 1920s, Margery the Medium (Mina Stinson Crandon), was from Princeton, Ontario. More than three hundred spirit photographs by Winnipeg's Dr. T. Glendenning Hamilton (1837–1935), documenting séances between 1918 and 1934, still exist.

By the late 1870s the innovation of dry-plate technology allowed photographers to accompany a British expedition through blinding snowstorms to the North Pole. Two members, Thomas Mitchell and George White, made more than 100 photographs, at least one at −45°C. In 1885 Captain James Peters also photographed action during the North-West Rebellion using a camera specially equipped to change plates quickly. After the release of the Kodak camera in 1888, the number of amateur photographers in Canada increased rapidly. A number of camera clubs formed, including the Toronto Amateur Photographic Association (1888) and the Toronto Camera Club (1891).

In 1916 the Canadian War Records Office was established. William Ivor Castle and William Rider-Rider, both of whom later worked for the War Record Office, were the only two major World War I photographers to circulate widely images portraying the brutality of trench warfare. Rider-Rider's photographs of Paschendale are particularly harrowing. The National Film Board (1939) and the Canadian Government Motion Picture Bureau established still-photo libraries in the 1940s, first with government access only but later supplying images to newspapers and magazines across the country. By the 1920s most newspapers had their own staff photographers; photo-essayists followed in the 1930s, including Walter Curtin (b. 1911) and John Vanderpant (1884–1939). After 1959 Kryn Taconis (1918–79), a former member of the Dutch resistance, took photographs of nature in Canada, First Nations, workers, immigrants, and children for the *Star Weekly* and the *Toronto Star*. Other magazines that promoted popular photography in the form of photo-essays included the *Montréal Standard*, the Winnipeg *New World*, the Montreal *Weekend*, and the Toronto *Star Weekly*.

In the late 1960s the National Film Board established a gallery in Ottawa, initiated a broad program of traveling exhibitions, and created a major publishing program to take photography to every corner of Canada. The National Film Board published *Canada: The Year of the Land* (1967), a book of photographs to celebrate the centennial. Roloff Beny (1924–84) also published *To Everything There Is a Season*. Both books drew attention to Canada's natural beauty and inspired innumerable similar coffee-table books. The Canadian Museum of Contemporary Photography was established in 1985 to continue to disseminate Canadian photography. The National Gallery and National Archives of Canada houses the historic photographs.

Canadian Ceramics

European earthenware pottery made from indigenous red firing clays has been produced in Canada since the mid-seventeenth century. It has been made by First Nations much longer. Utility pottery is the most common because it was inexpensive and readily replaceable.

In 1849 stoneware was produced in Canada with clay imported from Amboy, New Jersey. Canadian stoneware was identical to U.S. stoneware. The Enfield pottery was Canada's first true stoneware pottery. It started production in the nineteenth century when a local source of stoneware clay was discovered along the Shubenacadie River. The Medalta Pottery at Medicine Hat (Alberta) was another. Most potteries closed between 1890 and 1910 owing to the mass production of other tableware and the high spoilage rate of local potteries (as much as 50 percent).

In Quebec, pottery was produced between the 1850s and the 1900s. Quebec pottery imitated the forms (bowls, pitchers, and jugs) of imported French earthenware, but not the color. Quebec pottery had a transparent glaze over a brown slip coat. Maritime pottery was based on English and Scottish designs, but the earthenware was produced from the iron-rich clays of Nova Scotia whereas the inner lining was white slip. The most common vessels are crocks and bowls. Upper Canada pottery revealed various influences, especially the Pennsylvania Deutsch. Germanic pottery from Ontario was made in a variety of forms and shapes. Generic North American pottery such as slip-cast tablewares and canning vacuum jars of the 1870s became popular, but individually crafted objects gave way to the machine age in the 1880s.

In 1760 the ceramic objects used most often in Canada came from England, which considered its colonies a natural market for its products at a time when English potters aggressively promoted their wares. By the mid-nineteenth century, although Canadians had access to many markets, they continued to purchase English pottery. William Taylor Copeland, the Staffordshire potter, supplied ceramics to the Hudson Bay Company in the 1830s for distribution throughout the Northwest. Josiah Wedgwood's Queensware was popular with the French Canadian government, merchant households, and farming residences throughout the eighteenth century. In the 1840s Parian porcelain, which enabled manufacturers to simulate small marble sculptures very inexpensively, flooded the Canadian market. Examples include the busts of John A. MacDonald and Edward Hanlan.

Two glass companies, the Canada Glass Works (Quebec, 1845–51) and the Ottawa Glass Works (Como, 1847–57), produced glass that was either free blown or mold blown. A third company, the Foster Brothers Glass Works (St. Jean, 1855–58), produced medicine bottles with Como. Between 1860 and 1880 four companies produced jars and lamp chimneys, including the Canada Glass Works (Hudson, 1864–72) and the Hamilton Glass Company (Hamilton, 1865–96). Finer "flint" glass—the colorless glass for lamps and tableware—was produced at the St. Lawrence Glass Company (Montreal, 1867–73) and the Burlington Glass Company (Hamilton, 1874–98). By the 1880s several smaller flint glass companies started producing a wide range of glass tableware pieces with molded decorations.

Engraving or "cut" glass production started between 1900 and 1930. The four major companies were George Phillips (Montreal, 1904–71), Gowans, Kent and Company (Toronto, 1900–1918), Roden Brothers (Toronto, 1907–54), and Gundy-Clapperton, later Clapperton (Toronto, 1905–72), which employed fifty glass cutters in 1912. Each company established its own brand identity with designs and named patterns.

Canadian Jewelry

Most Canadian jewelry is the work of First Nations craftspeople and is sold through small retail outlets. A few European Canadians have made jewelry, but mostly on a commission basis. There has been no large-scale retail tradition in Canada comparable to Tiffany and Company in the United States.

RESOURCE GUIDE

PRINT SOURCES

Ainslie, Patricia. *Images of the Land: Canadian Block Prints, 1919–1945.* Calgary: Glenbow Museum, 1986.

Allodi, Mary. *Printmaking in Canada.* Toronto: Royal Ontario Museum, 1980.

Baigell, Matthew. *A Concise History of American Painting and Sculpture.* New York: Icon, 1996.

Berlo, Janet Catherine, and Ruth B. Phillips. *Native North American Art.* New York: Oxford University Press, 1998.

Bjelajac, David. *American Art: A Cultural History.* New York: Abrams, 2001.

Brandt, Frederick R. *Designed to Sell: Turn of the Century Posters.* Richmond, VA: Virginia Museum of Fine Arts, 1994.

Brody, J. J. *Beauty from the Earth: Pueblo Indian Pottery.* Philadelphia: University Museum of Archaeology and Anthropology, 1990.

Brown, Milton W. *The Story of the Armory Show.* New York: Abbeville, 1988.

Cheetham, Mark. *Remembering Postmodernism: Trends in Recent Canadian Art.* Toronto: Oxford University Press, 1991.

Colgate, William. *Canadian Art: Its Origins and Development.* Toronto: Ryerson, 1943.

Collard, Elizabeth. *Nineteenth-Century Pottery and Porcelain in Canada.* Montreal: McGill-Queens, 1984.

Corn, Wanda M. *The Great American Thing: Modern Art and National Identity, 1915–1935.* Berkeley: University of California Press, 1999.

Craven, Wayne. *American Art: History and Culture.* Madison, WI: Brown and Benchmark, 1994.

———. *Colonial American Portraiture.* Cambridge: Cambridge University Press, 1986.

———. *Sculpture in America.* Newark: University of Delaware Press, 1984.

Davidson, Abraham A. *Early American Modernist Painting, 1910–1935.* New York: Da Capo, 1994.

Doss, Erika. *Twentieth-Century American Art.* Oxford: Oxford University Press, 2002.

Duncan, Alastair. *Louis Comfort Tiffany.* New York: Abrams, 1992.

Evans, Godfrey. *Souvenirs: From Roman Times to the Present Day.* Edinburgh: National Museum of Scotland, 1999.

Fales, Martha Gandy. *Early American Silver.* New York: Dutton, 1970.

Fane, Diana, ed. *Converging Cultures: Art and Identity in Spanish America.* New York: Abrams, 1996.

———. *Objects of Myth and Memory: American Indian Art at the Brooklyn Museum.* Seattle: University of Washington Press, 1991.

Finch, Christopher. *American Watercolors.* New York: Abbeville, 1986.

Fort, Ilene, ed. *The Figure in American Sculpture: A Question of Modernity.* Los Angeles: Los Angeles County Museum of Art, 1995.

Frelinghuysen, Alice Cooney. *American Porcelain, 1770–1920.* New York: Metropolitan Museum of Art, 1989.

Gerdts, William H. *American Impressionism.* New York: Abbeville, 1984.

Greenhill, Ralph, and Andrew Birrell. *Canadian Photography 1839–1920.* Toronto: Coach House, 1979.

Grier, Katherine C. *Culture and Comfort: People, Parlors, and Upholstery, 1850–1930.* Rochester, NY: Strong Museum, 1988.

Groseclose, Barbara S. *Nineteenth-Century American Art.* Oxford: Oxford University Press, 2000.

Harper, J. Russell. *Painting in Canada. A History.* Toronto: University of Toronto Press, 1977.

Hart, James D. *The Popular Book: A History of American Literary Taste.* New York: Oxford University Press, 1950.

Haskell, Barbara. *The American Century: Art and Culture, vol. 1: 1900–1950.* New York: W. W. Norton, 1999.

Heckscher, Morrison H., and Leslie Greene Bowman. *American Rococo, 1750–1775: Elegance in Ornament.* New York: Metropolitan Museum of Art, 1992.

Hirsch, Robert. *Seizing the Light: A History of Photography.* Boston: McGraw Hill, 2000.

Koltun, Lilly, ed. *Private Realms of Light: Amateur Photography in Canada 1839–1940.* Markham, ON: Fitzhenry and Whiteside, 1984.

Langford, Martha, ed. *Contemporary Canadian Photography from the Collection of the National Film Board.* Edmonton: Hurtig, 1946.

Lee, Ruth Webb. *Early American Pressed Glass.* Pittsford, MA: Author, 1946.

Loring, John. *Louis Comfort Tiffany at Tiffany & Company.* New York: Abrams, 2002.

Marien, Mary Warner. *Photography: A Cultural History.* New York: Abrams, 2002.

Marzio, Peter C. *The Democratic Art: Pictures for a Nineteenth Century America.* Boston: Godine, 1979.

Meet Your Neighbors: New England Portraits, Painters & Society, 1790–1850. Sturbridge, MA: Old Sturbridge Village, 1992.

Mellen, Peter. *Landmarks of Canadian Art.* Toronto: McClelland and Stewart, 1978.

Miles, Ellen G. *The Portrait in Eighteenth-Century America.* Newark: University of Delaware Press, 1993.

Milroy, Elizabeth. *Painters of a New Century: The Eight & American Art.* Milwaukee, WI: Milwaukee Art Museum, 1991.

Montclair Art Museum. *Precisionism in America, 1915–1941: Reordering Reality.* New York: Abrams, 1994.

Mott, Frank L. *A History of American Magazines* (4 vol.). Cambridge, MA: Belknap, 1957.

Perry, Barbara. *American Ceramics: The Collection of Everson Museum of Art.* New York: Rizzoli, 1989.

Phipps, Elena. *The Colonial Andes: Tapestries and Silverwork 1530–1830.* New York: Metropolitan Museum of Art, 2004.

Pohl, Frances K. *Framing America: A Social History of American Art.* New York: Thames and Hudson, 2002.

Rapaport, Brooke Kamin, and Kevin L. Stayton. *Vital Forms: American Art and Design in the Atomic Age, 1940–1960.* New York: Abrams, 2001.

Reid, Dennis. *Our Own Country Canada.* Ottawa: National Gallery of Canada, 1979.

———. *A Concise History of Canadian Painting.* Toronto: Oxford University Press, 1973.

Reynolds, Donald M. *Masters of American Sculpture: The Figurative Tradition from the American Renaissance to the Millennium.* New York: Abbeville Press, 1993.

Rubinstein, Charlotte Streifer. *American Women Sculptors: A History of Women Working in Three Dimensions.* Boston: Hall, 1990.

S/10 Sculpture Today. Toronto: Visual Arts Ontario, 1978.

Saunders, Richard A. *American Colonial Portraits: 1700–1776.* Washington, DC: Smithsonian, 1987.

Stacey, Robert. *The Canadian Poster Book: 100 Years of the Poster in Canada.* Toronto: Methuen, 1979.

Swinton, George. *Sculpture of the Inuit.* Toronto: McClelland and Stewart, 1992.

Weinberg, H. Barbara et al. *American Impressionism and Realism: The Painting of Modern Life, 1885–1915.* New York: Metropolitan Museum of Art, 1994.

Wilson, Richard Guy et al. *The Machine Age in America 1918–1941.* New York: Abrams, 1986.

Winnipeg Art Gallery. *Sculpture on the Prairies.* Winnipeg: Winnipeg Art Gallery, 1977.

Worcester Art Museum. *American Traditions in Watercolor: The Worcester Art Museum Collection.* New York: Abbeville, 1987.

Zayas, Marius de. *How, When, and Why Modern Art Came to New York.* Cambridge, MA: MIT Press, 1996.

Zurier, Rebecca et al. *Metropolitan Lives: The Ashcan Artists and Their New York.* New York: W. W. Norton, 1995.

WEBSITES

Art Institute of Chicago. Chicago, IL. http://www.artic.edu.

Brooklyn Museum. Brooklyn, NY. http://www.brooklynart.org.

Henry Francis du Pont Winterthur Museum. Winterthur, DE. http://www.winterthur.org.

Los Angeles County Museum of Art. Los Angeles, CA. http://www.lacma.org.

M. H. De Young Memorial Museum. San Francisco, CA. http://www.thinker.org.

Metropolitan Museum of Art. New York, NY. http://www.metmuseum.org.
Museum of American Folk Art. New York, NY. http://www.folkartmuseum.org.
Museum of Fine Arts. Boston, MA. http://www.mfa.org.
National Gallery of Art. Washington, DC. http://www.nga.org.
National Gallery of Canada. Ottawa, ON. http://www.gallery.ca/.
New York Historical Society. New York, NY. http://www.nyhistory.org.
Philadelphia Museum of Art. Philadelphia, PA. http://www.philamuseum.org.
Royal British Columbia Museum. Victoria, BC. http://www.royalbcmuseum.bc.ca/.
Royal Ontario Museum. Toronto, ON. http://www.rom.on.ca/.
Smithsonian American Art Museum. Washington, DC. http://www.nmsa.si.edu.

DANCE

LIBBY SMIGEL

Many of the major trends in popular dance practices and entertainments of the United States and Canada are quite similar. A shared western European heritage of the colonizers imprinted many of the inherited country, folk, and social dances on the ballrooms and dance spaces of both countries. Tours that showcased famous artists and shows also exposed people in the major cities of both countries to similar entertainments in stage dancing of the burlesque and ballet styles, dances in minstrelsy, and dance entr'actes. But because of the vast sizes of both countries, different governments and policies in each, the historical absence of slavery in Canada, differences in immigration demographics, and internal regional variations in both nations, the "popular" dance practices of both nations are not easily stereotyped and cannot be fully enumerated.

Furthermore, it should be noted that prevailing terms for categorizing dance are often misleading. Folk dance, country dance, social dance, and ethnic dance are all terms that have been broadly applied to similar dance practices or forms. Ballroom dance often encompasses forms that arose from folk or ethnic forms, and ballroom dance is also practiced outside of ballroom spaces. So-called street dance, a term used in the twentieth century and thereafter for dances that developed outside dance studios or concert dance spaces, have more freedom for improvisation, but these may acquire a codified vocabulary when taught within dance studios. Dances that take their names from their corresponding music forms may vary in style from one community to another, or from one dance space or context to another. In theatrical contexts, a dance named after its music form may have been so theatricalized or dramatized that the steps bear virtually no relationship to its popular origin.

VERNACULAR, OR SOCIAL, DANCE

European Vernacular Dance Traditions

Colonists from Europe brought their native dance forms when they established their communities across North America. Typical of eighteenth-century dances at parties and balls (often termed "assemblies") were the "set dances" (dances for a specified "set" or group

47

of people). "Figure" is the term for the patterns danced in set dances. Also called contra dances (in French, *contredanses*) or longways dances, in parallel lines with partners facing partners, couples danced geometrical figures with their partners and adjacent couples. At private gatherings and as theatrical entr'actes, solo dances such as the hornpipe or jig might also be performed. On formal occasions, the minuet, in which a sole couple executed specified figures and repeated a "z" pattern using minuet traveling steps, was typical.

Changes to the prevalent social dance practices in nineteenth-century Europe were soon reflected in urban cultures in North America (rural areas typically were slower to adopt new dances). The quadrille, the set dance that supplanted the contra dance in ballrooms, retained the figures, but the set formation was a square, with the backs of each of four couples delineating the four sides. Initially, special traveling or skipping steps were used to dance the figures, but by the end of the century it was more common to walk the patterns. Couple dances of the early to mid-nineteenth century were inspired by "folk" or "national" dances (which shared their names with the accompanying music) of northern and eastern Europe, but they were refined for western European ballrooms. The most enduring were the polka, waltz, and galop, although the mazurka, schottische, redowa, polka mazurka, and others enjoyed periods of popularity. A major innovation of these dances was the way the man held his partner in his arms, called the "closed ballroom hold." The man placed his right hand on his partner's back, while she placed her left hand on his shoulder or upper arm; the free hands were clasped palm to palm. It was the man's responsibility to lead the woman, circumnavigating the dance space counterclockwise while dancing the steps in a clockwise direction. Versions of these eighteenth- and nineteenth-century dances are still practiced in parts of Canada and the United States, especially where traditions have been retained or immigrant groups have reintroduced them.

U.S. Vernacular Couple Dances, Late 1800s to 1940s

In the 1880s the two-step dance was invented to accompany the popular march-time music of John Philip Sousa. This music and dance fashion marks the point where the influx of European culture to the United States was reversed, with the United States becoming a dominant exporter of popular music and dance. Ragtime, a new African-American musical form, and the energetic dances that accompanied this new music style (such as the cakewalk and animal dances like the grizzly bear, monkey glide, and turkey trot) thrived in urban dance halls, especially those with surging African-American and immigrant populations common around 1900 to 1920. The Charleston of the 1920s broke from the ballroom hold, and women freed from corsets and lengthy skirts literally kicked up their heels and swung their knees apart. Evidence suggests that Canada's urban centers were not as swift as U.S. cities to respond to African-American music and dance innovations, perhaps because of the stronger ties to British culture or because the Great Migration of African Americans north to U.S. cities more directly and immediately impacted U.S. urban culture. In the United States, public dancing spaces were segregated during this period. African Americans were often relegated to off nights at nightclubs or private clubs such as the black Elks club arranged dances or rented halls.

While dancing as a social pastime was widely practiced in North America, some Protestant Christian sects in Canada and the United States banned dance entirely or only permitted dance within a liturgical setting or under specified restrictions. In Quebec, Canada, the Catholic Church issued anti-dance edicts. Dancing masters countered these criticisms by publishing their own treatises on dancing, which included an "apology" (or defense) of dancing that cited the benefits to a person's physical health and mental well-being.

By the end of the nineteenth century, organizations such as the National Association of Teachers of Dancing (of which there were local chapters across the United States and Canada) tried to legitimize the profession by creating professional standards and a support network. Most of these dance teachers taught refined versions of other newly introduced dances (the maxixe from Brazil, the tango from Argentina, a gentrified fox-trot, the one-step, and others) rather than the earthy "animal" dances. Dance teachers standardized the steps, which made them easier to teach as well as facilitated exhibition and competition events. Over the years, different dances were designated as the official vocabulary of ballroom dances. The Boston was a U.S. version of the waltz with a leisurely pace and a zigzag path. The tango, which had countless variations when it was first introduced before World War I, became standardized. Standardization also removed the improvisatory characteristics of the African-American and Latin-American dances.

Swing music of the 1930s and 1940s provided the inspiration for the swing dances that developed. The Lindy Hop (described in some sources as "jitterbugging"), characterized by acrobatic movements, breakaway moves, and encouragement of improvisation, was one of the first dances associated with swing music. "Hand dancing" is a contemporary term for swing that is used widely in the African-American community. Styles of swing differ on the East and West coasts, with the East Coast version having a more relaxed and simple footwork and the West Coast version offering more opportunities for breakaways and Lindy variations. Though swing dance fell out of fashion, it enjoyed a healthy revival in the 1990s.

Imported Latin-American couple dances such as the mambo, samba, merengue, and others joined the ranks of popular couple dances in the 1940s and 1950s. These dances had the attractions of interesting rhythms, along with predictable and simple dance movements. Many of these were adopted by dance teachers for codification and competition. Salsa dancing of the 1990s resurrected many of these older dances.

Twist

With the introduction of the twist, first in the late 1950s among African-American youths and later in white communities, social dance in the United States changed. Hip action became an essential part of social dance, even though white dancers twisted more with their knees than with their torsos. Also, the twist changed traditional partnering: touching between partners was inessential, so the accepted one-to-one heterosexual pairing was destabilized. Both of these innovations meant that improvisation of the individual became possible, even encouraged, and the path to the solo dances, such as the swim and pony of rock 'n' roll, was set. Dance band television shows such as Dick Clark's *American Bandstand*, *Hullabaloo*, and *Soul Train* all popularized the contemporary music and dance styles. Significantly, these shows promoted live music, much as the variety shows did with more conventional music entertainments. In the 1960s young people tended to identify themselves under labels such as "mod" (which tended to prefer rock music and adopt psychedelic fashions) and "soul" (which followed Motown music and Afrocentric fashion).

Country-Western Dancing

The pervasive popularity of country-western music has spawned complementary dances. Country music singing has a long tradition, but dancing to country-western music achieved widespread popularity in the 1980s, a movement that was spurred on by the movie *Urban Cowboy* (1980), which showcased "Cotton-eyed Joe" (a country line dance) and the country-western two-step (an embellished form of the ragtime partner dance of the same name). Country-western dancing has been popular in honky-tonks, dance halls, clubs, and restaurant-bars in both rural and urban areas. The ubiquitous radio stations that specialize in country-western music have extended the music and its dance culture as far north as rural upstate New York and the mountains of Pennsylvania, and in Canada country-western dancing is a much-enjoyed pastime in the prairie and western provinces. The dances themselves are accessible through cable network stations, as well as in how-to videotapes and DVDs.

Some line dances are attributed to specific choreographers. Jimmy Ruth White designed "The Traveling Four Corners" and the "J. R. Hustle" in the 1980s. In the 1990s Melanie Greenwood is credited with the dance associated with Billy Ray Cyrus's "Achy Breaky Heart," which may have helped propel line dancing into popularity among English-speaking countries worldwide. Over the years, line dances have increased in difficulty, and as a result there are now two groups of line dancers—social dancers who prefer easier steps and patterns, and line dance competitors who enjoy the challenge of harder dances.

Country-western dancing style has been fairly resistant to the impact of African-American dance forms; however, country swing has some of the steps of East Coast swing but adds variations from country-western dancing. The signature country attire, including heeled boots, belts, and trim-cut jeans, adopted by many devoted country-western dancers tends to restrict hip actions characteristic of African-American style, and the two-step and other couple dances hold the torso vertically as is more typical of earlier Eurocentric couple dancing.

Club Dance

A return to partner dance in the late 1970s with the popularity of disco dancing changed the face of dance nightclubs in urban North America. Instead of live local bands, a disc jockey (also, DJ or deejay) at a sound station with at least two turntables would use long versions of popular disco releases, cross-fading from vinyl album to another without a break. Both the film and the soundtrack *Saturday Night Fever* (1977) achieved icon status among the disco set. Young people took lessons in the Hustle and Latin Hustle, the mainstays of disco couple dancing, and ballroom dance teachers added technical lifts, spins, and other moves to compete in clubs for prizes. Disco line dances were also trendy. Since the disco fad, the club culture has expanded, reflecting the increasing diversity of musical heritages in the cities as well as the broad range of musical styles and genres marketed by the commercial music industry. Although disco as a dance form faded, the fashion of spinning records and mixing tracks with DJs continued.

Hip-hop music and dance culture has been considered to have been born in the African-American community in the Bronx, New York, around the same time as the disco craze. The athletic dancing included basic steps as well as inverted balances and freezes; spins on head, back, or shoulders; and clean slicing leg movements. *B-boying* is the term that practitioners prefer, although the media ascribed the term "break dancing" (because they dance on the "break") to the dance form. As in earlier forms where dancers challenged each other to take the center of a circle to outdance the others, hip-hop crews would prepare new moves for dance battles. Individuality and improvisation, the mark of many street dance forms, also spurred on the development of new moves and styles. Pop and lock is considered to be an early form of hip-hop, or an individual specialty, in which movements are jerkily passed along the limbs at different speeds. Martial arts have also influenced hip-hop moves.

On the West Coast, the Chicano community has contributed to the hip-hop movement, both to the music (which includes Spanish lyrics and Latino rhythms) and to the dance (popular Latino dance moves). In addition, hip-hop dance has influenced club dance in cities in Europe and Africa. In the 1990s more aggressive forms of hip-hop dancing developed, one of the most recent being "krumping" in south-central Los Angeles. An outgrowth of clowning, this form has now expanded to Houston, Detroit, and Atlanta. Krumping and other U.S. hip-hop developments may signal hip-hop's original importance in diffusing aggression and frustration in a performative way and may show that hip-hop has a resilience that permits it to respond over time to urban culture.

What began as a techno music and dance subculture in Great Britain and northern Europe, with a strong following of unemployed working-class white males, extended to high school and young adults in the United States and Canada in the 1990s. Rave music is created on the spot, with DJs who use their own collection of music, sounds, and rhythms to create styles of danceable electronic music, a process that puts the DJ into a category of artist-musician. The rave culture avows its affinity to the values of peace, love, unity, and respect (PLUR), but when commercial interests appropriated raves, from music distribution to dance arenas, some of the original energy of the underground movement was diluted.

The dance style most associated with raving is "liquid," smooth or wavy movements of the hands, which may have developed from the waving of break dancing. Popping and break dancing footwork are observed at raves, but hard-core ravers prefer to find original ways to respond to the impulse of the music. Glow sticks are often used as props; some wear white gloves that enhance liquid movements under black lights. Police and community leaders have attempted to regulate or prohibit raves because of illegal drug use (especially ecstasy) that has been linked to dehydration and accidental deaths at these all-night-long parties. Raves continue to happen, though they have reverted to their underground status.

The variety of club dance across North America defies complete categorization. From city to city, even from neighborhood to neighborhood within a city, a genre of club dance (such as hip-hop) may be quite different in music (the impact of the DJ's choices in mixing or scratching) and in dance style (the impact of different cultural preferences, ages, and many other factors). Sometimes a club style will seem particularly linked to one city, as in the reggae-inspired go-go clubs in Washington, D.C. Some dances are fleeting: in the early 1990s the lambada, a highly promoted import from Brazil via France, was a sexualized version of merengue moves that failed to secure an ongoing following despite media hype. On its heels, the macarena seemed appealing for its catchy identifiable tune and simplicity of movements, but except for its brief fame at the U.S. presidential conventions, it fizzled. Salsa dance, on the other hand, seems to be sustaining energy, with its simple couple-dance partnering and the prevalence and popularity of Latin-inspired music in North America.

PERCUSSIVE DANCE FORMS

Popular dance forms characterized by the dancers' ability to create rhythms with their feet have been practiced in both Canada and the United States. Variously termed step-dancing in Canada or clogging, buck-dancing, or flat-footing in Appalachia, settlers from northern England, Ireland, and Scotland brought their native forms with them. African-influenced rhythm dances that emerged among U.S. slaves evolved into tap. All of these examples have occurred in both community and performance contexts, but the context often affects the form, attributes of movement, or other characteristics of the dancing.

Step-Dancing and Clogging

The practice of step-dancing on Cape Breton, off the coast of Nova Scotia, Canada, is considered to reflect more of the traditional Scottish qualities because of this community's relative isolation from outside cultural influences. Appalachian clogging, found in communities in the mountains of the same name, is often done in boots or heeled shoes that can withstand the robust weighted attack of its movements. Arms respond to the footwork, and the torso often leans slightly forward from the hips. In French Canadian step-dancing, in contrast, the same "time step" is done with more economical footwork, with less weight, and with an upright torso and the arms fairly relaxed at the sides of the vertical torso. It is important, however, to avoid over-stereotyping regional dance styles, especially as exhibition step-dancing and precision clogging teams have modified or exaggerated characteristics of local execution. For example, "flat-footing" is characterized by some sources as not raising the foot more than 6 inches off the ground and in other circles the practice is characterized as having more shuffling movement (lateral) than up and down.

Southern Appalachian old-time clogging was and is primarily a solo dance: buck dancers might form a circle in which they would take turns showing off their footwork and rhythms. "Freestyle" clogging involves groups of dancers who flatfoot their way through geometric figures, but the steps are improvised, giving an outlet for individuality. The effect is like jazz, with individuals dancing in the same style but with their own rhythmic interpretations of the music. James Kesterson is credited with developing in the 1950s what is known as precision clogging. "Precision" means that each person in the group performs the same synchronized steps; other innovations include the choice of music (which can be drawn from pop music), the style of footwork (which encourages kicks and feet raised higher from the floor), an emphasis on speed, and introduction of new figures. Both freestyle and precision clogging styles are exhibited at festivals as well as at competitions. Despite opposition, advocates of precision style believe the form's response to cultural changes ensures an appeal to young people. These styles now coexist in North Carolina, and the dancer's choice of style makes a personal statement about innovation and tradition.

The popularity of the professional troupe Riverdance and its star Michael Flatley may be responsible for some of the increased interest in step-dancing and clogging. An exhibition and competition form of Irish step-dancing was codified decades ago. Riverdance's style is not limited to Irish but involves precision clogging and tap styles as well.

Tap

The origin of tap dancing, attributed to African-American slave communities, is less clear. Tap's energy and appeal derive from its being an improvisational form. Street dancers would group to take turns showing off their newest moves and rhythms. African-American tappers such as Honi Coles, LaVaughn Robinson, and the Nicholas Brothers developed the form into a complex display of percussion artistry, so that tap dance became a frequent feature of minstrel shows, vaudeville acts, and film divertissements, and in the film industry white tap artists such as Gene Kelly and Fred Astaire developed their own routines and style. Tap fell out of favor as an improvisational and vernacular practice sometime in the 1950s and was seen mostly in regimented performances in variety shows, Broadway revivals, or the performances of the Radio City Rockettes, an all-female ensemble replicating the aesthetic of Busby Berkeley's chorus lines. Improvisatory tap disappeared when codified tap steps and routines became standard fare in local children's dance studios alongside generic jazz and ballet. An interest in tap as a creative and expressive form surfaced in the 1980s, with the formation of innovative companies that specialized in new tap choreography (for example, Jazz Tap Ensemble or Balletap U.S.A.). The dance-off between ballet star Mikhail Baryshnikov and tap artist Gregory Hines in *White Nights* (1985) and the 1989 film *Tap* (which showcased Hines, as well as a number of historic tap greats) returned tap's creativity to the public eye. Contemporary tap artist Savion Glover further advanced public popularity and recognition of tap with his original Broadway show *Bring in 'da Noise, Bring in 'da Funk* (1996), which danced out African-American history through tap. At the beginning of the twenty-first century, tap had regained its dual following as participatory pastime and audience entertainment.

Steppin' and Drillin'

Stepping in African-American college fraternities and sororities has become an entertainment and a form of cultural expression. Precedents of marching in-line in the Greek societies of historically black U.S. colleges date to the 1940s and 1950s in pledging rituals. In the 1960s and 1970s indoor and outdoor step shows commemorated the occasion of the new members' induction into the fraternity or sorority. Elements of these shows included signature steps or gestures specific to that fraternity, saluting (emulating the steps or style of another fraternity), cracking (that is, making cracks or put-downs, or mocking) other fraternities, freaking or "show dogging" (breaking from the synchronization of the group), call and response, special props (like canes), and costumes. These shows were rarely done to instrumental music; instead, the rhythms of the steps and hand claps, as well as singing or chanting, furnished the accompaniment to the movement. As the shows became more elaborate, competitions were set up in the 1980s.

SPECIAL OCCASIONS

Because of the myriad cultures across North America and the variations in practice from region to region, every occasion for dance cannot be documented. Following is a sample of special occasions at which dance occurs.

Pageantry

Popular across North America and in Europe, the pageantry movement of the first and second decades of the twentieth century provided many opportunities to present folk dances, historical dances, and the revived Greek dances in community pageants and masques. In the United States, the pageantry movement had as its objective the development of a dramatic art form for the entertainment, education, and participation of the masses. In the New York City masque to commemorate the Shakespeare tercentenary, for example, Percy MacKaye's *Caliban by the Yellow Sands* (1916) featured young women in Greek aesthetic dancing and a chorus of young men in a Greek interlude, episodes that appealed to the participants as well as the spectators. For pageants that commemorated a historical event, choreographers attempted to design dances that reflected the practices during that time period, but the historical accuracy of these efforts was not great.

North American Rites of Passage

For upper-class young women in the U.S. South, on the East Coast, and in the Midwest, their introduction to society had traditionally been marked with a cotillion or formal ball in their mid- to late teens. The African-American elite in many cities adopted this social ritual and created clubs to sponsor debutante balls. Though this rite of passage is still observed among some communities, to a great extent the high school prom dance has replaced this festivity across all classes. The high school prom event, like its predecessor "promenade," a formal walk or an opening processional dance at a ball, is an opportunity for the community to see its young couples at their social best. Formal wear for men and women is still the usual required attire, and professional photographers capture the couples in traditional staged poses. The music band or DJ choice typically reflects the popular dance music preferences of the high school crowd, rather than nodding to social dance precedents. This social ritual extends beyond the timeline of the dance itself, oftentimes with chauffeured limousines engaged to ferry the students to pre-dance dinners or after-parties that last until dawn.

The Quinceaños is a rite of passage marked for young Latinas and Puerto Rican girls at age 15. The Quinceañera ceremony dates from the 1930s in the United States, and its traditional components have assimilated some of the attributes of the North American "sweet 16" party. In its traditional form, there is a Catholic Mass or religious ceremony followed by a party or fiesta. The father changes the young woman's shoes from flats of childhood to high-heeled shoes, an action that represents her initiation into womanhood. He dances with her, and then she dances with her mother. Sometimes the dance is choreographed to include her "court," other young men and women who are included in the ceremony and festivities.

The wedding reception is another tradition that has adapted to changing cultural mores and social preferences. The bridal industry dictates much of the fashion and jewelry trends, but the reception itself, the social event or party following the wedding ceremony, provides a greater range to reflect the culture and individual preferences of the couple, especially in the selection of the dance band or DJ. Strong religious or cultural affiliations may dictate some choices. For example, a Jewish wedding reception may have a requisite hora for the whole group even when popular music is chosen for the rest of the dancing. Mexican-American wedding receptions may have a mariachi band or a group that plays a repertory of current Latin-American dance music. Where Anglo tradition had previously dictated that the dancing begin with a waltz of the bride and her groom, followed by other prescribed pairings of the couple's family and wedding party, the opening dance may now be a different ballroom dance or a contemporary dance of the bridal couple along with their wedding party.

Specific to the African-American community is the practice of stepping to mark important events. From its initial use of indicating that pledges had been accepted by their fraternity, stepping as a form of African-American identity and community expression now may be seen at festivals such as the Philadelphia Greek Picnic, at wedding receptions and funerals, and in Christian liturgy and fellowship gatherings.

Cultural Festivals and Exhibitions

Whereas rites of passage have precise meanings for members of a culture, festivals often have to fulfill two objectives. Often festivals provide a means for cultural expression for participants and spectators, but—especially when the occasion is open to outsiders or to tourists—sometimes the event introduces commercial or voyeuristic values to cultural events. At the annual summer folk festival organized by the Smithsonian Institution on the Mall in Washington, D.C., one or more nations or states are selected for special feature. These cultures bring representative arts, crafts, and performances, including dance. Some of the dance programming is participatory, with the intention of offering tourists a firsthand opportunity to experience the dance; others show dances through lecture-demonstrations or short performances. Performances of indigenous or traditional dance often change the forms of the dance, because of the adaptations needed to accommodate an audience. In the last 40 or 50 years, exhibition and festival organizers have increasingly taken more care that the culture of the subject group is presented in a way that is not demeaning to the participants.

Other festivals continue to help celebrate and preserve traditions. The Calgary Stampede includes chuck wagon races, livestock displays, and dancing troupes in celebration of its western heritage. In Cape Breton, Nova Scotia, the decline of the Gaelic language and the migration of residents out in search of employment have undermined the traditional arts. The Cape Breton Celtic Festivals help to preserve the diverse cultures of the British, the French Acadians, the Mi'kmaqs, and the Celts, which make up more than 80 percent of the island's population.

Mardi Gras

In the French cultures in Quebec and in Louisiana, the observation of Mardi Gras (literally, "fat Tuesday," meaning the Tuesday before the beginning of Lent, a period of penance, fast, and abstinence in Catholic practice) involves some combination of carnival and parades, parties and costume balls, masked pranks or entertainments. In about two dozen rural Cajun and Creole communities in Louisiana, revelers make a run (*courir*) from house to house to dance, sing, or cajole until the resident donates a piece of chicken or other ingredient for gumbo. The Mardi Gras of New Orleans has become a tourist attraction with wild parades and masked revelries. Quebec's counterpart to Louisiana's Mardi Gras is Winter Carnival, which involves carnival parades, dogsled and canoe races, and snowmobiling by day, with traditional couple dancing at formal balls in the evening.

Cinco de Mayo

Literally "the fifth of May," Cinco de Mayo is celebrated to commemorate the victory of the Mexican army against the French at the Battle of Puebla in 1862. Mexican Americans, who make up about 9 percent of the population in the United States,[1] continue to mark the date with celebrations of their heritage and culture. The festivities often include parades, salsa or folk dancing, traditional Mexican food, and performances by mariachi bands. In Los Angeles, the celebration takes place in front of city hall, and the city's mayor may address the public and notable Mexican guests in Spanish. In other cities, the festivities may be more commercialized and attract tourists or people who do not have Latino heritage.

Christian Liturgy

Because so many of the religious sects of the American colonists prohibited dance, dance has been slow to be integrated into Christian liturgy. This uneasy relationship between Christianity and dance is not typical of most other historic religions, which have used traditional dances to commemorate religious events or milestones. From the midpoint of the twentieth century, however, a widespread movement toward incorporating dance into Christian liturgy has influenced Christian dance practice worldwide.

DANCE MARATHONS

A contest form where stamina is the only criterion for winning is the dance marathon. The dance marathon of the 1920s and 1930s, which developed into a kind of circus sideshow in the United States, held little appeal outside the United States. Estimates place the number of contestants and organizers at 20,000, with audiences numbering in the millions.[2] Dance marathons measured dancers' physical endurance to be the last dancer standing. At the first recorded marathons that date from 1910, when the rules permitted an individual to dance on with a new partner, the winners were women. Later rules pitted couple against couple; the longest endurance matches lasted 6 weeks to months. In the Depression (after 1929), the contests became widely known as "walkathons" because there was more walking than dancing. As the events became dominated by professional dancers, announcers, and promoters, prize money was offered, and entertainment acts included performances by out-of-work vaudevillians. By the early 1940s the appeal of these formulaic events waned.

In the 1990s a new breed of dance marathon emerged. Canadian and U.S. colleges across North America, from private to public, small to large, north to south, became the sites for fund-raising dance marathons. These dance marathons imitate the model of walkathons, bikathons, or jumpathons, in which participants solicit monetary sponsorships for their participation. However far the contestant can travel, or in the case of the dance marathon however long the participant can dance, the sponsor agrees to contribute a certain amount per mile or hour to a designated charity. The new dance marathon serves philanthropic as well as social ends.

DANCE COMPETITIONS AND CONTESTS

Throughout Western history, dance has been a vehicle for competition. Individuals in tap, stepping, hip-hop, or capoeira show off steps before a group. Partners in couple dances (ballroom, country-western, disco, salsa) compete for prizes. Formalized competition in dance has attracted avid participants and audiences in North America and elsewhere. Competitions and contests seem to be a viable strategy and incentive for increasing interest in a dance form.

Competition Couple Dancing

Competition ballroom dancing, along with other forms of dance contests for couples, is a natural outgrowth of exhibition ballroom dancing and related partner dances. The first world competition was held in 1909 in Paris, with the Boston, the grizzly bear, the turkey trot, and the one-step constituting the dances. International organizations set the standards for and approve the list of competition dances for professional-level competitors. In 1924 the Imperial Society of Teachers of Dancing (ISTD), based in Great Britain but with chapters in the United States and Canada, formed a ballroom branch that codified ballroom dance technique. Today, the USISTD sets and maintains standards for International Style Ballroom (Standard), Latin-American dancing, American Style Ballroom (Smooth), and rhythm dancing. Competition ballroom has enjoyed a small but dedicated following worldwide, with the audience broadened and encouraged in North America because of public television programming that showcases exhibitions and contests. When interest and participation in partner dancing is high (whether ballroom, disco, country-western, or other partner forms), there is a corresponding visibility of dance contests and competitions in those forms.

DanceSport is perhaps the most recognizable name for amateur competitive ballroom dancing in North America and Europe, especially because the International Olympic Committee granted the International DanceSport Federation full IOC membership in 1997 when ballroom was under consideration as an Olympic event. On college campuses across North America, DanceSport teams are active and compete in intercollegiate meets. Competition ballroom dancing has also been introduced into the school systems, notably through a pilot program in New York City called Dancing Classrooms. Although some of the judging criteria resemble the categories of ice dancing, ballroom dancing also requires the technique of "floorcraft," because couples simultaneously show their choreographies while navigating around their competition.

Country-western dance also has competitions throughout both Canada and the United States.

Competitive Step-Dancing and Stepping

For Anglo- and African-American forms of percussive dance, there is historical evidence that solo performers would alternate exhibiting their best steps and rhythms before the group in friendly competition. Irish schools of step-dancing have long standards against which participants have been rated or compete. In the last decades, competitions for some forms have become more institutionalized, such as the African-American step and drill conferences and contests hosted by black fraternities or the regional and continental clog or step-dancing competitions sponsored by various step-dancing organizations.

Contests in Powwows

Dances of the Native Americans, sometimes termed Indians, Native Peoples, and—in Canada—First Nations, have rarely been considered "popular dance," in part because these traditional forms have culturally specific significance and are open only to participation by Native Americans. Wild West shows and other nineteenth-century popular entertainments exploited Native American characters or identity: these dances were not authentic representations but instead were stereotypes adapted for commercial entertainment purposes before a predominantly white audience. More recently, some reservations (or "reserves" in Canada) that have courted tourist trade have opened certain ceremonies and dances to outside spectators. However, in the last few decades all across North America, one dance in particular has achieved a popularity for practitioners as well as spectators: the intertribal powwow.

The first of these ceremonies seem to have occurred sometime around the 1870s. Powwows had been recorded as war dances, celebrations of trips completed, or recreational picnics, among other cultural markings, and traditionally participation at a powwow was restricted to the community in which it occurred. Nowadays, powwows are viewed as sacred and recreational celebrations of Native American culture. The "intertribal powwow," which encourages participation by members of any Native American nation and includes all ages, has as its purpose inclusion and cultural affirmation across tribal demarcations. Powwows are sponsored by different Native groups across the North American continent, from the Tiinowit Powwow in Yakima, Washington, or the Rousseau River Powwow in Manitoba, Canada, to the Walpole Powwow in Ontario or the Beaver Creek Powwow in Belvidere, New Jersey. Intertribal powwows are attended by thousands of people, many of whom travel across the continent following the powwow circuit. The Native American nations are represented by tribal leaders, dancers and drummers, vendors, and others, but the powwow event also attracts non-Native spectators from all over the world.

Powwows include informal dancing as well as formalized contest dance events. The Grand Entry, a component of all powwows, is an example of noncompetitive dancing. The host determines who leads the entry processional; often war veterans or the owner of a traditional Eagle staff leads the way, with flag bearers, princesses, tribal leaders and honored guests, and dance competitors organized in groups. Elders often receive a place of importance in this procession. The contests are formal displays of dancing in various categories, including for men traditional, fancy, and grass and for women fancy shawl dancing, traditional, and jingle. The host nation establishes the parameters of the contests—whether the dancers in a specific category will dance together or individually or how long the dancing may last, for example.

STAGE DANCING AND POPULAR DANCE FOR SPECTATORS

Imported stars from Europe on the professional stages in North America during the 1800s had overshadowed native performers, although ample evidence documents appearances of North American dancers in entr'actes and specialty acts, as well as in minstrelsy, on vaudeville stages, and in opera houses. Much of the staged dance, whether discrete dance numbers or musical theater dances, had some connection to the dances of the ballroom. This relationship had been true in the nineteenth-century theaters of Western Europe, where national (or character) dances such as the polka or cachucha were theatricalized and performed within the plots of the ballets, melodramas, or burlettas. Because dancing masters usually taught dances to society people as well as choreographed for the stage, this dialogue between social dance practice and stage dance was facilitated. Advertisements in newspapers reveal that North American dancing masters similarly crossed the line between social and theatrical dance by offering lessons in ballroom dances as well as character dances, clogging, acrobatics, and other stage dance forms. In the early 1900s acrobatics were an element of many stage dance acts, with Harriet Hoctor in pointe shoes performing backbends or eccentric dancer Al Coogan adding splits and pratfalls to his humorous solo dances. Blackface minstrel groups, whose acts included solo and group dance numbers including the cakewalk, found popularity on the stages of North American and Canadian cities, through the 1920s. Exotic dances loosely inspired by Mexican, southern European, Middle Eastern, or Asian cultural stereotypes also found favor.

U.S. Musical Theater

Out of the tradition of music hall and vaudeville, the U.S. musical with its combination of music, song, and dance has become a popular dramatic form that frequently showcases dance. Dance in musicals such as *Oklahoma!* (1943) could be designed to advance the plot, as well as create mood and reveal characterizations. The U.S. musical form has developed to the point that some examples are built almost entirely around the dance, as for example *A Chorus Line* (1975). In Canada in the 1980s, notably in downtown Toronto, large performance halls began to import Broadway and London musicals with great commercial success, but Canada has not created similarly large-scale musical theater shows.

Exhibition Ballroom Dancing

Around 1910 exhibition ballroom dancing became a spectator sport in dance clubs as well as on vaudeville programs. Many exhibition teams have gone on to perform within musicals and films. Tied closely to competition ballroom dancing, often exhibition choreographies are included as entertainment on the program of ballroom competitions.

DANCE REVIVALS

At various times throughout the twentieth century, interest in the music and dance of previous generations would be rekindled and a kind of revival or resurgence of the dance practice would occur. Also, three examples (country dance, swing, and tango) included below show different conditions under which dances have been embraced again or reinvented.

Revivals, Early 1900s

Arguments for dance's benefit to a person's health were more culturally persuasive than were appeals to the value of art. Coincident with a broader movement supporting women's physical education and health at the end of the nineteenth century, those who recognized the healthful benefits of recreational dance worked toward integrating supervised folk dance instruction in the U.S. public school systems. In 1916 the American Folk Dancing Society was established. Although within the field of physical education dance is appreciated more as an activity or exercise rather than as an art, dance thus achieved a foothold in curricula in urban U.S. schools, a status that helped to advance it into physical education departments in higher education. There was a similar movement to teach and preserve Canada's traditional dances. Square dances were taught through the Toronto Board of Education schools and in events promoted by the Canadian Old-Tyme Square Dance Callers Association. The interest in documenting and teaching North American folk dances mirrored the work in collecting indigenous folk music and dance in Great Britain, a movement largely credited to Cecil Sharp's work in England. "International" folk dances were also standardized and taught in the school systems, but the versions preserved in this way were greatly simplified and the varieties of practice and style were sanded away.

Coinciding with a growing interest in archaeological excavations, the revived Olympics, and the study of Athens as the world's first democracy, the so-called revived Greek dances that arose in the early 1900s were regarded as healthful physical pursuits by U.S. proponents such as Louis Chalif. Isadora Duncan's dance innovations—her rejection of the period's corset in favor of a free-form Greek-inspired tunic for dancing, her assimilation of Greek poses from friezes and vase paintings in her dances—also captured the imaginations of young white women across North America, even though most of Duncan's success lay in tours of Europe and Russia. At women's colleges across the United States, groups of women imitated the essentials of her natural "aesthetic dancing," as it was called: the skipping steps, the swinging arms, the ease of movement. That this pastime was widely practiced and recognized is demonstrated by the parody of Greek aesthetic dancing in Charlie Chaplin's film *Sunnyside* (1919).

Country Dancing

The Country Dance and Song Society (CDSS) was established in New England in 1900 to ensure that the practice of English and U.S. country dancing did not become erased by ragtime music and accompanying dances. This interest in sustaining country dance practice was also triggered by concern over the shift in population away from rural regions. Many of the people who spearheaded the effort to revive U.S. country dance were well-educated city-dwellers aware of the European movement in collecting their music and dance heritage. Another wave of interest in country dancing occurred in the 1960s and 1970s, perhaps as a response to the perceived lack of community in rock 'n' roll dancing or in the superficial culture of the 1970s discos. The CDSS facilitated country dance practice by issuing membership lists, contact information for groups that meet regularly to learn or practice different kinds of country dance or music, and information on costume balls and festivities, and by organizing annual weeklong summer workshops that bring experts in the music and dance of different North American and British regions. Some of the more popular country dance bands have achieved a cult following, where dancers will travel many miles across state or provincial lines to participate in dance weekends where a favorite dance band is featured. The CDSS has reached across the 42nd parallel to welcome memberships and participation of individuals and dance groups from Canada, who had an interest and delight in their rural Canadian country dance practice as well as the historical country dances inherited from the mother country. A number of prominent country dance leaders in Canada have served among the organization's board members.

The range of dance and music groups listed by CDSS demonstrates the variety of U.S. and Canadian country dance practice: clogging and step-dancing, New England contras, Southwest squares, Appalachian groups, barn dances, and midwestern squares. Although some dance groups have attempted to preserve what the community thought were "authentic" dances, "living traditions" can be expected to respond (even in subtle ways) to the shifts in the culture that houses them. Some fiddlers and callers have designed new dances, creating an entirely new regional contemporary country dance repertory.

Swing

Swing dance is another historical social dance that has received a renewed respect and interest. The height of the swing dance revival roughly corresponded to the 1998 "Khaki Swing" Gap commercial in which swing dancers gleefully exhibited the Gap fashions as they moved to the jazzy accompaniment. The film *Swing Kids* (1993), which dramatized the Nazi ban on swing dance, displayed the dance as fun and energetic, and the prohibition by the Nazis only made it the more alluring. Although a causal link is impossible to establish, dance studios nationwide received an increase in inquiries about swing dance lessons, and swing dance bands formed and began to compose their own swing tunes. Many urban areas, especially in the Northeast area and California cities, have regular swing events in ballrooms, civic halls, or outdoor spaces, such as the weekly swing dance with live music in the ballroom at Glen Echo Park, Maryland. The teeming attendance at these events justifies their treatment as popular, though revived, dance events. East Coast and West Coast swing is characterized by different rock-step footwork.

Tango

The tango, whose original form dates from mid-nineteenth-century Argentina, has also undergone periodic revivals in North America. First popularized in North America in the 1910s by Vernon and Irene Castle, who smoothed the sultry Latin-American dance to win its acceptance in middle- and upper-class dance salons, the tango reasserted its traditional sensuality in the film tangos of Rudolph Valentino. Stereotypical tango movements in exotic films became exaggerated and then burlesqued: a red rose clenched between the teeth, the peacocking of the tango hold and promenade walk, the snapping head movements. Parodies of the tango popped up throughout the century: a Laurel and Hardy silent film, a *Flintstones* cartoon, a Ballet Trockadero burlesque, a *Frasier* television episode, to name a few.

With the Broadway success of the imported musical *Tango Argentino* (1985), which was followed by tango touring shows and Broadway imitators, as well as clever tango scenes danced by film stars Al Pacino in *Scent of a Woman* (1992) and Arnold Schwarzenegger in *True Lies* (1994), the tango received renewed attention by social dancers as well as by spectators. The difficulty of the dance movements is an obstacle for dance dilettantes, but the intricacy of the movements and the dramatic connection between partners make it especially appealing to spectators. The identifiable rhythms of the tango have intrigued concert dance choreographers: notably, New York–based modern dance choreographer Paul Taylor chose the tango for music and movement inspiration for his 1997 dance *Piazzolla Caldera*, named for the famed tango poet-composer. The tango is also among the dances that have challenged the contestants on the television reality show competition *Dancing with the Stars* (2005–).

DANCE IN FILM, TELEVISION SHOWS, COMMERCIALS, AND THE INTERNET

With the advent of the film industry, dance styles and steps of the best-known vaudevillian performers, ballroom dancers, specialty-act performers, and actor-dancers were more consistently available to a wider audience. The relationship between dance and film in the days of silent filmmaking was a symbiotic one: film dance drew inspiration from popular practice, and popular dance practices imitated theatricalized versions shown on screen.

Recorded dance on film, videotape, DVDs, television, and the Internet now provide easy access to dance worldwide, and live dance performance has largely been superseded by recorded media. Recorded dance, however, has had an enormous impact on influencing preferences for participatory forms.

Dance choreographed specifically for recorded media is considered by many to be a separate hybrid form distinct from dance as live performance. The Moving Pictures Festival of Dance on Film and Video in Toronto and the Banff Film and Video Festival in Alberta both have international stature in exhibiting and promoting outstanding national and international mediated dance works. The Dance Films Association in New York City annually sponsors an international festival honoring Dance on Camera, with a tour of selected works to other venues in the United States.

Film

The medium of Hollywood filmmaking brought many dance forms more efficiently to a broader audience across the United States and Canada, as vaudeville houses converted to cinema. Vaudevillians who specialized in dance and physical comedy found silent films a hospitable medium. Films from the early 1900s preserve noteworthy examples of choreography and performance, including the social dance and comic physical choreographies of Charlie Chaplin, tap dances featuring the likes of Bill "Bojangles" Robinson and Shirley Temple, pageantry dances of Ruth St. Denis for D. W. Griffith's *Intolerance*, or ballroom dance exhibitions of Vernon and Irene Castle. In the 1920s and 1930s the promise of long-running contracts with major motion picture studios lured vaudevillian song-and-dance performers such as Fred Astaire and his sister Adele to Hollywood, where film story formulas were shaped to showcase the performance skills of notable dancers and singers. Busby

Berkeley chorus line extravaganzas, Astaire's partnership with Ginger Rogers, the Nicholas Brothers' virtuosic tap numbers, Gene Kelly's athletic dancing, the gymnastic humor of Donald O'Connor's and Ray Bolger's eccentric dances—all achieved a popularity and an international recognition impossible without the mechanism of film distribution. Russian dancer-choreographer George Balanchine, who established the first U.S. ballet company, contributed dances in popular films from 1938 to 1942. Film musicals of the 1950s and 1960s tapped the talent of ballet dancers and choreographers, including American Ballet Theatre (ABT) dancers in *Seven Brides for Seven Brothers* (1954) and Jerome Robbins's choreography for *West Side Story* (1961).

Hollywood films have continued to exploit the popularity of dance. *Flashdance* (1983) and *Fame* (1980) are predecessors to later films such as *Save the Last Dance* (2001) and *Center Stage* (2000) that follow the paths of aspiring dancers. *Dirty Dancing* (1987) has a similar theme to *Shall We Dance?* (the 2004 remake of the Japanese film) in that the protagonists discover themselves through the experience of dancing.

Except for the category of "Best Dance Direction" in 1935 to 1937, choreography in film has been overlooked at the U.S. Academy Awards, and historically choreographers have often not been listed in credits of early films. The Academy of Dance on Film was formed in 1998 to document and preserve popular filmed dance. To that end, the organization gives annual American Choreography Awards to outstanding choreography in popular forms, including films, television programs and commercials, and fight choreography.

Television

When U.S. commercial television transmission began in the 1940s, some of the programs included dance. In most cases, these shows were televised versions of concert dance forms, whether ballet danced by notable artists or modern dance innovators: this kind of programming employed a mass communications medium to transmit what were considered elite cultural forms. The 1950s introduced variety programs, which offered a range of entertainments in the hour-long shows. Although an occasional excerpt from classical ballet—a pas de deux (dance for two) from famous ballets or other short scene that could be adapted to the small screen of television—was included, dance programming on variety shows tended toward more accessible styles. The show's resident choreographer would devise one or more dances for each week's program; the choreography for these dances reflected popular dance styles (such as tap or jazz) and was designed spatially for television's small screen. Where variety shows included a range of unrelated entertainments, some shows focused on a specific genre. From 1950 to 1960 *The Arthur Murray Dance Party* taught social dance moves and staged dance demonstrations, and—a feature added in 1956—hosted a dance contest. Popular dances and dance parodies also could be seen within half-hour situation comedies. Many television shows drew from film formulas that showcased a star's special theatrical abilities by building them into characterizations and plots. For example, a show like *I Love Lucy*, which gave real-life mambo king Desi Arnaz a role as manager of a nightclub, had ample opportunities to design dances that could substantially advance the sitcom plots.

In the 1980s the development of music videos that could be broadcast on television transformed the way popular music and dance accessed its public. MTV, a pilot television station devoted to promoting the popular music industry, created a separate entertainment industry through the short music videos that promoted a pop artist's latest song. The choreography for Michael Jackson's music videos made his moves (including the "moonwalk") and costumes (the glove) as famous as his songs. Since MTV's success, additional cable stations and television programming have been created to promote music products using music videos in a number of dance music genres.

Aside from music videos, dance programming has largely remained in three categories: programs on concert dance and its artists sponsored by the public television stations, dance within updated variety-show formats, and exhibition ballroom dancing programs on public television and cable-access stations. With the popularity of reality television shows, dance-offs have emerged as watchable television entertainment. *Dancing with the Stars* (2005–), an American Broadcasting Company (ABC) show, paired nationally recognized figures—from soap opera star Kelly Monaco to boxer Evander Holyfield and former *Seinfeld* actor John O'Hurley in the first season—with ballroom champions. For each weekly episode, the champions would coach their partners in one or two new dance styles. Judges were drawn from the community of international ballroom competition, but the network also permitted home viewers to vote by phone or Internet. The dances were drawn from the international ballroom repertory: fox-trot, quickstep, waltz, Viennese waltz, rumba, tango, jive. The contestant with the lowest combined score would be eliminated from competition. (Pitting stars against each other in televised dance contests is not without precedent: much of the audience appeal of *The Arthur Murray Dance Party* television show of the 1950s was the celebrity dance contest. From 1978 to 1988 *Dance Fever* offered money prizes for the winning couple in a hybrid dance competition of disco-ballroom-acrobatics.) Another recent dance show, *So You Think You Can Dance*, based on the hugely successful Fox-network *American Idol* competition among singers, draws many of its dances from contemporary "styles" (such as hip-hop or "Broadway") or from a competitive category familiar to girls' dance competitions ("lyric"). As of 2006, *Dancing with the Stars* remains highly popular and is said to have spurred new interest in ballroom dancing.

Canadian Dance in Mass Media

After World War I, Canada began to develop its own sense of identity, which the arts and dance have been instrumental in advancing. In a significant departure from the free enterprise market in the United States, the Canadian government set up public control of the mass media, which became a way of using arts to disseminate Canadian culture and information. In an episode titled "Ballet Festival" (1949), the National Film Board of Canada used dance, specifically a competition of amateur ballet students from across Canada, as part of its series *Canada Carries On* to demonstrate exemplary characteristics of the Canadian citizen: hard work, determination, and self-discipline, according to the voice-over. This film series, inaugurated in 1940 during the years of World War II with stories about the Canadian war effort, continued until 1959 with other features that defined aspects of Canadian national identity and achievement.

Years later, an excerpt of this film was used in a parodic video that showcased Canadian abstract dance achievement (*A Very Dangerous Pastime/Un Passe-temps terriblement dangereux*). Produced by the Canadian Dance Festival, the video used a mockumentary style with commentary of recognizable Canadian pop culture figures (a rap artist, a snowboarder, an Olympic swimmer, a comedienne, for example) to explicate the "mysteries" of abstract dance. The excerpts chosen for inclusion demonstrate the diversity of contemporary concert dance practice (including *La Petite Musée de Velasquez* by Edouard Lock, *Tari Rickshaw* by Peter Chin, *Birth* by Alvin Erascqu Tolentino, and *Lodela* by José Navas), although some Canadian dance artists and critics have questioned what they perceive as a preponderance of mainstream anglo- and francophone dance choreography. Nonetheless, the video serves as evidence that the traditional discipline and style of classical ballet shown in "Ballet Festival" has yielded some fifty years later to new directions and new expressions in dance that reflect the concerns and changes of contemporary Canadian culture.

Dance on film and video has been a significant creative pursuit and a growing industry in Canada. Notably, governmental funding of innovative choreography and media experiments has put Canadian talent to the forefront. Director Norman McLaren's collaboration with choreographer Ludmilla Chiriaeff on the 1967 seminal film *Pas de Deux* applied sophisticated filmic techniques and special effects to movement design to create stories and metaphors. The CBC/SRC (respectively, Canadian Broadcast Company and Société Radio-Canada) have regularly offered arts programming, despite dwindling public funding. The Canadian arm of Bravo, a U.S. company that licenses the use of its name for Canada's independent company, sponsors the creation of arts-related shorts (including dance pieces) through Bravo!FACT (A Foundation to Assist Canadian Talent).

How-to Videos and DVDs

In keeping with the abundance of how-to and self-improvement books and tapes on practical skills and personal development, videotapes and DVDs that teach forms of couple dancing from ballroom to disco, hip-hop, dancercise, martial arts, and body systems such as yoga or Pilates are ubiquitous. Published dance manuals date back to the Renaissance, and today instruction books on contemporary popular dances can be found. Printed instructions, however, have never replaced the subtleties of personal instruction. Dance and movement instructions on videotapes and DVDs supply the much-needed visual cues as well as the musical soundtrack and encouraging words of the demonstrator.

Commercials

It is possible that the most watched dancing in North America is the choreography for television commercials, when frequency of airtime is added to the numbers of television viewers nationwide. Well-crafted dance scenes in commercials use the moving body to create a visual sign for the product that is marketed. A 2005 Volkswagen Golf GTI commercial combined the head of Gene Kelly with the pop-and-lock style of Elsewhere, also known as David Bernal, in an updated sequence inspired by *Singin' in the Rain*. For a Spicy V-8 commercial (2004), tap maestro Savion Glover danced atop washing machines and down an aisle lined with dryers, finally morphing into an attractive white woman sipping from the V-8 Juice bottle. The Gap, Target, and eBay have recently used dance or movement for their messages, while Verizon's regular spokesperson, actor James Earl Jones, accomplished some hip-hop moves for one commercial. A 2002 Saturn commercial placed individuals and small groups on residential streets and highways, to use their simple pedestrian traveling movements to create a metaphor for Saturn's consideration of its customers.

Because advertisements capitalize on recognizable signs, dance in commercials reflects everyday life and plays off of popular perceptions, just as The Gap's swing commercial capitalized on the swing dance revival in 1998. In 2006 a television ad for Oreo cookies had three little girls clad in pink ballet tutus trying to dip their cookies in milk to an orchestral Strauss waltz. Since 1995 the American Choreography Awards has included the category of "dance in commercials" to acknowledge the proliferation of strong dance choreography in this medium. It is not new to use dance to sell products: a comic film short titled "Wash Your

Step" (1928–29) showed a traveling vacuum salesman using dance first in door-to-door pitches and then in film commercials to advance his marketing objectives. What *is* new is the recognition that the condensed dramaturgy of these dance advertisements shows skill, entertains, and communicates effectively.

Internet

The presence of dance on the Internet creates a space for dance that is not organized by or restricted by geography, because anyone with Internet access can search for dance across borders. Dance created for the Internet is a by-product of the digital age and the increasing effects of globalization. Web dances are plentiful; a search with English keywords yields examples primarily of anglophone choreographers and designers. Animation techniques and computer-graphics programs, as well as digitized recordings of live dance and movement, play to the contemporary aesthetic of entertainment. Although plentiful, choreography on the Web sometimes has a short shelf life: Website addresses or hosts change, yielding to new fashions.

Dance Video Games

As video games are a major North American pastime for children and adults, it is not surprising that games involving dance have been designed. Perhaps because television reality shows have raised interest in dance competition, or perhaps because video-cam interaction with game players has become widespread, dance video games now permit players to perform or imitate dance moves. Karaoke games, which measure players' ability to sing popular songs into a microphone connected to the game equipment, now accommodate the hookup of a video-cam that records and rates the contestants' dance or performance skills. From among a variety of dance video games, Dance Dance Revolution (DDR) has achieved the greatest following to date (May 2006). This Japanese-made game, known as Dancing Stage in the United Kingdom, debuted in Tokyo video arcades in 1998 and quickly found a following in North America. Now available in many home video game formats, DDR cues players with screen symbols to execute steps in a specified order and rhythm on a dance pad floor. DDR aficionados fall into two types: the "technical" or "PA" (perfect attack) players, whose objective is to execute the specified footwork and rhythm as cleanly as possible; and the "freestyle" players, who may play lower difficulty levels so they can add personal embellishments to the required footwork.

Home versions of DDR are popular, but the lure of playing before a crowd draws players to the arcade sites. Some players enjoy showing off special skills or getting to know regular players. Arcade tournaments or dance-offs usually attract more PA participants than freestyle. Interest in DDR has been heightened (or perhaps mirrored or parodied, in some cases) by the game's being featured in television shows such as *Will & Grace* and *Malcolm in the Middle*, in cartoons such as *King of the Hill* and *South Park*, in commercials, and in music videos by Madonna and other pop artists.

While DDR and other games like it are designed primarily to measure precision footwork, others measure arm movements (such as ParaParaParadise). Some (EZ2Dancer or Dance Maniax) require both footwork and arm movements. Samba de Amigo registers how well the player shakes a set of maracas in a movement pattern. Slated for release in the fall of 2006, Dance Factory boasts it will free players to use music tracks from their personal collections rather than restrict them to installed music selections.

DANCE CULTURE IN CANADA

Dance culture in Canada is affected by the size of the country (3.8 million square miles, which exceeds the area of the United States), over which a mere 31.8 million people have settled, of which more than 40 percent reside in one of six urban centers (the bilingual capital of Canada, Ottawa, in the province of Ontario, with its twin city Hull, Quebec; the primarily English-speaking cities of Toronto in Ontario, Edmonton and Calgary in Alberta, and Vancouver in British Columbia; and the predominantly French-speaking Montreal in Quebec). The country is officially bilingual, and the dance culture has developed differently in Quebec than in the English-speaking provinces, whether within rural or urban communities. As the principal minority culture of Canada, the French-speaking population constitutes about 23 percent of the total population, versus 45 percent for the anglophone residents, according to statistics from 2005.[3]

Through the nineteenth century, dance in Canada was largely influenced by the two major colonizers that had settled it: the British in Ontario and parts of the English-speaking Maritime Provinces, and the French in Quebec and "Acadia" (the French settlements in the Maritimes). The dances of the European ballrooms and the European and Russian ballet repertory and performers were the most fashionable imported cultural objects in urban centers throughout Canada. Where there were pockets of English-speakers among the Quebecois, as in Montreal, Anglophones were served by English-speaking dancing masters.

Anglophone Culture

Canadian occasions for great festivities often reflected the influence of British rule, such as the Victorian Era Ball in Toronto in 1897, which celebrated the 50 years that Victoria had ruled as queen of England. Hosted by the wife of the governor-general, who had held a similar ball in the nation's capital, Ottawa, in 1896, the Victorian Era Ball was a costume ball with a Canadian history theme for its 3,000 guests. Dances at this occasion included society dances from throughout her reign, from early Victorian couple dances such as the waltz, schottische, and polka (the queen's favorite when it was introduced to London in 1844) to late-century favorites such as the two-step (a dance inspired by John Philip Sousa's march music) and the lancers. Most of the dance academies in Ontario cities such as Toronto or Hamilton in the mid- to latter part of the nineteenth century offered classes in ballroom dancing as well as stage dancing. Stage dances might include those that had been featured at popular international exhibitions or those featured on the vaudeville stages. Canada's best-known dancing master at the turn of the nineteenth to the twentieth century was Toronto's John Freeman Davis (1835–1916), who published a book of dance instructions in 1878 and who held the office of vice president for both the American National Dancing Association and the National Association of Teachers of Dancing of the United States and Canada. His academy taught both stage and social dance. Advertisements in Toronto newspapers and theater programs of this era show that dance lessons were offered in ballroom dances, British national dances such as the hornpipe and Highland fling, acrobatics, and etiquette. At this time, music for ballroom dancing oftentimes was composed by Canadians, though popular European and U.S. melodies were also in fashion. In rural areas, a tradition of Ontario step-dancing and country dancing (longways dances and square dances) that were influenced by the traditional dances of Scotland, England, and the United States became popular. In some areas, U.S. squares were also introduced.

Social and theatrical dancing was not always considered favorably. In the 1800s some Christian sects objected to dancing for entertainment purposes. Evidence in newspapers offers examples where Christian fundamentalists managed to close public performances and ballroom soirées. Hugh Thomas Crossley's 1895 treatise titled *A Practical Discussion of the Parlor Dance, the Theatre, the Cards* is representative of the objections against dance published in Canada. The contemporary dance practices of the twentieth century have also earned censure from some Christian communities, notably private colleges operated by fundamentalist sects. Most Canadian institutions of higher education are public institutions, so anti-dance campuses are few. Also, with the emergence of Christian rock and rap groups, some campuses have softened their policies in the past decade to permit social dances if the song lyrics and style of dancing meet defined standards of decency. Recently, Trinity Western University in British Columbia permitted the first of a series of six probationary dance events as well as swing and salsa lessons.[4]

The documentation of popular dance in the Maritimes, which consists of the provinces of Labrador, Newfoundland, Prince Edward Island, New Brunswick, and Nova Scotia, is far from complete. Most of the area was settled initially by Irish and Scottish, but some remnants of French language and culture remain in the area from France's claim to Acadia, Nova Scotia, in 1605. The tradition of Scottish music and dance has been especially enduring in Nova Scotia for many reasons: communal entertainments solidified the community identity, the impoverished fishing communities had no money for nor access to formal concert and theatrical performances, among other factors. There are records of French dancing masters in Cape Breton in the mid-eighteenth century, and in Halifax British officers enjoyed balls and light entertainments. In the early 1900s through the 1940s dance teachers taught a variety of social dances, ballet classes, vaudeville dance styles, and versions of the revived Greek dances, but none of these supplanted the strong traditional dances for any length of time.

In the Yukon, a coexisting tradition of longways (contra dance) sets as well as square dance exists. This dual country-dance practice is attributed to the migrations of prospectors from areas of the U.S. South and West (where U.S. squares were prevalent), as well as from regions of anglophone Canada, to the Yukon during the gold rush.

Francophone Culture

In francophone Canada, traditional dancing was a form of French community identification. Quebec became isolated from direct influence of the mother country after the French and Indian War (1763), but its encapsulation on both sides by English-speaking provinces and by New England to the south introduced Anglo influences on the dance practice. The conservative Catholic Church in Quebec had officially prohibited all dancing as sinful, until 1952 when Cardinal Léger designated folk dancing as an acceptable pastime. Evidence, however, suggests that social dances such as quadrilles (often with the longways "country quadrille" formation), contra dances, *gigues* (from Irish jigs), *ronds* (circle dances), and *danses carrées* (U.S. squares) have had long traditions in Quebec. U.S. squares were introduced when Quebecois who worked in New England industries brought the social activities back home. The gigue was traditionally a man's solo dance: with an upright posture and relaxed legs, the giguer tapped rhythms with his heels and toes. Giguing steps have also been used as traveling steps or as a way to mark time while waiting for the next figure in a contredanse. In an effort to support continuing dance traditions, La Féderation des Loisirs-Danses du Québec sponsors well-attended workshops and dance camps on traditional francophone dance and maintains an archival resource of traditional dance.

In the major urban center of Montreal, the French Catholic and English Protestant cultures and languages existed side by side, a factor that supported the presence of social and theatrical dance despite Catholic dance prohibitions. In the 1930s to 1980s the Morenoff Studio offered classes in social dance and acrobatics, the latter perhaps a precedent to the athletic physicality embraced by French Canadian concert dance and Cirque du Soleil. A number of protégés of the Morenoff Studio danced on the stage of Les Variétés Lyriques before heading to New York City and elsewhere to better their dance careers, and one dancer (Fernand Nault) returned to Montreal to choreograph for Les Grands Ballets Canadiens, achieving international notice with his rock-opera *Tommy*.

Governmental control of broadcast media has served to create a popular following for ballet in Quebec lacking elsewhere in North America. The francophone Canadian network Société Radio-Canada (SRC) and its television station CBFT in Montreal inaugurated a weekly arts program called *L'Heure du concert* (the concert hour) in 1954. This program developed and broadcast what might be considered "elite arts" to the general populace. For ballet, Ludmilla Chiriaeff, a Russian ballet-trained immigrant, created about three hundred ballets suited specifically for the boxy screen of television broadcast. When she founded Les Grands Ballets Canadiens, her potential audience had already been introduced to ballet through television. Furthermore, her work along with the work of others choreographing specifically for television in this period contributed to the advancement of Canadian choreography in new media.

Les Ballets Jazz de Montréal adapted aspects of the popular jazz genre, employed ballet technique, and created an artful dance company with popular appeal. The ethnic origins of the three founders of Les Ballet Jazz—Haiti, Hungary, and France-Morocco—have supported the company's development of indigenous and nontraditional forms of jazz-ballet. Montreal's dance scene continues to be an international creative mix of concert performances and festival events.

Canada's Cultural Mosaic

Canadian policies regarding the acculturation of immigrants differ significantly from the approach in the United States. As a result, the cultural traditions brought to Canada have been encouraged to coexist alongside the dominant practices of Anglophones and Francophones, especially in Canada's urban areas. Where the metaphor to describe the integration of immigrant groups and their cultures into the United States has been a "melting pot" of cultural assimilation, the Canadian image has been a "mosaic" of culture, where the incoming groups are encouraged to practice the arts, cuisine, religion, and other aspects of their homelands. Although this idealized vision of cultural richness and appreciative coexistence has not always been achieved, music and dance have been ways that immigrant communities resist assimilation or exercise aspects of their native culture within the dominant English and French cultures. For example, recently Latin Americans who have immigrated to Montreal have begun to learn, dance, and promote salsa and other Latin dances *after* coming to Canada, as a confirmation of their identify. In the 1990s South Asian youth, who no longer wear traditional clothing and whose families have dispersed to the suburbs from Toronto's India Village, have found a cultural connection through bhangra dances. Hungarian communities in Toronto participate in *tanchaz*, a tradition of Roma-style music and improvisational dancing, to retain their ethnic connections. Two additional examples—Ukrainians and West Indians—highlight the ways that dance and dance events have been used by immigrant communities as a popular pastime or event that reinforces their heritage and cultural continuity.

Ukrainian Dance

Although their numbers in the larger population may seem small (in 2005 about 1.8 percent of Canadian residents named Ukraine as their ethnic heritage),[5] Ukrainians have maintained a strong presence in Canada since the 1900s, with additional waves of Ukrainian immigrants arriving throughout the twentieth century. Coming from a country with severe winters, the climate of Canada in the prairies did not seem inhospitable. Ukrainian community centers provided a common focus for cultural events, and traditional dance and music became a favored pastime. The earliest recorded instance of the staging of Ukrainian dance is 1904, in Winnipeg as a commemoration of a Ukrainian poet. Ballet dancer-choreographer Vasył Avramenko, who emigrated from Ukraine in 1925, codified the Ukrainian folk repertory. His approach reflected the USSR's influence on the classical ballet and folk practice of Soviet satellite republics, a markedly more balletic style and more technical execution than the traditions brought by earlier immigrants. Furthermore, he encouraged the design of new Ukrainian dances based on the codified steps and styles, the result being the creation of a Ukrainian stage dance rather than a folk or social dance form. In the provinces of western Canada, popularity of Ukrainian stage dance has increased, alongside opportunities to demonstrate skills in competition. The majority (about 70 percent) of participants are girls, who adopt the traditional embroidered blouses and braided hairstyle as part of the traditional costume. The judging system approximates that of the 1990s Olympic figure skating criteria.

Until 1984, when the Cheremosh Dance Festival in Edmonton, Alberta, was established, none of the Ukrainian festivals was devoted solely to dance competition. There are now six Ukrainian dance competitions in Saskatchewan, and three more in Alberta. Although these competitions are amateur events, the festivals are organized with professional lighting and sound systems on proscenium stages and they draw participants from afar. Significantly, the forms of Ukrainian dance that have developed through the influence of Avramenko's ballet aesthetic and the encouragement of new Canadian-Ukrainian choreographies are not intended to be "authentic" Ukrainian dance but represent efforts to forge a Canadian-Ukrainian community with an identity and culture of its own.

West Indian Caribana

Toronto, Ontario, and Montreal, Quebec, had attracted a significant inflow of West Africans during the 1950s and 1960s. With the hundredth anniversary of Canada in 1967 and the involvement of Montreal's West African community in contributing representative cultural programming to Expo '67 in Montreal, Toronto's West African community became motivated to create a West Indian carnival event in Toronto that would honor their contribution to Canada's cultural mosaic. Called Caribana, in its first year the festival included performances of seven masquerade bands and a ball, a boat cruise, and an island picnic (Toronto has several small islands offshore). The summertime festival, though widely heralded, was marked by petty political infighting in the 1970s and by conflicts between West Indians and Toronto police in the 1980s. The event, complete with Website, continues to be a tourist attraction, but the content of the festival has evolved to include aspects of North

American youth culture, such as hip-hop music and dance, that have been adopted by West Indian young people in Ontario. Caribana has become the largest Caribbean festival in North America.

Youth Culture

With the explosion of the U.S. commercial music industry and increasing access to a worldwide range of popular music genres, Canada's youth culture has been much affected by trends that come from outside the country's borders. The late 1970s saw an influx of mainstream U.S. disco dancing into urban clubs, but other music and dance genres were represented, such as reggae clubs in downtown Toronto, which reflected the increase in West Indian immigration. Raves and their corresponding techno music achieved a following in Toronto, Halifax, Montreal, and other cities, but city officials concerned with the associated drug use (ecstasy and other drug cocktails) tried—albeit unsuccessfully—to ban or restrict them. Bhangra, the popular Punjabi music and dance party that blends traditional music with Bollywood (the nickname for Bombay, the home of India's film industry) and Western pop sound, has also found popularity in urban centers with Indian settlements. Both raves and bhangras in Canada bear greater similarities to parallel British dance events than to those in the United States. By the close of the century, Latin-American dances such as the salsa became ubiquitous in Toronto and Montreal, especially among college-age and young professionals.

DANCE CULTURE IN THE UNITED STATES

The United States lacks a single national or folk dance because of the myriad forms of popular dance that were inherited or developed. The U.S. Congress has been lobbied by proponents of Western square dancing to adopt it as the national dance; however, in practice no one popular or traditional U.S. dance seems to represent a national character or geography.

Historically, imported European and African dances have shaped the development of popular dance in the United States. British "country" dances (including contras and step-dancing) and European folk-based social dances (such as the waltz, polka, and quadrille) took shape as U.S. forms of contra dance, square dancing, and clogging and U.S. adaptations of ballroom couple dances. However, the indigenous rhythms and dance movements brought by enslaved Africans interacted with the imposed dance cultures of the white plantations to produce new kinds of entertainment, music, and dance. Following the Civil War, as freed African Americans left the South to find opportunities in northern cities, African-American influence on popular dance and entertainment became the pervasive and dominant practice. Although white entertainers and dance teachers may have diluted the new movements and rhythms to culturally acceptable forms for mainstream white culture, the widespread appeal of these dances prepared U.S. culture to acquire a taste for syncopation and polyrhythms of future influxes of music and dance from the Caribbean and South America, as well as additional innovations of African-American jazz, swing, and rap. Thus, couple dances with a version of the ballroom hold (a European invention) would survive in U.S. social dance practice, but the most popular couple dances would show influences of African-American culture (Lindy and swing) or Latin America (in tango, salsa, and others).

The importance of U.S. innovation in, and ultimately domination of, the music industry cannot be underestimated in characterizing the development of popular dance forms and practices that have influenced popular dancing worldwide. The export of dances born in the United States began in the nineteenth century with the two-step that accompanied John Philip Sousa's marches, but the commercial music industry in the twentieth century converted from sheet music to phonograph records, radio airwaves, and—with talkie film—movie soundtracks, all of which facilitated the transmission of U.S. dance and music. With digital music files available on CD or on the Internet, dance bands and club recordings are available everywhere. At the end of the twentieth century, hip-hop dance and rap from African-American culture and country-western music and dance of white America were the two prominent U.S. forms that could boast an extensive influence and presence both in North America and worldwide. The impact of Latin-American rhythms on club culture and popular dance—especially in salsa dancing, which continues to grow—has not fully been appreciated or assimilated; however, with the current population of Spanish-speaking residents, Latino culture will likely continue to impact the popular dance across the United States. The globalization of the entertainment industry has not meant that dominant strains of U.S. culture prevail but rather—at least in the United States—that smaller pockets of vernacular dance-music culture (techno-rave, traditional country, or Cajun, for example) are able to sustain themselves through independent labels that can market on Amazon.com or the Internet.

Many of the genres of popular U.S. social dance and club dance have line dances among their practices. Participants stand individually and execute the same steps or gestures. From the Electric Slide, to Cotton-eyed Joe, to the disco line dances, these dances have established movement patterns and steps that the community recognizes and perpetuates. Line dances also break down inherited pairings of heterosexuals in European couple dances. Instead, as many as wish to dance may participate, no matter what the gender balance or sexual preference. These recognizable dances may be incorporated into festive community events, such as weddings, parties, fairs, and community festivals, as well as dance clubs.

The African-American forms of percussive dance—tap and stepping—also set the precedent in North America for people of the same gender to dance together socially. In fact, tap circles and stepping groups tend to be organized around a single sex when they dance together, though the audience for these demonstrations is usually mixed. Break dancing and capoeira have similarly been split along gender lines, as the forms initially were practiced by men and only later taken up by women. Some of the gender divisions have been blurred as more women participate and achieve a level of expertise on par with men.

Imported Dances

Although the United States takes credit for many of the popular dance styles (and their corresponding music forms) exported worldwide in the twentieth century, some vernacular dance forms have found followings elsewhere before catching on in U.S. clubs. Latin-American dance fads have included the tango and maxixe in the first two decades of the twentieth century, followed by the Cuban rumba and Brazilian samba through the 1940s, and the mambo craze of the 1950s. The disco Latin Hustle showed a continued Latin influence, and the salsa craze that swept the United States during the late 1990s and into the twenty-first century is an amalgam of Latin rhythms and steps. As the population of Latino-Americans increases, it is no longer accurate to categorize Latin-American-flavored dances as imports.

The rave phenomenon of northern Europe and British white-male working-class culture, with its distinctive techno music, began as an underground practice but became commercialized and mainstream through part of the 1990s. Although some of the musical features of techno music may find their origins in the predecessor disco genre, its development as a dance-music culture must be attributed to European innovations and practice. Moshing and ska, both punk-influenced dance cultures, were imported from Great Britain. In the 1980s, in moshing, also called slam-dancing, dancers pulsed forcefully to the fast beats and slam-dancers rammed against other dancers or threw themselves off the stage edge onto the crowd. Ska became popular in Anglo cultures worldwide before finding a following in the United States. In the 1960s ska music had developed from a combination of Jamaican music and blues; a second wave of ska created a hybrid form with British influences, in the late 1970s to early 1980s. The third wave of ska, which added influences from different rock styles including punk, found American fans in ska dance clubs of the 1990s. Described as punk-influenced, the movements typical of third-wave ska dance style (called "skanking") involved keeping knees and elbows bent, with an angular pumping of the legs and arms.

In the United States, immigrants from European countries in the early twentieth century and thereafter were encouraged to embrace the prevailing cultural practices—from food to entertainment—of their new country. Although many groups did assimilate, some determinedly created urban cultural centers at which they could keep their language and culture alive. For example, the Polish community, which settled along the "Rust Belt" (the northern cities from Buffalo and Cleveland to Chicago and Detroit), has retained much of its culture with polka bands and celebrations of traditional Polish festivities. The practices of these European immigrant communities, however, never influenced music and dance fashions outside of their small cultural community.

Ballroom

Social ballroom dancing of the early twentieth century has largely disappeared with its survivors being exhibition and competition ballroom dancing, with its codified movements and standards of execution. Arthur Murray (1895–1991) may be the best-known American teacher of social and ballroom dancing. Born in New York City as Murray Teichman, he created a mail-order business for his dance lessons and re-created diagrams for floor plans and instruction books with footprints showing the order and direction of the dance steps. In 1925 he used his name for a dance-lesson franchise business. Initially, he trained teachers who gave lessons for the Statler Hotel chain, but he expanded the business into dance studios in 1938. The first studio franchise opened in Minneapolis, Minnesota. At the height of popularity, the studios numbered in the thousands, but in the twenty-first century there remain fewer than 200. Competition dances that had formerly been danced socially, like the quickstep and jive (the transformation of jitterbug to the competition ballroom arena), have had their names restored by reality-television dance contests such as *Dancing with the Stars*. Whether these shows will have a long-term impact on ballroom dance forms remains to be seen.

Christian Dance

Christian liturgical dance might well be considered a form of ethnic dance for the Protestant groups that practice it in the United States. Many of the Christian sects that had banned dance now permit liturgical dance, also called "praise dance," because its function is to confirm the community's religious values. The lyrical movement quality, especially in the choreography for women, shows some affinity with the elegance of classical ballet vocabulary and U.S. forms of early modern dance (Doris Humphrey's or Isadora Duncan's style). Schools of liturgical dance have been established in some regions; these have developed their own codified systems of positions and dance movements. In some major metropolitan areas (including Chicago, the District of Columbia, and cities in the South), the communities of dancers identifying themselves as professional praise or liturgical dance practitioners are extensive. Among the African-American churches with liturgical dancers, aspects of contemporary hip-hop movement and athletic dancing are permitted for the male dancers. Movements that are deemed to be sexualized are not part of the Christian dance canon.

Youth Culture

The twenty-first century marks a trend toward more opportunities for dance instruction in popular forms, for children as well as for adults. Most urban and suburban community dance studios that had offered instruction in the triumvirate of ballet, tap, and jazz now add other movement forms such as hip-hop, Latin-American dances such as salsa or tango, belly dancing as an aerobic activity, or dancercise influenced by martial arts. The dance forms at local studios, which hope to appeal to popular tastes in dance and recreation, are often merged with jazz or other studio dance material in a commercialized form. Competition ballroom dancing has also recently been embraced in the K–12 school systems. Piloted by veteran ballroom dance champions Pierre Dulaine and Yvonne Marceau of American Ballroom Theater, this after-school program for fifth graders in New York City uses ballroom instruction to foster self-esteem, social skills, physical coordination, concentration, and self-discipline, and the program ends with a citywide competition. The 2005 documentary of this program in the film *Mad Hot Ballroom* has generated interest nationwide. Additionally, the 2006 dramatic feature film *Take the Lead* features Antonio Banderas as Pierre Dulaine.

Precision dancing has achieved widespread appeal among young people. In addition to the teams that have been formed in Irish step-dancing and African-American step and drill, high school and college dance teams compete in a hybrid form of ballet, jazz, and hip-hop set to pop music. Preparing for these events fosters a strong sense of community and also functions as a social activity. In addition to contests, school dance teams often demonstrate their routines at sports events. Forms that initially served one cultural group have often been taken up by others. The practice of African-American stepping at Greek societies on college campuses has been adopted by student groups of other minority cultures. Both Latino and South Asian Greek groups have taken to stepping, each adding elements characteristic of their own cultures. The Latinos added phrases in Spanish, used Latin dance movements, and performed to Latin-American tunes and rhythms. Bhangra music was used in some cases of the South Asian step shows.

Concert Dance Choreographers in Popular Forms and Media

Ballet and modern/postmodern dance have had rarefied existences in the United States. *The Nutcracker* (1892), a recognizable Christmas staple for ballet companies, is perhaps the only classical ballet to have achieved a popular audience. Ballet and modern dance choreographers have contributed choreography for popular entertainments. New York City Ballet founder George Balanchine choreographed for Broadway, film, and even a circus elephant dance, and modern dance choreographer Agnes de Mille is best-known for her film choreography for *Oklahoma!* (1955). Jamaican-born Garth Fagan, founder of Rochester's Bucket Dance turned Garth Fagan Dance, garnered a Tony Award for his choreography for *The Lion King* on Broadway (1998). Twyla Tharp's movement experiments of the 1970s bear little resemblance to the film choreography she contributed to *Hair* (1979) and *Amadeus* (1984) or to the Broadway production of *Movin' Out* (2002). Much of the modern dance choreography of Louis Falco (1943–93) is rarely performed, but his style of choreographed chaos is preserved in the group dances of *Fame* (1980).

Several major motion pictures have inadvertently popularized classical ballet while using it as a context for a Hollywood formulaic story, often meeting with some commercial and critical success. *The Turning Point* (1977) featured dancer-turned-film-star Shirley MacLaine and actress Anne Bancroft in roles where the characters played out ballet rivalries from their youth. International ballet star Mikhail Baryshnikov made his film debut in this movie, among a bevy of American Ballet Theatre dancers in roles of aspiring company members. Neve Campbell, a former Canadian ballet dancer before her film career, conceived the screenplay for and starred in *The Company* (2003), in which the physical and emotional hazards of ballet life were dramatized. *Center Stage* (2000) with ABT star Ethan Stiefel and *Save the Last Dance* (2001) both followed teen drama formulas.

African-American choreographers in modern dance have more consistently used vernacular forms on the concert dance stage. Alvin Ailey, who founded the world-class modern dance company that bears his name, and his colleague Talley Beatty incorporated African-American club culture, jazz and swing dance, and other vernacular elements into their choreographies, dating from the 1950s, a practice that continues in the Ailey company now under the direction of Judith Jamison. Since the 1990s, Philadelphian Rennie Harris has used his expertise in hip-hop for his company PUREMOVEMENT. His choreography uses the appeal of vernacular dance to show urban conflicts, dangers, and attitudes in a different way. Some of his work is autobiographical, such as the voice-over narrative for his solo *Endangered Species* with pop-and-lock and West African movement. Group dances are sometimes heavily mimetic or incorporate recognizable urban club styles. Acknowledging the importance of the connection between social and staged dance, Edward Villella, artistic director of Miami City Ballet, chose to use recognizable social dances from the waltz to the mambo for his newest work, *Neighborhood Ballroom*. The positive reception that these two artists have garnered from mainstream dance critics suggests that the boundaries between genres of ballet-modern-postmodern concert dance and vernacular dance practice are relaxing.

RESOURCE GUIDE

PRINT SOURCES

Bain, Ted. "Moving Past Words: Choreographed Parody in Popular Film." *The Mid-Atlantic Almanack* 13 (2004): 3–16.

Best, Amy L. *Prom Night: Youth, Schools, and Popular Culture*. New York: Routledge, 2000.

Billman, Larry. *Film Choreographers and Dance Directors: An Illustrated Biographical Encyclopedia with a History and Filmographies, 1893 through 1995*. Jefferson: McFarland, 1997.

Calabria, Frank M. *Dance of the Sleep-Walkers: The Dance Marathon Fad*. Bowling Green, OH: Bowling Green State University Popular Press, 1993.

Comeaux, Malcolm L. "The Cajun Dance Hall." *Material Culture* 32.1 (2000): 37–56.

Dawson, Jim. *The Twist: The Story of the Song and Dance That Changed the World*. London: Faber and Faber, 1995.

Dodds, Sherril, *Dance on Screen: Genres and Media from Hollywood to Experimental Art*. Basingstoke: Palgrave, 2001.

Emery, Lynne Fauley. *Black Dance from 1619 to Today*, 2nd edition, revised. Princeton: Dance Horizons, 1988.

Fine, Elizabeth C. *Soulstepping: African American Step Shows*. Urbana: University of Illinois Press, 2003.

Fisher, Jennifer Joyce. "The Annual 'Nutcracker': A Participant-Oriented, Contextualized Study of 'The Nutcracker' Ballet as It Has Evolved into a Christmas Ritual in the United States and Canada." Ph.D. dissertation, University of California, Riverside, 1998.

Flores, Juan. *From Bomba to Hip Hop: Puerto Rican Culture and Latino Identity.* New York: Columbia University Press, 2000.

Gerard, Morgan. "The Molecules of Ritual: Promoting, Producing, and Performing Raving and Clubbing in Toronto." Ph.D. dissertation, University of Toronto, 2004.

Golinowski, Jason O. "Gold, Silver, Bronze: Reflections on a Ukrainian Dance Competition." M.A. dissertation, University of Alberta, 1999.

Groppa, Carlos G. *The Tango in the United States.* Jefferson: McFarland, 2004.

Hazzard-Gordon, Katrina. *Jookin': The Rise of Social Dance Formations in African-American Culture.* Philadelphia: Temple University Press, 1990.

Heth, Charlotte. "Native American Aesthetics: Music and Dance." Pp. 410–414 in Jacob Ernest Cooke (ed.), *Encyclopedia of the North American Colonies*, Volume 3. New York: Scribner's, 1993.

Macpherson, Susan, ed. *Encyclopedia of Theatre Dance in Canada/Encyclopédie de la danse théâtrale au Canada.* Toronto: Dance Collection Danse, 2000.

Malnig, Julie. *Dancing till Dawn: A Century of Exhibition Ballroom.* Westport: Greenwood, 1992.

Malone, Jacqui. *Steppin' on the Blues: The Visible Rhythms of African-American Dance.* Urbana: University of Illinois Press, 1996.

Mathews, Lita. "The Native American Powwow: A Contemporary Authentication of a Cultural Artefact." Ph.D. dissertation, University of New Mexico, 1999.

Mishler, Craig. *The Crooked Stovepipe: Athapaskan Fiddle Music and Square Dancing in Northeast Alaska and Northwest Canada.* Urbana: University of Illinois Press, 1993.

Nahachewsky, Andriy. "The Kolomyika: Change and Diversity in Canadian Ukrainian Folk Dance." 2 vols. Ph.D. dissertation, University of Alberta, 1991.

Odom, Selma Landen, and Mary Jane Warner, eds. *Canadian Dance: Visions and Stories.* Toronto: Dance Collection Danse, 2004.

Phillip, Lyndon Andrew. "The Caribana Festival: Continuity, Change, Crisis and an Alternative Music." M.A. dissertation, York University, 1998.

Pietrobruno, Sheenagh. "Salsa and Its Transnational Moves: The Commodification of Latin Dance in Montreal." Ph.D. dissertation, McGill University, 2001.

Shadd, Ruth Ann. *Breaking Loose: A History of African-Canadian Dance in Southwestern Ontario, 1900–1955.* Windsor, Ontario: Preney Print, 1995.

Simon, Bradford Scott. "Entering the Pit: Slam-Dancing and Modernity." *Journal of Popular Culture* 31.1 (1997): 149–176.

Sommer, Sally R. "Social Dance: Twentieth-Century Social Dance since 1960." In Selma Jeanne Cohen (ed.), *International Encyclopedia of Dance.* Oxford: Oxford University Press, 1998.

Spalding, Susan Eike, and Jane Harris Woodside, eds. *Communities in Motion: Dance, Community, and Tradition in America's Southeast and Beyond.* Westport: Greenwood, 1995.

Tomko, Linda. *Dancing Class: Gender, Ethnicity, and Social Divides in American Dance, 1890–1920.* Bloomington: Indiana University Press, 1999.

Voyer, Simonne. *La Danse traditionnelle dans l'est du Canada: quadrilles et cotillons.* Québec: L'Université Laval, 1986.

Wagner, Ann. *Adversaries of Dance: From the Puritans to the Present.* Urbana: University of Illinois Press, 1997.

Warwick, Jacqueline C. "Can Anyone Dance to This Music? Bhangra and Toronto's South Asian Youth." M.A. dissertation, York University, 1996.

WEBSITES

American Memory Project. Library of Congress, Washington, DC. http://www.memory.loc.gov/ammem/index.html. This project includes facsimiles of historic dance manuals through the 1920s and other dance history resources.

Bravo!Fact (A Foundation to Assist Canadian Talent). Toronto, Ontario. http://www.bravofact.com.

Gibson, Chanda, Mary Ingram, Celeste Warren, and Nicole Magson. *Step Dancing: A Canadian Tradition*. Accessed November 28, 1996. http://www.fiddle.on.ca/fiddle/valley.htm.

Landry, Michel. *La danse au Quebec*. http://www.cvm.qc.ca/mlandry/folklore/histo-1.htm.

Munger, John. *Dance/USA Research*. http://www.danceusa.org/facts_figures/research.htm.

Popular Balanchine. George Balanchine Foundation, New York, NY. http://balanchine.org/.

Quebec Winter Carnival. http://www.carnaval.qc.ca.

Toronto Caribana Festival. Toronto, Ontario. http://www.caribana.com/.

VIDEOS/FILMS

Breakin' In—The Making of a Hip Hop Dancer (National Film Board of Canada, 2005). Produced by Silva Basmajian, written and directed by Elizabeth St. Philip. DVD.

Burn the Floor (Duet Entertainment, 1999). DVD.

Mad Hot Ballroom (2005). Directed by Marilyn Agrello, written and produced by Amy Sewell.

Rize (Lions Gate Films, 2005). Directed by David LaChapelle.

The Story of Vernon and Irene Castle (RKO, 1939).

Talking Feet: Solo Southern Dance: Flatfoot, Buck, and Tap (El Cerrito, CA: Flower Films, 1988). Directed by Mike Seeger and Ruth Pershing. VHS.

Un Passe-temps terriblement dangereux [A Very Dangerous Pastime] (Grimm Pictures & Canada Dance Festival, 2000). Directed by Laura Taler.

ORGANIZATIONS

The Academy of Dance on Film (DOF), Hollywood, CA. http://www.danceonfilm.org/.

Country Dance and Song Society of America, Haydenville, MA. http://www.cdss.org/. The CDSS Library and Archives is a collection of dance, tune, and song books; recordings; manuscripts; microfiche records; and archival material dating from the Society's founding (1900). It is available to researchers at the New Hampshire Collection of Traditional Music & Dance of the University of New Hampshire Library, Durham.

Dance Collection Danse, Toronto, Ontario, Canada. http://www.dcd.ca.

Dance Heritage Coalition, Washington, DC. http://www.danceheritage.org.

Fédération des loisirs danses du Québec, 4545 av. Pierre-De Coubertin C P 1000, Succ. M, Montreal, Quebec H1V 3R2 Canada.

International Tap Association. http://www.tapdance.org.

Library of Congress, Washington, DC. http://www.loc.gov.

Ministry of Canadian Heritage. http://www.pch.gc.ca/pc-ch/org/mission/index_e.cfm.

National Library and Archives of Canada, Ottawa, Ontario, Canada. http://www.collectionscanada.ca.

New York Public Library, Jerome Robbins Dance Collection, New York, NY. http://www.nypl.org/research/lpa/dan/dan.html.

York University Library, Toronto, Ontario, Canada. http://www.library.yorku.ca/ccm/jsp/homepage.jsp.

NOTES

1. U.S. Census Bureau. http://factfinder.census.gov/servlet/DatasetMainPageServlet?_program=ACS&_lang=en&_ts=9 2837068834.
2. Frank M. Calabria, *Dance of the Sleep-Walkers: The Dance Marathon Fad* (Bowling Green: Bowling Green State University Popular Press, 1993), p. 1.
3. "Canada," *Encyclopedia Britannica Almanac 2006*.
4. Shanda Deziel, "Disco—without the Inferno," *Maclean's* [Toronto] (Mar. 6, 2006): 24–25. Accessed through ProQuest, May 1, 2006.
5. "Canada," *Encyclopedia Britannica Almanac 2006*.

FASHION AND APPEARANCE

PATRICIA A. CUNNINGHAM

UNITED STATES

Women's Fashion

Today Americans consume fashion and appearance products in amounts never dreamed of by their forebears. As with other developed and developing nations, Americans participate in a fashion system. In 2003 Americans spent $311.2 billion on apparel and shoes. Figures for 1999 show that Americans spent $8.0 billion on cosmetics. The business of fashion in the United States includes men's, women's, and children's apparel manufacturers; fiber, yarn, and fabrics producers; importers; retail stores; advertisers; marketers; and related accessory industries. Clothing styles worn by Americans today reflect a wide global scene. Innovations in fashion filter through a broad spectrum of influences. They are inspired by entertainment—film, television, theater—sports, celebrities, politics, religion, technology, and the genius of designers from all over the world.

Americans have a preference for practical, sporty clothes that suit their lifestyles. Stylish clothes are now available to all thanks to cheap materials and labor. The supply of clothing far exceeds demand. There are more venues for shopping per capita in the United States than anywhere in the world. Yet U.S. fashion is distinctive. U.S. style has developed around attitudes and values that reflect the thinking of a majority of citizens and reflects individual and collective identities.

U.S. fashion began long before the dawn of the twentieth century. At first, clothing reflected styles worn in countries of emigration. English, Dutch, and French influence was strong in the colonial period on the East Coast. Spanish culture influenced missions in the West. Trade with Native Americans altered the material culture of both. In the eighteenth century regional tastes developed in the settled port towns of Philadelphia, New York, and Boston. There was heavy dependence on British, French, and Dutch imported merchandise and style direction. Information about the latest fashion came from travelers and communications sent from abroad, fashion dolls, and fashion plates. Differences between social strata were largely based on wealth, with distinction being made between yeoman farmers, merchants, servants, and laborers. During and following the Revolutionary period, Americans often sought to distinguish themselves by revealing their belief in democracy and liberty by wearing homespun, clothing made of cloth of their own manufacture.

As the nineteenth century progressed, America's aspiration for decent clothing for everyone was realized through advances in mass manufacturing. Population growth was aided by increasing numbers of immigrants who made up a large portion of the labor force. It was important for new immigrants to look American, even if circumstances forced them to wear secondhand clothes. The fashion industry grew with increasing numbers of manufacturers, mail-order companies, retail outlets, and print sources for fashion news. Eventually the United States excelled at producing vast quantities of basic fabrics such as calico and denim that could be made into serviceable clothing for the country's expanding population. Ready-made men's suit production began in earnest in the 1830s and by the 1890s half of the male population wore ready-made suits. This rise in democratization of menswear supported the idea of democracy. The new ready-made suits replaced homespun, and in many respects symbolized the new industrial age.

The westward movement and change from a largely agrarian society to one with an economy also centered on manufacturing, retailing, and commerce resulted in not only a growing middle class but also an economy dependent on consumption. Fashion magazines such as *Godey's Lady's Book* (1830–98), *Peterson's Magazine* (1849–92), *Harper's Bazaar* (1867–present), *Vogue* (1892–present), and *The Delineator* (1873–1937) communicated the latest Parisian styles, which were then interpreted by U.S. dressmakers, department stores, and manufacturers. Other sources of new fashion ideas were dressmakers who offered patterns of their latest fashions on a limited basis. The dominant U.S. leaders in the development of paper patterns—sized, cut, and ready to use—were Ellen and William Demorest and Ebenezer Butterick, both of whom had thriving businesses in the 1860s. While the Demorests geared their offerings to the trade and a stylish middle-class audience, Butterick appealed to the general public. Etiquette books provided needed advice on how to behave properly as a middle-class American, including what to wear for different occasions and times of day.

Women's dress during the nineteenth century became increasingly elaborate, requiring large amounts of fabric and trimmings, all of which aided the consumption of goods.

The accumulation of great wealth by some Americans created a new leisure class that became known for its display of expensive, often Parisian, custom-made clothing to distinguish itself from the growing middle class. Although the turn of the twentieth century is clearly marked by conspicuous consumption of fashion, since the mid-nineteenth century there had been a growing concern for health and physical well-being. Dress reform efforts beginning in the early 1850s—motivated by politics, economics, and social issues, as well as aesthetics, comfort, and health needs—saw concerned women adopting trousers to replace long full skirts and then, beginning in the 1870s, replacing corsets with less restrictive reform underwear. From the 1870s through the first decade of the twentieth century women adopted artistic reform gowns based on historic styles, especially classical Greek and medieval clothing.

Women's reform movements promoted the need for less restrictive, more comfortable and reasonable dress styles, which materialized in the so-called Gibson Girls of the 1890s, who wore simple skirts and blouses. From these beginnings came the United States' reputation for well-made basic styles. Later, U.S. designers such as Claire McCardell, Norman

Norell, and Bonnie Cashin became known for simple, practical clothes that fit the active lifestyle of U.S. women.

1900–1920

In the first decade of the century, high fashion designers Paul Poiret in Paris and Mariano Fortuny in Venice countered the prevailing corseted S-curve silhouette by promoting the historically inspired, simple, aesthetic, high-waisted gowns of the artistic dress reformers. Both designers were popular with U.S. women. The U.S. dancer Isadora Duncan wore Fortuny gowns and promoted dress reform.

At the turn of the century New York City was the fashion hub of the United States. Imported goods that streamed into the ports found a ready market in the department stores and shops, many now frequented by a growing number of women and men working in the trades. Women worked in many occupations such as importers, as owners of dressmaking and milliner's shops, and as editors of magazines. In cities they were the major labor force in the fashion industry, working as mannequins, buyers, salespersons, milliners, and seamstresses. The less fortunate, such as new émigrés, toiled in the city's factories. Women's work required simple garments. The most popular were a shirtwaist (a blouse) and an ankle-length gored skirt, which became the uniform of the working woman during the first decade. A simple tailored suit likewise was popular. These garments were available in stores that sold ready-made clothing.

Although there was an identifiable fashion industry in New York City—importers, wholesalers, retailers, tailors, dressmakers and milliners, and footwear manufacturers—the styles worn by most Americans were largely determined by European fashion setters. For women this meant Paris couture—Worth, Callot Sisters, Mme. Paquin, Pioret, as well as Fortuny. London's Saville Row determined styles for men. New York's designers barely received recognition for their efforts. They included Herman Patrick Tappé, Miss E. M. A. Steimmetz, and the many designers working in the custom salons of department stores.[1]

Shopping in department and specialty stores of major cities became a popular pastime for those who could afford to be so entertained. The store names between New York and Chicago became household words—Gimbel's, Arnold Constable, B. Altman, Franklin Simon, Wanamakers, Scruggs, Vandervoort and Barney, Stix, Baer and Fuller, Marshall Field's, and Carson Pirie Scott. Some remained in business for much of the twentieth century; others are still in business—Bloomingdale's, Macy's, Lord and Taylor, Carson Pirie Scott, and Famous Barr. Specialty stores Bergdorf Goodman, Henri Bendel, and Saks Fifth Avenue likewise continue to shape U.S. fashion.

Clothing for families who lived outside of major cities was provided by small department stores and retail shops, catalogs (Sears and Montgomery Ward), and local dressmakers or was made by women themselves. Many shops and department stores offered fabrics and trimmings to meet the needs of seamstresses. Of course, wealthy women who did not travel abroad to procure a European wardrobe could have clothes made at the elite custom houses such as those of Mrs. Dunston and Mrs. Osborn in New York City. Many of the custom houses also provided imported goods. Other opportunities to shop for European fashion goods were in their New York branches of the English designer Lucile, Lady Duff Gordon, the Boué Soeurs, Redfern, and Revillion.

In addition to the previously mentioned shirtwaist, skirt, and tailored suit, the styles worn by women in the first two decades of the twentieth century changed significantly from a garment often described as having an S-curve silhouette, a shape defined by a similarly formed corset, to a reliance on the Directoire high-waisted style that was a mainstay of the artistic dress reformers and promoted by both Poiret and Fortuny. By 1907 the skirt became narrower and shorter and the monobosom (full gathered bodice front) disappeared. Paul Poiret even introduced trousers for a gardening outfit in 1908. Hats were oversized with wide brims and heavily trimmed. By 1910 the high collar was replaced by a softer look, a new look spurred on perhaps by the influence of exotic Eastern dress and peasant blouses that were seen in Paris shops. Dancer Irene Castle and silent film stars such as the Gish sisters helped create a new standard of beauty. Short hair was first worn by Irene Castle in 1914. By this time women's daytime clothes became looser, shorter, and more comfortable. Shorter skirts (calf length) were worn with blouses on the outside and low-slung loose belts. A sweater or long jacket might be worn over this combination.

1920s

The 1920s was a period of remarkable change in U.S. culture. New art forms appeared—art deco, cubism, and futurism. New forms of entertainment—the movies, music, and the radio—reached more and more Americans. Motorcars, the telephone, and electric power had changed the world. Mass communication and marketing increased and with it came a rise in the mass marketing of fashion.

The new simple styles that emerged from the relaxed look of the late teens were easier to mass-produce; thus more ready-to-wear women's garments became available. Women wanted the new, easy-to-wear, freeing styles that were promoted by a new crop of Parisian designers—Coco Chanel, Jean Patou, M. Vionnet, and Elsa Schiaparelli. The look was sporting and it fit especially well with young women's newfound freedoms—cropped hair, bright lipstick, dancing to the latest jazz music, and smoking in public. These freedoms complemented the newly won right to vote. The clothes were simple chemises that were cut straight, were slim, and by mid-decade rose to above the knee. The chemise, a boyish look, often had a lowered waistline secured with a belt. Chanel had introduced costume jewelry, fake pearls and gems, as well as jerseys for women's wear and the little black dress. A hip-length sweater worn over a matching pleated skirt was another popular style. A cloche hat worn over the close-cropped hair and T-strap heels completed the daytime look.

The flapper was the ideal; she wore the shortest of dresses and if she could afford it one of the beaded dresses with fringe that moved when she danced to the new music called jazz. Other styles had uneven hemlines or pleats. Loose-fitting pajamas replaced tea gowns as at-home ensembles, a style introduced by Poiret. A spirit of reckless abandon seemed to prevail with college students, at least as judged by their elders. Even the wearing of galoshes unfastened so that they flapped (the origin of the term *flapper*) was deemed alarming.

In the twenties the number of stores increased, selling styles created by both European and U.S. designers. The American Hattie Carnegie built an art deco–style store for her business in 1925. Although made-to-measure clothing was still popular, ready-to-wear clothing increased and was produced by still-anonymous manufacturers such as Davidow, Max Meyer, Max Grab, and Edward Mayer. Prices could be kept low by using the new fiber rayon rather than silk for dresses. Other stores of note were Milgrim, where Sally Milgrim was the in-house designer, and Jay-Thorpe, which sold imported goods as well as their own in-house designs and accessories. Tappé was popular as the "Poiret" of New York, as was Jessie Franklin Turner, who continued to produce tea gowns for her New York customers. New designers appeared on the New York fashion scene: Valentina opened a couture house in 1925; Charles

James, a transplanted Englishman whose mother was an American, established a millinery business in the late 1920s; and Elizabeth Hawes founded a custom house in 1928. Jo Copeland and many other designers became known within the fashion industry through their work as in-house designers for stores or for manufacturers.

1930s

During the 1930s there was a shift away from the boyish flapper ideal to one that was more feminine, with style cut on the bias that revealed the natural shape of a woman's body. The style was more grown-up, elegant, and sophisticated. Although the Depression continued to affect the economy, an interest in fashion prevailed. It seemed that the stores were thriving. The glamour of the movies was beginning to translate into an American style. Film stars became the new ideal. Every woman wanted to look like a movie star or at least wear star fashions.

The bias-cut gowns had low backs and were made to look like bathing suits, and vice versa (suntanning was popular). Daytime looks included longer and narrower slim skirts and blouses close fitting to the body. They might have a new zipper or be cut from a man-made fabric, rayon. The ready-to-wear industry obliged by producing copies of dresses seen in the movies. The Lettie Lynton dress designed by Adrian for Joan Crawford seems to have been the singularly most popular copy. Even pattern companies offered "movie star" styles. Along with influencing fashion, the film industry was beginning to create excitement as a fashion center for the production of sportswear. Movie lifestyle had influenced Americans as well, for swimming, skiing, tennis, and other sports became popular with the middle class. Averill Harriman created Sun Valley in Idaho as the first destination ski resort. It became a popular vacation spot for movie stars and wealthy Americans. With the rise of sports and sportswear and the popularity of the bias-cut gown, the slim silhouette became the ideal look.

Newspapers and magazines more often mentioned U.S. designers. Saks Fifth Avenue and other stores promoted their in-house designers; Sofie Gimbel, the wife of the owner, was the designer for Saks's *Salon Modern*. Other stores with in-house designers of note were Bergdorf Goodman, Jay-Thorpe, and Henri Bendel. Wholesale designers included Nettie Rosenstein, Clairpotter, and Hattie Carnegie.

Claire McCardell, a new designer in the thirties, created a look that was simple and youthful. Her timeless, casual style caught on and came to represent U.S. style throughout the forties and fifties. Sportswear had become more popular through the efforts of Hollywood and was increasingly made in ready-to-wear styles. The sport of swimming increased in part because the Depression forced Americans to have more leisure time. In the 1920s women had adopted the figure-hugging maillot of men. So it was not surprising to see swimwear become more revealing during the thirties, with rayon acetate and Lastex being used to create shiny, body-hugging styles. Swimwear manufacturers such as Jantzen, Catalina, and BVD competed by promoting new styles that featured textured knits, exotic prints, or new man-made fibers. Movie stars were frequently seen in advertising for swimwear. BVD featured Johnny Weissmuller, who went on to become Tarzan in the movies.

1940s, the War Years

The beginning of the 1940s found many Americans still struggling to regain Depression losses. Throughout the decade movies and movie stars continued to inspire fashion. New

York couture, ready-to-wear, and sportswear designers gained more recognition, and California designers also pushed for greater media exposure. The fashion industry was beginning to see the future of "chemistry" in textiles with DuPont heavily promoting plastics in fashion. The coup was "N" Day—December 15, 1940—when nylon stockings went on sale in stores simultaneously throughout the United States. DuPont successfully promoted its new product to such an extent that by "N" Day crowds waited at entrances of department stores to rush to the hosiery counter at the moment the doors flew open. The supply of three-quarters of a million pairs quickly ran out. Nylons were marketed as a new wonder fiber and product of science. Nylons succeeded in removing the stigma of artificiality from the minds of Americans.

With most young men recruited for the war effort, shortages of labor became critical. Women quickly filled the gap, taking over typical male jobs in building ships and airplanes. Between 1941 and 1945, 6.5 million women entered the workforce. Others escaped from low-paying menial or servile jobs to higher-paying industrial jobs.

New jobs for women meant new clothes—work clothes. Factory work often necessitated safe clothing, which required women to wear some sort of trouser or even overalls in the workplace. Comfort was also an issue. Uniforms worn by women in the military, for Red Cross volunteers, and for other war-related positions offered women a new look that served as a symbol of their patriotism. All job-related clothing gave status to the women who wore it, a status they may never have achieved through fashion. Some workers were, in fact, wearing clothes created by top designers. Both Muriel King and Vera Maxwell designed coveralls and easy-to-wear wraparound dresses for women to wear for factory work or for working in the home. King's "flight blue" coordinated pieces for aircraft workers were taken up by Boeing, Lockheed, and Douglas.

The war created shortages of the wool, silk, cotton, and nylon fibers often used in men's, women's, and children's clothing. In order to control the production of textiles, the WPB established limited wartime production control of textile products. The WPB also put forth a set of rules regarding the use of materials used for clothing. These were the General Limitation Order L-85, which restricted the amount of fabric used, and Order L-217, which placed limits on leather used for shoes. The regulations affected every type of clothing made with the exception of wedding gowns, maternity clothes, infants' wear up to age 4, religious vestments, and burial shrouds. The purpose of the restrictions was to prevent fashions from changing—that is, to freeze the silhouette and prevent any changes in machinery or technique that might be costly.

The sportswear designer Claire McCardell set an example for wartime clothing by creating simple, no-frills clothing for women workers and by using inexpensive utilitarian fabrics: mattress ticking, children's prints, and even lingerie fabrics made their way into her designs. She also used surplus weather balloon cotton, butchers' apron linen, and rayon faille. She regularly ordered menswear fabrics for her popular shirtwaist dresses. Her appealing and innovative wrap-and-tie designs eliminated the need for zippers and metal closures. She experimented with closures that fell outside of wartime restrictions; she thus became known for her unusual fasteners, such as brass tabs and hooks, and continued to use them after war's end. Her wartime experiment to cover unrestricted ballet slippers with fabric to match her dresses created a fashion for flats.

Many designers who had been in business for decades finally gained name recognition during World War II. Fashion magazines, general magazines, and newspapers with a fashion section increased their coverage of fashion shows put on by department stores and manufacturers and often credited designers by name. They saw the opportunity to promote U.S. fashion and give recognition to designers, whose names were never seen on garment labels or mentioned by the press. The most important designers during the war years were well established. They included Hattie Carnegie, Claire McCardell, Claire Potter, Vera Maxwell, Norman Norell, Nettie Rosenstein, and the movie designer Adrian. Most surprising is that many of them were not well known by the U.S. public. Promoting these designers and many others during the 1940s were several champions of American fashion design: Dorothy Shaver, vice president of Lord and Taylor; the fashion publicist Eleanor Lambert; Virginia Pope, fashion editor for the *New York Times*; and Lois Long of the *New Yorker*. Dorothy Shaver, then vice president of Lord and Taylor, began actively promoting U.S. fashion by including U.S. designer names and photographs in store advertisements in 1932.

The predominant female silhouette continued to have square shoulders, a natural waistline, and a knee-length skirt. The suit was a staple of every wardrobe. A typical suit had a neat, close-fitting jacket with padded shoulders and a flared, pleated, or straight skirt. Worn with high heels and an interesting hat, these suits gave women an air of sophisticated glamour that is still admired today. Skirts and tops provided a popular ensemble for women of all ages. The movies offered the image of pinups of sweater girls, who wore matching short-sleeved sweaters and cardigans. Dirndl skirts became fashionable in the 1940s. In general skirts were fuller and shorter. Hats were small, miniature hats, worn forward on the head. They suited the upswept hairdos, or hair rolled or in a chignon at the nape of the neck. Cartwheel hats were also available. Hat could be straw or felt and trimmed creatively with bows, feathers, flowers, beads, and sequins. Veils draped across eyes gave women an air of mystery. Many women went hatless. Headscarves, turbans, or snoods were worn to cover hair in factories. Prior to the war, trousers and slacks were worn for sports activities. During the war, retailers promoted functional work slacks, overalls, and coveralls for women in the defense industry. Formal dresses were often long versions of suits and dresses. Wedding dresses for the often quick marriages also became the ubiquitous suit. Common features on dresses were sweetheart necklines, shirring, sequins, and other decorative treatments.

1947–50s

In 1947 the premier French courtier Christian Dior introduced the "New Look" in fashion. The look shook the fashion world from its complacent postwar doldrums. Dior offered women an alternative to the masculine styles of the forties. He presented a feminine style that consisted of a natural shoulder jacket with a very small waist and a long full skirt. The effect emphasized the bust and hips. Sometimes this was shown with a long straight skirt. The jacket might have padding in the hip area for emphasis. Americans quickly picked up the styles and purchased copies readily available in U.S. department stores and shops. The House of Dior went on to introduce other new styles: the A-line, the H-line, the trapeze, and the spindle, which became known as the sack trip. The new look persisted through much of the 1950s and was seen in all markets—women's, teens', and children's wear. Teenagers were especially fond of the poodle skirt version and the many full petticoats that could be worn with the look.

Although high fashion magazines focused on couture, publications for the younger college set promoted separates and ready-to-wear dresses. New York City was the center of ready-to-wear production, with designers creating junior and misses garments. Claire McCardell continued to offer her comfortable styles through Townley. New talents were Scassi, Sarmi, and Galanos, who found a market for their high-end ready-to-wear. Pauline Trigere became known as a designer's designer for her innovative style. Hats continued to be worn; Lilly Daché, John

TELEVISION: AN EMERGING INFLUENCE ON FASHION

Notwithstanding the influence of films on both youth culture and fashion, in the 1950s television was soon to emerge as an important source of visual persuasion. Television programs of the 1950s created fads, such as those associated with Davy Crockett, and fashions such as those seen on *I Love Lucy*. The show remained popular throughout most of the decade and featured Lucille Ball wearing maternity clothing, a first for television. Her styles caught on for maternity wear, but so did her other clothing. California manufacturers promoted these television styles using appropriate labels to identify their source. California designers are also credited with the poodle skirt as seen on Annette Funicello and pedal pushers as seen on Doris Day.

Fredericks, Sally Victor, and Mr. John were the most well-known milliners.

Although Christian Dior and Jacques Fath began to produce ready-to-wear clothing in the United States for the U.S. market, consumers were asking for fashions made by U.S. designers too. The styles they wanted were at first based on the "New Look" introduced by Dior. The long full skirt, nipped in the waist, was popular and then was replaced by a long narrow look. Picking up on couture designs, U.S. ready-to-wear designers introduced the sack, a loosely worn tube style, a close-fitting sheath, and the A-line. Suits retained a narrow skirt but the jackets became looser, often with Dolman sleeves and less structure. The short cocktail dress, sundress with matching jacket, and strapless evening gown all came into their own during this period. Costume jewelry was also popular. Although there was a somewhat more relaxed fit, the rules of etiquette still required women to try for matching purse and shoes (stilettos with a pointing toe) and to wear a hat and gloves.

Ready-to-wear sportswear was targeted toward students. Bermuda shorts, toreador pants, and pedal pushers were popular, as well as jeans. New stretch pants came on the scene after being introduced as skiwear. Cashmere sweater sets, detachable collars (sometimes fur), felt circle skirts, especially the poodle skirt, crinolines, saddle shoes, and penny loafers were all worn. Although cotton, linen, and wool continued to be used in clothing, new fibers, especially nylon and polyester, began to be used widely in both women's and men's apparel. After mid-decade, pastel polyester and cotton shirtwaist dresses with lace inserts in the bodice front were a particularly popular style, continuing the influence of the new look. Soon after, however, the sack dress came into fashion.

Movies and movie stars continued to provide ideals for the female audience. Films in the 1950s were not solely based on alienation of youth. The industry continued to provide fashion-focused films and wooed Paris designers to aid its cause. Christian Dior's "New Look," which descended on fashion from Paris following the city's release from German occupation, caught on fast. It was a relief for war-weary woman of the world. Interestingly, Dior quickly made changes to the style, but Hollywood retained the look for many films. This phenomenon may be the root of the retention of the look by many Americans throughout the 1950s, for many manufacturers reproduced the line. The style, named the sweetheart style, lives on for proms and wedding gowns and in an occasional burst of nostalgic fashion.

1960s

The 1960s were turbulent years. Fashions of the time served to broadcast the social, political, and artistic unrest of a growing youth culture. Among the many factors influencing dress of the period were young designers in Britain, France, and the United States, radical groups protesting the Vietnam War, new music genres, and explorations in space. The decade began with John F. Kennedy's presidency. His wife, the beautiful and charismatic Jackie Kennedy, became a fashion icon. Her style was *the* style. It was simple, easy, fresh, colorful, and elegant. Most of all it was youthful. Jackie's favorite American designers were Oleg Cassini, Chez Ninon, Gustave Tassell, and Donald Brooks. Her styles were youthful and simple, based on a princess cut with no defined waistline and no sleeves. The skirt shape was A-line, and the dresses just skimmed the body. There was little decoration, but the colors could be quite vivid. Her

HIPPIE STYLE

It was during the 1960s that the United States saw the growth of the counterculture hippie movement. It began in the mid-sixties but died out in the early seventies. Hippie style for women included jeans (the older and more ripped, the better), T-shirts, sandals or boots, and Indian gauze blouses and skirts. Imported clothing from India, Pakistan, and Afghanistan was popular, as was vintage clothing.

suits usually had boxy jackets. She mostly wore low-heeled shoes and gloves, carried a small purse, and kept jewelry to a minimum.

A youthful style, the sack dress, emerged in fashion in the late 1950s largely in reaction to adult styles that young girls were expected to wear. Yves Saint Laurent introduced the trapeze when he took over after Dior's death. Although the young look was apparent in the Kennedy style, the real revolution was seen in a short, loose-fitting gray shift introduced by English designer Mary Quant in the 1950s. She wore the shift with yellow tights. In 1955 she opened a store in London named Bazaar. Her designs were sold in the United States at J. C. Penney in the mid-1950s. Mary Quant, in fact, is often credited with taking fashion to the next level with the introduction of the mini. The youthful look gained credence in the 1960s. Some styles had puffed sleeves and so took on the term "baby-doll." The entire world now associates the mini with the English supermodel Twiggy, who clearly became the fashion icon of the youth movement.

The youthful short shift mini and boots also was introduced by a new Parisian designer, André Courrèges, in 1964. The short skirts were worn with tights and low-heeled shoes. By the mid 1960s Courrèges had appropriated a space-age, futuristic look. Other Parisian designers such as Pierre Cardin and Emanuel Ungaro followed with similar youthful styles and a more avant-garde look, including baby-doll styles. Paco Rabanne used plastic discs and metal. Pop art and op art designs began to be appropriated by designers as well. Yves Saint Laurent paid homage to Mondrian with his dress named "Broadway Boogie-Woogie."

Designers in the United States who offered their own versions were avant-garde designer Rudi Gernreich, who introduced a topless swimsuit, Stephen Burrows, Betsy Johnson, and Giorgio San'Angelo. The new kinky clothes were first seen at such boutiques in New York City as Paraphernalia, Serendipity, and Abracadabra and boutiques in Bonwit Teller (Safari shop) and Bergdorf Goodman (Biba). These stores featured paper and plastic minis, pantsuits, jumpsuits, leather and suede skirts and jackets, bell-bottom trousers, and skinny sweaters. Parisian designers began to offer youthful ready-to-wear to Americans. Dior introduced Dior Sport, and Yves Saint Laurent opened his own boutique, Rive Gauche. Clearly fashion had moved from the sacred salons of Paris couture to the boutiques and streets of London and New York. The shorter hemlines and younger fashion look also were picked up by the U.S. designers offering high-end fashion. These included Geoffrey Beene, Norman Norell, Bonnie Cashin, Anne Klein, Chester Weinberg, and Ann Fogarty.

The 1960s saw a change in movie fashion. Rather than designing costumes, the designers "shopped" for film costumes at ready-to-wear departments of couture and high fashion, choosing Yves Saint Laurent, Givenchy, and Mary Quant. Designed film costumes were sometimes minimalist, such as those by Hardie Amies for *2001: A Space Odyssey*, or erotic, such as Paco Rabanne's outlandish styles for Jane Fonda in *Barbarella*. Viewers could find similar styles in department stores. Elizabeth Taylor, Audrey Hepburn, and Marilyn Monroe were movie stars who could easily influence fashion: designers often knocked off what they wore in films.

1970s

Fashion in the seventies retained elements of sixties style. Young women were active participants in the various social movements of the sixties and seventies. They were involved with counterculture movements, dressed as hippies, and adopted the dress of their favorite music group or wore a T-shirt emblazoned with its name. The fashion industry also provided them with "the look," often copying clothing styles seen on the streets. The 1970s started out with the micromini skirt and hot pants, as well as the much debated mid-calf-length midi skirt as an alternative to the mini. By 1975 the mini was out. By mid-decade the skirt settled to just below the knee, but not before designers offered women trousers as a comfortable alternative to the skirt for daytime use.

The era, named the "me decade," was just beginning to see the efforts of the feminists and environmentalists come to fruition. Young protesters and returning Vietnam veterans were competing for scarce jobs. Looking good became important for success, for both men and women, who were now entering the workplace in full force.

The natural look of the late sixties and the colorful, ethnic styles of the hippies influenced many designers, who referred to them as nostalgic or folkloric. Knits also became popular and fit well with the long, lean, narrow aesthetic of the period. Women embraced the newly offered exercise programs on television and thus adopted leotards and stretch pants. An interest in leisure wear led to more wearing of sweat suits by women. They began breaking the rules for appropriate dress for evening wear—almost any long skirt was acceptable—and traditional evening gowns all but disappeared. Women began to wear pantsuits for all occasions. They came in velvet, corduroy, tweed, georgette or silk, and polyester.

Other casual garments popular with Americans, especially college students, were down jackets and vests, army fatigues, turtleneck shirts and sweaters, clogs, Frye boots, Earth shoes, cowboy boots, and the Adidas brand of sneaker. This clothing was similar to hippie dress but more down-to-earth. Yet, although the look of worn or used jeans was popular, it was during this decade that the "designer jean" began its long-held place in the United States' fashion system.

Although antifashion styles and the move toward casual dress influenced what women wore, other factors became more important in setting their clothing needs. Women were entering the workplace. The most important look for women early in the seventies was the pantsuit and blazer. Ready-to-wear apparel companies that provided a menswear look, a trousered look, were Calvin Klein, Perry Ellis, Liz Claiborne, Jones of New York, Anne Klein, later Donna Karan, and Ann Taylor, among others. Although not meant for the workplace, designer jeans by Calvin Klein and Gloria Vanderbilt came to the forefront of casual fashion.

The influence of women in the workplace and their new professional clothing soon was apparent to the fashion industry. Women were engaging in investment dressing. The designer Geoffrey Beene noted the change, saying that he did not dress dolls but rather "Tilly the Toiler." He further observed that women were influenced by Katherine Hepburn and Carole Lombard, who played lady executives in the films of the thirties and forties. These actors, of course, wore pants.

The proliferation of styles—trousered casual dress, pantsuits, long slim knit skirts, and folkloric-styled clothing—left some questions in the minds of some women about what was appropriate in the workplace and opened the door for John Molloy to provide an answer. John Molloy had written an influential book titled *Dress for Success for Men* (1975). Women had seen the book for men and wanted Molloy to do the same for them. He published *The Woman's Dress for Success Book* in 1977. In it Molloy stressed the need for women to have an appearance of authority. Molloy argued that the jacket filled that need. Yet, he thought, women needed to strike a balance between appearing too masculine in a suit and seeming too feminine and ladylike, which could lead to condescension. Molloy's compromise was to advise women to wear a conservative skirt, not trousers, with their jackets. This was serious clothing that would lead to an atmosphere of equality in the workplace. Certainly John Molloy's *Woman's Dress for Success Book* supported the same standards and methods used in his book for men; that is, women should dress as if they were already powerful and successful. The skirt provided balance for the woman's business suit. The skirt made it clear: this suit was a female garment.

Molloy's edict, however, did not stop women from wearing trousers. Late in the 1970s the preppy look, menswear styles for women, gained prominence when Diane Keaton appeared in Woody Allen's movie *Annie Hall* (1977). The preppy look was based on traditional clothing worn at East Coast prep schools. Shetland sweaters, hand-knit sweaters, tweed jackets, blue blazers, blue oxford cloth button-down shirts, Lacoste polo shirts, Weejuns, and khaki pants were the essential elements. The look was supported by new designers of women's wear: Ralph Lauren and Calvin Klein. Perry Ellis also provided the look. The style was also worn by men in most East Coast Ivy League colleges. Labels began to be placed on the outside of garments following perhaps the success of the crocodile on Lacoste shirts, an emblem of the new preppy.

1980s

In the early 1980s the movie *Flashdance* was the inspiration for the casual look of the decade—sweatshirts, leg warmers, stirrup pants, and tights, a look that fit right into the fitness movement that spawned the still popular aerobics workouts and the ubiquitous warm-up suit worn everywhere. Bodysuits and "catsuits" took center stage. Countering this look was one more opulent and extravagant that conformed to the descriptor of the decade, ostentation. Television offered a lifestyle model with its evening soaps, *Dallas* and *Dynasty*, both of which were immensely popular. *Dynasty* was the only television show with a resident designer, Nolan Miller. The look of *Dynasty* became the style of the decade. The producers took great care with the look, making sure that the colors of the clothes matched the mood of each episode. The popularity of the show convinced Miller to create a ready-to-wear line based on the garments created for its main female characters, Krystle, played by Linda Evans, and Alexis, played by Joan Collins. "The Dynasty Collection" included furs, lingerie, hosiery, shoes, blouses, suits, linens, sheets, chinas, glassware, tuxedos, and dolls. Ideological readings of *Dynasty* often compare the Carringtons to the Reagans and see the show as almost a parody of the United States in the 1980s. It seems that the 1980s had more than a little bit of Hollywood style.

During the 1980s money and power were clearly denoted by fashion. Status symbols were commonly used. Chanel, Hermés, fur, gold chains, cashmere, silk, and Rolex watches were in demand. The yuppies (defined as young urban professionals) desired a look of power in their dress that included broad shoulders, narrow skirts, bright colors, oversized bows, and designer labels.

U.S. designers of the seventies continued into the 1980s. Prominent 1980s designers were Calvin Klein, Ralph Lauren, Galanos, Mary McFadden, Diane von Furstenberg, Alber Nipon, Oscar de la Renta, Arnold Scassi, and Bob Mackie. European designers, especially Armani, remained popular with Americans. The English designers Zandra Rhodes and Vivienne Westwood provided avant-garde styles connected to punk music, while Issey Miyake combined high fashion with comfort and utility in garments that relied on high-tech fabrics. Designers for the most part were selling an image.

A popular style of the eighties was culottes for sportswear, and even suits. Norma Kamali provided casual loose-fitting garments made of sweatshirt fabric. European designers making an impact on fashion included Christian Lacroix, with his puff short-skirted evening dress.

When not brandishing the power of large shoulder pads in the workplace, women sought out spandex laced body-hugging clothing for working out and lace and sheer fabrics for evening. Designs of the eighties reveal an abundance of historical influences—paisleys, cabbage roses, tartans, polka dots, and animal prints. Styles from almost every decade of the twentieth century reappeared in the 1980s, including short skirts of the 1960s.

High-end designers offered lower-priced stylish "bridge" fashions for women desiring to upgrade their clothing, especially women in business. In the same vein, off-price shopping was a great success. These stores offered quality brand-name goods for less. Catalogs were also popular, especially with working women who now had less time to spend shopping in stores. By the 1980s Limited Stores, based in Columbus, Ohio, was the hottest retail store in the market catering to young women. Specialty stores increased in number in this decade, as they proved beneficial to meet the needs of the new businesswomen who desired sensible clothes. Besides The Limited, Ann Taylor, the Gap, Banana Republic, and J. Crew provided stylish and reasonably priced fashions for the economy-minded consumer. These stores offered more casual styles that were acceptable for dress-down days in the workplace. In 1989 John Molloy again turned to women with the *New Women's Dress for Success Book*. Dress codes in the workplace had changed considerably. In this new edition Molloy discussed casual dress in the workplace.

Television and music influences loomed larger than ever before with new media—the introduction of MTV in 1981. Punk and rock music styles clearly influenced the dress of their youthful admirers. Manufacturers obliged by producing clothing that mimicked the styles worn by musicians. Rock fashion became big business. Young girls desired to dress like Madonna and Cyndi Lauper, two of the early female musicians on MTV with "girl" appeal. It did not take manufacturers and retailers long to discover that the carefully cultivated images of rock stars created consumer desire. The shopping mall and department store were sites for female leisure culture. One mall in California took on the moniker "Madonna Mall" because so many girls who shopped there tried to look like her. The Associated Department Stores recommended that its member stores open FTV (fashion television) departments. With rock videos blaring, Macy's opened in-store boutiques with a Madonna connection: "Madonnaland" and "Girls Just Want to Have Fun," where they sold cropped sweaters ($30) and cropped pants ($21). The appearance of music video displays in Junior Departments in shopping malls and department stores across the country served as testament to the conversion of teenagers into MTV junkies.

Although there were many popular culture moments reflected in changes in fashion, it was new technology that brought permanent changes to the fashion industry. The use of computers in design, manufacturing, and retail would forever alter the way business is carried out. The development of microfibers allowed the miracle fibers of the sixties—polyester and nylon—to regain prominence in apparel products in the years to come.

1990s

The look of the 1990s was in stark contrast to the opulent eighties. Style centered on minimalism. Black was the color of favor. Yet revivals continued of earlier styles. Fads and high points of 1990s style centered on casual dress that included overalls, T-shirts, tennis shoes, fanny pack purses, Doc Martens shoes and boots, bell-bottom jeans, and cargo pants. Skirt length ranged from very short to varying longer lengths. There was not one set length for the skirt until later in the nineties when a short full skirt appeared. Pants and skirts in the early nineties were worn tight until later when a fuller style came into fashion. Almost all styles of dresses were available in the marketplace. Women continued to wear tailored suits in the workplace.

Casual clothing continued to invade and replace the hallowed walls of the salons of the

ONLINE SHOPPING

The electronic age for retail began in the 1990s. People had been able to order products promoted on their television screens. But then shopping became even more versatile when stores began to create Websites to offer their customers an alternative means to shop. Although some stores existed only on the Internet, others, especially department and specialty stores, went online to boost their sales. Catalogs were still around but mostly for traditional sports clothing such as L.L.Bean and Eddie Bauer, and they likewise expanded to the Internet. Further expansion of retail came with the development of the mega mall and superstores with entertainment and goods for every segment of the market. Some new malls created an alternative entertainment package that imitated a small-town atmosphere with an open-air design. Changes were also seen in the merger of many old department stores and the demise of others. Smaller specialty stores were better able to keep up with the diversified needs of the U.S. public.

past. The number of stores offering casual, upscale, comfortable clothing increased. A women's store that became popular was Chicos, which provided their own brand of stylish comfort for boomer women beyond age thirty-five. Yet casual styles also could be purchased in Wal-Mart and Target stores. Specialty stores such as Abercrombie & Fitch, the Gap, and Banana Republic appealed to different segments of the market. The mass marketing of clothing really took off with the growth of Ralph Lauren and Tommy Hilfiger, both competing for the middle-class American dollar. In many instances the high-tech fabrics produced for sports were adopted for casual ready-to-wear clothing. Lycra stretch yarns appeared in more and more clothes for added comfort. Jeans, often with Lycra, remained at the forefront of sales in almost every market segment, although cargo pants competed for their share.

Casual dressing expanded to the point where many businesses accepted dress-down clothing every day. Youthful but sophisticated fashion found a niche in the marketplace by catering to young women who were entering the workplace after college. They desired serious but not traditional clothing styles. The U.S. ready-to-wear casual market became a very large business in the nineties. Yet Europeans still appealed to Americans' need to impress with luxury leather goods. Prada, Gucci, Hermes, Celine, and Louis Vuitton become household words. Luxe was in for handbags and shoes. France and Italy remained leaders in fashion luxury goods but extended their markets by advancing ready-to-wear lines.

High-end U.S. fashion continued, with some designers providing both couture and ready-to-wear models. Many new names appeared in the pages of *Women's Wear Daily*, the newspaper of the fashion industry. Both Narciso Rodriquez and Ralph Rucci, for instance, came onto the radar screen of fashion in the 1990s. Retailers continued to provide business-women with attractive work clothing. Department stores with brands such as Liz Claiborne and chain stores such as Ann Taylor, Talbot's, and Brooks Brothers filled their needs.

The most impressive phenomenon of the nineties that was linked to the rise of casual dress was, of course, the influence of youth and music on dress. U.S. youth formulated a look that had its roots in music. This pairing of cultural phenomena—youth style and music—first appeared with the rise of jazz music and quickly moved into rock and roll, punk, and then, in the nineties, grunge and hip-hop. Since the 1980s MTV has bolstered the phenomenon by making the music styles accessible to television viewers worldwide. In addition to the grunge music look, the 1990s saw the rise of a new musical form—rap—and the hip-hop culture that developed around it.

Rap was the original music of the hip-hop culture. It initially emerged among African Americans from the Bronx as early as the fifties and sixties. It took root and flourished among the gangs of the city and eventually spread downtown and to Brooklyn. The first popular rap song, "Rappers Delight" by the Sugar Hill Gang, was released in 1979. Tasha Lewis noted that hip-hop fashion is not just one style but a mixture of influences from both the street and high fashion designer labels.[2] At first preppy labels, such as Tommy Hilfiger and Polo Ralph Lauren, were popular with hip-hop followers. Hip-hop style can include name-brand baggy clothes, baseball caps, sneakers, sports jackets and jerseys and other sport clothes such as hooded track suits, and puffer vests. To this mix of masculine styles female rappers added "door knocker" earrings. By the nineties the female stars had switched to a sexually provocative bombshell look of Lycra-tight and skin-revealing clothing, stilettos, and high fashion hair. Branded merchandise was such an important aspect of hip-hop that rap stars soon created their own successful brands of clothing. Sean Jean, Phat Farm, Baby Phat, and Rocawear are just four that have been moneymakers. Female stars such as Jennifer Lopez, Beyonce, Eve, and Lil' Kim have become "fashionistas" by adopting and promoting couture and by creating their own fashion lines as well.

2000–2006

The early years of the twenty-first century saw a continuation of the influence of hip-hop culture and music on fashion. Although the hip-hop artists promoted their own styles, many of the performers themselves adopted French- and Italian-made luxury goods. The term *bling* became a household word manifested in a proliferation of bold jewelry and metallic and rhinestone, and sequin applications on women's clothing. Glitter—hip-hop's bling—had found its spot in the ready-to-wear market. Glitter was on shoes, handbags, blouses, skirts, sweaters, and more. The look of the nineties continued with bare midriffs, low-rise jeans, cargo pants and shorts, sweater sets, and strapless evening and daytime dresses. Revivals of past fashions continued, with 1970s tights and 1980s big shoulders showing up on the runways. Even skinny pants returned.

Luxury leather goods continued to grow, as did the corresponding knockoff market for these products. Branding of products became the central theme for manufacturers as they geared their products toward consumer lifestyles. New discount stores emerged to appeal to the youth market desiring the latest styles. Most notable was the H&M stores' entrance into the U.S. market; these stores offered trendy fashions to young women. Yet mergers of department stores have allowed that segment of the retail market to remain in place, while smaller stores focus on their niche markets. Indeed, the mass market for women's fashion continues to unfold, with new designers and new stores appearing every week. Still the U.S. fashion industry, through its publications, keeps the public aware of offerings of the international fashion industry. The twenty-first century has seen China and other Asian markets compete with the Americans, Europeans, and Japanese.

In first years of the twenty-first century the relationship between fashion and film was solidified with superstars of the screen becoming the new faces on that other form of fashion media, the fashion magazine. *Vogue* and *Harper's Bazaar* featured Debra Messing, Gwyneth Paltrow, and Nicole Kidman. And then, of course, there is the ever-changing face of Madonna, who, like Barbie, can easily alter her persona. Madonna slid nicely from the world of pop music to film, and she even graced the ads for the ultimate casual store, the Gap, and later H&M. It was Madonna, with the French designer, Gaultier, who set the stage for women's underwear to become outerwear.

The merger of popular culture with fashion has revealed many influences on U.S. dress. The most influential may be Hollywood. There is no doubt that movies have influenced what we wear on many occasions, but mainly in the direction of comfort and casual dress. Hollywood has shown us what to wear and how to play. What has become the most popular of American clothes—jeans and T-shirts—we owe to California with the help of Hollywood's moving pictures. For well over a century it has been through visual persuasion, or rhetoric of the moving image, that Hollywood has helped to influence the many transformations that fashion has taken. Taking ordinary work clothes and underwear and making them fashionable could only happen in Hollywood. Perhaps it has been the steady movement toward casual dress in U.S. culture that fuels the clothing debates most intensely. Certainly "dress-down Fridays" have moved to "dress-down every day" in some segments of the business world, especially in the high-tech fields. Although financial institutions do retain their conservative dress codes, even they allow some dress-down days. Whether the suit remains or not, certainly the U.S. public will always understand what is meant by "dressing for success," and it may not be a suit.

Men's Fashion

The turn of the twentieth century saw menswear becoming increasingly simplified. Suits more often than not had short jackets. Men had begun to shun the longer morning jacket or frock coat. Many of these changes were introduced in England. Rather than formal wear, men began to wear flannel trousers, blue blazers, and straw hats—all sportswear—to sporting events. A looser-fitting jacket, the Norfolk, was introduced for gentlemen to wear for bicycling, shooting, and other outdoor sports. These sporting styles soon found their way into more formal occasions. Arrow shirt advertisements in the United States depict the ideal young male out of doors in sporting attire—tweed jacket, loose trousers or plus fours, a club tie blowing in a breeze. Usually sporting equipment—a tennis racket or golf club—was nearby or in hand. World War I military dress, especially the trench coat, became a classic and is still worn today by both men and women.

1920s–30s

Menswear in the twenties is often defined by the clothing worn by college men. A big change came in 1924 with the introduction of very loose wide trousers called Oxford bags, named for their student origin. These replaced the previously worn narrow trousers and were popular mostly with college students. The other notable collegiate style was the wearing of a raccoon coat, also worn by young women. The young Prince of Wales endorsed a sporting life and accompanying clothing. His casual style influenced menswear for more than 30 years.[3]

Menswear also became more elegant during the thirties. The Prince of Wales was still setting style. His abdication of the British throne to marry a divorced American, Wallis Simpson, did not negatively affect his fashion influence. Now known as the Duke of Windsor, his double-breasted midnight blue dinner jackets, with their wide collar and use of plaid, changed the look of fashionable men. The Windsor knot became a classic. Men everywhere adopted his style, which continued to whittle away at formality. Casual dressing for nonwork occasions had increased during the prewar years but especially during the thirties, when casual trousers worn with sweaters, tweed jackets, and blazers became the prescribed look for many.

1940s

Military dress styles continued to be worn following the war—khaki pants, Eisenhower and field jackets, bomber/flight jackets, Ray-Ban "aviator" sunglasses, pea jackets, the double-breasted boxy jackets of U.S. sailors, and the Royal Navy's duffle coat. Civilian dress suits were cut leaner to conform to L-85 regulations. The latter also did not allow waistcoats and eliminated cuffs and pleats on trousers. Wartime restrictions required dinner jackets to be single-breasted.

The zoot suit, which appeared during this decade, was in opposition to wartime restrictions. The zoot had been adopted by Latino and African-American youth early in the decade as a status symbol. It was associated with music, especially jitterbugging. It was an exaggerated style with a long, loose jacket with extremely wide shoulders and long, wide lapels. The pants were long and fully pleated but narrowed at the ankle. It was sometimes worn with a very long, heavy watch chain. In the late forties the menswear silhouette began to show signs of loosening. It had broad shoulders, suggesting that women clothing copied it, yet it remained the same drape suit from the 1930s, only longer. Checkered shirts were popular, as were colorful Hawaiian shirts as seen on the coasts of Florida and California. Clothing worn in these warm climates was beginning to influence warm-weather styles in Europe and other parts of the United States. Splashy ties also entered the market.

1950s

The mind-set of the fifties became one of conformity, symbolized best, perhaps, by the image of a man in a gray flannel suit. That image was soon shattered by the Beats, who protested against conformity and gendered expectations. In the 1950s sales of undershirts had a renaissance when the lowly undershirt, the T, gained ground as outerwear. It happened when Marlon Brando in *The Wild One* and *A Streetcar Named Desire* and James Dean in *Rebel without a Cause* appeared on the big screen wearing clothing that represented postwar teenage alienation. Brando's Levi jeans, T-shirt, leather jacket, and boots became "the look" for teenagers who needed guidance and a model for how to dress to express their own feelings of frustration with society. These films sparked the beginnings of the wholesale consumption of jeans and denim clothing by U.S. society. It was not far removed from the look set by male members of the Beat Generation that took root in the 1950s. Beat dress consisted of beards, loose turtleneck sweaters, soiled slacks or jeans, and berets.

Disenchantment with the status quo and rebelliousness took different paths. One led to the growing subversion of dress codes by work clothes, expressed best through the consumption of jeans as noted above. Another route sent young men on a trip toward mass consumption and a renewed interest in fashion. The latter group was aided on their journey by magazines such as *Playboy* and *GQ* and advertisements that promoted the pleasure of consumption and the virtues of living and dressing well. There was a lightening up of the work ethic. The new morality of the times embraced the virtues of pleasure. At the same time, menswear manufacturers were gearing up to provide suits and sportswear that reflected this new young man with an appetite for clothes. New looks were coming from Europe: the neo-Edwardian from London (a style adopted by East End hooligans called the Teddy boys, or Teds) and narrow pants (copied no doubt from the narrow look of U.S. jeans and chinos), to be worn with a single-breasted three-button short jacket with sloping shoulders. The latter was an Italian style. They became the standard look for a young man. By 1956 the Italian style became known as the "Continental Look" in the United States and gained ground as a serious rival to the "Ivy League Look," the standard gray flannel suit. The latter was Brooks Brothers' best-selling suit.

1960s

The new interest in consumption by young men came to fruition with the Peacock Revolution in menswear that occurred during this decade. The sixties also saw a great upswing in stores and boutiques for the male consumer and a proliferation of styles offered by new menswear designers. Young men especially were attracted to the designs being offered by European designers. Shirts started coming in more colors than white and blue. In England the dress of the youthful mods, as worn by the Beatles, consisted of a Continental-inspired collarless short jacket worn with skinny trousers, a shirt with Edwardian collar and pin, and short boots, called booties. Their look was in opposition to the look of the leather- and jeans-wearing rockers. By 1964 Carnaby Street in London became the hub of youthful male fashion and thus the center of the Peacock Revolution. The new male consumerism and accompanying style was quick to be absorbed by Americans, especially followers of the sounds of the Beatles.

However, it was during the 1960s that several other phenomena occurred that greatly altered menswear. The first was the adoption of antifashion by numerous cultural groups, the most notable, of course, being the hippies. Another example of antifashion, worn to express political beliefs, was the adoption of clothes from the past, old clothes called vintage. Other types of music and sartorial strictures entered the picture. Glam rock influenced the dress of the young, as did punk music, which had origins with economically repressed youth in England. These subcultural styles were in many respects a great uprising against consumerism and, thus, the world of retail and fashion.

The best known of the subcultural styles, of course, was the dress of the hippies. In the late sixties many young people began to turn away from clothing traditions to express their sentiments about the Vietnam War, nuclear power, or the environment. They stepped away from anything that suggested plastic, authority, or tradition. The hippie movement created a decline in the menswear market. Hippie clothing is often described as antifashion, created from patched clothing and mixed together with castoffs and flamboyant accessories. It might include a mixture of rumpled past styles and ethnic clothing. The movement generated many merchants selling clothing from Africa, India, Afghanistan, and the like. Hippies disdained new clothing and anything made of synthetic fibers or with wrinkle-free finish. In fact, they liked wrinkles. And they especially liked worn jeans.

1970s

By the early 1970s U.S. men had already experienced the rise of men's fashion with the Peacock Revolution and were now being regaled with a still wider assortment of casual styles; the leisure suit is still available in a confusing array of styles, colors, and fabrics that ultimately led to its demise. The hippie and other counterculture movements of the sixties and early seventies had left a whole generation of young people with a wardrobe of jeans and vintage clothing but little knowledge of appropriate business attire. Sportswear had gained a greater share of the menswear industry than ever before. Traditional suit production was down.

It is clear that in the early part of the 1970s the hippie style continued to influence what young men wore. Also, young people continued to emulate the look of whatever music group they were attracted to. In the seventies this could be the outlandish costumes of the larger-than-life glitter rock bands or, later, the stark and sometimes offensive clothing adopted by punk musicians. There was a greater interest in dressing vintage that reflected a sense of romanticism that was certainly connected to hippie style but also was a rejection of the glitter rock style. Even though vintage was old, it was old enough to seem new.

The idea of more comfortable menswear gained support with Yves Saint Laurent, who in 1969 began to promote styles that would "free men from their shackles." His safari jackets with Russian belts and sailor tunics were offered for both men and women in his Rive Gauche store. Other French menswear designers offered new looks that became elements of 1970s men's fashion. Gilbert Féruch created suits with the Mao collar, also called the Nehru, Oriental, Lenin, and Zhivago collar. Although at first their influence did not appear significant, when they switched from woven fabrics to knits they took off. Between 1968 and 1973 manufacturers successfully produced soft, wrinkle-free suits with no linings.

In the beginning, the leisure suit was a legitimate casual garment. It was worn by gentlemen of distinction. However, on the manufacturing end, producers sought ways to cut costs by eliminating many of the traditional construction details of suits. In seeking out knits, they discovered polyester, which had been used extensively in mod clothing of the 1960s. Knitted polyester, however, was new to the leisure suit market. The makers of knit polyester apparently sought to create colorful fabrics that would appeal to the young. However, the overproduction of polyester led to a drop in price that immediately allowed the lower end of the market to produce polyester suits in great numbers in colors that were far from traditional. The effect of these lower-priced casual styles was to undermine the suit industry. Indeed, the leisure style began to dominate men's fashion and the marketplace, replacing the traditional suit.

As former hippies and other young people grew older, they realized that there were alternative ways to "change the world," and they sought to enter the established workforce. At the time, however, jobs were scarce. And to make things worse, the many options in clothing caused some confusion about appropriate attire for business. Former hippies and wearers of the leisure suit realized that in order to be taken seriously they needed to learn how to dress appropriately. Managers were looking for young men they could relate to, and that was not a guy in jeans and a Levi jacket. Appearance had become a factor in competition and advancement up the corporate ladder. John Molloy came to the rescue with his best-selling book *Dress for Success*.

Prior to writing *Dress for Success*, John T. Molloy had been an image consultant to major corporations, advising them on problems of dress. Molloy stated that the suit was the most important garment in a man's wardrobe. He stressed this point because his research revealed that suits are authority symbols. He offered advice on how to buy a suit, noting that the fabric, patterns, fit, color, and style must be appropriate to the job and the person. He advised against the high style of Cardin for just anyone. Shirts, he felt, were a way to maximize power. That meant all cotton, or cotton-poly, just plain or striped fabrics (no fancies), and long sleeves. Ties, he believed, were a great status symbol and should be selected with care. He discussed the importance of accessories and went into detail on correct dress for different sports and casual wear. Molloy also offered suggestions for lawyers on how to dress for a judge, for executives on how to create a corporate image, and for job seekers on how to dress for an interview. Finally he offered suggestions on how to dress for women.

1980s

Television greatly influenced fashion in the 1980s. A new casual look emerged for men in the television show *Miami Vice*. The elements that made it popular were the look of its main characters, especially the male star, Don Johnson, who dressed in designer sports coats frequently worn with a T-shirt. Johnson's T-shirts, however, were far removed from the alienated, lowly white undershirt worn by Brando and Dean in the 1950s. Johnson's character, Crockett, always dressed in casual trousers and T-shirts in pastel shades of turquoise, pink, or lavender. Crockett's penchant for wearing no socks with his loafers became a fashion statement. Suits had broad shoulders and had a looser fit owing to Italian menswear influence. Indeed, the Italian designer Armani often showed his suits with T-shirts, a style apparently first used by the designer Versace in the 1980s.

In fact, the show provided a new and enduring casual look for men. In 2004 men continued to wear a crew neck T-shirt or a polo shirt with a sports coat for "dressing up" for informal occasions. The T-shirt might cost $100 at Saks Fifth Avenue. The pastels were still around. Lavender was a popular dress shirt color for men, easily purchased at Brooks Brothers. *Miami Vice* also was a milestone in that it confirmed for the networks the potential of fashion and music in appealing to an audience. The truth of this lies in the history of television since the 1980s.

Although businessmen continued to wear the important suit, their wardrobe also consisted of navy blue blazers and sports jackets, sweaters, and, in summer, linen slacks, jackets, and shirts in bright colors. Dress shirts were available in a wide variety of colors. Clothing for golf took on bright colors. There was, however, a growing trend toward casual dress in the workplace, and soon khakis and polo shirts would become the standard dress in many offices.

Yet even with this trend, or perhaps because of it, new books came out that continued to stress the importance of dress in the workplace, especially for those on the executive track. These included Mortimer Levitt, *The Executive Look: How to Get It—How to Keep It* (1981); Alan J. Flusser, *Clothes and the Man: The Principles of Fine Men's Dress* (1985); Lois Fenton, *Dress for Excellence* (1986); and Paul Keers, *A Gentleman's Wardrobe: Classic Clothes and the Modern Man* (1987). Not to be outdone by his imitators, Molloy published *New Dress for Success* in 1988.

1990–2006

Men's sports and suit jackets were being made with spandex (Lycra), which offered a bit closer fit than men's clothing in the eighties. Soft colors in checks were popular for linen jackets. Blue jeans became even more popular, as did casual khaki pants and cargo pants. Polo shirts and T-shirts continued to be worn for casual wear and to the office on casual days. T-shirts might carry a message or reflect the wearer's favorite music group. Everyone wore baseball caps. More men adopted high-tech activewear—jackets and wind pants—for casual dress.

Media and television coverage of the popular music scene of the 1990s took young men's clothing to a new place. Although jeans adorned the bodies of everyone, starting with grunge, rap, and hip-hop fashion, these pants were worn extremely loose and baggy and often defied gravity as they appeared to barely float over the derrieres of many young men. At first preppy labels, such as Tommy Hilfiger and Polo Ralph Lauren, were popular with hip-hop followers. Hip-hop style included name-brand baggy clothes, baseball caps, sneakers, sports jackets and jerseys and other sport clothes such as hooded track suits, and puffer vests. Many hip-hop musicians had great success in developing their own clothing lines. These sold well in department stores.

Health and Beauty

However, ideal beauty prior to the twentieth century did not depend solely on exercise, dress, and nature. Women experimented with home-brewed products to improve their complexions, that is, to make their faces fit the prevailing natural ideal, a pale complexion with rosy cheeks as seen in *Godey's Lady's Book*. The use of cosmetics was not a concern, because their use only assisted nature. Paints, on the other hand, were viewed as masks meant to hide the truth. Paints were deemed harmful, and indeed, if made of lead, they were.

Before the turn of the century the ideal woman was portrayed by the U.S. illustrator Charles Dana Gibson; she became the Gibson girl, and her image was the ideal American beauty. The ideal lasted well into the twentieth century but began to change as women achieved success in the workplace and attended college, where they would have more opportunities to become aware of new trends. Women did not need to rely on home-brewed beauty products for long. Businesses providing cosmetics soon offered many cosmetics products for skin and hair care. The beauty parlor came into existence. A number of women were extremely successful entrepreneurs in the beauty business, most notably two African-American women, Annie Turnbo Malone and Madam C. J. Walker. Helena Rubenstein and Elizabeth Arden are names from the early years that are still recognizable. These women and others created a market for beauty products that paralleled the growth of U.S. consumer culture. After World War I the acceptance of beauty techniques and products became a mass market. The introduction of beauty products and techniques and ways to promote them created an industry that has never ceased to expand.

In the 1920s the face, like the body, was susceptible to ongoing changes in trends that were being influenced by the cinema and popular entertainers. Shapes, color, and styles could change at any time. The 1920s also saw a craze for a suntan. The pale beauty of the turn of the century was now passé. Advertisers promoted the latest look. It was not unusual for young socialites and movie stars to be featured in ads for Ponds, Maybelline, or Woodbury soap. The value of beauty products rose tenfold by 1929. In that year, Americans spent $700 million on cosmetics and beauty services.[4]

By the 1930s and 1940s the painted face, achieved using Hollywood tricks, was the prevailing look. The ideal was still natural. However, if the makeup was too obvious, then it was considered inappropriate. Eventually the use of makeup was considered a natural feature of the face. Only the very young could go without it. The use of grooming aids had become fundamental. Even men were encouraged to use beauty products and toiletries during this period.

The war years drew on the ideal look of movie stars such as the long pageboy of Veronica Lake. With nylon being taken for war use, women adapted their face makeup for their legs, painting a long line down the back of their legs to create the look of seams.

The 1950s ideals of beauty continued to be based on the looks of popular movie stars. Elizabeth Taylor, Grace Kelly, Audrey Hepburn, and later Marilyn Monroe were watched by all. Fashion models were just beginning to have influence. The fifties emphasized makeup; bright red lips and arched brows were relished. An adult, sophisticated look and a curvaceous body were the ideals, helped in part by the new look in dress that emphasized a small waist, a large bust, and large hips. Hairstyles were long, worn in a ponytail, or, in copying Audrey Hepburn, worn in a short pixie cut. Perfumes had always been in use, and they appear to have been particularly popular in the 1950s. Men had their favorite colognes as well.

By the 1960s the ideal has shifted to a youthful appearance. The baby-doll dresses with short skirts gave the appearance of a youthful body. Makeup was pale, if worn at all. Long, straight hair was all the rage. Although movie stars remained an influence, the fashion model began to be promoted as the ideal. Certainly the model known as Twiggy led many to believe that a very thin body was the ideal. Fashion began a trend toward more revealing clothing, with bare midriffs appearing on some garments. The bikini became the rage for swimwear.

The top model of the 1970s was Lauren Hutton, who, while wholesome, set an ideal for a slim, willowy body. A healthy lifestyle became part of the environmentally aware seventies culture. With that came an interest in working out. Many Americans took up tennis and joined in various exercise programs on television. *Jane Fonda's Workout* was particularly influential. Although Lauren Hutton had long hair, a new hairstyle was the Afro for both men and women. The look could be achieved by using a permanent. Yet a more classic look for hairstyles was promoted for people who desired to dress for success, especially for those men who allowed their beards and mustaches to grow.

During the 1980s hairstyles were large—that is, the hair was long, curled, and puffy, a far cry from the sleek sixties. Hairstyles revealed the influence of female television stars. The styles matched the exuberance of 1980s dressing. Makeup also was used in excess. Tattooing and mutilating the body with scars began to become popular with both men and women, but the trend was most apparent with men. The trend for exercising with machines and free weights became a popular alternative to aerobics. Many clubs opened to meet the needs of Americans, and universities expanded their recreation centers. Health professionals promoted the health benefits of exercising, and the aging baby boomers joined in.

The health club boom continued into the nineties and the first years of the twenty-first century. Men and women were working out. Yet there were problems. Young women, teens and preteens, were increasingly diagnosed with eating disorders such as anorexia nervosa and bulimia, and more and more Americans—men, women, and children—were deemed overweight. The importance of healthful diets gained media attention, but not before bad eating habits had taken their toll. The ideal of thinness for young women, as seen on the fashion pages, had been around for some time, even with the media offering countering views of a healthy muscled body. In the 1990s, and especially in the early 2000s, a shift in the ideal from fashion models to movie stars occurred. Movie stars began to appear more frequently on the covers of *Vogue* and *Harper's Bazaar*. In many respects they altered the thin ideal, for not all movie stars bought into the concept of extreme thinness. The ideal look now included long, wavy hair, a more natural look than that of either the sixties or the seventies. Television shows continued to influence fashion. Jennifer Anniston's hair on *Friends* is a good example, but even more influential was the show *Sex and the City*, which focused on the clothing, particularly the sexy clothes, worn by one of its stars, Sarah Jessica Parker. The body continued to be more exposed, with low-slung tight pants and short, revealing tops, but the trends were beginning to change to a more covered look. The popular top—a short, colorful high-waisted tunic (sometimes strapless)—was growing longer and had sleeves.

CANADA

Growth and development of the clothing industries and retail establishments occurred later in Canada than in the United States, taking off with the industrial revolution in 1875. As in the United States, clothing businesses started small with tailors, dressmakers, milliners, shoemakers, and other craftspeople offering custom and in some cases ready-made articles of dress. For the most part, businesses were centered in the major cities, with Montreal considered the fashion capital of Canada. When mechanization was introduced in the nineteenth century, Canadian textile and fashion entrepreneurs, as in the United States, began to employ female operatives. There were thriving small-scale manufacturers in places as far afield as Halifax, Nova Scotia, and St. John, New Brunswick. The Canadian fashion industry today includes textile manufacturing, furriers, fashion designers, clothing manufacturing, and allied industries, as well as the retail trades for men's, women's, and children's clothing. The clothing industry has kept up with new technology, incorporating computers and high-speed sewing techniques to increase production. In this labor-intensive industry, apparel accounts for 5.7 percent of employment and 2.2 percent of manufacturing gross domestic production. Exports amounted to $4 billion in 1997. The retail business, although it has undergone many changes over the years, remains strong. In 2005 Canadians spent Can$19,742,000,000 on apparel products.[5]

Background

For all of the similarities between the two countries, there are elements within both the United States and Canada that provide distinctions for each. Although Canada has a western culture similar to that of the United States, it cannot claim jeans as a distinctly Canadian garment. That claim is purely American. Canadians have one very important apparel item that is distinctively Canadian—the blanket coat. The blanket coat is made from trade blankets such as those originally provided by the Hudson Bay Company. The blankets are thick and warm. When made up into coats, they provide casual alternatives to fur. For Canadians blanket coats are a symbol of their rugged outdoor past. They were immensely popular in the nineteenth century, yet they continue to be made and are worn with pride.[6]

Shopping

All of the major cities in Canada have department stores and shopping districts.

The first department store was the Hudson Bay Company, which started as a trading company in 1670. When men ceased wearing top hats made of beaver, trade in fur dropped significantly. The company diversified its business but held on to its trading posts by turning them into stores with more products than those they traded for furs. In 1912 it established six department stores across Canada, known today as the Bay.

Another famous department store was the Toronto-based Simpson's, established in 1896. By 1943 Simpson's was enormous, with 5500 employees in its Toronto store alone and with 1000 in mail order. In 1951 they merged their catalog department with the U.S. store Sears, which eventually took over in 1978. At that time the Hudson Bay Company bought many of Simpson's original department stores; other Simpson's stores became Sears.

For many years Montreal was the fashion leader, with stores clustered along St. Catherine Street, "the Fashion Mile." Stores that began locating there in the 1890s were Henry Morgan's Colonial House (1891), a dry goods palace; Henry Birks and Sons (1894), jewelers and silversmiths; John Murphy's (1894), fashionable assortments; James Ogilvy (1896), department store; Carsley's (1909), general store. The architecture of many of the buildings was impressive, as were the interiors with conveniences and services meant to appeal to customers and add to their comfort. In the early decades of the twentieth century these stores began to move toward the realm of fashion merchandising and away from general goods; they saw the success of the Colonial House, which had always offered more high-priced goods. When the Robert Simpson Company of Toronto took over the John Murphy Company in 1905, the Simpson-run Murphy's store began importing Paris fashions and focused solely on women's needs and fashion merchandising. Eventually Carsley's store became Goodwin's, which likewise focused on fashion merchandising in an environment that included a French Room, which purported to carry all of the latest Paris and American models. Changes were always occurring. One dramatic buyout was the purchase of Goodwin's by the Toronto-based T. Eaton Company in 1925. This added to the store rivalry, which remained keen, on St. Catherine Street, with competing advertisements for the latest of Paris couture until the Great Depression came along in 1929. The Depression altered or destroyed many venues for retail and manufacturers in North America. Then, World War II shifted manufacturing to wartime needs. Although postwar recovery was slow and later cultural changes affected the retail scene, St. Catherine Street remains a vital shopping district. The French couture may be absent, but the customers remain.[7]

One of the premier stores in Canada today is Holt Renfrew. The store began as a hat and fur shop with the name Henderson in Quebec City. Canadians have always embraced furs to keep them warm during their harsh winters. From the very beginning Holt Renfrew provided exquisite furs and gained a royal warrant from Queen Victoria. They too had a store on St. Catherine Street in Montreal. In the 1930s and 1940s they added international designers to their already prestigious line, including Christian Dior. Today they are still known for their furs, as well as cosmetics and perfumes. They have added their own private label to clothing products as well. They consider themselves a style leader in Canada. They have stores in all of the major Canadian cities.

Shopping for couture fashions in Canada as elsewhere was a great pastime for many women, but it was also essential to identity, for, of course, apparel reflects status and supports individuality. As Alexandra Palmer points out in *Couture & Commerce*, during the 1950s Toronto women purchased Dior and other Parisian-made clothing for their prestige. In certain segments of society it was expected of them. Yet they often altered the garments to conform to local etiquette regarding display and modesty. Some customers let their clothes hang in the closet for at least a year before they dare wore them. Such reticence was not apparent in the United States during the 1950s. New Yorkers ran to Lohman's to purchase the latest Dior or Balenciaga knockoff.

Trade, Manufacturing, and Design

In addition to the grand stores that developed in the late nineteenth century, there have been a number of successful high-end dressmakers (couturiers) with their own salons, especially in Montreal. Publications about them include a biography of Gaby, a 1930s couturier,

Jackie Beaudoin-Ross's essay on Marie-Paule, and most recently Lydia Ferrabee Sharman's work on Jean Harris's Salon in *Fashion: A Canadian Perspective*. Gerald Baril's *Dicomode: dictionnaire de la mode au Québec de 1900 à nos jours* includes information on twentieth-century Canadian fashion designers.

Ready-to-wear manufacturers have likewise been successful, but their names have not become household words. A similar anonymity has been the fate of the large numbers of ready-to-wear manufacturers of children's, women's and "junior" frocks who were active in the United States in the mid-twentieth century. Many of their names are now lost. In Montreal a number of designers sought to remedy the problem of anonymity. In *Fashion: A Canadian Perspective* Alexandra Palmer observed that some designers and manufacturers have been successful in gaining international recognition. Yet they have had little recognition within Canada, and their designs are not clearly identified as being of Canadian origin. In an effort to remedy the situation, in 1954 a group of Montreal designers formed the Association of Canadian Couturiers. Editors at the Canadian fashion and textile trade magazine *Style* were the instigators of the concept. The designers were to make up fashions using Canadian textiles, even Canadian woolen blanket material. The first collection was shown to the press in the Ritz-Carlton in Montreal. It traveled to Ottawa, Vancouver, and New York City. The success in New York gained some publicity for the group.[8]

The favorable response was deemed a positive effect for the less well-known designers in the group, not the better-known couturiers. Criticism of the collections was that they were of inconsistent quality compared to European fashions. The advantage of the show was that it allowed these designers to have greater exposure, even with only a few garments in each collection. Their individual businesses were too small for them to afford such a showing of their collections each season. Each designer had a salon that catered to elite customers, and now with the public collection using Canadian fabrics, they had the opportunity to develop links with ready-to-wear manufacturers providing garments that were less expensive. Unfortunately, the timing was wrong. When the youth quake occurred in the sixties, young women began to move away from looking like their mothers and wanting to wear couture garments. A new market opened for more youthful clothing inspired by English designers, such as Mary Quant. It appeared that Canadian fashion would be left out in the cold.[9]

There have been numerous exhibitions of Canadian-made and Canadian-worn fashion in major museums in the provinces. In many cases these serve to educate the public about the history of Canadian dress. The Bata Museum in Toronto provides a venue for the discussion of shoes and boots. In 1997 Alexandra Palmer of the Royal Ontario Museum set out to show the diversity of Canadian fashion with the exhibition "Au courant Contemporary Canadian Fashion." Yet for all of the exhibitions and fashion activities, it appeared that a Canadian identity in fashion design was not yet achieved. The lack of recognition of the Canadian-ness of Canadian designers persists. As Palmer notes, few people know that Elizabeth Arden, Rose-Marie Reid, and the early-twentieth-century "English" designer Lucille were Canadians. There is reason to believe, however, that these perceptions will change.[10]

In more recent years it has become apparent that trade between the United States and Canada is not a one-way street. In fact, all types of ready-made Canadian-designed and Canadian-manufactured clothing find their way to stores in the United States. Roots, although started by two Americans, is a Toronto-based sportswear manufacturer that caught the public eye during the Olympics. They have their own stores scattered throughout the United States, as well as in Canada. Apparel designed by Canadians is found in many popular boutiques in the United States, as well as in exclusive stores such as Saks Fifth Avenue. The list includes the designers Alfred Sung, Ron Leal, Dan and Dean Caten of D'Squared2, Linda Lundström, Lida Baday, Sunny Choi, David Dixon, and John Hardy, as well as Annie

Thompson, Franco Mirabelli, Denis Gagnon, Arthur Mendonca, Tracy Watts (an accessory designer based in New York City), and many others producing sportswear, outerwear, evening wear, and so on.

In order to remedy the situation the Canadian Apparel Federation has been active in promoting Canadian fashion. Materials for their 2006 *Wear? Canada!* marketing project (http://www.wearcanada.ca) asked, "Why buy Canadian?" and then proceeded to answer the question by first remarking on their success in the past but also by noting the quality and craftsmanship of the products, their ability to respond quickly, and their long-standing partnership in the North American Free Trade Agreement. They also observed that the companies are of manageable size, a characteristic that allows them to work with retailers as partners. They note that Canadian women's wear manufacturers are represented at every major international trade show, in showrooms in the United States, and at the Fashion Weeks held in Montreal, Toronto, and Vancouver in the spring and fall.

RESOURCE GUIDE

PRINTED SOURCES

Agins, Teri. *The End of Fashion: The Mass Marketing of the Clothing Business.* New York: William Morrow, 1999.

Arthur, Linda Boynton. *Aloha Attire: Hawaiian Dress in the Twentieth Century.* New York: Schiffer Publishing, 1999.

Ash, Juliet, and Elizabeth Wilson, eds. *Chic Thrills: A Fashion Reader.* Berkeley: University of California Press, 1993.

Ball, Joanne Dubbs. *The Art of Fashion Accessories: A Twentieth Century Retrospective.* West Chester, PA: Schiffer Publishing, 1993.

Baril, Gérald. *Dicomode: dictionnaire de la mode au Québec de 1900 à nos jours.* Quèbec: Fides, 2004.

Barnes, Ruth, and Joanne B. Eicher. *Dress and Gender: Making and Meaning.* New York: Berg Publishing, 1993.

Beck, Jane Farrell, and Colleen Gau. *Uplift: The Bra in America.* Philadelphia: University of Pennsylvania Press, 2002.

Berry, Sarah. *Screen Style: Fashion and Femininity in 1930s Hollywood.* Minneapolis: University of Minnesota Press, 2000.

Blau, Herbert. *Nothing in Itself: Complexions of Fashion.* Bloomington: Indiana University Press, 1999.

Blum, Stella, comp. *Victorian Fashions and Costumes from Harper's Bazaar 1867–1890.* New York: Dover Publications, 1975.

———, ed. *Fashions and Costumes from Godey's Lady's Book*, reprint edition. New York: Dover Publications, 1985.

Bond, David. *The Guinness Guide to 20th Century Fashion.* Enfield: Guinness, 1988.

Borrelli, Laird. *Stylishly Drawn: Contemporary Fashion Illustration.* New York: Harry N. Abrams, 2000.

Boston, Lloyd. *Men of Color: Fashion, History and Fundamentals.* New York: Artisan, 1998.

Brumberg, Joan Jacobs. "Fasting Girls: The Emerging Ideal of Slenderness in American Culture." In Linda K. Kerber and Jane Sherron DeHart (eds.), *Women's America: Refocusing the Past*, 4th edition. New York: Oxford University Press, 1995.

Bruzzi, Stella. *Undressing Cinema: Clothing and Identity in Movies.* London: Routledge, 1997.

Brydon, Anne, and Sandra Niessen. *Consuming Fashion: Adorning the Transnational Body.* New York: Berg Publishing, 1998.

Burman, Barbara. *The Culture of Sewing.* New York: Berg Publishing, 1999.

Burnston, Sharon Ann. *Fitting & Proper.* New York: Scurlock Publishing Co., 2000.

Buttolph, Angela, Alice Mackrell, Richard Martin, Melanie Rickey, and Judith Watt. *The Fashion Book.* London: Phaidon Press Limited, 1998.

Buxbaum, Gerda. *Icons of Fashion: The 20th Century.* New York: Prestel, 1999.

Calasibetta, Charolette Mankey. *Fairchild's Dictionary of Fashion.* New York: Fairchild Books, 1998.

Callan, Georgina O'Hara. *The Thames and Hudson Dictionary of Fashion and Fashion Designers.* London: Thames and Hudson, 1998.

Cassini, Oleg. *A Thousand Days of Magic: Dressing Jackie Kennedy for the White House.* New York: Rizzoli, 1995.

Cavallaro, Dani, and Alexandra Warwick. *Fashioning the Frame: Boundaries, Dress and the Body.* New York: Berg Publishing, 1998.

Chenoune, Farid. *A History of Men's Fashion.* Paris: Flammarion, 1993.

Clancy, Deirdre. *Costume Since 1945: Couture Street Style and Anti-Fashion.* New York: Drama Publishers, 1996.

Cole, Shaun. *Don We Now Our Gay Apparel: Gay Men's Dress in the Twentieth Century.* New York: Berg Publishing, 2000.

Cook, Daniel. *The Commodification of Childhood: The Children's Clothing Industry and the Rise of the Child Consumer.* Durham, NC: Duke University Press, 2004.

Cooper, Cynthia. *Magnificent Entertainments: Fancy Dress Balls of Canada's Governors General 1876–1896.* New York: Goose Lane Editions, 1998.

Costantino, Maria. *Men's Fashion in the Twentieth Century: From Frock Coats to Intelligent Fibres.* London: BT Batsford, 1997.

———. *Designers.* London: Batsford, 1997.

Countryman, Ruth, and Elizabeth Weiss Hopper. *Women's Wear of the 1920's: With Complete Patterns.* New York: Players Press, 1998.

Crane, Diana. *Fashion and Its Social Agendas: Class, Gender, and Identity.* Chicago: University of Chicago Press, 2000.

Craughwell-Varda, Kathleen. *Looking for Jackie: American Fashion Icons.* New York: Hearst Books, 1999.

Cunningham, Patricia A. *Reforming Women's Fashion, 1850–1920, Politics, Health and Art.* Kent, OH: Kent State University Press, 2003.

Cunningham, Patricia A., and Susan Voso Lab. *Dress and Popular Culture.* Bowling Green, OH: Popular Press, 1991.

———. *Dress in American Culture.* Bowling Green, OH: Popular Press, 1993.

Cunningham, Patricia A., and Linda Welters. *Twentieth Century American Fashion.* Oxford: Berg, 2005.

Darnell, Paula Jean. *Victorian to Vamp: Woman's Clothing 1900–1929.* New York: Fabric Fancies, 2000.

Davis, Fred. *Fashion, Culture and Identity.* Chicago: University of Chicago Press, 1992.

De Castelbajec, Kate. *The Face of the Century: 100 Years of Makeup and Style.* New York: Rizzoli, 1995.

De La Haye, Amy. *Surfers, Soulies, Skinheads, and Skaters: Subcultural Style from the Forties to the Nineties.* Woodstock: Overlook Press, 1996.

Downey, Lynn, Jill Novack Lynch, and Kathleen McDonough. *This Is a Pair of Levi's Jeans: The Official History of the Levi's Brand.* San Francisco: Levi Strauss & Co. Publishing, 1995.

Edelman, Amy Holman. *The Little Black Dress.* New York: Simon & Schuster Editions, 1997.

Eisner, Lisa, Roman Alonso, and Amy Spindler, eds. *Height of Fashion.* New York: Grey Bull Press, 2000.

Entwistle, Joanne. *Dress, Bodies and Business: Fashioning Women at Work.* New York: Berg Publishing, 2001.

Ewing, Elizabeth. *History of Twentieth Century Fashion.* Lanham, MD: Barnes and Noble Books, 1992.

Finlayson, Iain. *Denim: An American Legend.* New York: Simon & Schuster Inc., 1990.

Fontanel, Beatrice, and Willard Wood, trans. *Support and Seduction: A History of Corsets and Bras.* New York: Harry N. Abrams, 1997.

Fox, Patty. *Star Style: Hollywood Legends as Fashion Icons.* Santa Monica, CA: Angel City Press, 1999.

Fraser, Kennedy. *The Fashionable Mind: Reflections on Fashion, 1970–1981.* Boston: D. R. Godine, 1985.

Gan, Stephen. *Visionaire's Fashion 2000: Designers at the Turn of the Millennium.* London: Laurence King Publishing, 1997.

Gan, Stephen, and Alix Browne. *Visionaire's Fashion 2001: Designers of the New Avant-Garde.* New York: Universe Publications, 1999.

Glynn, Prudence. *In Fashion: Dress in the Twentieth Century*. New York: Oxford University Press, 1978.

Grafton, Carol Belanger. *Fashions of the Thirties: 476 Authentic Copyright-Free Illustrations*. New York: Dover Publications, 1993.

Haddock, Miranda Howard. *Darning the Wear of Time: Survey and Annotated Bibliography of Periodical Literature of Costume, Conservation, Restoration, and Documentation Published in English 1980–1996*. New York: Rowman & Littlefield, 1996.

Handley, Susannah. *Nylon: The Story of a Fashion Revolution: A Celebration of Design from Art Silk to Nylon and Thinking Fibres*. Baltimore, MD: Johns Hopkins University Press, 1999.

Harris, Kristina. *The Home Pattern Company 1914 Fashions Catalog: The Home Pattern Company*, reprint edition. New York: Dover Publications, 1995.

Haynes, Michaele Thurgood. *Dressing Up Debutantes: Pageantry and Glitz in Texas*. New York: Berg Publishing, 1998.

Hilfiger, Tommy. *All American*. New York: Universe Publishing, 1997.

Hilfiger, Tommy, Anthony Decurtis, Richard Martin, and James Henke. *Rock Style: How Fashion Moves to Music*. New York: Universe Publishing, 1999.

Hollander, Anne. *Sex and Suits: The Evolution of Modern Dress*. New York: Kodansha International, 1995.

Howell, Georgina. *In Vogue: 75 Years of Style*. London: Conde Nast Books, 1991.

Hunt, Marsha. *The Way We Wore: Styles of the 1930s and '40s and Our World Since Then*. Fallbrook, CA: Fallbrook Publications, 1993.

Kelcey, Barbara E. "Dress Reform in Nineteenth-Century Canada." Pp. 229–248 in Alexandra Palmer (ed.), *Fashion: A Canadian Perspective*. Toronto: University of Toronto Press, 2004.

Khornak, Lucille. *Fashion 2001*. New York: Viking Press, 1982.

Kidwell, Claudia Brush, and Valerie Steele, eds. *Men and Women: Dressing the Part*. Smithsonian Institute, 1989.

Lambert, Eleanor. *World of Fashion: People, Places, Resources*. New York: R. R. Bowker, 1976.

Lee, Sarah Tomerlin, ed. *American Fashion: The Life and Lines of Adrian, Mainbocher, McCardell, Norell, Trigere*. New York: Quadrangle/New York Times, 1975.

Lipovetsky, Gilles. *The Empire of Fashion: Dressing Modern Democracy*. Princeton: Princeton University Press, 1987.

Lobenthal, Joel. *Radical Rags: Fashion of the Sixties*. New York: Abbeville Press, 1990.

Lynch, Annette. *Dress, Gender and Cultural Change*. New York: Berg Publishing, 1999.

Malossi, Giannino, ed. *The Style Engine: Spectacle, Identity, Design and Business: How the Fashion Industry Uses Style to Create Wealth*. New York: Monacelli Press, 1998.

Martin, Richard. *Fashion and Surrealism*. New York: Rizzoli, 1987.

———. *Contemporary Fashion*. New York: St. James Press, 1995.

———, ed. *The St. James Fashion Encyclopedia: A Survey of Style from 1945 to the Present*. New York: Visible Ink, 1996.

———. *Khaki: Cut from the Original Cloth*. Santa Fe: Tondo, 1999.

Martin, Richard, and Harold Koda. *Jocks and Nerds: Men's Style in the Twentieth Century*. New York: Rizzoli, 1989.

———. *Fashion Today*. New York: Phaidon Press, 2000.

McRobbie, Angela, ed. *Zoot Suits and Second-Hand Dresses: An Anthology of Fashion and Film*. Boston: Unwin Hyman, 1988.

Mendes, Valerie D. *20th Century Fashion*. London: Thames and Hudson, 1999.

Milbank, Caroline R. *Couture, the Great Designers*. New York: Stewart, Tabori and Chang, 1985.

———. *New York Fashion: The Evolution of American Style*. New York: Harry N. Abrams, 1989.

Muggleton, David. *Inside Subculture: The Postmodern Meaning of Style*. New York: Berg Publishing, 2000.

Mulvagh, Jane. *Vogue History of 20th Century Fashion*. New York: Viking, 1988.

Mulvey, Kate. *Decades of Beauty*. New York: Checkmark Books, 1998.

Murray, Maggie Pexton. *Changing Styles in Fashion: Who, What, Why*. New York: Fairchild Publications, 1989.

Newman, Karoline, Gillian Proctor, and Karen Bressler. *A Century of Lingerie*. New York: Book Sales, 1998.

Nicholson, Kathleen. *WWD Century: One Hundred Years of Fashion*. New York: Fairchild Publications, 1998.

Oliver, Valerie Burnham. *Fashion and Costume in American Popular Culture: A Reference Guide*. Westport, CT: Greenwood Press, 1996.

Osma, Guillermo de. *Fortuny: Mariano Fortuny, His Life and Work*. New York: Rizzoli, 1980.

Owen, Elizabeth. *Fashion in Photographs 1920–1940*. London: Batsford Ltd., 1993.

Palmer, Alexandra. *Couture & Commerce, the Transatlantic Fashion Trade in the 1950s*. Toronto: Royal Ontario Museum and UBC Press, 2001.

———, ed. *Fashion: A Canadian Perspective*. Toronto: University of Toronto Press, 2004a.

———. "Introduction." Pp. 6–7 in Alexandra Palmer (ed.), *Fashion: A Canadian Perspective*. Toronto: University of Toronto Press, 2004b.

———. "The Association of Canadian Couturiers." Pp. 90–112 in Alexandra Palmer (ed.), *Fashion: A Canadian Perspective*. Toronto: University of Toronto Press, 2004c.

Peacock, John. *Twentieth-Century Fashion: The Complete Sourcebook*. London: Thames and Hudson, 1993.

———. *The 1920s (Fashion Sourcebook)*. London: Thames and Hudson, 1997.

———. *The 1940s*. New York: Thames and Hudson, 1998.

———. *Fashion Accessories: The Complete 20th Century Sourcebook*. New York: Thames and Hudson, 2000.

Peiss, Kathy. *Hope in a Jar: The Making of America's Beauty Culture*. New York: Owl Books, 1999.

Queen, Sally, and Vicki L. Berger. *Clothing and Textile Collections in the United States. A CSA Guide*. Lubbock, TX: Texas Tech University Press, 2006.

Ray, Virginia Allen, and William H. Goetzmann. *Gordon Conway: Fashioning a New Woman (American Studies Series)*. Austin: University of Texas, 1997.

Robinson, Julian. *The Golden Age of Style*. London: Orbis Publications, 1976.

———. *Fashions in the 40's*. New York: St. Martin's Press, 1980.

Routh, Caroline. *In Style: 100 Years of Canadian Fashion*. Toronto: Stoddart Publishing, 1993.

Russell, Douglas. *Costume History and Style*. Englewood Cliffs, NJ: Prentice-Hall, 1983.

Schefer, Dorothy. *What Is Beauty?: New Definitions from the Fashion Vanguard*. New York: Universe Publishing, 1997.

Schnurnberger, Lynn. *Let There Be Clothes*. New York: Workman Publishing, 1991.

Severa, Joan L., Nancy Rexford, and Claudia Brush Kidwell. *Dressed for the Photographer: Ordinary Americans and Fashion, 1840–1900*. Kent, OH: Kent State University Press, 1997.

Sifton, Elizabeth. "Montreal's Fashion Mile: St. Catherine Street, 1890–1930." Pp. 203–223 in Alexandra Palmer (ed.), *Fashion: A Canadian Perspective*. Toronto: University of Toronto Press, 2004.

Stack, Eileen. "'Very Picturesque and Very Canadian': The Blanket Coat and Anglo-Canadian Identity in the Second Half of the Nineteenth Century." Pp. 17–40 in Alexandra Palmer (ed.), *Fashion: A Canadian Perspective*. Toronto: University of Toronto Press, 2004.

Steele, Valerie. *Fifty Years of Fashion: New Look to Now*. New York: Yale University Press, 1997.

Stegemeyer, Anne. *Who's Who in Fashion*, 3rd edition. New York: Fairchild Publications, 1996.

Tortora, Phyllis, and Keith Eubank. *Survey of Historic Costume: A History of Western Dress*, 2nd edition. New York: Fairchild Publications, 1994.

Vogue Company. *Vogue: 100th Anniversary Special*. New York: Vogue Company, 1992.

Warner, Patricia C. *When the Girls Came Out to Play: The Birth of American Sportswear*. Amherst: University of Massachusetts Press, 2006.

Watson, Linda. *Vogue: Twentieth Century Fashion*. London: Carlton, 1999.

Welters, Linda, and Patricia A. Cunningham, eds. *Twentieth Century American Fashion*. Oxford: Berg, 2005.

White, Nicola. *Reconstructing Italian Fashion: America and the Development of Italian Fashion Industry*. New York: New York University Press, 2000.

White, Nicola, and Ian Giffiths, eds. *The Fashion Business: Theory, Practice, Image*. New York: Berg Publishers, 2000.

Wilson, Sharmain. *The Evolution of Canadian Fashion (1997)*. A multimedia resource.

Wright, Meredith, and Nancy Rexford. *Everyday Dress of Rural America 1783–1800: With Instructions and Patterns.* New York: Dover Publications, 1992.

Yohannan, Khole, Nancy Wolfe, Irving Solero, and Valerie Steele. *Claire McCardell: Redefining Modernism.* London: Harry N. Abrams, 1998.

MUSEUMS

United States

Cincinnati Art Museum, 953 Eden Park Drive, Cincinnati, OH 45202–1596. http://www.cincinnatiart museum.org/.

Colonial Williamsburg Foundation, 313 First Street, Williamsburg, PA 23187–1776. http://www. history.org.

The Costume Collection, Chicago Historical Society, Clark at North Avenue, Chicago, IL 60614. http://www.chicagohs.org/.

The Costume Institute, Metropolitan Museum of Art, 1000 Fifth Avenue, New York, NY 10028–0198. http://www.metmuseum.org.

Fashion Institute of Technology, 227 West 27th St., New York, NY 10001–5902. http://www.fitnyc.edu.

Kent State University Museum, P.O. Box 5190, Kent, OH 44242. http://www.kent.edu/museum.

Museum of the City of New York, 1220 Fifth Avenue, New York, NY 10029. http://www.mcny.org.

Canada

Bata Museum, 327 Bloor St. West, Toronto, ON M5S 1W7. http://www.batashoemuseum.ca.

Canadian Museum of Civilization, 100 Laurier Street, P.O. Box 3100, Station B, Gatineau, Quebec J8X 4H2. http://www.civilization.ca/indexe.asp.

McCord Museum, 690 Sherbrooke Street West, Montreal QC H3A 1E9. http://www.mccord-museum.qc.ca.

Parks Canada, Edmonton, 145 McDermont Ave., Winnipeg, MB R3B 0R9. http://www.pc.gc.ca/index_e.asp.

Royal Ontario Museum, Toronto, 100 Queen's Park, Toronto, ON M5S 2C6. http://www.rom.on.ca/.

WEBSITES

AAFA (American Apparel & Footwear Association). http://www.apparelandfootwear.org/. Official Website of the AAFA, which represents apparel companies and their suppliers.

apparelbc. Apparel-BC. http://www.apparel-bc.org/. Official Website of the British Columbia apparel industry association, which promotes awareness of the fashion and design industry in British Columbia, Canada.

ca (Canadian Apparel). Canadian Apparel Federation. http://www.apparel.ca/. Website of the Canadian Apparel Federation, designed to promote communication across the Canadian fashion industry sectors.

Costume Society of America. http://www.costumesocietyamerica.com/. Designed to further study in the field of costume and fashion.

Costume Society of Ontario. Costume Society of Ontario. http://www.costumesociety.ca/. Promotes education in dress throughout history. Allows member chats about all aspects of fashion.

Council of Fashion Designers of America. http://www.cfda.com/flash.html. The CFDA is a not-for-profit trade association of over 250 of the United States' foremost fashion and accessory designers. Website features news and the CFDA Fashion Awards Program.

Fanshawe's Virtual Library: Art & Design. Fanshawe College. http://www.fanshawec.on.ca/vlibrary/art/fashion.asp. Includes listings about the fashion industry and organizations in North America.

Strategis. http://strategis.ic.gc.ca. A Website for business owners and consumers.

The Textile Society of America, Inc. Textile Society of America. http://textilesociety.org/. Official Website of the organization, providing a forum of the exchange of information about textiles worldwide, from artistic, cultural, economic, historical, political, social, and technical standpoints.

NOTES

1. For further discussion see Milbank 1989 (in Resource Guide), in which Caroline Milbank discusses the rise and development of the fashion industry in New York City.
2. Unpublished conference paper. Popular Culture Association Conference, 2004.
3. For further discussion of the history of menswear, see Chenoune 1993 (in Resource Guide).
4. For further discussion of the development of American beauty culture, see Peiss 1999 (in Resource Guide).
5. See http://strategis.ic.gc.ca.
6. Stack 2004 (in Resource Guide), pp. 17–40.
7. Sifton 2004 (in Resource Guide), pp. 203–223.
8. Palmer 2004c (in Resource Guide), pp. 90–112.
9. Ibid.
10. Palmer 2004b (in Resource Guide), pp. 6–7.

SCOTT L. BAUGH

WITH STARS IN THEIR EYES . . .

Hollywood is cinema; cinema is Hollywood. This tautology, though partly truthful, deserves close examination. In some significant respects, the rise of cinema since the 1890s has followed a pattern of worldwide domination of corporate and aesthetic models headquartered in Hollywood. In 2005 domestic box office topped US$8.9 billion from almost 1.5 billion admissions to 563 releases[1] across almost 39,000 indoor and outdoor screens.[2] Worldwide box office amounted to $23 billion.[3] In spite of a slight decline in gross after over a decade of steady growth, the big numbers equal big business, the vast majority of which remains Hollywood-owned and Hollywood-flavored.

To consider the cinema of North America (or the world, for that matter), then, requires retracing its path through the southern California hills. And yet, there have been strong alternative models—involving production and management as well as expressive, visionary, and independent aesthetics—that live and breathe outside of L.A.'s smoggy air, off Hollywood Boulevard, even beyond the shadows of Mulholland Drive. Mainstream culture and cinema of the twenty-first century are global and consumer-driven, where plastic likenesses of Mulan, Mushu, and six other characters from Disney's 1998 blockbuster, *Mulan*, could be collected from McDonald's Happy Meals in over 100 countries; or where the promotional T-shirt, lunch box, poster, and key chain of the latest sequel in the *Jurassic Park*, *Harry Potter*, or *Matrix* series could be purchased, along with the DVD of the movie itself and its video game extension for home use, in any one of the almost 6000 Wal-Mart stores across 16 countries, for example. Cinema's influence on mainstream culture and vice versa are not only huge business; they are equally culturally and socio-politically enveloping. One might argue that the legacy of Western imperialism across the continent and world historically wielded by U.S. politics finds its reflection in its mainstream cultural production, especially in moving pictures. Cinema (especially commercial cinema) possesses an apparatus that yields crucial representations, sometimes stereotypes, and a level of identification for viewers (a phenomenon called "spectatorship"), in which viewers vicariously embody the images, the story lines, and the characters they see and hear.

But against mainstream cultural and commercial flows rush crosscurrents and undertows. Distinguished film historian Thomas Cripps borrows an economic principle to describe and help explain the various tensions and contests surrounding North American cinema and its "countervailing forces."[4] Is cinema an art or a business? If cinema is primarily a business, should it be driven by technological and aesthetic innovation or by demographics, marketing trends, and expense reports? If cinema is primarily an art, should it aim at refined tastes like traditional "high" art, should it reflect a moral or political elite or give voice to "the people," should it include sensational topics, exploding helicopters, and all the spectacular "eye candy" that can fit, and can it be mass-produced? Do we as viewers align ourselves with these films, and how do the film heroes and villains influence our attitudes and views? Are the best methods creative and original or pragmatic and generic? And, can all these issues fit together and come in on time and under budget? "Countervailing forces" offer multiple answers to these questions, which have shaped the history of cinema in North America and throughout the world, from its beginnings just over 100 years ago in western Europe and the United States to its heyday in Hollywood and beyond.

The theme of domination succeeds in North American cinema today, as most productions are packaged deals cofinanced among the largest conglomerates such as Sony, Paramount, Universal, and Warner, and their limited partnerships; almost half of the theater screens in North America are owned by the five largest exhibitors in Regal Entertainment Group, AMC, Cinemark, Carmike, and Loews; and around 95 percent of domestic (U.S. and Canada) box office returns went to the top seven distributors, including Warner, Universal, and Buena Vista.[5] In 2003, for example, the domestic top five box office grossing films—first, *Lord of the Rings: Return of the King*, followed by *Finding Nemo*, *Pirates of the Caribbean*, *Matrix: Reloaded*, and *Bruce Almighty*—combined for over $1.6 billion box office gross (representing almost 17 percent of the $9.4 total from 2003's just under 500 commercial releases).[6] This third year of the new millennium is typical of most current trends, especially as it rounds off a decade of growth, reflecting studio cinema as another "return of the king." But have the bigger-as-better production and management models outgrown themselves, as latest box office declines suggest, and is the industry oversaturated with competing entertainment? Perhaps history will help enlighten what the future holds for North American cinema.

BEGINNINGS OF U.S. FILMS

East Coast, 1878–1926

A decade after Eadweard Muybridge's famous "instantaneous photograph" experiments in 1878, Thomas Alva Edison, best known then for his invention of the telegraph, the incandescent lightbulb, electricity, and the phonograph, with his assistant William K. L. Dickson set their sights on devising an instrument for the eye similar to what the phonograph was for the ear. Their kinetoscope, the first true movie camera, initiated the recording of short motion pictures, the earliest U.S. films. Some of this earliest history has been forever lost, as Frank Thomson and others point out, with material preservation only very recently gaining attention.[7] Subjects of the earliest shorts, though, consist of everyday events such as employees leaving work at the factory, a brief dance routine, a boxing match, or even news reports from the Spanish-American War. Sometimes the drama of these shorts was formalistically heightened with colored tints or histrionics. Film producers and vendors, though, recognized the need for something to gain the viewers' attention and to market the product, something beyond "The Kiss" (1896) between two lovers. Films needed a cinematic spectacle beyond mundane events, as the novelty quickly wore thin. The films themselves shifted away from "actualities" to fictional narratives, stories initially modeled after vaudeville's popular, if lowbrow, entertainment.

The convergence of art, enterprise, and ideology is a theme that repeats throughout cinema history, and one that, while it creates tensions and countervailing influences, places the U.S. film industry in a position of relative dominance in the world. In economic and aesthetic terms, countries throughout the Americas were dependent upon the United States, and within the United States independent producers tended to bow to the major studio forces. Filmmaking businesses became progressively more centralized, as corporate style, typically conservative in nature, already shaped the film industry at the century's turn. By 1897 three studio companies—the Edison Company, Vitagraph, and American Mutoscope and Biograph—dominated the East Coast industry with their "camera-man system" of production. By the early 1900s formulae already were becoming established: trains rolling into the frame or carrying the moving camera in travelogue, ocean tides and mountain vistas, predictable gags, and historical reenactments. As the films grew to one reel in length (about 1000 feet of 35mm film played at silent speed, sixteen frames per second) or about 15 minutes of visual material, greater possibility for storytelling increased.

In 1895 Alfred Clark, working for Edison's studio, added an important technological and aesthetic innovation while treating an otherwise unnoteworthy re-creation of the "Execution of Mary, Queen of Scots" (1895). At climax, Clark cleverly stops the camera, replaces the actress with a dummy, restarts the camera, and beheads the character, exposing the dummy head's fall to the ground. The stop-action special effect heightened the cinematic illusion and realistic representation of the execution. Over the next few years, Edwin S. Porter, also working with Edison, made perhaps the greatest advancement in filmmaking of this era. In his "Great Train Robbery," "Life of an American Fireman" (both 1903), and subsequent films, Porter used editing techniques to "intercut" near-simultaneous action at different locations into a unified story and, in so doing, offered a prototype of commercial cinema's language and style that would grow to dominance in years to come.

Hollywood, 1907–14

In 1907 the Chicago-based production of "The Count of Monte Cristo" by William Selig moved to southern California to finish shooting. This was the first of many such productions to take advantage of early-twentieth-century California's many resources: ideal weather and environment; versatile and pristine natural resources, from mountains to ocean and forest to desert in a day's drive; and (then) cheap real estate. One apocryphal story demands that the move to southern California allowed outlaw businesses to hide in Mexico from patent enforcers, but the patent officers loved California and moved there too. The cinema industry had started in the East, but its move to southern California was decisive. Studio production companies planted roots, taking advantage of the room for enormous soundstages and large tracts of land for back lots and facilities. Hollywood (Edendale, North Hollywood, Burbank, Culver City, and surrounding vicinities) became emblematic of U.S. film and, as a result, wielded a great deal of power through its cultural production and influence over mass audiences. Some of the eastern power brokers moved with the industry, but the migration to California also allowed a new generation of businessmen to take a risk with the growing industry. Gerald Mast and Bruce Kawin argue that the prominence of Jewish businessmen, especially, in Hollywood at this time was due to the industry's lack of structure and tradition, which did not lock them out, and the relative illegitimacy involved in the

"SILENT CINEMA"

Although the technological integration of synchronized sound (spoken word, music, and effects) was not adopted until 1927 as a result of the commercial success of *The Jazz Singer*, sound has always been a part of the movie text and the moviegoing experience. Since the earliest theatrical exhibitions, live accompaniment from piano or Wurlitzer to full orchestra and dialogue spoken by actors standing offstage or behind the screen enlivened the visual imagery of the film. Some silents were distributed with specially scripted dialogue and musical score. More than merely prelude to the talkie, the silent era featured significant conventions and the birth of the classical paradigm upon which modern commercial film would rely; it introduced influential genres and characters; it established business models around the prevalent studio structure; and it saw the rise of a number of important film artists to make their films.

Hits of the silent era include *Birth of a Nation* (1915), *Broken Blossoms* (1919), *Four Horsemen of the Apocalypse* (1921), *Way Down East* (1921), *Ten Commandments* (1923), *Ben-Hur* (1925), *What Price Glory?* (1926), and *The General* (1927). *Wings* (1927) won two Academy Awards, including the first ever Best Picture award.

entertainment field, which more established, respectable businessmen avoided and left to them.[8] And yet, there have been other groups and their stories that seem to have been locked out of the industry for most of its existence based on gender, racial/ethnic, and other biases. Clearly, political power and control always have been important factors in Hollywood.

In 1911 Thomas Ince helped move the New York Motion Picture Company to Santa Monica, California, founding Inceville, an early, significant studio. Key to the success of Ince's studio was a factory style with centralized power that set a standard for Hollywood studios to follow. If, in its infancy, cinema's art was shaped by its technological innovation, then in its move to Hollywood, art was shaped even more profoundly by business models. Three facets to the movie business—production; management and marketing; and exhibition—have grown over the years into a triumvirate. Financiers based in New York, politicians in Washington, and film executives in Hollywood would use these three arms of the film industry to vie strategically for control and power. As World War I broke in Europe and the Bolshevik Revolution took a grip on Russia through the last half of the 1910s and, as a result, energy, resources, and interests diverted away from cinematic cultural production, Hollywood was assured worldwide domination just as the studio system emerged. Parallel to the studio system's rise, the classical paradigm of film style was galvanized.

Hollywood, 1915–26

In the 1910s and 1920s, Hollywood grew into the film capital of the world, and even today, marketing, talent agencies, and other crucial aspects of the industry, if not always filming itself, remain there. Although the term *studio* refers to the building and the set where a film might be shot and sound recorded, it also significantly refers to the company that owns the facilities and to the types of operations there. That is, a studio film derives from a large-scale method of production with a hierarchical division of specialized labor. At the top, an executive producer, sometimes a studio head or mogul known for an egomaniacal drive and business acumen, supervised producers and cast and crew of that studio's individual projects, with the primary goal of keeping the company financially solvent and each film profitable. From producers, the decision-making power trickled down, generally from a film's director through its crew and top-billed cast. As the profit of any production depends on its box office returns (and, even more so since the 1980s, auxiliary sales and tie-in marketing), large production companies began accumulating their own distribution companies and theater chains to control marketing, management, and exhibition. In the 1920s the film industry was vertically integrated and "the Business" grew into what economists designate a mature oligopoly, whereby studios could finance their own productions and retain control over the three arms of the industry. Across the mechanisms of production, distribution, and exhibition, across a particular studio's slate of projects, and within a particular production, the Fordist division of labor made the industry more efficient, if potentially making the films themselves less artful and original. Crew and cast became highly specialized cogs on the gear of cultural production, for only rarely would a star or filmmaker achieve enough individual status to warrant decision-making power over or alongside the producer.

Beginning in 1911, like East Coast filmmakers in increasing numbers, D. W. Griffith took his Biograph productions to winter shoots in California, and this is where his most significant and influential work was made. One of the most controversial figures in cinema history, Griffith was also tagged the "father of Hollywood style," the classical paradigm. Modest, he was not, as an advertisement he himself took out in a 1913 issue of *The Dramatic Mirror* on the occasion of his split with Biograph attests:

> Producer of all great Biograph successes, revolutionizing Motion Picture drama, and founding the modern technique of the art. Included in the innovations which he introduced and which are now generally followed by most advanced producers, are: The large or close-up figures, distant views as represented first in *Ramona*, the "switchback [crosscutting]," sustained suspense, the "fade-out," and restraint in expression, raising motion-picture acting to the higher plane which has won for it recognition as a genuine art.[9]

Today there are still critical debates over whether Griffith made "innovations" in these areas or synthesized earlier accomplishments. Moreover, Griffith's departure from Biograph and his decision to make independent productions in his own name marked a profound moment for the role of the director-*auteur*, its autonomy and control within studio business operations and political structure. But perhaps his greatest controversy arose from his political views, the ideologies, especially racist and patriarchal, that revolve around his greatest works and stylistically the most profound in cinema history, especially *Intolerance* (1916) and *Birth of a Nation* (1915).

To be sure, *Birth of a Nation* stands as a landmark in U.S. and world cinema. Its original style and ambitious narrative structure rivals epic literary standards; its versatile shot types, sizes, movements, and perspectives afford a range of dramatic purpose far greater than what its audiences were accustomed; and perhaps greatest of all, its masterful use of intercutting not only depicts the continuity of a complex story across expansive locations and several years but also correlates symbolically the politics (from a southern, white supremacist viewpoint) of the U.S. Civil War to a family saga. Where Porter signaled the start of the Hollywood style, Griffith brought it to fruition.

In 1922 the correlation between Hollywood and the elite power base wishing to define mainstream values became institutionalized in the form of the Motion Picture Producers and Distributors of America (MPPDA, later the Motion Picture Association of America or MPAA). Popularly known as the "Hays Office" after its president, Will H. Hays, this "little State Department" started as a public relations mission to clean up the image of Hollywood after sex scandals (especially the Fatty Arbuckle affair) and avoid the need for external policing, but by the 1930s its industry-imposed regulation and censorship had become a staple force in the structure of the studio system, like another department in the studio, according

"THE WESTERN"

A film genre popular since the earliest days of cinema, the Western derives from the history and legends around the settling of the western United States in the nineteenth century, somewhere between lawlessness and social order; as such it represents an important link between cinema, its classical style, and U.S. imperialist conquest and in turn helps to shape a national imaginary. Beautiful, vast, untamed landscapes with panoramic views of expansive horizons; a ruggedly independent hero cowboy who holds true to his own code regardless of social pressure or personal loss, who is peaceful but quick to just violence, and who represents a natural intelligence over civilization and law; the holdup, the chase, and the resolving shoot-out: these are the ingredients of the classic Western film. White hats and black hats made clear distinction between the good and the evil in the first half-century of Westerns, but after World War II the characters developed a psychological depth and complexity that ponders whether goodness is even possible. Tom Mix and William S. Hart were silent stars; Gene Autry, Tex Ritter, Roy Rogers, Eddie Dean, and Rex Allen were among the musical Western's "singing cowboys." From Marshal Will Kane (Gary Cooper, 1952) in *High Noon*, through "Black" Bart (Cleavon Little, 1974) in *Blazing Saddles*, to Bill Munny (Clint Eastwood, 1992) in *Unforgiven*, "The Lady" (Sharon Stone, 1995) in *The Quick and the Dead*, and Jack and Ennis (Jake Gyllenhaal and Heath Ledger, 2005) in *Brokeback Mountain*, the cowboy and his (and her) genre have undergone revision, often paralleling significant cultural and political shifts.

Perhaps none were better in the classic Western than director John Ford and his star, John Wayne, who together created over two dozen films, including *Stagecoach* (1939), *Fort Apache* (1948), *She Wore a Yellow Ribbon* (1949), *Rio Grande* (1950), *The Searchers* (1956), and *The Man Who Shot Liberty Valance* (1962).

to Leonard Leff and Jerold Simmons.[10] By the 1930s the Production Code greatly curtailed the creative freedoms of film artists through a list prohibiting or prescribing material. Administratively, scripts and treatments passed close scrutiny in preproduction, and releases required a seal of approval.

The cinematic treatment of moral issues would only grow in complexity as the United States approached and survived World War II, especially as the lines between information and propaganda and between morality and political ideology blurred. In some ways, this might be seen as a loss of innocence for the film industry as the silent era came to a close. As the style of the classical paradigm became more firmly established, stories also followed more rigidly a pattern or "genre" (from the French for *kind* or *type*). Major genres of cinema break down into functions more than type: fictive-narrative, relating fictional stories around travails or glories of characters; nonfiction, documenting an actual subject matter; and experimental, expressing personal artistry and testing the limits of media. Yet *genre* is most often referred to as a group of narrative-based films sharing similar plots, character types, techniques, and conventions that are repeated so as to create familiarity, even to invoke mythic associations and certain national or cultural expectations, for their viewers, while also remaining fresh, not dull or clichéd. From the business side, the formula of the genre ensures an audience and, thus, a certain return on investment. In the silent era, the Western with its cowboy, melodrama and its invocations of nineteenth-century values and sentimentality, the social-problem film and its attention to Progressive-era politics and current affairs, and other genres made their start.

Though sharing the prevailing classical style and studio business model, Griffith's epic melodramas stood in striking contrast to the type of stories and characters in the silent comedies of Mack Sennett, Buster Keaton, and especially Charlie Chaplin. Audiences knew going in they could expect Chaplin's Tramp to appear with bowler hat, baggy and patched pants, too-tight and mismatched jacket, floppy clown shoes, cane, and cropped mustache; they came to expect that his clownish character in films from *A Dog's Life* (1918) and *The Kid* (1921) to *The Gold Rush* (1925) and *City Lights* (1931) would manipulate the space of the frame with prop jokes, minor pranks, sight gags, and balletic movements, while also revealing ingeniously the inner psychology of the down-and-out. Where Griffith plunged blindly into singular goodness, Chaplin (as actor, director, and independent producer) exposed the complexity of goodness and evil in his films' stories and in the viewers' real, classist world. His hero never succeeds in ways that viewers expect from tried-and-true heroes, but rather Chaplin's hero ends up giving his enemy a good "kick in the pants" and getting the last laugh, if not winning riches and the girl. Chaplin's artistic style modeled the invisibility of the medium to offer illusions of reality and magically transport viewers backward and forward in time and across space; he created a seamlessness in his shot selection and editing that put the spotlight on his and other actors' performances, on the exploration of the gag, and on the psychic tremblings behind that joke. This unfairly earned Chaplin the reputation for being "uncinematic," and as sound emerged on the scene, his hesitancy reinforced this judgment. But all of Hollywood was shaken initially by the coming of sound to the pictures.

RISE AND FALL OF THE U.S. STUDIO SYSTEM

Hollywood, 1927 to World War II

From the 1920s through World War II, the studio system engendered Hollywood as filmmaking capital for North America and the entire world. Sound in film, as well as the increase of projection speeds to 24 fps, reinforced the illusion of realism so crucial to the widespread appeal and popularity of the Hollywood fictive-narrative film and solidified the business and aesthetic models of the studio system. By 1927, landmarked by the successful reception of *The Jazz Singer*, the studio system anchored itself with the talkie.

Only a few years after the adoption of sound-film technology, studios gained interest in color. Although there had been color tinting and hand-painted frames since the 1890s in the earliest shorts and additive color processes as early as 1908, processed color was used sparingly for spectacles such as *The Toll of the Sea* (in 1922, the first to use a two-strip Technicolor process), swashbucklers, or musicals, where the garish colors fit. Technicolor was a trademarked monopoly, and the special equipment and consultants accompanying their use on a production carried with them secrecy; as such, Technicolor leveraged power like another small studio department built into the system. In 1932 Technicolor sealed its monopoly for the next three decades with the subtractive three-strip process. Studios moved cautiously into this new aesthetic and technological terrain in the mid-1930s, and at the end of the decade over two dozen projects had been filmed in Technicolor. *Snow White* appeared in 1937 as the first feature-length animation to incorporate synchronized sound and full color technologies, and *Fantasia* (1940), *Gone with the Wind* (1939), and *The Wizard of Oz* (1939) stand out as momentous for the use of the new Technicolor process to achieve unparalleled dramatic results. Not until after World War II, though, did color become pervasive in commercial cinema.

The year of 1927 serves as a threshold into the modern era. Sound technology presented a huge risk to the studios but paid off over the 1930s and 1940s, as the majors used this as leverage during the tumultuous Depression era following the crash of 1929, putting some distance between themselves and the minor and independent production companies. By

1930, 95 percent of all U.S. productions came from the eight biggest studios; these took 75 percent of the U.S. market with much of the remainder divided among other such notable companies as Disney, Monogram, and Republic.[11] There was a paradox that surrounded the studios, though: as part of the system, they shared business strategies, aimed at monopolistic control, utilized similar stables of contract talent, and relied on the classical paradigm for conventionalized storytelling; and yet, each strived for originality, mostly trying to create a niche market with the widest appeal. There were also bragging rights for which certain studio heads, producers, and directors competed. (We see this still today with the importance that certain critical praise and awards carry.)

The five majors each had, according to Ethan Mordden, their unique flavor of Hollywood, a "house style": Metro-Goldwyn-Mayer or M-G-M with gloss and glamour, high fashion under high-key lighting; Paramount's sophistication and light comedies; Warner Bros. with a gangster's underworld and low-lit working-class struggles; 20th Century-Fox's conservative aesthetic, which bought the way for the occasional defiant social commentary; RKO's late-blooming free spirit and commitment to the talkie.[12] Vertical integration was key to these five majors attaining their status, and, as Douglas Gomery's research indicates, studio production in the 1930s and 1940s accounted for only 5 percent of expenses, distribution management another 1 percent, leaving 94 percent investment in theater ownership and assured exhibition.[13] Three "minor" studios, which owned no theaters and were, as a result, dependent on the majors, included Universal with its darker emphasis on horror; Columbia with its low-budget Westerns and serials; and United Artists, founded in 1919 by Chaplin, Pickford, Griffith, and Fairbanks as a distribution outlet for independent producers, such as David O. Selznick, Samuel Goldwyn, among others.

The stability that the biggest players in the studio system attained before World War II translated into dominance in the world-system economy, an equal dominance in cultural production, and an according dissemination of cultural codes and tastes. Evidence for this one-way flow of money and cultural capital can be seen in the number of European directors lured to Hollywood, among them Ernst Lubitsch, F. W. Murnau, and Alfred Hitchcock. A number of directors were amazingly successful by working within the Hollywood system— business and art. William Wellman, William Wyler, Frank Capra, Howard Hawks, John Ford: all figured their own innovative and unique style into the monolith of the commercial film. Hitchcock, perhaps because he brought a biting English wit and working experience from both the British studios and the German expressionist movement with him to the United States, seemed to work alongside the studio system, affording his oeuvre a versatility rarely approached. Hitchcock moved to Hollywood in 1939, coinciding with the outbreak of war in Europe. Many of Hitchcock's films adapt the proven convention of the chase with a bizarre mix of dark humor, irony, macabre, and character vulnerability to offer viewers suspenseful action. Viewers might be upended by the banality of Hitchcock's characters and their situations set against a probing, hypnotizing psychological game. This psychological game in some of the earliest Hollywood work such as *Saboteur* (1942), *Lifeboat* (1944), and *Notorious* (1946) plays into an antifascist agenda, predominant in U.S. cultural production at the start of the 1940s.

Hollywood, World War II to 1967

Citizen Kane (1941) has received more acclaim than any other single film: in popular and critical circles, it is known as "the greatest film of all time." *Kane* represents a clear turning point in cinema history and has become over generations what some call a "textbook" for making and viewing the modern film. Part of this credit owes to its crew roster, several en route to amazingly prolific and influential careers—Robert Wise's editing, Bernard Herrmann's music direction, Herman Mankiewicz's scripting, Edward Stevens's costuming, Vernon Walker's special effects, and, among the actors, Joseph Cotten and Agnes Moorehead. Orson Welles and Gregg Toland, who share the film's final title card, deserve special discussion.

Gregg Toland served as cinematographer on *Kane* as well as on *Wuthering Heights* (1939), *The Little Foxes* (1941), and *The Best Years of Our Lives* (1946) with Wyler and *The Grapes of Wrath* and *The Long Voyage Home* (both 1940) with John Ford, instituting a style of cinematography called deep focus. Although deep-focus photography was available and sometimes used in the silent era with fast orthochromatic stock, the industrial conversion to more efficient panchromatic stock made deep focus technically difficult. Over the previous two decades, the classical paradigm had adopted editing techniques that glued together shallow-focus shots into a standard language, from Griffith's thematic to more associational styles of *montage*. Faster film stock as well as better wide-angle short-focus lenses and lighting available by the late 1930s allowed Toland and a select group of filmmakers to experiment with the depth of field and the *mise-en-scène* or composition of shots rather than rely solely on montage and the combination of thinly focused shots. Since this groundbreaking work, Hollywood aesthetics have tended toward combinations of deep and shallow frames with balanced cutting dependent on the narrative's requirements, all part of what style historian David Bordwell refers to as a "standard version" of cinema history that borrows from art history's appreciation for evolution of complex forms.[14]

Complexity is key for *Citizen Kane* and its director, Orson Welles. In his directorial debut at age twenty-four, Welles earned the reputation as "boy genius." Much has been said and written about the striking parallels between newspaper tycoon William Randolph Hearst and Kane, played brilliantly by Welles himself. Beyond that, *Citizen Kane* manipulates a seemingly simple story of American scandal and muckraking satire. The film's then-experimental narrative, its complicated shifting points of view, its search for the human condition around the enigmatic "Rosebud" and alongside a self-conscious exposition of the "American Dream" and individualism: all were parts of a story reinforced by cinematographic explorations of the frame's depth. Viewers after World War II were growing more conscious of the functions of cinema within popular culture in a mass-media age.

Even before the bombing of Pearl Harbor on December 7, 1941, the industry was keenly aware of the ideological underpinnings of the Hollywood studio film, war, and society. In the early years of World War II, the United States embarked on a policy of nonintervention, one that was debated throughout U.S. society and questioned throughout the world. Movies served a number of wartime purposes, not least significant of which was information exchange and propaganda about U.S. isolationism. Capra's "Why We Fight" series (1942–45), Ford's *December 7th* (1943) and *The Battle of Midway* (1942), Wyler's *The Memphis Belle* (1944), and John Huston's *The Battle of San Pietro* (1945) stand among the best documentaries of the period and the home-front campaign. Hawks with *Air Force* (1943) and Wellman with *Story of G.I. Joe* (1945) exemplify the stalwarts of the Hollywood system who used the classical style and the studio mechanism to promote pro-U.S. values. Offering more than merely escapist entertainment, much of the best early-1940s studio fare drove home the lessons of World War II, and perhaps none was better than *Casablanca* (1942), produced at Warner Bros., directed by Michael Curtiz, and starring Ingrid Bergman and Humphrey Bogart. Bogart's character, Rick, is a New Yorker living in Morocco, avoiding the war. Rick initially embodies U.S. isolationism: "I stick my neck out for nobody," delivered walking off left frame and, thus, already undercutting how "wise" is this "foreign policy." Later, having witnessed the kinds of deeply personal sacrifices others make to fight fascism, Rick decides that his problems "don't amount to a hill of beans" and that he has "a job to do," a message carefully reinforced by a subtly low-angle close-up within a shot-countershot with Ilsa. Most crucially, the film accommodates the conventions and style of the commercial film, while it uses the business mechanisms of the studio to promote the mainstream values and allow identification for viewers to form a lesson across the Americas and the world beyond mere entertainment. The ability of Hollywood to promote mainstream values, especially against a backdrop of war and cultural conflict, became especially problematic as the Cold War began.

One of the greatest cultural effects of World War II came in the form of renewed attention to humanity, to our existence and purpose in being. Though existentialism was not exactly a hallmark of prewar studio products, as European films grew progressively more philosophical, there was room for such soul-searching in U.S. cultural production, especially after the full disclosure of world-war devastation—over 55 million dead, as many as 6 million Jews and 5 million ethnic minorities due to Nazi genocide; much of Europe in rubble and ashes; Truman's decision to use atomic warfare on Japan—and consideration of European cultural production that came in response. Worldwide cultural crises after World War II met a number of technological and industrial crises that placed Hollywood in a state of paralysis and decline from the last half of the 1950s, through the demise of the studio system, and spun it into a series of transitions in the 1960s.

A number of causes might be cited for the demise of the studio system. Robert Sklar points out that movies grew progressively dull and unimaginative, saddled by the "increasingly unconvincingly artifice" of Hollywood style.[15] Another valid reason includes the antitrust decrees building up to the 1948 *Paramount* case, according to which major studies were forced to divest themselves of exhibition holdings. The divorce decrees scissored the vertical integration studios had for decades enjoyed and, along with increased federal tax burdens, undercut business leverage of the system. In 1945 the MPAA expanded to confront international issues related to Hollywood's global distribution and growing competition from other national cinemas and formed the MPEA (Motion Picture Export Association) and the International MPA (Motion Picture Association). Hollywood wished to regain foreign distribution and meet the competition from European arts. Lifestyle changes, too, shaped the market into which the studio film tried to fit. Americans, especially teenagers, enjoyed a significant relationship with their cars in the 1950s; as adults moved their families to the suburbs, driving was a part of their daily routine and their identity. Teens found in driving a kind of freedom and sense of personal space not necessarily afforded in the family's home. Although fewer people went to the theaters in this era and around 3000 hardtoppers closed, another 3000 drive-ins opened, perhaps with customers rolling into the drive-in as much for its flicks as for its "passion pit." But Hollywood's greatest financial competition in this period came not directly from foreign films or lifestyle changes as much as from the domestic growth of television programming.

Using CinemaScope—an anamorphic process designed around a special lens on the camera at recording that compresses the visual material onto 35mm film and another lens on the projector at screening that restores the image to a 2.35:1 aspect ratio—20th Century-Fox in 1953 released *The Robe*, and its commercial success won out. Warnerscope, Panascope, TechniScope, SuperScope, and Panavision rivaled as wide-screen processes, and so popular was the wider image that there were even some nonanamorphic processes (such as VistaVision at Paramount) that simply left unused the top and bottom of 35mm. By the early 1960s the classical-style, studio-backed commercial film had fully emerged in wide-screen, in color, and with sound.

In 1945 the ideologically laden struggle of the Cold War began. The U.S. government and an elite minority recognized the influence that cultural productions, especially cinema, held over mainstream attitudes and in the contentious times after World War II and through the Korean and Vietnam conflicts tried to shape the messages in U.S. movies. The House Committee on Un-American Activities, or HUAC, where in 1947 representatives investigated select filmmakers, aimed to disclose communists and communist sympathizers who promoted subversive and disloyal propaganda through cultural production such as cinema. In spite of the fact that the congressional hearings infringed upon the Constitutional rights of those being questioned, industry representatives acquiesced, testifying and even naming others suspected of being communist. A veritable "witch hunt" followed, especially by the early 1950s centered around Senator Joseph McCarthy's rhetoric of those who are "friendly" or "unfriendly," activities that are "American" or "un-American." Notably, a number of film artists refused to testify on the grounds that the hearings were unconstitutional, earning the badge of courage "Hollywood Ten" but also losing, beyond work in the industry, their rights and freedoms. Studios denied the existence of any "blacklist" or boycott against these filmmakers who had not been proven guilty of any wrongdoing, and yet the industry's response to the HUAC hearings is suggestive of Hollywood's need to craft its films with especially conscious political messages and meet mainstream audience's tastes and sensibilities, which would prove increasingly difficult as cultural upheaval grew into the 1960s.

Cinema of the 1950s had its fair share of escapist entertainment, the sexual enticement of Marilyn Monroe, and the spectacles of *The Greatest Show on Earth* (1952), *Around the World in 80 Days* (1956), and *Ben-Hur* (1959); and yet, looking at Hitchcock's *North by Northwest* (1959) suggests the manner in which ideology, specifically mainstream-tempered anticommunist sentiment, had filtered into U.S. popular culture. Ideological associations were fitted into the conventionalized stories, such as the classist issues in *How Green Was My Valley* (1941) to *On the Waterfront* (1954) or the racist issues treated in *The Defiant Ones* (1958) and *Giant* (1956) to *Guess Who's Coming to Dinner* (1967). Even more obliquely, consider the kinds of enemy forces, fear of the unknown, and paranoia to which Hitchcock's work alludes—in *Rear Window* (1954), *The Man Who Knew Too Much* (1956), or even *Psycho* (1960) and *The Birds* (1963). All place the viewers in a position of identification, even psychological and emotional perturbation, and in desperate need of some resolution.

In the erosion of studio-system control, a number of stars recognized opportunity for independent projects—Burt Lancaster, Kirk Douglas, Randolph Scott, and John Wayne all redirected their star status into attempts at forming "independent" studio companies.

EMERGENCE OF "INDEPENDENT" CINEMAS

"New" Hollywood, 1968–79

Bob Dylan's soulful lines, "the times, they are a-changin'"—as the text of Donn Pennebaker and Richard Leacock's 1966 direct-cinema profile of the artist, as the satirical backdrop to a late-1980s reminiscence of mid-1960s Bronx in *Five Corners*, or as the subtext to Michael Moore's anticorporate tirade in *The Big One* in 1997—reverberate across the decades marked by change. By 1968, North America as well as the rest of the world was undergoing social and cultural upheaval and political turmoil unlike any other time in the modern era, and U.S. cinema was obliged to respond. Activism in the late 1950s and 1960s characterized by passive resistance grew as a result of slow progress and frustration into militancy by the decade's end. The famous "March on Washington" in 1963 reflected populist support for equality for all and the attempts by President John F. Kennedy and Senator Robert F. Kennedy to institutionalize civil rights protections. The Southern Christian Leadership

Council (SCLC) spotlighted the Reverend Martin Luther King, Jr., who came to national prominence advocating a "beloved community." The Civil Rights Act of 1964 made illegal public and work-related discrimination; the Voting Rights Act one year later assured African Americans voting opportunities, especially in places where they had previously been denied their rights; and the 1972 Equal Rights Amendment passed Congress and incited greater discussions to follow over gender-based discrimination and civil rights. The formation of groups such as the United Farm Workers (UFW) in 1962, the National Organization for Women (NOW) in 1966, and the American Indian Movement (AIM) in 1968 indicated the level of indignation that fostered outright anger through more strident, nationalist groups such as the Black Panthers around the leadership of Malcolm X. Starting in 1963 the *Front de libération du Québec* (FLQ) launched terrorist attacks against government facilities to counteract North American Anglocentrism, restore French as the official language, and protect certain indigenous Canadian cultural trends. Riots in many large North American cities in 1966 and 1967, too, revealed in a very tangible way the rifts and fault lines of America's social landscape.

Hollywood (along with a number of strains of cinema throughout North America) was embroiled in the ongoing cultural crises and literal and figurative battles through the 1960s and 1970s. Its methods, its identity, and its purposes were in question as at no other time in its century-long history, especially as the studio structure had been dismantled. One response was for movie productions to imitate the studio company—pouring money into a lavish production with the hope of a return on the investment—but the influence of European and Asian cinemas grew on Hollywood films as the number and influence of independent, lower-budget package-unit productions increased. Many films of this flux period admitted to their own use of conventions, their own study and appreciation of classical style and even reverence to particular directors' styles; a self-awareness of stories and cinema-narrative devices emerged and an unabashed inclusion of ingredients that made cinema popular—sex and violence, in particular, and spectacle, in general. *Bonnie & Clyde* (1967), for example, offered moments that reveled in the cinematic quality of the cinema, even as our two dark-horse heroes are riddled with bullets, its montage layering one part of their fall atop another part of their fall in slow motion. This violence, intensely treated, thinly veils the antiwar and antiestablishment sentiment of a youthful counterculture on the rise. Robert Altman's 1970 *MASH*, too, disguised an anti–Vietnam War message in its seemingly informal and darkly comic treatment of an Army hospital in the Korean War, all while aleatory effects reflected the ambiguity, disorder, and uncertainty of life outside the theaters for the viewers. *All the President's Men* (1976) self-consciously treated Watergate events just two years after President Nixon's actual resignation, alluding to the suspicion of bureaucratic-government and institutional-corporate dominance throughout the U.S. mainstream.

The production code that censored certain subjects outright during the studio-system era gave way in 1968 to a rating system, in which the prescriptions of appropriate or prohibitions against taboo subjects were lifted. Still self-regulating, film producers then as now may cover controversial (sometimes merely and gratuitously salacious) material, carrying a rating—G, PG, PG-13, R, and NC-17 in the United States, for example; G, PG, 14A, 18A, and R in most Canadian provinces—for market consumption and audience expectations. Smaller budgets meant that niche markets could support a production and keep it out of the financial red. Particular productions aimed at specialized markets, giving rise to exploitation genres. The wildfire popularity and box office boon of Russ Meyer's work such as *Faster, Pussycat! Kill! Kill!* (1965) and *Beyond the Valley of the Dolls* (1970) in their X-rated mix of sex and violence and the stag-turned-features such as Gerald Damiano's *Deep Throat* (1972) and *The Devil in Miss Jones* (1973) initiated the "porno chic" era that would elide with disco and late-1970s club culture. Their popularity bespeaks that nature of post–World War II cinema to integrate the latest-and-greatest—from color and wide-screen, to 3-D, smell-o-vision, and risqué subjects—and the fleeting interest of moviegoers. It is crucial, though, to distinguish among aspects of 1960s and 1970s North American cinema that simply joined in the parade of gimmicks-as-spectacles as opposed to the long-standing influences on the business and art of cinema in the United States and abroad.

The Hollywood Renaissance is often contextualized around the work of a group of filmmakers, many of whom were film-school trained and aware of cinema's critical and historical schools of thought, much like their contemporary European counterparts. In their work, self-conscious styles and revisionist genres, sometimes with a cynical edge and sometimes with nostalgia for the halcyon days of bygone Hollywood, help to provide a venue through which provocative social and philosophical issues instigate a dialogue with their viewers. Roman Polanski's *Chinatown* (1974), for example, according to John Cawelti's famous reading, enacts a generic transformation of *film noir* in order to address crucial political and cultural issues of the mid-1970s.[16] Polanski along with Steven Spielberg, George Lucas, Francis Ford Coppola, Peter Bogdanovich, William Friedkin, and others formed a New Hollywood. Bogdanovich with Friedkin and Coppola negotiated with Paramount Pictures (then parented by the Gulf & Western conglomerate, until Viacom's purchase and reallocation with CBS companies in the early 1990s) for a program called the Directors Company, which allowed independent productions maintaining a low budget the use of its studio and out of which came *Paper Moon* (1973), *The Conversation* (1974), and *Daisy Miller* (1974).

Perhaps there were several "1960s," as cinema historian John Belton suggests: One "1960s" for the conservative, middle-class, middle-aged mainstream who frequented lavish musicals, Doris Day and Rock Hudson romantic comedies, Disney family shows, and James Bond spy thrillers, extending the 1950s a few more years. A second "1960s" for a still conservative, middle-class yet youthful mainstream that identified with the "radical chic" of the miniskirts and bikinis in *Beach Blanket Bingo* (1965) and the quashed rebelliousness in the likes of 1967's *The Graduate*'s Ben Braddock (Dustin Hoffman) or 1960's *G.I. Blues*' Tulsa (Elvis Presley). These were carryovers of *Rebel without a Cause*'s Jim Stark (James Dean, 1955) and *The Wild One*'s Johnny (Marlon Brando, 1953) even as they were updated for

"NEW HOLLYWOOD BRATS"

Steven Spielberg: *Jaws* (1975), *Close Encounters of the Third Kind* (1977), *Raiders of the Lost Ark* series (1981, 1984, 1989, scheduled for 2008), *E.T.* (1982), *The Color Purple* (1985), *Jurassic Park* series (1993, 1997), *Schindler's List* (1993), *Amistad* (1997), *Saving Private Ryan* (1998), *Minority Report* (2002), and *Munich* (2005); recipient in 1987 of the Irving Thalberg award, as well as three Oscars and nine more nominations from the Motion Picture Academy.

George Lucas: *American Graffiti* (1973), *Star Wars* series (1977, 1980, 1983, 1999, 2002, 2005); honored with four nominations and recipient in 1992 of the Irving Thalberg award from the Motion Picture Academy; founder of Industrial, Light and Magic at Skywalker Ranch.

Francis Ford Coppola: *The Godfather* series (1972, 1974, 1990), *The Conversation* (1974), *Apocalypse Now* (1979), *The Outsiders* (1983), *Rumble Fish* (1983), *Dracula* (1992); winner of five Oscars and nine more nominations from the Motion Picture Academy; founder of Zoetrope Studios.

Roman Polanski: *Rosemary's Baby* (1968), *Macbeth* (1971), *Chinatown* (1974), *Tess* (1979), *The Pianist* (2002); winner of one Oscar and four more nominations from the Motion Picture Academy.

American Graffiti in 1973 and television's *Happy Days* starting in 1974 with a small-screen hood-hero, Arthur "Fonzie" Fonzarelli (Henry Winkler). These versions of the era are reflected in a general decline in domestic movie attendance and studio releases, greater access to foreign films, and diversification of popular entertainment. And still, there was yet another "1960s" for a restless, even more rebellious sect that was growing more and more dissatisfied with anything associated with the mainstream and was willing to move "underground."[17]

One might do well to consider carefully the facial expression and body language of Benjamin Braddock (played masterfully by a young Dustin Hoffman) at the conclusion of Mike Nichols's *The Graduate* (1967). Ben and Elaine Robinson seem destined to be together, to be in love, as the Hollywood happy-ending and love-story mechanics would have it; and yet the film's penultimate medium two-shot betrays mainstream style and its audience's expectations by revealing the deeper sense of uncertainty and angst of the period. Did Ben benefit from the "tricks" he was to have learned "back East" on his way to being a college graduate? Consider also the countercultural message buried in *Easy Rider*'s easy riders, Peter Fonda's Captain America and Dennis Hopper's Billy, who ends up shot at the hands of defenders of U.S. mainstream conformism. The two heroin dealers, having completed their last transaction, expect to be able to pull up roots and leave 1969's southern California, venture back east, and find happiness in an idyllic American landscape. Their tragic end corresponds perhaps to the failings of the "golden age" or any return to it by a "New Hollywood"; it equally responds to the general cynicism of U.S. culture in the late 1960s and into the 1970s and beyond. In *Kramer vs. Kramer* (1979) and *Mommy Dearest* (1981) to *Mr. Mom* (1983), audiences recognized that the families, mothers, and fathers of the past were as much an illusion of perfection as the construction of a Hollywood montage; moviegoers were left with the ordinary people of *Ordinary People* (1980) and their depression, angst, and imperfect lives in this "New" Hollywood and Canada. Other notable New Hollywood directors retained their East Coast roots, especially Martin Scorsese and Brian De Palma, and in spite of this rich and contentious body of "new" material, alternative traditions that had slipped under the radar of mainstream viewership for decades were increasingly gaining attention in the postwar era within popular and critical circles.

Alternative Currents, Post–World War II and Beyond

The (old and "New") Hollywood tradition has followed in many respects the grand U.S. tradition of giving greater opportunities to individuals who fit the mainstream mold and uphold the conformist vision of right and wrong, truth, and beauty. The first set of questions arising from this discrepancy deals with representation, and critics have been successful in bringing awareness to the inequalities and dangerous influences of such stereotypes and representations as they have long been ingrained in the classical paradigm. Black characters, as filmmaker and critic Donald Bogle reveals, model "Tom" submission or "coon" and "mammy" buffoonery; Hispanic characters, according to art historian Gary Keller, embody the lower class as a "greaser," transgression as a "bandit," and out-of-control passion as a "cantina girl" or "Latin lover."[18] "Women's films" tend to evoke as a genre emotionality and "domesticity," whereas sexual objectification imbue the majority of female characters for the theoretically male-encoded audience, according to film theorist Laura Mulvey.[19] Films after World War II and especially in the 1960s and 1970s began working against traditional values in their subject matter, included previously marginalized voices (as in some rare cases minority filmmakers were green-lighted or scraped together themselves enough money to survive the project) and offered various experiences to their audiences. Consider, for example, John Cassavetes's *Shadows* (1961), a *vérité*-style love story that reverses stereotypes and preconceived cultural notions about race, ethnicity, and gender. While blaxploitation films such as *Cotton Comes to Harlem* (1970), *Superfly* (1972), *Cleopatra Jones* (1973), and *Shaft* (1971) sensationalized violence and invested unrestrained sexuality into their black characters, they provided inroads for African-American talent to the cinema industry, including as directors Ossie Davis and the Parks father and son. A film like *Sweet Sweetback's Baadasss Song* (in 1971, made with earnings from Columbia Pictures–backed *Watermelon Man* from a year earlier) not only employed a black director, Melvin Van Peebles, and showcased his vision but also put in relief the militancy of nationalism of the 1970s in a self-conscious story of racism and stereotyping, echoing Robert Downey's *Putney Swope* (1969) and portending Spike Lee's *Bamboozled* (2000). Since the beginnings of the classical paradigm in *Birth of a Nation* (1915), an alternative tradition such as the all-African-American production of *Birth of a Race* (1916) has resisted that model. When studios caravanned to the West Coast around the early 1910s, several black film companies remained in Chicago, New York, and Philadelphia, including Million Dollar Productions and the Oscar Micheaux Company, which produced Paul Robeson's first feature, *Body and Soul* (1924). As David Cook's research proves, profits for these productions were slighted by segregated theaters in the northern and midwestern United States and white-owned theaters in the South.[20]

Spike Lee's output and access to studio mechanisms are aberrations, to be sure, but there have been since the 1970s a number of African-American film artists to have their work reach a wide audience, including John Singleton, Charles Burnett, Ernest Dickerson, Robert Townsend, Mario Van Peebles, Keenan Ivory Wayans, Julie Dash, and Stan Lathan, with their radically wide range of styles and film types. Though with slower progress, Latino and Latina filmmakers have gained opportunities in the cinema industry, including the important work of Luis Valdez, whose *Zoot Suit* (1981) is regarded as the first Chicano studio feature film and one in which UFW agitprop aesthetics are adapted. Valdez would later stir a great deal of interest around the commercial success of *La Bamba* (1987) and the invocation of the "Hispanic Hollywood" boom alongside Ramon Menendez's *Stand and Deliver* (1988) and Cheech Marin's *Born in East LA* (1987). Even before then, Efraín Gutiérrez, Jesús Salvador Treviño, Sylvia Morales, Alejandro Grattan, Moctesuma Esparza, Lourdes Portillo, and Robert Young made fictive-narrative and nonfiction films with critically engaged and accurately sensitive portrayals of Latino and Latina characters, offering diversity to the mainstream experience of moviegoing; since then, Gregory Nava, Frank Zuniga, Severo Pérez, Paul Rodriguez, Marcus de Leon, and Joseph Vásquez have added to the corps. Edward James Olmos's acting career and his direction of *American Me* (1992) reflect a significant level of commercial success for Latinos, but perhaps Robert Rodriguez and his innovative filmmaking strategies best exemplify the future of cinema. And many women directors have made inroads to mainstream cinema, especially over the last three decades as film artists, including Dede Allen, Penny Marshall, Joan Micklin Silver, Nora Ephron, Elaine May, Jodie Foster, Susan Seidelman, Amy Heckerling, Kathryn Bigelow, Martha Coolidge, Mary Lambert, Penelope Spheeris, Randa Haines; as producers, including Midge Sanford, Sarah Pillsbury, Debra Hill, Gale Anne Hurd; and even as studio executives, including Dawn Steel at Columbia and Sherry Lansing at Columbia, 20th Century-Fox, and Paramount. Lansing's influence extends beyond the cinema industry, as demonstrated by her winning of the Jean Hersholt Humanitarian Award from the Academy in 2007.

More often, the alternative current shifted entirely away from the mainstream text and its classical style, opting instead for experimental narratives or even nonnarrative avant-garde forms. Experimental techniques have frequently been cited as merely fresh injections to the mainstream film—Salvador Dali's dreamscape in Hitchcock's *Spellbound* (1945), Bruce Conner's mediated psychedelia inducing *Easy Rider*'s (1969) LSD-tripping scene, or Stan

"NEW YORKER BRATS"

Martin Scorsese: *Mean Streets* (1973), *Italianamerican* (1974), *Alice Doesn't Live Here Anymore* (1974), *Taxi Driver* (1976), *New York, New York* (1977), *Raging Bull* (1980), *The King of Comedy* (1983), *The Color of Money* (1986), *The Last Temptation of Christ* (1988), *Goodfellas* (1990), *Cape Fear* (1991), *The Age of Innocence* (1993), *Casino* (1995), *Gangs of New York* (2002), *The Aviator* (2004); honored with eight nominations from the Motion Picture Academy and receiving his first Oscar for *The Departed* (2006).

Brian De Palma: *Sisters* (1973), *Carrie* (1976), *The Fury* (1978), *Dressed to Kill* (1980), *Blow Out* (1981), *Scarface* (1983), *Body Double* (1984), *Wise Guys* (1986), *The Untouchables* (1987, scheduled for 2008), *Casualties of War* (1989), *Bonfire of the Vanities* (1990), *Carlito's Way* (1993), *Mission: Impossible* (1996), *Snake Eyes* (1998).

Spike Lee: *She's Gotta Have It* (1986), *School Daze* (1988), *Do the Right Thing* (1989), *Mo' Better Blues* (1990), *Jungle Fever* (1991), *Malcolm X* (1992), *Crooklyn* (1994), *Clockers* (1995), *Get on the Bus* (1996), *4 Little Girls* (1997), *He Got Game* (1998), *Summer of Sam* (1999), *Bamboozled* (2000), *25th Hour* (2002), *Inside Man* (2006); honored with two nominations from the Motion Picture Academy.

Brakhage's scratched and light-burst fingerprints across the opening credits to *Se7en* (1995)—though they represent their own traditions. Often working in 16mm, 8mm, video, or more recently digital media has allowed cinema artists freedom outside of studio business schemes. One tradition, often called New American Cinema, is distinguished by the "visionary film," conceived around the personal-artistic expressions of the film artist and the lyrical quality of the works themselves, according to P. Adams Sitney's important study.[21]

Documentary, too, has historically appeared on the margins of Hollywood and mainstream cinema. Although newsreels were quite popular in the studio-system era, television inherited that service responsibility, and nonfiction film production had to warrant distribution investment outside of itself. Starting in the 1960s, the direct cinema style of the Drew & Associates' films and the cinéma vérité of Michel Brault's "Quiet Revolution" studies exemplified a heightened sense of awareness of the power of media and uses of the latest technologies, especially lightweight cameras and mobile setups that allowed filmmakers to engage their subjects in ever closer proximity. More recently, documentary makers from Barbara Kopple to Ken Burns and Michael Moore have used the nonfiction film as a pulpit from which political and socially active statements have met a popular audience and relative commercial appeal. Ken Burns brings production value to his work that is atypical of most nonfiction, covering somewhat traditional subject matter (jazz music, the U.S. Civil War, Manifest Destiny, and baseball, for example) but with rapid cutting across "animated" still photographs and well-known actors narrating. Moore, with his critical and commercial success in the anticorporate and working-class message of *Roger & Me* (1989) and even more so in the investigation of violence and fear in U.S. politics and culture in *Bowling for Columbine* (2002, winning that year's Academy Award for best documentary feature) and *Fahrenheit 9/11* (2004), exposes provocative topics and has revitalized the documentary as a form of expression and persuasion.

Back East, Post–World War II and Beyond

Perhaps New York City, art capital and metropolitan grounding force in North America, and New Yorkers working in the alternative currents suggested above deserve a special discussion. Among the New Hollywood, Brian De Palma, Martin Scorsese, Woody Allen, Spike

Lee, and others retained a sense of their East Coast spirit that would be lost if transplanted to a California scene. Scorsese's oeuvre exemplifies this lineage as well as that of any filmmaker, from the director's own birth in Queens and NYU graduation to the films *Mean Streets* (1973), *Taxi Driver* (1976), *New York, New York* (1977), *Raging Bull* (1980), *Goodfellas* (1990), *The Age of Innocence* (1993), and *Gangs of New York* (2002). Scorsese's work explores *Italianitza*, masculinity, and violence in U.S. society, especially as it travels New York's city streets, and his work's success has carried Robert De Niro, Harvey Keitel, Joe Pesci, and others along for the ride. In Woody Allen's quirky and neurotic comedies, almost as self-consciously about comic genre and psychoanalysis as they are about their themes and characters, Allen's New York reappears more as a character and icon than as backdrop or scenery: *Annie Hall* (1977), *Interiors* (1978), *Manhattan* (1979), *Hannah and Her Sisters* (1986), *Crimes and Misdemeanors* (1989), *Manhattan Murder Mystery* (1993). A recent film, *Match Point* (2005), manipulates the iconic city, as London substitutes for New York, a transnational departure in locale but not in Allen's offbeat style. John Schlesinger's *Midnight Cowboy* (1969), Brian De Palma's *Sisters* (1973), and Spike Lee's *Do the Right Thing* (1989), among others, in their orientation to New York represent the curious blendings and contests of popular cultural production as alternatives to Hollywood's version of the mainstream. And New York harbored filmmakers even further removed from the mainstream such as those involved in Andy Warhol's "Factory" and Jonas Mekas's Film-Makers' Cooperative (FMC) and Anthology.

Hollywood, 1980–99

Sifting the ashes of the studio system, multinational corporations incrementally acquired collapsed production companies over the 1970s and 1980s. With this business model in tow—marked by a "boom-or-bust" attitude, saturated releases of enormously budgeted films, extravagant special effects, and sophisticated promotion and marketing to include tie-ins such as T-shirts and lunch boxes—the age of the blockbuster began. The early commercial success of these business methods in 1975's *Jaws* fueled the fire for corporate conglomerates supported by diversified investments. *Star Wars* (1977) heralded this age in a number of telling ways: first, its aesthetics and mythologizing of "film brat" George Lucas; second, its blockbuster business model implemented by the coordinated efforts of Lucasfilm and 20th Century-Fox production companies (the latter now divorced from the Zanuck legacy but facing shifting executive management and on the verge of being gobbled up by the growing Murdoch empire); third, its illusionism and realistic fantasy through effects (out of which Lucas's pet project–turned–industry giant, Industrial Light and Magic, would emerge); fourth, its use of innovative sound technology, Dolby noise reduction and four-track optical stereophonics; fifth, its status as highest-grossing film of all time at over $1 billion alongside 1939's *Gone with the Wind* (without inflation adjustment, James Cameron's $200 million *Titanic* in 1997 took first spot, grossing over $600 million in the United States from 129 million admissions, adding another $900 million in worldwide home rentals); sixth, its commercial success launching a string of equally successful sequels, a strategy Hollywood would adopt ad nauseam; and last but not least, its groundbreaking tie-in of action figures, toy lightsabers, posters, et cetera, also ad nauseam.[22]

The period of the 1980s and 1990s also sees the rise of the multiplex, as one or two screens per theater simply could not recover enough profit for the greater operating expenses of the times. Multiplexes generally have as many as sixteen to thirty screens, with multiple showings of a particular blockbuster movie; a single box office and concession to consolidate those operating costs; enormous parking lots to accommodate rush hours; and, more recently, the addition of auxiliary services, such as restaurants and a range of dining options, gourmet coffee, stadium seating with large reclining chairs, even massages, all of which accompanied a return of the patrons to theaters since the 1980s. The auxiliary sales— $5 popcorn, $4.75 Coke, $10 valet parking—provided theaters a profit against increased print costs. Conservative politics merged in the returns of Hollywood dominance and the Republican presidencies through the 1980s and early 1990s. Reagan-era politics demanded a strong national defense (carrying illusory bravado and New Hollywood nomenclature, "Star Wars") that ran aground the national deficit; a repositioning of the United States in the world order, though ignoring pressing social problems domestically (e.g., welfare, unemployment, labor-law reform, universal health care, Social Security); and the appearance of transparently "clean" government, with a shadow regime running armaments to our enemies. Not least significantly, Cold War paranoia through 1989 (when the Soviet state finally crumbled) translated into an enormous industry in nuclear-age weapons development and manufacturing. Reagan's persona (partially crafted by the studio structure during his acting days and refined as he led anticommunist sweeps through the industry) exuded confidence and security for Americans and much of Western culture.

Reagan-era cultural production, then, promised reassurance through a return to the "happy days" in new age optimism, especially around the family, traditional values, and faith, and it promoted the reclamation of individualism, especially around masculine ideals and consumption. *The Right Stuff* (1983) revels in Chuck Yeager's (Sam Shephard) right/"right" stuff of American manhood, as it is built into conventionalized historical treatment of the U.S. space program; John Rambo's (Sylvester Stallone) *First Blood II* (1985) refights the Vietnam War (and the Cold War), this time single-handedly winning by avenging a personal lost love and the various national losses and saving abandoned POWs; *Commando* (1985) reinstitutes retired Colonel John Matrix (Arnold Schwarzenegger) and his sidekick/love interest to save his daughter, leaving behind "just bodies" and a U.S. kick-ass spirit; John McClane (Bruce Willis) and his *Die Hard* (1988) attitude overturns terrorists who have taken his wife and her corporate cohorts hostage in a whirl of explosives and helicopters; *Top Gun*'s (1986) Pete "Maverick" Mitchell (Tom Cruise) overcomes the ghost of his father while temporarily defeating "unknown forces" in Russian MiG jets over the Middle East at "Mach two with his hair on fire." It is worth noting how many of the action heroes answer a craving for thrills and a "need for speed" while reinforcing America's identification with right-wing political agendas (antifascist, anticommunist, pro-capitalist) and restoring the figurations of the American family. *Back to the Future* (1985) continually plays, in sequel and reiteration (part II in 1989, part III in 1990, animated television series in 1991, amusement park ride and science-fair simulator in 1991, video game in 1991, video game–slot machine in 2004), with the idea of looking "back" to secure a better, safer "future." Ironically, the son saves himself and his own family with brains and brawn, paradoxically moving ahead by looking to the past to fix the future. In a similar vein, performers aspired to become "triple threats," with one eye on screen success and another set on other entertainment fields. Eddie Murphy, Steve Martin, Robin Williams, Bill Murray, and, more recently, Jim Carrey and Adam Sandler parlayed comic talents into star-actor status. Tom Hanks, John Travolta, Johnny Depp (from starter television roles), and Will Smith (from his music career) attract a great deal of attention in their movie work. Among the current crop of popular movie actors, many deserve credit for their range of abilities and depth of characterization: Kevin Spacey, Harrison Ford, Morgan Freeman, Julia Roberts, Meryl Streep, Jodie Foster, Geena Davis, Holly Hunter, Susan Sarandon, Bette Midler, Anjelica Huston. Will the ages be kind to Pamela Anderson? To Cameron Diaz, Scarlett Johansson, and Natalie Portman? To

Nicole Kidman, Gwyneth Paltrow, and Hilary Swank? To Colin Farrell, Jude Law, Orlando Bloom, especially in an industry prone to fickle tastes?

Brisk countercurrents complicated the starkly contrasted good and evil and the simplistic lessons of faith and family of Reaganite Hollywood. *A Few Good Men* (1992) transfigures the gung ho fighter pilot of *Top Gun* into an equally cocky but counter-establishment lawyer in Tom Cruise's Kaffee, also struggling against his own past and father's ghost. The film acknowledges the U.S. public's need for men "on that wall" for national security, for our own safety, and for the freedoms we enjoy, while questioning the "code" and means by which those freedoms are secured. Such, in a Hollywood nutshell, is the contest between the individual and the community, between wanting to know the truth and not being able to "handle the truth," suggestive of countervailing forces at the end of the twentieth century. Ron Howard, Lawrence Kasdan, and Robert Redford stand among the most successful filmmakers who have accommodated Hollywood's pressures alongside their own visions. Oliver Stone's body of films try to expose a type of truth typically shielded from the mainstream, across a spectrum of topics from the nagging JFK assassination and Vietnam conflict to corporate culture. David Lynch's film work often exposes hidden and unsavory depths to the surface of middle-class suburban U.S. lifestyles. Quentin Tarantino has tested the limits of mainstream audiences with his nonlinear story lines, graphic violence, and memorably quirky characters. Cinema style can create an alternative world in the film's story, such as the dystopia of David Fincher's work and the fantasy of Tim Burton's. Gus Van Sant and, even more on the fringes, Jim Jarmusch and Todd Haynes, cover topics from which 1980s mainstream cultural production tended to shy. Sofia Coppola, the first American woman to be nominated by the Academy for best direction, has drawn a particular perspective to century's-end angst through her female characters. And the Coen Brothers turn this critical knife edge into blunt comedy with cutting wit and razor-sharp dialogue. Over the course of the 1980s to the present, mainstream viewers and cinema theorists have acknowledged a similar idea, though in very different terms and in different ways: cinema's representation and viewer identification can offer a range of experiences and can be based on a range of preconceptions, across a wide market for a business executive and across diverse communities for scholars, as Robin Wood and others prove.[23]

The television, desktop home computer, and the VCR became home "appliances" over the 1980s and 1990s, and alongside cable programming and the rise of video games, the entertainment industry offered great choice and interactivity to their consumers. These instruments shape not only our lifestyles but also the cinema and entertainment industries, even revealing themselves as crucial, self-reflexive tropes in turn-of-the-century Hollywood products. *The Matrix* (1999) spawned sequels, each trying to outdo the last, with the earliest energizing the art-business matrix with innovative "bullet time" photography. Mr. Anderson (Keanu Reeves), a data-entry clerk by day, is as ordinary as the "Johns," "Chucks," and "Petes" who saved the decades before, but remove the guise, and (*Wizard of Oz* meets high-tech *Superman*) he is also "Neo"—new and "the chosen one."

CANADIAN FILMS

Beginnings

While Edison and Dickson experimented in New Jersey with the first film recordings, a farmer in Canada was producing shorts to capture the beauty of Manitoba's natural landscape, hoping to entice Europeans to visit the Canadian prairies. Jim Freer's "Ten Years in

Manitoba" was shown in England in 1897 on a tour of fairs. Similarly, in 1903 when Porter and Edison were showing their first story films, Englishman Joseph Rosenthal shared his Canadian-produced adaptation of *Hiawatha*, a fifteen-minute silent short, which led to longer and more complex narratives. Just a year before Griffith would release his epic, *Birth of a Nation*, another Longfellow-inspired narrative, *Evangeline* (1914), was produced by William Cavanaugh and Edward Sullivan. A long-standing trend in North American cinema saw Canadian talent, from Mary Pickford and Mack Sennett to Norman Jewison and David Cronenberg, emigrate from Canada to work in Hollywood. Nell Shipman, after stints in vaudeville and at several early Hollywood studios, attained brief commercial and critical success back in Canada with *Back to God's Country* (1919).

As Hollywood increasingly steered toward fictive narratives produced by corporate studios, however, Canada devoted energy to the one-reel "scenics" that advertised the pristine natural beauty of the northern landscapes. Canadian film production historically has favored the realistic aspects of cinema's visual discourse and the documentary mode, especially as they were particularly well suited to disseminating information that sustained government policy and English-Canadian agendas. The British-owned Canadian company, Associated Screen News (ASN), for example, specialized in producing short documentaries aimed at English-speaking audiences in Canada and other countries, while handling imports from the United States. Even feature-length productions, such as *Madeleine de Verchères* (1922) and *The Viking* (1931), revealed aesthetic subordination to the United States and political and ideological dependence on England. There are some parallels between the maturing cinema industries north and south of the U.S.-Canadian border. Perhaps one of the most significant of these parallels with Hollywood is the extent to which the emerging style of Canadian cinema reinforced the nation's cultural identity—especially considering Anglocentric imperialism and conflicts due to its past as first French and later British colony. Having been confederated in 1867 by British rule, the Dominion of Canada expanded westward over the next three decades in a sweep that mirrored the U.S. "Manifest Destiny," taking native populations and indigenous cultures with it. Like in the studio Western, a trend in Canadian movies glorified English colonialism as it pit heroic Mounties and hardworking lumberjacks against dark French or savage Indian villains. The issues of race/ethnicity, bilingualism, and religion split English-speaking Protestant Canadians from Catholic French-speakers and First Nation/Native Canadians, divisions which would grow more discernible in the mass-media age, alongside the issue of indigenous rights and similar separatist movements.

Perhaps more crucially, though, differences set Canada and its cultural production apart from the Hollywood tradition. Most notably, Canadian cinema was state-sponsored and state-regulated in 1918 through the auspice of the Canadian Government Motion Picture Bureau and its better-known successor, the National Film Board (NFB), starting in 1939. After the Imperial Conference in 1926, where several western European countries set in motion the Cinematographic Films Act (CFA), a quota system to guard against the influx of Hollywood products and promote domestic fare, the provinces of Ontario, Alberta, and Quebec would implement only loose restrictions on U.S. business. By the early 1930s, Canada served Hollywood studios as a launching ground for "quota quickies," using a loophole to target British and other European markets and circumvent the CFA. Film historian Peter Morris points to the collusion of the Canadian government with Hollywood studios and to the insistence on making documentaries and leaving fictional narrative feature production to the United States and Europe as a turning point in the history of North American cinema.[24] Given its relative size, population, and wealth in the world system at the turn of the twentieth century, Canada advanced the establishment and innovation of cinema in marked ways, especially through documentary, but its own state enforcements as well as the rising dominance of Hollywood stunted the economic and aesthetic growth of Canadian cinema indelibly.

World War II to 1967

Even before the National Film Board of Canada (NFB) was established in 1939, the Canadian government steered its cinema industry away from the commercially viable and artistically versatile field of narrative features and toward animated shorts and documentary, especially those that served the public good through social service or political propaganda. These included the animation work of Evelyn Lambert, the first female animator at the NFB, and several productions by Judith Crawley with her husband, including the English/French parenting pieces *He Acts His Age* (1949), *The Terrible Twos and Trusting Threes* (1951), and *The Frustrating Fours and the Fascinating Fives* (1953). Canada would not be in the "entertainment" business. Under the directorate by British rule of John Grierson, an English documentary maker, theorist, and proponent, the NFB and the Massey Commission developed a program of production that over the next three decades would aim to help Canadians understand their own culture and share that culture with the rest of the world. The search for a unified national identity, especially given Canada's legacy of colonialism, and the grounding forces of place, language, and heritage define Canadian cinema and exemplify the "countervailing forces" that make up North American cinema.

Grierson retained a talented pool of documentary makers, including Stuart Legg, Stanley Hawes, Raymond Spottiswoode, John Fernhout, Irving Jacoby, and notably Joris Ivens, known as "international man of causes," who had tried to work in Hollywood's wartime studio machine but sought refuge in Canada. Ivens's *Action Stations* and *Corvette Port Arthur* (both 1943) diverge from typical NFB documentaries of the day, as they mix experimental aspects into their tribute to the Royal Canadian Navy. Other NFB documentaries earned a great deal of attention both domestically and internationally, such as the direct-cinema offshoots *Lonely Boy* (1961) and *Warrendale* (1967). In *City of Gold* (1957), filmmakers Wolf Koenig and Colin Low reinvent the documentary as their film inaugurates the animation of still photographs, now an accepted cinematic convention, earning the NFB an Academy Award nomination. Even more than the "Why We Fight" series, the "Canada Carries On" (1940–45) and "World in Action" (1942–45) series reflected North America's Allied propaganda and a crucial link back to western Europe. Other significant "public information" films included *Universities at War* (1944) and the Academy Award–winning *Churchill's Island* (1941). Stylistically, following a pattern in Grierson's earlier British productions, voice-over narration "preaches and teaches" in both English and French and across a spectrum of regional attitudes and cultural values. As integral to the World War II "March of Time" newsreel series was the voice-of-god narration by Westbrook Van Voorhis, so too was the famously soothing Lorne Greene voice-over to mid-century Canadian nonfiction shorts in their universal appeal.

Norman McLaren's "V for Victory" (1941) and "Five for Four" (1942) war-bond promotionals (as part of the NFB's mobilization efforts) implement experimental paint-on-film animation he would later make famous in "Fiddle-de-dee" (1947), "Blinkity Blank" (1955), "Around Is Around" (1951), and the even more self-reflexive *Animated Motion* series in the late 1970s. McLaren received an Oscar for his *Neighbors* (1952) and nominations for *Pas de Deux* (1968) and *Ballet Adagio* (1971). After the war, Grierson returned to England and the NFB structure laxed slightly, still emphasizing documentary and animated shorts but also allowing a few significant fictive-narrative features to reach screens, and this aesthetic shift would follow closely the state's reinvestment in the cinema industry in the 1970s. The questions of a unified national cultural identity amid glaring regional differences and divisions continued to nag at Canada's cultural production approaching the twenty-first century.

1968 and Beyond

If in *The Graduate* Ben Braddock with his disquietude, vulnerability, and exposed uncertainty represents one of North America's "1960s," then perhaps his Canadian "little brother," Peter (Peter Kustler), from *Nobody Waved Goodbye* (1964) represents yet another. Originally commissioned by the NFB as an after-school docudrama on juvenile delinquency, the feature utilizes then-cutting-edge documentary techniques, black-and-white 16 mm, and improvisation to give a crisp realism that Canadian cinema seldom possessed. Peter, rather than "graduate" as does the Californian, skips his final exams and fails, must pick up a menial job, degrades to stealing, and, discernibly, is left alone and shaken at the end of the film. Its director, Don Owen, would in some respects usher in a new age of English-Canadian cinema, using state investment to produce and internationally distribute feature films—*Ladies and Gentlemen, Mr. Leonard Cohen* (1965), *The Ernie Game* (1967), and *Cowboy and Indian* (1972). Established in 1967 and in full effect by the late 1970s, the Canadian Film Development Corporation (CFDC), later known as Telefilm Canada, added commercial robustness to Canada's cinema industry through business models more closely aligned to late-twentieth-century corporate culture. Although the bulk of the movies subsidized by the CFDC were largely derivative of commercial cinema, including the "maple-syrup porn" of *Valérie* (1968) and *Love in a Four Letter World* (1970), grants also made possible the breakthrough *Goin' Down the Road* (1970), energizing a new generation of Canadian filmmakers. Although headquartered in Ottawa, Canadian production units appear scattered throughout Canada, and so just as cultural identity has been defined in regional terms, so has cultural production. One strategy of the CFDC was to centralize the cinema industry and more effectively coordinate state departments, making the NFB a type of studio executive producer, in Hollywood terms, and putting budget in the makers' hands. Perhaps most importantly, state sponsorship and regulation seemed to limit, even neglect, the cinema industry over its first 75 years, and so through tax incentives, the federal government lured private-sector investment to balance financial obligations in Canada's cultural production.

Having slept with an elephant for so long, according to Prime Minister Pierre Trudeau's famous analogy, the Canadian film industry was attempting to awaken and compete with its hulking neighbor, recognizing the historical commercial limitations of nonfiction mode and short program. In the latest waves of feature films, there remains a style that harkens back to Canada's documentary and animation traditions as well as its search for identity—unified or diverse across regions, races/ethnicities, classes, genders, and sexual orientations—with a close connection to place and language. Anne Wheeler's *Great Grandmother* (1975) and *A War Story* (1981) align her family history with the regional culture of Alberta. Paul Almond's *Act of the Heart* (1970) and *Journey* (1972) personify the environment of Quebec alongside strong female characters, just as do Claude Jutra's *Kamouraska* (1973) and *Mon Oncle Antoine* (1971), the latter around a boy's coming of age. More recently, Manon Briand has updated these relationships in *2 Secondes* (1998) and *La Turbulence des Fluides* [Chaos and Desire; 2002] in French-Canadian, especially as Quebec's state-culture interaction initiated federal agenda. Denys Arcand, too, stirred interest in *cinéma Canadien* with the critical and commercial success of *Le Déclin de l'Empire Américain* [The Decline of the American Empire] (1986), its sequel, *Les Invasions Barbares* [The Barbarian Invasions] (2003), and *Jésus de Montréal* [Jesus of Montreal] (1989). Narrative innovation and a resulting international commercial viability characterize this era of Canadian cinema, from Bruce Elder's *The Book of All Dead* 40-hour program (1975–95) to Atom Egoyan's *Exotica* (1994) and Ted Kotcheroff's Oscar-nominated *The Apprenticeship of Duddy Kravitz* (1974) and *Joshua Then and Now* (1985) and from Guy Maddin's *Twilight of the Ice Nymphs* (1997) to Denis Villeneuve's *Un 32 Août sur Terre* [August 32nd on Earth] (1998). An "Ontario New Wave" led by "outlaws" Bruce McDonald, Don McKellar, Peter Mettler, Ron Mann, and Patricia Rozema, among others, arose in the early 1980s but slipped away almost a decade later.

Quebec has witnessed its own wave of filmmaking, beginning with the transitional work of Jean-Claude Lauzon, *Un Zoo la Nuit* [Night Zoo] (1987) and *Léolo* (1992). This body of cinema can be characterized as secular, francophone, inclusive, and especially working-class oriented, and it critiques provincialism and drives social satire deep into the ages-old examination of Canadian national identity. Quebec cinema in this latest period strikes a careful balance between local concerns and global issues, particularly around the international economics of NAFTA (North American Free Trade Agreement), and between progress and tradition, especially in its self-conscious approach to film story, genre, and character. Charles Binamé's *Seraphin* (2002) remakes a 1950s hit, while his latest, *Maurice Richard* (2005), explicitly treats the story of Quebec's most famous hockey player, "The Rocket," entering the Anglo-dominant National Hockey League. André Turpin, Lynne Stopkewich, and Catherine Martin turn small budgets into the freedom to experiment with unconventional narratives and eccentric characters. Robert Lepage has performed in several significant contemporary films—*Jésus de Montréal* [Jesus of Montréal] (1989) and *Stardom* (2000) under Arcand's direction; *L'audition* (2005) under Luc Picard—and has written and directed *Possible Worlds* (2000) and *The Far Side of the Moon* (2003). Before this work, Lepage wrote and directed *Le Confessional* [The Confessional] (1995) in which Alfred Hitchcock appears as a character; references look back to Hitchcock's 1953 *I Confess*, indelibly drawing Quebec and contemporary Canadian cinema into world popular culture and cinema.

In the transnational mix, Canadian filmmakers have begun another generational exodus to Hollywood. Likewise, Hollywood and other national cinemas have, since the start of the "tax shelter boom" in the late 1970s to today, brought productions to Canada: Claude Lelouch's *Us Two* (1979), Louis Malle's *Atlantic City* (1980), and Ettore Scola's *A Special Day* (1978). In particular, Vancouver has grown rapidly over the last two decades as a home and site of film production. Important international coproductions include *Margaret's Museum* (1996) with the UK and *The Red Violin* (1998) with the United States. This latest period of Canadian cinema reflects its entrance to the "entertainment" industry, showcasing U.S. style starting with the likes of *Murder by Decree* (1979) and *Meatballs* (1979) for mass appeal and converting Canadian cinema into a "Hollywood North." Still, critical issues surface in some well-received films: Native culture, for example, has taken center stage in some well-respected work, revealing the latest round of Canada's "countervailing forces," from *The Grey Fox* (1983) and *Cold Journey* (1975) to *The Fast Runner* (2002). *Mambo Italiano* (2003), grossing just under $8 million at the domestic box office, is one of the most commercially successful Canadian films in history in its lighthearted exploration of sexual identity, immigration, and other current American affairs. *C.R.A.Z.Y.* (2005), Canada's 2006 selection for the Academy Award's foreign film entry, too, addresses gay themes within the male bonding of a comic family drama, while *Familia* (2005) explores sisterhood and individuality within family culture.

Most recently, the Canadian feature film production has taken a backseat to the national television industry, as Canada Telefilm 2005 investment reports indicate; the latest special projects at Telefilm, in fact, reveal media diversification and attention to international coproduction.[25] Alliance Atlantis, for example, is a leading distributor and producer of films in Canada and in limited partnerships worldwide, yet, since the late 1990s, this corporate giant has placed over half of its business in broadcasting thirteen specialty channels—including national outlets for BBC, Discovery, IFC, and National Geographic—and producing TV shows.[26] Several of the most critically and commercially successful filmmakers to emerge from the last few decades have chosen a path toward television as well. And in the world of animation and computer graphics, Nelvana, which gained attention in 1985 with the *Care Bears* movie and the mid-1990s with a *Star Wars* television animation series, joined the Toronto media group Corus Entertainment; and Softimage of Montreal, which gained attention with its *Jurassic Park* graphics through the 1990s, was purchased by Microsoft, exemplifying strengths in Canada's entertainment industry. To what extent these might pay off in the long run is yet unclear, but given Canada's tradition in experimental cinema, animation, and short programs, its industry might be poised for the new-media revolution and technological convergences at the dawn of the twenty-first century.

Y2K AND BEYOND

Nearing the end of the twentieth century, many North Americans, like many others throughout the world, acceded to a general apprehension over the *fin-de-siècle* transition and humanity's ever increasing reliance on technology. Theories of massive shutdowns and widespread panic due to digital dates rolling back to the 1900s and resulting toilet paper and bottled water shortages seemed like Hal from *2001* (1968) taking over, as if we were all destined to become the "copper tops" in "the great matrix." And yet, the third millennium rang in without any greater event than the typical *Dick Clark's New Year's Rockin' Eve* of yesteryear. Or did it?

Titanic (1997) has grossed a total of $1.8 billion worldwide; all three parts of the *Lord of the Rings* trilogy (2001, 2002, and 2003) remain in the all-time top ten, combining for over $3 billion worldwide.[27] The "bigger-is-better" philosophy of Hollywood over the last few decades clearly amounts to big business for a few. Reports reveal that North American cinema made $9.5 billion at the box office in 2004,[28] with an estimated additional $24.5 billion in home sales and rental.[29] Warner Bros. was the only studio to boast four $100 million productions, and Sony Pictures led all studios in box office tallies with over $1.3 billion in sales.[30] That these numbers have continued to grow over the last five years indicates the vibrancy of North American cinema domestically and globally and suggests the prominence and influence North American cultural production retains today. As Internet-based and other on-demand technologies and handheld devices allow even greater flexibility, the power of cinema in these new mediated forms seems limitless. And although there has not been a remarkable surge of interest in what has been traditionally associated with the film avant-garde, the interest in media-savvy and socially and politically aware documentaries such as *Control Room* (2004), *Outfoxed* (2004), *The Fog of War* (2003), *The Corporation* (2003), and *Super Size Me* (2004), following on Michael Moore's success perhaps, shows a breadth of interest and commercial appeal atypical of the U.S. mainstream tradition.

Capturing the Friedmans (2003), capturing an Academy Award nomination, and *Control Room* (2004) were both products of 2929 Entertainment. Worth noting, *Enron: The Smartest Guys in the Room* (2005), which was also produced by HDNet Films and distributed by Magnolia (both under the care of 2929 Entertainment with Internet pioneers Mark Cuban and Todd Wagoner at the helm), became the first movie simultaneously released in theaters and to subscribers on high-definition television, and then only one day later in pay-per-view, on-demand, and DVD formats. Alongside these innovative business models are innovative aesthetics, where *Pi* (1998) and *Requiem for a Dream* (2000) directed by Darren Aronofsky, *Leaving Las Vegas* (1995) and *Timecode* (2000) by Mike Figgis, *Being John Malkovich* (1999) and *Adaptation* (2002) by Spike Jonze, *Memento* (2000) and *Insomnia* (2002) by Christopher Nolan, and *Eternal Sunshine of the Spotless Mind* (2004) and *The Science of Sleep* (2006) by Michel Gondry, among others, represent a body of work appealing to a relatively wide audience through their experimental narratives and nontraditional characters. Moreover, recent landmarks as Jamie Foxx receiving two nominations and one win in 2005 and Halle Berry one win (the first African-American best actress) in 2002 at the Oscars suggest a wider perspective by the mainstream and the members of the Motion Picture Academy.

Perhaps the greatest change in North American cinema in the last few decades involves its changing identity, its relationship to digital technology, and what media theorist Lev Manovich calls the "computerization" of cinema and the resulting "new language" and "alternative aesthetics of continuity."[31] Not all theorists advance such an optimistic view, as this changing role of new-media technology in cinema might represent an "end" to cinema's medium specificity.[32] With improvements to high-definition digital video, filmmakers turning to digital production include Robert Rodriguez with *Spy Kids 2* (2002) and *Once Upon a Time in Mexico* (2003), Gary Burns with *Waydowntown* (2000), and George Lucas with the later *Star Wars* episodes, starting with *Attack of the Clones* (2002). *Revenge of the Sith* (2005), the last of the six-part project, included a distribution contract for a block of theaters to install digital projection. Of the 544 releases in 2005, around 90 were digitally shot; moreover, the number of theaters with digital projection more than doubled in 2005 to 849.[33] Comparable to what cinema history witnessed with the coming of sound, color, and wide-screen in the modern film text, there will need to be a commitment and financial investment toward this conversion of production and distribution. And yet consumers already indicate their acceptance of new-media Hollywood at the box office. Computer techniques have been adopted successfully into traditional cinema works, such as the digital painting in *Forrest Gump* (1994) and digital composite and virtual graphics in *Titanic* (1997); Internet promotions with parallel story lines, such as the exceptional case of the *Blair Witch Project* (1999); comic book and video game aesthetics in cinematic texts, and vice versa, such as the *Tomb Raider* series (2001, 2003) and *eXistenZ* (1999), in which the media feed off one another. Computerization and digital graphics have factored into a range of mainstream movies from *Monsters, Inc.* (2001) and the *Lord of the Rings* (2001, 2002, 2003) and *Harry Potter* (2001, 2002, 2004, 2005, 2007) series to *The Matrix: Reloaded* (2003), in which today's viewers have a distinct identification through this updated cinematic illusion, a blending of realism and fantasy, in a new-media Hollywood.

RESOURCE GUIDE

PRINT SOURCES

Barnouw, Erik. *Documentary: A History of the Non-Fiction Film*, 2nd edition. New York: Oxford University Press, 1993.

Belton, John. *American Cinema/American Culture*, 2nd edition. Boston, MA: McGraw, 2005.

Bordwell, David, Janet Staiger, and Kristin Thompson. *The Classical Hollywood Cinema: Film Style and Mode of Production to 1960*. New York: Columbia University Press, 1985.

Braudy, Leo, and Marshall Cohen, eds. *Film Theory and Criticism*, 6th edition. New York: Oxford University Press, 2004.

Cook, David A. *A History of Narrative Film*, 4th edition. New York: Norton, 2004.

Cripps, Thomas. *Hollywood's High Noon; Moviemaking and Society before Television*. Baltimore, MD: Johns Hopkins University Press, 1997.

Ellis, Jack C. *The Documentary Idea*. Englewood Cliffs, NJ: Prentice, 1989.

Grant, Barry Keith, ed. *Film Genre Reader II*. Austin: University of Texas Press, 1995.

Holtzclaw, Robert P., and Robert A. Armour. "Film." Pp. 649–687 in M. Thomas Inge and Dennis Hall (eds.), *Greenwood Guide to American Popular Culture*, Vol. 2. Westport, CT: Greenwood, 2002.

Mast, Gerald, and Bruce F. Kawin. *A Short History of the Movies*, 9th edition. New York: Pearson, 2006.

Melnyk, George. *One Hundred Years of Canadian Cinema*. Toronto: University of Toronto Press, 2004.

Morris, Peter. *Embattled Shadows: A History of Canadian Cinema, 1895–1939*. Montreal: McGill-Queen's University Press, 1978.

Nadel, Alan. "Film." Pp. 457–467 in Mary Kupiec Cayton and Peter W. Williams (eds.), *Encyclopedia of American Culture and Intellectual History*, Vol. 3. New York: Scribner's, 2001.

Nowell-Smith, Geoffrey, ed. *The Oxford History of World Cinema*. Oxford: Oxford University Press, 1996.

Sitney, P. Adams. *Visionary Film: The American Avant-Garde, 1943–1978*, 2nd edition. New York: Oxford University Press, 1979.

Sklar, Robert. *Movie-Made America: A Cultural History of American Movies*, revised edition. New York: Vintage, [1975] 1994.

Tyler, Parker. *Underground Film: A Critical History*. New York: Da Capo, [1969] 1995.

WEBSITES

Baseline Hollywood. Hollywood Media Corporation. http://www.baseline.hollywood.com. A data-on-demand information tool on the entertainment industry. Currently contains over one and one half million records on film and television.

Box Office. *Boxoffice* magazine. http://www.boxoffice.com. Website sponsored by print magazine *Boxoffice*, a leading source on the movie business for over seventy-five years. Includes archive of past and current issues, news on current movie listings and returns, sales in the home market, and related industry links.

Drew's Script Archive. http://www.script-o-rama.com. Independent Website that has accrued thousands of film and television scripts since 1995. Includes continuity scripts, shooting scripts, and final transcripts. Additional links as well.

Greatest Films. Tim Dirks, editor. http://www.filmsite.org. Interpretive and background historical material on U.S. cinema. Categorizes information into articles and lists according to decade, year, film style, genre, and other elements.

Internet Movie Database. Amazon.com. http://www.imdb.com. Searchable collection of information on almost one-half million film and television titles and over 2 million names. Collected by international team of experts from on-screen credits and other sources and checked for consistency by site's editors.

EVENTS

Academy Awards (Oscars). Los Angeles, CA. Annually, one evening in March. http://www.oscars.com.

Berlin International Film Festival. Berlin, Ger. Annually, two weeks in February. http://www.berlinale.de/en/HomePage.html.

Canadian Academy Awards (Genies). Toronto, ON. Annually, one evening in March. http://www.genieawards.ca.

Cannes International Film Festival. Cannes, Fr. Annually, two weeks in May. http://www.berlinale.de/en/HomePage.html.

Film Independent Awards (Spirits). Los Angeles, CA. Annually, one evening in March. http://www.filmindependent.org.

Montreal World Film Festival. Montreal, QC. Annually, late August through early September. http://www.ffm-montreal.org.

New York Film Festival. New York, NY. Two weeks, annually in September/October. http://www.filmlinc.com.

San Francisco International Film Festival. San Francisco, CA. Two weeks, annually in April/May. http://fest06.sffs.org.

Sundance Film Festival. Park City, UT. Ten days, annually in January. http://www.sundancechannel.com/festival.

SXSW (South by Southwest) Film Festival. Austin, TX. One week, annually in March. http://2006.sxsw.com.

Telluride Film Festival. Telluride, CO. One week, annually in September. http://www.telluridefilmfestival.org.

Toronto International Film Festival. Toronto, ON. Ten days, annually in September. http://www.e.bell.ca/filmfest/2005/home.asp.

UNIVERSITY CINEMA STUDIES

New York University. http://cinema.tisch.nyu.edu/page/home.
Queen's University. http://www.film.queensu.ca.
University of California, Los Angeles. http://www.filmtv.ucla.edu/dof.cfm.
University of Montreal. http://cri.histart.umontreal.ca/grafics.
University of Southern California. http://cinema.usc.edu.
University of Toronto, http://www.utoronto.ca/cinema.

ORGANIZATIONS

Academy of Canadian Cinema and Television. http://www.academy.ca.
American Film Institute (AFI). http://www.AFI.com.
American Indian Film Institute. http://www.aifisf.com.
Anthology Film Archive. http://www.anthologyfilmarchives.org.
Atom Films home-movie archive. http://www.atomfilms.com.
Association of Independent Video and Filmmakers (AIVF). http://www.aivf.org.
Electronic Arts Intermix (EAI). http://www.eai.org.
Facets retailer. http://www.facets.org. Distributor of hard-to-find videos, including cult films, documentaries, foreign and art films.
Film Connection. http://www.thefilmconnection.org.
iFilm home-movie archive. http://www.ifilm.com.
Internet Archive. http://www.archive.org. A nonprofit organization providing archives of more than 44,000 mainly public domain movies, along with other media.
Library of Congress, American Memory. http://lcweb2.loc.gov/papr/mpixhome.html.
Library of Congress, National Film Preservation. http://www.loc.gov/film.
Motion Picture Academy of Arts and Sciences. http://www.oscars.com.
Motion Picture Association of American (MPAA). http://mpaa.org.
Motion Picture Association-Canada. http://mpaa.org/inter_canada.asp.
Museum of Modern Art. http://www.moma.org.
National Film Board of Canada. http://www.nfb.ca.
Pacific Film Archive, University of California, Berkeley. http://www.bampfa.berkeley.edu/pfa_library.
Society of Cinema and Media Studies (SCMS). http://www.cmstudies.org.
University Film and Video Association (UFVA). http://www.ufva.org.
Video Data Bank, Art Institute of Chicago. http://www.vdb.org.

NOTES

1. Statistics are from the Motion Picture Association of America (MPAA), as reported in the "U.S. Entertainment Industry: 2005 MPA Market Statistics," MPA Worldwide Market Research (2006): 4, 8, 11.
2. Theater statistics are from the National Association of Theater Owners (NATO), http://www.natoonline.org/statisticsscreens.htm, accessed May 2006. See also Nielsen EDI statistics as

reported in the MPA's "U.S. Entertainment Industry: 2005 MPA Market Statistics," MPA World-wide Market Research (2006): 22.

3. Statistics are from the Motion Picture Association of America (MPAA), as reported in the "U.S. Theatrical Market: 2005 Statistics," MPA Worldwide Market Research (2006): 6.

4. See Cripps 1997 (in Resource Guide), p. 17.

5. See Richard W. Latella, "The Motion Picture and Theatre Industry Overview," *Retail Real Estate* (December 2004): 6.

6. Statistics are culled among a number of sources including the MPAA reports; Nielsen EDI reports; the Internet Movie Database, http://www.imdb.com, accessed May 2006; and the Box Office Report, http://www.boxofficereport.com, accessed May 2006.

7. See Frank Thomson, *Lost Films* (New York: Citadel, 1996). Also consult the period volumes of the "History of American Cinema" series out of the University of California Press. Readers may also consult one noteworthy study of the production logs at Biograph: Paul C. Spehr, "Filmmaking at the American Mutoscope and Biograph Company, 1900–1906," *Quarterly Journal of the Library of Congress* 37 (1980): 413–421.

8. See Mast and Kawin 2006 (in Reference Guide), p. 125.

9. See Harry M. Geduld's Introduction, *Focus on D.W. Griffith*, edited by Harry M. Geduld (Englewood Cliffs, NJ: Prentice, 1971), p. 6.

10. See Leonard J. Leff and Jerold L. Simmons, *The Dame in the Kimona: Hollywood, Censorship, and the Production Code from the 1920s to the 1960s* (New York: Grove-Weidenfeld, 1990), p. xiii.

11. See Cook 2004 (in Resource Guide), p. 239; Mast and Kawin 2006 (in Resource Guide), p. 268.

12. See Ethan Mordden, *The Hollywood Studios* (New York: Knopf, 1988).

13. See Douglas Gomery, *The Hollywood Studio System* (New York: St. Martin's, 1986).

14. See David Bordwell, *On the History of Film Style* (Cambridge, MA: Harvard University Press, 1997), p. 9.

15. See Sklar 1994 (in Resource Guide), p. 280.

16. See John G. Cawelti, "*Chinatown* and Generic Transformation in Recent American Films," in *Film Genre Reader II*, edited by Barry Keith Grant (Austin: University of Texas Press, 1995), pp. 227–245.

17. See Belton 2005 (in Resource Guide), pp. 344–345.

18. See Donald Bogle, *Toms, Coons, Mulattoes, Mammies, and Bucs: An Interpretive History of Blacks in American Films* (New York: Continuum, [1973] 1989), pp. 4–9; and Gary D. Keller, *Hispanics and United States Film: An Overview and Handbook* (Tempe, AZ: Bilingual Review, 1994), pp. 40–67.

19. See Laura Mulvey, "Visual Pleasure and Narrative Cinema," in *Film Theory and Criticism*, 6th ed., edited by Leo Braudy and Marshall Cohen (New York: Oxford University Press, 2004), pp. 837–848. For additional discussion, consult E. Ann Kaplan, *Women and Film: Both Sides of the Camera* (New York: Methuen, 1983); and, Annette Kuhn, *Women's Pictures: Feminism and Cinema* (London: Routledge, 1986).

20. See Cook 2004 (in Resource Guide), p. 252.

21. See Sitney 1979 (in Resource Guide). Readers may also consult Tyler 1995 (in Resource Guide); and, Scott MacDonald, *Avant-Garde Film: Motion Studies* (New York: Cambridge University Press), 1993.

22. Statistics are from Nielsen EDI, as reported by http://www.the-numbers.com/movies/records, accessed May 2006.

23. See Robin Wood, *Hollywood from Vietnam to Reagan* (New York: Columbia University Press, 1986), pp. 137–139; readers may also consult important scholarship that updates Mulvey's feminist conceptions of spectatorship, including Manthia Diawara, "Black Spectatorship: Problems of Identification and Resistance," in *Film Theory and Criticism*, 6th ed., edited by Leo Braudy and Marshall Cohen (New York: Oxford University Press, 2004), pp. 892–900.

24. See Morris 1978 (in Resource Guide), p. 181.

25. See the "2005 Investment Reports" and "Special Projects," available from Telefilm Canada, http://www.telefilm.gc.ca/accueil.asp, accessed May 2006.

26. See Melnyk 2004 (in Resource Guide), pp. 252–254.

27. Statistics are from Nielsen EDI, as reported by http://www.the-numbers.com/movies/records, accessed May 2006.

28. Statistics are from the Motion Picture Association of American (MPAA), as reported in the "U.S. Entertainment Industry: 2005 MPA Market Statistics," MPA Worldwide Market Research (2006): 4.

29. Statistics are from Mike Snider, "DVD Continues Spinning Success," *USA Today* (2005, January 6).

30. Statistics are from Nielsen EDI, as reported by http://www.boxofficeguru.com/studio_2004.htm, accessed May 2006.

31. See Lev Manovich, *The Language of New Media* (Cambridge, MA: MIT Press, 2001), pp. 143–145; readers may also consult Manovich's fuller discussion and extension of the "computerization" effect, pp. 287–333.

32. See especially Anne Friedberg, "The End of Cinema: Multimedia and Technological Change," in *Film Theory and Criticism*, 6th ed., edited by Leo Braudy and Marshall Cohen (New York: Oxford University Press, 2004), 914–926; readers may also consult John Belton, "Digital Cinema: A False Revolution," in *Film Theory and Criticism*, 6th ed., edited by Leo Braudy and Marshall Cohen (New York: Oxford University Press, 2004), pp. 901–913.

33. Statistics according to *Screen Digest* research, as reported in the "U.S. Entertainment Industry: 2005 MPA Market Statistics," MPA Worldwide Market Research (2006): 24; and in the "Digital Cinema" report, May 2006, http://www.screendigest.com/reports/06digcin, accessed May 2006.

FOOD AND FOODWAYS

BEVERLY TAYLOR AND EDMUND REISS

From the beginning, European settlers in the New World, hungry for the familiar, copied the diets of their homelands, mainly Great Britain. Suspicious of the food possibilities in the new land, they accepted corn from Native Americans only when they were starving and pumpkins only because of their resemblance to familiar squash. They imported plants and seeds from Europe, including apples, which, fortunately, flourished. Other indigenous vegetables and fruits such as the potato and tomato became part of the North American diet only after they had become accepted in Europe. The dependence on British culinary tradition continued for at least another hundred years, not only throughout most of Canada but also throughout the United States, even after the country achieved political independence from Britain.

The North American diet was dominated by meat, especially beef, although poultry, mutton, and pork were also consumed in large amounts. Roasting, of large fatty joints, was the preferred method of cooking, though frying, in lard and butter, became increasingly popular, and in Canada meat pies became a staple. Stewing chopped meat with vegetables and spices was not common, except in New England and Canada, which favored meat and vegetables boiled all together in an iron pot. Although cod and clams were popular along the Northeast coast, lobsters and oysters were so abundant that they were scorned as a poor man's food. The other main element in the North American diet, the filler, was bread, made from a variety of grains. Vegetables, if eaten at all, were boiled and then mashed to paste, becoming in effect sauces accompanying the meat—like applesauce with pork. Even potatoes were overboiled, presumably to rid them of their inherent poisons. Although onions, peas, beans, and turnips appeared occasionally on the table, root vegetables were grown primarily for fodder, and apples—the preferred fruit—were similarly overcooked and served mainly in pies.

Hardly a barren continent when Europeans arrived, North America was full of wild berries. Contemporary commentators were amazed at the quantity of raspberries, strawberries, and huckleberries growing everywhere; and later writers such as Henry David Thoreau marveled at the foolishness and impracticality of the new settlers, not only for turning their backs on nature's bounty in favor of imported foodstuffs from Europe, but also for clearing

137

the land of these berries so that they could "devote themselves to the culture of tobacco, slavery, and a thousand other curses for that purpose."

The early American diet was both monotonously unvaried and largely tasteless. Herbs were grown only for medicinal purposes, and spices other than salt were most often viewed with suspicion and used sparingly. Newer, more exotic spices, brought from Asia and increasingly available in the nineteenth century, were thought to cause cravings for alcohol and sex. The daring might use "curry powder," but a pinch was more than enough. On the other hand, the demand for sweet and sour condiments—various vegetables preserved in sugar, salt, and vinegar—increased to such an extent that American food was unrivaled in its reliance on sweetness. Spices used in desserts—cinnamon, cloves, ginger, and mace, along with beet or cane sugar—were exceptions to the general abstinence from seasonings. Both Americans and Canadians shared the British love of sweets, which appeared in an amazing variety of cakes, pies, and puddings—so much so that by the mid-eighteenth century, North America and Britain led the world in consumption of sugar. In Quebec maple syrup was added to everything from meat glazes—hams were frequently boiled in maple sugar—to desserts. But although the sweetness of the desserts might counter the blandness and saltiness of the rest of the meal, it did not relieve its heaviness. The emphasis on meat and starch, combined with the lack of fresh fruits and vegetables, resulted in widespread constipation (called in the United States the national curse) by the first half of the nineteenth century.

THE LAND OF PLENTY: NORTH AMERICA

Although by the late eighteenth century Americans were the best-fed people on earth, with an abundance of food unmatched anywhere else, overeating was endemic. Foreign visitors regularly commented on the amount of food Americans consumed. With the advent of the "American Plan," including meals in the price of a hotel room, the food offerings were at times overwhelming. The breakfast tables of American hotels—which groaned under steak, lamb chops, liver and bacon, kidneys, chicken, and fish—looked to foreign travelers like dinner tables, and the items available on dinner menus commonly numbered in the hundreds. As might be expected, such an abundance of food led both to enormous waste and to a widespread unconcern with the quality of preparation. The dishes were too frequently bland and overcooked, with sauces that were little more than liquid grease. For most Americans, the dinner table was not a place for socializing, and eating was not an experience to savor but a time to "gobble, gulp, and go."

Although the particular foods consumed by Americans varied somewhat by region, as well as by economic class, meat remained through the nineteenth century the main food, followed by sweets. New milling processes resulting in cheaper white flour allowed Americans to consume breads and rolls as never before. In the Northeast salted meats, potatoes, cabbage, and beans were commonplace; in the South "hog 'n hominy," that is, bacon or salt pork and corn meal; and in the Midwest and much of Canada, beef and, after the 1870s, corn. Coffee, sweetened with molasses, was the preferred nonalcoholic drink, replacing the tea of the British homeland. The rural poor generally ate no better than the urban poor, although the Mason jar, invented at mid-century, making it possible to preserve fruits and vegetables in something like their natural form, gave an advantage to farm families. With the expansion of dairy farming in the Northeast and Midwest by the 1880s, fresh milk, butter, and cheese increasingly became staples in the diet of these regions, resulting in Canada in the creation of the famous Oka cheese.

Given these gastronomic tendencies, fine dining was exceptional in eighteenth- and nineteenth-century North America. Although cooks in Quebec and Acadia preserved much of their Norman French culinary heritage, their fare was more peasant than aristocratic. Although Thomas Jefferson was known for his love of French food and wines, he was hardly typical. And although New Orleans, a refuge for exiled French Canadians, was an early bastion of French cooking in the United States, it was hardly a typical American city. In the prospering New World, however, French restaurants tended to go hand in hand with new wealth. New York City had its Delmonico's, which opened in 1832, and, after 1849, the gold rush brought French chefs to San Francisco. By the 1870s, the number of newly rich miners was such that fine French restaurants had even sprung up in frontier boom towns such as Virginia City, Nevada; Tombstone, Arizona; and Georgetown, Colorado. Striking it rich apparently meant indulging in *haute cuisine.*

By the 1880s, the number of very wealthy Americans had grown significantly, and with the new wealth came a concern for sophistication and elegance. Visiting Europe, particularly Paris, they saw how the *beau monde* lived and especially how they dined. As *nouveaux riches* families sought to consolidate their social positions, they gave elaborate dinners of unprecedented luxury, events that became the basis for determining social position. Guests, often ten to twenty, would arrive punctually in full evening dress. After taking their seats at the table, they perused a handwritten menu listing the courses of the elaborate meal to come. The dinner commonly began with raw oysters and champagne, followed by a choice of white or brown soup accompanied by sherry. Then a course of fish with Chablis preceded an entrée such as green peas or sweet corn. After this came a slice or two of roast beef, accompanied by champagne or claret. Then Roman punch (*sorbet*) would be offered to prepare the palate for the courses to follow—first, game, such as canvasback duck, accompanied by Madeira and port, then salad and cheeses, followed by an array of puddings, pastries, and ices. These desserts would be followed by fresh fruit, such as grapes, pears, and peaches, accompanied by sherry or claret, and finally, the meal in the dining room concluded with nuts, raisins, sugarplums, and dried ginger. The ladies would then leave the room, though the gentlemen might remain at the table for another quarter hour with their wine, liqueurs, cognac, and cigars before joining the ladies in the drawing room for demitasse, bonbons, and other dainties, as well as more brandy. The meal would likely last two hours.

Although women typically ate less than men, the appetites of both sexes were, by our standards, voracious. Along with their formal dinners wealthy women commonly hosted sumptuous lunches and teas. These multicourse lunches often featured elaborate oyster and lobster dishes, as well as others of grouse and turkey, and the late-afternoon teas commonly included items such as *pâté de foie gras*, mushrooms on toast, partridge, and fried chicken. The concern for sophistication and elegance apparently could not restrain the native inclination toward excess. To visiting Europeans the remarkable luxuries of the upper-class American table called up images of the grossly lavish banquets of decadent ancient Rome.

Despite the habits of the *nouveaux riches,* fancy French ways never became part of the mainstream in nineteenth-century America. When President Martin Van Buren hired a French chef for the White House, his aristocratic tastes were used against him, perhaps contributing to his election loss in 1840 to William Henry Harrison, whose preferred food was said to be raw beef and salt. By the 1880s, following the opening of new cattle lands in the West, beef became both cheaper and more plentiful and, in the form of porterhouse steaks as well as roasts, became the favorite food of even more Americans, replacing pork, which fell in popularity below chicken and lamb. For many middle-class Americans, their heavy, greasy diet of beef and potatoes, bread, and pies, along with their fondness for alcohol, frequently led to indigestion and various stomach disorders, all commonly referred to as "dyspepsia," which gradually replaced constipation as the national affliction.

ADVANCES IN FOOD

Technological Innovations in American Food, Late Nineteenth to Early Twentieth Century

By the end of the nineteenth century the westward expansion of the railroads made food available across the continent as never before. The Canadian Pacific Railway offered in its dining cars and hotels a range and quality of dining previously unimagined. Moreover, with the advent of refrigerated railroad cars, beef, newly slaughtered and dressed in Chicago, could be shipped fresh to the East and South. New vegetables and exotic fruits, grown in Florida and California, could reach markets in the Midwest and Northeast. The availability of oranges, lemons, pineapples, and bananas led to new fruit-flavored drinks made with soda water. New strains of foods developed by scientists, such as iceberg lettuce, made available to everyone foods so perishable that they had previously been enjoyed only by the wealthy.

Other technological advances of the late nineteenth century changed the nature of the middle-class American kitchen. Although after 1827 the icebox gradually replaced the cold cellar, little else changed in North American kitchens until the 1880s. Then iron stoves, replacing open hearths, made it possible to regulate heat and to cook several dishes simultaneously, and an amazing number of new metal utensils—including various corers, needles, churns, strainers, and copper molds—encouraged more variety in meals and made their preparation less time-consuming.

Also by the 1880s, the consolidation of food processors led to giant conglomerates that were able to control and influence the marketplace. For instance, the advertising campaign for Domino sugar made Americans think that refined white granulated sugar was superior not only to brown sugar but to homemade sorghum and molasses as well. All of America was convinced that white sugar not only was more sanitary than the other sweeteners but also conferred higher social status. Earlier in the century, the response to the newly affordable white flour was much the same. Status, as well as lightness, was increasingly important, as the later packaged white bread would demonstrate once again. Likewise, Quaker Oats' success with its individual packages of cereal gave consumers the status of not having to scoop it from the merchant's bin. And Nabisco's soda cracker, Uneeda, wrapped in colorful, sanitary-looking packages, seemed superior to the crackers picked from the cracker barrel—which soon became obsolete.

The power of the food processors to determine food preference was just beginning to be felt in late-nineteenth-century America, but no success for the industry was greater than that of the cereal manufacturers, who persuaded consumers to change the entire nature of their breakfast. The American breakfast had featured bacon or ham, eggs, potatoes, beans, porridge, and breads—much like the traditional English breakfast. Even the desire to follow French ways did not extend to replacing this breakfast with the traditional Gallic bread and butter. But the success of Kellogg's with its Corn Flakes and Post with its Grape-Nuts and Toasties meant that Americans rejected meat in favor of grain, in effect reversing the usual trend in economic development, where prosperity brought a change in people's diets from grain to meat. Taking advantage of the discovery of bacteria in the 1880s and the resulting fear of germs, these cereal makers stressed how healthy and how sanitary their products were. Their marketing success showed as never before just what innovative advertising, promotion, and packaging could accomplish.

Similarly, Heinz achieved great success in replacing food traditionally made at home with mass-produced items. Though Americans had always preserved and pickled their fruits and vegetables, storing them in airtight crocks or, later, in glass jars, by 1880 a new method using steam pressure made it possible to mass-produce this glass-jarred food. Through innovative advertising and promotion on a scale unprecedented, including the first use of electric signs, Heinz persuaded housewives that its pickles and condiments were not only as tasty as their homemade ones but also safer and more convenient. Heinz expanded the budding canned-food industry so much that the company was soon able to feature "57 Varieties," introducing bottled ketchup in 1908.

By 1900 the invention of crimped cans, replacing soldered ones, boosted the food industry, as did the development by Campbell of condensed soup. Before this, soup was not significant in the American diet, for it took an inordinate amount of time to make at home and was heavy and bulky when canned. The discovery of condensing it (1898) so that it could be transported in small cans changed American diets. Similarly, foods that housewives traditionally "put up" were now available in cans, as were combinations of foods, such as pork and beans and corned beef hash, as well as pressed meats (Armour, Swift), so that increasingly one could prepare a meal simply by opening cans, making the can opener indispensable in early-twentieth-century American kitchens.

Whereas the early years of the twentieth century brought a host of new foods to Americans, most—or at least most that still exist—were candies or sweets of some sort, such as cotton candy (1900), the Hershey Bar (1900), Animal Crackers (1902), peanut butter (1904), jelly beans (1905), Tootsie Rolls (1905), and the hot fudge sundae (1906). The sweet tooth was still significant in determining what new foods would succeed. In the same period two of America's favorite foods entered the national consciousness—the hot dog and the hamburger. The first hot dog, then called a frankfurter, may have been sold on a bun at a New York Giants baseball game in 1901, though according to some authorities it first appeared at the St. Louis Universal Exposition in 1904. (The term *hot dog* seems to have originated from a cartoon drawing of dachshunds in 1906.) The St. Louis fair may also have been the setting for the advent of the hamburger, as well as iced tea. But if the two meat items represent versions of German sausages—the one from Frankfurt, the other from Hamburg—it is likely that they existed in German-American communities for some time before entering the mainstream.

Food and Health

The new emphasis on convenience in food went hand in hand with the concern for sanitation. But whereas Americans historically had tended to view all food as more or less equal fuel for the body—that is, what one ate did not matter—the discovery of proteins, carbohydrates, fats, and minerals made people realize that it was not enough simply to eat what they liked. To be healthy, they had to eat what was good for them. Whereas apples had long been regarded as a healthy food, most people never thought to distinguish between meat and bread except in economic terms. People who could afford it could enjoy meat; those with only a little money could always eat bread.

This new concern with health led to an amazing amount of food faddism. Every kind of diet imaginable had its supporters—not only vegetarians, but more specifically, fruitarians, nutarians, and lacto-ovarians; also those who ate only uncooked food or only beef, others who shunned fermented foods, and still others who never ate breakfast. One widespread fad required the thorough mastication of food—each bite had to be chewed until it had no taste and only then could be swallowed. The advocates of all these diets viewed eating as a way to attaining good health. Losing weight was not an issue—unlike later, in the twentieth century, when dieting became synonymous with trying to be thin.

More important than these faddists, the new home economists and their ideas about nutrition most reshaped American attitudes toward food. Not only did these new experts stress smaller, well-balanced meals, they created what in effect became the standard American dinner: meat or fish accompanied by potatoes or rice, a vegetable, and rolls or bread, followed by dessert and coffee, which was viewed as a healthy stimulant and encouraged as an antidote to alcohol. Because vitamins had not yet been discovered, most fruits and vegetables, regarded as composed of mostly carbohydrates and water, were neglected.

The traditional diets of immigrants after the 1880s proved especially challenging to the home economists' view of proper eating. Whereas the older immigrants to North America had come largely from northern Europe, that is, from Anglo-Saxon and other Germanic and Celtic countries, the newer immigrants were mainly from southern and eastern Europe. Although the traditional meat and potato diet of the older immigrants was not far from the ideal extolled by the home economists, the diet of the newer immigrants consisted of mixtures of foods and spices that appalled them. The strange smells of their stews, goulashes, and thick soups suggested that these foods were both unpalatable and difficult to digest. Similarly, their strong seasonings were thought to cause a craving for alcohol. And whereas the sauces used in American food—bland white and brown sauces composed essentially of flour, butter, and milk—were innocuous, the immigrants' tomato sauces full of garlic and onions were considered dangerous, designed to hide inferior products.

The point of the home economists was not to show the immigrants how their cuisine could be adapted to fit that of America, but to persuade them that for their own well-being they had to renounce their traditional foods. Similarly, the food stalls, open-air markets, and delicatessens where these immigrants bought their food were condemned by the home economists as unsanitary, and the unusual staples they bought—for instance, olive oil, pasta, and tomatoes—were thought to lack any food value. Unsurprisingly, programs established to teach immigrant housewives the American way of cooking and housekeeping enjoyed only limited success.

Although immigrants imported unpasteurized cheeses from the old country, it took a long time for cheese to be accepted across the United States. By the 1880s, milk had become affordable and available to American households in glass bottles, and after 1910, with the introduction of pasteurization, it was regarded as a safe food. But for many infants who needed a substitute for mother's milk, cow's milk would not do. Scientists had created dried and powdered formulas since the 1860s, and companies such as Nestlé and then Gerber competed to fill this niche. After the advent of condensed milk in the 1870s, other companies, such as Borden's, joined the competition. But these new milk substitutes did little to change the habits of immigrants, who traditionally breast-fed their babies. Even with appalling infant-mortality rates, the urban poor continued in their old ways. Ironically, artificial formulas and canned infant foods, though designed to help the poor, appealed mostly to the upper and middle classes, who, influenced by advertising, came to view these products as superior to mother's milk. It was the discovery of vitamins in 1912 and the recognition of their importance in diet that dramatically changed the way Americans regarded milk. Because milk was found to be an ideal source of vitamin A, discovered to be essential for growth and good eyesight, milk became more than ever a staple of the American diet, especially for children and young adults.

During the years of World War I, as people consumed less beef, butter, wheat, and sugar, they realized that this patriotic gesture of eating less made them feel better. At the same time, increased recognition of the existence of harmful bacteria led to the perception that various ailments could be cured by avoiding certain foods. Though in one sense the idea that illness was caused by certain foods was the opposite of the recognition that good health resulted from consuming foods rich in certain vitamins, the two attitudes reflected a new consciousness of nutrition. Food not only provided fuel for the body; it was the way to avoid disease. Because vitamins were not yet available in pill form, they had to be ingested through food. And not only milk was necessary; so also were grains, vegetables, and fruits, all of which took on new importance in the American diet.

The food industry in the 1920s responded by extolling the healthfulness of their products, launching promotional campaigns on a scale never seen before, with each sector proclaiming its product the most nutritious and most necessary for healthy bodies. Sealtest and Borden's insisted that milk was the essential food and that everyone should drink a quart a day; Post argued that its Grape-Nuts cereal contained all the iron, calcium, and phosphorus children needed in their diets; Fleischmann's maintained that its yeast was the richest known source of vitamins; Morton's, that its new "health salt" gave children vim and vigor; Welch's, that its Grape Juice contained essential vitamins and minerals; Sunkist that its lemons and oranges prevented acidosis; and General Mills, that its white bread was an important energy food. Food producers introduced new foods, such as asparagus, and promoted others, such as raisins, as unique sources of energy. The consumption of many of these foods, especially those which, like milk, won public recognition as "protective foods," reached new highs in the 1920s.

Food and the Modern Housewife, Early Twentieth Century

Despite the new interest in food properties, the national diet promulgated by nutritionists and home economists did not change. It was still resolutely Anglo-Saxon, not at all reflecting the melting pot the United States had become, and after the Immigration Act of 1924 effectively put an end to immigration from southern and eastern Europe, there was a greater insistence than ever on the need to Americanize foreign tastes and ways of cooking. Food companies assisted in this task with their fictional spokespersons, such as General Mills' Betty Crocker, who came to represent the face and voice of the American way of eating. Likewise, the many women's magazines that had increased in number after the war, such as *Good Housekeeping* with its Seal of Approval, provided additional testimonials supporting the American diet.

Incongruously, despite all the interest in nutrition, cooking actually declined in middle-class households. In part this may have been due to the replacement of the live-in servant with the cleaning woman, whose duties did not readily include preparing food. It may also have been due to the increased number of housewives working outside the home. And even though new stoves and refrigerators, along with various other appliances such as electric toasters and skillets, made life easier in the kitchen, informal meals increasingly replaced more elaborate dining, giving the food preparer less than ever to do. In 1908 the invention of tea bags meant not only that consumers could brew tea in a cup simply by pouring hot water over the bag, but also that they had no leaves to clean up. And in 1912 the mass production of mayonnaise in glass jars by Hellmann relieved housewives of the chore of whipping their own. Rather than spend time in the kitchen or at the table, families increasingly pursued leisure activities outside the home. The modern woman of the 1920s played tennis and other sports and, as families moved farther from urban centers, drove herself to shop and see movies. Enjoying this newfound mobility, she lacked the time and the inclination to cook. And the new appliances and increasingly widespread availability of canned, processed, and prepared foods made it possible for her, and other members of the family, to eat and run as never before.

While stating their preference for fresh food and "home cooking," Americans were more willing than ever to sacrifice both taste and nutrition if they could reduce the time and effort spent on food preparation. New construction of houses and apartments with smaller kitchens and dining rooms reflected this attitude, as did the new pastime of eating out in restaurants. For the first time, middle-class housewives could make dining out a holiday from cooking. New chains of family restaurants, such as Child's, featured healthy food at modest prices in an elegant setting. Though the décor of other eateries might evoke the interior of a sailing ship, a Roman grotto, a Mediterranean port, or a Polynesian village, the food generally remained standard American. Ambience, not unfamiliar tastes, provided the sense of adventure.

In the United States the advent of Prohibition in 1920 caused the closing not only of saloons but also of many good restaurants that depended on the sale of alcohol for their profit—establishments with mostly male clientele. But with more women entering the workforce and with people beginning to live farther from their work, different kinds of eating establishments, catering to respectable women and to the lunch trade, came into existence. Lunch counters, which had originated in railway stations in the 1880s, provided one option. Soda fountains, which simply used the existing bar stools of former saloons, offered soups and sandwiches, along with desserts and drinks—with Prohibition, ice cream sodas, soft drinks, and coffee became more popular than ever. Later, the soda fountain became a fixture in drugstores and variety stores, such as Woolworth's, contributing significantly to their profits. Like these, the new luncheonettes, where the consumer could watch the food preparation, thrived, especially after the invention of the automatic toaster in 1927 made the club sandwich possible. For fuller meals, tearooms enjoyed a vogue, but these could not compete with the new cafeterias, such as the Waldorf chain, that not only offered quick, cheap meals but also allowed the consumer to see the food before making a choice. "Automats," notably Horn and Hardart, also emphasized convenience. They displayed food items in separate containers, and all one had to do was to insert a coin. These were all safe, clean establishments where women could go to eat, even by themselves.

As women's fashions changed, reflecting the new emphasis on physical and social activity, clothes revealed more flesh than ever before. Slimness thus became the ideal for both men and women, and dieting became a middle-class obsession. Recipes in newspapers, magazines, and a host of new cookbooks stressed not the tastiness or even the convenience of a dish but the number of calories it contained. Meals thus became simpler than ever: breakfast commonly included only juice, dried cereal with milk, and coffee; lunch was little more than a sandwich; and dinner consisted of meat, potato, and vegetable, followed perhaps by a simple dessert. Salads featuring molds of Jell-O, which had been invented in the late nineteenth century, set on beds of lettuce and other vegetables or fruits, became main-course dishes—the Caesar salad, voted the most important dish to originate in America, was invented in 1924 and the Cobb salad in 1926. The earlier antipathy of home economists to mixing foods yielded to the popularity of one-dish meals, which ironically were often Americanized versions of immigrant dishes previously held in contempt. And the tomato became accepted more than ever with the advent of canned tomato juice in 1925.

The postwar era saw a great increase in the number of women's magazines, and their recipes and cooking advice aimed at housewives across the country meant that women in the South were often preparing the same dishes as women in New England and the West. The result was a greater homogenization of the North American diet, even in immigrant households. As the children of immigrants learned about nutrition in school and copied the habits of their American friends, they tended to reject the traditional foods of their parents in favor of the packaged and prepared foods preferred by their peers. Old-country food might be fine for festivals and even for Sunday dinners, but for daily consumption it was important to eat American, and this meant following the diet of the middle class. Banquets—no matter whether served in Connecticut, Kentucky, Kansas, or California—typically began with fruit or shrimp cocktail, followed by chicken or roast beef with potatoes and peas and accompanied by a salad, and concluded with pie or ice cream and coffee. This menu came to represent both the standard American dinner and the epitome of fine dining, at home and in restaurants, for the next several decades.

PROLIFERATING FOOD CHOICES IN THE 1930S THROUGH 1950S

Even the Great Depression of the 1930s did not significantly alter the way most Americans ate. As the unemployed lined up at soup kitchens, eating options proliferated for the more fortunate. Whereas full-service restaurants suffered, diners and lunch counters expanded, along with new chains that catered to the working class. White Tower, open day and night at trolley and subway stops and opposite factories, offered identical clean, well-lighted places where the working man could enjoy a hamburger, doughnut, and coffee. Also in urban areas, coffee shops, such as those in the Chock Full O' Nuts chain, which peppered Manhattan from the 1930s to the 1960s, served quick fixes to office workers. Likewise, neighborhood restaurants, notably Italian and known for their checkerboard tablecloths and candles in Chianti bottles, offered filling food at inexpensive prices. Outside the cities, taking advantage of the increasing attraction of the automobile and the Sunday drive to the country, roadside restaurants appeared. The most successful was Howard Johnson's, whose orange roofs provided a beacon to hungry drivers looking for somewhere safe to stop. Noted for its fried clams and rich ice cream, Howard Johnson's was so successful that after its first roadside restaurant opened in 1935, by the end of the decade it had grown to number 125 on East Coast highways.

Americans were driving more often and farther than ever and discovering that different regions of the country featured distinct and sometimes very good food. Though some regional specialties were already known and available nationwide—Maine lobster, Long Island duckling, Chesapeake Bay crabs, Virginia hams, Gulf shrimp, Columbia River salmon—the country offered less well-known delicacies for those willing to go beyond what was available on the highways—for instance, broiled scrod in Boston, scrapple in Philadelphia, chicken potpie in Pennsylvania Dutch country, Brunswick stew in the Southeast, burgoo in Kentucky, catfish in Mississippi, carne adobada in New Mexico, cioppino in San Francisco. Travelers discovered that even familiar dishes—say, barbecue or fried chicken—took on entirely different incarnations in different parts of the country. North Carolina barbecue differed from that of Memphis, Kansas City, or Texas. To know eating in the United States, one had to experience not only a Texas barbecue but also a New England clambake, a Maryland crab boil, and a Carolina oyster roast. For breakfast one had to experience country ham with red-eye gravy, grits, and biscuits, as well as lox and bagels. Moreover, eating in New Orleans or Santa Fe was like eating outside the United States. Similarly in Canada, a huge country larger than the United States, without even taking into consideration the Inuit dishes of the far north, one could cross the continent enjoying Canadian bacon and maple syrup, as well as traditional seafood dishes in the Maritime Provinces, Québécois specialties such as *tourtière* and yellow split pea soup, smoked sausages and *schnitz* pies in Ontario, whitefish and *pierogi* in the Prairie Provinces, and Pacific Rim delicacies in Vancouver.

For all the hardships of the poor and the unemployed during the Depression, lower prices and improved transportation made some foods more available than ever—the consumption of beef, for instance, actually increased during the decade. Shelves in the larger chain grocery stores, such as the Great Atlantic and Pacific Tea Stores (A&P), were full, offering the same choices to consumers, regardless of where in the country they lived. The distinction between summer and winter foods, which had marked North American food habits from the beginning, virtually disappeared, as all sorts of produce, including fruits from the tropics, became available year-round. What could not be had fresh was available in cans, including spinach, which, despite its bad taste, was successfully marketed as a miracle food by the *Popeye* comic strip. Condensed cream of mushroom soup, brought out by Campbell in 1934, became the basis for a remarkable number of dishes nationwide, in rich as well as poor households. Similarly, differences between urban and rural diets became less noticeable than ever as even farm households, not wanting to seem old-fashioned, increasingly succumbed to the high status, as well as the convenience, of packaged and processed foods. New items, including Sanka Decaffeinated Coffee (1921), Kool-Aid (1927), Velveeta Process Cheese Spread (1928), Ritz Crackers (1934), and Nestlé's Nescafé (1939), the first instant coffee, had wide appeal. And few households could resist the convenience represented by the new wax paper (1927) and sliced bread (1928).

One major change of the Depression years was the return of the American housewife to the kitchen. The repeal of Prohibition in 1933 had little effect on family life. In part because of budgetary pressures and in part because of the media's celebration of home cooking, the middle-class wife came to view her role as preparer of food as central to her marriage and her work in the kitchen as both satisfying and important. Even the advent of World War II did not significantly alter this perception. Despite the large increase of women in the labor force, three out of four married women remained at home, doing their part for the war effort in the kitchen. Significantly, when U.S. servicemen were asked to describe their dream girl, they cited her cooking skills first, even ahead of intelligence.

Despite an increase in food prices and the rationing of certain foods, World War II did not significantly alter the food habits of Americans. In fact, the U.S. Army was the best fed army in the history of warfare. Although it was thought that firsthand encounters with the foods of unfamiliar cultures in Europe and Asia might well change the eating preferences of Americans, in actuality servicemen had little opportunity to taste the culinary delights of foreign countries. Little food was available to the civilian population, and few restaurants remained open in the ravaged countries where Americans were fighting. Servicemen ate almost all their meals in mess halls, which, eschewing regional or foreign dishes, served plain, familiar American food. In fact, on any given day anywhere in the world, these mess halls were serving the same menu to all, regardless of ethnic origin or rank: meat, potatoes, one or two vegetables, salad, dessert, and milk. This diet became for servicemen synonymous with home and with what dinner should be. Even after the war when restaurants had reopened and foreign food was available, few of the occupying troops were tempted to eat away from their bases.

The millions of pounds of food items shipped overseas—second in bulk only to petroleum products—were offset by various efforts at home. Food rationing helped, though it was onerous to many Americans who did not believe that food shortages really existed, and who found it painful to do without their usual amounts of meat, butter, and sugar. At the same time, the program encouraging the planting of Victory Gardens in backyards and empty lots was remarkably successful both in compensating for the canned produce being sent overseas and in giving urban and suburban Americans the opportunity to eat more fresh vegetables than ever. The parallel campaign to revive home preserving was equally successful. Though once a major activity in the American kitchen, messy and time-consuming "canning" had been made virtually obsolete by the ready availability of jarred and bottled pickles and condiments. To encourage people to do their own preserving once again, the government diverted steel from the war effort to manufacture pressure cookers, which could facilitate the process. Despite innumerable difficulties and accidents, the program became a great success, resulting in more food being preserved at home than ever before.

Although the war did not change the U.S. diet in significant ways, it gave some dishes a new popularity, especially those functioning as meat substitutes. Macaroni and cheese, a Depression favorite, was accepted by people of all classes, especially after it was adapted and marketed by Kraft Foods in 1937. Similarly, beans, along with other legumes, were discovered to be a ready source of protein. Some people tried previously neglected vegetables such as eggplant, squash, and broccoli and found them more than palatable. Others turned to horsemeat, as well as innards and other parts of animals previously eaten only by the poor or by foreigners. Hormel, which had introduced canned ham in 1926, brought out Spam in 1937. Despite giving rise to countless jokes, this "miracle meat" became a favorite of many Americans, including servicemen. But after the war, when food supplies returned to normal, the ideal meal for most Americans was shrimp cocktail, steak, and baked potatoes, with pie à la mode for dessert.

Despite an innate distrust of foreign foods, the assimilation of the immigrant populations by the 1950s made their foods seem less threatening. For the middle-class Americans who migrated to the suburbs after the war, the Chinatowns and Little Italys of the inner cities came to represent exciting destinations with alluringly exotic smells and tastes. For those who sought spiciness, ketchup, Worcestershire sauce, and curry powder had long been available, and more recently garlic powder had appeared in grocery stores. But one did not have to venture into the ghettoes to indulge a taste for variety. One could try an exotic dish such as chow mein in the sanitary surroundings of one's own kitchen simply by opening a can of the new vegetable, bean sprouts, mixing it with canned fried noodles, and adding the new flavoring, soy sauce. It did not really matter that neither chow mein nor the other popular "Chinese" dish, chop suey, represented authentic Chinese foods—their tastes were sufficiently foreign to the typical palate to satisfy most Americans' sense of daring and adventure.

These foods were also available in ethnic restaurants, though after the war, especially with the advent of television in 1948, Americans tended increasingly to stay home in the evening, often snacking on potato chips, introduced by Lay in 1934. Most restaurants, to cut prices, had turned to frozen and processed food. When Americans did go out to eat, their favorite

SPAGHETTI: THE NEW AMERICAN STAPLE

The first foreign food to enjoy widespread acceptance in the United States, back in the 1920s, was spaghetti, which, as made in middle-class kitchens, was topped with canned tomato sauce and packaged grated cheese. Though the sauce was bland and the noodles overcooked, the dish was praised by Betty Crocker and favored by those learning to cook, and it became a staple of both Depression households and World War II mess halls. By the 1950s it was no longer regarded as foreign but as American as pork and beans. And when Chef Boyardee made spaghetti and meatballs available in a can, American diners could enjoy the dish simply by warming it up.

foods were those they generally did not get at home: deep-fried dishes, mainly potatoes. To address America's love for both convenience and the automobile, drive-in restaurants, using processed foods and techniques of mass production, sprang up across the country, often in small towns lacking real restaurants. Without getting out of the car, patrons could order simple food such as hamburgers, French fries, and milk shakes, served by scantily clad carhops often wearing roller skates. The appeal was complex—on the one hand, the drive-ins offered speed of service and convenience; on the other, they made a subliminal association of food with sex. Drive-ins became the setting for what amounted to *rites de passage* into adulthood for millions of American teenagers.

IN SEARCH OF CONVENIENCE IN THE 1950S AND 1960S

The 1950s brought a revolution—frozen food. Although invented in 1929, the process was not successful until developed by Clarence Birdseye and later marketed by General Foods as Birds Eye Frosted Foods. Birdseye had to overcome not only the popular association of freezing with low-quality food—which he did by calling his product "frosted"—but also the considerable difficulty of storage, in both the grocery store and the home, problems that kept frozen foods from the consumer for years. Only with the advent of the suburban supermarket, much larger than the urban grocery store, was there space for frozen foods to be properly displayed, and only after home freezers became reasonably priced and widely available could these foods be stored at home. Whereas frozen green peas and strawberries were immediately very popular—in appearance alone, canned vegetables could not compete with them—the great success was Minute Maid's frozen orange juice in 1948, in the form of a concentrate that could be thawed and mixed with water. Also increasingly popular were individually packaged meals, especially as developed by Swanson's in 1954 and termed "TV dinners." The first of these—turkey with dressing, gravy, peas, and sweet potato in a partitioned metal tray—was still the most popular fifty years later.

Other favorite convenience foods of the period included the newly introduced Minute Rice (1950), Mrs. Paul's fish sticks (1952), and Swift's Butterball turkeys (1954). The success of Lipton's dehydrated onion soup mix, introduced in 1952, depended less on its being a soup than on its being the base for onion dip. Called California Dip, it became such a staple at parties that Lipton eventually included the recipe on the package. Convenience was clearly the dominant concern of the day. Tupper had introduced resealable food containers made out of virtually indestructible plastic in 1946; Reynolds Wrap aluminum foil appeared in 1947, followed by Saran Wrap in 1953. And products that could reduce the chores of cooking—such as cake mixes, first introduced in 1947, which required little more than the addition of water—were virtually guaranteed success. Choosing among proliferating brands (Betty Crocker's cake mixes, for instance, faced competition from those of Duncan Hines and others) challenged shoppers, who in the new supermarkets, where self-service was the norm, did not have a friendly clerk to offer advice. Advertising and products' visual appeal often determined selection, especially since three-quarters of all supermarket purchases were unplanned.

Although supermarkets made the corner grocery store a relic of the past—by the late 1950s they accounted for 90 percent of all food sales in the country—in presenting the consumer easy access to a seemingly unlimited choice of foods, they seemed to support the American ideal of a classless society. Without offering the shopper human interaction, they also supported the sense of loneliness or disaffection that began afflicting many suburban housewives by the end of the decade, and that could not be relieved by the Tupperware parties popular since 1951. Meanwhile, the wife's role in the kitchen was celebrated as a norm on television sitcoms. In the most popular shows of the decade, *Father Knows Best* and *Ozzie and Harriet*, the kitchen provided the familiar setting for much of the action. Likewise, the women's magazines of the time glorified the wife's role in the kitchen—pie was the dish thought to best reveal her cooking skills, even though Pillsbury had introduced pie crust mix in 1946. Ironically, however, the housewife's diminishing degree of involvement in the preparation of food seemed to correlate directly with her flagging interest in the process. The less there was to do, the less she was inclined to do it. Beyond television, it appeared that all the convenience foods and work-saving appliances had diminished the creativity in cooking, making food preparation for many women less a skill than a chore much like housecleaning.

Whether or not the boom in barbecuing of the late 1950s and early 1960s responded to the disaffection of the housewife, it allowed the man of the house to share her responsibilities. Previously, the husband had been all but banished from the American kitchen, the wife's domain, at least until the meal was ready—afterward he could carve the meat on festive occasions and help by drying the dishes. With barbecuing, he was still outside, in the backyard, without any modern conveniences, cooking over an open fire the simplest of foods— primarily hot dogs and hamburgers. The accompanying items—potato salad, coleslaw, relishes and other condiments—could be bought already bottled or prepared. Wearing a large apron and wielding oversized utensils, the husband appeared as a caricature of a real cook whose charred achievements underscored the wife's culinary superiority more than they promoted him to cook.

In the 1960s the new fast-food restaurants began to spread across the country. White Towers still existed for the working class in the inner cities, and the small-town drive-ins for teenagers, but Ray Kroc targeted middle-class families in the suburbs for his innovative McDonald's restaurants. The first McDonald's had opened as a drive-in just after World War II. But it was only after the owners fired the carhops, cut prices in half, and had customers order at a walk-up window that the business became a success. After Kroc bought out the McDonalds and started his chain under their name, his concern was to make mealtime a special, fun experience for children and their families. His clown mascot, Ronald McDonald, was, by the end of the 1960s, recognized by more U.S. children than any figure other than Santa Claus. And the golden arches symbol he devised was the most successful restaurant icon since Howard Johnson's orange roofs. Although when he opened his first McDonald's restaurant in Des Plaines, Illinois, in 1955 Kroc was primarily interested in making milk shakes with his special machine, his hamburgers and French fries quickly became the basis of his success; more accurately, success arose from the quickness of food delivery combined with an emphasis on hygiene and openness—one could see the food being prepared—plus the appeal to families. A similar formula enabled Harlan Sanders's success with Kentucky Fried Chicken, begun in 1954. And again, a recognizable icon presided over the restaurant, in this case the goateed Confederate Colonel Sanders in his white suit. It is hardly accidental that even in the early years of the twenty-first century, McDonald's and Kentucky Fried Chicken should represent to the rest of the world the essence of American food. Moreover, it is not surprising that among the largest and most popular restaurants in 2005 Beijing were franchises of these two companies.

The other great American success of the time was pizza. Though not a fast food, it enjoyed its success at the same time as McDonald's and KFC. From as early as the first decade of the twentieth century, pizza existed in the Little Italys of U.S. cities, but it was not until the 1950s that pizza parlors began to flourish and that pizza became a popular item at drive-ins and take-out counters. What kept pizza from becoming a legitimate *fast* food was its crust, but, as the process of making it developed, chains such as Pizza Hut, which started in 1958, cut the time necessary to make and bake it, and, with their pizza buffets, rivaled the hamburger and fried chicken outlets. Moreover, unlike the others, pizza was popular not only for lunch but also for supper and late-night snacks. The only other ethnic food to become a major player in the fast-food restaurant business was the taco, first created by Glen Bell at his hamburger and hot dog stand in 1951 and subsequently marketed as Taco Bell.

Chemicals and the Search for Quality

Even as fast-food chains flourished, the assumption that food from the family kitchen must be superior became increasingly dubious. The attractive appearance and packaging of mainstream food supplies disguised the unseen additives within. From as early as the 1920s Americans had applauded while food chemists created marvelous substances that tasted like real food, forecasting a revolution in which the creations of science would replace nature's bounty. A favorite trope in science fiction represented meals of the future as nutritional pills or instant powders—a fantasy sustained in later decades by such developments as the instant drink Tang (1958), which accompanied astronauts on every venture into space from 1965 on. Marketed as a substitute for orange juice, it was considered by some to be superior.

Over subsequent decades the successes of the chemical laboratories multiplied, until by the 1950s—not even counting all the growth vitamins, antibiotics, and vaccines that were regularly administered to poultry and cattle—more than seven hundred chemicals were being added to food to improve its appearance, shelf life, and flavor. At the time, however, consumers were so blinded by the marvels of freezing, dehydrating, condensing, and packaging that they came to view food scientists as wizards, the giant supermarket with its seeming infinity of packaged and processed foods as the epitome of the American way of life, and themselves as the best-fed people on earth.

The Lure of Good Cooking

It was only with the rise of middle-class travel to Europe, beginning in the 1960s with the introduction of jet planes on transatlantic routes, that Americans first began to realize what was missing from their food. They found in hole-in-the-wall shops freshly baked bread that, despite being unsliced and unwrapped, tasted better than the soft, squeezable product sold at home. They likewise discovered in open markets fresh fruit that, though not as pretty as that in supermarkets, was superior to any they had previously tasted. Despite the lack of convenient, one-stop shopping, Europe gave these travelers a sense of comparative culinary deficiency in the United States, and they returned home less impressed with the quantity of food offered by supermarkets and more concerned with finding food of quality.

They found it first in the new French cooking that from 1961 on enjoyed a renaissance in the United States. Although Henri Soulé's Le Pavillon in New York City had been offering haute cuisine to well-to-do Americans since the 1940s, it was not until the 1950s that imitators, often trained by Soulé, began opening a host of other notable French restaurants, again modeled on *cuisine classique*. And after John F. Kennedy appointed a French chef—another Soulé protégé—in the White House, French restaurants sprang up as never before, not only in major cities but also in fashionable rural areas. Although many of these imitated Le Pavillon, others were more casual bistros and brasseries, offering not complex food in the style of the famed French chef Auguste Escoffier, but the bourgeois cuisine and regional dishes that most native Frenchmen ate.

Also in 1961, serendipitously, a cookbook, *Mastering the Art of French Cooking*, offered middle-class Americans a demystified view of bourgeois French cooking and became one of the most successful cookbooks ever written. The following year, 1962, one of its three authors, Julia Child, a native-born American, began hosting a weekly television program, *The French Chef*, that likewise enjoyed unprecedented success. Child repeatedly insisted in both the book and the TV show that French cooking was much simpler than people thought and that Americans did not need to eat tasteless food. While teaching proper techniques, she showed that cooking could be fun.

This attitude not only ran counter to the contemporary notion that cooking was little more than drudgery but also differed from the intentions of other American cookbooks. Although originally cooking was a skill Americans learned from their mothers and grandmothers, the earliest cookbooks aimed to function as forces for morality and propriety. The very popular *Boston Cooking School Book* by Fanny Farmer (1896) stressed the need not only to eat simple foods but also to avoid the sin of living to eat. Similarly, *The Joy of Cooking* by Irma Rombauer, which became a best seller in 1943 and again in 1951, while adapting traditional midwestern cooking for busy housewives stressed the need for meals to be wholesome and admonished the food preparer to realize that what she creates "decisively influences family health and happiness." The fun that reading and viewing audiences found in Julia Child was just what contemporary American cooking needed, since other forces at the time were alarming people more than ever about the food they were consuming.

Particularly unsettling were the concerns being raised by government agencies and consumer advocates about the safety of much of the food eaten in the United States. In 1961 Rachel Carson's *Silent Spring* showed the dangers of pesticides, notably DDT, and made people aware that these poisons could get into their food supply and then into human tissues. Carson's views found support in the 1967 revelation that mercury levels in freshwater fish were so high as to pose a threat to humans. By the end of the decade a majority of Americans felt that chemicals used in agriculture definitely endangered their health. Likewise unnerving was the news that some growth hormones, as well as some common food colorings, were suspected of causing cancer. Though industry spokesmen tried to calm fears by saying that tests had dealt only with animals, not humans, consumers were more wary than ever, especially as later investigations into the contents of popular foods revealed a host of possibly carcinogenic chemicals. Also in the early 1960s the first cholesterol scare caused an additional outcry as people realized that their standard diet, the one promoted by home economists and health professionals, might actually be deadly. If their most common, and favorite, foods—milk, butter, cheese, and beef—could be killing them by clogging their arteries and precipitating heart attacks, what should they do? And whom should they believe?

As Americans demanded increased government regulation of the food industry and full disclosure of their foods' contents, growing numbers were turning to chemical-free organic food and profiting from the advice of J. I. Rodale's magazine *Organic Gardening and Farming*, and, later, the *Mother Earth News*. Following Euell Gibbons's *Stalking the Wild Asparagus* (1962), many sought nutrition in wild foods. Health foods such as granola, a naturally sweetened mixture of grains, nuts, and dried fruits, became increasingly popular. As nutritionist Adelle Davis demonstrated in her several best-selling books, the modern American diet promoted illness, and if one wanted to be healthy, it was necessary to eat right. Of particular concern were all the sweets and junk food with little or no nutritional value that the food companies had long been pushing on unwary consumers. Much of the criticism targeted refined white sugar. Although celebrated as a food since the seventeenth century, in the late 1960s it was blamed for causing arthritis, diabetes, hair loss, heart disease, hemorrhoids, impotence, mental illness, tooth decay, ulcers, and varicose veins. The dry cereals commonly consumed by Americans for breakfast also reaped criticism. These, it was demonstrated, had less nutritional value than the boxes in which they were packaged. The cereal industry responded with a host of new products, which mostly amounted to versions of granola.

Many representatives of the food industry seemed to give their critics what they wanted, while continuing to market the other questionable food as well. They felt that the adverse criticism came from relatively small segments of the population: hippies, wealthy liberals, and older people concerned with looking young. They believed that most Americans preferred snacks, fast food, soft drinks, and beer and would not change their eating habits to avoid sugar, salt, and fried foods. Thus the food industry made available both diet soft drinks and regular soft drinks, both traditional beer and "light" beer. Though Stouffer's Lean Cuisine initiated a new age of frozen food in 1981, it was not at the expense of "Fat" Cuisine. Food companies designed for their traditional products new labels featuring the terms "natural" and "pure." Although as employed, these terms had little meaning, they offered consumers the glimpse of a guarantee of what many felt was missing from their food—safety.

THE NEW GOURMETS: THE 1970S TO THE PRESENT

The health-food stores and food cooperatives that sprang up to answer this need did not satisfy most Americans, who wanted more from their food than granola, brown rice, sprouts, and yogurt. For many, the ready alternative was ethnic foods, not yet ruined by industrial food processors, and both urban and suburban shoppers gave new life to ethnic grocery stores in old immigrant neighborhoods of major U.S. cities. For these shoppers the particular cuisine did not really matter. They tried what was at hand, whether French croissants and pâtés; Italian pasta, olive oil, and fresh Parmesan cheese; Portuguese bread; Greek olives and feta; Middle East couscous; Polish pierogi; Mexican frijoles; Indian pickles and chutneys; or Chinese bok choy and hoisin sauce. The important thing for these shoppers was that the foodstuffs differ from what was featured in the supermarkets. They discovered new herbs and spices and wondered how they had ever gotten along without basil, oregano, and saffron. Among new cookbooks of the 1960s and 1970s several seminal ones not only offered the techniques needed to cook foreign dishes but also revealed riches of the cuisine hitherto unimagined. These included the *Joyce Chen Cook Book* (1962), Diana Kennedy's *The Cuisines of Mexico* (1972), Marcella Hazan's *The Classic Italian Cookbook* (1973), and Paula Wolfert's *Couscous and Other Good Food from Morocco* (1973). Gourmet food stores, which had previously featured such expensive French specialties as *pâté de foie gras* and *escargots* became more international in scope, expanding their selection of both local and imported goods, as well as their fresh breads, cheeses, and vegetables. By the 1980s stores such as Whole Foods were providing viable alternatives to shoppers seeking a wide range of organic and ethnic foods. Although many of the items in these stores commanded higher prices than those in the supermarkets, their customers—mainly educated people with disposable incomes—were ready to pay them.

Traditional regional foods of the United States, but only those uncorrupted by the food industry, similarly fascinated these shoppers. City dwellers, both white and black, discovered such "soul food" as ham hocks, collard greens, black-eyed peas, and grits, as well as such treasures of Creole and Cajun cooking as gumbo and red beans and rice. James Beard, known as the father of American gastronomy, assisted this exploration. Not only did he offer the first cooking program on television (1946) and operate a cooking school for the next forty years, but his cookbook *James Beard's American Cookery* (1972) addressed the diversity of American tastes and the ethnic backgrounds of the people as no other American cookbook had before.

The interest in ethnic foods led also to an interest in a host of foreign kitchen utensils previously unknown in the United States—from mandolines, couscousiers, and pasta machines, to woks and bamboo steamers. For the new upper- and middle-class cooks cuisine was a determiner of status, much as it had been at the end of the nineteenth century. The single most important item to facilitate this new gourmet cooking was the food processor, especially as manufactured by Cuisinart. Now American cooks could duplicate the wonders of French *cuisine classique* with a flick of their wrists, mastering *pâté à chou* (puff pastry) for dauphiné potatoes or *pâté brisée* for tart crusts. Home chefs learned how to cook their pasta and vegetables *al dente* and how to garnish their dishes with baby vegetables and edible flora. They valued cookbooks ranging from introductions to previously neglected foreign cuisines, such as Turkish and Thai, to those celebrating regional American cooking, such as Cajun and southwestern. In the late 1960s and early 1970s, Time-Life Books published a successful series called Foods of the World, in twenty-seven volumes featuring twenty-five different cuisines—including eight volumes on regional American cuisines. The interest in good cooking remained so keen that in the late 1970s and early 1980s, Time-Life produced still another series, this one called The Good Cook: Techniques and Recipes. At the same time, gourmet cooking could be combined with fast cooking, as reflected in the *New York Times 60-Minute Gourmet* books authored by Pierre Franey. Clearly the new home cooking of the late twentieth century differed dramatically from that of mid-century which had featured dishes made with processed cheese, cream of mushroom soup, and Jell-O.

Preoccupation with quickness explains why the microwave oven so rapidly became the most indispensable item in U.S. kitchens in the 1980s—and with good reason. By the early 1980s more than 50 percent of married women were working outside the home. The status of the full-time housewife had sunk so low that it approximated that once reserved for the spinster. Now husbands were brought in from the backyard barbecue to contribute to household maintenance as never before. Along with helping to clean the house, they were expected to work in the kitchen, even to make meals. Ironically, as more males cooked in the home, the status of home cooking rose. At the same time, the breakdown of the traditional family structure accelerated until, by 1980, half of all households were composed of singles or people without children, with most working outside the home. Dining out daily was commonplace for these people, but so was eating at home—with a modern twist. Takeout was available, not only from ethnic restaurants but also from supermarkets, which offered both a wide variety of dinners needing only to be thawed or heated in those new microwave ovens and also a wealth of fully prepared foods, including barbecued meats, pastas, and salads. In fact, by the late 1980s more than 80 percent of U.S. households regularly purchased take-out food to be eaten at home.

Restaurant dining had also been dramatically affected by the quest for healthy food. In 1972 Alice Waters created a national stir by opening her restaurant, Chez Panisse, in Berkeley, emphasizing fresh, organic foods, grown and produced locally. This food, free from additives and chemicals, was prepared by her as simply as possible to retain its healthfulness and emphasize the natural taste of its ingredients. The restaurant achieved enormous success, but even with the Café added to offer Waters's fare at cheaper prices, her clientele remained affluent people who were willing to pay for the kind of food not readily available to them in other restaurants. These were not the ordinary Americans who needed to be educated about how real food could taste. Still, Waters's success spawned a host of imitators across the country, offering New American food that was the equivalent of the *nouvelle cuisine* that was replacing the overly rich artery-clogging *cuisine classique* both in France and in this country.

Food Writers and TV Cooks

Before the late twentieth century the evaluation of restaurants in the United States had generally been left up to the food writers of local newspapers. On a national scale, with the publication of his *Adventures in Good Eating* in 1936, Duncan Hines became the country's leading restaurant critic for the next two decades—though he knew little about food. He accentuated finding restaurants that were clean and served traditional American food, preferring chains that offered the same dining experience across the country, avoiding both local cooking and adventure. Similarly, the anonymous evaluators for the Tour Books made available to members of AAA (the American Automobile Association) rated restaurants as they did hotels, by ranking cleanliness, then value, as the most important factors. In 1958, when Craig Claiborne began reviewing restaurants for the *New York Times*, New York City got a critic who knew food in general and foreign cuisines in particular, but the nation's restaurant patrons got equivalent guidance only after 1979, when the Zagat Survey began. Using the assessments of actual patrons, the survey covered more than seventy metropolitan areas by the early years of the twenty-first century. For the nonmetropolitan areas, from the 1980s on, the restaurant-goer had the several books on road food and regional cooking by Jane and Michael Stern, who also wrote a well-received column for *Gourmet* magazine.

Diners increasingly had a wealth of restaurant choices. In 1979 Paul Prudhomme, formerly a chef at New Orleans' Commander's Palace, opened his own restaurant, K-Paul's Louisiana Kitchen, where he combined traditional, sophisticated Creole foods with spicy, backcountry Cajun cooking. The result was a regional cuisine that, boosted by Prudhomme's entrepreneurial skills, took the country by storm. In 1984, after he introduced what became his signature dish, blackened redfish—which quickly made its way into home kitchens—and published his cookbook, *Chef Paul Prudhomme's Louisiana Kitchen*, Cajun food became widely popular and imitated. Similarly, Wolfgang Puck's restaurant Spago, which opened in Los Angeles in 1982, introduced Americans to novel blendings of foods of different cuisines. Despite the occasional bizarre combination, Puck's fusion cuisine dramatically influenced the subsequent course of American cooking. Also, his enormously successful gourmet pizzas showed what could still be done with a tried-and-true favorite. Another celebrity chef, Daniel Boulud, whose French restaurant Daniel won awards as the best restaurant in New York City, later performed a similar kind of makeover on the traditional hamburger.

While innovative restaurants continue to reinterpret mundane dishes of middle America, the influence flows in the other direction as well. Sushi now sells briskly in school cafeterias and grocery chains. Food courts at shopping malls and airports have become international in scope and even include outlets featuring the creations of celebrity chefs. The success of cooking shows spawned an entire Food Channel on cable TV, which somewhat dispels the snobbish aura of *haute cuisine* by featuring cooks such as Rachel Ray alongside Emeril Lagasse—figures whose TV exposure fuels brisk sales of cookbooks and cooking equipment. The long tradition of the local cooking contest continues unabated: the Food Channel features the contest of the Iron Chefs, newspapers sponsor chili competitions, and the formidable Betty Crocker/Pillsbury Bakeoff (now in its forty-second year) offers a top prize of $1 million. Moreover, the food sections of newspapers regularly print recipes from local restaurants alongside others that have won as much as $100,000 in national competitions.

Food festivals—focused on regional fare, ethnic varieties, or even single food items such as garlic, spam, or strawberries—continue to proliferate across the continent. Popular food memoirs help satisfy the nation's appetite for food news, as illustrated by Anthony Bourdain's best-selling exposé, *Kitchen Confidential* (2000). The growth of Martha Stewart's multimedia empire (television programs, books, magazine, kitchen equipment, and decorating items), built largely on the presentation of food and the accoutrements of entertaining, has made her a force in the history of American cooking comparable to Fannie Farmer and Julia Child.

In the early twenty-first century Americans want to savor the entire world's bounty while remaining thin and fit. To address widespread concerns with avoiding junk food, too much salt, sugar, and red meat, fast-food establishments now sell salads and low-calorie sandwiches, and supermarkets stock more low-fat, sugar-free food than ever, though both continue to sell their traditional fare as well. Incongruities abound: eight-ounce bottles of mineral water share shelves with sixty-four-ounce bottles of soft drinks. And in Quebec, healthy, locally grown foods participating in a new culinary movement designed to give *une vrai gout de terroir*—a true taste of the land—exist side by side with *poutine*, an immensely popular artery-clogging dish invented in 1964 consisting of french fries and cheese curd covered in gravy.

Current Trends in North American Food

By the year 2000, an average of twenty-five thousand new food products were being introduced to Americans every year, and, not unexpectedly, supermarkets were larger than ever. So were Americans themselves, with 50 percent of the population overweight. Around the world Americans are noted for obesity and overindulgence in burgers, fries, Cokes, Twinkies, and pork rinds, as well as foods with foreign cachet but domestic calorie quotients, such as chocolate truffles and all-you-can-eat Brazilian meat feasts. Portion size plays a huge role in spiking health problems such as diabetes; the practice of supersizing fast food inflates health costs as much as clothing sizes. But even with all this eating, Americans continue to have the lowest food costs in the world, spending an average of only 10 percent of their income on food. And the mid-2006 announcement that the giant discount chain Wal-Mart will be stocking more organic food demonstrates a growing grassroots preoccupation with fresher, healthier eating.

Discussions of the alarming rise in health problems directly associated with diet reveal that food concerns—such as the placement of soft drinks and fast food in school cafeterias, the culpability of food manufacturers in individuals' health crises, and the health and environmental impact of commercial fish farming (introduced in the 1980s)—are highly charged political and economic issues. Practices in the cultivation, production, and distribution of food raise a host of ethical issues, including the role of large corporations in eliminating the family farm; the uses of pesticides, fertilizers, and genetic engineering to improve harvest yields; the impact of waste lagoons on livestock farms; and the compassionate slaughter of animals.

Despite such vexing issues, in the first decade of the twenty-first century the stature of American cuisine has grown tremendously from what it was a mere fifty years ago. At its best it equals Europe's finest. More good restaurants than ever exist across both the United States and Canada, with very good food available not only in big cities but also in out-of-the-way spots. It is not at all strange that what has been widely considered the best restaurant in the United States, Thomas Keller's French Laundry, should be a French restaurant run by a self-trained American, situated in rural Napa Valley north of San Francisco, or that for the past five years, according to *Gourmet* magazine, the eleventh-best restaurant in the entire country should be in Durham, North Carolina. The variety of cuisines that American cooking has accommodated, if not absorbed, is unequaled in any other country, though the range of ethnic restaurants in Toronto and Vancouver rivals that in the most cosmopolitan U.S. cities.

Notwithstanding the amount of foreign food increasingly available in the United States (albeit much altered from its origins), American food habits have been even more influential in permeating and altering traditional eating habits in other nations. Along with hamburger, fried chicken, and Tex-Mex fast-food restaurants, others such as Hard Rock Café and Planet Hollywood, though they may have lost their allure in the United States, continue to open around the world, offering what purports to be an American experience appealing to the young people of all countries. With Budweiser selling briskly in places long respected for producing fine beer, such as Munich and Prague, and with Starbucks already ensconced alongside traditional coffeehouses in Vienna, it appears only a matter of time before Pizza Hut is flourishing in Rome and Taco Bell in Mexico City. The Americanization of the world's food and drink has definitely reached a new level, arousing considerable ire in other countries resentful of American economic and cultural imperialism, and spawning a rebellious "slow food" movement. As national foods are being replaced, homogenization of the international diet appears to be already happening. This multifaceted globalism may be what is most distinctive about American food today.

RESOURCE GUIDE

PRINT SOURCES

Avakian, Arlene, ed. *Through the Kitchen Window: Women Explore the Intimate Meanings of Food and Cooking.* Boston: Beacon Press, 1997.

Benoäit, Jehane. *The Canadiana Cookbook: A Complete Heritage of Canadian Cooking.* Toronto: Pagurian Press, 1970.

Bundy, Beverly. *The Century in Food: America's Fads and Favorites.* Portland, OR: Collectors Press, 2002.

Camp, Charles. "Food in American Culture: A Bibliographic Essay." *Journal of American Culture* 2 (1979): 559–570.

Counihan, Carole M., ed. *Food in the USA: A Reader.* New York: Routledge, 2002.

Cummings, Richard Osborn. *The American and His Food: A History of Food Habits in the United States,* revised edition. Chicago: University of Chicago Press, 1941.

Davidson, Alan. *The Oxford Companion to Food.* Oxford: Oxford University Press, 1999.

Finkelstein, Joanne. *Dining Out: A Sociology of Modern Manners.* New York: New York University Press, 1989.

Food and Foodways (periodical, New York: G&B/Harwood), 1985–.

Gabaccia, Donna R. *We Are What We Eat: Ethnic Food and the Making of Americans.* Cambridge, MA: Harvard University Press, 1998.

Gotlieb, Sondra. *The Gourmet's Canada.* Toronto: New Press, 1972.

Grover, Kathryn, ed. *Dining in America, 1850–1900.* Amherst: University of Massachusetts Press; Rochester: Margaret Woodbury Strong Museum, 1987.

Haber, Barbara. *From Hardtack to Home Fries: An Uncommon History of American Cooks and Meals.* New York: Free Press, 2002.

Hess, John L., and Karen Hess. *The Taste of America.* Urbana: University of Illinois Press, 2000.

Humphrey, Theodore C., and Lin T. Humphrey, eds. *"We Gather Together": Food and Festival in American Life.* Ann Arbor: UMI Press, 1988.

Inness, Sherrie A., ed. *Kitchen Culture in America: Popular Representations of Food, Gender, and Race.* Philadelphia: University of Pennsylvania Press, 2001.

Kiple, Kenneth F., and Kreimhild Conèe Ornelas, eds. *The Cambridge World History of Food.* 2 vols. Cambridge: Cambridge University Press, 2000.

Langdon, Philip. *Orange Roofs, Golden Arches: The Architecture of American Chain Restaurants.* London: Michael Joseph, 1986.

Latham, Jean. *The Pleasure of Your Company: A History of Manners and Meals.* London: Adam and Charles Black, 1972.

Levenstein, Harvey A. *Paradox of Plenty: A Social History of Eating in Modern America.* New York: Oxford University Press, 1993.

———. *Revolution at the Table: The Transformation of the American Diet.* New York: Oxford University Press, 1988.

McWilliams, James E. *A Revolution in Eating: How the Quest for Food Shaped America.* New York: Columbia University Press, 2005.

Mintz, Sidney W. *Tasting Food, Tasting Freedom: Excursions into Eating, Culture, and the Past.* Boston: Beacon Press, 1996.

Murcott, Anne, ed. *The Sociology of Food and Eating.* Aldershot: Gower, 1983.

Paston-Williams, Sara. *The Art of Dining: A History of Cooking and Eating.* New York: Harry N. Abrams, 1993.

Pillsbury, Richard. *No Foreign Food: The American Diet in Time and Place.* Boulder, CO: Westview, 1998.

Rappoport, Leon. *How We Eat: Appetite, Culture, and the Psychology of Food.* Toronto: ECW Press, 2003.

Root, Waverly, and Richard de Rochemont. *Eating in America: A History.* New York: William Morrow, 1976.

Scapp, Ron, and Brian Seitz, eds. *Eating Culture.* Albany: SUNY Press, 1998.

Schlosser, Eric. *Fast Food Nation: The Dark Side of the All-American Meal.* Boston: Houghton Mifflin, 2001.

Schwartz, Hillel. *Never Satisfied: A Cultural History of Diets, Fantasies and Fat.* New York: The Free Press, 1986.

Shapiro, Laura. *Perfection Salad: Women and Cooking at the Turn of the Century.* New York: Farrar Straus & Giroux, 1986.

Shortridge, Barbara G., and James R., eds. *The Taste of American Place: A Reader on Regional and Ethnic Foods.* Lanham: Rowman and Littlefield, 1998.

Smith, Andrew F., ed. *Oxford Encyclopedia of Food and Drink in America.* 2 vols. Oxford: Oxford University Press, 2004.

Villas, James. *American Taste: A Celebration of Gastronomy Coast-to-Coast.* New York: Arbor House, 1982.

Williams, Susan. *Savory Suppers and Fashionable Feasts: Dining in Victorian America.* Knoxville: University of Tennessee Press, 1996.

Witt, Doris. *Black Hunger: Food and the Politics of U.S. Identity.* New York: Oxford University Press, 1999.

WEBSITES

Food Network Canada. November 9, 2006. Alliance Atlantis Communications, Inc. 2006. http://www.foodtv.ca. Schedule of TV cooking shows, recipes, meal planner, listing of contests.

Food as Popular Culture. November 9, 2006. Thomson Nelson. 2004. http://www.popularculture.nelson.com/issues.html#food. Supplement to Canadian publisher's textbook *Popular Culture: A User's Guide* by Susie O'Brien and Imre Szeman; brief essay on food as commodity fetish, food porn, food, and media.

Food Reference Website. Food Festivals. November 9, 2006. TheFoodWorld.com Database of Food Producers & Exporters. 1990–2006. http://www.foodreference.com/html/us-food-festivals.html. Listing of food festivals.

Gourmet Spot. November 9, 2006. StartSpot Mediaworks, Inc. 1997–2006. http://www.gourmetspot.com/foodtv.htm. Guide to TV shows on 3 food channels: CNN Food, Food Network, and MSNBC; cookbooks, recipes, articles, food magazines, kitchen tips, food trivia.

Headline Spot. November 9, 2006. StartSpot Mediaworks, Inc. 2001–6. http://www.headlinespot.com/subject/food/. Guide to food items in newspapers, magazines, radio, TV.

Nutrition and Well-Being A to Z. Food and Popular Culture. November 9, 2006. Thomson Gale. 2006. http://www.faqs.org/nutrition/Ome-Pop/Popular-Culture-Food-and.html.

Questia: Food and Culture. November 9, 2006. Questia Media America. 2006. http://www.questia.com/library/science-and-technology/food-and-culture.jsp. Listing of books and articles on food and culture.

2 Camels Festivals and Events: Food Festivals. November 9, 2006. 2Camels. 2006. http://www.2camels.com/festivals/food-festivals.php.

FILMS/VIDEOS

Big Night (Samuel Goldwyn Films, 1996). Directed by Campbell Scott and Stanley Tucci, starring Stanley Tucci and Tony Shalhoub.

Dinner Rush (Access Motion Picture Group, 2001). Directed by Bob Giraldi, starring Danny Aiello and Sandra Bernhard.

Eating (International Rainbow Pictures, 1990). Directed by Henry Jaglom, starring Nelly Alard and Mary Crosby.

The Last Supper (Sony Pictures, 1995). Directed by Stacy Title, starring Cameron Diaz, Courtney B. Vance, and Bill Paxton.

Pieces of April (MGM/United Artists, 2003). Directed by Peter Hedges, starring Katie Holmes, Patricia Clarkson, and Derek Luke.

Sideways (Searchlight Pictures, 2004). Directed by Alexander Payne, starring Paul Giamatti and Thomas Haden Church.

Simply Irresistible (Twentieth Century Fox, 1999). Directed by Mark Tarlov, starring Sarah Michelle Gellar and Sean Patrick Flanery.

Spanglish (Sony Pictures, 2004). Directed by James L. Brooks, starring Adam Sandler and Téa Leoni.

Super Size Me (Roadside Attractions, Samuel Goldwyn Films, 2004). Directed by Morgan Spurlock, starring Morgan Spurlock.

Tortilla Soup (Samuel Goldwyn Films, 2001). Directed by Maria Ripoll, starring Hector Elizondo, Jacqueline Obradors, and Tamara Mello.

What's Cooking (Lions Gate Films, 2000). Directed by Gurinder Chadha, starring Joan Chen, Julianna Margulies, Kyra Sedgwick, and Alfre Woodard.

ARCHITECTURE

ARCHITECTURE: No need to travel to New York—the Brooklyn Bridge can be found in this Las Vegas hotel, along with a whole assortment of sights and attractions. Courtesy of Carroll Van West.

ARCHITECTURE: Gas stations have gone through a multitude of designs, reflecting the changing times of the country. Once bustling with travelers, this Texaco in Texas has been converted into a library and museum. Courtesy of Carroll Van West.

ART

ART: Mount Rushmore was the creation of American artist and sculptor Gutzon Borglum. The original plans were drawn up to have full-length portraits of the four men. Courtesy of Shutterstock.

ART: *Washington Crossing the Delaware* (1851), by Emanuel Leutze. © Art Resource, NY.

DANCE

DANCE: Karen Lynn Gorney and John Travolta star in *Saturday Night Fever* (1977). This film helped to usher in the return to partner dance in the late 1970s and the popularity of disco dancing. Courtesy of Photofest.

DANCE: A woman in an elaborate costume dances during the Caribana street festival in Toronto, 1992. Caribana has become the largest Caribbean festival in North America. Courtesy of Shutterstock.

FASHION AND APPEARANCE

FASHION AND APPEARANCE: Rosanna Arquette (as Roberta Glass) and Madonna (as Susan) in Susan Seidelman's *Desperately Seeking Susan* (1985). Madonna's semi-trashy and very colorful fashion style of the 1980s was widely copied. Courtesy of Photofest.

FASHION AND APPEARANCE: Lil' Romeo with Master P at the Amercan Music Awards (ABC) 2002. The hip hop culture began to figure heavily in fashion for young people in the 1990s and continues today. Courtesy of Photofest.

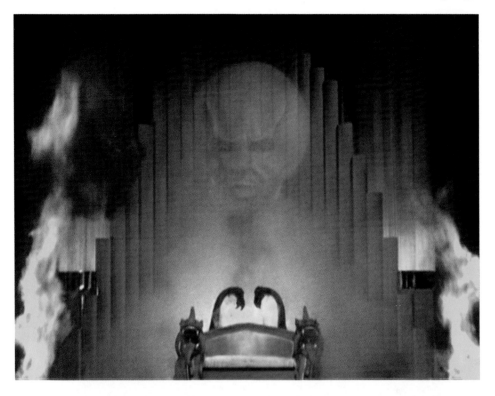

FILM: The Great Wizard appears in a cloud of smoke in the 1939 film, *The Wizard of Oz*, based on the novel by L. Frank Baum. This film was considered momentous for the use of the new Technicolor process to achieve unparalleled dramatic results. Courtesy of Photofest.

FILM: Neil and Adrian Rayment in Andy Wachowski and Larry Wachowski's film, *The Matrix Reloaded* (2003). Some considered *The Matrix* to be *The Wizard of Oz* meets high-tech Superman. Courtesy of Photofest.

FOOD AND FOODWAYS

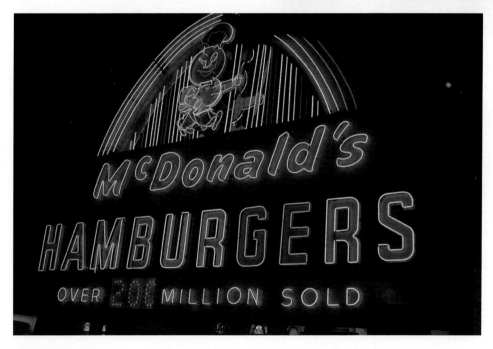

FOOD AND FOODWAYS: Chef Paul Prudhomme displays a batch of jambalaya outside his K-Paul's Louisiana Kitchen in New Orleans, Louisiana. Americans began enthusiastically trying ethnic foods in the latter half of the twentieth century. © Owen Franken/CORBIS

FOOD AND FOODWAYS: Vintage McDonald's sign. By the end of the 1960s, Ronald McDonald was recognized by more American children than any figure other than Santa Claus. Courtesy of Shutterstock.

GAMES, TOYS, AND PASTIMES

GAMES, TOYS, AND PASTIMES: Ouija boards rose from nineteenth-century spiritualism, and still create controversy today. Pictured is a Ouija board made by Milton Bradley. Courtesy of Shutterstock.

GAMES, TOYS, AND PASTIMES: Barbie dolls line the shelves at a toy store in Torrance, California, 1995. In spite of continuing controversy over whether or not she makes a good role model, Mattel makes about 90 different versions of the Barbie doll. © AP Photo/Eric Draper.

GAMES, TOYS, AND PASTIMES:
Monopoly was originally designed to illustrate the evils of price gouging and monopolistic ventures. Instead, it became practice for establishing them. © photographer: Razvan Cosa; agency: Dreamstime.com

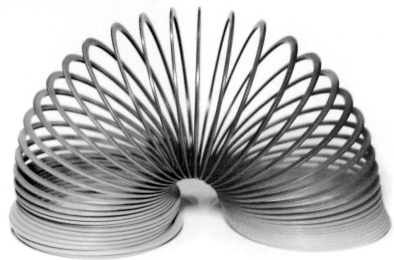

GAMES, TOYS, AND PASTIMES: A modern plastic "slinky," originally an accident stumbled on by Richard and Betty James who became overnight superstars of the American dream. Courtesy of Shutterstock.

GAMES, TOYS, AND PASTIMES

SHARON SCOTT, WITH MARY CAROTHERS

LEISURE TIME IN NORTH AMERICA

The unofficial history of North America can be understood by surveying the toys, games, and hobbies enjoyed by its people. In the moments outside of work or family obligation, individuals are free to indulge themselves. With no consequence beyond the immediate play and no responsibility other than to win, games allow people to behave differently than they might in *real life.* Cautious people can act surprisingly reckless in games. Refined people may participate in the most deplorable sports. From bad form to bad etiquette, outlandish behavior can be forgiven or forgotten with the conclusion of the play. For both children and adults in North America, playtime allows people to explore different activities, escape difficult realities, and envision new possibilities.

Classified ads across the continent prove that in addition to age, sex, and height, pastime activities are among the essential features that both Canadians and Americans want to know about potential mates. The way an individual entertains himself or herself during the moments outside of work might be considered an accurate indicator of his or her deeper personality. Healthy people are thought to play sports, for instance, inquisitive people may read, and sensitive people might take strolls in the park.

Just as a person's extracurricular interests may reflect one's personality, pastime activities can also reflect the personality of a country. Fads capture the ingenuity and like-mindedness of a society. Playthings that endure reveal the heart of a people. North America was discovered by explorers, settled by pioneers, and conquered by capitalists. North America is built upon immigration and invention. So are its toys.

The North American universe of toys, games, and activities is virtually infinite. A constant and unlimited supply of playthings includes everything from ancient marbles to space-age robots. Games with Native American roots such as King of the Hill and Pick-up Sticks are played alongside international imports such as mah-jongg and Nintendo. Among the millions of hobbies cultivated in North America are stamp collecting, competitive eating, and space tourism. The diversity of pastimes and playthings enjoyed by the inhabitants of the New World attests to the economic prosperity and social freedom that has developed across the continent.

Despite individual differences, North Americans share a collective vocabulary of play. From the Atlantic Ocean to the Pacific, new trends are promoted by talkative children and borderless media. A single item can easily take the entire continent by storm. Teddy bears, hula hoops, and Sudoku are among phenomena of the twentieth century that have hit Toronto and New York at virtually the same time. These fads attest to the ingenuity and camaraderie that lie at the heart of North American society.

Like good sisters, the United States and Canada have shared their toys since birth. An open border, a common language, and a legacy of free trade agreements have allowed the development of a vast toy industry in North America in the twentieth century. Among the citizens of the continent, little distinction is made between Canadian and U.S. toys. Silly Putty, Trivial Pursuit, Superman, and many other playthings that seem classically American are truly products of Canadian ingenuity. In North America, regional differences such as climate and economy prove more important than national boundaries in the development of pastimes and playthings.

In both countries, toys are considered instruments for building one's personality. They encourage the imagination and liberate it from the limitations of the real world. Toys direct thought and introduce new ideas. At the beginning of the century, toys in North America were precious, rare, and handmade. They were made by families and sold in local stores. As the economy grew, so did the number of toys and toyshops. Inventions such as plastic and the assembly line eventually made domestic toys more accessible than European imports. After pushing smaller shops out of business, Wal-Mart and Toys "R" Us have become the largest toy retailers on the continent. These mega-shops carry the products of toy manufacturing giants such as Mattel and Hasbro.

Once children enter school, playtime becomes structured and work becomes introduced as the most important part of the day. Suddenly play is not free. It is something a child must work to achieve. It is a prize for good behavior, a reward for work well done. Children are gradually weaned away from imaginative play and into games of skill and strategy. As children mature they are provided with rules to follow and given goals to attain during their play. The concept of winning is introduced at an early age, and even in their games North American children are expected to excel.

As children grow older playtime is increasingly filled with competitive games. Parents involve their children in a variety of competitive activities from organized sports to beauty contests. During these contests parents may relay an old saying to their children: "It is not important if you win or lose, but how you play the game." Regardless of this positive banter, the importance of winning is demonstrated by the poor behavior of some parents when their child loses.

Imaginative play is the property of children. Adults in English-speaking North America are forbidden from revisiting the fantastic worlds they knew as children. Pretending to be different people in impossible situations is an activity preserved for actors or those with mental health issues. Literature, cinema, and television are popular substitutes for these sorts of role-playing games. Instead of *becoming* the heroic characters of their own playful fantasy, adults become spectators to the play of others. The experience of becoming an astronaut or an Aztec warrior is still possible to adults but usually only through the observance of professional actors who are paid to do so.

Games in North America are rarely limited to a single demographic group. With the exception of certain sports, men and women of all races, religions, and economic backgrounds regularly compete with and against one another. From the schoolyard to the casino, both sexes are encouraged to participate in games.

In North America there are games for memorization, games for cognition, games for survival, and games for financial gain. Although ancient games such as checkers, chess, and go fish continue to be played frequently in both the United States and Canada, personal computers, PlayStations, and cell phones have made high-tech gaming a standard feature in most North American homes.

In contrast to the various items found in the American marketplace, many toy, game, and hobby traditions have been successfully passed down through the generations. Many American children still spend a great deal of time playing outdoors, scratching out chalk-outlined hopscotch grids onto asphalt, running around feverishly in games of freeze tag and dodgeball. Marco Polo, hide-and-seek, Punch Bug, and spin the bottle are games North Americans instinctively know.

Although both Canada and the United States have their share of fervent sports fans, the types of sports that engage each country differ. The primary national pastimes of Canada are hockey and lacrosse. Although each of these sports can be downright vicious compared to most pastimes in the United States, these team sports are dependent on cooperation as well as competition. Baseball, shopping, and watching TV might all vie for the title of America's pastime, but none has united her citizens in a way that hockey has the Canadians.

In their spare time individuals across North America enjoy activities that involve automobiles, athletics, arts, pets, outdoor activity, music, cuisine, and technology. Hobbyists generally do not have Olympic aspirations, nor do they expect to see their artwork hanging inside the Smithsonian. Instead, they strive toward a sense of individual accomplishment that arises from the fulfillment of personal goals. Still, the seriousness with which people approach their hobbies is exhibited by millions of dollars spent annually on private lessons and pastime equipment.

Appealing to the competitive spirit of the Americas, many hobbies involve some sort of contest. Collectors compete for the most extensive or the most valuable collection. Gamers race for the highest score. The competition is usually considered friendly, and a sense of good sportsmanship is expected—if not always exhibited—within the playing field.

As the Internet and the airplane continue to make the world smaller, more and more international toys, games, and pastimes introduce themselves to the North American vocabulary. Sudoku, feng shui, and Pilates are just a few examples of recently imported pastimes that have become wildly successful in Canada and the United States.

For centuries, ideas and activities have migrated to North America from other parts of the world. Marbles and checkers have roots in ancient Greece. Hacky Sac was called Jian Zi when it was played in ancient China. Parcheesi is based on the game *Ludo* that has been played in India since 4 AD. Tiddlywinks is slang for an unlicensed pub in England where the game of the same name was invented. Toys, games, and pastimes have arrived in America by foot, by boat, and by airplane from nearly every corner of the globe. Like the people who carried them in their pockets and suitcases to the New World, many of these imported playthings have adapted to suit the melting pot culture of North America.

Although many pastimes and playthings have immigrated to the Americas, many are indigenous to the land. Shrinky Dinks, Sea-Monkeys, and Mr. Potato Head are characteristically North American. It would be impossible to imagine the Big Wheel or Nerf Football coming from any other place on the globe. Intersecting cultures, competing technologies, and an undying belief in the New World have made the United States and Canada fertile ground for oddly progressive playthings.

HISTORY OF NORTH AMERICAN PASTIMES

Forging a society out of the wilderness required the constant effort of all settlers. Children worked along with their parents to plant, build, and create a new civilization. The continent was unified by its will to work and its need to survive. Activities such as gardening, sewing, and home improvement were methods of survival that demanded constant attention. Children had spinning tops, kites, dolls, and other toys. Certain games such as hoops or horseshoes were played freely. Puritan morals did not prohibit play, but adults were expected to spend most of their waking hours productively. In many communities it was sinful to play with toys on Sunday, with the exception of those that taught a religious lesson. Gaming, especially gambling, was considered immoral, and idleness was often punishable by law. Cards and dice were not tolerated by the Puritan colonists nor was any sort of acting. In Jamestown, bowling was forbidden, and the trespasser of this law could be sentenced to the galley.[1]

Archery, wrestling, and footraces were pastimes the colonists and the native populations had in common. The indigenous Americans introduced the settlers to string games such as cat's cradle and children's toys such as the Pickup Sticks. Requiring little or no equipment, native games traveled lightly across geography and generations. Many games played by contemporary American children such as hide-and-seek, blind man's bluff, and king of the hill are descended from the traditions of Indigenous America.

As pioneers expanded into the lawless West, distance from Puritan values allowed gaming to prosper. Frontier children learned to make dolls out of cornhusks, and adults made wooden puppet toys to dance around campfires. When the card game poker was developed, gaming parlors not only were legal but also were the center of society.

By the mid-nineteenth century an affluent class flourished on the eastern shore of the United States. Anxious to prove a European sophistication, wealthy Americans imported fashionable games from the Continent. German tin toys dominated the toy market. Exquisite porcelain dolls, dollhouses, toy carriages, and rocking horses were fashionable accessories for the Victorian home. At the end of the day, family and friends gathered to play indoor games. Parlor games were both intellectual and fun. They included acting games, treasure hunts, and history quizzes. The introduction of chromolithography in the 1870s ignited an explosion of colorful board games, and New England publishers Milton Bradley and George Parker quickly became household names.

State fairs, midway carnivals, and amusement parks became important features upon the social landscape of the continent. These community-building events broke the routine of work and offered rides, shooting games, and theatrical shows to citizens of all financial situations. Gypsy fortune-tellers, both real and mechanical, became favorite items at the midway fair. Famous magicians such as Houdini and mediums such as Cora Scott would travel across the country astonishing audiences with their supernatural powers. Nineteenth-century Spiritualism birthed a fascination in magic and the occult that crept into American drawing rooms. Séances and spirit rapping became some of the more bizarre games incorporated into evening parlor activities.

Planchettes, small platforms holding writing utensils, were often used in parlor séances to transcribe messages and pictures from the spirit world. According to mythology, it was Maryland cabinet and coffin maker E. C. Reiche who removed the pencil from the planchette and placed a board underneath it. On the surface of the board he etched the letters of the alphabet, numbers one through ten, and the words "yes," "no," and "goodbye." Reiche claimed the name Ouija had been spelled out to him while using the instrument. He speculated incorrectly that the name means "good luck" in Egyptian.

The "Talking Board" was patented on February 10, 1891, by Reiche's business-minded friend Elijah J. Bond. Bond then sold the invention to the Kennard Novelty Company. The Kennard Company made the Ouija boards commercially available in 1891. The story goes that while Kennard's office manager William Fuld was experimenting with the board, he received instructions for building his own Ouija factory.

After a hostile takeover of the Kenner Company, Fuld claimed to have invented the board and established trademarks on the concept and the Ouija name. Fuld sold thousands of boards and shipped them across the country. He adamantly refused to pay taxes on the Ouija sales, stating that the boards were scientific instruments, not games, and therefore not taxable. Fuld's battle against the IRS went all the way to the Supreme Court, whose 1920 decision legally categorized Ouija as a game. In 1927 Fuld fell from the roof of the very factory the Ouija had purportedly instructed him to build. Weather accident or suicide, William Fuld's death heightened the macabre tone of the boards and increased sales.

Fuld's children successfully ran the family Ouija business until 1966 when it was sold to Parker Brothers. Parker Brothers moved Ouija production to Salem, Massachusetts, and it immediately began to outsell Monopoly.

Because it has survived the century, the Ouija board is an interesting example of the changing landscape of American toys. During the early part of the century, handmade inventions were shared between individuals. It was common to copy or improve upon the ideas of others. Many ideas that had once belonged to the general public have since become private property. The owner of a toy or game patent often masquerades as its inventor.

The true story of a toy may be lost and its actual origins hidden in tall tales and marketing schemes. Fact or fiction, the stories that endure are often as intriguing as the playthings themselves. The mythology surrounding the toys and games of North America reveals the values and aspirations of its inhabitants. Surprising revelations arise during the study of North American toys. The popularity of the Ouija board, for instance, indicates that Americans may not be as materialistic as they pretend. The success of the game reveals a persistent fascination with the occult that Americans do not often admit.

OUIJA: "IT'S ONLY A GAME—ISN'T IT?"

Although the United States Supreme Court has ruled that the Ouija is a game, there is a surprising sentiment among the North American public that it is not. Many religious groups forbid playing with the Ouija, and some parents will not allow the item inside the home. The Ouija Mystifying Oracle Talking Board of today is a Masonite imitation of William Fuld's 1920 design. Although there is some skepticism of the newer, cheaper, glow-in-the-dark boards, there remains a general consensus that the game "works."

Over the course of a century, the board has been used to attempt to channel everyone from Abraham Lincoln to Houdini. Emily Grant Hutchins claimed to have used the board to transcribe Mark Twain's posthumous novel *Jap Herron* in 1916. During World War II using the Ouija board became popular with women attempting to contact husbands who were fighting overseas. In times of national tragedy, Ouija sales have increased. Individuals having difficulty coping with the loss of a loved one have been known to consult the game.

Although Christians may believe the movement of the planchette is the work of the devil, skeptics say someone else pushes the object. Psychologists often explain that Ouija messages are a product of the subconscious. Scientists have speculated that the nervous energy of participants propels the moving planchette. Despite its reputed power, professional psychics are hesitant to use the board for fear of opening a door to the "dark side."

There is no instruction booklet for the Ouija. There is only one rule that everyone knows: never play alone.

The Ouija board may be the most mis-placed item in Toys "R" Us. Somehow it never seems right to see a device for spirit communication stuffed in between Candyland and the Hungry Hungry Hippos. Despite its dark reputation, however, Ouija has been one of the best-selling games in North America for over a century.

THE EARLY TWENTIETH CENTURY: 1900–40

The following toys are selected from among millions of North American playthings. In addition to being exemplary of the age in which they were created, these toys are commercially successful today. In order to succeed through multiple generations, playthings must stay young. Classic toys are constantly repackaging and renewing themselves. Updates in materials, production methods, packaging, and advertising campaigns keep the same objects selling. As diverse and complex as the population of North America may be, almost everyone has owned a teddy bear.

Toys

In 1902 President Roosevelt had bad luck hunting. In an attempt to preserve his rugged reputation, the presidential staff tied a domestic bear to a tree as an easy target. The president refused to shoot, and the story became well-known in a political cartoon by Clifford Berryman. Upon seeing the drawing, Morris Michtom, a Russian immigrant and Brooklyn shopkeeper, asked his wife, Rose, to sew toy bears that resembled the cub in the cartoon. Morris sent one of the completed bears to President Teddy Roosevelt along with a note requesting permission to name the lovable animals after him. Roosevelt agreed, and Rose Michtom's bears were placed in the shop window with a sign that read "Teddy's Bears." Mania ensued. Despite her seamstress abilities, Rose Michtom could not keep up with the demand for Teddy's Bears. In 1903 the enterprising couple joined with the Butler Brother's wholesalers to establish The Ideal Toy and Novelty Company as the first teddy bear company in the United States.

America's continued fascination with European toys, however, would soon threaten domestic teddy bear production. In 1903 Margarete Steiff introduced a line of plush bears from Germany. Her bears were more realistic than Rose Michtom's, and they had the benefit of movable limbs. When the Steiff bears were released in North America, the patriotic roots of the teddy bear were quickly forgotten. The Steiff name was in demand, and Michtom's sales plummeted. The Michtoms managed to keep their business alive by adapting their bears to mimic the Steiff bear. The attraction of toys from Europe continued to be a problem for domestic toy makers until the onset of World War I.

In the nineteenth century, children played with toys that were made for them by neighbors and members of the family. Mothers sewed dolls and soft animals for their children. Fathers built miniature houses, toy boats, and pull toys. At the dawn of the twentieth century, industrial productivity was high, and children provided the labor necessary for keeping up demand. Playtime and playthings were rare and valuable treats. To the emerging upper class, European toys were symbols of wealth and sophistication. When toys were bought, they generally came from overseas.

Many of the toys that were invented at the beginning of the century exhibited a shift from handmade toys into assembly-line products. The original red wagons were handcarved by Italian immigrant Antonio Pasin in his cabinet shop. As demand for his Liberty Coaster Wagon outgrew his ability to produce, Pasin was drawn to the low cost and high output of stamped steel. In 1927 Pasin replaced his assistant carpenters with assembly-line machines. The metal wagon was given a new name, and soon the Radio Flyer was an international success.

The first Raggedy Ann dolls on the market were handmade by Johnny Gruelle and his wife, Myrtle. They were based on a rag doll their daughter, Marcella, had owned before her untimely death at 13. The couple sewed a candy heart inside each doll, hoping to give other children the love they could no longer give to their own. Johnny, a political cartoonist for the *New York Herald*, wrote stories about the doll and dedicated them to his daughter. Eventually the P. F. Volland publishing group bought the rights to the Gruelles' Raggedy Ann books and oversaw the manufacturing of the Raggedy Ann and Andy dolls. Because the candy was fragile, it could not withstand the assembly line. Volland executives replaced the heart with cardboard. In a relatively short time, the assembly-line items proved as lovable as those handmade items that went before.

Invention: Steam and the Lionel Train

The Age of Invention sparked a new wave of international progress. Delightful products were emerging from America. The telephone, the phonograph, electricity, and the automobile had captured the attention of the entire world. Toys in North America both mimicked and influenced the progression of technology. Model cars were born alongside the automotive industry, replicating and sometimes predicting its changes. Toy airplanes celebrated the successful flight of the Wright brothers in 1903.

Before the advent of television and radio, stores depended on interesting window displays to attract customers. Movement, color, and the latest technology were used to draw shoppers inside. In 1901 Joshua Lionel Cowen introduced shopkeepers to a wooden crate called the Electric Express that moved products around the showcase window on an electric track.

Instead of purchasing the items the Electric Express tried to promote, customers outbid one another for the display items storekeepers were reluctant to sell. Cowen's invention was mesmerizing because it made the new and mystifying power of electricity visible. When Cowen realized the demand for his invention, he quickly replaced what shopkeepers sold from their window displays. The next season Cowen added a steam engine and a trolley car and remarketed his product as the Lionel Train. Within a few years, full railroad sets came equipped with working lights, steaming engines, and heart-stopping sounds.

As the nation grew more urban-minded, so did its toys. Magician and Olympic pole-vaulter A. C. Gilbert marketed the Erector Set in 1913. This steel building toy allowed children to mimic the skyscrapers that were appearing in U.S. cities. John Lloyd Wright patented Lincoln Logs in 1916. His wood beam building toys were modeled after construction materials that his father, Frank Lloyd Wright, was using within the Imperial Hotel, an "earthquake-resistant" tower in Japan. The industrial progress of the United States was captivating, and it was common for children's toys to mimic real-life inventiveness.

World War I: American Dolls

Expensive, beautiful, and sweet turn-of-the-century girls cherished the porcelain dolls that came from Europe. But porcelain is as fragile as little girls' hearts, and in all of New York City there was only one place that could fix both: Maurice Alexander's Doll Hospital.

World War I cut off the European supply that was needed to repair the porcelain dolls. When the existence of the hospital seemed threatened, it was Maurice's daughter Beatrice Alexander who proposed that she and her sisters make new dolls as replacements. No one knew dolls better than Maurice's daughters, and soon they were hiring local tenement women to help keep up with demand. In 1923, less than three years after women in the United States received the right to vote, Beatrice took out a $1600 loan to create the Alexander

Doll Company.[2] Beatrice adopted the name "Madame," and her dolls quickly gained a distinguished reputation. America's first doll hospital was saved.

By the time European dolls returned to the market, they found it difficult to compete with the popularity of the Alexander dolls. In 1933 Madame Alexander released her Alice in Wonderland dolls to coincide with the cinematic release of Lewis Carroll's fairy tale. This move introduced the concept of media tie-ins that would eventually characterize the North American toy industry.

Madame Alexander influenced the media as much as it influenced her. In 1936 she produced a Scarlet O'Hara doll that was the spitting image of Vivian Leigh. Remarkably, it was not until 1939 that the actress was chosen to play the role.

To date, the Alexander Doll Company has produced close to 5000 different dolls and licensed hundreds of media characters that range from Gidget to Queen Elizabeth. Recently, Madame Alexander dolls made a surprise appearance inside McDonald's Happy Meals.

Depression Bingo

During the Depression the toy industry boomed. With more than half of the United States and Canada out of work, there was no choice but to play. Inexpensive games such as bingo and crossword became popular means of escaping boredom and despair. Homemade copies of board games were played regularly.

In 1931 retired Dartmouth professor Frank Austin invented the Austin Ant House as a means for occupying kids who had been pushed out of factory jobs. The bankrupt professor used a wooden frame, two pieces of glass, and a heap of soil to create an observable ant habitat. When he noticed that the busy ants also captivated the imagination of his out-of-work neighbors, Austin began selling the kits as a novelty. Dartmouth University reports that Austin was eventually able to pay local children $4 for a quart of ants. One hundred fifty ants were mailed with each kit.[3]

Monopoly

Monopoly experts agree that the original concept for "America's favorite game" was patented in 1904 as the Landlord's Game by a woman named Elizabeth Maggie. The object of the play, "to obtain the most wealth or money as possible," was to illustrate the evils of price gouging and monopolistic ventures. Instead, it became practice for establishing them.

Students at the top business schools such as Wharton and Yale began playing the Landlord's Game on homemade boards. Although Maggie approached Parker Brothers several times for publication, she was consistently rejected. The popularity of her game, however, continued to spread across the continent.

Ruth Haskins, a teacher at the Quaker Friends School, made a simpler version of the Landlord's Game for her students to play. In so doing, she renamed the properties according to the local Atlantic City streets.

Charles Darrow, an out-of-work plumber, was introduced to the Atlantic City version of the Landlord's Game in 1932. Darrow redrew the board and began selling copies of it in Philadelphia department stores. Meanwhile, he shopped the game to Parker Brothers and Milton Bradley. Both publishers initially rejected Monopoly on the grounds that it took too long to play. What the game executives failed to realize, however, is that during the Depression, people were desperate for ways to spend their time. When Parker Brothers finally published the game in 1935, Monopoly sold 1.8 million copies and Darrow's progression from rags to riches became legendary.[4]

Although it is generally agreed that Darrow stole the Monopoly concept, he can be credited with giving the game its unique look. The lightbulb, the train, and the jailbird make Monopoly unforgettable. Darrow's creation Rich Uncle Pennybags (now Mr. Monopoly) is one of the most widely licensed characters in the States.

Presently there is an edition of the game to suit every interest. There is a Dale Earnhardt Monopoly, a Napa Valley Monopoly, and just about every Monopoly in between. A large number of North American universities have their own version of Monopoly, as do most cities. In its constant revisions, street names are altered and the board is given a slightly new look.

Monopoly has been published in twenty-seven languages, including Braille, and 200 million sets have been sold worldwide. When Castro gained power 1959, he vehemently destroyed all Monopoly sets in Cuba. The same year in Moscow, all six sets on display at the American National Exhibition vanished.[5] With its play money, expensive real estate, and cold business practices, it is obvious: Monopoly is the official game of capitalism.

Leisure Pursuits for Children and Adults

Comic Book Heroes

DC Comics introduced their first picture books in 1934 when the continent was increasingly unemployed and disillusioned. The easy-to-read, easy-to-share, and easy-to-enjoy comics gave Americans a constantly updated escape from their increasingly difficult lives.

Superman first appeared in 1938 in DC's *Action Comics #1*. Toronto's Joe Schuster drew the Superman cartoons while Cleveland's Jerry Siegel wrote the script. Together they proved the strength of a unified Canada and America. Upon the birth of the superhero, North Americans shifted from playing with reality—cars, skyscrapers—into a world of fantasy—kryptonite, golden lassos. Superhero culture continues to thrive in the Americas. Batman, Wonder Woman, and the entire League of Justice are recognized by the youngest children and remembered by the oldest adults.

Radio in the 1930s and 1940s

Through the new technology of the radio, people in the 1930s tuned into quiz shows and other on-air contests. Vacation packages were awarded by the broadcast media to the "real-life" contestants who participated in the live games. The concept of reality programming attracted listeners who hoped to win a way out of their desperate situations. Many early radio programs such as *Information Please* and *Professor Quiz* distributed game booklets such that listeners could play in conjunction with the broadcast. In 1938 Milton Bradley released a board game version of the popular radio program *Paul Wing's Spelling Bee*. Throughout the 1940s NBC marketed a slew of products related to the *Quiz Kids* show.

The *Little Orphan Annie Radio Show* invited children to send away for decoder pens that could help them interpret cryptic messages read during the program. A beverage called Ovaltine sponsored the Orphan Annie show, and to get the pens, children sent in proofs of purchase from the chocolate-flavored product. The 1983 classic movie *A Christmas Story* immortalizes the excitement with which American children anticipated the arrival of their Little Orphan Annie Decoder Pin.

WORLD WAR II

Eventually, the continent made its way out of the Depression and into the conflict overseas. Canada entered World War II in 1939 in defense of Great Britain. The United States remained neutral until the 1941 attack on Pearl Harbor. During the war, domestic productivity increased for both countries. The toy industry exploded, and the invention of plastic gave manufacturers the ability to make toys that were both inexpensive and realistic.

During the war the United States government sought a synthetic rubber that could be used to manufacture military items such as tires, boots, and grenades. James Wright was a chemical engineer working on the project for General Electric. When Wright mixed boric acid with silicone oil, it appeared as if he had accomplished his goal. The compound looked, felt, and bounced like rubber. To Wright's dismay, it also broke easily and had a tendency to melt. GE scientists spent the next five years researching practical applications for the product. Ultimately, they concluded it was useless.

In 1949 an unemployed Canadian by the name of Peter Hodgson attended a party at the house of a GE executive. During the course of the evening, Wright's chemical reaction was demonstrated by the host. Hodgson was thrilled with the resulting compound and soon convinced his shop-owner friend Ruth Fallgatther to sell it in her toy store. The putty did not succeed as they had expected, and Fallgatther eventually dropped the product. The chicken, or in this case the putty, actually did come first. The following Easter, Hodgson had the idea to package the product within a plastic egg. The whimsical idea stuck and the product was renamed Silly Putty. It has sold remarkably well ever since.

Somewhere near the Boundary Waters of Minnesota, Herb Sharper got the Cooties. As if possessed, Sharper began whittling bug-like fishing lures. In 1948 the first official year of Cootie production, Sharper is said to have carved 40,000 bugs by hand. Catching more children than fish, Sharper decided to sell his creations as toys. The following year Herb was introduced to plastic casting techniques and soon the W. H. Sharper Toy Company began infesting the world—first Cooties, then Tickle Bees, Thumbugs, and Ants in the Pants.

Toys are often the accidental inventions of scientists. Richard James, a nautical engineer, was building a navigational system that would maintain its balance on rough seas when he knocked a coil spring off his workbench. When he showed his wife how the spring miraculously stepped down to the floor, she named it *Slinky*. Together in 1945 the couple introduced the Slinky at Gimbel's department store in Philadelphia. The toys sold out in an hour, making the Slinky an immediate success. With a lucky idea and a good name, Richard and Betty James, the hardworking middle-class couple, became superstars of the American dream.

The technologies of one age become the toys of another. In the days of coal heating, soot was removed from the walls by stamping it with a tacky bread-like product called Kutol. The invention of radiators eliminated the need for wallpaper cleaner. Joseph McVicker, proprietor of the family business Kutol, was nearly bankrupt when his daughter-in-law Kay Zufall read in a teacher's magazine that making Christmas ornaments out of wallpaper cleaner was a good craft activity for kids. She repackaged Kutol and saved the family business. Since 1955 children all over the continent have become familiar with the salty taste and unique smell of Play-Doh.

THE FALLOUT ERA: 1945–60S

Upon the surrender of Hitler in May of 1945, America and Canada were enjoying the respect of the entire world. The flag-waving euphoria lasted just 2 months. In July of the same year, the United States defeated Japan in two gruesome blasts of light caused by bombs with toylike names. Little Boy, Fat Man, and the threat of further nuclear war sent America into a paranoid fit. The children of the nuclear age began doing strange things, such as cramming telephone booths and throwing Frisbee pie tins. Hula Hoop, Slinky, Magic 8 Ball, and Mr. Potato Head are the fallout of science and suburbia.

Norm Stingley was the chief chemist for the Bettis Rubber Company when he was given a compound that executives were hoping to develop for use in the oil industry. Instead, Stingley was fascinated by the way the new polymer bounced. By pouring the compound into a round mold, Stingley produced the world's first Superball. The original ball was compressed at 2,500 pounds per square inch, which made it highly unstable. Certain bounces would cause the ball to explode into tiny pieces. It took Stingley and Wham-O product developer Ed Hedrick months in the laboratory to render the Superball indestructible.

Harold von Braunhut first sold Sea-Monkeys as a mail-order item in the back of comic books. The original kit included an aquarium, a "purifier package," and an "instant egg package." Combining the contents of the two packages in the aquarium full of water magically brought creatures to life. Scientifically speaking, the toy reanimates *Artemia salina*, a species of brine shrimp that becomes dormant in dry conditions. In order to extend the life span of the toy, the New York Ocean Sciences created a brine shrimp hybrid called *Artemia NYOS*.[6] The Transcience Toy Company presently guarantees the life of the Sea-Monkeys for 2 years.

Toys from TV

Unlike the Mr. Potato Heads produced today, George Lerner's 1948 "Funny Face Man" did not include a plastic potato. Instead, it provided plastic facial features that kids could push into any fruit or fresh vegetable. Adults who recently had been subject to food shortages during the Depression and rationing during World War II objected to Mr. Potato Head on the grounds that it taught children to be wasteful and play with their food. The toy survived the criticism to become a national favorite. In 1952 Mr. Potato Head became the first toy to have his own television spot. Sales skyrocketed, and the marketing of toys was changed forever.

By the time television was introduced to American households, children and adults had well-established habits of purchasing items directly related to broadcast programming. The Disneyland Game was released in conjunction with the Mickey Mouse Club in 1955. It is considered the first TV tie-in game.

Miniature versions of Roy Rogers and his horse Nellybell were released by Ideal in 1956. These plastic figures started a tradition of toy production that allowed North American children to play along with their favorite television shows. The success of the TV-inspired line was perpetuated through a bandwagon of toy companies that began producing plastic versions of prime time's favorite characters.

Science and Toys

After working at Los Alamos on the development of the atomic bomb, physicist Willy Higinbotham began research at the Brookhaven National Laboratory, a nuclear facility on Long Island. To calm the nerves of residents who lived near Brookhaven, scientists invited locals to open house events. Hoping to "liven up the place" for these events,[7] Higinbotham and his colleagues invented a game using a piece of laboratory equipment called an oscilloscope.

The game was called Tennis for Two, and the simple graphics resembled a side view of a tennis court. Players operated paddle controllers to angle their shot and pushed a red button

UGLY TOYS AND DEROGATORY IMAGES

Many toys created throughout the early portion of the twentieth century are now considered derogatory toward African Americans. It is still common to find examples of "darkie" toys in U.S. antique stores. The toys created racial stereotypes by exaggerating the physical features of darker-skinned Americans and diminishing their intellectual capacities. Characters such as "Sambo" and "Mammy" were so common that white adults rarely questioned the implications such toys would have on the perceptions of their children.

At one time it was not unusual for American businesses to place lifelike black dolls in their window displays. The "darkie" toys were meant to be fun, friendly, and welcoming to customers. Today they are considered racist, dehumanizing, and obscene. Little Black Sambo is a character that belongs to this time in history. For many contemporary adult Americans it is impossible to look at the Sambo toys in a fun way. Still, these items have a strong resale market. Certain collectors appreciate the financial value of these out-of-production items. Other Americans believe that the racist toys should be destroyed. They feel that the display of such items perpetuates the racism that is implicit within them.

David Pilgrim is the curator of the Jim Crow Museum of Racist Memorabilia at Ferris State University. He is among those who believe these toys should remain in the public eye. He has collected 4,000-plus derogatory pieces for his museum. "I collect this garbage," Pilgrim says, "because I believe and I know to be true that items of intolerance can be used to teach tolerance."[8] Whatever their fate, it is hoped that the knowledge of these ugly dolls from the past will help future generations avoid history's mistakes.

on the handset to hit the digital ball. Though it sounds rudimentary today, the game attracted large crowds to the Brookhaven open houses, and they waited hours for the opportunity to play. Invented in 1958, Tennis for Two is considered the world's first video game.

Barbie

When a day at the lab was over, men returned to well-kept suburban wives who had prepared dinner, cleaned house, and slipped into a pair of stockings to welcome their husbands home. Women of the 1950s were expected to take care of the home and children. They typically sacrificed professional ambition in support of men who pursued cutthroat careers. From this unlikely environment emerged the most powerful woman in the North American toy industry.

Ruth Handler was on vacation in Europe when she spotted an erotic toy that the German men called Lilli. Lillis were small but voluptuous dolls that were sold in tobacco shops and given as sexy presents at bachelor parties. Although the toys were intended for an adult male audience, Handler bought several Lillis to give to her daughter Barbara. After observing her little girl's enjoyment of the doll, the Handlers' toy company Mattel contacted the German company Weissbrodt/Hausser to acquire rights to the Lilli. Remodeled and renamed, Barbie made her dramatic debut at the International Toy Fair in New York in 1959.

Unlike the prim and proper Madame Alexander dolls, Barbie was shapely and scantily clad. In contrast to the historical baby doll, Barbie's physique was that of a well-developed woman. Instead of nurturing Barbie, young girls tended to idolize her.

Today, Barbie is a rock star and an astronaut. She is a soldier and a model. She can be a politician or a McDonald's employee. Whatever her job, she can hardly move. Barbie's joints have minimal flexibility in order to preserve the shapeliness of her arms and impossible legs.

Exaggerated sexuality and an unattainable physique make Barbie dolls questionable role models for little girls. Parents and feminists agree that Barbie may be responsible for body image problems in young girls. In a 1977 interview with the *New York Times*, Handler stated her opinion that Barbie's voluptuousness would improve the self-esteem of girls anticipating the development of breasts. In 1975, sixteen years after the debut of Barbie, Handler introduced her newest product, the "Nearly Me" prosthetic breast implants.

G.I. Joe

1. Dolls are for girls.
2. G.I. Joe is not a doll.

Hoping to imitate Mattel's success with Barbie, Hasbro began shaping a similar item for boys in 1964. Hasbro coined the term "action figure" for G.I. Joe and subsequently established a new genre of playthings. The G.I. Joe character had originally been developed for a cartoon in a military newspaper during World War II, "G.I." standing for "**G**overnment **I**ssue," which was ubiquitously stamped on military equipment in World War II.

Joe represents the ultimate American soldier. He is in the Army, Navy, Air Force, and Marines. He is every race and any background. His face, hair, and outfit change, but his fearless strength remains the same. Like Barbie, G.I. Joe is sold inexpensively, but his accessories—assault vehicles and ninja hovercycles—are not.

G.I. Joe action figures do well when public support for the military is high. When Americans grow weary of the conflict, G.I. Joe sales plummet. During the later years of the war in Vietnam, Hasbro saved G.I. Joe's career by pulling him out of the jungle and sending him into outer space.

COUNTERCULTURE: 1960s–70s

Mattel introduced Christie and Brad, the first American fashion dolls with dark skin and ethnic features, in 1968. In the same year the Miss Black America Pageant and a network of local contests such as Miss Black Alabama were created for women who were not permitted in the Caucasian pageants.

Twister was released just one year prior to the legalization of the Pill. Denounced by competitors as "sex in a box," Twister became a popular party game when Johnny Carson played against the sultry Eva Gabor on a 1966 episode of the *Tonight Show*. That year Milton Bradley sold 3 million copies of Twister and established a new connection between the game industry and late-night television.

Wild-eyed and naked, Troll Dolls became popular in the mid-1960s. Thomas Dam's Trolls were friendly and magical creatures in a world of increasing conflict. Honest and unaggressive, the Trolls' nudity, free love, and wild hair predicted the emergence of hippie culture.

Games

TV Game Shows

Game shows were extremely popular in the early 1970s. Hosted by Bob Barker, *The Price Is Right* asked contestants to guess retail prices of prizes and products through a series of games. (An earlier version of the TV show had begun in 1956 and continued until 1965, hosted by Bill Cullen. Barker began hosting the show in 1972.) Blinking lights and velvet curtains set the stage for America's hopeful public to take a shot at winning new cars and exotic travel vacations. Women hosting the show became known as "Barker's Beauties" and ranged from Playboy models to Miss America winners. Bob Barker's "Come on down!" is a phrase that has become immortalized in popular culture and now, more than 30 years later, Bob Barker has announced his retirement. With dreamy someday desire, people still enjoy a television game show that reflects America's obsession with fame and fortune.

Chuck Barris, another famous game show host, introduced reality TV in the 1970s. *The Dating Game, The Gong Show,* and *The Newlywed Game* were three of the most popular television game shows during the late 1970s and early 1980s. These games played on Americans' desire for fame. Before becoming celebrities, Suzanne Sommers, Arnold Schwarzenegger, and Paul Rubens, the future Pee-Wee Herman, appeared as contestants on Chuck Barris's unusual game shows.

Although Barris's shows developed a reputation for being tacky and crass, the current reality TV game shows are far more brutal in comparison. People eat cockroaches and sit in tanks of leeches on NBC's *Fear Factor.* Contestants face grueling challenges and "tribes" play for blood on CBS's *Survivor.* In the newest television reality games, sportsmanship is often thrown out the window and players are sometimes voted out of the game by the "disapproval voting" of other contestants.

1980s–90s

Video Games

Ralph Baer developed "the Brown Box"—a prototype for the first home video game console, the Odyssey—while working for the military contractor Saunders Associates. In 1972 he convinced Magnavox to manufacture the product, promising it would help sell television sets. Although it was a commercial flop, the Magnavox Odyssey opened the doors to home video gaming.

PONG was introduced in November of 1972. Available as home consoles and coin-operated machines, PONG is considered the first commercially successful video game. Atari's Nolan Bushnell and Al Alcorn developed the digital game as an update of Higinbotham's Tennis for Two.

In the 1970s and early 1980s electronic gaming centers sprang up in shopping malls, bowling alleys, and movie theaters. The arcade provided both a place to escape and a place to be seen. Amid blinking lights and electronic sounds. coin-operated games that had been popular since the 1930s penny arcade, such as pinball and skee ball, were now played alongside highly technical, quarter-driven machines. America's pinball youth quickly mastered the terms and maneuvers of slam tilt, slingshot, and slap save while video gamers faced their screened challenges with joysticks and guns in either cockpit (sit-in), cocktail (sit-down), or cabaret (stand-at) formats.

At some point during the Age of the Arcade, video gaming establishments developed a seedy reputation. Nightly news reported drug use and violent behavior among teens at the arcade.

The Atari 2600 brought the video arcade safely home. The console operated plug-in software cartridges that allowed owners to constantly update their video library. Breakout, Donkey Kong, Pole Position, Space Invaders, Pac-Man, and hundreds of other games were developed for the Atari. Competitive systems such as Mattel Intellivision and ColecoVision forced Atari to upgrade. The 5200, however, could not save the company from the 1983 video game crash. The oversaturated video game market and the proliferation of the personal computer ruined U.S. console manufacturers.

IBM, Texas Instruments, Apple, and Atari had been competing with one another for dominance in the personal computer market when the Commodore 64 became the best-selling personal computer in the world. For one low cost, the C64 was both a personal computer and a home gaming system. As the gaming possibilities of the home computer improved, it was speculated that the video game industry would never recover.

The Japanese company Nintendo found opportunity amid the bankruptcy of Silicon Valley. During the mid-1980s the NES became the dominant console on the market. In 1989 Nintendo updated America's landscape with the introduction of the Game Boy. Suddenly boys were seen playing video games in some of the most remote, most irritating places, from deserts to dinner tables.

In the mid-1990s Sony developed the Playstation, a line of console and handheld gaming devices that proved wildly successful. The Playstation stepped into the third dimension and ushered in a new era of gaming that was more realistic and more popular than ever.

Microsoft, the world's largest software company, introduced the Xbox in 2001 in an attempt to diversify their product line. Enhanced graphics, a wide variety of games, and the addition of nongaming features such as a CD/DVD player made the Xbox the new standard in home equipment. In 2002 subscriptions to Xbox Live were made available to allow competition between international players via the Internet.

Alternatives to Video Games

Trivial Pursuit

As if in protest to the isolating world of cable TV and video games, there was a sudden resurgence in parlor games across North America in the 1980s. Tests of knowledge, which had been popular diversions in the Victorian era, became favorites again. Scott Abbott, an editor for the *Canadian Press*, and Chris Haney, a photo editor at the *Montreal Gazette*, invented Trivial Pursuit in 1979. The self-proclaimed "revolt against television,"[9] Trivial Pursuit sold 20 million copies in the year of its United States release. To date, there have been innumerable versions of the game produced: Trivial Pursuit Kids, Trivial Pursuit Book Lovers, Trivial Pursuit Star Wars, and so on. Hasbro acquired Trivial Pursuit in 1992, and contrary to the intentions of its inventors, the latest versions of Trivial Pursuit come with a supplemental DVD/TV version of the game.

Dungeons & Dragons

Gary Gygax and Dave Anderson introduced the role-playing game Dungeons and Dragons in 1974. The tabletop war game combined skill, chance, and character development to become fantastically popular among teenage boys in the 1980s. Parental advisory panels were alarmed by the amount of time adolescents were spending on the game. The supposed threat of D&D seems strangely laughable when compared with today's violent video games; still, conservative churches warn against playing a role-playing game that is ruled by dragons, goblins, and dungeon masters.

Role-playing became popular with a wider public in the late 1990s in the form of Murder Mystery parties, board games, and interactive theater. In 2000 role-playing also proved successful among video gamers. The hack-and-slash game Diablo II sold more than a million copies in two weeks to become the fastest-selling PC game ever.[10] Recently, online role-playing games such as Second Life have attracted thousands of users. In these online communities, users create characters that interact with one another in a digital arena that bears a striking resemblance to the real world.

Collection vs. Craze, Mid-1980s to Mid-1990s

Among the most memorable Christmas scenes from the 1980s were televised fistfights between mothers vying for plastic-headed baby dolls. No two Cabbage Patch Kids were alike, and each one came with a birth certificate and adoption papers. Xavier Roberts credits a "magical cabbage patch hidden behind a beautiful waterfall" with the creation of the Cabbage Patch Kids.[11] In reality, Roger Schlaifer, an advertising expert from Atlanta, had a lot to do with it. Schlaifer connected Roberts, a craftsman from rural Georgia, with Coleco, a New England manufacturing company that was nearly bankrupt after the failure of its home video game console ColecoVision. Each Cabbage Patch Kid was loved for its unique qualities, and it was Coleco's high-tech capabilities that made the mass production of individuality possible. Random computer applications changed hair and eye color, dimple and freckle location, name, and style of clothes.

The Cabbage Patch phenomenon reminded North American toy companies that the most sought-after audience may not be children at all. The most loyal, reliable, and affluent toy consumers, it turns out, are adult collectors. In 1996 the Beanie Baby craze struck the American continent. Failed actor but savvy businessman Ty Warner created an air of exclusivity about his dolls by introducing them in limited quantities. He sold them at boutiques instead of department stores. As a result, millions of Americans became convinced the dolls would become valuable over time. Buying and selling Beanie Babies became as serious as trading stocks. The value of the toys, however, never did yield the return some had expected. With or without the heart-shaped tag intact, very few Beanie Babies have gained on the dollar. Ten years after the peak of the craze, Ty Warner is among the wealthiest men in the world and millions of American attics contain large plastic trash bags filled with small bean-filled dolls.

TWENTY-FIRST CENTURY

Today the shelves of every Toys "R" Us, Wal-Mart, and online warehouse are swelling with bright shiny boxes containing the latest and greatest toys, games, and hobby kits. There are toys and games of virtually every conceivable sort, and they are suitable for just about everyone—fast-moving dice games and slow strategic board games. There are toys to cuddle and toys to throw.

Toys, games, and action figures have been developed to commemorate all aspects of American popular culture, from athletics to political campaigns. These historically significant items are important to collectors.

During his presidency, George W. Bush inspired a boom in business of political toys. "From bobbleheads to talking action figures" said D. Parvaz in the *Seattle Post*, "he's well on his way to becoming one of the most action-figured presidents ever."[12] Bush dolls sell well to Americans on both ends of the political spectrum. Whether in celebration or mockery, the ability to have fun with politics is a fundamental American right that is protected in the United States by the Constitution. North Americans cherish their right to poke fun at national leaders and employ it frequently.

As media continues to infiltrate the play-time of American families, licensing becomes increasingly important for toy companies. By stamping media-related logos and characters upon products, the toy manufactures allow Hollywood to do their advertising for them. When new games are developed, the industry finds they are magically successful with a media tie-in. *The Desperate Housewives* board game and the Britney Spears doll were best sellers. The endurance of a television show or a licensed character promises toy companies an extended financial success. Instead of sitting on the forefront of ingenuity, the toy companies seem to follow lazily on the coattails of culture.

The Internet and high-speed connections have made World Wide Web developer Tim Berners-Lee the most important toy inventor in the world. North American children and adults of all ages, sexes, and backgrounds spend a portion of the day playing games on the computer. Every memorable game of the past from Rubik's Cube to PONG has been rescripted in HTML and posted on the Net. Sites such as gprime.net allow users to publish and play homemade video games. Despite the growing influence of the Internet in American life, it is not yet common to model toys after Websites. The most popular toys do have their Web pages and online fan clubs. G.I. Joe's homepage looks like a war-based video game, and Barbie's Website resembles a MySpace profile.

The popularity of computer and video games, as well as electronic toys, has been increasing steadily ever since the 1983 drop-off. Electronic games are aimed at both sexes and at all age groups. Today's electronic toys can roar, sniff, and bite; they can walk, run, and hunt. Some of them, if left alone long enough, will roam freely. Popular electronic toys such as I-Dogs are marketed with personalities that change with the music. Hasbro's interactive musical companions "groove to the beat of your iPod" and act out emotions ranging from joy to loneliness. Neo-Pets are another variety of robotic animal that sing, obey commands, and communicate with one another.

GAME THEORY

Prior to being immortalized by the 2001 Ron Howard film *A Beautiful Mind*, Princeton University mathematics professor John Nash and his colleagues John Harsanyi and Reinhard Selten won the 1994 Nobel Prize in Economics for their work in game theory. The theory suggests that all human behavior from science to sexuality can be understood in terms of game playing. According to this idea, humans are in constant competition with one another. Decisions to gain points (money, love, etc.) are made by one individual in response to the moves of others. In the game of life, players develop strategies, make alliances, and abandon territories in order to secure the greatest payoff. Game theory began as an economic application, but it is now used to describe behavioral patterns in sociology, political science, and biology.

Games

The North American mind is a storehouse of games. Collective games are the subconscious material that weaves society together. There are games for special occasions such as weddings and birthdays. There are games for specific places such as the beaches or roller rinks.

The rules to these games are deeply embedded within the psyche, where they can survive for years untouched. When the occasion arises, the rules are remembered and the play begins again. Collective games teach strategy, teamwork, and conflict resolution. Through games we express emotions and develop personalities.

Hopscotch and hangman are among the hundreds of games the entire continent knows how to play. Where did games such as tic-tac-toe and Simon Says come from? Televisions, activity books, and cereal boxes teach games. So do parents, friends, and circus performers. New games are acquired in social clubs, campgrounds, schools, gymnasiums, playgrounds, and casinos. In short, games are everywhere. Once a game is learned, it is difficult to forget. Even the most stern-looking individual is a treasury of games, and the attempt to catalog the games within the collective memory would be a lifetime endeavor. The following examples are but a few of the games North Americans instinctively know.

"Kingdom"

In the United States, wishes are made on dandelions as the seeds are blown into the air. Children play with sunlight using mirrors, watches, and magnifying glasses. They make friends with little creatures such as caterpillars, roly-polies, and lightning bugs. In the winter American children build snowmen and have snowball fights. At the beach everyone collects seashells and makes sandcastles. Children live in the world of play, and everything around them is a toy. From babies to bumblebees, children learn that something is not a plaything only when it hurts or becomes boring. Using found materials, children build clubhouses and forts. These become the center of their imaginary kingdom.

"House"

The game of life is consistent throughout human society. As if by instinct, boys and girls mimic the actions of the adults around them. In the playful world of American children, even the greatest dreams are possible. Some children pretend to be movie stars, whereas others fly airplanes. Becoming imaginary adults is a favorite activity whereby children first express career ambition. While young comedians often make up routines for their families, young accountants may be found playing games with calculators and pretend money. Pantomiming adults allows children to experiment with a variety of personalities as they develop their own.

In North America boys are given plastic versions of saws and other hand tools for playthings. Girls are still likely to receive pretend vacuum cleaners and Betty Crocker Easy-Bake Ovens. It is common for young boys and girls to pretend to be married in the ever-popular activity of "playing house." Boys generally shy away from the game as they learn from other boys that playing house is for girls. Girls may continue playing at domesticity in later childhood years, whereas older boys turn to action games such as Cops and Robbers.

School Games

Children are adept at finding new uses for school supplies. While elementary school girls make paper fortune-tellers, boys make paper footballs. Competitive in-school sports include Pencil Wars and paper clip bouncing. Paper airplanes are still common in classrooms, as are spitballs.

In most elementary schools children are given a recess. During this time, the children are allowed to play freely in the schoolyard. Most adult Americans would confess that they did most of their learning during the recess hours. On the schoolyard, younger children play group games such as Red Rover, London Bridge, ring-around-the-rosy, and Simon Says.

Simon Says is a game where one child is Simon. The players must do what Simon says, but only if the phrase "Simon says" is used.

Older boys and girls play against one another in Four Square, keep-away, and dodgeball. Although these games are exceptionally competitive during recess, they are not taken seriously beyond the schoolyard. Many games are learned during physical education classes, and schools have designated field days where children compete for awards in the sack race, the three-legged race, the tug-of-war, and various egg-carrying contests.

It is common for elementary schools and churches to host weekend festivals. At these community events, old-fashioned carnival games are revived. Silent auctions, cakewalks, and dunking booths are standard features at these events. Bobbing for apples is a game in which a washtub is filled with water and loose apples. The apples float, and the player's arms are tied behind his or her back. The player then kneels in an attempt to capture an apple with the teeth.

Hand Wrestling Games

The negotiation game Rock, Paper, Scissors is often used to solve friendly disputes in North American society. In this game, contestants make fists with one hand. The players then pound their fists on the opposite palm while counting "one," "two," "three," and on "four" the players make their hand into one of three shapes: rock, paper, or scissors. Rock smashes scissors. Scissors cut paper. Paper covers rock.

Thumb war is a more physical form of hand wrestling. Players grasp hands such that their thumbs are in the air. On the count of "one, two, three, four . . . I declare a thumb war," opponents try to capture the other player's thumb and hold it down for the count of three.

Travel Games

Several games have developed in relationship to the American road. Punch Bug is a classic. This game is played while driving or riding in a car. The players are constantly looking for a Volkswagen Bug. The player who first spots the automobile gets points by calling out "punch bug" or "buggy." He or she then punches another player in the arm.

In the License Plate Game, players seek examples of car tags from other states and provinces. The player who has spotted the most distant location wins. The Alphabet Game, Mad-Libs, and Battleship are among the many popular games for the car. Games to play on airplanes remain virtually unknown.

Holiday Games

At Easter there are Easter egg hunts. On Halloween there are pumpkin carving and costume contests. At Christmas there is a game requiring lovers to kiss beneath the mistletoe. Wishing on a blazing cake is one of America's most anticipated games, and birthday candles extinguished in a single breath fulfill any dream.

At birthday parties, young children often play Pin the Tail on the Donkey. In this game, a large image of a tailless donkey is posted on the wall. The birthday child is the first to be blindfolded and handed a tail. After being spun in a circle several times, the child is pointed at the donkey, which is several steps away. Dizzy and blind, the child walks toward the animal and tries to attach the tail in the proper position. Each child at the party is given a turn, and the one who puts the tail in the most appropriate position wins.

At birthday parties for older children, papier-mâché piñata's are common. In this game the birthday child is blindfolded, spun in circles, given a bat, and asked to hit the hanging piñata. When the bat finds the piñata, candy and toys explode throughout the room. Despite Mexico's proximity to the United States, piñata is one of the few Mexican games that are played in the English-speaking Americas.

Adolescent Games

Adolescents play flirtatious games such as spin the bottle and Seven Minutes in Heaven. Many American children receive their first kiss while playing one of these two games. To play spin the bottle nervous youngsters sit in a circle around an empty wine bottle that is turned on its side. Players take turns spinning the bottle and kissing the person it lands on. The player can spin again if the bottle points to a person of the same gender.

Seven Minutes in Heaven is a riskier adolescent game than spin the bottle. In the game, couples are selected randomly and locked in a dark closet for a specified amount of time, 7 minutes being the maximum. During this time, the pair is expected to kiss and touch. For many young American teenagers, this game is their first experience with physical intimacy.

Truth or Dare is another game popular among adolescents. The game starts with the question "Truth or dare?" If the respondent says, "Truth," he or she has to answer a personal question; if the respondent says, "Dare," he or she must accept a challenge of a more physical nature. After the player gives the truth or accomplishes the dare, he or she restarts the game by asking, "Truth or dare?"

Grown-up Games

Whatever bizarre situations teenagers find themselves in during sessions of Truth or Dare, none are as humiliating as seeing their parents doing the Hokey Pokey. Like the Macarena, this participatory song asks listeners to play along. Although teenagers know the Hokey Pokey dance, most will refuse to participate. Meanwhile, baby boomers, wedding planners, and roller skaters seem to think the Hokey Pokey *is* "what it's all about."

Drinking Games

Pool and darts are games descended from European pubs that are frequently played in American bars. Foosball, karaoke, and trivia contests are also popular in North American drinking establishments. Games that involve alcohol are common among college age adults. Quarters is the most popular of these. In this game coins—usually quarters—are bounced off the table into a shot glass. If the coin does not land in the glass, the player must have a drink. Players become inebriated quickly.

Shotgunning beers is a drinking race popular with young adults. Beer funneling and keg stands are among the more dangerous drinking games. These are generally played by young men, although young women often participate. Such games are regularly played at fraternity parties where the amount of alcohol a person can consume is considered a sign of strength.

With thousands of alcohol-related deaths in the United States and Canada every year, these games are among the most deadly played in North America today.

Wedding Games

At a wedding shower the engaged couple is required to play a homespun version of *The New Newlywed Game*. The pair is separated and asked a series of questions designed to show how well acquainted they are with one another. The woman is asked a different set of questions than her husband. The answers are recorded on paper, and the couple is brought together in front of the party. The questions are asked a second time. This time the man answers the questions his fiancée was asked previously and vice versa. The couple is given points when the answers match. The crowd playfully chides them into arguments when they do not.

Immediately following the wedding, the bride turns her back and tosses her bouquet to a crowd of assembled single women. She who catches the bouquet is said to be the next bride. The bride and groom then play a game of stuffing wedding cake into one another's mouths. Finally, the groom removes a garter belt from his new wife's leg and throws it to an assembly of single men. The fellow to catch the garter, likewise, will be the next to catch a wife.

Gambling Games

After periods of significant prohibition, casino gambling is now legal in twenty-seven of the fifty United States and in all eleven of the Canadian provinces. According to the World Casino Directory, there are just over one hundred legal gaming establishments in Canada. Meanwhile, the United States has nearly fifteen hundred! The Foxwoods Resort Casino in Connecticut is the largest casino on the continent. Even when prohibited by state law, legal gambling takes place on extravagant riverboats and Native American reservations. Millions of dollars are annually won and lost on the roulette wheel and in the slot machines. Bets on cards are made at blackjack and poker tables. Keno is also a popular casino game. In the 1960s millionaire Howard Hughes had the idea to plant a strip of casinos in the arid Nevada desert. The seductive landscape of Las Vegas has since become the gaming capital of the world.

At homes throughout the continent, dice games and card games are played in competitions for money between friends. North Americans frequently bet on sports. Lottery games are played with scratch cards and pull tabs that are purchased at convenience stores. Lotto and Powerball winners are announced nightly on TV.

Poker is America's card game. Although the precise history of poker is unclear, most credit the smoky saloons of the American frontier with its development. For over a century, poker has been the most popular card game on the continent. It comes in hundreds of variations, from lowball to Texas hold 'em. The play consists of assessing property, speculating on the actions of others, knowing how much to invest, and understanding when to fold. Poker teaches its players that to win, it is necessary to risk. The game illustrates the benefits of cooperation and the value of competition. Most importantly, however, poker teaches the difference between bluffing and lying.

The antique game of poker has adapted with the technological revolution. Although most high-stakes tournaments are still played with cards, large amounts of real money are won and lost through computerized competitions. Poker faces are no longer obligatory as online and cellular phone tournaments allow players to compete internationally from the privacy of their own homes.

HOBBIES AND PASTIMES

all work and no play makes jack a dull boy all work and no play makes jack a dull boy all work and no play makes jack a dull boy all work and no play makes jack a dull boy all work and no play makes jack a dull boy all work and no play makes jack a dull boy all work and no play makes jack a dull boy

—Jack Nicholson as Jack Torrance in Stanley Kubrick's *The Shining*

In the 1950s many treatises were written to encourage the development of hobbies. The cultivation of interests, it was said, would produce a happy individual and a healthy nation. The proliferation of television, however, drew time and attention away from the improvement of personal talents. This trend has continued steadily as media has become increasingly prevalent in the American landscape. Certain television programs such as *This Old House*, *The Joy of Painting*, and *Monster Garage* are marketed as instructional programming for hobbyists, but they are most often viewed as pure entertainment. With the exception of cooking shows, Americans rarely put the skills they have learned from TV into practical use.

The Internet, on the other hand, has proven infinitely useful to the hobbyist. Cyber clubs and chat rooms allow the people in North America the opportunity to connect with people of similar interest around the world. Virtually every passion can be enhanced by information on the World Wide Web. With the increasing availability of personal computers and high-speed connections, information, ideas, and a general sense of camaraderie are now shared instantaneously among international communities of aficionados.

In the infancy of the twenty-first century, technological hobbies have reached a level of popularity that few science fiction writers could have imagined. Podcasting and the creation of personal Websites have become prevalent activities among a diverse population. Opposing opinions are frequently posted upon the Internet. The polarity of Web users and programmers reached substantial proportions during the 2004 presidential election in the United States. Despite their position on the political spectrum, voters were united in the activity of attaining and adding to information on the Net.

In the United States and Canada there are relatively few hobbies that are gender-specific. Men and women are free to participate in any activity that is of interest. Still, a division persists; certain activities are more appealing to men, whereas others are more interesting to women. Hobbies reflect the physical location and financial status of a person. Regional variation in North American hobbies depends more on climate than it does on cultural heritage. In colder areas activities such as ice fishing, sledding, and snowmobiling are popular. In warmer climates people enjoy swimming, hiking, and miniature golf. The diversity of pastime activities available within the United States and Canada reflects the immense diversity of the people who inhabit North America.

Reading is among the most respected hobbies across the continent. The reader cultivates knowledge, exercises the mind, and expands her imagination. Writing likewise is considered a great talent whose development is to be taken seriously. Since 1992 the nature of reading has shifted from printed text to digital media. Although Americans continue to use books, magazines, and newspapers, the majority of their reading time is online. Interpersonal written communication has seen a massive resurgence through electronic mail and cellular phone text messaging.

Downloading music and posting profiles on the Net have become controversial online pastimes. The music industry has tried to put an end to illegal file sharing. Thousands of arrests and millions of dollars in fines, however, have been unable to contain the growth of the peer-to-peer networking.

Teenage Americans are now spending extraordinary amounts of time cultivating profiles and online friendships on the Web. Sites such as MySpace.com allow individuals to construct online personalities that may or may not resemble the person they are at home. Despite the potential for identity fraud, many friendships and romantic partnerships now begin online.

Hobbies of Collection

Virtually every North American has a collection. Hunting, gathering, and preserving specific items are games that adults and children enjoy. Whereas youngsters are satisfied collecting pretty items such as rocks and seashells, adults generally develop collections that promise financial or intellectual rewards. Enthusiasm is the primary prerequisite for collecting. The investment of time and energy is more imperative than money. Garage sales, thrift stores, and antique malls are the hunting grounds for the collector. From fine art to wooden buttons, collectors often become experts in their field. Local collectors know one another and regularly share information within clubs and societies. International collectors connect through the Web and at annual conventions.

Star Wars items, Smurfs, metal lunchboxes, nautical equipment, baseball cards, antique coins, Barbie dolls, scent bottles, grandfather clocks, postage stamps, playing cards, matchbooks, and phonograph records are among thousands of items Americans collect. It is common to collect paraphernalia related to a specific movie, superhero, or television series. Robert and Patricia Leffler of the United States, for example, boast the world's largest collection of *Conan the Barbarian* memorabilia. They have spent over 30 years collecting 2,418 items including posters, comic books, action figures, and toy weapons related to the 1982 film starring Arnold Schwarzenegger.[13]

Miniature Hobbies

Model cars, trains, and airplanes are built, collected, and driven by fathers and sons in North America. Die-cast metal automobiles are becoming increasingly popular among collectors on account of their exquisite detail. Die-cast cars often have opening doors and functioning steering wheels. More expensive models have leather interior, wooden detail, and working brake lights.

Radio-controlled cars are generally powered by electricity or gas. They often mimic high-performance street vehicles and can reach speeds of 100 mph.

Model airplanes come in a variety of shapes, sizes, and capacities. Static models are generally scaled-down versions of actual airplanes. Aeromodeling, or the art of flying model airplanes, is a popular activity for grown-ups and children. Local model airplane clubs host air shows, where hobbyists compete against one another for prizes in speed and dexterity.

Creative Hobbies

Arts and crafts remain popular among a wide range of individuals. Painting, drawing, and printmaking are among the most popular two-dimensional arts. Woodworking, pottery, and metal smithing are common three-dimensional pursuits. Technological advances and the recent availability of home editing equipment have made videography and digital photography among the most common artistic pastimes practiced by North Americans.

In the late 1970s spray-painting walls, bridges, billboards, and train cars emerged as the artistic expression of urban youth. Graffiti soon became popular with California surf and skateboard culture. Although graffiti is illegal across the continent, it is considered a developed art form. Anonymous artists participate in this rebellious activity, which has been featured in exhibitions at the MOMA and the San Francisco Museum of Modern Art.

Freestyle rapping, beatboxing, and break dancing are creative forms that emerged from inner-city gang conflict in the 1970s. Street competitions between rappers and dancers are called "battles." They were initially used to settle gang disputes. Today rap culture is easily criticized for glorifying drug trade and commodifying women, while hip-hop expresses a more socially conscious voice of urban youth.

Musical ability is considered a great asset in North America. Parents register their children for piano or violin lessons hoping to establish a lifelong involvement with music. Elementary schools have mandatory music classes.

Mesa/Boogie Amp and the Punk movement encouraged teenagers with little or no musical experience to form their own rock 'n' roll bands. Practice in suburban basements makes perfect for gritty downtown clubs.

Karaoke culture was imported from Japan during the late 1980s, making the spotlight, the microphone, and the audience accessible to all. Karaoke bars are one of the few places, outside of church, where passionate singing is encouraged. The spirit of good fun is a welcome alternative to a society that is often critical of public performance.

In the information age, collecting and broadcasting music has become increasingly popular. Through computer technology, connected individuals have access to infinite online music databases. Streaming audio technologies transform the personal computer into an international radio receiver. Podcasting enables individuals to produce their own radio shows and distribute them electronically through the World Wide Web. Blogs, or online journals, allow individuals to post real-time thoughts with the international community. Bloggers have become such important resources for immediate information that several of them have reached a level of celebrity. The blogosphere has elevated the power of the individual voice within mainstream media.

The Stage and Performance

Amateur writers, actors, dancers, directors, and scene designers enjoy the spotlight at community theaters. Long hours are spent after work and on weekends preparing the opening night of seasonal plays and Shakespeare in the Park performances. Readings and poetry "slams" are regularly hosted at coffee shops, allowing young writers to share their work with one another.

For those who develop an interest in dance, there is a wide range of options available in most communities. Art centers, religious establishments, and community colleges offer lessons in ballet, tap, ballroom dancing, modern dance, and more. Courses usually conclude with a public recital.

Puppets

Puppeteering arts became popular with North American hobbyists in the 1950s. Today many individuals and groups enjoy creating puppets, writing scripts, building scenery, and performing for local audiences. The Bread and Puppet Theater in Vermont and the Burning Man Festival in Nevada are two festivals that push the hobby into the realm of art.

A ventriloquist is a puppeteer who makes a "dummy" appear to talk. Comedic ventriloquism emerged as a part of vaudeville shows in the mid-1800s. Edgar Bergen and his sidekick Charlie McCarthy brought ventriloquism to the unlikely medium of radio and later made it a popular act on TV. Every summer hundreds of these "belly-talkers" gather for a ConVENTtion near Cincinnati, Ohio, at the Vent Haven Museum, "the world's only museum dedicated to the art of ventriloquism."

Television and Film

Literature, cinema, and television are popular substitutes for children's role-playing games. Instead of *becoming* the heroic characters of their own playful fantasy, adults become spectators to the play of others. The experience of becoming an astronaut or an Aztec warrior is still possible for adults but only through the observance of professional actors who are paid to play for the television or on the silver screen. Many North Americans consider themselves film aficionados.

Intellectual Hobbies

At any given time American libraries and historical archives are filled with individuals who spend their free time learning. Genealogists, history buffs, and pop culture experts enjoy digging through books and old papers, piecing together clues from the past.

Amateur astronomers can spend thousands of dollars on personal telescopes that are powerful enough to view craters on the moon. Members of local astronomical societies gather together to view important celestial events.

North America's cultural materialism is balanced by a spiritualistic counterculture. Aspiring psychics practice activities such as reading palms, stars, tarot cars, auras, and crystal balls. Psychic fairs and metaphysical conferences are held throughout the United States and Canada. Ghost-hunting clubs are available in most North American cities.

VEHICLE HOBBIES

Even when they are not traveling, Americans are obsessed with the instruments of locomotion. Vehicles that provide mobility through land, air, and water have become a part of the American family. Names and personalities are given to cars, airplanes, and boats. Considerable amounts of both time and money are invested in them.

Boats are popular among the private sector, but they are rarely used for practical transportation. Boating is a popular hobby across the continent. It often incorporates other water activities such as skiing, fishing, and tubing. Fishing boats are small, fun, and affordable recreational vehicles for many families. Speedboats and pontoon boats are common accessories at middle-class vacation homes. Yachts and houseboats are symbols of affluence.

Airplanes are likewise the property of the upper class. On top of the obvious expenses of purchasing and maintaining a plane, one must acquire a pilot's certificate. In order to qualify for such a license, a person invests between $5,000 and $9,000 in flight training courses. Since the early 1970s it has been possible for Americans to purchase kits for building airplanes in their own garage.

All-terrain vehicles (ATVs) became popular with Americans in the 1980s. Fat wheels and a low center of gravity allow users to travel quickly over rugged land that is impossible for automobiles and motorcycles. Farmers and hunters use ATVs for utilitarian purposes. While Daredevils use them to outdo one another at the motocross track, other ATV motorists simply enjoy rugged trail riding.

Americans love their cars and wear them like shells. The make and model of a person's vehicle is considered a reflection of his or her personality. Most households have at least one car. Many families have a car for each eligible driver. Exceptional amounts of recreation time are spent inside these personal automobiles. Teenagers enjoy "cruising," and older adults enjoy the "Sunday drive." Whether circulating through downtown streets or enjoying nature through the windows of a car, Americans often drive to see and be seen.

Custom cars are most often expressions of male identity. Restoring antique automobiles and caring for new vehicles are popular activities for a diverse cross section of North American men. High-performance vehicles make their annual debut at the Canadian International Auto Show in Toronto and at the United States Auto Show in Detroit. These are two of the most well-attended events on the continent.

Hot rods are heavily modified "vintage tin" cars that tend to be popular among the older generations. Hot rod enthusiasts add powerful engines, modern transmissions, and flashy paint jobs to nostalgia cars made between 1945 and 1965. Weekend meetings, annual reunions, and noisy drag racing unite the hot rod community.

Owners of muscle cars tend to be younger and rougher than the fun-loving hot-rodders. The Ford Mustang, the Chevy Impala, and the Pontiac Trans Am are among the classic varieties of American muscle cars. The age of the muscle car begins with the Pontiac GTO and the introduction of the V8 engine in 1964. Vintage muscle cars are among the most desirable items within the North American landscape. Younger muscle car enthusiasts have begun adorning these antique cars with "candy paint," chrome wheels, and expensive electronic accessories, including DVD players and video games.

A lowrider is a truck or muscle car whose suspension system has been modified to drop the body of the car as close to the road as possible. The lowrider culture began with Chicano youth and quickly attained popularity within hip-hop culture. In addition to wet T-shirt contests, lowrider rallies include competitions for the trickiest hydraulics, flashiest paint, and loudest stereo.

High-performance motorcycles imported from Japan are commonly known as "rice rockets" in the United States. These motorcycles are favored by young men who live for speed. These cycles travel over a hundred miles an hour in organized races at drag strips and in impromptu contests between competitors on public streets.

Over the course of the century gangs of Harley riders became known for their rowdiness, illegal activity, and general sense of lawlessness. Bikers gradually developed an underground network of gangs and bike clubs. The American fear and fascination with bikers has been portrayed by movies such as *The Wild One* starring Marlon Brando and *Easy Rider* with Dennis Hopper and Jack Nicholson.

The culture of leather and loud pipes which once belonged to the outlaw culture of biker gangs such as the Outlaws and Hell's Angels has become the part-time attire of wealthier Americans seeking a weekend escape from their daily routine. In addition to selling motorcycles, Harley-Davidson now sells an image of rebellion. In recent decades American women have stepped out of the "bitch seat"—the backseat on a motorcycle—onto their own Harleys. Motorcycle maintenance has become increasingly popular among young independent women.

ATHLETIC HOBBIES

Outdoor sports that are played across the continent include basketball, golf, baseball, tennis, soccer, fencing, rowing, rugby, lacrosse, and football. On the coast, Americans enjoy snorkeling, scuba diving, windsurfing, and the art of sunbathing. In rivers they canoe, kayak, and whitewater raft. Winter sports such as skiing and snowboarding are popular in northern regions. Ice-skating rinks are located throughout the continent, allowing people in warmer climates to skate. Hockey is the national sport of Canada, where men, women, and children of all ages are passionate about the game.

Ever since the Wright brothers took off from Kitty Hawk, Americans have followed suit. Hot-air ballooning, parachuting, hang gliding, soaring, and gyrocopting are among the ways hobbyists enjoy the sky.

In the mid-1990s young adults began pushing the boundaries of already dangerous sports. The Xtreme Games made their debut in Providence, Rhode Island, in 1995, and for over a decade ABC and ESPN have provided live coverage of the annual daredevil competitions. As a result, skateboarding, snowboarding, whitewater rafting, caving, rock climbing, and mountain biking have become faster, trickier, wilder, and more popular than ever before. Over the past decade many American cities have developed "play at your own risk" Xtreme BMX trails and skate parks. The Xtreme competition is balanced by a sense of camaraderie among competitors, who generally consider themselves united against the mainstream.

The development of martial arts is popular with many American men and women. Local clubs offer lessons in karate, judo, jujitsu, aikido, and kung fu to prepare students for regional competitions. Boxing clubs generally cater to men, but in recent years they have begun opening their doors to women. Regional boxing competitions pitch fights between boys as young as eight. The movie *Fight Club* starring Brad Pitt drew media attention to a growing culture of illegal bare-knuckle boxing.

Although yoga is not considered a religious practice as it is in India, it is practiced daily by many Westerners as an alternative to high-impact exercise. Recently, Pilates has also become popular among Americans, primarily women.

GUN HOBBIES

Hunting is popular in both the United States and Canada. The year is divided into seasons for deer, quail, and duck hunting. Strict rules regulate the hunting of buffalo and birds of prey. Killing an American eagle or even possessing a feather from one is punishable by U.S. law.

In the United States, boys never seem to outgrow guns. Pretend hunt games including laser tag and paintball are popular activities for children's birthday parties. Gun ranges and annual gunshots allow children and adults to handle high-power specialty weapons such as machine guns and flamethrowers. Guns and knives are among the top collectables for American men. Gun shows are among the nation's most profitable events. Michael Moore's 2002 film *Bowling for Columbine* exposes the popularity of recreational guns in the United States compared to their relative nonuse in Canada.

ANIMAL HOBBIES

Americans love their pets. Dogs, cats, and furry rodents are among the most common animals kept in homes across the continent. Considerable amounts of time and money are

THE BARBIE LIBERATION ORGANIZATION

On Christmas morning 1989 hundreds of children in the United States and Canada received an unexpected surprise. Boys were horrified when their talking G.I. Joe action figures said in a high-pitched voice, "Let's plan our dream wedding!" Little girls were equally confused when their Barbie dolls grumbled in a mannish tone, "Dead men tell no lies!"

The Barbie Liberation Organization, an artist-activist group headquartered in San Diego, California, bought several hundred talking G.I. Joe and Barbie dolls. They switched the doll's voice boxes and then returned them to toy store shelves. Stickers were placed inside the packaging of the altered dolls instructing surprised parents to call the local news stations and alert them of the prank.

During the following media sensation, the BLO announced their goal to disrupt the violent lessons taught by G.I. Joe and subvert the brainless materialism of talking Barbies. Additionally, the Barbie Liberation Organization sought to expose and potentially eliminate gender-based stereotyping in toys. Hasbro Inc., G.I. Joe's parent company, called the stunt "ridiculous,"[14] whereas Mattel, the manufacturer of Barbie, did not comment on the project.

The Barbie Liberation Organization continues to prank the consumer market and encourages individuals all over the world to participate in the voice box switch using the Official BLO Barbie/G.I. Joe Home Surgery Instructions, which are readily available online at http://users.lmi.net/~eve/barbie.html.

spent caring for these creatures, which are usually considered part of the family. Exotic birds, fish, and reptiles are imported to North America from all corners of the globe. American pets are taught to do tricks. Birds speak and dogs jump through hoops. Americans train their animals to perform for competitions ranging from the incredibly serious international dog shows to the completely ridiculous Stupid Pet Tricks on David Letterman's late-night television.

HOBBIES OF THE HOME

In 1950 *Time* magazine named "do-it-yourself" home repair "America's new 50-million-dollar hobby." Men across society continue to enjoy renovating their homes on weekends. The television show *This Old House* has provided construction instruction for the hobbyist since 1979. Saws, drills, and other items bought at the hardware store are often referred to as "toys."

Cultivating home fashions remains a primary pastime of the American woman. The home décor magazine *Better Homes and Gardens* has sold consistently to women since 1922. In recent years knitting, needlepoint, and scrapbooking have seen a resurgence in popularity. North American women with a strong grasp on the corporate ladder have begun revisiting their domesticity.

THE ART OF BEAUTY

American women spend significant amounts of time cultivating their appearance. They attend classes and read magazines to keep current with the latest fashions and methods of makeup application. Women attend beauty workshops and hire cosmetic consultants to improve their beauty skill.

At formal beauty contests or "pageants" women and young girls promenade across a stage in evening gowns, bikinis, and high-heel shoes to be judged on physical beauty. The winner of local pageants travels to statewide and then national competitions such as Miss America. According the *Guinness Book of World Records*, P. T. Barnum organized the first international beauty pageant after staging similar contests for babies, animals, and birds.

Weight lifters began competing against one another when the National Amateur Body-builders Association (NABBA) initiated the Mr. Universe contest in 1950. Competitive bodybuilding quickly became popular throughout the world. At the Mr. Universe Championship men are judged on muscle tone rather than facial appearance. Although a relatively small percentage of American men officially compete, bodybuilding is a daily activity for many North American men.

Ms. Universe contests were added by the NABBA in 1966; it is common at any gym to see women lifting weights. The present "thin is in" aesthetic generally motivates women to be skinny instead of strong. The resulting tendency is that women prefer calorie-burning activities, such as aerobics, jogging, and swimming, at the gym.

RESOURCE GUIDE

PRINT SOURCES

Arnold, Peter. *The Book of Card Games.* London: Christopher Helm, 1988.

Baudrillard, Jean. *America.* Translated by Chris Turner. London: Verso, 1988.

Burns, Brian, ed. *The Encyclopedia of Games.* New York: Barnes and Noble, 1998.

Drew, Robert. "'Anyone Can Do It': Forging a Participatory Culture in Karaoke Bars." Pp. 254–269 in Henry Jenkins, Tara McPherson, and Jane Shattuc (eds.), *Hop on Pop: The Politics and Pleasures of Popular Culture.* Durham: Duke, 2002.

Driver, Ian. *A Century of Dance.* London: Octopus, 2000.

Emrich, Linn. *The Complete Book of Sky Sports.* London: Collier Macmillan, 1970.

Gibbs, Brian, and Donna Gibbs. *Teddy Bear Century.* London: David & Charles, 2002.

Harbin, E. O. *The Fun Encyclopedia.* Nashville: Abingdon, 1960.

Hofer, Margaret. *The Games We Played.* New York: Princeton Architectural Press, 2003.

Holstrom, Darwin. "Sturgis: Freak Show Lite." Pp. 300–303 in Darwin Holstrom and Brock Yates (eds.), *The Complete Story: Harley Davidson.* St. Paul: Crestline, 2005.

Horowitz, Judy, with Billy Bloom. *Frisbee: More Than a Game of Catch.* New York: Leisure Press, 1983.

Kennedy, Rod Jr. *Monopoly: The Story behind the World's Best Selling Game.* Salt Lake: Gibbs Smith, 2004.

Koepsell, David R. "Online Poker: Is it Bluffing When No One Sees You Blink?" In Eric Bronson (ed.), *Poker and Philosophy.* Chicago: Open Court, 2006.

Levy, Richard C., and Ronald O. Weingartner. *The Toy and Game Inventor's Handbook.* Indianapolis: Alpha, 2003.

Linn, Susan. *Consuming Kids: Protecting Our Children from the Onslaught of Marketing and Advertising.* New York: Anchor, 2004.

Page, Linda Garland, and Hilton Smith, eds. *The Firefox Book of Appalachian Toys and Games.* Chapel Hill: University of North Carolina, 1993.

Quirin, William L. *Winning at the Races: Computer Discoveries in Thoroughbred Handicapping.* New York: William Morrow & Company, 1979.

Rich, Mark. *Toys A to Z.* Iola, WI: Krause, 2001.

Richard, Dan. *Ventriloquism for the Total Dummy.* New York: Villard Books, 1987.

Roosevelt, Theodore. *Outdoor Pastimes of an American Hunter.* New York: Charles Scribner's Sons, 1905.

Schwartz, David, Steve Ryan, and Fred Wostbrock. *The Encyclopedia of TV Game Shows.* New York: Zoetrope, 1987.

Townsend, Charles Berry. *The Curious Book of Mind-Boggling Teasers, Tricks, Puzzles and Games.* New York: Sterling, 2003.

Walsh, Tim. *Timeless Toys.* Kansas City: Andrews McNeel, 2005.

Waters, T. A. *The Encyclopedia of Magic and Magicians.* New York: Facts on File, 1988.

WEBSITES

Atari Museum. http://www.atarimuseum.com/.

Barbie Collectors Official Website. http://www.barbiecollector.com/.

Bob Ross Incorporated. The Joy of Painting Website. http://www.bobross.com/.

Brookhaven National Laboratory. The First Video Game. http://www.bnl.gov/bnlweb/history/higinbotham.asp.

CandyRific. http://www.candyrific.com/.

Fun and Games in Virtual Museum of Canada. http://www.virtualmuseum.ca/English/Games/index.html.

G.I. Joe Official Website. http://www.hasbro.com/gijoe/.

GPRIME. http://gprime.net/. Homemade online games.

IBM. IBM Research-Deep Blue-Overview. http://www.chess.ibm.com. Deep Blue vs. Garry Kasparov.

Internet Teddy Bear Museum. http://www.teddies-world.net/.

Lionel Train Company. http://www.lionel.com/.

Museum of the Talking Boards. http://www.museumoftalkingboards.com/.

Nolo.tv: Toys, Games, and Hobbies Online Resources. http://www.nolo.tv/toys/.

Pong-Story.com. http://www.pong-story.com/.

Superman Homepage. http://www.supermanhomepage.com/news.php.

World Casino Directory. http://www.worldcasinodirectory.com/.

VIDEOS/FILMS

40-Year-Old Virgin (Universal Studios, 2005). Directed by Judd Apatow, starring Steve Carell and Catherine Keener. The plot partly involves collecting and selling action figures on eBay.

2001: A Space Odyssey (Warner Brothers, 1968). Directed by Stanley Kubrick, starring Keir Dullea and Gary Lockwood. http://www.kubrick2001.com/. The computer HAL plays a deadly game of chess.

Beach Blanket Bingo (American International Pictures, 1965). Directed by William Asher, starring Frankie Avalon and Annette Funicello. A game best played by two! A group of teenagers parties, surfs, sings, and takes up skydiving. Possibly the most famous of the Beach Party films.

A Beautiful Mind (Universal Studios, 2001). Directed by Ron Howard, starring Russell Crowe, Jennifer Connolly, Paul Bettany, and Ed Harris. Film about game theorist John Nash.

Bladerunner (Warner Brothers, 1982). Directed by Ridley Scott, starring Harrison Ford, Sean Young, Daryl Hanna, and Edward James Olmos. The future of robotic toys?

Christmas Story (MGM Studios, 1983). Directed by Bob Clark, starring Darren McGavin, Melinda Dillon, and Peter Billingsley. Features classic American toys of the 1940s such as the Roughrider BB gun and Little Orphan Annie Decoder Pens.

Clue (Paramount Pictures, 1986). Directed by Jonathan Lynn, starring Ellen Brennan and Tim Curry. Movie based on the board game of the same name.

Dodgeball: A True Underdog Story (MGM Studios, 2004). Directed by Rawson Marshall Thurber, starring Ben Stiller and Vince Vaughan. A group of underachievers enters a Las Vegas dodgeball tournament in order to save their local gym from a corporate fitness chain.

The Exorcist (Warner Brothers, 1973). Directed by William Friedkin, starring Ellen Burstyn, Jason Miller, and Linda Blair. A young girl is possessed by the Devil after playing with a Ouija board.

Mr. Universe (Zeitgeist Films, 1951). Directed by Joseph Lerner, starring Jack Carson, Janis Page, and Vince Edwards. Includes actual footage from 1950 Mr. Universe contest.

Okie Noodling (Little League Pictures, 2001). Directed by Bradley Beesley. Documentary about the sport of hand-fishing.

Toy Story (Disney-Pixar, 1995). Directed by John Lasseter, starring Tom Hanks, Tim Allen, Don Rinkles, and Annie Potts. Animated. A group of toys must work together to return home after being separated from their owner.

Tron (Walt Disney Pictures, 1982). Directed by Steven Lisberger, starring Jeff Bridges, Bruce Boxleitner, and Cindy Morgan. A video game programmer is trapped inside a video game.

WarGames (MGM Entertainment, 1983). Directed by John Badham, starring Matthew Broderick, Dabney Coleman, and Alley Sheedy. A young computer whiz inadvertently hacks into a military central computer, engaging in a strategic game that nearly initiates World War III.

EVENTS

American International Toy Fair, Jacob J. Javits Convention Center, 11th Avenue at 34th Street, New York, NY. http://www.toy-tia.org. Largest and most important American toy industry trade show.
Comic-Con International, San Diego Convention Center, 111 W. Harbor Drive, San Diego, CA. http://www.comic-con.org. The world's largest comic book convention.
Electronic Entertainment Expo (E3), Los Angeles Convention Center, 1201 Figueroa Street, Los Angeles, CA 90015. http://www.e3expo.com/. Most important annual exhibition of new video games.
International Consumer Electronics Show (CES), Las Vegas Convention Center, 3150 Paradise Road, Las Vegas, NV 89109. http://www.cesweb.org. Largest trade show for consumer technology.
International Model and Hobby Expo, Donald E. Stevens Convention Center, 5555 N. River Road, Rosemont, IL. http://www.ihobbyexpo.com.
Vent Haven ConVENTion, Vent Haven Museum, 33 West Maple Avenue, Fort Mitchell, KY 41011. http://www.venthaven.com. Oldest and largest annual gathering of ventriloquists.
Western States Toy & Hobby Show, Fairplex, 1101 W. McKinley Avenue, Pomona, CA 91769. http://www.wthra.com.

ORGANIZATIONS

Board Game Players Association. http://www.boardgamers.org/.
International Federation of Bodybuilding and Fitness (IFBB), 2875 Bates Road, Montreal, Quebec, Canada H3S 1B7. http://www.ifbb.com/.
Video Arcade Preservation Society. http://www.vaps.org/.
Women in Toys. http://www.womenintoys.com/.

MUSEUMS

Babyland General Hospital, 73 Underwood Street, Cleveland, GA 30528. http://www.cabbage patchkids.com/.
Computer History Museum, 1401 N. Shoreline Blvd., Mountain View, CA 94043. http://www.computer history.org/. Strong collection of antique computer games.
Delaware Toy and Miniature Museum, P.O. Box 4053, Wilmington, DE 19807. http://www. thomes.net/.
Elliott Avendon Museum & Archive of Games, University of Waterloo, 200 University Avenue West, Waterloo, Ontario N2L 3G1. http://www.gamesmuseum.uwaterloo.ca/.
Joe Ley Antiques, 615 East Market Street, Louisville, KY 40202. http://www.joeley.com/. Bizarre collection of antique toys and carnival objects.
Kruger Street Toy and Train Museum, 144 E. Kruger Street, Wheeling, WV. http://www. toyandtrain.com/.
Liman Collection of American Board Games, New York Historical Society, 170 Central Park West @ 77th, New York, NY 10024. https://www.nyhistory.org/.
Madame Alexander Heritage Gallery, 615 W 131st Street, New York, NY. 212-283-5900 x7128. http://www. madamealexander.com/.
Marx Toy Museum, 915 Second Street, Moundsville, WV. http://www.marxtoymuseum.com/.
Raggedy Ann and Andy Museum, P.O. Box 183, 110 East Main Street, Arcola, IL 61910. http://www. raggedyann-museum.org/.
Strong Museum: National Museum of Play, One Manhattan Square, Rochester, NY 14607. http://www. strongmuseum.org/. Home of the National Toy Hall of Fame.

The Teddy Bear Museum, 2511 Pine Ridge Road, Naples, FL. http://www.teddymuseum.com/.

Toy and Action Figure Museum, 111 S. Chickasaw Street, Paul's Valley, OK 73075. http://www.action figuremuseum.com/.

Zeum, 221 Fourth Street (@Howard), San Francisco, CA 94103. http://www.zeum.org/. San Francisco's hands-on arts and science exploratory museum.

DOLLS

Madame Alexander. http://www.madamealexander.com/contact/. For information on 1936 Scarlet O'Hara doll, the original doll that predicts Vivian Leigh in the movie. Contact Madame Alexander Doll Company, 212-283-5900.

BARBIE

http://www.mattel.com/contact_us/default.asp. For information on Lilli doll (precursor to Barbie), or original Barbie. Also see http://www.theculture.net/barbie/. "Suicide Bomber Barbie." Artwork by Simon Tyszko. London Institute of Contemporary Arts (ICA). August 2002.

ANT HOUSE

Austin & His Ant House, 1930s. Dartmouth University, Special Collections. http://www.dartmouth. edu/~library/Library_Bulletin/Apr1993/LB-A93-Cramer.html.

VIDEO GAME

Brookhaven National Laboratory. William Higinbotham, inventor. Tennis for Two. First video game. http://www.bnl.gov/bnlweb/history/higinbotham.asp. Great picture of the first video game "instrumentation."

OUIJA BOARD

Bilingual Ouija board or other antique talking boards. http://www.museumoftalkingboards.com/ gal7.html.

NOTES

1. Foster Rhea Dulles, *A History of Recreation: America Learns to Play* (New York: Meredith, 1965), p. 354.
2. Women's Archive, "JWABeatrice Alexander Career Beginnings," http://www.jwa.org/exhibits/wov/ alexander/career.html (May 15, 2006).
3. Kenneth C. Cramer, "The Austin Ant House." *Notes from the Special Collections.* http://www. dartmouth.edu/~library/Library_Bulletin/Apr1993/LB-A93-Cramer.html (April 27, 2006).
4. Tim Walsh, *Timeless Toys* (in Resource Guide), p. 52.
5. Hasbro Website, "Monopoly Fun Facts." http://www.hasbro.com/monopoly/pl/page.funfacts/dn/ default.cfm (May 21, 2006).
6. Walsh, p. 129.
7. Brookhaven National Laboratory, "The First Video Game: Brookhaven History." http://www.bnl. gov/bnlweb/history/higinbotham.asp (May 23, 2006).
8. David Pilgrim, *The Garbage Man: Why I Collect Racist Objects.* Jim Crow Museum Website. http:// www.ferris.edu/jimcrow/collect/.

9. Trivial Pursuit Website, *The Most Popular Trivia Game in the World*. http://www.trivialpursuit.com/trivialpursuit/about.html (April 17, 2006).

10. *2003 Guinness World Records* (New York: Bantam Books, 2003), p. 234.

11. Cabbage Patch Kids Website, *The Legend*. http://www.cabbagepatchkids.com/pages/History_folklore/Legend/legend.html (April 6, 2006).

12. D. Paravaz, "Action Figure Makers Are Toying with President Bush." *Seattle Post-Intelligencer* (2003, October 20).

13. *2003 Guinness World Records*, p. 172.

14. Bridgette Greenberg, *The BLO—Barbie Liberation Organization*. The Associated Press, San Diego. http://www.etext.org/Zines/UnitCircle/uc3/page10.html.

LITERATURE

PATRICIA KENNEDY BOSTIAN

North Americans are readers. In 2004 there were 24,243 stores carrying books in the United States and Canada, with almost 6000 of these classified as general bookstores.[1] According to the American Library Association (ALA), the United States alone has an estimated 117,664 libraries, with Canada adding an additional 3,153 branches and mobile book units. Libraries in both the United States and Canada offer Internet connectivity as well as the traditional reading and research tools. In Canada public libraries are the most frequent point of access to the Internet for those without home Internet service. Of public libraries in the United States that have access to the Internet, 95.3 percent offer this access to the public. With the explosion of book, e-book, and audiobook formats on the North American publishing scene, the number of people buying or borrowing reading materials has reached phenomenal numbers. According to the *Book Industry Trends* report of 2005, Americans spent $39 billion on books in 2004. Canadians spent $2.8 billion (in Canadian dollars) on books in 2004. A 2002 ALA survey of American library usage found that 46 percent of patrons used the library for education purposes and 46 percent used the library for entertainment. Americans' book-buying trends are not so different from their reasons for using the library: sales of fiction titles amounted to 54 percent of sales in 2000; 36 percent were nonfiction and poetry/drama.

UNITED STATES

As the standard of living improved at the dawning of the twentieth century, books became more valued than ever. The large U.S. middle class encouraged publishers to pour more money into their publishing ventures. Unlike other countries, the United States experienced an economic boom after World War I, and the number and quality of publishers grew as well, increasing the publishers' profits. Universities and their demand for books grew as well, increasing the publishers' profits. Improved postal and transportation systems led to the development of book clubs where customers could purchase inexpensive titles through the mail. Their popularity did not decrease until paperback publishing became widespread.

Rank	Population
1. Minneapolis, MN	382,618
2. Seattle, WA	563,374
3. Pittsburgh, PA	334,563
4. Madison, WI	208,054
5. Cincinnati, OH	331,285
6. Washington, DC	572,059
7. Denver, CO	554,636
8. Boston, MA	589,141
9. Portland, OR	529,121
10. San Francisco, CA	776,733

Source: University of Wisconsin-Whitewater, 2004, http://www.uww.edu/advancement/npa/special_reports/cities/allrank.html.

Most Literate U.S. Cities

In the late 1800s American paperback books were cheaply made and were often reprints of pirated British works. Their popularity declined until Penguin began its paperback line in 1935. In 1939 Pocket Books was established in the United States and was extremely successful. Books, with their new easy-to-tote format, began appearing in a variety of retail establishments, drugstores, train stations, airports—anywhere anything else was sold. It was no longer necessary to find a bookstore to buy a book. Paperbacks, after a brief period of being associated with steamy fiction, such as Mickey Spillane's *I, the Jury*, regained their respectability and by the 1960s were outselling hardcovers. Paperback reprints of hardcover titles were eventually joined by original releases.

Technological advances in the late twentieth century have further expanded the market for published works. Readers can choose to listen to their favorite authors on audiotape or DVD. They can download e-books to their computers. Books long out of print, or at least no longer covered by copyright laws, can be found on the Internet at such sources as Gutenburg.com. Readers can follow their favorite serial installments on the Internet as well. Anyone can become an author with the on-demand printing services of the self-publishing industry. In short, Americans have access to the written word in myriad ways unknown to and undreamed of by readers as recently as 25 years ago.

Americans are willing to spend increasingly large sums of money to support their reading habits. The suggested retail price for adult hardcover titles in 2004 was $27.52; mass-market paperbacks ring in at an average cost of $7.35 according to a 2004 media release by Bowker. Mystery novels were $6.94 and romances were the best bargain at $5.57 in 2006. But who is reading the most in the United States? The most literate cities, based on education, number of bookstores, libraries, newspaper circulation, and so on, are Minneapolis, Minnesota, and Seattle, Washington.

Book Clubs and Reading Groups

The Literary Guild was created in 1922 mainly to appeal to female readers and offered mostly commercial or popular titles. The largest book club, the Book-of-the-Month

Club (BOMC), was established by Harry Scherman in 1926. Sherman's motivation to begin the book club was twofold: he wanted to ensure that quality books received the attention they deserved and that people in remote areas not served by bookstores would have access to them. A selection committee, often made up of literary scholars, culled books from the ever-increasing numbers published each year to offer its members. Until 2000 the major players in the book club field included Bertelsmann Doubleday Direct and the BOMC. These two companies combined, and the resulting company now offers dozens of clubs as part of Bookspan, a venture owned by Time-Warner and Bertelsmann, providing members with offers for everything from history books to Hispanic titles. Most book clubs offer members discounted prices and dividends toward future purchases. Others are a loose membership of readers interested in similar genres, for instance the African-American Literature Book Club and Oprah Winfrey's book club. Market information from the Ipsos-NPD Group for 2000 shows that 24 percent of trade book sales are through book clubs. A title promoted by a book club, therefore, can catapult an author onto the best seller lists.

Reading groups are popular and also help book sales. Groups can be quite small or very large, as some online reading groups/discussion boards can be. Members read the same book and meet, online or in person, to discuss their current title. Most large publishers, for example Random House, and bookstores, such as Barnes and Noble, offer reading guides for groups, containing discussion questions and background information on the author and the work.

FICTION

Preliminary 2005 reports show that 23,017 titles were published in the United States that year.[2] Approximately 5,500 of these were fiction titles. The sales of books in 2000 amounted to $15.3 billion. It is difficult to

OPRAH WINFREY'S BOOK CLUB

Television talk show host, author, actress, and billionaire Oprah Winfrey (1954–) also has an impact on publishing and book-buying trends in North America. In 1996 Winfrey launched the Oprah Book Club to promote new authors whose books she felt merited attention. After a brief hiatus, she relaunched the club in 2003 with the intention of promoting classic authors, catapulting Tolstoy's *Anna Karenina* (1875–77) and Elie Wiesel's *Night* (originally published in 1958, rereleased in 2006 with a new preface) to the top of the best seller lists. Her online book club, at 800,000 members, mostly female, is the largest of its kind in the world. Winfrey's ability to draw attention to often unknown authors and create literary sensations has been dubbed the Oprah Effect.

Kathleen Rooney has authored *Reading with Oprah: The Book Club That Changed America* (2005) in which she examines the Oprah Book Club phenomena and the impact the choices Winfrey makes has had on both the publishing industry and the reading habits of millions of Americans. Cecilia Konchar Farr's *Reading Oprah: How Oprah's Book Club Changed the Way America Reads* (2004) places Winfrey at the heart of the lowbrow versus highbrow debate in American literature. Winfrey's admirers praise her efforts to bring good reading choices to the American public via her high-profile media presence and for creating communities of readers through her online book clubs. Winfrey's book club does have its detractors, though. Most criticism rests on what have been considered uneven selections. Classics such as Steinbeck's *East of Eden* (originally published in 1952) have been featured alongside such controversial works as James Frey's *A Million Little Pieces* (2003). Frey's memoir was subsequently found to be based on falsehoods and Winfrey confronted the author on her show, pulling *Pieces* from the book club.

estimate how much of this amount is due to the sales of fiction titles. Sales of general fiction account for 12 percent of fiction sales; popular fiction amounts to 40 percent of Internet sales for companies such as Amazon.com or the online arm of Barnes and Noble. The Romance Writers of America (RWA) organization boasts that $1.2 billion of North American book sales comes from the sales in the romance fiction genre. Genres, or categories of books based on subject matter, are rather slippery things, however. A novel that is primarily historical, with a romantic subplot, may be shelved in the general fiction section in one bookstore, yet promoted as a romance title in another. Publishers, too, market their books to particular audiences under the guise of genre. John Grisham has written primarily legal fiction, a subgenre of mystery. Yet his 2001 *A Painted House*, a historical novel set in the 1950s, appeared in the catalog of the Mystery Guild in hopes of capturing fans of Grisham's mystery novels.

General Fiction

Although there is a market for regional authors, most locally published writers or authors of books depicting a very localized setting generally do not sell well beyond their intended locale. Some titles are exceptions, though. For example, *Midnight in the Garden of Good and Evil* by John Berendt was published in 1994. Its setting is Savannah, Georgia, and it is about the town and one of its murders. The book took off and spent 216 weeks on the *New York Times* best seller list, was nominated for a Pulitzer Prize, and was released as a film in 1997. Regional authors who appear on the best seller lists, for example, southern writers Clyde Edgerton, Rebecca Wells, or Lee Smith, may sell slightly better in their home states, but the regional best seller lists show that, in general, Americans across the United States are fairly consistent in their book buying. Patricia Cornwell and John Grisham, again, both southern authors, sell as well in New York as they do in Charlotte, North Carolina, and Mississippi. Carolyn Mott Davidson, whose mysteries are set in Colorado, sells well all over the country.

The general fiction category is swarming with subcategories including historical fiction, adventure stories, psychological suspense, futuristic, Hollywood, and the rich and famous; the categories are never-ending and expand daily. Although many authors' titles could as easily be marketed as romance or science fiction or some other genre, most best-selling authors are marketed as popular fiction. Among the most-read authors are Patricia Cornwell, John Grisham, Michael Crichton, Danielle Steel, Dean Koontz, Anne Tyler, and James Patterson.

Romance

The success of the romance novel was based in part on the development of mass-market publishing. By the 1920s romance stories were being published in periodicals such as *Ladies' Home Journal*. These stories closely resembled more modern romance fiction: young heroines being saved by heroes with the requisite happy endings. Georgette Heyer, the first lady of romance fiction, popularized the Regency romance and was later joined by the prolific Barbara Cartland. In 1949 Harlequin, a Canadian company, began reprinting titles from its British arm, Boons and Mills. In 1960 America's Phyllis Whitney's *Thunder Heights* and Britain's Victoria Holt's *Mistress of Mellyn* ushered in the age of the Gothic romance. The modern Gothic dominated paperback sales from 1969 to 1974, outselling all other categories.

In the 1970s the gentle romances were joined by more sophisticated sexually explicit romances, which came to be dubbed bodice rippers. Avon published *The Flame and the Flower* by Kathleen Woodiwiss in 1972, and the British stranglehold on romance novel sales was broken. By the end of the 1990s, Harlequin's contemporary romances were outselling all other genres of romance fiction. Other companies began their own imprints of romances as well. In the late 1980s the romance heroine was beginning to change, and more mature characters were beginning to appear in the novels. The readers of romances in the 1990s were largely college-educated and had careers. Heroines reflected the new woman and had careers, friends, and sometimes children and occasionally were even divorced.

According to the RWA, the largest professional romance organization with over 9,500 members, today's romantic fiction accounts for $1.2 billion in sales in North America.[3] This amounts to the lion's share of the fiction category with 38.8 percent of the market. Romance readers between the ages of 25 and 44 account for 46 percent of all romance readers. Surprisingly, in a genre seemingly dominated by women (both readers and authors), 22 percent of readers are male. Romance readers are spread fairly evenly throughout the United States, making up 26 percent of the Midwest, 27 percent of the West, and 29 percent of the South. Only 12.6 percent of northeastern readers read romances. Customers make most of their book purchases at mass-market retailers such as Wal-Mart and Target.

Romance writers are extremely prolific, catering to their loyal readers' desire for frequent releases by their favorite authors. It is not unusual for an author to have several ongoing series of titles, along with single titles not featuring series characters, releasing one to two titles a year, often in different subgenres. Catherine Coulter, for example, has the FBI series (a contemporary series) and the historical Sherbrooke series, both of which have nine titles. Nora Roberts, who also writes mysteries under the name J. D. Robb, has over 128 romance titles, 7 of which were released in 2006 alone. Some romance authors publish titles under separate names. For instance, Jayne Anne Krentz has a strong list of titles under her own name but has also adopted seven pseudonyms, the most prolific being Amanda Quick, Jayne Castle, and Stephanie James.

The subgenres of romance fiction seem endless: contemporary, historical, series, multicultural, and even fantasy and futuristic titles proliferate. The genre producing the most titles in 2004 was contemporary, which is 80 percent larger than the next three largest categories combined: historical, inspirational, and paranormal. Readers responding to an RWA 2005 survey indicated that they favor romances featuring mystery and suspense (48 percent); historical novels set in Colonial America (27 percent), England (24 percent), and Scotland (21 percent) and in the medieval period (21 percent); stories with paranormal (18 percent) and futuristic (14 percent) elements; and inspirational titles (31 percent).

Contemporary Romances

Contemporary romances are set in the present time with heroines ranging from stay-at-home divorced moms to businesswomen juggling their careers and love lives. One subgenre in this category is "chick-lit." Chick-lit authors present young, unmarried businesswomen who have difficulties maintaining their careers and finding love (and sex). The titles cater to the market created by the successful television series *Sex in the City*, launched in 1998. One such successful chick-lit author is Meg Cabot, who also writes for teenagers. Glitzy romances, those novels filled with the jet set of the rich, often make it to the best seller lists. Jackie Collins, Danielle Steel, and Fern Michaels have all penned these romances. Other contemporary authors include Judith McNaught and Nicholas Sparks, one of the few male writers in the romance field.

Historical Romances

Historical romances flooded bookstore shelves after the 1972 release of Kathleen Woodi-wiss's *The Flame and the Flower*. Disparagingly termed bodice rippers for their explicitly rough sexual encounters, historical romances have story lines set in a specific historical period, often including royalty, or are family sagas spanning generations. The novels are often meticulously researched, and authors frequently adhere to a particular time and place. For instance, Amanda Scott situates most of her romances in the Scottish Highlands. Readers of historical novels often have favorite subgenres, such as cowboys, pirates, or medieval royalty. Although less sensual, Regencies fall into the historical category as well. They are set in the Regency period of English history and are often brimming with historical accuracy.

Inspirational Romances

Christian romances are a popular subgenre. From the early novels of Grace Livingston Hill to Janette Oke and Jan Karon, inspirational or Christian romances have flourished. Hannah Alexander offers gentle romances with a touch of suspense. In 1999 the Christian book industry established the Christy Award, naming the award, which is given to outstanding fiction incorporating a Christian worldview, after a character created by Catherine Marshall.

Paranormal and Futuristic Romances

One of the most popular segments of the paranormal subgenre in recent years is the time travel novel. The most successful author of time travel novels is Diana Gabaldon with her Outlander series. In a time travel romance, the heroine finds herself in a historical time period and falls in love with a man there. The novels combine elements of both contemporary and historical romances as the characters adjust to life in the period in which they have landed and their lives in the present time.

Other paranormal lines include ghosts and other supernatural forces of good and evil. Romantic suspense often has elements of paranormal activity: Barbara Michaels and Phyllis Whitney, grand mistresses of the romance genre, frequently incorporated inexplicable phenomena into their novels. Futuristic titles could as easily be marketed as science fiction with their emphasis on the technology.

Other Categories

Category (or series) romances, such as those released by Harlequin, a Canadian company, and Silhouette, an imprint of Simon and Schuster, have vast appeal and have seen a number of subgenres in recent years. These romances are traditionally shorter than single-volume romances (250 pages on average), less expensive, and released every month. Category authors frequently use this genre as a stepping-stone to noncategory publishing contracts. One of the most famous (and prolific) of Harlequin authors was Janet Dailey; her Harlequin titles included the American series of fifty novels. She later entered the mainstream romance field and has published scores of novels, both historical and contemporary, set mostly in the

American West. Some of the current lines of Harlequin are Harlequin Romance, with mildly sensuous titles, and Blaze, with titles having a high level of sensuality. Other lines are American Romances, Historical, Intrigue, Medical Romances, and two series in Spanish (Deseo and Bianco). Silhouette stretches the genre a little further, including in its line a series called Bombshell featuring women having dangerous adventures.

The romance market has expanded to meet the reading desires of multicultural audiences. There are several lines of African-American romances. According to *Essence Magazine*, Arabesque/BET published seventy titles in 2001 alone. Kensington's Dafina line releases romance titles as well as general fiction and nonfiction. Sandra Kitt and Kayla Perrin, along with erotica/romance author Zane, are particularly successful in the romance genre.

The most important award given to romance fiction is the RITA Award, given by the RWA. RITA entrants are judged by fellow romance novelists. Winners of the RITA are frequently recognizable names (Nora Roberts won two RITAs in 2004), but newcomers take home awards as well.

Science Fiction and Fantasy

Although considerable debate about the origins of speculative and fantasy literature exists, science fiction has long been a strong genre in the American book industry. Since Herbert Gernsback founded the pulp fiction magazine *Amazing Stories* in 1926, the science fiction and fantasy market has grown to include 7.3 percent of the fiction book market in the United States. In the past thirty years, the hard-science writers of space exploration have been joined by authors who explore fantastic realms of myth and magic. Other related genres are alternate histories, epic fantasies, and space operas. The themes of contemporary science fiction are far-reaching: utopias and dystopias, post-nuclear disasters, plagues or other medical disasters, alien invasions, alternate histories, and robots and cyborgs are just a few.

Fantasy novels offer worlds peopled with legendary or mythical creatures, often set in a fanciful version of an earlier time period on Earth (the medieval time period is a frequent setting). Novels such as J. R. R. Tolkien's *Lord of the Rings* (1954–55), Ursula K. Le Guin's *Earthsea* (first volume published in 1968) series, and C. S. Lewis's *The Chronicles of Narnia* (first volume published in 1950) are perennial favorites and still rank high in sales. Subgenres in the fantasy category include tales of sword and sorcery, the comic fantasy worlds of Piers Anthony's Xanth series, the hidden worlds of vampires, witches, and other magical creatures, and retellings of classic fairy tales. One of the most popular topics of fantasy has been retellings of the King Arthur legends. Novels have focused on King Arthur himself (as both child and adult) and on other players from the legends such as Morgan LeFay and Merlin.

Currently, the genre has opened up to include crossovers from general fiction, techno-thrillers, and the horror genre. Philip Roth's *The Plot against America* (2004) posits an alternate America where Charles A. Lindbergh is president and anti-Semitism is rampant. Michael Crichton's thriller *State of Fear* (2004) lays bare the awesome power of technology in the wrong hands. British author Susanna Clark's *Jonathan Strange and Mr. Norrell* (2004) is a historical fantasy set in nineteenth-century London (and *Time* magazine number one title of 2004). These nontraditional speculative fiction titles share space on American best seller lists with more familiar science fiction and fantasy authors such as Neal Stephenson, Gene Wolfe, Patricia McKillip, David Eddings, Terry Goodkind, Orson Scott Card, George R. R. Martin, Raymond E. Feist, Sara Douglas, Robert Jordan, Terry Brooks, and Mercedes Lackey, all of whom have published several titles each since 2000.

Readers of speculative fiction are loyal, purchasing titles by new authors in the genre but also keeping classic titles in print. The Science Fiction Book Club, established over 50 years ago, offers science fiction classics (their biggest sellers) along with newcomers to the field such as Stephen King, who is better known for his horror fiction, and chick-lit crossovers, for instance Charlaine Harris's southern vampire novels. Books based on hard science fiction epics, such as *Star Wars* and *Star Trek*, are still popular.

The world of science fiction offers several awards for outstanding titles published each year. Two American awards are presented by the Science Fiction and Fantasy Writers of America: the Nebula Award and the Andre Norton Award for Young Adult Fiction. Recent Nebula Awards for the novel category include Joe Haldeman's *Camouflage* and *Paladin of Souls* by Lois McMaster Bujold. The first Andre Norton Award went to Holly Black for *Valiant: A Modern Tale of Faerie* in 2006. The Philip K. Dick Award is given to the author of an original paperback published in the United States (M. M. Buckner's *War Surf*, 2006).

Mystery

The mystery genre is an old, and a prolific, one comprising many subgenres. Many novels sold in the mystery category could as easily be sold as general fiction. However they are categorized, though, as of 2000, mystery sales made up 24.7 percent of all fiction sales in the United States as reported by the market research group Ipsos-NPD Group.

The extent of the popularity of the mystery genre can be seen by the numerous search options on the Barnes and Noble Website. Customers can search for their favorite subgenre (and there is no end to the subgenres), historical time period, or author. Mysteries, thrillers, or suspense novels are often at the top of the *New York Times* best seller lists.

The current proliferation of television crime shows that feature mysteries often solvable only when particular forensic techniques are used has been accompanied by the trend of forensic mystery novels. These include characters who are medical examiners such as Kathy Reichs's Temperance Brennan (recently the impetus for the television series *Bones*) and Patricia Cornwell's Kay Scarpetta. Other characters are experts in particular forensic techniques or are psychological experts, such as profilers. Both James Patterson's Alex Cross and Jeffrey Deaver's Lincoln Rhyme are the forensic detectives of a popular series of titles.

Historical mysteries continue to be popular. Elizabeth Peters's series character Amelia Peabody (*Tomb of the Golden Bird*, 2006, is the eighteenth in the series) is a woman whose Egyptian archaeological adventures span the late Victorian age to the end of World War I. Steven Saylor's readers cannot get enough of his Roman character Gordianus the Finder, who solves mysteries under the rule of Julius Caesar. And the mysteries of Walter Mosley are set in 1948 Los Angeles and are solved by World War II veteran Easy Rawlins.

The authors of police procedurals show a group of police officers at work, frequently on several cases at a time. The popularity of such television shows as *Law and Order* (on the air in various spin-offs since 1990), the 1980s' *Hill Street Blues*, and *NYPD Blue* (1993–2005) has fueled the demand for mysteries with similar characters and situations. Ed McBain leads the pack with fifty-five titles in the 87th Precinct series. J. D. Robb, pen name of Nora Roberts, who has written dozens of romance novels, has penned twenty-two extremely popular novels about police lieutenant Eve Dallas and her husband, Roarke, set in a futuristic New York. Characters Jim Chee and Joe Leaphorn appeared together for the first time in Tony Hillerman's 1986 novel *Skinwalkers*. The most recent installment of the Navajo sleuths is *Skeleton Man* (2004).

The private eye mystery began as a strongly male genre: characters, authors, and audience. One of the most consistently popular authors in this genre is Lawrence Block, who has created several sleuths, all of whom continue to appear in the 2000s. Women broke on the scene and now command a huge portion of private eye sales with Sara Paretsky's V. I. Warshawski and Janet Evanovich's Stephanie Plum. Marcia Muller leads in sales with twenty-three Sharon McCone titles, and Sue Grafton is close with her nineteenth Kinsey Millhone title, *S Is for Silence*, released in 2005.

The 1991 film release of Thomas Harris's *Silence of the Lambs*, starring Anthony Hopkins and Jodie Foster, created a market for plots featuring murders committed by serial killers. Ridley Pearson and Michael Connelly are both contributors to this market. Other popular subgenres include cooking mysteries that often include recipes (Diane Mott Davidson), cat or dog fanciers (Lillian Jackson Braun), bookstore owners (Joan Hess and Carolyn Hart), legal proceedings, especially courtroom drama (John Grisham and Alex North Patterson), and capers or humorous mysteries (Donald Westlake). Authors who have created ethnic characters such as the African American Walter Mosely's Easy Rawlins or Tony Hillerman's Native American police are seeing strong sales as well. Suspense novels, including those of Mary Higgins Clark and her daughter Carol Higgins Clark, often cross boundaries and can be considered part of general fiction.

More so than most general fiction, the often regional nature of many mysteries, especially those written with series characters, appeals to readers in various geographic regions. Joan Hess's characters appear in Arkansas, Diane Mott Davidson writes about Colorado, Carolyn Hart's Death on Demand series is set in South Carolina, and Lawrence Block's turf is New York City.

New England

Boston figures prominently as a locale for a number of mystery writers. Jane Langton's series about Homer Kelly includes Cape Cod and other Massachusetts environs, while Linda Barnes's Carlotta Carlyle investigates crimes in Boston. Other popular Bostonians are Robert B. Parker and Jeremiah Healey. Dennis Lehane's series featuring private investigators Kenzie and Gennaro is set in his hometown of Dorchester, Massachusetts.

Mid-Atlantic

New York City has been cited as the U.S. city most frequently serving as the setting for mystery novels. Ed McBain, Rex Stout, and Donald Westlake have all set mysteries in New York. Lawrence Block lends a strong air of realism to his several series of mysteries, including the popular Matthew Scudder series, by evoking New York both pre- and post-9/11. Rachel Alexander and her Akita, Dash, walk New York's streets in Carol Lea Benjamin's series. Janet Evanovich sets her wildly popular novels about bond agent Stephanie Plum in New Jersey. Gillian Roberts's Amanda Pepper series is set against the backdrop of Philadelphia, as are those of Lisa Scottoline and Jane Haddam. K. C. Constantine created the mythical Rocksburg, Pennsylvania, and Tamara Myer depicts the Pennsylvania Dutch country. Margaret Truman's Capital Crimes series is set in Washington, D.C., as are George P. Pelecanos's Derek Strange novels.

The South

Florida and Louisiana are the most frequent settings of crime novels: Carl Hiaasen, James Lee Burke, and Julie Smith use both of these locales. Patricia Houck Sprinkle and Kathy Hogan Trochek both use Atlanta and its environs as settings. Charlotte, North Carolina, is the setting for both Kathy Reichs's Temperance Brennan series and for Patricia Cornwell's Kay Scarpetta titles (other series are set in Richmond, Virginia, and Miami). Joan Hess's characters live in Arkansas, and Sharyn McCrumb's best sellers are set in the Appalachian Mountains. Rita Mae Brown (*Rubyfruit Jungle*) has been writing her popular mystery series featuring the cat Sneaky Pie Brown set in Crozet, Virginia, since 1990.

The Midwest

William Kienzle's Father Koesler mysteries and Loren D. Estleman's Amos Walker novels are both set in Detroit. Ellen Hart's Jane Lawless and John Sandford's Lucas Davenport both operate in Minnesota.

The West and Southwest

Rudolfo Anaya, better known for his coming-of-age novel *Bless Me, Ultima*, joins the ranks of mystery writers with his series featuring Sonny Baca set in New Mexico. The *Scene of the Crime* Website lists several hundred mysteries whose authors or settings are Texas-based, including Kinky Freidman, Bill Crider, Rick Riordan, and Jim Thompson. The novels of Susan Wittig Albert are set in small-town Texas, and the environmental mysteries of Nevada Barr, focusing on national parks, have been set in New Mexico and Texas, among other southwestern locales. Tony Hillerman's Jim Chee and Joe Leaphorn are Navajo detectives investigating crimes primarily in Arizona and New Mexico. Walter Mosley's Easy Rawlins prowls the streets of Los Angeles along with Michael Connolly's Harry Bosch.

Awards

The MWA gives the Edgar Award (named for Edgar Allan Poe) for the best mystery writing in several categories including fiction, crime reporting, and critical or biographical book. The 2005 winner for best novel was T. Jefferson Parker. The MWA also presents the Grand Master Award to mystery writers who have made great contributions to the genre and have a history of great writing. Marcia Muller was named the 2005 Grand Master. The Agatha Award is presented by Malice Domestic, an organization established to promote mysteries in the tradition of Agatha Christie. These mysteries have little overt violence and are generally solved by an amateur detective. The 2005 award was presented to Katherine Hall Page for her latest installment in the Faith Fairchild series, *Body in a Snowdrift*. The Anthony Award, named in honor of Anthony Boucheron, who helped found Malice Domestic and was a renowned mystery critic, was given to *Blood Hollow* by William Kent Krueger. *Prince of Thieves* won the Hammett Award for Chuck Hogan, and *While I Disappear* by Edward Wright won the Shamus Award.

Horror

Early horror fiction was based on the supernatural and featured ghosts, hauntings, and otherworldly creatures such as vampires and werewolves. Stephen King's and John Saul's novels often revolve around a historical evil, usually an unavenged murder, and the spirits stirred up in the process. In recent decades many writers have moved away from the strict adherence to the ghost story and have incorporated elements of splatterpunk into their writings. This subgenre revolves around sociopathic characters, and their plots include graphic physical violence. Clive Barker and Poppy Z. Brite are writers in the splatterpunk tradition. Established in 1987, the Horror Writers Association began awarding the Bram Stoker Award. In a field filled to overflowing with authors, a select few own the market in the United States, including Stephen King, Dean Koontz, Poppy Z. Brite, Anne Rice, and John Saul.

Ethnic Authors

Although American authors of every nationality and ethnicity publish their titles in the mainstream book market, some categories of multicultural authors are making a strong impact on books sales.

African-American

Female authors such as Bebe Campbell, Toni Morrison, Alice Walker, Terry McMillan, and Gloria Naylor have been joined by Walter Mosley and Eric Jerome Dickey.

A genre of African-American fiction that has been popular in recent years is ghetto fiction (sometimes marketed as urban or hip-hop fiction). A resurgence of popularity of Donald Goines's graphically sexual and violent titles from the sixties and seventies has been prompted by this trend.

Native American

Louise Erdrich, Sherman Alexie, Leslie Silko, and M. Scott Momaday are well-known Native American authors. They are joined by poets Joy Harjo, Linda Hogan, and Paula Gunn Allen in bringing a wider appreciation of Native peoples to the American public.

Hispanic-American

According to a Simba Business Brief, the United States today is the fifth-largest Spanish-speaking country in the world. Yet fictional Hispanic characters are still not widely seen. Authors such as Sandra Cisneros, Julia Alvarez, Cristina Garcia, and Oscar Hijuelos have contributed much to the increased sales of Hispanic

CENSORSHIP, BANNED BOOKS WEEK, AND PLAGIARISM

In 2003 Dan Brown's *The Da Vinci Code* was published, spawning a host of titles purporting to offer the "real" history of Leonardo da Vinci's paintings, the Templar knights, and the Holy Grail. It also sparked great controversy among religious leaders, especially with the imminent release of the film. It is not the first film based on a book to be attacked by conservative Christians: Nikos Kazantzakis's 1952 novel *The Last Temptation of Christ* (film version, 1988) and the films based on J. K. Rowling's Harry Potter (the first released in 2001) books have felt the sting of opposition as well.

Held the last week of September since 1982, Banned Books Week celebrates Americans' fundamental freedom to read and to remind Americans not to take this freedom for granted. Each year the American Library Association Website updates its list of the 100 most frequently challenged books in America (usually in classrooms and public and school libraries). Many of these titles are classics or children's titles, such as *The Adventures of Tom Sawyer* by Mark Twain, Steinbeck's *Of Mice and Men*, and several Judy Blume titles.

Another controversial issue in today's book news is that of plagiarism—authors stealing ideas from other authors or failing to accurately report their sources. Historian Stephen Ambrose, the author of many best-selling titles, has been attacked for his many instances of plagiarism or sloppy crediting of sources. Dan Brown won his court battle against the authors of *Holy Blood, Holy Grail*, who accused Brown of stealing their ideas for his novel *The Da Vinci Code*. Several journalists at major newspapers have also come under fire for plagiarism in recent years.

authors in the United States. The oldest and largest publisher of U.S. Hispanic authors is Arte Publico Press, based at the University of Texas, Houston.

Asian-American

Gish Jen, Amy Tan, Maxine Hong Kingston, and Frank Chin are at the forefront of Asian-American book sales in the United States.

Film

Books in the United States achieve high sales in a number of ways: self-promotion, word of mouth, publisher or author marketing, and author television appearances are the most common routes to high sales. When a book is made into a film, however, especially if the lead role is a famous star, public interest in, and of course sales of, a title increases. Sales of the first three titles in the Lemony Snicket series for children, *A Series of Unfortunate Events*, each increased over 60 percent upon the movie's release with actor Jim Carey playing Count Olaf. The release of the film version of Chris Van Allsburg's children's classic *The Polar Express* increased sales of that title by 157 percent (*USA Today*). According to the author's Website, as of 2005 Dan Brown's controversial and wildly successful *The Da Vinci Code* (2003) had sold over 50 million copies, making it one of the most successful books of all time. It was released on film in 2006, grossing over $220 million on its opening weekend.

Literary Fiction

What is considered literature is a slippery proposition. Battles between highbrow and lowbrow literature have always been the center of debate in the literary world. Bookstores regularly shelve literature, classic and modern, with regular mass-market fiction, making it difficult for consumers to tell the difference. The distinction is also blurred by crossover literature titles, which have received the endorsement of the Oprah Book Club or some other media tie-in. Most definitions of literature in bookselling terms are appended with the idea that literature has artistic value, as opposed to solely commercial or entertainment value. Literature titles are often marketed by university presses or by specific imprints of larger publishing houses. Buyers tend to be more educated and include college students and academics.

Literature is generally considered more carefully written with an eye toward appealing to a better-read audience, one with a college education or with an interest in books that transcend sheer entertainment, offering a deeper reflection on life. The battle over the moniker "literature" is a long-standing one, stretching back to the early days of publishing history, and one that has not yet been settled. For the sake of convenience, literary fiction is here defined as that produced by authors of short story collections; those published most frequently in literary magazines, by university publishing houses, or by literature imprints of commercial publishing houses; and those who are winners of literary prizes, such as the Pulitzer Prize, the Nobel Prize for Literature, the Booker Prize, and so on.

In 1918 friends of the celebrated American short story writer O. Henry (William Sidney Porter) established the O. Henry Award, given to writers each year who have published their fiction in a U.S. or Canadian journal. Since 1919 the winners have been published in a yearly anthology, *The O. Henry Memorial Award Prize Stories*. Among the notable O. Henry Award winners have been Ray Bradbury, James Thurber, Katherine Anne Porter, Chaim Potok, and Tom Wolfe. An equally prestigious yearly collection of short fiction is *The Best American Short Stories* series, published by Houghton Mifflin since 1915. Each year a special guest editor selects twenty pieces to publish in that year's volume, selecting from a seemingly endless number of literary periodicals.

Established in 1917 with funds earmarked in journalist Joseph Pulitzer's will, the Pulitzer Prizes have been awarded to writers in an ever-increasing number of categories every year since. Various prizes are given to newspaper articles and photography, as well as to biographies, history, poetry, and literary fiction. The Pulitzer Prize, awarded by a committee, is a highly sought-after, though often controversial, prize. Awards often go to titles that have not been on the best seller lists or that have flown under the radar of popular fiction readers. The Pulitzer is accompanied by a gold medal and a monetary award of $10,000. Winners over the past decades have included James Michener, Herman Wouk, Michael Chabon, and Jhumpa Lahiri.

The National Book Award was established both to create awareness of books by American authors and to promote reading in America. The prize, which is accompanied today by $10,000, has been awarded since 1950 to writers of fiction, nonfiction, poetry, and young adult/children's literature. Nelson Algren's *The Man with the Golden Arm* won the fiction award in 1950; William T. Vollman won the 2005 award with *Europe Central*.

Most large commercial publishing houses release literary fiction under a separate imprint. Random House Trade Paperbacks publishes serious fiction and nonfiction. Alfred A. Knopf publishes both classic and contemporary literary fiction under the Vintage imprint. Small independent publishers are still the greatest supporters of literary authors. Algonquin Books, for example, was founded in 1982 by Louis D. Rubin Jr. to publish "worthy fiction." Their list of authors ranges from North Carolinian Clyde Edgerton to Nigerian Chimamanda Ngozi Adichie. Nonprofit publishers, such as Coffee House Press, have been instituted to produce books by underrepresented writers.

Drama

The theater has had a long history in the United States. From the early imitations of British drama to the melodramas of the early nineteenth century to the realism of the twentieth century, drama has been a persistent part of the American literary scene. The most forceful plays of the twentieth century have been those addressing social issues such as Sam Shepard's *True West*, David Mamet's gritty Pulitzer Prize–winning *Glengarry, Glen Ross* and his frightening exploration of sexual harassment, *Oleanna*, Tony Kushner's controversial *Angels in America* about AIDS, and Wendy Wasserstein's *The Heidi Chronicles*.

Poetry

In the early years of the United States' founding, poetry was read with as great a frequency as essays and fiction, accessible in every newspaper and periodical. For the past fifty years, though, poetry sales have been weak: along with literature and books on art, sales of poetry titles accounted for only 3.3 percent of American book purchases in 2000. April is National Poetry Month, which was created to celebrate the joys of poetry and does boost sales of poets during that month. Although doomsayers predict the death of poetry as a genre in the United States, Internet sites such as *Poetry Daily* may prove them wrong: the site attracts 15,000 to 20,000 viewers a day, and the *Atlantic Monthly* online poetry pages count

100,000 hits a month. More accessible poets such as Billy Collins, former poet laureate, continue to sell titles. Sales of *Picnic Lightning*, for example, have passed 40,000 copies. Poetry slams, spoken word poetry competitions, are increasing sales as teenagers discover poetry through this venue. Barnes and Noble reported in 2001 that it saw sales of poetry titles increase by 30 percent over a three-year period.

Another venue for public access to poets is the Geraldine Dodge Poetry Festival. The festival has a twenty-year history of offering a wide diversity of poets with its biennial gatherings. The four-day-long festival offers dozens of readings and events featuring international poets and involving upwards of 20,000 attendants. Such luminaries as Yehuda Amichai, Jimmy Santiago Baca, Amiri Baraka, Robert Bly, Rita Dove, and W. S. Merwin have graced the Dodge stages.

If American poets do not sell as many books as they would like, the appreciation of Americans for poetry is offered in the way of dozens of poetry prizes. The Yale Younger Poets prize, awarded since 1919, is the oldest literary award in the United States, and winners include such notables as W. S. Merwin and Carolyn Forché. Although poetry was not one of the original categories established by Joseph Pulitzer, by 1920 the Pulitzer Prize included a category for poetry. The oldest poetry journal in the United States, *Poetry*, printed its first issue in 1912 and has not missed an issue since. The pharmaceutical heiress Ruth Lilly endowed the Ruth Lilly Prize in 1986, and its award of $100,000 is one of the largest annual poetry awards.

CHILDREN'S BOOKS

According to the American Booksellers Association, two-thirds of the total number of trade books sold are adult books; one-third are children's books. The best-selling children's books of all time include titles with amazing staying power: *Goodnight Moon* by Margaret Wise Brown, published in 1947, spent 539 weeks on the best seller lists; Lois Lowry's young-adult novel *The Giver* stayed 440 weeks. Sales of classics remain strong in a market that is overwhelmingly huge. Projected sales of juvenile titles in 2005, according to *Book Industry Trends 2005*, were $3.2 billion.

There is no disputing the dominance of quality British children's books that have been the mainstay of the American children's book market for decades: Kenneth Grahame's *The Wind in the Willows*, Lewis Carroll's *Alice in Wonderland*, A. A. Milne's Winnie the Pooh books, C. S. Lewis's *The Chronicles of Narnia*, Beatrix Potter's Peter Rabbit books, Frances Hodgson Burnett's *The Secret Garden*, and Roald Dahl's *Matilda* and *James and the Giant Peach* are just a few of the classic British children's books that still sell regularly in American bookstores.

The most recent British novelist to invade America's shores is J. K. Rowling. Rowling's Harry Potter books have taken American children (and adults) by storm, and the American market has been flooded with new fantasy titles and series in unprecedented numbers. Older titles, such as Madeleine L'Engle's *A Wrinkle in Time* and Lois Lowry's *The Giver*, are enjoying new sales as well. Dozens of new fantasy series have appeared, peopled with witches, dragons, vampires, and other marvelous creatures.

Series, branded titles, and media tie-ins make up the biggest sector of children's publishing. Branded titles are those that capitalize on a character's success, for instance the Curious George books. Publishers release new titles extending the adventures of these classic characters. Any television show or movie now has accompanying books and merchandize. For example, the Disney industry has spawned hundreds of titles, many focusing on the "princesses," particularly Cinderella, Jasmine, and Belle. *Dora the Explorer* and *The Magic School Bus* have all been developed into books; in the case of *The Berenstain Bears*, the television show has increased sales of the books.

Series books, however, have been the backbone of children's book sales in America throughout much of its publishing history. Often criticized for their formulaic plots and lack of "classic" style, children's series titles, from the Bobbsey Twins, to Cherry Ames, to *The Babysitters Club* and the scary fiction of R. L. Stine and Christopher Pike, have nonetheless had an impact on children's reading habits, often encouraging poor readers to take up and/or continue reading. The Stratemeyer Syndicate (of Hardy Boy and Nancy Drew fame) dominated the market with its various series, marketed to girls and boys separately, for decades. The popularity of the Nancy Drew mysteries is such that new titles, with an updated Nancy, have been released. Marc Brown's Arthur books appeal to the younger crowd, as do those in the ever popular Encyclopedia Brown series by Donald Sobol.

American children's books have a history of featuring children who are rebellious and unwilling to submit gracefully to authority. Louise Fitzhugh's *Harriet the Spy* (1964) is one of the most popular and long-selling examples. Other popular characters include Judy Blume's Fudge and Lois Lowry's Anastasia Krupnik.

For the younger crowd, Dr. Seuss (Theodore Geisel) is a household name. *The Cat in the Hat* was published in 1957, and children have been wild for Dr. Seuss ever since; he holds twenty-two spots on the *Publishers Weekly* Bestselling Children's Books of All Time list. Other all-time classics for younger children include E. B. White's *Charlotte's Web*, Maurice Sendak's *Where the Wild Things Are*, Eric Carle's *The Very Hungry Caterpillar*, Shel Silverstein's poetry collections, particularly *Where the Sidewalk Ends*, Richard Scarry's *Best Word Book*, Laura Numeroff's *If You Give a Mouse a Cookie*, Robert McCloskey's *Make Way for Ducklings*, and Audrey Wood's *The Napping House*.

Authors of books for older readers include Katherine Patterson, Mildred Taylor, Cynthia Voigt, Paul Danziger, Judy Blume, Robert Cormier, Richard Peck, and Paula Fox, many of whom have won the prestigious Newbery Medal Award for excellence in children's writing.

HARRY POTTER

There is no denying the force with which British author J. K. Rowling's Harry Potter series has exploded on the American publishing scene. Rowling has created, in the young boy attending Hogwarts School of Witchcraft and Wizardry, a character that has reached millions of readers, both children and adult. Harry has also grabbed the attention of the media, the courts, and promoters and critics of all stripes.

Often attacked for its setting in a magical world of magic and fantasy, the six novels in the Harry Potter series (the American edition of *Harry Potter and the Sorcerer's Stone* was published in 1997) are also praised for inviting millions of young readers to join the boy wizard and his friends as they face the problems and the joys of growing up. Harry is "everychild"—he has problems with relationships, with teachers, with girls, and with sports and homework. The difference is that Harry is also embroiled in a battle for good and evil with his nemesis, Lord Voldemort. In his hands ultimately lies the fate of the entire wizarding community.

Along the way, Harry and his friends learn about themselves and life in the magical world Rowling has created. The novels are credited with getting children, especially boys, to read not just the Harry titles but other books as well—quite a feat for an author who is creating 900-page books for her young audience. The demand for Rowling's titles is unprecedented in the publishing industry. The latest installment, *Harry Potter and the Half-Blood Prince* (2005), sold 6.9 million copies in the United States on the first day of sales.

9/11

September 11, 2001, will not be forgotten by Americans. The day the Twin Towers of the World Trade Center in New York and the Pentagon in Washington, D.C., were attacked by Islamic terrorists continues to be at the center of American consciousness. The attacks have been discussed and memorialized in dozens of books: photographic essays, interviews with survivors and family members, biographies, and historical and political speculation. The attacks have also prompted an increase in the production and sales of books about the Middle East in general and about Islam in particular as Americans try to understand both why the attacks happened and the people who committed them. Muslim Americans have also been anxious for their neighbors to understand them, and to break stereotypes that have solidified since 9/11. Many nonfiction titles focusing on Muslims, Afghanistan, and the Taliban, including discussions of Islam such as Karen Armstrong's *A Short History of Islam*, have been joined by innumerable titles by fiction authors as well. The most popular have been Khaled Hosseini's *The Kite Runner*, Azar Nafisi's *Reading Lolita in Tehran: A Memoir in Books*, and *The Bookseller of Kabul* by Asne Seierstad.

A growing trend is that of celebrities writing books for children. Recent titles have been released by Jimmy Buffett, Madonna, Henry Winkler, Katy Couric, Whoopi Goldberg, and Edward M. Kennedy.

NONFICTION

General nonfiction titles accounted for only 7.8 percent of books sales in 2000. After the September 11, 2001, attacks, however, the nonfiction market has been saturated with titles covering the fighting in the Middle East, hefty tomes speculating on the world economy in general and the U.S. outlook in particular, and books on terrorism and other political topics. Titles such as Steven D. Levitt's *Freakonomics*, Thomas Friedman's *The World Is Flat: A Brief History of the Twenty-first Century*, and books about the Enron scandal are riding the wave of American readers who are clamoring to understand the world around them, including economics and politics. General self-help books have been pushed aside but have not dropped out of sight altogether: Americans are still reading for edification and growth.

Diet and Exercise

Several recent titles have focused their lenses on the rising obesity rates in the United States spurred by the Oscar-nominated documentary *Super Size Me* (2003). Statistics indicating that 61 percent of Americans are overweight and 20 percent are obese and other frightening facts about the food industry are at the heart of Greg Critser's *Fat Land: How Americans Became the Fattest People in the World*, Eric Schlosser's *Fast Food Nation*, and *Want Fries with That?: Obesity and the Supersizing of America* by Scott Ingram. Sales of diet books, consistent sellers for decades, have exploded along with sales of exercise videos. The most popular diet books have been the *Atkins Diet* and *South Beach Diet*, riding the no- and low-carbohydrates diet trend. Yoga adherents have increased, spawning both books and videos for novices and experts alike.

Cooking

The immense popularity of the Food Network channel has created cooking stars far beyond what Julia Child ever experienced. Television chefs such as Rachael Ray, Emeril Lagasse, Giada De Laurentiis, Bobby Flay, and Paula Deen, to name just a few, have fueled

Americans' desire to cook. Sales of cookbooks have never been stronger, due in large part to the release of titles by all of these stars. Of the top twenty-five cookbooks for 2004 at Borders and Waldenbooks, twelve titles were produced by just five Food Network stars.

Ethnic cooking has seen a surge as well. Cookbooks for the ever popular Italian and the traditional French cookery books by Julia Child have been joined by books on cuisines from every continent.

Home Improvement and Decorating

As with cookbook titles, sales of home improvement, gardening, and decorating books have skyrocketed due to titles released by hosts appearing on the Home and Garden and Do-It-Yourself networks. Martha Stewart, the doyenne of home management, has released dozens of titles, including cookbook and decorating titles. Both Christopher Lowell and Lynette Jennings, popular television decorating gurus, have released several home design books. Books addressing cleaning and de-cluttering have proliferated as well, in part due to television shows such as *Mission: Organization* and *Clean Sweep*. Longtime cleaning expert Don Aslett continues to release new books on managing cleaning and organization. A surprise seller in 2005 was the paperback release of *Home Comforts: The Art and Science of Keeping House* by Cheryl Mendelson, a hefty 896-page guide to housecleaning and management.

Self-Improvement

Americans have long had a desire for self-improvement. The late-1800s book market was flooded with books by Horatio Alger, whose heroes rose from the lowest ranks of society to become successful men on the strength of their own hard work and determination. Dale Carnegie's *How to Win Friends and Influence People* is one of the best-selling self-improvement books in American bookselling history. The success of such business titles as *Dress for Success* and *What Color Is Your Parachute?*, child-care best sellers *Dr. Spock's Baby and Child Care* and the *What to Expect When You're Expecting* series, and the physical and sexual improvement books *Thin Thighs in Thirty Days* and *The Joy of Sex* speak to the desire Americans have for improving themselves and the world around them. Hundreds of *Dummies Guides* how-to titles cover every category imaginable, from spirituality to learning computer programs to improving public speaking skills.

As important as Oprah Winfrey has been to the careers of many authors of fiction, she has been instrumental in launching the career of several self-improvement experts as television personalities and authors. Phil McGraw's tough-love attitude and straight talk made his appearances on *Oprah* well received. Now he has his own show and is the best-selling author of books on weight loss and relationships. *Emerge* magazine hailed Iyanla Vanzant, an inspirational speaker, as the "most dynamic African-American speaker in the country." She was a popular guest on *Oprah* and launched her own talk show in 2001. Her appearances keep her book titles selling as well. Suze Orman, also a popular *Oprah* guest, is consistently on the best seller lists for her personal finance titles.

The newest television fad affecting book purchases is the makeover industry. One of the most popular programs is *What Not to Wear*, the British version of which was hosted by Trinny Woodall and Susannah Constantine, who released their own accompanying titles in 2003. American hosts Stacey London and Clinton Kelly have also released a style guide, one of many that are currently flooding the market.

Religion

A growing category of books is religion, both fiction and nonfiction. According to *Trends 2005*, sales of religious titles (including Bibles, hymnals, and prayer books) increased by 11 percent in 2004, reaching $1.9 billion in sales. The increase is due in part to a series of novels by Tim LaHaye and Jerry Jenkins entitled *Left Behind*. The series follows the lives of those left behind to battle the Antichrist after the Rapture. New Age and alternative-religion authors are moving into the mainstream as well. Authors such as Deepak Chopra are no longer seen as being on the fringes but are placing books on the best seller lists. Shambala, a long-standing publisher of books on Eastern philosophies, is seeing gains as the post-9/11 readers are searching for answers in very confusing times. Another established New Age publisher, Llewellyn, has seen a new market for teens, and the Left Behind series has a spin-off for children titled *Left Behind: The Kids*.

Self-help books have boosted sales in the religion category as well. *The Purpose-Driven Life* by Rick Warren, as well as titles by Eric and Leslie Ludy, and Scott Peck's best seller *The Road Less Traveled* are strong favorites. Even diet books have been given a spiritual spin. The first religious diet book was Charlie Shedd's *Pray Your Weight Away* (1957), but the current market is becoming saturated with weight-loss titles.

Memoir

The publication of Mary Karr's *The Liars' Club* in 1995 opened the floodgates for the publication of memoirs. Some of the recent best-selling titles have been *The Year of Magical Thinking* by Joan Didion, *Marley & Me: Life and Love with the World's Worst Dog* by John Grogan, and *Tuesdays with Morrie* by Mitch Albom. James Frey's *A Million Little Pieces*, discredited as a fictionalized memoir, has shone the spotlight on memoirs and their levels of truthfulness.

History

Americans love books about U.S. history. David McCullough is one of the most popular and prolific scholars of U.S. history, and his titles range from *1776* to *Johnstown Flood*. Titles about the founding fathers and the period of American history from the colonial days to the years of the early republic are strong sellers. Recent titles include *Mayflower: A Story of Courage, Community, and War* by Nathaniel Philbrick and *American Gospel: God, the Founding Fathers, and the Making of a Nation* by Jon Meacham. Titles about George Washington (Paul Johnson's *George Washington: Founding Father*), Thomas Jefferson (Joseph Ellis's *American Sphinx: The Character of Thomas Jefferson*), and Benjamin Franklin (Joyce Chaplin's *The First Scientific American: Benjamin Franklin and the Pursuit of Genius*) are released on an almost yearly basis. Other recent best sellers have been Erik Larson's *Devil in the White City* about the Chicago World's Fair, Kenneth C. Davis's *Don't Know Much about History*, and James Loewen's *Lies My Teacher Told Me*.

CANADA

Of Canada's inhabitants, 11.7 million are Canadian, 5.9 million are English, and 4.7 million are French. According to the Canadian Arts Council, approximately 60 percent of Canadians read books each year, 25 percent of whom borrow them from the library. Canada shares the United

States' northern border. It also shares many of the same authors and book trends. Dan Brown and J. K. Rowling are read as avidly by Canadians as by Americans. That being said, this section will focus, although not exclusively, on those authors of Canadian citizenship (francophone or anglophone) who are popular mainly in Canada and may not be as familiar to U.S. readers.

According to *Publishers Weekly*, the Canadian book industry reported Can$2.4 billion ($1.5 billion) in book sales, with 15,744 new titles published in the period 2000–2001. Of these new titles, 72 percent were produced by Canadian authors. The largest book chain is Chapters, which merged with Indigo in 2001. Mirroring the trend in the United States, the large "big-box" superstores pushed out many Canadian independent booksellers, reducing readers' choices to blockbuster titles and reducing the number of small press and backlist titles. Several online venues emerged, one of them Amazon.ca. The Canadian Booksellers Association lodged a complaint against the online merchandizing giant, citing Canadian laws that bookstores be owned by Canadians, but was unsuccessful in stopping the creation of a Canadian arm of Amazon.com. In a 2002 study of Canadians' book-buying habits, researchers found that Amazon.ca was visited by 43 percent of online book shoppers, with the online branch of Chapters-Indigo capturing 35 percent of Canada's book customers.

Fiction

In general, Canadian best seller lists for fiction feature many of the same authors as best seller lists in the United States. There are more Canadian authors, though, in the genres of romance, science fiction, and mysteries.

Romance

Canada is the home of Harlequin Romances, a category fiction line that has been on the romance fiction scene since 1949 and publishes over a hundred titles a month. The Toronto-based company acquired the rights to the British Mills & Boons in 1957 and by 1964 was publishing romances exclusively. Many of the Canadian romance authors write for Harlequin.

Jo Beverly, one of the most popular Canadian romance writers, is also well received in the United States; she has won many RITA Awards from the RWA. Karyn Monk sells well in the United States as well. Canadian authors are as varied in their interests as U.S. authors. Gordon Aalborg (Victoria Gordon) and wife and fellow romance writer Denise Dietz team up to write romantic suspense novels along with their own romance and mystery projects. Carrie Chesney is another writer of romantic suspense. Catherine Kean writes medieval historical romances, and Laura Paquet pens Regency romances. Lynn Turner writes historical fiction as well, using eighteenth-century Nova Scotia as her settings. Judy Gill, veteran author of dozens of romance novels, has recently incorporated the paranormal into her romances. Kayla Perrin has topped the Romance of America's Top 10 list as well as *Essence Magazine*'s best seller lists with her contemporary romances, published by Harlequin, BET, and other publishers.

Mystery

As in the mystery tradition of any country, Canada has its share of authors who have developed a character through a series of novels. Canadian author Alisa Craig lived in the United States but was born in Canada and situated her Madoc Rhys mysteries there. Laurali

Wright (L. R.) created another series of Royal Canadian Mounted Police with Sergeant Karl Alberg. Eric Wright's mysteries feature Toronto police inspector Charlie Salter. Canadian mysteries incorporate their respective environments within their settings; locale is at the heart of many authors' offerings. Howard Engel sets his Benny Cooperman detective novels in the Niagara Region, and Gail Bowen's Saskatchewan settings help propel her mysteries.

Other successful Canadian mystery writers, many of whom have been awarded the Arthur Ellis Award, are Peter Robinson, Giles Blunt, William Deverell, and Rosemary Aubert. Awarded by the Crime Writers of Canada, the Arthur Ellis Award, named for Canada's official hangman, is bestowed for excellence in crime writing.

Science Fiction

Robert Sawyer, a leading Canadian science fiction writer and critic, argues that there is no real difference between Canadian and U.S. science fiction authors. He does say that there are two different kinds of science fiction writers in Canada, and the difference does not fall along linguistic lines (French or English). The difference lies in their publication goals: those who sell exclusively in U.S. markets and those whose fictional voices and themes are more distinctly Canadian. The dominant theme in Canadian speculative fiction is that of science in relationship to environment. Sawyer's 1992 *Far-Seer* is representative of the theme of the inhospitable Canadian landscape. Artificial intelligence is a frequent theme as well, embodied by William Gibson's blockbuster *Neuromancer* (1984), in which the term *cyberspace* was coined.

Clearly identified Canadian landscapes are more common in fantasy fiction than in science fiction. Charles de Lint, Tanya Huff, and Edo van Belkom all set some of their work in Canadian locales. The dearth of authors using recognizable Canadian regions may be due in part to the sheer number of science fiction writers who are transplants from elsewhere (William Gibson hails originally from South Carolina, for example). Since the book market in Canada is less reliant on genres as a marketing tool than the book market in the United States, authors who are seen as generally more mainstream often write in other genres. For example, Margaret Atwood's *The Handmaid's Tale* (1985) was considered science fiction based on its speculative nature.

Successful contemporary science fiction and fantasy novelists publishing in Canada include Charles de Lint (*Widdershins*, 2006), Donald Kingsbury, Spider Robinson (*Callahan Con*, 2003), Tanya Huff (*Smoke and Ashes*, 2006), and the mother of Canadian science fiction, Phyllis Gottlieb (*Mindworlds*, 2001). Canada's foremost publisher of science fiction, Tesseract Books, merged with EDGE Science Fiction and Fantasy in 2003; the house publishes English titles. Francophone titles are published mostly by Québec/Amérique.

Literary Fiction

Many of Canada's most notable and best-selling authors are women. The late Carol Shields, 1995 Pulitzer Prize winner for *The Stone Diaries*, Margaret Atwood (*Surfacing*, *The Handmaid's Tale*), and Alice Munro are among the best-known internationally. Jane Urquhart is better known in Canada, where her 1992 *The Whirlpool* was the first Canadian book to win the Prix du Meilleur Livre Estranger, France's foreign book award. Robertson Davies, Malcolm Lowry, and Timothy Findley are writers whose works have won much acclaim. Yann Martel's *Life of Pi* won the Booker Prize for Fiction in 2002 and propelled him into international fame. Michael Ondaatje, a poet and essayist, is best known for his novels, *The English Patient* (1992) in particular.

Alice Munro is one of the best short story writers of all time; her newest collection, *Runaway*, is on the best seller lists. Elizabeth Smart has an almost cultish following for her novel *By Grand Central Station I Sat Down and Wept*. Barbara Gowdy has been nominated for a Governor General's Award for her 1995 novel *Mister Sandman* and for *White Bone*, published in 1998.

Canada's ethnic voices are as well recorded in fiction as their counterparts in the United States. Japanese Canadian Joy Kogawa's *Obasan*, East Indian Canadian Himani Bannerji's *The Other Family*, Rohinton Mistry's *Swimming Lessons*, M. G. Vassanji's *The London-Returned*, and Jewish Canadian A. M. Klein's *The Second Scroll* are just some of the novels exploring Canada's multicultural nature.

Drama

Canada is renowned for its theaters, many dozens of which are in Toronto and other major cities, and its many festivals, including the Edmonton International Fringe Festival and the Stratford Festival of Canada. Don Hannah's *The Wooden Hill*, based on the journals of L. M. Montgomery, was the winner of an AT&T OnStage Award, and his drama *The Wedding Script* won the Chalmers Award. George F. Walker, along with Michel Tremblay, is one of Canada's most prolific and widely produced playwrights. One of his best-known works is *Zastrozzi: The Master of Discipline*, which is set in 1893 and tells the story of the European mastermind of evil and his plan for vengeance. Tremblay's first play, *Les Belles Soeurs*, set new standards for both franco- and anglophone theater. Three of Michael Cook's plays are grouped as the Newfoundland trilogy—*Colour the Flesh the Colour of Dust* (1970), *Head Guts and Soundbone Dance* (1973), and *Jacob's Wake* (1974)—and were produced by the Open Group, a popular Canadian troupe. Set in Quebec, Robert Lepage and Marie Brassard's "play noir" *Polygraph* weaves together the fact and fiction surrounding a murder. Women have made their mark in Canadian theater as well. Anne-Marie McDonald has won awards for both her fiction (*Fall on Your Knees*) and her plays (*Goodnight Desdemona [Good Morning Juliet]*). Award-winning playwright and actress Sharon Pollock's wide reputation is based on many works including *Walsh* and *Blood Relations*.

Poetry

One of Canada's finest poets, James Reaney is best known for his dramatic *Donnelly* trilogy. From the 1960s onward, the Canadian poetry of E. J. Pratt, whose interests included Canadian mythmaking, was joined by the more personal poetry of Earle Birney, Irving Layton, Dorothy Livesay, and Al Purdy. Some of Canada's most popular poets are novelists as well, for instance Margaret Atwood and Michael Ondaatje. Leonard Cohen, now more popular as a songwriter, received high praise for his 1961 book *The Spice-Box of Earth*.

French-Canadian poetry has a long tradition as well, beginning with Emile Nelligan. Alain Grandbois, St-Denys-Garneau, Anne Hébert, Rina Lasnier, Gaston Miron, Roland Giguère, Michel Beaulieu, and Nicole Brossard all write in French.

The Scream Literary Festival, held in Toronto, is a popular venue for contemporary poets to read their work. Paul Vermeesh—whose *Burn*, with poems reflecting rural Ontario, was a finalist for the 2001 Gerald Lampert Award—has been a featured speaker. John Stiles is another poet whose work is located in Canada's countryside. *Scouts Are Cancelled: The Annapolis Valley Poems* is reminiscent of Edgar Lee Masters's *Spoon River Anthology* and is narrated by characters in rural Nova Scotia.

Canada's indigenous writers have produced a number of poets. Rita Joe is often called the poet laureate of the Mi'kmaw people. Gary James Richardson is of Ojibway and Irish descent. Daniel David Moses hails from southern Ontario. And probably the best-known Okanagan Indian poet is Jeanette Armstrong, the first Native American woman to publish a novel in Canada.

Children's Books

Canadian Children's Book Week is held in late November. It was organized in 1976 to highlight Canada's authors and illustrators of children's books and to promote reading.

Along with the typical themes of children's literature (growing up, fears, social situations), many Canadian authors situate their books for children in historical settings that educate readers about the frontier existence of Canada's pioneers. Lucy Maud Montgomery, the best-known Canadian author, children's or adult, has won the hearts of readers all over the world for her *Anne of Green Gables* series, first published in 1908. The books feature Anne Shirley, adopted by a couple and brought to live at Green Gables on Prince Edward Island.

Other authors focus on the indigenous peoples of Canada, their way of life and their relationships and conflicts with settlers. Maria Campbell writes of the Métis and Plains Indians. Having grown up in a log cabin in British Columbia, Christie Harris uses western Canada as the settings for her books. Her most successful title has been *Raven's Cry*, a critique of the unfair treatment of the people of the Haida Nation.

According to a recent listing of top sellers in Canada, Robert Munsch held nine of the fifteen slots. He is as well-known in the United States as he is in Canada. *Love You Forever*, about a mother's unending love for her son, is a perennial favorite, having sold upwards of 15 million copies since it was published in 1986. Munsch's books frequently come under fire for their use of "vulgar" language (such as *pee* and *bum*), but children love his characters and the situations they get themselves into. Titles such as *I've Got to Go* and *I'm So Embarrassed* are attuned to the everyday experiences of kids, and he is a sought-after author for school visits.

Popular authors of various types (contemporary, historical, science fiction, and fantasy) are Mary Blakeslee, author of the popular Lemon Street Gang books, Karleen Bradford, Phoebe Gilman, Margaret Buffie, Julie Johnston, Gilles Tibo, and Budge Wilson.

Paulette Bourgeois, author of dozens of books for children, is most famous for her titles about Franklin, a turtle who overcomes many fears and difficult situations. The books are popular in the United States as well. Gordon Korman's books, featuring the adventures of rowdy little boys, are also strong sellers in the United States. Paul Kropp is the author of fifty books for younger readers and young adults; his book for parents, *How to Make Your Child a Reader for Life*, has become a mainstay across North America.

Nonfiction

Canada's nonfiction publishing industry is a strong one and demonstrates Canada's fiercely independent nature. A number of titles celebrate the lives of Canadians, offering insight into a society that is often regarded, by outsiders, as indistinguishable from its U.S. counterpart to the south. This independent spirit is often in conflict with the more commercial drive of the United States, and many Canadian nonfiction books are written to persuade the Canadian public to reexamine its relationship with the United States.

Douglas Coupland, author of the popular novel *Generation X*, has created two collections of images and reminiscences, often humorous, of life as a Canadian, *Souvenir of Canada 1* and *2*. Kerry Colburn is another popular writer whose lighthearted book about Canada, *So You Want to Be Canadian: All about the Most Fascinating People in the World and the Magical Place They Call Home*, answers questions Americans have about their northern neighbors. In Will Ferguson's *How to Be a Canadian* and *I Hate Canadians* and Ann Douglas's *Canuck Chicks and Maple Leaf Mamas*, readers from the United States are given lively insight into the world of Canadians.

Other writers, though, are more serious about the state of the nation in Canada and are quick to point fingers at the United States, laying the blame for many of Canada's woes on its southern neighbor. Andrew Cohen's *While Canada Slept: How We Lost Our Place in the World*, Mel Hurtig's *The Vanishing Country: Is It Too Late to Save Canada?*, and *Fire and Ice* by Michael Henry Adams are three titles that offer insight into the economic and political ills plaguing Canadians. On the lighter side, yet still cognizant of the split between French Canadians and Anglo-Canadians, are two memoirs: *American Ghosts* by David Plante and *Sacré Blues: An Unsentimental Journey through Quebec* by Taras Grescoe.

Cookbooks

Canada's best seller lists are graced with many of the same cookbooks that are popular in the United States. There are, however, many cookbooks specific to Canadian cuisine and culture. Julian Armstrong, a food writer for the *Montreal Gazette*, penned *A Taste of Quebec*, which features foods from various regions of Quebec. Anita Stewart's *The Flavours of Canada: A Celebration of the Finest Regional Foods* and Dorothy Duncan's *Nothing More Comforting: Canada's Heritage Food* explore the rich diversity of Canada's culture and cooking history. Marcy Claman offers recipes from Canada's inns in *Rise and Dine Canada: Savory Secrets from Canada's Bread and Breakfast Inns*, and top Canadian chef Jamie Kennedy provides tips for cooking Canada's seasonal foods in *Jamie Kennedy's Seasons*.

History

One of the most popular Canadian historians has been Pierre Berton. Berton's pleasing writing style made best sellers of many of his titles. *Marching to War* looks at how war has shaped Canada. *The National Dream* and *The Last Spike* both examine the history of the Canadian railway. *The Arctic Grail, Klondike Fever: The Life and Death of the Last Great Gold Rush*, and *Niagara: A History of the Falls* tell the story of some of Canada's great explorers and adventurers.

Other popular history books are Christopher Moore's *1867: How the Fathers Made a Deal*, about the Canadian Constitution, *Book of Letters: 150 Years of Private Canadian Correspondence*, the first in a series designed to connect Canadians to their past, and *Canada: A People's History*, volumes 1 and 2, based on the epic CBC television series.

RESOURCE GUIDE

PRINT SOURCES

Atwood, Margaret. *Strange Things: The Malevolent North in Canadian Literature*. Toronto: New York: Oxford Press, 1995.
Bleiler, Richard J. *Reference Guide to Mystery and Detective Fiction*. Libraries Unlimited, 1999.

Clute, John, and Peter Nicholls, eds. *Encyclopedia of Science Fiction*, 2nd edition. New York: St. Martin's Press, 1993.

Herbert, Rosemary, ed. *The Oxford Companion to Crime and Mystery Writing*. New York: Oxford University Press, 1999.

James, Edward, and Farah Mendelsohn, eds. *The Cambridge Companion to Science Fiction*. Cambridge: Cambridge University Press, 2003.

Jones, Raymond E., and Jon C. Scott. *Canadian Children's Books: A Critical Guide to Authors and Illustrators*. Oxford: Oxford University Press, 2000.

Ketterer, David. *Canadian Science Fiction and Fantasy*. Bloomington, IN: Indiana University Press, 1992.

Landrum, Larry. *American Mystery and Detective Novels: A Reference Guide*. Westport, CT: Greenwood Press, 1999.

New, William H., ed. *Encyclopedia of Literature in Canada*. Toronto: University of Toronto Press, 2002.

Paradis, Andrea, ed. *Out of This World: Canadian Science Fiction and Fantasy Literature*. Kingston: Quarry Press, 1995.

Priestman, Martin. *The Cambridge Companion to Crime Fiction*. Cambridge: Cambridge University Press, 2003.

Regis, Pamela. *A Natural History of the Romance Novel*. Philadelphia: University of Pennsylvania Press, 2003.

PERIODICALS

Magazines are listed with their publishers and Websites.
Asimov's Science Fiction. Dell Magazines. http://www.asimovs.com/.
Black Issues Book Review. Target Market News Co. http://www.bibookreview.com/.
Booklist. American Library Association. http://www.ala.org/ala/booklist/booklist.htm.
Bookmarks. Bookmarks Publishing LLC. http://www.bookmarksmagazine.com/.
Books and Culture: A Christian Review. Christianity Today. http://www.christianitytoday.com/books/.
Fantasy and Science Fiction. Fantasy & Science Fiction. http://www.sfsite.com/fsf/.
Historical Novels Review. Historical Novel Society. http://www.historicalnovelsociety.org/.
Locus (Science Fiction). Locus Magazine. http://www.locusmag.com/About/LocusOnline.html.
London Review of Books. London Review of Books. http://www.lrb.co.uk/.
Mystery Scene. Mystery Scene Magazine. http://www.mysteryscenemag.com/.
New York Times Book Review. New York Times. http://www.nytimes.com/pages/books/.
Pages. Advanced Marketing Services. http://www.pagesmagazine.com/.
Publishers Weekly. Reed Business Information. http://www.publishersweekly.com/.
Quill & Quire (Canadian Book Reviews). St. Joseph Media Inc. http://www.quillandquire.com/.
Romantic Times Book Review. Romantic Times Book Review Magazine. http://www.romantictimes.com/.
The Strand Magazine (Mysteries). The Strand Magazine. http://www.strandmag.com/.
The Times Literary Supplement. The Times Literary Supplement Ltd. http://tls.timesonline.co.uk/.

WEBSITES

Brian, Paul. *Science Fiction Research Bibliography: A Bibliography of Science Fiction Secondary Materials in Holland Library, Washington State University*. Updated March 6, 2006. Washington State University. Accessed April 29, 2006. http://www.wsu.edu/~brians/science_fiction/sfresearch.html.

Brown, David K. *Children's Literature Web Guide*. Doucette Library of Teaching Resources, University of Calgary. Accessed May 12, 2006. http://www.ucalgary.ca/~dkbrown/index.html.

Canadian Children's Book Centre. Accessed May 15, 2006. http://www.bookcentre.ca/index.shtml.

Charlebois, Gaetan. *Canadian Theater Encyclopedia*. Accessed June 17, 2006. http://www.canadian theatre.com.

Crime Fiction Canada. Brock University. Accessed May 29, 2006. http://www.brocku.ca/crimefiction canada/.

Crime Thru Time. Accessed May 18, 2006. http://crimethrutime.com/. Website devoted to historical mysteries.

Derie, Kate. *The Mysterious Home Page.* Accessed May 20, 2006. http://www.cluelass.com/MystHome/index.html.

Grost, Michael E. *A Guide to Classic Mystery and Detection.* Accessed May 15, 2006. http://members.aol.com/mg4273/classics.htm.

Impressions: 250 Years of Printing in the Lives of Canadians. Library and Archives Canada. Accessed May 12, 2006. http://www.collectionscanada.ca/2/10/index-e.html.

Lewis, Steve. *The Crime Fiction Research Journal. Mystery*File.* Accessed May 20, 2006. http://www.mysteryfile.com/.

Made in Canada: The Homepage for Canadian Science Fiction. Accessed May 18, 2006. http://www.geocities.com/canadian_SF/index.html.

Publishing Central: Book, Magazine, Newsletter, and Electronic Publishing Industry Information. Accessed May 29, 2006. http://www.publishingcentral.com/subject.html?sid=122&si=1.

Publishing Trends: News and Opinion on the Changing World of Book Publishing. Accessed May 12, 2006. http://www.publishingtrends.com/.

Pyrcz, Heather. *A Digital History of Canadian Poetry.* League of Canadian Poets. Accessed May 20, 2006. http://www.youngpoets.ca/history/history.php.

Runté, Robert, ed. *The NCF Guide to Canadian Science Fiction and Fandom.* 4th ed. Accessed May 20, 2006. http://www.uleth.ca/edu/runte/ncfguide/cansf.htm.

Sawyer, Robert J. *Canadian Science Fiction Homepage.* Updated 1995–2006. Accessed May 14, 2006. http://www.sfwriter.com/index.htm.

ORGANIZATIONS

Academy of American Poets, 584 Broadway, Suite 604, New York, NY 10012–5243. http://www.poets.org/.

American Booksellers Association. http://www.bookweb.org/.

The American Library Association, 50 East Huron Street, Chicago, IL 60611. http://www.ala.org/.

Canadian Booksellers Association, 789 Don Mills Rd., #700, Toronto, ON M3C 1T5. http://www.cbabook.org.

Canadian Library Association, 328 Frank Street, Ottawa, ON K2P 0X8. http://www.cla.ca.

Malice Domestic, P.O. Box 31137, Bethesda, MD 20824–1137. http://www.malicedomestic.org/. Mystery writers' organization.

Mystery Writers of America, 17 E. 47th Street, 6th Floor, New York, NY 10017.

Romance Writers of America, 16000 Stuebner Airline Rd., Suite 140, Spring, TX 77379, 832–717–5200.

Science Fiction and Fantasy Writers of American. http://www.sfwa.org.

NOTES

1. All figures retrieved from the *American Book Trade Directory*, the Ipsos-NPD Group, the American Library Association, the Canadian Library Association, *Book Industry Trends*, and *Statistics Canada.*
2. Figures retrieved from Bowker and the U.S. Department of Commerce.
3. Figures retrieved from the Ipsos-NPD Group and Romance Writers of America.

LOVE, SEX, AND MARRIAGE

VICTOR C. DE MUNCK

The cultural and demographic landscape of the United States has changed significantly over the last half a century.[1] In 1950 the U.S. Census reported a population of 151,325,798. The U.S. Census Bureau estimates that in October 2006 the population of the United States climbed above the 300 million mark. Forty percent of the annual growth rate of the United States is attributed to immigration, primarily from Central and South America and Asia. It is estimated that 33 million, or 11 percent, of the total 2006 population is foreign-born. Though there has been a significant change in the demographics of the U.S. population since the 1950s, it is perhaps surprising to note that whites still constitute 81 percent of the U.S. population, African Americans 13 percent, American Indians 1 percent, and Asians and Pacific Islanders 5 percent. If we disaggregate "whites" into Hispanics and non-Hispanics, then non-Hispanic whites constitute 69 percent of the population and Hispanics 14 percent (the percentage for Hispanics also includes de-aggregating African Americans and Asians).

HOUSEHOLDS

Though the population is increasing, the size of the average household is shrinking. The reduction in household size is found mostly among whites and African Americans and is a result of smaller family size and divorce. In the 1970s the size of the average non-Hispanic white family was 3.1 and in 2002 it was 2.5. However the size of Hispanic families is increasing over time. Over that same period of time the size of the average Hispanic family has increased from 3 to 3.5 per household. The reason for this increase is due to the acceptability of extended families, particularly relatives who immigrate to the United States after the household has been established and also due to the fact that most Hispanics are Catholics.

On a smaller scale we find similar changes occurring in Canada as in the United States. However, these changes occur at a much higher order of magnitude in Canada than in the United States because of the lower population of Canada. For example, in 1950 the population of Canada was 13.7 million, and in 2006 it was estimated to be 32.5 million; this marks a 237 percent increase in a 56-year period. Further, 18.5 percent of Canadians in 2002 were foreign-born, with most immigrants coming from Asia (58 percent) rather than Mexico and Latin America, as they do for the United States.

MARRIAGE RATES

For all ethnic groups, there has been a general trend to postpone marriage; the average age in the United States for men to marry in 2003 was 27 and for women 25, whereas in 1950 it was 24 and 21, respectively. The annual rate of marriages, calculated by the percentage of all unmarried citizens over the age of 15 who marry in the year, has dropped by a third since the 1970s despite the rise in the population. From 1950 to 2005 the marriage rate per 1,000 people decreased from 11.1 to 7.5. The current marriage rate of 7.5 per 1,000 has remained stable since the 1990s and the aforementioned decrease is not indicative of a long-term trend but of a trend triggered by changes in divorce law, acceptance of cohabitation as a substitute for marriage, increasing number of women in colleges, and the invention and accessibility of the birth control pill in the 1960s.[2] In addition, the U.S. Census Bureau's American Community Survey, released in October 2006, states that a minority of households now have married couples. Of the 111.1 million U.S. households in 2005, 49.7 percent, or 55.2 million, were composed of married couples—with and without children. However, the total number of married couples is higher than before; it is just that there is more cohabitation and divorce.[3] In Canada the current marriage rate is 5.0, two-thirds that of the U.S. rate.[4]

Canadian marriage rates are lower than those of the United States, primarily because the average age for marriage is significantly higher: the average age of first-time brides in Canada is 31.7 years, and for first-time grooms it is 34.3 years. Since the 1960s there has been a dramatic shift from two-parent to one-parent households in Canada; at present 19 percent of all children live in one-parent households, and 80 percent of these are households headed by the mother.

DIVORCE RATES

There was also a jump in the divorce rate in the 1970s due to changes in the divorce law, but this rate has remained stable since the 1980s to just under 50 percent. The divorce rate is typically calculated in terms of the number of marriages that ended in divorce. However, if one does not take into account the frequency of divorce by individuals, then 41 percent of men who have married and 39 percent of women who have married have also divorced. The divorce rate is often associated with a deterioration of family values, but it is more likely caused by economic and legal factors. Women, who make up 46 percent of the U.S. workforce, are no longer economically dependent on a spouse for their livelihood. Legal procedures for divorce, particularly for couples without differences, have become much easier over the last 40 years. Just as "being in love" is a primary motivation for marriage or cohabitation, "falling out of love" is the most frequently cited explanation for separating.

Canadian divorce rates have followed the same pattern as those in the United States; there was a major increase in the late 1960s due to the easier divorce laws that were put into effect, and then the divorce rate leveled off in the 1980s, peaking in 1987 to 362 per 100,000 and decreasing to 262 per 100,000 marriages in 1994. In that same year, the U.S. rate was 460 per 100,000 (the highest in the Western world, with the UK second and Canada third); the lowest rate was for Japan at 130 per 100,000. Among all living adults who have been married the divorce rate is actually 30 percent.

COHABITATION RATES

Cohabitation has become an important step that unmarried couples choose in preference to or as a substitute for marriage. Fifty percent of females have participated in cohabitation before turning 30, thus postponing marriage. Relative to marriage, cohabitation is much less stable, with 49 percent of couples who are cohabiting separate within 5 years compared to 20 percent for married couples. The trend toward cohabitation prior to marriage is the main reason for the increase in the mean age for first marriage. Seventy percent of premarital cohabitations that last 5 years make a transition to marriage (NCHS 2002:21). Cohabitation rates for Canada are comparable to those of the United States. As in the United States, cohabitation is much less stable than marriage in Canada.

SAME-SEX MARRIAGES

Only Massachusetts recognizes same-sex marriages; domestic partnerships are permitted in a number of states, and in nineteen states there are state constitutional amendments that bar same-sex marriages. The number of same-sex marriages or domestic partners in the United States is difficult to determine but is indirectly counted by the U.S. Census Bureau by asking "sex and relationship" questions to the "main householder." Estimates of same-sex households have risen from an estimated 600,000 (1 percent of households) in 2001 to 708,000 in 2004 (1.16 percent) (http://gaydemographics.org/usa/usa.htm).

In Canada same-sex marriage was approved by Canada's House of Commons on June 28, 2005, with 158 MPs voting in favor and 133 against. The definition of marriage was changed shortly thereafter, and same-sex marriage became legal as of July 19, 2005, with hardly a word of protest.

Despite the population statistics cited above that emphasize that marriage is a dynamic institution sensitive to economic and population shifts, there are two general ideal cultural blueprints that typically guide the development of a relationship from meeting to falling in love to marriage for almost all Americans, regardless of gender, class, ethnic differences, or sexual orientation (Sobo 1997; Lee 1998). These two general cultural blueprints will be referred to as standard cultural models and are discussed below. The components and variations from the components are described after a general introduction to these two models.

COHABITATION

In the early 1960s cohabitation was considered an alternative lifestyle engaged in by bohemians and hippies. By the 1970s it had become a cultural norm. Why did this happen? It was a result of three converging factors: (1) in Canada and the United States new divorce laws in the late 1960s were adopted that made obtaining a divorce simpler and allowed for no-fault divorces; (2) the emergence of a feminist movement; and (3) low tuition rates at state universities and the increase in high school graduates entering college, particularly women. These three factors led to greater tolerance for premarital sex and cohabitation among older adults (who had experienced divorce) and college students. The percentage of couples in cohabitation in Canadian is 16 percent, nearly twice as high as the 8.2 percent rate in the United States. However, much of the Canadian rate is attributed to Quebec, the predominantly French-speaking area, where the rate of cohabitating among all couples is 30 percent. The cohabitation rate for French couples is also around 16 percent, but for Italy it is only 4 percent. Thus, legal, economic, and secular-cultural, rather than religious, factors are the determining factors in varying rates of cohabitation in the United States and Canada and in other countries.

POLYAMORY MARRIAGE

A new form of marriage that has gained some fame is *polyamory*, meaning "many lovers." Polyamory marriage came out of the anti-monogamy rhetoric of the 1960s and was written about in the best-selling novel *The Harrad Experiment* as well as practiced in hippie communes. It is not like the Mormon practice of polygyny (e.g., one man, many wives), which is tacitly allowed in Utah and Idaho, where the general legal policy is "don't ask, don't tell." Polyamory permits all sorts of combinations of people into a group marriage unit. Polyamory groups may consist of heterosexuals, bisexuals, all-lesbian groups, and so forth (see Deborah Anapol's authoritative text on polyamory titled *Polyamory: The New Love without Limits*). As in hippie communes and polygynous relationships throughout the world, such relationships are inherently unstable unless emotional attachment is not an important aspect of the relationship. Once emotional connection becomes important, such forms of partnering inevitably lead to jealousy and conflict and are unstable.

THE TRADITIONAL CULTURAL MODEL OF DATING, LOVE, SEX, AND MARRIAGE IN NORTH AMERICA

Despite changes in the ethnic composition and rates of divorce, the rise of out-of-wedlock births and matrifocal households, the prevalence of cohabitation, and the postponement of marriage, there remains a standard cultural model for marriage and family in North America that has remained virtually unchanged since the time of independence in its most basic and fundamental components. The standard cultural model is a simplified, idealized scheme that is used as a blueprint for the relationship between dating, sex, love, and marriage. Contemporary studies reaffirm that this model represents a cultural ideal that is known but not necessarily practiced by most Canadians and Americans. The traditional ideal standard cultural model (hereafter referred to as scm1) of the American courtship process was succinctly captured in the well-known ditty "Love and Marriage Go Together like a Horse and Carriage." The key components of the scm1 are the following:

> Boy and girl meet.
> Boy and girl date.
> They like each other and begin to date exclusively.
> They think of themselves and are seen by others as boyfriend and girlfriend.
> They declare love for each other.
> They continue to date until the boy proposes.
> They marry.
> They have sex.
> They have children.

The elemental stripped-down temporal and causal sequence can be further reduced to the following: date → fall in love → marriage → sex. This scm remains an ideal model adhered to and practiced particularly by religiously devout North Americans. A second standard cultural model (scm2) has become more popular both as an ideal and as a practiced standard cultural model. This model is essentially a variant of the traditional model. It is considered a second model because when sex can occur "is" in free variation, occurring anywhere in the above sequence after meeting and prior to marriage. Also cohabitation precedes and is usually preferred as a substitute for marriage. Except for cohabitation the components of this model are the same as in scm1; however, there is even more significant variation in those components in scm2 compared with scm1. The key components of this model are as follows:

> Boy and girl meet.
> Boy and girl date.
> Boy and girl fall in love.
> Boy and girl have sex.
> Boy and girl cohabit.
> Boy and girl postpone marriage.
> Eventually they break up or marry or continue to cohabit without marriage.
> If they marry, they do so to have children.

In scm2, components 2, 3, and 4 are interchangeable. The connection between love and marriage is also much more ambiguous in scm2 than it is in scm1. There are also a number of variations on each of these two standard cultural models. Despite all these differences, scm2 can really be seen as an update or as the secularized alternative to scm1. The major differences between the two models lie in the place and status of sex in courtship and the acceptance of cohabitation prior to and often as a substitute for marriage.

TECHNOLOGICAL CHANGES AFFECT DATING

The mode of dating has shifted largely as a result of technological changes. The car gave couples increased mobility and sexual freedom. Serving as a mobile bedroom that was controlled by the male, the car put the female at a great power disadvantage. Because the male was the driver, and thus the controller, of the car, male interests were advanced in car dates and there was always the fear that the boy would not drive the girl home if she did not comply should he make unwanted advances. Car dating greatly increased the frequency of date rape and the risk of putting females in psychologically traumatic if not abusive situations. Hence, double-dating and horde dating were typically advanced by young women because they are considered safer modes of dating. Economic conditions, the rise in gas prices, and the proximity of places to "hang out" have greatly increased the popularity of horde dating on college campuses.

A BRIEF HISTORY OF THE STANDARD CULTURAL MODEL OF LOVE, SEX, AND MARRIAGE

Since the sixteenth century, North America was fertile soil for a love-marriage cultural model of courtship. The early waves of immigrants came to the New World because it was a land of opportunity where through hard work they could live their dreams. It was and continues to be a land of vast natural resources that, relative to Europe and Asia, was underexploited and underpopulated. Thus the ratio of population to natural resources offered comparatively greater opportunities for individuals in the New World than in the Old World, where population densities were much higher and natural resources had long been exploited. Even today, the population density of the United States is much lower than that of all European countries (with the exception of the Scandinavian countries).[5]

"Self-reliance" was cited as the number one value held by Americans in an extensive qualitative study of American culture (Bellah et al. 1985). This value is associated with the immigrant spirit and also with the importance of love as the primary criteria by which individuals self-select a mate. Jankowiak and Fisher (1992) found that romantic love is a cultural universal, thus present in every culture, but it is not always an important criterion for selecting a mate. As late as the turn of the twentieth century, arranged marriages were common among the upper classes of Great Britain. The cultural values of self-reliance and rugged individualism, as well as the social, spatial, and economic mobility of Americans, laid the groundwork for the "love and marriage" model of courtship. It is important to note that fundamentally the scm has not changed significantly since the

1700s if we only take into account the presence of its most elemental and necessary components.

In the 1960s there was a sexual revolution in both the United States and Canada, which led to the rise in importance of scm2. The two key reasons for the sexual revolution of the 1960s were the invention of the birth control pill in 1960 and the increasing numbers of women who went to college after high school. In 1900 only 19 percent of all college students were women; in 1960 men constituted 54 percent of all college students, and 46 percent were female. By 1984 the percentage of females enrolled in college had risen to 49 percent, and by 2005 females made up 57 percent of all college students.[6] In 1963 Betty Freidan's *The Feminine Mystique* was published and is commonly seen as a main impetus for the women's movement and as giving a feminist stamp of approval to the sexual revolution. In the following sections the main components of scm 1 and 2 are described; they are described in order of their most typical sequence in the courtship process, from meeting to marriage. Sex (stage 4) would occur after marriage (stage 5) for scm1 and may occur before love for scm2.

Stage 1: Meeting a Potential Mate

Meeting a potential mate is defined as any form of interaction where one or both parties decide whether they are interested in the possibility of developing a romantic relationship with the other. The meeting may take place in person or via letters, the Internet, or phone. If both decide positively and one of them takes the initiative to ask the person out, then the meeting leads to a date. Meeting for the purpose of developing a romantic relationship usually begins in the teenage years but can occur earlier. If the meeting is virtual rather than actual, then the couple will usually exchange a number of emails or instant messages in which they make inquiries about each other, exchange photos, praise each other, and let the other know that they are interested in a face-to-face encounter. If the meeting is an actual face-to-face meeting and it is a precursor to dating, then it usually involves the following:

A period of interaction in which the potential couple reveal personal information about themselves
Gaze
Gestures or expressions of pleasure and approval
Attentiveness
Synchronic behavior

The above attributes are components of flirting. The gaze refers to prolonged eye contact, and usually the eyes are dilated. Gestures or expressions of pleasure and approval include frequent nodding of the head, gazing and seemingly unintentional touching, leaning forward toward the person, smiling, softened voice, and frequent statements of assent and affirmation such as the simple "uh-huh" or "yes" to "exactly what I thought," "how clever," "you really are _____" (include any positive trait such as smart, funny, kind, attractive, etc.). Attentiveness refers to listening as well as gazing at the person and responding to the person's statements or gestures rather than shifting to other topics of conversation or action. Synchronicity is one of the strongest signals of reciprocal interest and affection and refers to the couple mirroring each other's behavior. Dancing is a key romantic activity because the couple are expected to mirror each other's movements while embracing or in proximity of each other. Synchronicity extends to less obvious mirror actions such as when one person drinks from a glass and the other follows suit.

The gaze, the accidental touch, and increasing synchronicity of movement between a couple who have just met signal interest in one another. This sequence is found in all cultures according to Timothy Perper (1985). The male taking the woman to a restaurant and showing that he can feed her is also a prominent universal dating activity. It has even been discovered that, like their human counterparts, male fruit flies will offer morsels of food, usually meat or fecal matter, to prospective mates as part of their courtship ritual.

Stage 2: Dating

Dating is a prescheduled meeting between two people with the goal of exploring the possibility of developing a romantic relationship with each other. There are many forms of dating, from historical-traditional to classical, to horde, dating service, Internet, and speed-dating. Each of these will be discussed in turn.

Historical-Traditional Dating

The forms of dating have changed significantly since the 1900s. Prior to the advent of the car, teenage couples were typically chaperoned by family members on their dates. Again, prior to the car, dating had two functions: the first was to explore whether the couple would establish a romantic relationship, and the second was to gain the approval of the parents of both the boy and the girl. Historical-traditional dating had two functions: (1) developing a romantic relationship and (2) integrating the couple into their respective familial households.

Classical Dating

The invention of the car and its affordability to most Americans by the 1930s significantly transformed these traditional dating practices. The car gave the couple increasing autonomy from their respective families as well as friends. Chaperoning was not required. However, the boy was obligated to meet with the parents prior to dates and ideally was to bring the girl home at a prearranged time, while the parents were still awake. After World War I there were more women in the workplace, and with the increasing rise of working women, meeting with parents diminished in importance. As a result of the availability of automobiles and increasing economic independence and social autonomy of women, the social, familial function of dating decreased and the romantic function of dating increased. The automobile, as its name suggests, also served as a sort of mobile bedroom that served to increase the possibility of sexual adventures by the couple. The car isolated the couple and emphasized the idea that the couple was a dyadic social unit, removed and separated from the larger world. Market forces also accentuated this by offering getaway retreats, isolated booths for romantic dining, drive-in movies, and so on.

By the 1950s teenagers not only had access to the family car but also were often able to buy and repair their own car. As a consequence, teenagers gained even more independence and the classical dating pattern of the couple going out in a car and finding secluded spots to "make out" (i.e., kiss extensively) after a movie or date emerged. Movies such as *American Graffiti* are paeans to the car and the freedom it offered teenagers to meet for romantic encounters. The basic form of this pattern was as follows:

The boy was expected to take the initiative and telephone the girl for a date after having become acquainted with her.
The primary activities for dates were going out to eat, to sports events, to movies, to drive-ins, to amusement parks, or to romantic places such as the beach or a park.

If it was a first date, the boy and girl were expected to spend the night in trying to develop an intimate relationship through talking about their personal lives, feelings, and hopes. A successful first date would end with a kiss, when the boy walked the girl to the front door of her house.

If the couple were dating regularly, then they often found a safe, secluded spot where they could park and make out or "neck." They were not expected to engage in oral or vaginal sex, but how far the boy could go was usually left up to the girl. He was also expected to walk the girl to the front door of her house.

The baseball metaphor of "hits" was often used to score the sexual success of a date. A single indicated that the couple "made out," that is, kissed extensively; a "double" indicated that the boy was able to feel the girl's breasts; a "triple" typically meant that the boy was able to feel her vagina; and a "home run" meant that the couple had sexual intercourse. Oral sex was not included in this baseball analogy, implying that it was not a common part of the sexual repertoire traditionally.[7] Although there was undoubtedly an increase in date rape and teenage pregnancy at this time, there are no reliable statistics on this. Ideally scm1 was the model that both the boy and the girl adhered to.

Two common variants of the classical dating pattern were double dates and blind dates. In both cases the male still took the initiative and also paid for the date, but in a double date two couples went on a date together. They did this for three reasons: social comfort, as usually the two boys or two girls were close friends of each other; only one of the males had access to a car; and the parents of the girls were more likely to approve of a double date, assuming there was safety in numbers. A blind date is when a mutual friend of the boy and girl acts as a matchmaker and encourages the boy to ask the girl out for a date. If the boy phones or asks the girl on a date, then the date follows the classical dating pattern.

When a couple continued to date, they were expected to stop dating or showing interests in others. For teenagers it was common to make a formal declaration of dating each other exclusively, and this often was accompanied by a declaration of love. This was referred to as "going steady," and the couple would begin to refer to each other as "boyfriend" and "girlfriend" respectively. "Boyfriend" and "girlfriend" were also used as teknonyms by others. A teknonym is when you refer to someone indirectly through their relationship with someone else; for example, "He is Jill's boyfriend" or "She is Tom's boyfriend." Although the phrase "going steady" is not much used today, the terms "boyfriend" and "girlfriend" remain common currency and refer to a mutually exclusive enduring romantic relationship.

Dating Services

After World War II, dating services became popular. The basic procedure of the early dating services was to obtain personal information that was used to establish compatibility indices between men and women in terms of age, social, economic, religious, political, and various psychological variables. Newspapers and magazines also became outlets for individuals to place personal ads presenting personal information and usually a brief description of the kind of person they were looking to date. Dating agencies replaced the traditional matchmakers and catered predominantly to 25- to 45-year-old professionals. The video industry changed dating services in the 1970s and 1980s, when it became common for clients to make a video at the dating agency and prospective dates would come to view these videos.

Online Dating

By 1995 most teenagers and adults had access to computers and to the Internet. In April 1995 match.com began one of the first online dating services. It remains one of the most successful dating services, and by 2004 match.com registered 20 million members world-wide. Approximately 10 percent of unmarried North Americans have tried online dating services to find a match (*Canadian Business*, February 2002). In 2003 it was estimated that 40 million North Americans had visited, but not necessarily used, dating sites (Hitch et al. 2004). The number of Internet dating services continues to grow; the exact figure is impossible to estimate due to the ease of setting up such services, but there are probably 300 to 400 online dating services in the United States alone.[8]

Online dating services usually include a compatibility survey much as the precomputer dating services. In addition they usually request that the individual set up a profile and personal statement about who they are and what kind of person and relationship they are looking for. Some services compartmentalize dating into three or more categories: those who are looking for a serious relationship, those seeking sex, and those who are looking for friendship. Services may also cater to homosexuals, ethnic and religious groups, and those with alternative sexual orientations (e.g., swingers, fetishes). A word of warning: many of these sites may simply be masquerading as dating services and are, in reality, porn sites.

A video or photo of the online dater often accompanies the profile of online members. After signing up as a member, the client can browse through the regionally available online matches. Contact with other singles is initiated by the individual rather than the service, though the service may provide one with lists of singles who are most compatible with the data you provided in the questionnaire and on your profile. Males are usually overrepresented on online dating services and respond at an 80 percent rate to every contact initiated by a woman; women, on the other hand, respond to about 30 percent of all contacts initiated by men.

The goal of online dating is to establish a romantic relationship, though it is not uncommon to use online dating to pursue a sexual relationship. After a couple has established contact, they will email each other regularly and often "date" outside the online service Website using instant messenger services or cell phones. The goal is to meet for a date. Unlike the classical dating scheme where the male picks up the female, in online dating the couple usually plan to meet at a neutral site, such as a coffee shop, park, or other public place, and use their own cars to come there. Often, the first date is brief and the couple will go "dutch," with each paying for their own expenses. Online daters frequently prefer dutch dating in order to minimize mutual obligations of any kind and to retain one's independence in case the date does not go well. Even when a man pays for a drink or a cup of coffee, the woman will often feel sexually obligated to him.

Contact through the computer is always suspect, and both parties may feel a bit wary, wondering whether the person they are to meet has represented himself or herself honestly. Prior to a date, both parties may demand verification of the appearance of the other by asking to view them via a Web cam or to look them up on other Internet sites such as myspace.com or facebook.com.

Horde Dating

Horde dating is reminiscent of Lewis Henry Morgan's (1965) claim in *Ancient Society* that the modern human family structure developed from unregulated group marriages during the "savage stage" of society to the patriarchal monogamous form of marriage of modern "civilized" society. He referred to unregulated sex as "horde marriage."

Horde-dating is common among college students where the frequency of classical dating (one man and one woman) has declined in frequency, probably caused by economic factors and the prevalence of forming residential "hordes," or "gangs," in dormitories or in off-campus housing. Students will go out with roommates and friends to a bar or to a popular public area to simply "hang out." When hanging out, they will then often separate into couples. As a couple begins to establish themselves within this "horde context," they will begin to visit each other at their respective residences, at school, or at popular "hangouts" in the vicinity of the school. There is never an acknowledgment of "dating" per se. What is emphasized in this form of informal dating is friendship and sex. When the couple establishes a sexual relationship, they will usually bond as a mutually exclusive sexual couple and be recognized as such by their peers. If the couple declare love for each other, they are likely to cohabit when the economic opportunity becomes available. Cohabiting following the horde-dating practice is usually framed in terms of friendship and mutual economic benefits rather than romantic ideals. Horde dating is a contemporary twist on traditional dating practices, as social and economic considerations play an important part in the establishment of the relationship and dating is seldom a private affair.

Speed-Dating

The most recent innovation in dating styles has been speed-dating. A Jewish rabbi, Yaacov Devyo, is credited with having invented speed-dating as a way to encourage single Jewish men and women in large cities to meet each other. The first speed-dating event was organized by the rabbi in Los Angeles. Speed-dating is based on findings that show that people often decide whether they will date someone or not in less than a minute. Speed-dating is a new twist on traditional matchmaking. An equal number of males and females are invited to meet at a restaurant, bar, coffee shop, or other public place. There are usually age, ethnic, religious, educational, or other criteria that determine who is eligible to attend. Speed-dating works best in large urban settings where people can meet others of similar backgrounds or sexual orientations. Often up to one hundred people attend a speed-dating meeting. Individuals are usually assigned about ten people to speed-date. Assignments are usually done randomly, as there is not enough time prior to the speed-dating meeting to arrange dates according to a compatibility index. As a result, after the speed-dating officially ends, there is a period where people just "hang around" to chat, and this is often a time when someone can meet another potential date.

The typical speed date lasts 8 minutes and then one meets someone else. The rules of the speed-dating encounter are that one cannot gain personal contact information during the period they are speed-dating. Individuals should never reject their partner during a speed-date. Usually both individuals have a set of questions to ask their partner. At the end of the speed-dating encounters, individuals meet with an administrator of the speed-dating service and give them the names of the people who can contact them. When there is a match, the personal information is given to both parties.

Speed-dating is becoming very popular because it is a way to maximize contacts with people of the same social background without the fear of being rejected by them in a face-to-face encounter. It also minimizes the amount of time spent on an unsuccessful date. Individuals also report that the experience of speed-dating is in itself "fun."

Stage 3: Romantic and Companionate Love[9]

Helen Fisher et al. (2002) discovered thirteen universal psychophysiological characteristics that are associated with romantic love: (1) one thinks that the beloved is "unique";

(2) attention is paid to the positive qualities of the beloved; (3) contact or thought of the beloved induces feelings of "exhilaration," "increased energy," "heart pounding," and intense emotional arousal; (4) in adverse times, feelings of connection to the beloved are magnified; (5) one experiences "intrusive thinking"; (6) one feels possessive of and dependent on the beloved; (7) one feels a desire for "union" with the beloved; (8) one feels a strong sense of altruism and concern for the beloved; (9) one reorders priorities to favor the beloved; (10) one feels sexual attraction for the beloved; (11) "emotional union" takes "precedence over sexual desire"; (12) the feeling of romantic love is "involuntary" and not controllable; and (13) romantic love is generally temporary (416–417). These thirteen indicators reflect psychological states of the individual.

De Munck (2006) reviewed the scholarly ethnographic literature on romantic love and discovered a second set of universal features. The key component of this second list is that lovers around the world consider romantic love to be a transcendental "striving for unity" that is motivated by the desire for "perfection" or "wholeness" or "possessing perpetually the absolute good." In other words, in requited romantic love the two lovers complete each other and become a perfect whole. This accords with the platonic view of love in which lovers had been separated and love was the reunification of two halves that were once indivisible. Romantic love is viewed as the steady and perfect state of humans.

THE CHEMISTRY OF LOVE

In *Why We Love* Helen Fisher cites much of the research on love, noting that there are two basic chemical systems at work. The first chemical system releases adrenaline chemicals—a primary one being phenylethylamine, an amphetamine-like chemical also dubbed the *love molecule*—into the bloodstream whenever one comes into proximity or thinks about the person he or she is attracted to; this excites the brain neurotransmitters and creates a feeling of elation and surge of energy that is translated as "being in love." Chocolate, thought to be an aphrodisiac, is known to contain a high level of this chemical. This initial chemical system is said to last for 2 to 4 years and then gradually wears off, being replaced by endorphins and vasopressin—attachment chemicals—that lead to feelings of quiet contentment and security when one is in proximity of one's lover. This chemical system begins to fade after 3 to 4 years, and thereafter the couple are on their own.

The platonic view focuses on the idealistic expectations for romantic love, whereas Fisher et al. focus on the more pragmatic aspects of romantic love, those that are observable and measurable. Nonetheless, there is overlap between the two models, in particular with the concept of unity. However, the concept of unity has different connotations; for Fisher et al. (2002) it is a "craving for emotional union," but in the "higher" platonic sense union leads to an absence of any emotional feeling since the two are now permanently indivisible (hence romantic love lasts forever) and so there is no reason to "crave" union. The striving for unity is transcendent because the feeling of unity "cannot be broken down into attributes" (Soble 1990:38).

Swidler and many others have noted that romantic love seldom endures and typically is transformed into "true" or "companionate" love, which is more enduring and stabilizes the couple. Companionate love is important to establish a stable marriage and to "get on with the business of raising a family." However, the desire to marry someone is usually predicated on romantic love, and when all romantic love disappears in a marriage, one or both parties are likely to become dissatisfied in the relationship. Hence, romantic love is a double-edged sword in that it triggers a highly aroused psychosocial state in both parties that is the motive for marriage, but it also does not last when a relationship becomes stable and mundane;

hence the reason for marriage is often eliminated during marriage, thus providing a reason for divorce.

Stage 4: Sex

A Brief Cultural History of Sex in America

In the 1700s "bundling" was frequently practiced as a form of courtship. Bundling was practiced only during winter when houses were cold and there was not enough fuel to heat the rooms. The woman's family would invite a man over, and the family would bundle both the man and the woman in separate blankets and they would share a bed. It was understood that they would not have sexual intercourse and would talk during the night. The goal was both pragmatic—to get warm on cold nights—and to encourage the development of intimacy between the man and woman. Bundling was not practiced during summers. A study of marriage practices of colonial New England indicated that at least one-third of the women were pregnant at the time of marriage; thus abstaining from sex may not always have been practiced during "bundling."

By the 1920s the majority of Americans lived in towns and cities, and with the Industrial Revolution in full swing there also emerged a "liberal sexual ethic" of enjoying sex and that sharing sexual pleasure was a hallmark both of a love relationship and of marriage. With the emphasis on sex in both love and marriage, it became only a matter of time before people began to question why sex should be confined to love or marriage relationships.

Increasing social experimentation actually increased more as myth than as actuality. In the most comprehensive survey of sexual practices in the United States to date, Michael, Gagnon, Laumann, and Kolata (1994) reported that more than 80 percent of adult Americans age 18 to 59 had zero or one sexual partner in the past year (106). Sixty percent of those surveyed between the ages of 18 and 59 reported that they had between zero and four sexual partners in their lifetimes, and only 15 percent of men and 2.7 percent of women reported having had twenty-one or more sex partners in their lifetimes (109). Although cohabitation is much less stable than marriage, rates of fidelity for both types of relationships are around 80 percent. Thus most sexual activity occurs before and between steady romantic relationships.

The myths that people are having lots of sex and that one is "missing out" leads to dissatisfaction for both men and women who are in stable relationships. Thus metaphors of the woman as a "ball and chain" or relationships as a "prison" and the thought that one is "missing out" are common themes among couples who are in committed and satisfying relationships. The myth that many people are engaged in free-sex/love relationships that are somehow more satisfying than one's own also leads to a cultural acceptance of those who are in such relations. Thus there is a general tolerance in the United States for sexual relations among consenting adults of any variety as long as there is consent and there is no intent to injure.

Paul Robinson (1976) and Christine Stansell (2000) posit that the conflict between myth and reality reflects a larger conflict between Victorian romanticism and "sexual modernism." Romanticism idealizes the erotic but as cultivated in, essential to, and confined to the love dyad (that is, the couple themselves). This relationship is perceived as both a physical and spiritual union along the lines of the platonic model of romantic love. The "sexual modern" acknowledges the romantic ideal but also considers the satisfaction of "innocent physical need" as natural and thus morally acceptable and justifiable (Robinson 1976:194).

The general cultural acceptance of sex as "natural" and that its expression can be distinct from love and not immoral if acted upon outside a couple relationship is associated with the sexual modern culture and with scm2 rather than scm1. Its corollary, however, is that sexual fidelity is a product of repression and a person's voluntary or involuntary internalization of old-fashioned Victorian sexual mores. One 30-year-old male respondent in Michael et al.'s survey of sex in America said that "in my worst moments the spur posse makes me feel like an uptight, hyper-cautious square." The "spur posse" was a group of male high school athletes who competed for the most sexual conquests.

Sexual Practices and Preferences

Most of the following data were taken from the "Sex in America" survey by Michael et al. (1994:146–147). When we refer to sex, we are referring to any act that involves receptive penetrative relationships between two or more people.

Vaginal Intercourse

Vaginal intercourse is the universal sexual practice and preference common to women and men of all ages, ethnicities, and religious persuasions. Vaginal sex is also the default image that is triggered in the minds of people by the term *sex*. That vaginal intercourse stands out as the most preferred and practiced sexual practice is not surprising as it is the only sexual act that leads to the birth of a baby. Approximately 70 percent of individuals reported spending between 15 minutes to an hour on vaginal intercourse; this includes foreplay. Twenty-three percent reported spending more than an hour, and 7 percent reported spending less than 15 minutes.

Oral Sex

Oral sex is the most varied and complicated of the sexual practices. It is directly related to ethnicity and to education. Forty-one percent of women with less than a high school education report practicing oral sex in their lifetimes, compared to 78 percent of women with any college education. Similarly, 81 percent of white men and 75 percent of white women report having engaged in oral sex in their lifetimes, whereas 51 percent of African-American men and 34 percent of African-American women report having engaged in oral sex in their lifetimes.[10] It is probable that oral sex came into vogue as a general technique for arousing one's partner in the 1960s on college campuses. The dormitory experience, particularly at the time of the "sexual revolution" of the 1960s, paved the way for students to engage in and experiment with sexual practices without being under the supervision or watchful eye of their parents. Further, these college students formed social networks in which sexual partners circulated within the network. If some group in the social network was participating in oral sex, others were likely to follow. These social networks and the conditions of being in an unsupervised context with other singles of one's peer group do not exist outside the college campus. Thus those who did not go to college, mostly African Americans, did not have access to the social networks of sexual partners and the social contexts that spurred the sexual revolution.

Newspapers and popular magazines have reported a sharp rise in oral sex among teenagers. However, there is no reliable empirical data to verify this. The rise is thought to be connected both with oral sex as a strategy by which girls can keep their virginity and with increasing social pressures by males to demand fellatio. Cunnilingus is practiced much less frequently (Remez 2000). Surprisingly, in a 1991 survey conducted at a midwestern university,

59 percent did not think oral sex constituted sex. A Gallup poll conducted after the Monica Lewinsky scandal came to light found that 20 percent of their respondents agreed with President Clinton and said that oral sex was not sex.

Anal Sex

Approximately a quarter of Americans have tried anal sex in their lifetimes; again there are much higher frequencies among whites and higher-educated Americans than among blacks and those who have never gone to college.

Orgasm

In a recent survey of 10,000 people, 18 percent of women and 49 percent of men said that they attain orgasm every time they have sex; 39 percent of both genders said that they attain orgasm most of the time, and 13 percent of women and 2 percent of men said they seldom if ever have an orgasm.[11] The most popular position for sexual intercourse is with the man on top. Rear entry was considered to be animal-like during the medieval period and thus was stigmatized. Further, unlike chimpanzees, bonobos, and our primate ancestors, humans walk erect, and for the human female the vagina has dropped down and is further from the buttocks, making it more difficult to reach from behind than from the front.

Safe-Sex Practices and Barriers to It

Despite the public's increased awareness about the modes of HIV transmission and the widespread adoption of AIDS prevention programs in hospitals and schools, there has been little consequent change in people's sexual practices. There are four main reasons for this. First, AIDS was thought to be a disease that was mostly found among homosexuals and drug users; hence non-drug-using heterosexuals often thought of themselves as immune. Second, many people thought that condoms, which is the primary safe-sex practice, diminish sexual pleasure. In an unpublished study conducted by the author of 180 respondents between the ages of 18 and 45 who were recruited in public parks and bus stands around New York City, 71 percent thought that condom use diminished the pleasure of sex for men and 55 percent thought it diminished the pleasure of sex for women. Males are much more reluctant to use condoms than females, according to studies of U.S. and Canadian male sexual behavior (Fullilove, Fullilove, Haynes, and Gross 1990; Bogaert and Fisher 1995; Mosher and Tomkins 1988). The researchers concluded that adherence to masculine ideology acts as a barrier to safe-sex practices. The negotiation over and use of a condom goes against the "hypermasculine" ideology that views men as dominant and women as "sexual conquests."

In her study of inner-city black women in Cleveland, Ohio, Elisa Sobo (1995, 1998) found that adherence to a monogamous model of romantic love was the single most important factor explaining why a woman would choose to practice unsafe sex. Condomless intercourse symbolized trust and fidelity, whereas condom use symbolized distrust and infidelity. Sobo writes, "Unsafe sex deflects attention from adultery and deceit and focuses it instead on . . . trust and honesty. It helps women maintain the belief that theirs are monogamous, caring, satisfying unions that leave neither partner desirous of sex or love from outside sources, as it is prescribed by the popular U.S. conjugal ideal" (1995:121). The hypermasculine ideology and the prevalent belief that condoms reduce sexual pleasure dovetail with Sobo's findings of an idealized model of romance that is prevalent among the poor to lead to unsafe sex practices despite knowing that unsafe sex can lead to STDs and unplanned pregnancies.

That romantic love is an important factor in deciding to engage in safe or unsafe sex is demonstrated in the study by Regan (1998). In her study, Regan gave both male and female college students an identical scenario of a male physically forcing a female into sexual intercourse though she verbally rejected his advances. However, she framed the scenario as a couple "in love" for one college student sample and as dating, but not in love, for the other sample. The majority of male and female college students rated the male's behavior in the "in love" scenario as acceptable, whereas only a small minority rated it as acceptable for the "not in love" scenario.

Stage 5: Marriage

Marriage is an enduring union between two people that establishes economic rights and obligations between the two and social and economic obligations for the care of offspring born from this union. The average marriage lasts 25 years, and most adults spend most of their lives in a marriage relationship. Though approximately 40 percent of Americans divorce and the rate of divorce is close to 50 percent, still 60 percent of Americans do not divorce.[12] The rate of divorce has stabilized, and there are indications that the trend is reversing slightly. Divorce rates are related to class and ethnicity, as economic difficulties are the primary underlying cause for conflict between husband and wife and for divorce. African Americans are more likely to divorce and less likely to remarry than whites. It should be noted that this is probably due to economic differences between whites and African Americans rather than to ethnic differences.

The preferred and predominant marriage practice in the United States is heterosexual monogamy—that is, the union of one man and one woman. Polygyny, one man and many wives, was practiced by some Mormons and Muslims but is now illegal, though it remains surreptitiously practiced in areas with large Mormon communities. There are no statistics on polyandry, in which one woman has many husbands. Anthropologists have noted that with the high divorce and remarriage rates, many Americans practice serial monogamy. That is, they move from one monogamous union to another.

Approximately 1 percent of Americans have open marriages, which are monogamous unions in which husband and wife permit each other to have sexual encounters outside marriage. However, the overwhelming majority of Americans disapprove of adultery and most remain faithful in marriage.

There are three main tensions that destabilize marriage. The first is economics. Economic difficulties are the primary cause of conflict in a family, and in most families the husband and wife both have full-time jobs. If they do not, then it is expected that eventually both will be employed and financially contributing to the household. The economic pooling of resources leads to conflict over how the money should be used. With both spouses working full-time, Hochschild (2003/1983) pointed out that no one is responsible for the quality of the family life.

In an extensive qualitative survey of married life in America, Swidler (2001) observed a transformation of "romantic love" to "true love." She concluded that "romantic love" served as the fuel to motivate people to marry but that it was inherently unstable, and so the "companionate" form of love referred to as "true love" was necessary to stabilize the couple in marriage. True love is based on friendship, mutual respect, and sexual fidelity. A problem with the "true love" model of American marriage is that it can lead to discontent when the couple wonders what happened to "romance."

233

A third tension that occurs in marriage is that the popular media and advertisement create the myth that other couples are having more exciting and romantic lives than you are. This leads to a sense of relative deprivation in which couples, even if they are satisfied with their spouse and family, still feel that they are not leading full and exciting lives.

Marriage is also related to a variety of benefits and positive outcomes. First, it is a union usually based on romantic love. Romantic love, as a platform for marriage, serves to develop a sense of intimacy, uniqueness, and permanence that is necessary for a stable and satisfying union. Romantic love does not disappear but can be conjoined with "true love" as it is maintained through vacations, nights out, and other activities aimed at keeping romance in the marriage. Second, married men and women live longer, are at a lower risk for HIV/AIDS and other STDs, have higher wages, have higher frequency of sex, and rate themselves as having more satisfying sex lives than unmarried men and women (Bramlett and Mosher 2002).

RESOURCE GUIDE

PRINT SOURCES

Ambert, Ann-Marie. "Divorce: Facts, Figures and Consequences. Report for the Vanier Institute of the Family of Canada." Occasional paper, 1998.

Anapol, Deborah. *Polyamory: The New Love without Limits.* San Rafael, CA: Intinet Resource Center, 1997.

Bellah, R. L., Richard Madsen, William M. Sullivan, Ann Swidler, and Steven M. Tipton. *Habits of the Heart.* Berkeley: University of California Press, 1985.

Bogaert, A. F., and W. A. Fisher. "Predictor of University Men's Number of Sexual Partners." *The Journal of Sex Research* 32 (1995): 119–130.

Bramlett, M. D., and W. D. Mosher. *Cohabitation, Marriage, Divorce, and Remarriage in the United States.* Series Report 23, Number 22. 103 pp. (Phs) 98-1998. Hyattsville, MD: Center for Disease Control and Prevention, National Center for Health Statistics, 2002.

De Munck, Victor C. "Romantic Love, Sex and Marriage Lithuania Style." *Journal of Baltic Studies* 4 (2006): 44–59.

Fisher, Helen, *Why We Love:* The Nature and Chemistry of *Romantic Love.* New York: Henry Holt. 2004.

Fisher, Helen, et al. "Defining the Brain Systems of Lust, Romantic Attraction and Attachment," *Archives of Sexual Behavior* 23 (2002): 92–97.

Fullilove, M., R. Fullilove, K. Haynes, and S. Gross. "Black Women and AIDS Prevention: A View towards Understanding the Gender Rules." *Journal of Sex Research* 27.1 (1990): 47–64.

Hitch, Gunther J., Ali Hortascu, and Dan Ariely. "What Makes You Click: An Empirical Analysis of Online Dating." Working paper, 2004.

Hochschild, Arlie. *The Managed Heart: The Commercialization of Human Feeling.* Berkeley: University of California Press, 1983. (Reprinted with new afterword, 2003.)

Hurley, Dan. "Divorce Rate: It's Not As High As You Think." *New York Times* (2005, April 19: 46).

Jankowiak, William R., and Edward F. Fischer. "A Cross-Cultural Perspective on Romantic Love." *Ethnology* 31 (1992): 149–155.

Lee, John Alan. *The Colours of Love.* Toronto: General, 1976.

———. "Love and Sex Styles." Pp. 33–76 in V. De Munck (ed.), *Romantic Love and Sexual Behavior.* Westport, CT: Praeger, 1998.

Michael, Robert T., John H. Gagnon, Edward O. Laumann, and Gina Kolata. *Sex in America: A Definitive Survey.* New York: Warner Books, 1994.

Morgan, Lewis H. *Ancient Society.* Cambridge, MA: Belknap Press of Harvard University Press, 1965.

Mosher, D. L., and S. S. Tomkins. 1988. "Scripting the Macho Man: Hypermasculine Socialization and Enculturation." *The Journal of Sex Research* 25.1 (1988): 60–84.

Mosher, William D., Anjani Chandra, and Jo Jones. "Sexual Behavior and Selected Health Measures: Men and Women 15–44 Years of Age, United States." *The Journal of Sex Research* 34 (2005): 39–55.

Newcomer, S. F., and J. R. Udry. "Oral Sex in an Adolescent Population." *Archives of Sexual Behavior* 14.1 (1985): 41–46.

Perper, Timothy. *Sex Signals: The Biology of Sex.* Philadelphia: ISI Press. 1985.

Regan, Pamela. "Romantic Love and Sexual Desire." Pp. 91–112 in V. DeMunch (ed.), *Romantic Love and Sexual Behavior*, Westport, CT: Praeger, 1998.

Remez, Lisa. Oral Sex among Adolescents: Is It Sex or Is It Abstinence? *Family Planning Perspectives* 32.6 (Special Report, 2000): 298–304.

Rimmer, Robert. *The Harrad Experiment.* New York: Doubleday, 1966.

Robinson, Paul. *The Modernization of Sex.* New York: Harper & Ross, 1976.

Sanders, S. A., and J. M. Reinisch. "Would You Say You 'Had Sex' If . . . ?" *Journal of the American Medical Association* 281.3 (1999): 275–277.

Soble, Alan. *The Structure of Love.* New Haven, CT: Yale University Press, 1990.

Sobo, E. J. *Choosing (Un)Safe Sex.* State College, PA: University of Pennsylvania Press, 1995.

Stansell, Christine. American Moderns: Bohemian New York and the Creation of a New Century. New York: Metropolitan, 2000.

Swidler, Ann. Talk of Love: How Culture Matters. Chicago: University of Chicago Press, 2001.

Weis, David L. "Basic Sexological Premises (USA)." Pp. 246–273 in Robert T. Francouer (ed.), *The International Journal of Sexuality*. New York: Continuum Press, 1997.

WEBSITES

American Social Health Association. http://www.ashastd.org/learn/learn_statistics.cfm. A site that gives statistics and basic information on socially transmitted diseases.

Bridal Guide. http://www.bridalguide.com/. One of the many commercial traditional wedding planning Websites.

Divorce net. http://www.divorcenet.com/. An excellent site for extensive information on divorce.

The Kinsey Institute For Research in Sex, Gender, and Reproduction. http://www.indiana.edu/~kinsey/. A major resource, the Kinsey Institute promotes interdisciplinary research on sex, gender, and reproduction. It was founded in 1947 by the pioneering work of Dr. Alfred C. Kinsey at Indiana University.

Sex Info. http://www.soc.ucsb.edu/sexinfo/. An excellent site, sponsored by the University of California at Santa Barbara and run by graduate students who are doing research on sexuality. It has extensive and reliable information in plain language on human anatomy and reproduction, abortion, pregnancy, love and communication, sexual violence, sex and the law, sexual difficulties, sex under the influence, and so on.

Smart Marriages; The Coalition for Marriage, Family, and Couples Education. http://www.smartmarriages.com/. A good Website on marriage, with information on how to have a strong and happy marriage, the importance of marriage and why it matters, main reasons for divorce and how to avoid and fight divorce, what to do in the case of domestic violence, and how to put the romance back into marriage.

NOTES

1. Population statistics are drawn from U.S. Census Bureau data; sources are cited in the reference section.
2. http://www.gendercenter.org/mdr.htm (rate of marriage 1950–95).
3. Sam Roberts, "To Be Married Means to Be Outnumbered." *New York Times* (2006, Oct. 15). http://www.nytimes.com/2006/10/15/us/15census.html?em&ex=1161230400&en=a26705a7fc88bdec&ei=5087%0a.
4. Most of the Canadian statistical data on marriage, divorce, and cohabitation rates come from http://atlas.nrcan.gc.ca/site/english/maps/peopleandsociety/immigration/imfb_01/1.

5. The United States ranks 171st in population density (with 33 per square mile) out of 230 countries; Canada ranks 219th (a population density of 3.0 per square mile). This is significantly different from European countries such as the Netherlands, which has a population density of 392, or the United Kingdom, with a population density of 246 (http://education.yahoo.com/reference/factbook/countrycompare/pd/1a.html).
6. http://nces.ed.gov/programs/digest/d99/d99t187.asp (percentage of women in college in 1960).
7. There have been no comprehensive statistical data on the prevalence of oral sex prior to 2005.
8. http://www.onlinedatingmagazine.com/history/history-of-online-dating.html (this site has information on both online dating and speed dating).
9. I am placing romantic love in stage 4, but in scm2 sexual intercourse often precedes romantic love.
10. See Mosher et al. (in Resource Guide), pp. 1–56. http://www.cdc.gov/nchs/data/ad/ad362.pdf.
11. See http://www.queendom.com/sex-files/passion/passion-gender.html (data on frequency of orgasm and preferred sexual positions).
12. See http://www.cdc.gov/nchs/fastats/divorce.htm (data on divorce and marriage rates).

MUSIC

DON CUSIC

The popular music industry is the product of musical performances and recordings in a market-based economy. At its most commercial level it is big business, dominated by four major multinational corporations (Universal, EMI/Capitol, Warner Brothers, and BMG/Sony). Independent labels—defined as those privately owned and without major label distribution—accounts for approximately 15 percent of total recording sales, whereas the major labels account for around 85 percent in any given year, although these figures fluctuate a little year by year.

The global music recording industry accounted for approximately $40 billion in sales in 2005; the United States was responsible for about a third of that or $12.269 billion. This is roughly the same amount the United States received a decade ago ($12,533 billion in 1996). The high point was 1999 when $14.584 billion in recordings were sold; since that time, illegal downloads and file-sharing have significantly decreased the amount of income from recording sales.

CD album sales accounted for 87 percent of total sales in 2005, whereas digital downloads accounted for 5.7 percent of revenues. Although digital downloads are the fastest-growing segment of recording sales, by the end of 2005 they only accounted for approximately 6 percent of mainstream music sales, although some independent labels see a significantly higher percentage of sales from downloads.

Latin music sales accounted for $463.8 million (wholesale) and $753.7 million retail in 2005. This is an area of growth in the music industry, with a sales increase of 16 percent over 2004; mainstream music sales decreased over $1 billion during the same time period.[1]

There are three basic revenue streams in the mainstream music business: (1) sales of recordings where the money goes from the consumer to the retailer to the distributor and record company, who pays artists, songwriters, and publishers a royalty on each recording sold; (2) broadcast and nonbroadcast of songs where the radio and television stations pay the performance rights organizations (BMI, ASCAP, and SESAC), who then pay songwriters and publishers; and (3) personal appearances where consumers pay concert promoters, who then pay booking agents, artists, and managers. Merchandise sales (T-shirts, caps, etc.) are usually connected to personal appearances. Studios, engineers and musicians are generally paid by either the record company or publishers for sessions in the mainstream recording industry. For legal downloads, the money goes from the consumer to a collecting agent to the recording company.

For independent artists who press their own CDs and pay studio costs themselves, their major revenue stream comes from the sale of CDs and merchandise during their personal appearances.

In terms of genre, "rock" accounts for approximately 31.5 percent of total sales; second is rap/hip-hop with 13.3 percent followed by country (12.5 percent), R & B/urban (10.2 percent), pop (8.1 percent), religious (5.3 percent), classical (2.4 percent), children's (2.3 percent), and jazz (1.8 percent).[2]

The Canadian music industry is the sixth largest in the world, behind the United States, Japan, the UK, France, and Germany, accounting for 2 percent of the world's total recordings sold or 946.6 million in Canadian dollars (US$575 million) on 58.6 million units sold in 2005.

The Canadian music industry differs from that of the United States because Canadian radio is required to play at least 35 percent of Canadian product. This is defined as (1) music composed entirely by a Canadian, (2) an artist who is Canadian, (3) music recorded in Canada, or (4) lyrics written by a Canadian.

Canada also differs from the United States in that it has both English- and French-language music industries; in the Canadian Broadcasting Corporation (CBC) there are two English-language and two French-language radio stations; the English language stations are required to program 50 percent Canadian content, whereas the French-language stations are required to program a minimum of 65 percent French-language music. The Canadian French-language music industry is located primarily in the province of Quebec, and its major city is Montreal.

Because the majority of the Canadian population resides within 200 miles of the U.S. border, most Canadians have access to U.S. entertainment, from radio to television to concert tours. Although Canadians have a long history of producing top musical acts, the tastes of Canadian consumers generally mirror that of consumers in the United States, with rock being the dominant genre and country music also having a strong presence.

Because the population of Canada is approximately 10 percent that of the United States (roughly 30 million vs. 300 million), Canada must depend on exports for a profitable music industry; of the sales of Canadian music, approximately 72 percent are international and 22 percent are domestic.

Canadian acts span the gamut from country music pioneers to rock icons to current hit-makers. Canadian performers past and present include Bryan Adams, Paul Anka, April Wine, Alanis Morissette, Bachman Turner Overdrive, The Band, Barenaked Ladies, Blue Rodeo, Wilf Carter, Terri Clark, Tom Cochrane, Bruce Cockburn, Leonard Cohen, Stompin' Tom Conners, The Cowboy Junkies, Crash Test Dummies, Burton Cummings, Céline Dion, Maynard Ferguson, Nelly Furtado, Glenn Gould, Robert Goulet, The Guess Who, k. d. lang, Andy Kim, Diana Krall, Daniel Lanlois, Gordon Lightfoot, Guy Lombardo, Loverboy, Sarah McLachlan, Joni Mitchell, Anne Murray, Nickleback, Ocean, Oscar Peterson, Rush, Buffy Sainte-Marie, Robbie Robertson, David Clayton Thomas, Hank Snow, Shania Twain, Ian and Sylvia (Ian and Sylvia Tyson), Gino Vannelli, Michelle Wright, and Neil Young.

Popular Music before the Twentieth Century

Early in the nineteenth century an "American voice" emerged in music; prior to this time, North Americans saw themselves—at least in terms of the arts—as an extension of Europe. The roots of American popular music are the eighteenth-century broadside ballad and the ballad opera. The broadside led to sheet music; the ballad opera led to musical comedy. Broadsides were generally written about current events using everyday language, using satire, wit, and ribald stories, usually printed on small sheets of paper without a musical score and sung to popular tunes or folk melodies. They achieved wide circulation because they were printed on a single folio sheet and sold cheaply.

The first ballad opera was *The Beggar's Opera*, written by John Gay and J. C. Pepusch, which premiered in 1728. This opera led to others that used the folk tradition in an opera context, lampooning society, politics, and other events with singers singing in the Italian opera tradition.

The term *folk music* may be defined as music of the "common" folk—black and white—who later became known as the "working class." It is music from those who are generally musically illiterate but have musical talent and are musically accomplished. This music is developed outside the circles of the musical elite and represents the basis of popular culture, where music comes from the bottom up to the mainstream. This early folk music was usually played on stringed instruments, and the musicians were, by and large, self-taught; the songs were passed down through the oral tradition.

By 1800 the guitar had evolved in Europe from lute-like instruments with paired strings into a six-stringed instrument. In 1850 C. F. Martin of Nazareth, Pennsylvania, perfected a flat-top guitar, and in the 1890s Orville Gibson of Kalamazoo, Michigan, perfected the archtop guitar. By the 1890s guitars and mandolins came into wider use after they were offered in the Sears, Roebuck and Montgomery Ward mail-order catalogs.

Hawaiian music first became popular in the United States in 1909 when Joseph Kekuku played a slide guitar in exotic dancer Toots Paka's troupe in New York. In 1913 Walter Kolomoku with the Hawaiian Quintette recorded Hawaiian music for Victor Records, and these recordings popularized the genre; the "sound" of Kolomoku playing a slide on a guitar would influence the sounds of the slide and steel guitar in blues and country music.

By the end of the nineteenth century the most popular folk instruments were the fiddle and the banjo; the guitar and the harmonica were available, but their popularity occurred during the 1930s.

The history of North American folk music in both the United States and Canada begins with the early folk songs from Scotland, Ireland, Wales, England, and France. The roots are not "pure" folk music—songs composed anonymously and handed down through oral tradition. Rather, from the beginning, folk music comprised a mixture of songs from anonymous sources as well as those a singer rewrote or changed, as well as songs composed by songwriters who composed new songs from this old tradition.

The Piano in America

"Parlor songs," or songs that were played—usually by young ladies—on pianos in parlors, tended to be romantic and sentimental. Pianos had to be imported from Europe in the early nineteenth century and therefore were prohibitively expensive, but during the 1820s the first domestically manufactured upright pianos were produced in the United States. The popularity of the piano created a demand for sheet music, and the music publishing business was born and grew.

Minstrel Shows

The development of minstrel shows—whites in blackface imitating blacks—became popular before the Civil War. Minstrel songs achieved their effect primarily through their lyrics, which were in black dialect; musically the songs were an extension of theater songs and folk melodies. The first full-time minstrel group was the Virginia Minstrels, formed in early 1843 in New York, which consisted of banjo, fiddle, bone castanets, and tambourine. It was led by Daniel Decatur Emmett, who is credited with writing the song "Dixie." This group generally performed between acts in plays or circuses but never as a whole show.

Perhaps the most significant pre–Civil War minstrel group was E. P. Christy's Minstrels, which eventually totaled seven members, led by Christy on banjo and singing, and provided a whole evening's entertainment, generally in three parts. The full band performed skits and dances and sang a dozen or more songs.

The most historically significant fact about Christy's Minstrels is that, in addition to being the first to present a full evening's program, they introduced many of Stephen Foster's songs to the American public.

Stephen Foster

Stephen Foster was the first American to make a living through his songwriting. Foster's first success came in 1847, and he achieved his fame and income primarily from minstrel songs such as "Oh! Susanna," "Old Uncle Ned," "The Lou'siana Belle," "Old Folks at Home," "Nelly Was a Lady," and "My Old Kentucky Home."

Foster's songs had full choruses with three- and four-part harmony, in the tradition of the family singers who toured the country during Foster's time. Other minstrel songs before Foster generally had refrain lines, or a line at the end of each verse the whole troupe sang in unison or perhaps a brief chorus sung in unison.

The Music Business during the Civil War

The U.S. Civil War has been called "the singin'est war ever." Twenty-two years after the war ended, in 1887, a 640-page collection containing 438 songs called *Our War Songs, North and South* was published. However, this was only a portion of the songs written during the Civil War; over ten thousand were published during the conflict, mostly in the North. In the South, songs were published under the control of the Board of Music Trade, which existed until the end of the nineteenth century. After the Civil War, the music publishing industry continued to thrive.

After the Civil War, audiences increasingly wanted variety shows, a departure from minstrel shows, although variety shows included a number of minstrel numbers and a number of acts still performed in blackface. But audiences also wanted comics, acrobats, jugglers, dancers, skits, tragicomic plays, animals, freaks, singers, and anyone else who could entertain a crowd.

In the "varieties" of the latter 1800s, a banjo was an important instrument, accompanying dances of jigs, clogs, and solo numbers, as well as serving as a prop for comics and to fill any gaps during the show. In the better theaters in larger towns, there was often an orchestra, usually consisting of three pieces—piano, cornet, and drums—for the show. A drum was used for percussive sounds—drumrolls, cymbal crashes, and rim shots—to accompany falls of comics, the flight of an aerialist, and jumps through rings of fire. In seven-piece orchestras, the group generally consisted of violin, cornet, piano, clarinet, trombone, string bass, and drums.

The music performed was generally minstrel show numbers and comedy songs. The comedy of the varieties depended heavily on stereotypes, with the Irish being buffooned the most, followed closely by blacks. The varieties continued throughout the nineteenth century but were changed by Tony Pastor, who had a theater in New York in the 1880s. Because Pastor struggled to fill his theaters, he developed the idea of a "clean" variety show that would appeal to all people.

During the latter part of the nineteenth century the term *vaudeville* was increasingly used to describe varieties. The person most responsible for popularizing the term *vaudeville* in North America was B. F. Keith, who, with partner E. F. Albee, eventually dominated the world of vaudeville, owning or controlling theaters all over the country.

The Phonograph

Recorded music was made possible by the invention of the phonograph by Thomas Edison in 1877. The Edison Speaking Phonograph Company, which may be considered the first recording company, was formed on January 24, 1878; Edison's invention played cylinders.

Two other inventors, Charles Tainter and Chicester Bell, who worked at Alexander Graham Bell's laboratory (Chicester was Alexander's nephew), worked on the phonograph and in 1885 filed a patent for a "graphophone," which also played cylinders. This company eventually became Columbia.

A third inventor, Emile Berliner, patented the "gramophone" in 1888; it played "plates" or discs instead of cylinders. By 1896 there were three firms competing for the market: Columbia was the leader, followed by the National Phonograph Company owned by Edison, then Berliner's Gramophone Company.

The first commercial music recording for Edison was made in 1888 by 12-year-old pianist Josef Hofmann; commercial cylinders began in the spring of 1889. The first recordings were made by people in and around New York because Edison's laboratory was in that area. Edison sought out theater performers as well as opera singers; recordings were made of arias, popular songs from vaudeville and the musical theater, and minstrel numbers.

In 1891 Columbia issued its first catalog of recordings, which contained twenty-seven marches, thirteen polkas, ten waltzes, and thirty-four items listed as "miscellaneous." The vocal recordings were divided into categories such as "Sentimental," "Topical," "Comic," "Negro," and "Irish." There were also twenty "speaking" records. Their most popular act was the Marine Corps Band, headed by John Philip Sousa; they were the first act to sign an "exclusive" recording contract, when they agreed to record only on Columbia.

John Philip Sousa was America's first musical superstar. Known as "The March King," Sousa's marches were hit songs; people danced to them as well as marched. His biggest hit during his lifetime was "The Washington Post March"; other hits included "The Stars and Stripes Forever."

POPULAR MUSIC: 1900–1930S

The Victor Company

Victor Records was begun in 1901 by Eldridge Johnson and Emile Berliner after a series of lawsuits involving patent infringement between Berliner's company and Columbia. The first Victor star—and the first international recording star—was Enrico Caruso, whose greatest hit, "Vesti la gibba," from Act I in *Leoncavallo* by Pagliacci, was first recorded in 1902. This song, and subsequent recordings of it, sold over 1 million copies during Caruso's lifetime.

Although recordings became increasingly popular during the early twentieth century, sheet music sales were more indicative of popular music in the late nineteenth and early twentieth century, and some of the most popular songs were "coon songs," which took rag-time rhythms and added lyrics in black dialect.

Ragtime began with "ragging" existing songs, adding rhythm and syncopation to known songs until new songs developed with distinctive rhythm and syncopation. African Americans were the primary developers of ragtime, and the earliest ragtime songs were developed by piano players in brothels and sporting houses. However, as the music was published and caught on with audiences, a large number of white songwriters adapted the rhythms and incorporated them into their own work. There are two major black ragtime composers—Scott Joplin and James Scott—but the greatest number of ragtime songs came from white Tin Pan Alley songwriters in New York. Ragtime evolved from marches, minstrel numbers, and espe-cially the syncopated "coon songs" popular in the 1890s. In time *ragtime* denoted any song with a snappy, up-tempo melody, especially if it was connected to some new fad or dance.

Ragtime achieved its greatest fame from 1910 to 1920. Probably the single most impor-tant song for ragtime was "Alexander's Ragtime Band" (1911), which was really not a rag-time song but had "ragtime" in the title and became a major hit. It was the first hit written by Irving Berlin, who would eventually be recognized as the greatest American songwriter in the twentieth century. Ragtime led directly to the development of jazz.

Radio

During the early years of the twentieth century, radio was developed, and it would have a profound effect on music and musical recordings. The event that spurred the development of wireless broadcasts was the sinking of the *Titanic* in April 1912. After the *Titanic* disaster, Congress enacted legislation requiring the navy to develop radio communication. During World War I the Navy took over all amateur and commercial radio stations, declared a moratorium on radio patent litigation, and set up schools for radio operators to train young men in the use of radio.

After World War I, radio grew rapidly. Live music was performed on early radio stations in both the United States and Canada, but it was primarily "conservatory music," with vocal and instrumental music generally alternating. One program director called it "potted palm" music; this type of music would dominate on radio throughout the 1920s.

Broadway and American Popular Music

The center for American popular music during the 1920s was in New York on Broadway. Here Tin Pan Alley writers wrote songs for vaudeville performers, music revues, and musical theater. Great American composers such as Irving Berlin, Jerome Kern, Cole Porter, Richard Rodgers and Oscar Hammerstein, and George Gershwin all wrote songs for the live audi-ences who attended vaudeville or theater shows. These songs were also recorded as the recording industry increasingly became the dominant means to preserve performances. Sheet music remained important during the 1920s, but increasingly a hit song was measured by how many records it sold.

There were approximately eighty theaters in the Broadway area during the 1920s, and forty to fifty musicals were produced each year. It was during this period that the pop song reached a standard form: thirty-two bars consisting of four segments of eight bars each.

The dominant themes for songs during the 1920s were escapism and a pseudosophistica-tion. Because they wrote for musicals, songwriters wrote "outside" themselves, composing songs for characters and situations; the purpose of their writing was to fit a story or appeal to the public—not to express their own private emotions. They wrote on demand and with deadlines—they could not wait for inspiration.

The songwriters were usually divided between "lyricists" and "composers" with only a few writing both melodies and words. Broadway was the anchor—and aspiration—for these writers. The area where music publishing companies congregated in New York on West 28th Street between Broadway and Fifth became known as Tin Pan Alley, a term coined by journalist Monroe H. Rosefeld (who was also a part-time songwriter), who noted that the cacophony of sounds coming from the open windows of the publishing companies with their tinny upright pianos sounded like "tin pan alley." The term caught on in the 1903–10 period and came to mean manufactured songs.

During the 1920s these Tin Pan Alley songwriters directed their energies toward Broadway; however, after the Wall Street crash in 1929, and the ensuing Depression, the relative decline of Broadway coincided with the rise of talking pictures in Hollywood, so songwriters shifted from New York to California, where they wrote for movies.

The biggest star of the 1920s was Al Jolson, who first achieved fame in vaudeville.

Jazz

Jazz is a direct descendant of ragtime, which descended from brass band music. But although jazz is a child of ragtime, its ancestors also include the rhythms of West Africa, classical music from Europe (with its harmonic structure), American folk music, gospel or religious music, work songs, blues, and minstrel show music.

The term *jass* was originally used as a verb to describe the sex act. And so the term for the music became *jass*, which became a popular fad in Chicago, New York, and New Orleans, replacing the term *ragtime*. Musically there was not much difference between ragtime and jazz at this time, other than the new name.

The first jazz recording was made in February 1917 by the Original Dixieland Jazz Band for Victor. "The Livery Stable Blues" soon became a million seller. Although a follow-up jazz hit would not occur for several years, this marks the beginning of the history of recorded jazz.

Also in 1917 a federal order closed the Storyville area of New Orleans; this was the red-light district where jazz musicians performed and developed their craft. When Storyville closed, most jazz musicians were forced to go elsewhere to perform; musicians found work on the Mississippi riverboats and in Chicago, New York, Los Angeles, and other large cities.

Society orchestras and dance bands in large hotels and ballrooms also contributed to the development of jazz and big band music. Paul Whiteman's group was one of many who played in these hotels, ballrooms, and resorts, but Whiteman was an ambitious man and his musical tastes increasingly leaned towards jazz.

Whiteman had a talent for making jazz commercial and fashionable and was a forerunner of the big band era. His most famous contribution to the history of jazz occurred in 1924 with his concert at Aeolian Hall in New York. The concert mixed symphonic and jazz music and featured the debut of "Rhapsody in Blue" by George Gershwin. The Aeolian Hall concert, and the ensuing personal appearances, made Whiteman the "King of Jazz," the spokesman for popular music and jazz.

Blues

The roots of the blues go back to work songs African Americans sang in southern fields during the period of slavery in the United States. It includes field hollers, cries, calls, arhoolies, and spirituals, as well as washboard, jug, and string bands. As the blues developed in urban areas—when some blacks moved out of the rural South after the Civil War—this music became more rhythmic, later becoming rhythm and blues; this sound included songs from marching bands, ragtime, blues, gospel, minstrel shows, vaudeville blues, and classic blues.

The first commercially successful recording of blues was "Crazy Blues" by Mamie Smith, released in August 1920. This recording, by an African-American singer released nationally, proved that there was a large market for "race" music (as it was called at the time).

Prior to Mamie Smith's recording, Tin Pan Alley songwriters had written songs derived from blues and African-American folk songs, particularly after W. C. Handy moved from Memphis to New York in 1915. Before 1920 Handy had published his most famous blues compositions, including "Memphis Blues" and "Saint Louis Blues."

Handy's success showed Tin Pan Alley the commercial potential for blues songs, and a number of songs came off the assembly line to satisfy the demand in vaudeville theaters, dance halls, and cabarets. By 1920 this form was generally referred to as "vaudeville blues," which was based on commercial, rather than folk, tradition. Among the vocalists who popularized vaudeville blues were Ma Rainey, Ida Cox, Sara Martin, Alberta Hunter, Sippie Wallace, and Bessie Smith. Composers included W. C. Handy, Perry Bradford, James and Rosmond Johnson, Spencer Williams, Porter Grainger, Clarence Williams, and Thomas Dorsey. Most of these composers and performers were connected to the South and traditional black folk music.

Country Music

"Country music" before World War I comprised fiddling contests, home entertainment, and local dances in rural areas in both Canada and the United States. The basic instruments had been developed: the violin or fiddle, the banjo, and the guitar.

The first commercially successful recording of country music occurred when Fiddlin' John Carson was recorded in Atlanta by Ralph Peer on June 14, 1923. Carson recorded two songs: "Little Old Log Cabin down the Lane" and "The Old Hen Cackled and the Rooster's Gonna Crow." Copies of the recording were originally sold at the Georgia State Fiddling Convention. The success of Fiddlin' John Carson's recording demonstrated a demand for hillbilly music, so more recording companies entered the field.

In 1924 Vernon Dalhart recorded "The Prisoner's Song," and the success of this recording led other labels to enter the country recording market. This recording also led to the historic recording session in Bristol, Tennessee, where Ralph Peer recorded the Carter Family and Jimmie Rodgers.

The Carter Family, consisting of A. P. Carter, his wife Sara, and Sara's cousin and A.P.'s sister-in-law, Maybelle, recorded a repertoire of songs that established the Carters as one of the most influential groups in country music. Among the more than 300 songs they recorded for Victor were "Keep on the Sunny Side," "Wildwood Flower," "I'm Thinking Tonight of My Blue Eyes," "Wabash Cannonball," "Worried Man Blues," "Anchored in Love," "John Hardy Was a Desperate Little Man," "You Are My Flower," and "Hello, Stranger."

Jimmie Rodgers became the first solo recording star in U.S. country music and influenced several generations of country artists with his "blue yodels" and songs such as "T for Texas," "Waiting for a Train," "Daddy and Home," "In the Jailhouse Now," "Miss the Mississippi and You," "Mother the Queen of My Heart," and "Peach Pickin' Time in Georgia." Jimmie Rodgers died in 1933.

Wilf Carter was a pioneer of Canadian cowboy and country music, appearing first on the radio in Calgary in 1930 and recording such songs as "The Capture of Albert Johnson," "The Fate of the Old Strawberry Roan," "There's a Love Knot in My Lariat," and "You Are My Sunshine." Also important in the 1930s and 1940s in Canadian country music was Hank Snow, who, like Wilf Carter, often sang in a yodeling style. Both men were inspired by Jimmie Rodgers.

Music in Movies

The success of the first movie with sound, *The Jazz Singer* starring Al Jolson in 1927, eventually led to the filming of musicals and a shift from New York to Hollywood for Tin Pan Alley writers; most of the early movie musicals were adaptations of Broadway musicals.

As the power base of the American popular music industry shifted from Broadway to Hollywood, movies became the main avenue for a hit song. The Broadway musical was also replaced by radio with its network shows, bands that performed on radio, and recording labels. Thus by the end of the 1920s Tin Pan Alley was moving to Hollywood; during the 1930s Hollywood would replace New York's Broadway as the center for entertainment. Not only was popular and big band music popular in the movies, but country and western music became popular through movies by the "singing cowboys" Gene Autry, Roy Rogers, Tex Ritter, and others.

Recording Companies

At the end of World War I the recording industry was dominated by three giants: Victor, Columbia, and Edison; however, a number of early patents ran out, resulting in the formation of about two hundred recording companies during the 1920s. By this point, discs dominated the industry, but cylinders were still manufactured. Edison had reluctantly agreed to disc production in 1914, but his company continued to manufacture cylinders until 1928; recordings sold on average about 150 million a year during the 1920s.

Electrical Recordings

In recording technology, the advent of electrical recording introduced the microphone to the recording process. Microphones replaced the old horns that people sang or spoke into and made it possible to regulate and control sound as well as enhance it. For singers this meant an end to the vaudeville-type singer who could belt out a tune so that people in the last row could hear and marked the beginning of the era of the "crooner." The first to successfully make this transition was Gene Austin, whose 1927 hit "My Blue Heaven" ushered in this new era. The ultimate crooner would be Bing Crosby, whose fame began in the 1930s.

Dance Bands

The golden age of radio, roughly 1929–54, produced the big band era. Big band music, popular in both Canada and the United States, was an extension of jazz, and as the popularity of big bands grew they had to become bigger for a simple reason: because they played larger and larger dance halls and hotel ballrooms, they needed to be heard throughout larger areas, but there were no effective sound systems.

Bing Crosby

The pop music singer who best personified the 1930s was Bing Crosby, whose relaxed, easygoing persona and singing style were soothing influences on those faced with the wrenching hard times of the Great Depression. His recording of "Brother, Can You Spare a Dime?" (1931) served as an anthem for that era.

With the development of electrical recording and the microphone, a new style of singing evolved where the singer used the microphone as an instrument. This "crooning" style allowed a singer to sing more softly and develop vocal inflections and an intimacy with the audience. Nobody did this better than Bing Crosby.

Bing Crosby dominated the recording industry during the 1935–54 period like no other singer. He was the most commercially successful and influential recording artist, and the public found him to be one of the most likable stars.

The era of "swing" music lasted from around 1938 through World War II. Top swing bands during this time included Benny Goodman, Glenn Miller, the Dorsey Brothers, Artie Shaw, Count Basie, and numerous others who played for the teenage market.

The Golden Age of Radio Begins

The Depression cut deeply into the record business; in 1928 there had been 34 million records sold, but in 1931 only 10 million were sold. If families had to choose between buying a phonograph or buying a radio, they bought a radio. There were 14 million radio sets in the country by 1930—seven times as many as there had been in 1925—and over six hundred stations.

In both Canada and the United States, radio exposure created a demand for live performances, and musical artists often played on a radio program for free in order to get bookings within a listening area. The most popular performers found sponsors who wanted to reach an audience. Sometimes a sponsor paid the performer, but usually a sponsor paid the radio station so that the performer could have time on the air.

For performers, radio also had a profound impact; no longer were amateurs who played music on the side part of the game. Professional entertainers emerged, and many musicians had careers instead of an avocation. Also, because radio demanded a huge repertoire, no longer could a musician, or a group, get by with a few tunes. Audiences would no longer accept the songs they had been hearing for years; performers had to either compose new songs or find new songs from professional songwriters.

Big band music was the most popular music heard on the radio during the 1930s; however, live country music shows, called "barn dances" were also popular, whereas blues was virtually never heard on the radio. Country music was influenced by the jazz age and the big band movement with the development of western swing; the most important pioneer in western swing was Bob Wills and His Texas Playboys.

The development of radio throughout the 1930s provided employment for big band dance groups because sponsors realized that audiences liked music on the radio. Because the young audience wanted fast, beat-driven music, the bands soon adapted to this, which created the "swing" craze at the end of the 1930s. Swing became the theme music for a generation of teenagers entering adulthood during the Great Depression and World War II.

The music of blues and hillbilly found a market in the Great Depression on jukeboxes in "joints" and "honky-tonks." These "juke joints" or barrooms became popular after Prohibition was repealed in 1933 when President Franklin Roosevelt took office. Hillbilly recordings accounted for about a fourth of record sales during the Great Depression, and a significant number of them were sold to jukeboxes. In fact, jukeboxes were the major purchasers of recorded music during this time.

Fiftieth Anniversary of the Recording Industry

In 1939 the recording industry celebrated its unofficial fiftieth anniversary. The major labels were Victor, now owned by RCA, which also had the NBC network; Columbia, now owned by CBS; and Decca, whose 35¢ records had rejuvenated the music business. In 1939, 50 million phonograph records were sold in the United States.

Radio was now the carrier of the most popular music of the day, and the music they played was "national" music as the electronic media, via radio, linked the nation. Radio had become a vital part of the music business and so had recordings; meanwhile sheet music publishing was in a sharp decline.

GUY LOMBARDO

Guy Lombardo (1902–77), from London, Ontario, along with his brothers and other performers in the area, formed the big band The Royal Canadians in 1924. The band's career spanned well into the 1970s, playing what they famously called "the sweetest music this side of heaven." Popular on radio and through their best-selling recordings, they became associated most with New Year's Eve. Their New Year's Eve concerts from New York City, often from the Waldorf-Astoria Hotel, were broadcast throughout North America until 1976. A recording of their "Auld Lang Syne" is still played at Times Square on New Year's Eve.

POPULAR MUSIC: THE 1940s AND 1950s

The World War II Era

American popular music provided the soundtrack for World War II; Americans at home and GIs abroad listened to the same music. In 1940 and 1941, the years before the United States entered World War II, the major hit recordings included "Take the 'A' Train" and "I Got It Bad and That Ain't Good" by Duke Ellington and His Orchestra, "Boogie Woogie Bugle Boy" and "I'll Be With You in Apple Blossom Time" by the Andrews Sisters, "God Bless the Child" by Billie Holiday, "Star Dust" by Artie Shaw and His Orchestra, "Chattanooga Choo Choo" and "Elmer's Tune" by Glenn Miller and His Orchestra, "New San Antonio Rose" by Bob Wills and His Texas Playboys, and hits by the bands of Tommy Dorsey, Charlie Barnet, Jimmy Dorsey, Sammy Kaye, Benny Goodman, Vaughn Monroe, and Kay Kyser.

For the record industry, the declaration of war meant a problem in getting shellac, which had been imported from India, and wax from Germany in order to press records. Still, in 1941, the industry produced 130 million records, their best year since 1921. Consumers had begun to purchase recordings. In 1940 the jukebox operators were responsible for purchasing 40 percent of discs manufactured; this percentage would decrease in the coming years.

The biggest pop hits from 1942 were "Chattanooga Choo Choo" by Glenn Miller and His Orchestra, which sold over 1 million units, "White Christmas" by Bing Crosby, and "Don't Sit under the Apple Tree (with Anyone Else but Me)" by the Andrews Sisters. Other pop hits included "A String of Pearls" by Glenn Miller and His Orchestra, "Tangerine" by Jimmy Dorsey and His Orchestra, "Blues in the Night" by Dinah Shore, "Jingle Jangle Jingle," by Kay Kyser and His Orchestra, which covered the country hit by Tex Ritter, "Deep in the Heart of

Texas" by Alvino Rey and His Orchestra, "Cow-Cow Boogie" by Freddie Slack and His Orchestra, "(There'll Be Bluebirds Over) The White Cliffs of Dover" by Kate Smith, "Flying Home" by Lionel Hampton and His Orchestra, and hits from the bands of Benny Goodman, Harry James, Vaughn Monroe, Tommy Dorsey, Johnny Mercer, and Bing Crosby.

Hit Songs and War Songs

A number of "war" songs were recorded and/or released in 1942: "Get Your Gun and Come Along (We're Fixin' to Kill a Skunk)," "Mussolini's Letter to Hitler," "Hitler's Reply to Mussolini," "It's Just a Matter of Time," and "Plain Talk," all written and recorded by Carson Robison; "Shh, It's a Military Secret," "When Johnny Comes Marching Home," and "She'll Always Remember" by Glenn Miller and His Orchestra; "Three Little Sisters" and "He Wears a Pair of Silver Wings" by Dinah Shore; "This Is Worth Fighting For" by Shep Fields and His New Music; "News of the World" by Cliff Nazarro; "Pearl Harbor Blues" by Doctor Clayton; "Wartime Blues" and "One Letter Home" by Jazz Gillum; "Little Bo Peep Has Lost Her Jeep" by Spike Jones and His City Slickers; "Obey Your Air Raid Warden" by Tony Pastor and His Orchestra; "Dear Mom" by Swing and Sway with Sammy Kaye; "Johnny Doughboy Found a Rose in Ireland" by Freddy Martin and His Orchestra; "From the Coast of Maine to the Rockies" by Vaughn Monroe and His Orchestra; and "(We'll Be Singing Hallelujah) Marching through Berlin" by Ethel Merman.

A song that became a standard during World War II was recorded in 1939 by Kate Smith. "God Bless America" was written by Irving Berlin for his World War I musical *Yip Yip Yaphank*. Berlin pulled the song out of the musical but remembered it 20 years later when Smith needed a song to commemorate the twentieth anniversary of the end of World War I. Berlin gave it to Smith to record and donated all income from the song to the Boy Scouts.

During World War II, Frank Sinatra would emerge as a star, capturing the hearts of teenage girls with his ballads. Virtually unknown when the war began, Frank Sinatra was one of the biggest pop stars of that era. An intense, determined, ambitious young man, Frank Sinatra was not easy to get along with and did not allow for anyone or anything to stand in the way of his climb to success and fame. Sinatra did not replace Bing Crosby as America's favorite singer; instead he gave audiences a different kind of singer to admire, one whose singing was an "art" and whose recordings captured the longings of love-starved teenage girls yearning for romance.

In January 1942 *Billboard* and *Downbeat* both named Frank Sinatra the top male vocalist, ending the six-year reign of Bing Crosby.

Elton Britt recorded "There's a Star Spangled Banner Waving Somewhere," which became one of the two biggest country recordings during World War II. The other was "Pistol Packin' Mama," recorded by Al Dexter. Other hit country songs during World War II included "You Are My Sunshine" by Jimmy Davis, "I'm Walkin' the Floor over You" by Ernest Tubb, and "Be Honest with Me" by Gene Autry.

Gasoline and tire shortages meant that most musicians could not do personal appearances during World War II; it also stopped crowds from coming to shows. Additionally, a number of musicians were drafted or enlisted, forcing the breakup of bands.

By 1944 the big bands had lost a lot of members to the armed services, and many groups had to disband. This loss of musicians to war manpower coincided with a shift in national tastes away from big bands and toward singers. The record industry had not quite caught up with these changes; there were no recordings made throughout 1943 and most of 1944 because of a musicians' strike called by the American Federation of Musicians. Hits that year included "The Trolley Song" by Judy Garland, "San Fernando Valley" and "I'll Be Seeing You" by Bing Crosby,

"Time Waits for No One" by Helen Forrest, "It Could Happen to You" by Jo Stafford, "It Had to Be You" and "Long Ago (And Far Away)" by Helen Forrest and Dick Haymes, "Mairzy Doats" by The Merry Macs, and "You Always Hurt the One You Love" by the Mills Brothers as well as hits from the orchestras of Guy Lombardo ("Speak Low When You Speak, Love"), Lawrence Welk ("Don't Sweetheart Me"), Harry James ("I'll Get By As Long as I Have You," and "Cherry"), and Duke Ellington ("Do Nothin' Till You Hear from Me"). There were also hits by African-American artists, including "Straighten Up and Fly Right" by The Nat King Cole Trio and two hits by Louis Jordan and His Tympany Five: "Is You Is or Is You Ain't (Ma' Baby)" and "G.I. Jive."

By the end of 1945 the year had seen pop hits such as "Till the End of Time" by Perry Como, "Ac-Cent-Tchu-Ate the Positive" and "On the Atchison, Topeka and the Santa Fe" by Johnny Mercer, "Rum and Coca-Cola" by the Andrews Sisters, "Don't Fence Me In" by Bing Crosby with the Andrews Sisters, as well as orchestras led by Vaughn Monroe, Les Brown, Russ Morgan, Harry James ("It's Been a Long, Long Time"), Benny Goodman, and Les Brown ("Sentimental Journey"). The beginning of what would become known as rock and roll a decade later was heard in songs on the pop charts such as "Caldonia" by Louis Jordan and His Tympany Five and "Dig You Later (A Hubba-Hubba-Hubba)" by Perry Como.

R&B and Post–World War II

During World War II several important independent labels began; these labels would be important to the development of rhythm and blues, although the recordings were generally referred to as "race" in the trade magazines. These labels would record artists the major labels ignored and market them to the jukebox industry.

The major African-American artist to emerge during World War II was Louis Jordan. Jordan, considered the "Father of Rhythm and Blues," was the pivotal figure in the development of rhythm and blues because his success on recordings, on the radio, in the movies, and in personal appearances inspired black artists and independent record producers by demonstrating that not only was there a market for black-oriented material and black-styled music, but it was a very big market that attracted both white and black fans.

Another artist who represented a new direction in music for African Americans was Muddy Waters, who moved from Clarksdale, Mississippi, to Chicago during World War II. Waters was part of the "Great Migration" of blacks leaving the South for northern cities; the movement began around World War I but accelerated during World War II and continued through the 1960s until Chicago had a large black population, which led that city to become a leader in developing rhythm and blues.

The music played by musicians in Chicago differed from the music played by black share-croppers in The Delta. The old rural blues of a single person with a guitar gave way to a small three-piece group with guitar, bass, and drums. As the music evolved, brass instruments and a harmonica were often added to the musical lineup. The music was louder and more belligerent, indicative of the "attitude" of blacks in Chicago. No one reflected this better than Muddy Waters.

The biggest impetus for independent labels recording R&B came with the hit single "I Wonder" (1945) recorded by Pvt. Cecil Gant in Los Angeles on Gilt Edge Records. Because this record sold over a million copies, entrepreneurs saw that rhythm and blues could be a lucrative field for a small record company; this led to a number of small labels starting and recording rhythm and blues.

After World War II, Chess Records was formed in Chicago; this label recorded Muddy Waters, Chuck Berry, and Bo Diddley. In New York, Atlantic Records was formed; this label recorded Ray Charles, Ruth Brown, and Clyde McPhatter. In Cincinnati, King Records was formed; this label recorded Hank Ballard and the Midnighters and James Brown. Imperial Records was formed in New Orleans, and that label recorded Fats Domino.

Country Music

Country music was popular on radio after World War II through broadcast of "barn dances" from Nashville, Chicago, Atlanta, Los Angeles, and other cities. But country music headed in several different directions after World War II.

Western swing was the most commercially popular type of country music after the war, led by band leaders Spade Cooley and Bob Wills, both groups based in Los Angeles. Also in Hollywood were the singing cowboys, led by Gene Autry, Roy Rogers, the Sons of the Pioneers, and Tex Ritter, whose movies and recordings were still popular.

The mountaineer image in country music had been replaced by the image of the cowboy, although the mountaineer image would continue through artists such as Roy Acuff, whose mountaineer-type singing was still popular. In Texas, honky-tonk music developed by artists such as Ernest Tubb, Ted Daffan, and Floyd Tillman was popular in beer joints.

Bill Monroe's band, the Bluegrass Boys, hired banjo player Earl Scruggs, whose three-fingered style of banjo playing defined the sound of bluegrass. However, the most popular type of country music would be a contemporary blend of country and pop music, exemplified by artists such as Red Foley and Eddy Arnold. This would be where country music would direct its energies after World War II.

The Disc Jockeys

An important reason for the rise in the sales of hillbilly and race records was the disc jockeys, particularly at small radio stations, who grew in stature and importance after World War II. Disk jockeys did not simply cue up records and play them anymore; now they made comments about the song or artist, thought about format and spacing, and had special programs for requests, new releases, a single vocalist, or oldies.

The music business began to take disc jockeys seriously after World War II; by the end of 1947 about 90 percent of radio stations had a disc jockey show. A survey showed that 24 percent of people said the disc jockey was the reason they purchased a record. At this point the biggest buyers of pop music were families with teenagers; teenagers directly accounted for 10 percent of purchases of records.

A major reason for the success of disc jockeys was the increased number of radio stations; in 1945, when World War II ended, there were 943 licensed stations in the United States.

Changes in Technology after World War II

Recording technology improved after World War II with the discovery of tape technology developed by the Germans. After World War II the industry began moving toward recording on tape, which allowed editing and, later, multitracking and overdubbing, instead of recording directly to disc.

Other changes in technology occurred when Columbia Records developed the 33⅓ rpm LP (long-playing) album in 1948 and RCA developed the single 45 rpm disc in 1949; these would eventually replace the 78 rpm record, which had been the staple of the music industry since the 1920s.

Rhythm and Blues

By the end of the 1940s rhythm and blues was good-time dance music in black sections of town in segregated America. The jukebox—and the shortage of discs in locations in the black sections of cities and towns—as well as the rising purchasing power of African Americans after World War II made rhythm and blues economically possible. Technologically, R&B was made possible by the development of tape and the relatively low cost of producing a single record. Musically it expressed a new sense of freedom for blacks; for whites it represented an exiting, vibrant new music.

Between 1948 and 1952 a number of "Negro" radio stations came on the air, playing rhythm and blues. WERD in Atlanta discovered that 20 percent of its listening audience was white. This would mark the beginning of a major influence of black music on pop and country music.

Several disc jockeys became extremely influential and important during the 1950s playing R&B. Alan Freed in Cleveland began broadcasting R&B on WJW in 1951; other DJs broadcasting R&B included Dewey Philips in Memphis; Gene Nobles and John Richbourg (John R) in Nashville; Zenas "Daddy" Sears in Atlanta; Ken "Jack the Cat" Elliott and Clarence "Poppa Stoppa" Hamman, Jr., in New Orleans; George "Hound Dog" Lorenz in Buffalo; "Jumpin'" George Oxford in Oakland–San Francisco; Phil McKernan in Berkeley; Hunter Hancock in Los Angeles; and Bob "Wolfman Jack" Smith in Shreveport and Del Rio, Texas.

Freed named his Cleveland show *The Moondog Show* and called himself "Moon Dog." In Philadelphia, Dick Clark began *Dick Clark's Caravan of Music* on WFIL in 1952. In 1955 Alan Freed was broadcasting in New York, where he named his radio program *The Rock and Roll Show*, which gave the music a new name. Dick Clark took over a local television show, *Bandstand*, and launched it nationally on ABC Television as *American Bandstand*. This show brought rock and roll into American homes each weekday afternoon.

The period 1950–55 was a blossoming of rhythm and blues, especially from independent labels. White singers on major labels often covered R&B hits from African-American artists, and the white recordings initially received more radio airplay than the African-American versions; however, as the 1950s progressed, the original versions of these records by black artists were increasingly heard on radio.

Rock and Roll

In mid-1955 Bill Haley's recording of "Rock Around the Clock" reached number one, marking the official beginning of the rock-and-roll era. The next year, Elvis sold 10 million records as teenagers became the dominant record market.

This shift in the music heard on radio and corresponding record sales hurt pop and country music, although it helped rhythm and blues. As the 1950s progressed, the top-selling albums were usually Broadway musicals but the music heard on radio was rock and roll. Country music increasingly centered its activities in Nashville.

From a business perspective, rock and roll was fueled by the growth of independent labels, who recorded music (primarily black music) that the major labels were not doing. The small labels were aided by AM radio, which had shifted to records from live talent after the introduction of television.

The audience that radio found in the 1956–58 period was young teenagers who wanted to hear rock-and-roll and rhythm and blues records. Many young country performers moved into rock and roll, and the young white working-class audience, who might have become country music fans, shifted over to rock and roll.

The rock-and-roll revolution was a revolution about individualism, rebellion, and a new world order. It was a new way of thinking that discarded the past and created a new future not bound by any restrictions of the past. This new individualism expressed itself in the younger generation breaking away from the previous generations for new forms of entertainment and new forms of music.

The teenagers of 1955 were beneficiaries of an economic boom that came after World War II; they could afford to buy recordings and wanted young stars to relate to. They also wanted their own individuality to shine through.

In 1956 the rock revolution hit full force when Elvis Presley sold 10 million records and appeared on a series of popular television shows. The music industry was quick to capitalize on the rock-and-roll movement, as evidenced by the number of young, attractive men signed to recording contracts the next year.

POPULAR MUSIC: THE 1960S AND 1970S

Country Music in the 1960s

During the 1960s country music moved from being a regional music, confined mostly to the South (with the exception of the singing cowboys in the movies), to becoming a national music, moving from a musical form on the fringes of U.S. society to part of mainstream U.S. popular music. A major reason for that success was the development of the "Nashville sound," which added strings and pop-type arrangements to country recordings, moving it away from its "twangy" sound into one palatable to the tastes of middle-class fans.

The importance of the "Nashville sound" in the 1960s was based on several things: (1) its commercial success, which helped make country music big business, and (2) its connection with the urban middle class with rural roots that emerged after World War II.

The Beatles and the British Invasion

In February 1964 the Beatles made their first U.S. television appearance on *The Ed Sullivan Show*. At this time "I Want to Hold Your Hand" became their first American single to reach number one. After their TV appearance, "Beatlemania" captured American teenagers and the Beatles became the most popular and most influential rock group. Their success sparked the British Invasion in 1964–66 when a number of British groups had hits on American radio.

This second rock revolution came from both the folk revival of the late 1950s, which inspired many young people to play guitars and sing, and the first rock revolution. The rock and roll of the 1960s covered a multitude of styles, everything from folk rock with protest lyrics—led by Bob Dylan—to the Motown Sound, which was pop R&B. As the 1960s progressed, soul became the music of blacks, led by artists such as Otis Redding and Aretha Franklin. The influence of drugs in rock music led to "psychedelic," music and the hippie movement that was centered in San Francisco. Leading psychedelic acts included Jimi Hendrix and the Grateful Dead.

Woodstock

In 1969 it was a summer of festivals for rock and roll. The "father" of these festivals was the Monterey Pop Festival, held in 1967; in 1968 the movie *Monterey Pop* was released and served as an inspiration for concert promoters, artists, fans, and film-makers to try to re-create the magic of Monterey. During 1969 there were rock music festivals in Palm Springs and Venice, California; in Denver, Toronto, and Atlanta; at Hyde Park in London; and then, in August, on a farm near Woodstock, New York. The Woodstock Festival suffered from too many fans and too little food, water, toilets, and security, as well as a thunderstorm. By the end of that weekend there had been many drugs consumed, three deaths, and three babies born. A film crew documented the event, and the movie, released the following year, provided the name for this generation: Woodstock Nation.

The final festival of 1969 occurred at Altamont, California, where the Rolling Stones performed before a crowd patrolled by Hell's Angels; one fan was killed in front of the stage during that concert.

TAPE

In terms of listening to music, the most revolutionary technology came in the mid-1960s and extended through the 1970s when tape—first eight-track and then cassette—was introduced, which made music portable. Prior to tape, a person could only listen to the radio in the car or on a transistor radio and had to sit in front of a stereo system to hear a recording at home. After tape, people could hear whatever artist or album they wished, whether they were driving in a car, walking across a campus, or jogging on a track.

The Fragmenting of Rock Music

During the 1960s, rock music—led by the Beatles—moved from being a force that challenged mainstream American culture to being part of mainstream American culture. By the time the Beatles broke up, in 1970, there was an acceptance of rock as the voice of American youth culture.

The first musical trend to emerge in the early 1970s, after the Beatles broke up, was singer-songwriters such as James Taylor, Carole King, and Don McLean who primarily wrote self-confessional lyrics. However, as the 1970s progressed, rock split into several different subgenres: hard rock, heavy metal, southern rock, art rock, country rock, disco, reggae, punk, and oldies.

Hard Rock and Heavy Metal

The improved sound systems made arena rock possible; the developments in amplifiers and electric guitars meant a group could play in huge stadiums and large arenas and be heard. Acts such as Lynyrd Skynyrd, J. Geils Band, Grand Funk Railroad, Aerosmith, and the James Gang all became big within the rock culture but never really had an impact in mainstream culture. These groups did not receive much radio airplay or appear on television, but through their constant touring they developed a core of faithful fans who consistently went to their shows and bought their albums.

Because radio had splintered into various rock formats, the album-oriented rock (AOR) format became popular. Acts such as Journey, Styx, REO Speedwagon, Rush, Kansas, Supertramp,

Ambrosia, Gentle Giant, and Nazareth—called "faceless bands" because individual personalities did not matter—became popular.

The most influential hard rock group was Led Zeppelin. In 1971 the group released the album *Led Zeppelin IV*, which contained what became the most requested rock song of all time, "Stairway to Heaven." Led Zeppelin played a blues-based rock, basic chords pounding behind a high-pitched male tenor. The lyrics were a combination of hostility, mysticism, and sex, and their primary audience was young males. Following Led Zeppelin were groups such as Aerosmith, Ted Nugent, Kiss, and Motley Crue, whose main connection to their fans was in high-decibel concerts.

Hard rock and heavy metal were woven together in this early stage, although later each would become more defined as new bands staked out either one territory or the other with their image and their sound. Heavy metal was also loud, arena rock music that attracted a core group of faithful fans who bought albums in large numbers. The best example is Pink Floyd's album *Dark Side of the Moon*, which was released in 1973 and remained on the rock album chart in *Billboard* for 15½ years.

A concert-based music that appealed primarily to young males, heavy metal music appealed to the 16–24 demographic. The music was loud, crude, and hostile and seemed to embody teenage rebellion. During the early 1970s, heavy metal was defined by groups such as Deep Purple, Black Sabbath, Humble Pie, Mahogany Rush, James Gang, Bad Company, and Blue Oyster Cult; later Ozzy Osbourne, formerly a member of Black Sabbath, and Metallica joined this lineup, replacing some of the earlier groups who had disbanded or had fallen by the wayside.

Heavy metal was linked to mid-1950s rock and roll because both appalled parents; indeed, this was one of the appeals of heavy metal. Heavy metal was a working-class music that combined the hippie attitude of "do your own thing" to create a music that was despised by outsiders but strongly embraced by those inside this world. This was not "nice" music, but that was the point—the term *heavy metal* itself indicated something hard, durable, and coldhearted. It was an apt description of a music intended to be offensive in everything from its decibel level to its lyrics, and heavy metal succeeded by adhering to a sound that shattered the sensibilities of the fans of soft rock.

Disco

Disco—the term derives from the French term *discotheque*—was a music designed and created to make people dance. Although disco returned music to clubs, it used the technologies developed for large concert halls and studios; there were elaborate sound systems that bathed the room with music. The rhythm and blues roots are obvious, but technological advances such as synthesizers and drum machines also played an important part of this musical subculture.

The star of the disco was the disc jockey, who used two turntables to create a music that was hypnotic and could manipulate a crowd on the dance floor to lose themselves in physical release. The disc jockey attempted to have the music build, creating a tension, until it peaked—like the sex act itself—letting the participants, sweaty and exhausted, scream in pleasure.

Disco developed in clubs patronized by gays, blacks, and women; the audience tended to be older than the rock audience, and the aura of the club lent itself to high fashion—sharp-dressed men and women—instead of the jean-clad, T-shirt-wearing audience for rock in the 1970s. Disco featured slick, polished production that was either up-tempo with a pulsing beat or in ballads with lush orchestral arrangements.

Disco originated in clubs, and the music spread club to club, disc jockey to disc jockey; it was not a music made for radio, although there were a few disco hits on radio. "Rock the Boat" by the Hues Corporation and "Rock Your Baby" by George McCrae in early 1974 were hits both on radio and in the dance clubs; so was "The Hustle" by Van McCoy and "Shame, Shame, Shame" by Shirley and Company, both in 1975. That year (1975) there were an estimated 200–300 disco clubs in New York and about 2,500 in the United States. The clubs and the music were an urban phenomenon; disco was a product of city life, a genre for the "beautiful people" who sought to be trendy and elegant.

Europe was an important source of early disco, and the biggest disco act to emerge, Donna Summer, recorded her initial disco hit, "Love to Love You Baby," in Munich, Germany, in 1976.

The center for disco was New York, and by the mid-1970s the disco industry accounted for $4 billion. The disco disc jockeys, like the early rock-and-roll disc jockeys, changed the music as they defined it, moving away from the three-minute singles and into long, extended versions of songs with special mixes, highlighted by a heavy bass and drums and accompanied by advanced lighting.

Disco music also affected technology. Because dancers wanted recordings that lasted longer than three minutes, disc jockeys used tape loops and other electronic wizardry to expand the length of a song. Soon artists recorded songs that lasted much longer than the typical pop record; out of this came the 12-inch single.

The white rock audience, initially put off by the cult following of disco in gay and African-American cultures, remained largely dismissive of it until the Bee Gees album *Main Course*, released in 1975, which featured the hit "Jive Talkin'." It was the Bee Gees, especially on the soundtrack to the movie *Saturday Night Fever*, released in 1978, that brought the music into the rock mainstream.

The backlash against disco reached its apex on July 12, 1979, when a Chicago disc jockey burned a pile of disco records in center field at Comiskey Park at a Detroit Tigers–Chicago White Sox game. By 1980 disco was finished as a commercial music.

The most visible reminder of the music came from the Village People, six well-built males who obviously appealed to the gay audience; their recordings, produced by Jacques Morali (1977–79), are still heard, particularly "YMCA," which has become part of mainstream American culture everywhere from sporting events, where crowds stand and sing along, to dance clubs.

Punk Music

The message of punk music was that "anybody can play this." In some ways, punk contained the essence of early rock and roll with its rebellious snarl shaking up the conservative music establishment. Because musical ability was not required or even desired—the attitude was more important than musical ability—it was more influential than commercially successful during the 1975–79 period.

The roots of punk can be traced back to the Velvet Underground in the 1960s. When that group broke up in 1970, Lou Reed signed on as a solo artist and made records through the 1970s. Reed was a street-smart New Yorker filled with cynicism, a rock star who was blatantly noncommercial.

In 1971 the New York Dolls began performing; Alice Cooper and Kiss both challenged the musical establishment with their stage shows.

In 1975 a club in New York, CBGB (which stood for "country, bluegrass, and blues"), opened its doors to the rock-and-roll avant-garde. Owner Hilly Kristol let Patti Smith perform, and she provided "new wave" (which was what the music was originally called) its first solid image. The club booked a number of new-wave acts: Tuff Darts, Blondie, Stumblebunny, the Ramones, Televison, and the Talking Heads. Richard Hell wrote "Black Generation" for his group, the Voidoids, in 1977, and the movement had an anthem. The Ramones made the definitive new wave/punk music with their 1976 debut album; they played loud, fast, and furious—most sets lasted only thirty minutes—but crowds were both exhilarated and drained at the end.

Meanwhile, in London the most famous punk band of all time, the Sex Pistols, was formed by manager Malcolm McLaren, who had a clothing boutique called Sex. The original band members were John Lydon, who changed his name to Johnny Rotten, Steve Jones, Glen Matlock, and Paul Cook; bassist Sid Vicious joined when Matlock dropped out.

The Sex Pistols were angry and intent on showing it. Their first single, "Anarchy in the UK" was performed by the group on the British TV show *Today*. Their next single, "God Save the Queen," was a straight-ahead attack on the monarchy during Queen Elizabeth's Silver Jubilee year of celebrations and was immediately banned in Britain. The Sex Pistols recorded only one album, *Never Mind the Bollocks, Here's the Sex Pistols*, released in 1977. Although the Sex Pistols were popular in the UK, they were never commercially successful in the United States.

The most commercially successful punk group to come out of England was the Clash, formed by Joe Strummer. In 1979 CBS in the United States released *London Calling*, which became a hit album, led by the single "Train in Vain."

Punk rock led to the creation of independent labels because the major labels steered clear of this music, which could be offensive both musically and lyrically. Punk openly condemned rock as big business and, for many young musicians, cleared the slate for the star-making machines. The end of the initial punk movement came on February 2, 1979, with the death of Sid Vicious in New York. The self-destructive music had claimed a victim, and the general public thought it was tasteless and useless to promote this music.

The movement was influential, though, especially in Los Angeles, where a post-punk scene emerged with middle-class teens who claimed punk in order to wear ragged clothes, put safety pins on their faces, and get hostile while they got drunk. Slam dancing became a trademark of hard-core punk; this dancing consisted of ramming into anyone in the dancer's vicinity.

This second wave of punk saw some genuine musical talent emerge, although most punk bands felt that snarls, sneers, and self-absorption constituted a musical statement. Punk acts who showed musical ability included Elvis Costello, Graham Parker, Chrissie Hynde and her band, The Pretenders, the Clash, and Devo.

Although the first punk era ended in 1979, the influence of punk continued because artists' look of defiance—from spiked hair, body piercings, and torn secondhand clothes to their attitude of rebellion and in-your-face rejection of mainstream music—continued to be an attribute of a number of acts during the rest of the twentieth century and into the twenty-first century.

POPULAR MUSIC FROM 1980 TO 2000

Digital Technology

In the late 1960s the Holland-based company Philips began experimenting in optical electronics. By early 1979 it had produced a compact disc system using digital technology.

Japanese-based Sony soon joined Philips as a full partner in the new technology and contributed research, marketing, and enhancements. In the fall of 1983 the compact disc was introduced to American consumers. By the end of the year it had about 4 percent of the market. By the end of the next year it accounted for about 16 percent of the market. Over the next 7 years it would virtually eliminate the vinyl LP from the market.

MTV

In 1981 MTV (Music Television) debuted on cable television. Created by Warner Communications, MTV benefited from the development of the cable TV system. The station popularized music videos and made music a visual as well as aural experience. As MTV progressed, the station added shows such as *Beavis and Butthead* in the evening to break up the constant showing of videos. Also, other music video channels and shows emerged; VH1, Country Music Television (CMT), and shows on BET (Black Entertainment Television) were all influenced by MTV.

MTV influenced the music industry because it made the visual as important as the audial. The medium served as an alternative to radio when it came to exposing new acts and new genres, such as rap and hip-hop. It added a significant cost to marketing a recording and provided a "cool" way for acts to be on television. Prior to MTV, musical acts appeared on variety shows, specials (such as ones at Christmas), and some late-night shows such as *Midnight Special*. However, prior to MTV, rock acts generally disdained TV appearances because of the compromises they were required to make in order to appear; MTV allowed rock acts to appear on TV on their own terms.

Rap and Hip-Hop

Rapping can be traced back to African-American preachers or the early black radio disc jockeys in the 1940s. Musically there were acts such as Barry White and Isaac Hayes in the early 1970s who "rapped" or talked in a low, sexy tone over music. But in terms of the late-twentieth-century music business, the origin of rap can be traced back to 1979 and the release of "Rapper's Delight" by the Sugar Hill Gang.

Musically it was a descendant of soul and funk music, especially the music of James Brown and George Clinton. Also influential were the *Soul Train* TV show hosted by Don Cornelius, the dancing of the Jackson Five, particularly Michael Jackson, and disco music. Hip-hop was a grassroots movement that was a product of technology as well as inner-city life and was the first music trend where blacks embraced the music of their past. Until hip-hop, African Americans saw the music of their past as representing something they wanted to forget.

Rapping was first popularized in New York by disc jockeys with portable sound systems in the 1970s. Disc jockeys, better known as DJs, such as Kool Herc, Afrika Bambaataa, and Grandmaster Flash, began to "toast" or celebrate their triumphs as lovers.

In October 1979 "Rapper's Delight" by the Sugar Hill Gang was released; it was a huge hit in the black community and entered the national charts. After "Rapper's Delight," the MCs became known as "rappers" and this music was labeled "rap." "Christmas Rappin'" by Kurtis Blow on Mercury was the next big hit from rap, and then Sugar Hill released "The Message" and "The Adventures of Grandmaster Flash on the Wheels of Steel." During these early years of rap, 1979–83, Sugar Hill became the dominate label in rap music.

Gangsta rap set the tone for much of the earliest rap recorded. Because of the popularity of crack cocaine in the early 1980s, violence was part of everyday life in inner-city ghettos, and gangsta rap reflected this.

The period 1981–85 was the developmental era for hip-hop. The records came mostly from small, black-owned record companies who could not get radio airplay or the support from African-American record executives with major labels.

"The Message" by Grandmaster Flash came in 1982; in 1983 Herbie Hancock released "Rockit," and this video was shown on MTV. "I Feel for You" by Chaka Khan with Melle Mel was the first time an established star collaborated with a rapper; the album went platinum and the single went gold.

Although hip-hop originated from the black culture, it was white entrepreneurial involvement that allowed this movement and music to survive and thrive. After the initial rap records from black-owned labels Sugar Hill, Enjoy, and Winley, the next stage required the input of white, mostly Jewish, entrepreneurs.

Although hip-hop started in New York, it was soon picked up by African Americans in California, who presented their own brand of the music to the world. In 1988 the landmark album *Straight Outta Compton* by NWA (Ice Cube, Dr. Dre, and Eazy-E) was released and became a major breakthrough; that same year Public Enemy released "It Takes a Nation of Millions to Hold Us Back."

Rap reached the large, general public in September 1988 when *Yo, MTV Raps!* premiered. Hip-hop is unique in the history of the recording industry because most "musicians" cannot play a musical instrument; their "instruments" are a large record collection, turntables, and a sampler. Since the E-mu Emulator was put on the U.S. market in 1981, hip-hop producers have learned to use this digital technology to store, manipulate, and play back any sound.

POPULAR MUSIC IN THE TWENTY-FIRST CENTURY

American music encompasses a wide variety of styles and sounds. In the twenty-first century, American music includes styles as diverse as rock, pop, jazz, country, urban, reggae, Cajun, blues, gospel, punk, hard rock, and a myriad of other offshoots. The most commercially successful music in terms of record sales is rock, country, and rhythm and blues or urban (rap and hip-hop). However, American radio continues to provide consumers with a wide variety of music, although newer technological developments such as the Internet and iPods have increasingly replaced radio as the primary way for young people to hear new music and new acts.

RESOURCE GUIDE

PRINT SOURCES

Baldwin, Neil. *Edison: Inventing the Century*. New York: Hyperion, 1995.

Barnouw, Eric. *The Golden Web: A History of Broadcasting in the United States, Volume II: 1933–1953*. New York: Oxford University Press, 1968.

———. *A Tower in Babel: A History of Broadcasting in the United States: Volume I: To 1933*. New York: Oxford University Press, 1966.

———. *The Image Empire: A History of Broadcasting in the United States: Volume III: From 1953*. New York: Oxford University Press, 1970.

Bergreen, Laurence. *Louis Armstrong: Extravagant Life*. New York: Broadway Books, 1997.

Carr, Patrick, ed. *The Illustrated History of Country Music*. New York: Dolphin, 1980.

Chang, Jeff. *Can't Stop Won't Stop: A History of the Hip-Hop Generation*. St. Martin's Press, 2005.

Clarke, Donald. *The Rise and Fall of Popular Music*. New York: Viking, 1995.

Cohadas, Nadine. *Spinning Blues into Gold: The Chess Brothers and the Legendary Chess Records*. New York: St. Martin's Press, 2000.

Collier, James Lincoln. *Benny Goodman and the Swing Era*. New York: Oxford University Press, 1989.

Conot, Robert. *A Streak of Luck*. New York: Seaview Books, 1979.

Dannen, Frederic. *Hit Men: Power Brokers and Fast Money inside the Music Business*. New York: Random House/Times Books, 1990.

Davis, Francis. *The History of the Blues: The Roots, the Music, the People from Charley Patton to Robert Cray*. New York: Hyperion, 1995.

Dearling, Robert, and Celia with Brian Rust. *The Guinness Book of Recorded Sound*. Middlesex, England: Guinness Books, 1984.

DeLong, Thomas A. *Pops: Paul Whiteman: King of Jazz*. Piscataway, NJ: New Century, 1983.

Emerick, G., and H. Massey. *Here, There, and Everywhere: My Life Recording the Music of the Beatles*. New York: Gotham, 2005.

Emerson, Ken. *Always Magic in the Air: The Bomp and Brilliance of the Brill Building Era*. New York: Viking, 2005.

———. *Doo-Dah! Stephen Foster and the Rise of American Popular Culture*. New York: Simon & Schuster, 1998.

Escott, Colin, with Martin Hawkins. *Good Rockin' Tonight: Sun Records and the Birth of Rock 'n' Roll*. New York: St. Martin's, 1991.

Fong-Torres, Ben. *The Hits Just Keep on Coming: The History of Top 40 Radio*. San Francisco: Freeman, 1998.

Gelatt, Roland. *The Fabulous Phonograph: From Tin Foil to High Fidelity*. Philadelphia: J. B. Lippincott, 1954, 1955.

Giddens, Gary. *A Pocketful of Dreams: Bing Crosby: The Early Years 1903–1940*. Boston: Little, Brown, 2001.

Goldman, Herbert G. *Jolson: The Legend Comes to Life*. New York: Oxford, 1988.

Goodman, Fred. *The Mansion on the Hill: Dylan, Young, Geffen, Springsteen and the Head-On Collision of Rock and Commerce*. New York: Vintage, 1997.

Guralnick, Peter. *Last Train to Memphis: The Rise of Elvis Presley*. Boston: Little, Brown and Company, 1994.

———. *Sweet Soul Music: Rhythm and Blues and the Southern Dream of Freedom*. New York: Harper & Row, 1986.

Harvith, John, and Susan Edwards Harvith. *Edison, Musicians, and the Phonograph*. New York: Greenwood Press, 1987.

Jackson, John A. *American Bandstand: Dick Clark and the Making of a Rock 'n' Roll Empire*. New York: Oxford University Press, 1997.

————. *Big Beat Heat: Alan Freed and the Early Years of Rock & Roll*. New York: Schirmer Books, 1991.

Lemann, Nicholas. *Promised Land: The Great Black Migration and How It Changed America*. New York: Vintage, 1992.

Lewis, Tom. *Empire of the Air: The Men Who Made Radio*. New York: Edward Burlingame Books, An Imprint of HarperCollins, 1991.

Malone, Bill C. *Country Music, U.S.A.* Austin, TX: University of Texas Press, 1968, 1985.

————. *Singing Cowboys and Musical Mountaineers: Southern Culture and the Roots of Country Music*. Athens: University of Georgia Press, 1993.

Norman, Phillip. *Shout! The Beatles in Their Generation*. New York: Simon and Schuster, 1981.

Passman, Arnold. *The Deejays*. New York: The Macmillan Company, 1971.

Picardie, Justine, and Dorothy Wade. *Atlantic and the Godfathers of Rock and Roll*. London: Fourth Estates, 1990.

Porterfield, Nolan. *Jimmie Rodgers: The Life and Times of America's Blue Yodeler*. Urbana: University of Illinois Press, 1979.

Romanowski, Patricia, and Holly George-Warren, eds. *The New Rolling Stone Encyclopedia of Rock & Roll*. New York: Fireside, 1983, 1995.

Rust, Brian. *American Record Label Book*. New Rochelle, NY: Arlington House, 1978.

Sanjek, Russell. *American Popular Music and Its Business: The First Four Hundred Years: Volume II: From 1790 to 1909*. New York: Oxford University Press, 1988.

————. *American Popular Music and Its Business: Volume III: From 1900 to 1984*. New York: Oxford University Press, 1988.

Sanjek, Russell, and David Sanjek. *American Popular Music Business in the 20th Century*. New York: Oxford University Press, 1991.

Shaw, Arnold. *Honkers and Shouters: The Golden Years of Rhythm & Blues*. New York: Macmillan, 1978.

————. *The Jazz Age: Popular Music in the 1920s*. New York: Oxford, 1987.

Shemel, Sidney, and William M. Krasilovsky. *This Business of Music*, 6th edition. New York: Watson-Guptill, 1990.

Shepherd, John, and Paul Kegan. *Tin Pan Alley*. London: Routledge, 1982.

Spitz, Bob. *The Beatles: The Biography*. New York: Little, Brown, & Co., 2005.

Ward, Ed, Geoffrey Stokes, and Ken Tucker. *Rock of Ages: The Rolling Stone History of Rock and Roll*. New York: Rolling Stone Press/Summit Books, 1986.

Whitburn, Joel. *Billboard's Top 1,000 Hits of the Rock Era 1955–2005*. Menomonee Falls, WI: Record Research, Inc., 2006.

————. *Billboard's Top Pop Singles 1955–2002*. Menomonee Falls, WI: Record Research, Inc., 2003.

————. *Joel Whitburn's Pop Memories 1890–1954: The History of American Popular Music*. Menomonee Falls, WI: Record Research, Inc., 1986.

————. *Pop Hits: Singles & Albums 1940–1954*. Menomonee Falls, WI: Record Research, Inc., 2002.

————. *Top Country Singles 1955–1994*. Menomonee Falls, WI: Record Research, Inc., 1995.

Wile, Frederic William. *Emile Berliner: Maker of the Microphone*. Indianapolis: The Bobbs-Merrill Company, 1926.

WEBSITES

American Federation of Musicians. http://www.afm.org.

American Society of Composers, Authors and Publishers. http://www.ascap.com. Performance rights organization for songwriters.

Billboard. http://www.billboard.com. Major trade magazine for the music industry.

Broadcast Music, Inc. http://www.bmi.com. Performance rights organization for songwriters.

Canadian Academy of Recording Arts and Sciences (CARAS). http://www.carasonline.ca/.

Canadian Country Music Assn (CCMA). http://www.ccma.org.

Canadian Recording Industry Association (CRIA). http://www.cria.ca.

Grammy.com. http://www.grammy.com. National Academy of Recording Arts and Sciences and the organization that awards the Grammys.

International Federation of Phonograph Industries. http://www.ifpi.org. The international recording industry trade organization.

Juno Awards. http://www.juno-awards.com. Canadian Academy of Recording Arts & Sciences (CARAS), which awards the Juno Awards.

Music Industries Association of Canada. http://www.miac.net.

Pollstar. http://www.pollstar.com. For information on live recordings.

Radio & Records, Inc. http://www.radioandrecords.com. Trade magazine for the music industry.

Recording Industry Association of America. http://www.riaa.com. The recording industry trade organization in the United States.

Society of Composers, Authors and Music Publishers of Canada. http://www.socan.ca.

MAGAZINES

Following is a collection of magazines dealing with popular music:

Acoustic Guitar Magazine
American Songwriter Magazine
ASCAP PlayBack Magazine
Billboard
Bluegrass Unlimited Magazine
Blues Access
Blues & Soul Magazine
CCM Magazine (Christian music)
College Music Journal (CMJ)
CultureFinder.com
Cybergrass (bluegrass)
Dance Magazine
DownBeat (Jazz)
Electronic Musician Entertainment Weekly
Flatpicking Guitar Magazine
Folk Alliance Newsletter
Goldmine Magazine (for collectors)
Gramophone (classical)
Hollywood Reporter
iBluegrass Magazine
iMusic
Jazz Guitar
JazzReview.com
Journal of Musicology
Just Jazz Guitar Magazine
Keyboard Magazine
Latin American Music Review
Living Blues
Mix
Modern Drummer
MPA Press (music publishers)
MTV Online
Muse Magazine
Music Row
Music World Magazine from BMI
Opera Magazine
Performing Songwriter Magazine
Pollstar—The Concert Hotwire
Pro Sound News

Professional Sound Magazine
Rhythm (world music)
RimShot! Magazine (for drummers and percussionists)
Rock & Pop
Rolling Stone
RootsWorld
RPM Online
Sing Out! Magazine
Spin
Static Magazine
Variety
Vibe

MUSEUMS

Canadian Music Hall of Fame (will open in new location in Toronto in 2007), Canadian Academy of Recording Arts and Sciences (CARAS), 355 King St. West, Suite 501, Toronto, Ontario M5V 1J6, Canada. http://www.carasonline.ca/HOF_home.php.

Country Music Hall of Fame, Nashville, Tennessee, 222 5th Ave. S, Nashville, TN 37203. http://www.countrymusichalloffame.com.

Experience Music Museum, Seattle, Washington, 325 Fifth Ave. North, Seattle Center, Seattle, WA 98104. http://www.emplive.com.

Rock and Roll Hall of Fame, Cleveland, OH, 1 Key Plaza, Cleveland, OH 44114. http://www.rockhall.com.

Rock and Soul Museum, Memphis, Tennessee, 191 Beale St., Memphis, TN 38103. http://www.memphis rocknsoul.org.

Smithsonian Museum (American History Museum), Washington, D.C., 950 Independence Ave. SW, Washington, DC 20560. http://www.si.edu.

Stax Museum, Memphis, Tennessee, 926 E McLemore Ave., Memphis, TN 38106. http://www.soulsvilleusa.com.

MOVIES

Note: There are numerous movies and documentaries of music; the below are a few that are especially notable, either for the music they introduced or because of the significance of the movie. Movies are listed in chronological order.

Holiday Inn (1942). Starring Bing Crosby and Fred Astaire. "White Christmas" was introduced in this movie, along with a number of other popular songs.

Blackboard Jungle (1955). Glenn Ford. High school movie that introduced "Rock Around the Clock."

Don't Knock the Rock (1956). Early rock-and-roll movie featuring DJ Alan Freed, Bill Haley and the Comets, the Treniers, and the Applejacks.

A Hard Day's Night (1964). The Beatles' first movie, with many of their songs, in a charming story based on their early popularity in England.

Help! (1965). The Beatles again appear as themselves, this time in a much more fantasy-like plot, but again featuring many of their songs of the time, including "Help!," "Ticket to Ride," and others.

Elvis: That's the Way It Is (1970). A documentary of Elvis Presley appearing in Las Vegas.

Bob Dylan: Eat This Document (1972). A very messy documentary, edited by Dylan himself, about Bob Dylan's historic 1966 tour of Europe with The Band, where he began to use electrical instruments.

Lady Sings the Blues (1972). Diana Ross stars as Billie Holliday in an overly sentimental story about her brief but brilliant career in the 1930s.

American Graffiti (1973). An iconic movie, directed by George Lucas before he went on to make *Star Wars*; it shows one night in the life of high school students in 1962 in a small California town.

The soundtrack includes such notables of the early 1960s as "The Great Pretender," "Come Go with Me," "Maybe Baby," "Ain't That a Shame," "At the Hop," and many more. Features Ron Howard, Harrison Ford, and Richard Dreyfuss in their early acting careers.

Nashville (1975). Robert Altman directed an ensemble cast including Lili Tomlin, Keith Carradine, Karen Black, Ronee Blakely, and others, featuring many country songs, some written by the actors for the movie.

Coal Miner's Daughter (1980). Sissy Spacek won an Oscar for her portrayal of Loretta Lynn, the country singing star, who began her career as a teenager. With Tommy Lee Jones as her husband and manager, Dolittle Lynn.

Tender Mercies (1983). Starring Robert Duvall as a down-on-his-luck country-western singer. Features songs by Duvall, Lefty Frizzell, and Charlie Craig.

This Is Spinal Tap (1984). A fake documentary about a loud, talentless English rock band, directed by Rob Reiner, written by Reiner, Christopher Guest, Michael McKean, and Harry Shearer (who also play the band members).

Almost Famous (2000). Directed by Cameron Crowe. Tells the story of a high school boy in the 1970s who gets the chance to write about rock groups (and groupies) for *Rolling Stone* magazine.

Ray (2004). The story of the great R & B singer, Ray Charles, with terrific singing and acting by Jamie Foxx, who won an Oscar for the role. Focuses on his early career in the 1960s and 1970s.

A Mighty Wind (2003). Written and directed by Christopher Guest, a fake documentary about a reunion of 1960s folk singers, which expertly satirizes, and re-creates, folk music of that era.

NOTES

1. http://www.riaa.com. Information on the sales of recordings is compiled annually by the Recording Industry Association of America.
2. http://www.riaa.com.

PERIODICALS

GARYN G. ROBERTS

Historians, librarians, and literary scholars often point to the Industrial Revolution—a sociocultural event spanning decades in the early and mid-nineteenth century—as the point in which mass and popular culture found definition in North America. Subsequently it is logical to trace the development of the popular periodical in North America from the time of the Industrial Revolution forward. Of course, in print form some North American periodical publications can be dated even earlier. "Periodicals," for the sake of discussion here, are defined as print and nonprint publications that are released and marketed to a mass public on a consistent timetable—daily, weekly, biweekly, monthly, quarterly, and so on. These publications have been and are made available to, purchased by, or consumed by thousands and millions of people. By definition, then, such mass-produced periodicals range from newspapers in the early 1800s to Internet periodicals of contemporary times.

The history of popular periodicals in North America over the last 200 years is rich. Publishing houses, editors, authors, story forms and genres, marketing strategies, innovations and technologies, successes and failures, and colorful personalities mark this history. There is much to explore and investigate further. Many reference books discuss these periodicals and related publications. What follows here is an overview of North American periodical publications since the early 1800s. Related topics of popular fiction genres, and specific geographic regions where periodicals have flourished, are also addressed. For example, the emergence of popular fiction types such as Westerns/frontier stories, mystery/crime/detective fiction, fantasy/science fiction, adventure stories, and more are detailed. Such is also the case of regions in North America where periodicals have thrived. For example, New York City has been the publishing capital of the world for hundreds of years. Publishers of newspapers, dime novels, slick magazines, pulp magazines, feature books, comic books, and paperbacks have often been based in New York. Similarly, such periodicals have been part of the Canadian cultural landscape. Cleveland was a publishing center for dime novels at the end of the nineteenth and beginning of the twentieth centuries. Chicago was, for years, the home of the most famous fantasy pulp magazine of all—*Weird Tales*. Along with New York City and California, Chicago has traditionally been one of the top newspaper publishing centers of the world. California, New York, and other regions saw the rise of newspaper mogul

William Randolph Hearst. From 1932 on, Racine, Wisconsin, was the home of Whitman Publishing Company, the creator of specialized periodical books marketed for children—Big Little Books.

In North America the Industrial Revolution not only brought mass-produced periodicals as entertainments and escapism, but also fostered literacy among those who previously had not had access to print and learning. From the start the popular periodical help to create and define a middle class, a popular culture, which had not been solidified earlier. People could discuss the adventures of their favorite dime novel and pulp magazine heroes with one another and share a common culture. Newspaper comic strips and comic books defined the twentieth century, and they told "our" story better than many works of literature. Though we tend to view the past more positively and romantically than is realistic or accurate, it was great time to be one of the great unwashed, dig into your pocket, fish out a coin, and buy— be part of—the adventures of Buffalo Bill, The Shadow, or Dick Tracy.

Newspapers and magazines continue to hold significant market shares in North America. Business, trade, and technical magazines are among the most popular. Internet/electronic periodicals have become significant companions to their print newspaper and magazine counterparts. Internet/electronic periodicals have also etched out their own unique markets. Children's magazines, now often tied to Internet/electronic Websites, continue to thrive. Also, English- and French-language periodicals published uniquely in Canada are thriving and expanding along with Internet use.

DIME NOVELS

The birth, rise, and reign of the dime novel were events whose likes the world has never seen before or since. Literally billions of dime novels were produced and sold in the latter half of the nineteenth century and early years of the twentieth. Dime novels ultimately featured a range of popular literary genres (i.e., categories or types), but in the early years of the form (roughly 1830 to the Civil War years, 1860–65), frontier stories that chronicled European America's expansion westward were dominant. These dime novel stories often featured social melodrama in the vast North American continent, and they most often included very "cardboard" or two-dimensional ethnic, gender, and related stereotypes. Like the print medium in which these stories appeared, characters and story lines were pretty "black and white."

In the years following the Civil War, frontier stories continued to thrive. They would continue their popularity, and remain one of readers' favorite genres until the twilight years of the medium about the time of World War I, 1917–20. But, shortly after the Civil War, frontier stories were joined by increasingly popular tales of crime, mystery, and detection. Such stories had been made popular by Edgar Allan Poe (1809–49) and Arthur Conan Doyle (1859–1930), who created Sherlock Holmes, the archetypal detective hero, in *A Study in Scarlet* (1887).

Newspapers and similar publications had documented social and popular culture history for centuries by the time the dime novel arrived on the scene, but with the arrival of the dime novel in American, Canadian, and English society, a mass audience was for the first time targeted by an inexpensive purely entertainment medium that was accessible to a large portion of the total populace. The dime novel was as important to people of the nineteenth century as television is to us today.

As might be expected, the dime novel claimed New York City as its birthplace. New York had established itself as the publishing center of the world long before. One of the most successful and popular of the dime novel (and later pulp magazine) publishers was the firm of Francis S. Street and Francis S. Smith. Street and Smith purchased *The New York Weekly Dispatch*, a newspaper, in 1855. Yet it was not until 1889 that Street and Smith got into the dime novel game. Beadle and Company (later Beadle and Adams) was the first firm to publish dime novels on a regular basis. Beadle and associates dominated the dime novel field for about three decades and had the finest staff of Western writers working in the medium. Beadle began publishing dime novels in 1860, but several irregularly formatted and sporadically published story newspapers had been marketed prior to this time.

The phrase "story newspapers" is a very accurate description of dime novels. The earliest dime novels, and the majority of all dime novels, were printed in a very similar fashion to newspapers of the day. They were roughly nine inches wide, twelve inches tall, and forty-eight to sixty-four pages long. Text was typeset in columns—usually two or three columns per page. Dime novels were sold in "Libraries" or "Series" as a marketing ploy to get readers to purchase future issues. Titles of stories resembled those of articles commonly found in newspapers. These titles attracted readers to the stories. Authors of dime novels frequently had their literary beginnings in journalism. The writing styles employed in dime novel stories, like those in newspapers, were filled with intense action and colorful wording. The dime novel was a sensual form that appealed to a variety of emotions—base and redeeming alike.

Beadle's first dime novel was published with a June 1860 cover date. Dime novel historians often cite this dime novel as the beginning of the medium. However, as earlier noted there were predecessors to the form that were irregularly sized and published. The first Beadle dime novel was entitled *Maleska, the Indian Wife of the White Hunter* and was written by Ann S. Stephens. Seemingly all histories and studies of the dime novel cite this one particular work as the starting point of the medium. There is a degree of justification in this claim, since Beadle was the first major dime novel publisher and since *Maleska* was Beadle's first published title. Interestingly, Stephens's novel had first appeared in 1839 in *Woman's Companion* magazine. It was not especially

WESTERNS

The structuring metaphor and primary narrative device of the Western is the setting for the story form—the wilderness, the vast frontier extending westward from the Atlantic coast—from which this literary genre (type) derives its name. More than any other genre of popular fiction, the Western is America's story; it is fantastic, reality-based fiction that chronicles European Americans' expansion westward. In popular culture, the Western has its roots in the early days of European arrival on the North American continent. The enormous, anomalous landscape of beauty and opportunity, and danger and the unknown, fascinated people arriving for the first time. This landscape subsequently became a primary subject matter of letters, histories, folklore, and stories by authors including Michel Guillaume Jean de Crevecoeur (1735–1813), Charles Brockden Brown (1771–1810), and Robert Montgomery Bird (1806–54). The first true writer of "Westerns" was James Fenimore Cooper (1789–1851), known for many contributions to the canon of American literature, but especially for his archetypal, romanticized stories of the frontier, which are known as his "Leatherstocking" tales: *The Pioneers* (1823), *The Last of the Mohicans* (1827), *The Prairie* (1827), *The Pathfinder* (1840), and *The Deerslayer* (1841). Other famous Western/frontier authors included Mark Twain (pseudonym for Samuel Clemens, 1835–1910), Francis Brett "Bret" Harte (1836–1902), Owen Wister (1860–1938), Frank Norris (1870–1902), Stephen Crane (1871–1900), Zane Grey (1872–1939), Willa Cather (1873–1947), Jack London (1876–1916), Jack Schaefer (1907–91), and Walter van Tilburg Clark (1909–71).

unique, enthralling, or inspiring—it seemed just one of many frontier narratives. With the success of *Maleska*, Beadle began to publish two dime novel titles per month. The eighth title in the series was written by a man who would become one of the most prolific and published authors of all time. The novel was entitled *Seth Jones, or The Captives of the Frontier*, the author was Edward S. Ellis, and the publication date was October 1860. While eighth in the series by the new and number-one dime novel publisher (i.e., Beadle), *Seth Jones* launched the dime novel era as mass marketing and big business success. E. F. Bleiler and others estimate that *Seth Jones* sold 400,000 copies.

In 1863 there was a division in the house of Beadle as Irwin Beadle and George Munro broke away from the publisher. Shortly thereafter, Irwin Beadle left the business, and George Munro became the chief competition for the Beadle Company. In 1870, Norman Munro (George's brother) entered the field with his own company, and in 1878, Frank Tousey started publishing dime novels. In 1899, thirty-four years after the purchase of *The Dispatch* (1855), Street and Smith began publishing dime novels. Around 1912, when the medium was in decline, Street and Smith was the only dime novel publisher to make the transition successfully to the era of the pulp magazine, where, of course, Street and Smith flourished.

Buffalo Bill and Deadwood Dick were the fictional stars of two of the most popular Western and frontier life dime novels. Buffalo Bill was also, of course, the name of a real-life frontier hero. William F. Cody ("Buffalo Bill") became a legend in his own lifetime largely because of the factual, fictional, always sensationalized stories of his life written by Colonel Prentiss Ingraham and others for the dime novels. Perhaps the most popular and assuredly the longest-running of all dime novel series, the Buffalo Bill tales first saw publication in 1869 (Ned Buntline was the author) and was the last series in print at the end of the dime novel era. Edward L. Wheeler's Deadwood Dick debuted in 1877.

Dime novel publishers were a highly competitive and an imitative lot. While it is estimated that fully three-fourths of all dime novels featured some sort of story of the frontier or Wild West, other genres of fictions emerged and prospered. Such was the case with crime, mystery and detective fiction. When Norman Munro's Old Cap Collier series (arguably the first important crime, mystery and detective dime novel series) achieved popularity, other dime novel publishers followed with similar genre fiction.

Detectives with rather two-dimensional personalities and incredible superhuman strength tracked and hounded rather two-dimensional, rough-sawn criminals in many of the dime novels of the 1880s and 1890s. Tales of Old Cap Collier, Old King Brady, Nick Carter, and Old Sleuth were the most celebrated. John R. Coryell's and Street and Smith's Nick Carter, who debuted September 18, 1886, in *The Old Detective's Pupil; or The Mysterious Crime of Madison Square*, made the transition from dime novels to pulp magazines to motion pictures to radio drama to paperback novel. At one point, Nick Carter was the longest-running series detective in fiction. Gary Hoppenstand's *The Dime Novel Detective* is the best collection and assortment of crime, mystery and detective dime novels ever assembled in one volume. In that book, Hoppenstand explains how the Avenger Detective story line or formula of crime and mystery fiction found its birth in the dime novels.

Although frontier stories and tales of crime and detection were the "bread and butter" for dime novels, other genres and formulas flourished in this medium. Edward S. Ellis produced the first "science fiction" for the dime novels in his 1865 *The Steam Man of the Prairies*. The story is magnificent and was so popular, inventive, and ingeniously crafted that it was reprinted, imitated (more accurately, stolen), and responsible for the launch of the most popular of dime novel science fiction series—the stories of Frank Reade, Jr. The invention—and story hook—in a good percentage of Reade stories is a "steam man" or variation of Ellis's steam man of some sort. Frank Reade, Jr., first appeared in Frank Tousey's *Frank Reade*

Library, September 24, 1892, in a story entitled *Frank Reade, Jr. and His New Steam Man; or The Young Inventor's Trip to the Far West*. The Reade stories were heavily cannibalized years later in Victor Appleton's (pseudonym for Howard Garis and others) Tom Swift series of young adolescent books (the first of which appeared in 1910). Science fiction was even blended with science fact in the dime novels. When Thomas Edison was receiving publicity for his inventions, a new dime novel library (series) appeared that starred Edison. At the close of the Civil War, Horatio Alger, Jr., produced the first of his very popular tales of poverty-stricken homeless waifs rising from "rags to riches" in *Ragged Dick*. The dime novels helped connect Alger to his consuming public for decades and generations to come. The Frank Merriwell stories of Burt Standish (a pseudonym)—foreshadowing children's adventure stories like those of Franklin W. Dixon's Hardy Boys and Carolyn Wells's Nancy Drew—employed a somewhat similar formula. Merriwell first appeared in dime novels in 1896.

After some sixty years of incredible circulations and unparalleled landmarks in publishing history, the dime novel as first established by Beadle and Adams faded into the sunset. As one might suspect, the decline of the dime novel occurred for a variety of reasons. Further, America's first purely entertainment medium died as it was born—over a period of years. The descent began about the turn of the century and continued after World War I into the 1920s. Formulas simply wore out. Conventions overshadowed inventions—story lines were too predictable and not creative enough. In addition, scholars at the turn of the century had declared that the western frontier was now closed; it had been conquered.

TOM SWIFT

Howard R. Garis (1873–1962), prolific novelist of adolescent novels and series, was the primary creative force behind the Tom Swift (TS) novels. The TS series was initially published by the (Edward) Stratemeyer Syndicate and is believed to be highly derivative of the immensely popular Frank Reade dime novel series (1892–98). Both were action adventures that featured scientific-invention-based fantasy. Under the "Victor Appleton" pseudonym, Garis wrote all but the last three of the initial thirty-eight-novel TS series, which appeared between 1910 and 1938. The first TS novel was entitled *Tom Swift and His Motor-Cycle; Or, Fun and Adventures on the Road*. Other early TS novels featured Motor-Boats, an Airship, a Submarine-Boat, and an Electric Runabout. Later adventures featured a House on Wheels and a Planet Stone. Today, the inventions in these stories seem quaint, but in there time were quite exciting. There were two TS Big Little Books: *Tom Swift and His Giant Telescope* (1938) and *Tom Swift and His Magnetic Silencer* (1941). A second series of TS books began in 1954 with *Tom Swift and His Flying Lab*. The byline/house name on this series of thirty-three novels, which ran until 1971, was "Victor Appleton II." There were a third series (begun in 1981 with *Tom Swift and the City in the Stars*) and a fourth series (begun in 1991 with *Tom Swift #1: The Black Dragon*) as well.

The United States Postal Service now increased the postage on "novels" sent through the mail. For years, dime novels had been mailed at the extremely low, subsidized second-class periodical rate. But in the early 1910s this changed. Perhaps influenced by book publishers, "moralists," and other influential constituents, the Post Office revoked dime novels' eligibility for the second-class rate. Postage costs went up. Profits had traditionally been measured (by dime novel publishers) by the cent and fraction of a cent. Revenue had previously been generated by selling thousands and hundreds of thousands of issues at low profit margins per issue. The increase in postage of one or two cents per issue was more than enough to destroy the profitability that had been inherent in dime novel publications for years.

Of the dime novel publishers, Street and Smith was one of the few to alter its product so that it adhered to postal regulations and still maintained its large market. Story newspapers (now more like magazines than like newspapers) retained their ten-cent cover prices in many cases and were still technically "dime novels." But the ten cent (and sometimes more expensive) fiction magazines that Street and Smith, and newly emerging companies, produced no longer featured the one novel that was so offensive to the Postal Service. Rather, these magazines provided collections of novels, novellas, short stories, and features—and advertising. They were still eligible for the old postal rate, and these new "dime novels"— now deemed "pulp" magazines because of the crude quality pulpwood paper upon which they were printed—were also marketed in more diverse ways (such as newsstand sales) than dime novels had been.

With as much certainty as it can be said that Beadle's *Maleska* was the first dime novel, *The New Buffalo Bill Weekly*, published through 1912, can be claimed the last original "dime novel" publication. (Old dime novels were reprinted in the 1920s, and several series of "digest format" dime novels appeared in the 1920s as well.) The Nick Carter series continued through it all.

There were several other contributors to the downfall of the dime novel. Almost from the start, individuals and groups emerged who condemned the content found in dime novel story lines. These "moralists" usually arose from the ranks of clergy and educators, but to state that all people of the cloth and teachers embraced a common revulsion for the dime novel would, of course, be erroneous. The usual point of contention was that these periodicals showcased ruthless violence and blatant disregard for human life of any form. Indians and villains were "picked off" by gunfire like so many bottles lined up on a wooden fence. Perhaps. But it is important to remember that dime novel publishers could ill afford to offend any portion of the spending public. In many ways, the medium monitored itself better than any outside interest group could. Ironically, as E. F. Bleiler points out, violence (extravagant as it was) was really the only vice of dime novel story lines. Inherently, dime novels (aside from violence) featured very "morally conservative" content. For example, there was nothing close to graphic sex or related social taboos found in any popular dime novels.

Some educators found something else very disquieting about the story papers—the dime novel typically, but not always, showcased fiction that was not "L"iterature. What many educators celebrated in fiction as Literature during this time did have redeeming value. However, until the advent of the Industrial Revolution and the advent of the dime, this material was not available to the masses. Those "classic" authors—Milton, Byron, Dickens, Cooper, and Twain included—found further and new audiences via the mass-produced medium of the dime novel. Prior to the advent of the Industrial Revolution and viability of mass marketing cheap story papers to hundreds of thousands and millions of people, books, and education and literacy, were expenses often afforded only by the wealthiest strata of society. (Today, figures of hundreds of thousands and millions seem impressive, but given a much smaller North American population 100 to 150 years ago; those figures are even more significant.)

The Industrial Revolution and the dime novel era did make two historically and culturally significant contributions to American society in the nineteenth century. Russel B. Nye hypothesized decades ago that the Industrial Revolution, and the dime novel form that arose from that event, created a mass culture—a popular culture—that was not previously possible. Dime novels reached a vast middle class and subsequently provided a common experience, a common tie, that bound that class and its members together. Most people could now afford to buy writing and "L"iterature in the inexpensive form of the dime novel. This led to Nye's second hypothesis. With the availability of print now available because of the Industrial

Revolution and the dime novel, many people who were previously illiterate could now learn to read. Literacy expanded exponentially in English-speaking North America. Books and writing were no longer the sole property of the privileged.

Eventually the term "dime novel" became so popular and generic that it survived its original medium. While the classic format of the dime novel expired in the mid-1910s, the term "dime novel' continues to this day to mean, in a larger sense, any form of inexpensive novel, pulp magazine, paperback-like story. Unfortunately, the term has a somewhat pejorative or negative type connotation, indicating (often unfairly) a subliterate form.

Dime novels pervaded American society like no other medium of the nineteenth century. Dime novel scholars Philip Durham, Bleiler, and others recount amazing stories of dime novels, estimating that several billion individual dime novels were published. As earlier noted, such scholars, and a survey of titles and press runs, also suggest that three-fourths of dime novel stories featured, in one way or another, adventures on the American frontier. In the mid-1890s, when the four-color process of mass printing became viable and affordable, Street and Smith was the first to publish color covers for front pages of dime novels. The four-color process had a profound influence on the early days of pulp magazines and newspaper comic pages.

For decades, a range of scholars has established themselves as authorities, recognized worldwide, on dime novels. Scholarship by Philip Durham, Charles Bragin, Edward T. LeBlanc, E. F. Bleiler, Daryl Jones, J. Randolph Cox, Gary Hoppenstand, Richard Bleiler, and others has been invaluable to our appreciation and understanding of this tremendously pervasive, important, and popular periodical medium. The three books on dime novels (identified in the Printed Sources section of the Resource Guide at the end of this chapter) by Jones, Bleiler, and Hoppenstand are cornerstones of dime novel scholarship.

PULP MAGAZINES

The mid 1890s was an important time in the history of mass produced periodicals. While dime novels remained extremely popular, a new print medium emerged. Historians generally agree that the first of these periodicals, later called "pulp magazines," was the October 1896 issue of *Argosy* magazine. With this issue, the Munsey Company changed the physical layout, content and format of its existing *Argosy*. The result was the prototype of pulp magazines to come. These magazines were approximately 8 inches wide, 10 inches tall, and about one-half to three-quarters of an inch thick. They sported action-packed color covers, made possible by the recent advent of the four-color process. Of course, as with the history of all media and periodicals, there were exceptions to seemingly everything. Some issues were oversized, for example.

Like dime novels, pulp magazines were designed as ephemeral entertainments—that is they were meant to be enjoyed, maybe shared with a friend or two, and then discarded. This periodical medium derived its name from the pulpwood paper upon which it was printed. Cheap, coarse, and acidic, this paper was not meant for long-term durability. Ultimately the term "pulp" became a pejorative, negative term indicating (both accurately and inaccurately) an inferior grade of story as well as paper. Because many were discarded, or recycled in World War II paper drives, relatively few original pulp magazines remain today. Of those that remain, most are in advanced stages of deterioration. The acidic pulpwood paper of yesterday is today most often yellowed, browned, and brittle.

Like their predecessors, pulp magazines relied on large circulations to compensate for low profits, measured in pennies and fractions of a cent per issue sold. Publishers of pulp magazines also diversified their marketing and revenue strategies. Though sold monthly and biweekly and even weekly, like dime novels, pulp magazines relied much less extensively on the U.S. Mail for their distribution. Pulp magazines were sold primarily on newsstands and at corner grocery stores and drugstores. Pulp publishers also sold advertising space in their periodicals. The products and services were wide-ranging and sometimes were as exotic, as weird, and as downright strange as some the story content found in these fiction magazines.

As was the case with dime novels, early pulp magazines lived off the "bread and butter" of the Western story. As the 1920s and 1930s approached, however, pulp stories featured a kaleidoscope of popular genres, not only Westerns. There were sea stories, love stories, social melodramas, and more. Famous Western pulp titles are numerous and are themselves now legendary, but a short list would include *Western Story Magazine*, *Western Rangers*, *Dime Western*, *Star Western*, *Masked Rider*, *Pete Rice*, and others. In the pages of the pulps, authors such as Max Brand (pseudonym for Frederick Faust, 1892–1944) and Luke Short (1908–75) flourished. Both Brand and Short had tremendously large readerships; Brand was one of the most prolific authors ever, providing the novel *Destry Rides Again* (1930) and many others. It was also in the pages of the pulps that a writer named Louis L'Amour (1910–75) first appeared. L'Amour was renowned for his "graphic style"—a sort of antithesis to the romantic style epitomized by Zane Grey in the 1920s. Some thirty years after his passing, L'Amour remains very popular today and is probably best known for his books about the Sackett family.

Argosy published Westerns and an array of other story types. Because of its wide range of offerings, *Argosy* appealed to a broad spectrum of people. Beyond Westerns, this pulp featured stories of action adventure, crime/mystery/detection, science fiction and fantasy, South Seas and pirate stories, and much, much more. The kind of action adventure stories found in *Argosy* was often reminiscent of nineteenth-century British fiction by H. Rider Haggard. Steven Spielberg paid tribute to these action adventures in his Indiana Jones movies. Some of Edgar Rice Burroughs's Westerns, Tarzan stories, science fiction, and romantic adventures appeared in *Argosy*. Other pulp magazines that showcased a wide range of action adventure stories included *Triple-X*, *Short Stories*, and *Blue Book*.

(*The*) *Black Mask* began in 1920 and at first was a pulp magazine that featured action adventures, Westerns, and crime fiction. It was in the pages of *The Black Mask* (later just *Black Mask*) that the frontier hero of the Western moved to the urban, asphalt jungle of the city and became the private investigator (PI, private eye) or hard-boiled detective. Authors included the very popular Erle Stanley Gardner (a highly prolific author best known years later for his Perry Mason stories), Carroll John Daly (considered by some the first author of PI stories), Dashiell Hammett (the ex-Pinkerton investigator turned crime writer), Raymond Chandler, and others. The famous editor of *Black Mask* who focused magazine content on the private detective was Captain Joseph T. Shaw. Other pulp magazines with crime, mystery, and hard-boiled detective fiction included *Dime Detective*, *Detective Story Magazine*, *Detective Fiction Weekly*, *Ten Detective Aces*, *Popular Detective*, and *Thrilling Detective*. In the 1930s a popular subgenre of hard-boiled detective fiction was the weird-menace story. Weird-menace stories were a sort of synthesis of PI detective fiction and horror stories. Four prominent weird-menace pulps were *Dime Mystery*, *Terror Tales*, *Horror Stories*, and *Thrilling Mystery*.

Detective pulps were the parents of what would become the very popular hero pulps. Hero pulps were each named for one series character and featured full-length novels of their respective character. Three of the most famous were Street and Smith's *The Shadow* and *Doc Savage* and Popular Publications' *The Spider*. As a character, the Shadow had begun on radio as an announcer of a mystery drama series. Famous newspaperman and magician Walter B. Gibson (of Pennsylvania) was hired to develop the character into a detective hero for an ongoing pulp magazine. The first full-length *Shadow* appeared in the summer of 1931 and was entitled *The Living Shadow*. In 1938 the Shadow returned to radio on his own program. *Shadow* radio dramas were now based on Gibson's stories. Ultimately, Gibson (under the pseudonym "Maxwell Grant") wrote 282 Shadow novels—a *Guinness Book of World Records* record for most novels written about a series character by one person. The Shadow became the archetypal avenger detective, reminiscent of avengers found in dime novels and predicting Bob Kane and Bill Finger's Batman in the comic books and comic strips.

In 1933 Street and Smith launched its *Doc Savage* magazine with the opening story, "The Man of Bronze." Lester Dent and other pulp veterans were the writers behind the superman (Clark "Doc" Savage, the Man of Bronze) who would presage Superman (Clark Kent, the Man of Steel) in comic books in 1938. For *Doc Savage*, Dent and others wrote under the "Kenneth Robeson" house name.

In 1933 also, Popular Publications debuted its competition for Street and Smith's immensely popular *The Shadow*. Popular's hero pulp was called *The Spider* and featured a very violent, apocalyptic avenger of the same name. R. T. M. Scott wrote the first two novels (*The Spider Strikes* and *Wheel of Death*), but he was soon replaced by Norvell Page, who wrote under the guise of "Grant Stockbridge." Like Scott, Page was a seasoned pulp veteran, but he specialized in lurid, weird-menace-type crime and horror stories. This résumé made Page attractive to executives at Popular Publications. He was hired to outdo Gibson's *Shadow*. Today, both the Shadow and the Spider remain lexicons of our popular culture, with the Shadow being the more famous of the two. While tales of the Shadow tended to be better plotted than those of the Spider, adventures of the Spider tended to be more action-packed and violent. For Norvell Page, plot could be (and often was) sacrificed for action. Gibson tended to employ both plot and action, but he made sure plot was in place first. *Weird Tales* first appeared in 1923. This Chicago-based pulp is considered the most

CATHERINE LUCILLE MOORE

Weird Tales published Catherine L. Moore's first story in its November 1933 issue. The tale, a wild space opera set on Mars and featuring a hero named Northwest Smith, was entitled "Shambleau." The story was well received by readers and became a turning point for science fiction (SF). Moore, born in Indianapolis in 1911, would soon become one of the most important and highly revered writers of the genre. As was the case with her contemporary, Leigh Brackett, Moore championed women writers of SF. Like Brackett, she was inspired by the popular pulp magazines of her youth—particularly *Amazing Stories* and Edgar Rice Burroughs. In turn, she influenced a whole new generation of writers. In the 1930s and 1940s, Moore was a regular contributor to both *Weird Tales* and *Astounding* (*Astounding Science Fiction*), and she published in other magazines as well, including *Unknown* (*Worlds*) and *Famous Fantastic Mysteries*. She had two primary series characters; one was Northwest Smith (introduced in "Shambleau") and the other was a strong-willed female warrior named Jirel of Joiry (introduced in "The Black God's Kiss" in the October 1934 issue of *Weird Tales*). From her earliest writings, Moore used her initials instead of her first and middle names to disguise her gender. (Mary Elizabeth Counselman did the same thing. Magazine editors knew that it was a fact, however unfortunate and unfair, that women authors did not sell as well as their male counterparts in those days.) During the years of her marriage (1940–58) to famous SF writer Henry "Hank" Kuttner (1914–58), Moore collaborated with Kuttner on a number of short stories and novels, often under the "Lewis Padgett" pseudonym. However, in 1957, Moore published her own novel, *Doomsday Morning*. After the death of Kuttner, Moore turned to writing for television. Her grand SF career was all but over. Like Leigh Brackett, Catherine L. Moore was dearly loved by her fellow authors and fans alike. She died in 1987.

important fantasy periodical of all time. *Weird Tales* featured stories of the strange and supernatural, of horror, mystery, fantasy, and science fiction. The three most famous *Weird Tales* authors were H(oward) P(hillips) Lovecraft, Clark Ashton Smith, and Robert E. Howard. Seabury Quinn, however, was the most prolific author in the magazine. There were many other famous authors. The table of contents pages often included the names Edmond Hamilton, M(ary) E(lizabeth) Counselman, C(atherine) L(ucille) Moore, Henry Kuttner, Robert Bloch, Ray Bradbury, and a young Richard Matheson. Before science fiction was given its own definition and specialty pulp magazines, *Weird Tales* and *Argosy* published "space operas" (for all practical purposes, Westerns set in outer space) and "scientific romances" in the 1920s.

Hugo Gernsback (August 16, 1884–August 19, 1967) and his Experimenter Publishing Company released the first issue of *Amazing Stories* in early 1926. (The magazine was dated April 1926.) Originally, *Amazing Stories* was an oversized (bedsheet-formatted) pulp magazine, and was for some time subtitled "The Magazine of Scientifiction." Although literary and other narrative elements of science fiction have existed almost as long as people have, it was Gernsback and *Amazing* that were ultimately responsible for identifying and celebrating these elements (e.g., regarding speculations about the nature of the universe and its inhabitants, space travel, scientific inventions and advances) that characterize and make unique the term and genre Gernsback would ultimately deem "science fiction."

In February 1904, Hugo Gernsback, a native of Luxembourg, came to the United States to market his newly invented form of battery. During the next several years, Gernsback, now a New York City resident, developed his talents as scientist, writer, and marketer. He soon discovered that fiction grounded in sound, up-to-date scientific fact and theory and published in catalogs and magazines advertising his products, increased sales of these products. Ultimately, Hugo Gernsback was responsible for a score of science fact- and fiction-related periodical magazine series. The most famous, though not his first, was *Amazing Stories*. Through the years, the pages of *Amazing* have featured an array of famous and not-so-famous authors. Early issues featured reprinted stories of Edgar Allan Poe, Jules Verne, and H. G. Wells; they also featured a range of established and new authors of the day—included in the former group were A(braham) Merritt and Murray Leinster, in the latter, Dr. David H. Keller and Jack Williamson. Landmark SF authors and stories and serials that appeared in *Amazing* included Edgar Rice Burroughs's *The Mastermind of Mars* (the sixth John Carter of Mars novel—1927), E. E. "Doc" Smith's *The Skylark of Space* (1928), Philip Francis Nowlan's *Armageddon 2419 A.D.* (the first Buck Rogers story), Edmond Hamilton's *The Universe Wreckers* (1930), and Jack Williamson's *The Green Girl* (1930).

Frank R. Paul (1884–1963) did many of the colorful, imaginative, larger-than-life paintings that graced the covers of *Amazing* and other Gernsback publications magazines in the 1920s and 1930s. Paul's portrayals of magazine story lines that featured speculations about futuristic technologies, alien races, space travel, monsters, and more were highlights for readers of Gernsback's magazines.

In the 1930s, *Astounding Stories* pulp magazine proved to be *Amazing Stories*' chief competitor. John W. Campbell (1910–61), a famed science fiction writer who had written for *Amazing*, became the editor of *Astounding* in 1937 and remained there until his death. *Astounding* was first published by the Clayton Company and then by Street and Smith. *Astounding* magazine is still published today, though for several decades it has been more recognizable as the digest-format *Analog Science Fiction/Science Fact*. George Lucas's *Star Wars* movies and Steven Spielberg's *Close Encounters of the Third Kind* and *E.T.* are highly derivative of the stories found in *Amazing* and *Astounding*. (Jack Williamson's *Legion of Space* series is heavily drawn upon in the *Star Wars* saga.) In the 1980s, Spielberg had a successful Sunday night television show named *Amazing Stories*, a tribute to the old pulp magazine.

Other science fiction pulps had titles such as *Startling Stories*, *Captain Future*, *Planet Stories*, and *Wonder Stories*. Though not as prolific as Western and mystery pulps, science fiction pulps were very popular.

Pulp authors came from all walks of life and from all areas of North America. Some came from international locations (e.g., Arthur C. Clarke), and some North Americans traveled internationally and wrote from personal experiences in exotic lands (e.g., Hugh B. Cave). Others lived in relatively the same places for most of their lives, and wrote about the regions in which they lived and real and imaginary places they discovered via reading (e.g., H. P. Lovecraft and Robert E. Howard). A small sampling of pulp authors, where they came from, and what types of fiction they specialized in follows. William Merriam Rouse lived in the Adirondack Mountains and wrote action adventure, horror, weird, folk tales, and frontier stories. Michigan authors included James B. Hendryx (Northern frontier and action adventure), James Oliver Curwood (action adventure, social melodrama, and moral allegory), Dan Cushman (action adventure, South Seas tales, and Westerns), and Elmore Leonard (Westerns and later detective fiction). Wisconsin authors included: T(heodore) V. Olsen (frontier and Western), H(arold) A. DeRosso (Western and other), and August W. Derleth (weird, science fiction, fantasy, mystery, and more). Ohio authors included Edmond Hamilton (science fiction, space opera, and weird) and Leigh Brackett (science fiction, fantasy, space opera, crime fiction, and Western). Brackett helped teach Ray Bradbury to write, and shortly before her death she wrote the screenplay for the second of George Lucas's *Star Wars* movies to be released, *The Empire Strikes Back* (1981).

Mary Elizabeth Counselman was from Alabama; she specialized in weird, fantasy, and Southern folk tales. Jack Williamson is from New Mexico, and he has specialized for eighty years—his first published story appeared in a 1928 issue of Hugo Gernsback's *Amazing Stories*—in science fiction, space opera, weird, and action adventure stories. California authors included Henry Kuttner (science fiction, weird, and mystery), Catherine L. Moore (science fiction, space opera, heroic fantasy, and weird), and Clark Ashton Smith (weird and science fiction). Ray Bradbury is from California, too, though many of his stories are based

LEIGH (DOUGLASS) BRACKETT

Author of numerous short stories, novels, motion picture screenplays and more, Leigh Brackett (1915–78) was one of the top woman writers of twentieth-century science fiction specifically and popular literature generally. Her SF stories were often, but were not limited to, space operas reminiscent of Edgar Rice Burroughs's John Carter of Mars tales. She also wrote Westerns and crime fiction. Influenced by past literary tradition, Brackett was an important teacher of aspiring authors. Ray Bradbury may have been her most famous student, and Bradbury himself acknowledges an extensive debt to Brackett. The pair collaborated on a new legendary short pulp novel, *Lorelei of the Red Mist* (1946). Brackett is remembered for contributions to pulp magazines including *Planet Stories*, *Startling Stories*, and *Thrilling Wonder Stories*; her Eric John Stark Mars adventures (which appeared in two series—one in the 1940s and one in the 1970s); her screenplays—including a 1946 adaptation (with William Faulkner) of Raymond Chandler's landmark of detective fiction, *The Big Sleep*; a John Wayne vehicle, *Rio Bravo* (1958); her last major work, the script for the second *Star Wars* movie, *The Empire Strikes Back* (1979); and more. Her novel *The Long Tomorrow* (1955) is a classic futuristic tale of Cold War–era America. Leigh Brackett married famous popular author Edmond Hamilton and both influenced and was influenced by his work.

RAY BRADBURY

An author who draws heavily upon personal experience and cultural inheritance, who relies on the history of ideas, free word association, and the potential of imagery and color through language, Ray Bradbury (b. August 22, 1920) has proven himself a magician of words and teller of universal tales that define both North American and world cultures. Bradbury's short stories, novels, stage plays, screenplays, poetry, radio plays and television plays appeal to all ages, and his dexterity with issues of youth and age, and coming of age, make his writing significant and meaningful to a wide-ranging public. He has always drawn heavily from personal experience, making autobiography the largest overriding thematic element of his work. Bradbury's first professional sale, "Pendulum," was co-authored with Henry Hasse and appeared in the November 1941 issue of *Super Science Stories*, a pulp magazine. Some of his early contributions to *Weird Tales* and other such periodicals were collected in his first book, *Dark Carnival*, published in 1947 by August Derleth and Arkham House. This list of his single-authored book publications is extensive and includes *The Martian Chronicles* (1950), an episodic novel based on a series of pulp and non pulp writing; *The Illustrated Man* (1951), a short story collection framed by the idea of the "Illustrated Man," a tattooed carnival worker; *Fahrenheit 451* (1953); *The October Country* (1955); *Dandelion Wine* (1957); and many, many more through contemporary times. In October 2006, he released *Farewell Summer*, a fifty-years-later sequel to *Dandelion Wine*. In the 1940s and 1950s Bradbury was writing intelligent, insightful stories about ethnicity and race relations and about gender long before such stories became fashionable. Stories like "The Big Black and White Game" and "The Other Foot" told more about racial harmony than many things before or since; stories like "I'll Not Look for Wine" and "Cora and the Great Wide World" featured women with great stamina, independence, and individual identity. Ray Bradbury is one of the twentieth and twenty-first centuries' most important storytellers and allegorists.

upon his childhood in Illinois and his travels in Mexico and Ireland. One of the single most important authors of the twentieth century, Bradbury has written speculative fiction, space opera, fantasy, science fiction, weird fiction, and crime, mystery, and detective fiction. G. T. Fleming-Roberts was from Indiana, though he also lived in Tennessee. Fleming-Roberts wrote for the detective fiction pulps, weird and weird menace pulps, and hero pulps. Nelson S. Bond is from Tennessee and has written space opera, science fiction, action adventure, and more.

Carl Jacobi (action adventure, south seas, weird, mysteries and more) and Donald Wandrei (science fiction, space opera, weird, and more) were from Minnesota. Isaac Asimov was from New York City, and, though he wrote mysteries and ultimately many other types of fiction and nonfiction, was best known for his science fiction. Robert E. Howard, pioneer of action adventure fiction and heroic fantasy and creator of Conan the Barbarian, also wrote weird fiction, frontier fiction, fight stories, South Sea stories, and more; he was from Texas. Famous detective fiction writer John D. McDonald wrote extensively for the pulps and was from Florida. He also wrote science fiction.

Some authors moved throughout North America. Frank L. Packard, famous action adventure author, had residences in both Canada and the United States. Robert Bloch (weird, mystery, western, science fiction, fantasy, humor, and more), the famous author of the novel *Psycho* (1959), was born and raised in Chicago, lived in Wisconsin for years, and spent most of his adult life in California. Frederick C. Davis, author of crime, mystery, and

ROBERT BLOCH

Best remembered as the author of the novel *Psycho* (1959), which Alfred Hitchcock made into the famous movie of the same title (1960), Robert Bloch (April 5, 1917–September 23, 1994) was more importantly the author of hundreds of short stories, novels, radio plays, movie screenplays, television dramas, and other popular writings of social criticism. His fiction made significant contributions to the popular genres of dark fantasy/horror, mystery and detective fiction, science fiction, and more. Many of Bloch's stories incorporate elements of comedy; many showcase the author's vast knowledge of world and literary history. A trademark of Bloch tales is the twist ending. Particularly in the short story format, this technique often earned Robert Bloch comparison to O. Henry. Although Bloch had stories published at age sixteen (such as "Lilies" in William L. Crawford's *Marvel Tales* in 1934), his first professional sales to a nationally renowned periodical included the short story "The Feast in the Abbey," which appeared in the January 1935 issue of the popular pulp magazine *Weird Tales*. Between 1935 and 1952, Bloch had sixty-seven short stories, novellas and novelettes appear in *Weird Tales* alone. In the 1930s and 1940s, he also had stories of various lengths and types published in an range of other magazines including, but not limited to, *Amazing Stories, Fantastic Adventures, Imaginative Tales, Unknown Worlds*, and *Unusual Stories*. Robert Bloch's first hardcover book was his collection of short stories published by August Derleth's Arkham House of Sauk City, Wisconsin, entitled *The Opener of the Way* (1945). There were many other short story collections to follow in both hardcover and paperback. Among the author's many novels number *The Scarf* (1948), *The Kidnapper* (1953), *Spiderweb* (1953), *Psycho* (1959), *Firebug* (1962), *The Star Stalker* (1968), *Psycho II* (1982), and *Psycho House* (1990). In addition, Robert Bloch's stories were the basis for several motion pictures, and Bloch himself wrote several screenplays that were made into movies. Of his many television plays written and produced, his three episodes for the original *Star Trek* series, "What Are Little Girls Made Of?" (aired October 20, 1966), "Catspaw" (October 27, 1967), and "Wolf in the Fold" (December 22, 1967) are perhaps most famous. Bloch was born in Chicago, spent his childhood and early adulthood there and in Wisconsin, and the rest of his life in Los Angeles. Numerous writers, including Ray Bradbury and Stephen King, have acknowledged the profound influence of Robert Bloch on their own styles.

detective fiction, Westerns, air stories, and much more, lived, at various stages in his life, in Ohio, Pennsylvania, New York, and Florida. The father of twentieth-century space opera, E. E. "Doc" Smith, lived in Wisconsin, Michigan, and both New England and the Pacific Northwest.

Famous Canadian pulp authors included Thomas P. Kelley (*Weird Tales* and many more), Harold Cruickshank (frontier, action adventure, Canadian Mounties story writer), and A. E. van Vogt (science fiction, fantasy, and weird). During the years of the dime novel and pulp magazine in North America, "penny dreadfuls" and "shilling shockers" were cousins or rough equivalents in Great Britain.

With the advent of World War II, the pulp magazine and pulp magazine market changed. Genre stories were becoming too predictable (much as they had fifty years earlier in dime novels). The war itself required Americans to conserve and rethink use of resources such as sugar, steel, rubber, and paper. Paper was not as disposable as it had once been. In 1938, paperback novels arrived as a response to the war. Paperbacks used less paper, and they could be sent overseas to soldiers for three cents postage. By 1948, network television became a reality in highly populated cities—radio dramas and movie serials, like pulp magazines, were now becoming obsolete and saw diminishing returns.

But the pulps were far from entirely finished. The sturdiest of titles carried on in smaller digest formats. These included *The Shadow*, *Doc Savage*, *Weird Tales*, *Amazing Stories*, and *Astounding* (later *Analog*), a range of Western and frontier titles, and others. Early paperbacks guaranteed themselves a significant beginning market share by reprinting the most successful of pulp magazine authors and stories, just as the pulp magazines had done in their early days with reprints of dime novel authors and stories. To this day, paperbacks reprint classic and not so classic tales from the Golden Age of the pulps.

And there is the hardcover book reprint market. Almost from the start of the pulp era, book publishers realized that the ephemeral pulp could be profitably preserved in book form. Street and Smith publishers even had their own hardcover line to reprint and preserve stories originally printed in their pulp products. This hardcover line was called Chelsea House. In the late 1930s, August Derleth (from Wisconsin) and Donald Wandrei (from Minnesota) created Arkham House publishers to preserve the weird, supernatural, horror, fantasy, and science fiction of H. P. Lovecraft. Their first book, published shortly after Lovecraft's untimely death, was *The Outsider and Others* (1939). In the next decades, Arkham House provided first book publications for pulp stories by Robert E. Howard, Robert Bloch, Ray Bradbury, and others. In the 1980s, Bowling Green State University's Popular Press provided a number of volumes of pulp reprints at the hands of Ray B. Browne and Gary Hoppenstand. Today, pulp reprints thrive in the specialty book market as well. John Gunnison's Adventure House is one leader in such publications. In Canada, George Vanderburgh's Battered Silicon Dispatch Box Press reprints beautiful volumes of pulp fiction. In Canada also, Leigh and Neil Mechem's Girasol Collectables specializes in equally beautiful pulp replicas and reprints.

NEWSPAPER COMIC STRIPS

The comic strip, as we know it, has been part of American culture since the late nineteenth century; the two-dimensional caricature, of course, dates back to beginnings of humanity and ancient cave paintings. In recent centuries, the single-frame political cartoon has evolved internationally with the newspaper, yet in North America it was not until the 1890s that the comic strip first appeared as a regular feature of newspapers. The comic strip is a logical sequencing of line drawings—often compartmentalized into panels—that tells a brief story or elicits a smile or even laugh. Hence, the term "comic." Originally, comic strips were designed as vehicles for humor. It was not until the early twentieth century that this new media form was employed to tell extended stories of adventure, mystery, and intrigue. Today, in the early days of the twenty-first century, the classic comic strip has been rediscovered with great fervor. Publishing houses have emerged that have specialized in reprinting these cultural products of decades past in hardcover and paperback formats, in color (as in Sunday comic strip pages), and in black and white (as in daily strips). Established academic and international publishers such as McFarland, the University Press of Mississippi, Oxford University Press, and Ivy League school presses such as those from Harvard and Yale are some of these publishers.

Most authorities on the American newspaper comic strip identify international and artistic precedents for the contemporary phenomenon that still is found in newspapers. Most authorities also vary in what they claim as the "first" American comic strip. Some cite

Richard Outcault's *Yellow Kid* (1896), created for the Hearst Syndicate, as the first comic strip. However, the newspaper strip that fulfills all the requirements delineated above was Rudolph Dirks's *The Katzenjammer Kids*. Hans and Fritz, the Katzenjammer Kids, appeared for the first time on December 12, 1897, in *The American Humorist*, the Sunday supplement of William Randolph Hearst's *The New York Journal*. Dirks was the creator and first story-teller of the Katzenjammer Kids saga. The strip, originally adapted from the German cartoon *Max and Moritz*, revolved around Hans and Fritz and their rebellion against any form of authority. Although several elaborate one-panel cartoons appeared during the years immediately preceding the arrival of *The Katzenjammer Kids* (including *The Yellow Kid*), no newspaper feature organized panels or cartoon art in a logical, lineal sequence to tell a story until the debut of Dirks's comic strip.

Shortly after the first appearance of Dirks's Hans and Fritz, Richard Outcault's *Buster Brown* (May 4, 1902) and Winsor McCay's *Little Nemo in Slumberland* (October 15, 1905) appeared, along with an array of lesser-known strips. The ideas of the mischievous child and the clownish innocent were not born, however, on the comic page. Such characters had pervaded folk culture centuries earlier. But the comic strip did become a vehicle that immortalized tales of such stereotypic characters.

The humanized animal arose almost simultaneously with the trickster and innocent. For example, Buster Brown was accompanied by his dog, Tige. Fred Opper, the comic strip artist most often remembered for *Happy Hooligan*, provided the public with Maud the Mule in *And Her Name Was Maud*, which began in 1904. J. M. Conde's Uncle Remus characters were part of a larger humanized animal community in *Uncle Remus Stories*. Yet, like the mischievous child and clownish innocent, the humanized animal had been a staple of folk tales since ancient times. At the turn of the century, many of the newspaper strips were adult-oriented. Largely because William Randolph Hearst was the primary publishing force behind these strips, newspaper comics at this time were designed so that they could be acceptable facets of Hearst's "aristocratic" productions.

Between 1907 and 1927 also, comic strips increasingly targeted larger audiences—audiences that included children. On November 15, 1907, H. C. "Bud" Fisher introduced *A. Mutt*, which was soon changed to *Mutt and Jeff*. One of the most famous vaudevillian teams of the comic page, Mutt and Jeff provided their audience with a form of comedy and satire that had been around for decades in other forms and that would continue to thrive and grow in a variety of media during the first half of the twentieth century. The narrative device for *Mutt and Jeff*—perhaps the single most important ingredient of the comic strip's success—centered on the interactions of the carefully drawn protagonists.

In 1917 Sidney Smith of Lake Geneva, Wisconsin, under the tutelage of William Randolph Hearst's biggest evolving competitor, newspaper mogul Captain Joseph Medill Patterson, produced a comic strip that parodied domestic, middle-class American families—*The Gumps*. Andy Gump, and later his son Chester, became enduring staples of *The Chicago Tribune*, the New York News Syndicate, and newspaper comic pages everywhere. At the close of 1918, Frank King of Tomah, Wisconsin, provided the *Chicago Tribune* and New York News Syndicate with another saga of middle class America, though King's strip did not appear in the established comic strip form until February 14, 1921. This was *Gasoline Alley*, and it featured Walt Wallet and his foundling son, Skeezix. And there were still other comic strips that arose and thrived. Frank Willard provided Patterson with *Moon Mullins* in 1923, largely as a competitive response to Billy DeBeck's *Barney Google*, which was a popular strip of *The Chicago Herald* and other Hearst syndicate newspapers.

Murat "Chic" Young created a fictitious heroine who at one time was the subject of the most widely read comic strip in the world. Her name is Blondie, and she debuted in the strip with the same name in 1930. *Blondie*, like its predecessors *The Gumps*, *Gasoline Alley*, and *Moon Mullins*, was and continues to be popular because it celebrates the human spirit and the trials and tribulations of the once traditional American family. Chic Young was a master at eliciting a laugh or a chuckle from his readers because he had a keen insight into middle-class America. While Blondie is the central character of this strip, her interactions with her husband, Dagwood Bumstead; her children, Alexander and Cookie; the dog, Daisy, and her pups; the Ditherses; and the Woodleys have carried the script.

By the mid-1920s the domestic-comedy newspaper comic strip had established itself as the dominant genre of the new medium. This particular comic strip genre has traditionally centered on the seemingly everyday activities of a family or pseudo-family group, and its focus is the daily social interactions of members of the family. Realistic settings, coupled with exaggerated stereotypes and events, provide a balance of reality and fantasy that is satisfying for the newspaper comic strip reader. The convention is the family group and its elaborate rituals. The invention is the response of group members to the new events of each day.

Andy Gump and Blondie, along with their family members, are extensions of everyday life. Their popularity is largely attributable to their creators' abilities to tap into social sentiment. Sidney Smith and Chic Young, for example, projected their own experiences onto the newspaper page. And since Smith, Young, and most other comic strip artists were products of middle-class America; their stories were credible to their readers. Each of these artists related events in history that molded their thinking and reflected the experience of most comic strip readers. Popular entertainment and media are a very reflective lot. If these masters of the comic strip could not cite specific influences from earlier comic art, they could reference vaudevillians, popular authors and works, and so on that they enjoyed and embraced, and then subsequently used to varying degrees in their own creative efforts. We all do this. Selected values and ideas that we use to construct our mindsets are modified based on new information. In the case of comic strip creators, artists, and writers, the result of this process is immortalized on the printed page.

In the 1920s and 1930s, variations and extensions of the domestic comedy genre began to appear. *The Gumps* and *Moon Mullins* were first stories of interaction within the confines of a family group, but each strip developed a strong spin-off story. In these two particular instances, the spin-off was a variation of the mischievous child and clownish innocent formulas. By the end of the 1920s, the exploits of Chester Gump, Andy's son, were as vital to *The Gumps* as were the interactions of the larger family—perhaps more vital. Similarly, Kayo became a central focus of *Moon Mullins*. In other cases, such as in *Blondie*, the humanized animal took center stage in the domestic comedy story: in *Blondie*, stories featured the antics of Daisy and her pups, the children, and so on.

The hallmark of the domestic comedy newspaper strip of the 1920s and 1930s was the character development that occurred in the better strips despite limitations of the medium. The comic strip is a two-dimensional medium that depends upon the linear progression of ideas, embodied in symbolic caricatures and settings, to relate a message. The most popular comic strip characters of this period grew, and the morality play they advanced was more detailed and complex than it is today. Trials and tribulations, and resulting moral growth, sometimes lasted for months. Comic strips of recent years are, with rare exception, reliant on short gags and superficial ideas that are limited to one day's telling. Space allocated to comic strips in newspapers today has become increasingly limited at the hands of editors and publishers.

In the 1920s and 30s, humorous comic strips were joined by the second and final major comic strip genre—the adventure comic strip. The action hero and the adventure story were not new; they had appeared in seemingly all of North America's (and the world's) popular media, including dime novels, pulp magazines, motion pictures, and radio drama. But the advent of the adventure strip was a new twist for a relatively new medium. What finer place for a fantastic adventure than next to even more fantastic accounts of real-life history and atrocities found in newspapers?

Probably the most legitimate claimant for title of first established adventure strip was Roy Crane's *Wash Tubbs*, though in the most general sense, there was a great deal of "adventure" in some of the earliest comic strip comedies. A few years after Wash Tubbs, a comedic little oaf, debuted on the newspaper page in 1924, he was joined by Captain Easy, a handsome, muscular adventure hero. With the introduction of Easy, Crane turned the story lines of the strip into larger-than-life adventures. So well received was this change that Crane re-titled his strip *Captain Easy*.

The most famous of all adventure strip heroines appeared for the first time on August 25, 1924, several months after *Wash Tubbs*'s debut. She was Harold Gray's Little Orphan Annie. *Little Orphan Annie* first appeared at a time when, in the relatively new medium of the newspaper comic strip, the role of central protagonist was left primarily to the male of the species. The little waif with the red mop of hair was a Horatio Alger–like figure spouting moral philosophy and struggling her way upward. While her adopted father, Oliver "Daddy" Warbucks, was a product of hard work, strict dogma, and the material wealth that was often equated with such attributes, Annie found herself most often on the other side of the tracks. She worked hard trying to improve the human condition as she found it. Harold Gray had been Sidney Smith's assistant on *The Gumps* from 1920 until the time that Captain Patterson accepted *Little Orphan Annie* for publication in 1924. *Annie* reflected

HAROLD GRAY AND LITTLE ORPHAN ANNIE

Harold Lincoln Gray (January 20, 1894–May 10, 1968) originally envisioned his little orphan as a boy. However, Captain Joseph Medill Patterson, comic strip mogul of *The New York News* and *The Chicago Tribune*, suggested that Gray make the character a girl and call her "Little Orphan Annie"—a name derived from the title of a once famous James Whitcomb Riley poem.

Harold Gray was born on his parents' farm in Kankakee, Illinois. He was a graduate of Purdue University, worked in *The Chicago Tribune* art department, and was a veteran of World War I. Gray's famous comic strip, with its legendary title character, her dog Sandy, her adopted father "Daddy" (always in quotes in the strip) Warbucks, and a myriad of friends and foes, was launched in the August 5, 1924, edition of *The New York Daily News*. Story lines featured Horatio Alger–like "rags to riches" themes, and celebrated moral goodness, hard work, and the inevitable (as Gray saw it) triumph of good over evil. *Little Orphan Annie* was particularly popular in the 1920s and 1930s, perhaps due to themes of hope for good people down on their luck (as many people were during the Depression). Annie herself was the star of a radio show sponsored by Ovaltine drink mix, and was the focus of a Broadway musical that debuted in April 1977. After Gray died in 1968, there several writers and artists tried unsuccessfully to carry the strip forward. Finally, as of the December 9, 1979, installment of *Annie*, Leonard Starr brought Harold Gray's comic back to prominence for 20 additional years, ending in February 2000.

the struggle upward that was so much a part of Gray's own life. Gray's comic embodied much of how America envisioned itself at that time. Such themes would find large audiences after the stock market crash of October 1929. Annie became the number-one adventure heroine of the funny pages.

Philip F. Nowlan and Dick Calkins's *Buck Rogers* provided another such adventure heroine, though the strip she appeared in was not named for her. Wilma Deering was Buck Rogers' female counterpart in the comic, and often it was Wilma who was the true star of

CHESTER GOULD

Chester Gould (November 20, 1900–May 11, 1985) was the descendant of Oklahoma Territory pioneers. During his childhood and adolescence, Gould lived in Pawnee, Oklahoma, the frontier town whose residents included world famous entertainers Buffalo Bill and Pawnee Bill (William F. Cody and Gordon Lillie), silent Western movie star Tom Mix, Iron Tail (the Native American whose image is found on the Indian-head/buffalo-head nickel started in 1913), Mose Yellowpony (Gould's good friend and the first Native American to play major league baseball on the Pittsburgh Pirates), and others from African-American, Native American, and European-American communities. Chet was an accomplished artist at an early age, publishing his drawings in local newspapers and painting his art for hire on the sides of local buildings.

From 1919 to 1921, Gould attended Oklahoma A&M (Agricultural and Mechanical—later renamed Oklahoma State University) in Stillwater. In 1921, with $50 in his pocket, he moved to Chicago to pursue a career as an illustrator and newspaper comic strip writer and artist. In 1923 he earned a degree in commerce and marketing from Northwestern University. Over the next 10 years Gould worked for all the major newspapers in Chicago. In 1931 he landed a contract with the *Chicago Tribune*—New York News Syndicate to write and draw his latest comic strip, *Plainclothes Tracy* (later *Dick Tracy*). Both William Randolph Hearst and Marshall Field (better known for his department stores than for his newspaper syndicate) would later, unsuccessfully, try to buy Gould away from the *Tribune*.

Responding to the culture of gangsterism and crime he found in Chicago, Gould brought frontier justice to urban rogues of Dick Tracy's not-so-fictional world. Developing and employing a story formula in which police procedure and science were conventions and physically and morally grotesque villains were inventions, Chester Gould provided a morality play in *Dick Tracy* that captivated audiences internationally. On Christmas 1977, he retired as the artist of his famous strip. However, *Dick Tracy* continues, at the hands of other artists and writers, to this day.

The violence found in gangland during the 1930s was a horrendous thing to depict in a newspaper comic strip. Only in America, where there is a free press and free speech, was this possible. One of the narrative and illustrative staples of *Dick Tracy* was the violent act. Though these acts are remembered more often and romantically than as they actually appeared, in the heyday of *Dick Tracy*, bullets went right through people, fires burned, water drowned and froze, and knives slashed rogues and innocents alike. Violence, though not new to the comic strip (it had appeared in various forms in the 1920s adventure continuities), had reached a new level of intensity and now became a staple, a central focus of the burgeoning medium. The extremes to which Dick Tracy employed violence were justified as being socially accepted and prescribed means of purging evil or regenerating cultural morality. These acts very quickly and permanently reinstated good over evil.

Gould's work on *Dick Tracy* was so effective a means of reflecting social mores and history that J. Edgar Hoover became interested. Hoover realized that *Tracy* enacted a wonderful ritual that reinforced, in a "black and white" fashion, the common American belief that "good" will ultimately triumph over "evil." The strip provided the public with a police force that worked, and one that could be idealized—something that was seriously missing in the real-life drama of the time. Hoover believed that, as a model of justice and moral goodness, *Dick Tracy* affected America's thoughts and behavior. As head of the FBI, Hoover praised Gould for his work toward the betterment of society through the medium of the newspaper comic strip. Ultimately, Hoover paid Gould one of the highest compliments possible when he tried to imitate Gould's work. Hoover hired a team of artists and writers, and the result was a comic strip called *War on Crime*. The strip featured

CHESTER GOULD (CONTINUED)

actual cases of the FBI. But it survived for only a short time, meeting with moderate success at best, quite possibly because it was too exclusively factual and consequently did not attain the necessary balance of fact and fantasy.

Dick Tracy was so successful that it inspired, influenced, engendered imitation in, and was parodied in other comic strips as well—such as the Hearst Syndicate's *Secret Agent X* and Fearless Fosdick in Al Capp's *Li'l Abner*. In the 1930s there were several *Dick Tracy* imitations in the newspapers, such as Dick Moore's *Jim Hardy* and Norman Marsh's *Dann Dunn*.

this newspaper-page space opera. This newspaper comic strip originally appeared in Hugo Gernsback's pulp magazine *Amazing Stories* in 1928. It first appeared as a comic strip on January 7, 1929. Nowlan and Calkins theorized what space travel would be like in the twenty-fifth century based on scientific knowledge and social perceptions of the day. Their strip met with tremendous success because it provided adventure and escapism for people of the Depression era. Buck Rogers was a futuristic All-American hero. Wilma Deering was more than the hero's love interest. She was a futuristic All-American heroine.

Less than two weeks after the debut of Buck and Wilma on the comic page, another hero emerged who, along with a colorful female foil, rose to epic proportions as a legend of the newspaper page. His name was Popeye, and he first appeared in Elzie Crisler Segar's *Thimble Theatre* on January 17, 1929. *Thimble Theatre* had first appeared over nine years earlier and had centered on a cast of improbable stereotypic characters and their daily routines. At that time, the hero of Segar's strip was Harold "Ham" Gravy. His girlfriend, Olive Oyl, and her brother, Castor Oyl, accompanied him. William Randolph Hearst was behind the promotion of Segar and his comic, but neither could have anticipated the success the comic strip would enjoy in the Great Depression after the introduction of Popeye the Sailor. Popeye soon replaced Ham Gravy as Olive's beau, and a number of other colorful characters were introduced in the 1930s. Lesser characters departed. The ageless ideology that good will ultimately engage and defeat evil became the mainstay for the now re-titled *Popeye*—Segar and his successors made that quite clear. Olive quickly became Popeye's companion and foil.

The 1930s, as in the case of several other American mass media, proved to be the "golden age" for the newspaper comic strip. Domestic comedies flourished. In the adventure comic strips, countless heroes and heroines appeared. Some endured, most grew as characters, and many disappeared in following years. It was a glorious time for comic-page justice.

No sooner had this era commenced than one of the most famous comic-strip and fictional detectives of all time appeared. He was Chester Gould's Dick Tracy, and he debuted in *The Detroit Mirror* on October 4, 1931. Today, *Dick Tracy* remains the most sociohistorically important newspaper comic strip of all time. The title character is second in fame and notoriety as a fictional sleuth only to Arthur Conan Doyle's archetypal Sherlock Holmes. In 1931, Gould and Captain Patterson recognized that the comics that were the most commercially viable were those that employed topics, situations, settings, and characters to which the reader could relate. Chester Gould made every effort possible to depict police procedure in as realistic a fashion as possible. He did this primarily by working with Chicago-area police forces; by studying ballistics and related sciences; by investigating criminal behavior, by riding with Chicago area police officers in their squad cars; and by reading accounts of gangsters

DICK TRACY

Chester Gould's *Dick Tracy* first appeared in *The Detroit Mirror* (a *Chicago Tribune*–owned newspaper) on October 4, 1931. The first continuities began eight days later on October 12, establishing the origin and justification for the detective hero and his cause. These continuities debuted in *The New York Daily News*, where they continued, on the front page, for 55 consecutive years. The famous comic strip has appeared in many hundreds of national and international newspapers. A hallmark of *Dick Tracy* has always been the grotesque rogues that populate the fictional world of Tracy. Chester Gould's ability to blend documented history and cutting-edge police procedure with these exaggerated, grotesque villains make *Dick Tracy* a very important cultural text and barometer. As the creator, writer, and artist of the comic strip, Gould believed that a symbolic portrayal of horrendous crime via the symbolic horrendous physiognomy of his villains emphasized the moral stance of detective hero, and of course, the artist/writer himself. In the panels of this comic strip appeared fictionalized, fantastic interpretations and portrayals of real-life people and events such as Al Capone (as "Big Boy," 1931–32), John Dillinger (as "Boris Arson," 1934–35), and the Lindbergh baby kidnapping (as the "Buddy Waldorf" case, 1932). There were thousands more. Of the many famous *Tracy* rogues, the most famous was probably Flattop (1943–44), a World War II racketeer and cold-blooded killer. Physically, Flattop literally had a flat-topped head, and was named for World War II aircraft carriers. There is reason to believe that this *Tracy* character was influenced by the real-life "Pretty Boy" Floyd.

By carefully studying police procedures and sciences, Gould was able to accurately and profoundly predict forthcoming advances in these procedures and sciences. His most famous prediction was probably the wrist radio, though he also accurately speculated about such things as open-heart surgery before they became reality. (Magnetic space coupes and Moon Maid did not, however, last long after the Apollo missions.) In popular fiction, Chester Gould's *Dick Tracy* provided the archetypal police detective hero and police procedural mystery formula. Gould's message, celebrating a high personal and social morality, has reflected and affected the mindsets of millions of people and has subsequently left an indelible legacy and mythology for generations past, present, and to come.

and their exploits in newspapers. Gould succeeded in his efforts because he employed a finely balanced blend of fact and fantasy in *Tracy*.

Adventure on the newspaper page of the Great Depression was not limited to *Captain Easy, Popeye, Little Orphan Annie,* and *Dick Tracy,* however. On October 22, 1934, Ohio's Milton Caniff provided *Terry and the Pirates* for the first time in newspaper pages. An incredible array of rogues and stereotypes populated *Terry* in the early years—dragon ladies, yellow perils, ruthless scoundrels, and the like. When World War II came around, *Terry and the Pirates* adjusted to the changing world culture. Dismayed at the way in which his comic strip had been taken over by the syndicate, Caniff left the work to pursue projects over which he had much more creative control. The most important result of this was his comic strip *Steve Canyon* (January 13, 1947 to June 5, 1988), a premiere adventure strip of the 1940s and 1950s.

A whole spectrum of adventure heroes and heroines populated the comic strips of the Great Depression. There were Vincent Hamlin's caveman, Alley Oop; Harold Foster's star of the Middle Ages, Prince Valiant; Lee Falk and Phil Davis's master prestidigitator, Mandrake the Magician; Alex Raymond's spaceman, Flash Gordon; Raymond's professional adventurer,

Jungle Jim; and Dashiell Hammett and Alex Raymond's crackerjack hard-boiled private investigator, Secret Agent X—to name but a few. The Adventure strip had established itself as the second and final comic strip genre. The cultural setting and the popularity of the comic strip as a periodic medium allowed this story form to flourish as never before—and never since. Today, as a result of a changing public, the arrival of new media to compete for public attention, and changing editorial policies of newspapers, the Adventure continuity is virtually extinct.

World War II saw the emphasis of the adventure story shift to themes of war and world conflict. At the same time, the domestic comedy presented family and pseudo-family life updated to accommodate domestic wartime concerns. The humanized animal remained a strength of this genre and in the 1950s continued to provide a vehicle for commentary on the day's events. In fact, in the 1950s, animals reached new heights in popularity as political crusaders during the postwar years. Perhaps the biggest contribution of the period was Walt Kelly's fictitious group from the Okefenokee Swamp.

The title character of Kelly's *Pogo* lived in a fantasy world where he was the moderator of a kaleidoscope of sociopolitical ideologies espoused by other animals. Pogo's first appearance was not in the newspaper comic strip medium, however. His was one of the rare cases of a character debuting in a comic book and then moving to a comic strip instead of the reverse. Walt Kelly's creation hit newspapers in 1948 and concluded July 20, 1975.

On October 2, 1950, a comic strip debuted that centered on a group of adults in children's bodies and on humanized animals. It starred the "everyman"—Charlie Brown—an autobiographical creation to whom we could all relate. Minnesota's Charles Schulz had produced the first of his famous *Peanuts* newspaper comic strips.

In the world of the newspaper comic strip

BIG LITTLE BOOKS

Whitman Publishing Company of Racine, Wisconsin published the first "Big Little Book" (BLB) in 1932. This book, about four inches wide, four a half inches tall, and one and one-half inch thick, was entitled *The Adventures of Dick Tracy* and featured a reprinted segment (although not the first) from Chester Gould's famous comic strip. In the course of the next sixteen years, hundreds of titles appeared (published by Whitman and about a dozen competitors), each of which sold thousands and hundreds of thousands of copies. Most BLBs adapted and reprinted famous newspaper comic strips. These books usually featured a page of illustration on the left page and text on the right. Many of these books numbered 424 pages or more in length. In some cases, BLBs were "All Pictures Comics" and simply reprinted one comic strip frame, in its entirety, on each page. The most popular BLBs reprinted comic strips featuring Dick Tracy, Orphan Annie, Mickey Mouse, Donald Duck, Flash Gordon, Buck Rogers, and Popeye. Less frequently, but still quite importantly, BLBs found their source material in motion pictures, movie serials, radio dramas, pulp magazines (such as *The Shadow*), and even early motion picture animation. The "Golden Age" for the BLB ran from 1932–38. In 1938, with its highly commercially successful product imitated and exploited by other North American publishers—in fact, the term "Big Little Book" now quite generic—Whitman decided to re-title its product "Better Little Books." Hence, the "Silver Age" of Big Little Books was ushered in; this lasted until about 1949. BLB history between 1950 and the late 1980s is divided into several smaller periods. Big Little Books were an important transitional medium between newspaper comic strips and comic books.

of the 1960s, Alex Raymond and Chic Young's Blondie, who had begun life as a flapper of the Roaring Twenties, was still an international favorite. Yet the world of the newspaper comic strip was changing. Comic strips were being allotted increasingly smaller spaces on the

FEATURE BOOKS

David McKay Publishers began its "Feature Book" series early in 1937. McKay's Feature Books were forerunners to what would eventually become recognized as a standard for comic books. They measured about $8^1/_4$ inches wide, $11^1/_4$ inches tall, and a quarter of an inch thick. It seems apparent that Feature Books took a great deal of their lead from Whitman Publishing's Big Little Books. The difference between the two print media was primarily in size and format and the fact that Feature Books reprinted comic strips largely unedited and unchanged. (Big Little Books were much more liberal in their editing of original comic strips and their presentations of these strips.) Like Big Little Books, McKay's product served as an important transitional medium between newspaper comic strips and comic books. In 1939, Dell Publishing introduced it oversized "Black and White" comic series, which, except for publisher, were essentially identical to McKay's product. Between 1941 and 1943, Dell continued its Black and White series as "Large Feature Comics." Prior to the advent of McKay's Feature Books and Dell's Black and White line, even the most avid of newspaper comic strip readers had had to wait months for their favorite newspaper strip story lines to reach completion, and it was very likely that in that period of several months the reader would miss some of the daily installments. In a sense, Feature Books and Black and White comics were the equivalent of today's trade paperbacks that reprint contemporary comic strips like Charles Schulz's *Peanuts*, Jim Davis's *Garfield*, and Patrick McDonnell's *Mutts*. Feature Books usually sold for ten cents apiece and featured famous comic strips like Chester Gould's *Dick Tracy*, Lee Falk and Phil Davis's *The Phantom* and *Mandrake the Magician*, E. C. Segar's *Popeye*, and Milton Caniff's *Terry and the Pirates*. These early forerunners of the comic book lasted until about 1948.

newspaper page. Gone were the days of the grandiose one-page color comics on Sundays. One of Schulz's innovations was his ability to perpetuate and create a comic strip that was designed for smaller spaces. Like *Blondie*, *Peanuts* enjoyed a period when it was the most widely read comic strip in the world. The heyday for *Peanuts* was the 1960s. Schulz's Charlie Brown made a television debut in *A Charlie Brown Christmas* on CBS in 1965.

Two new comic strips became immensely popular in the 1970s and 1980s. The first of these was Garry Trudeau's *Doonesbury*, which began on October 26, 1970, and continues to this day. The second was Berke Breathed's *Bloom County*, which ran from December 8, 1980 to August 6, 1989. *Bloom County* arose as a replacement for *Doonesbury* when Trudeau took a leave of absence from comics between January 1983 and September 1984. Trudeau and *Doonesbury* returned, but Breathed's very popular *Bloom County* continued also. In 1989, Breathed concluded his strip and replaced it with a new work called *Outland*, which continued some of the characters found in *Bloom County*. Trudeau and Breathed have been, as Walt Kelly was, political cartoonists with mastery of social satire.

In the 1980s and 1990s, the most popular comic strip was Bill Watterson's *Calvin and Hobbes*—a sort of hybrid of Crockett Johnson's *Barnaby* and Hank Ketcham's *Dennis the Menace*. Watterson's strip debuted on November 7, 1985, and concluded December 31, 1995. Like *Peanuts*, *Calvin and Hobbes* was tailored to make use of—rather than be hindered by—the constraints placed on comics in its time.

The comic strips of the early years of the twenty-first century that are popular are short gag strips. The most popular of these is Patrick McDonnell's *Mutts*—featuring Earl the dog and Mooch the cat.

COMIC BOOKS

The first comic book were collections of newspaper comic strips. In the broadest sense, some of these appeared as early as the 1890s, when newspaper strips were in their infancy. In a more strict sense, the periodic format that we recognize today as that of a comic book first appeared in the mid-1930s. At this time, comic books were recognized as saddle-stapled magazines with color covers and interiors and price tags of ten cents. Even though many still reprinted favorite newspaper comic strips of the day, they now also provided original stories that were scripted and drawn by people who worked exclusively for comic book publishers—not newspapers.

In the 1930s, pioneers of the comic book included M.C. Gaines, Will Eisner, Bob Kane, and Stan Lee. Like pulp magazines, comic books were sold on newsstands, at the corner store, and via subscriptions, delivered through the U.S. Mail. Like dime novels and pulps, comic books were sources of concern for the moral gatekeepers of society. Also like dime novels and pulps, comic books were considered ephemeral, disposable entertainments. Funny animals, detective heroes, Westerns, domestic comedies, adventure, romance, and a wide spectrum of other story types were the subject matters of these periodicals.

By the late 1930s, two of the most famous comic strip superheroes of all time made their respective debuts. In the pages of *Action Comics* #1, two Cleveland area high-schoolers named Siegel and Shuster introduced Superman. In the pages of *Detective Comics* #27, Bob Kane and Bill Kane introduced Batman. There were others. A few months later, Walt Disney studios marketed the first volume of *Walt Disney's Comics and Stories* with Dell Publishing. Soon there would be individual comic book titles for each of Disney's most popular characters from motion picture animation of the 1930s—Mickey Mouse and Donald Duck included. Almost all comic book publishers at this time were located in New York City.

When World War II came around, paper shortages were an issue for comic books as they were for pulp magazines and other periodicals. Comic books persisted, though some of their very famous creators—such as Will Eisner—left their work to serve in the military. Just prior to the war, Mickey Spillane got his start as a writer by authoring two-page fillers in comic books. These fillers helped make comic books eligible for distribution through the U.S. Mail. World War II comic books often featured military themes and story lines in which superheroes fought the Axis powers. These story lines were immensely popular at this time.

With the advent of the atomic bomb, the close of World War II, and the start of the Cold War, a new era in comic book publishing began. In 1945, industry pioneer M. C. Gaines established EC Comics (Educational Comics, later Entertaining Comics) to publish comic art adaptations from the Bible and from history. But the subject matter was too conventional, too familiar, and the company had to change its direction. Upon his father's death, Bill Gaines took over the company. A student of the Cold War, the vicious attacks of junior United States Senator Joseph McCarthy, and the overall popular culture of the day, Bill Gaines dramatically changed the content of his comic books, and the famous EC line of comic was born. Originally designed as forms of parody and entertainment, titles such as *Tales from the Crypt*, *Weird Science*, *Vault of Horror*, and more have been part of our lexicon ever since. Gaines introduced *MAD* comic book in 1952—the forerunner of *MAD* magazine. By 1954, some of Gaines's comic book publications were cited and reviled in Dr. Fredric Wertham's *Seduction of the Innocent*. In addition, at this time, Gaines appeared as a star witness at a U.S. congressional hearing convened to investigate the role of comic books in youth society at that time. Much like the Motion Picture Production Code of the Hays Office of 1930, the Comics Code was the result.

The comic book tales marketed by Bill Gaines are invaluable documents of their era. One very popular science fiction and fantasy writer of the day—Ray Bradbury—had a number of his *Weird Tales* pulp magazine stories adapted in Gaines's publications. Typically, many EC comic books contained four stories of about seven or eight pages apiece. The writers' and artists' use of plotting devices to develop story lines, build suspense, and leverage twist endings is an excellent study of and tribute to the short story form. Most of the famous EC line has been reprinted in recent years.

In the 1950s, Harvey Publishers brought us *Casper the Friendly Ghost* (begun by St. John Publishers in 1949), *Wendy the Good Little Witch*, *Little Audrey*, *Baby Huey*, *Herman and Catnip*, *Terrytoons*, George Baker's *Sad Sack*, and more.

By the late 1950s Dell, one of the pioneer publishers of comic books in the 1930s and 1940s, was finishing its four color series of comic books and giving way to Gold Key Publishers (an imprint Whitman Publishers in Racine, Wisconsin—creators of the Big Little Book in 1932). Gold Key titles included *Walt Disney's Comics and Stories*, *Walt Disney's Mickey Mouse*, *Walt Disney's Donald Duck*, *Walt Disney's Uncle Scrooge*, *Bugs Bunny*, *Porky Pig*, *Looney Tunes*, *Marge's Little Lulu*, *Doctor Solar*, *Magnus Robot Fighter*, *Tarzan*, and many others. By the early 1960s, Harvey and Gold Key were firmly entrenched as integral parts of American comic book culture, providing stories and art for readers who enjoyed funny animals and comedies as well as (or in place of) heroic adventures. The Comics Code was still firmly in place, and most high-volume, mainstream comic book publishers boasted adherence to it. (By the 1980s, on the other hand, flying in the face of the Code actually brought sales to smaller publishers.) Carl Barks was still the "Good Duck Artist" for Disney.

On the heroic adventure side, in the 1960s Stan Lee and his cohorts at Marvel seemed to be introducing smash hits at every turn. This was the era of the Fantastic Four, the X-Men, the Hulk, and many more. Meanwhile, it seemed that DC could produce, almost at will, Superman and Batman stories that were even better (if that was possible) than those of years past. Despite the world situation, it was a great time to be a kid, and a great time for comic books. For twenty-five cents, one could buy ten- or twelve-cent comic books and have change. Or one could buy a special twenty-five cent issue.

MAD magazine flourished in the 1960s, and so did extensions of the *MAD* ethos called underground comics. Such writers as R. Crumb and Art Spiegelman were establishing reputations for themselves that reflected the culture and subcultures of the day. By the late 1970s, direct marketing and specialized comic book shops became important avenues for comic book purchasing that remain vital today. Underground comics were and are sold through these venues. In the mid to late 1980s and early 1990s, Spiegelman's *Maus* stories received critical acclaim and earned him a Pulitzer Prize. In these stories, Spiegelman used animals (much as Aesop had millennia before) to comment on social issues. Specifically, the artist/writer addressed his heritage as the son of a survivor of the Nazi Holocaust.

Since about the 1970s, authors and editors such as Bill Blackbeard, Herb Galewitz, and Richard Marschall have collected and preserved classic newspaper comic strips in book form. Comic book stories have been preserved in books by other authorities. In the first decade of the twenty-first century, reprints of "Gold" and "Silver" age DC and Marvel comic book stories are very popular. DC has a very successful "DC Archive" series; Marvel has an equally successful "Marvel Milestones" series of archival/collectable-quality hardcovers. These command cover prices of $50 or more apiece. Less expensive paperback reprints of famous comic book stories are even more popular. For decades the popular EC Comics of the 1940s and 1950s have been reprinted in a variety of limited and mass-market formats. The last years have been a great time to purchase color facsimile reprints of very rare, very famous comic book stories.

Recent comic book stories have been collected in anthologies as well. Examples of these are Frank Miller's Dark Knight Batman sagas, Matt Groening's tales of the Simpsons, and Alan Moore's League of Extraordinary Gentlemen adventures. Original comic art and stories have debuted in such longer books. The term "graphic novel," which applies to all the above examples and more, is as broad and general as were terms such as "Big Little Book" and "Feature Book" during the Great Depression. One of the most successful graphic novels of recent years is Max Allan Collins and Richard Piers Rayner's *The Road to Perdition*, which was the basis for the 2002 blockbuster movie starring Paul Newman, Tom Hanks, Jude Law, and Daniel Craig. In recent decades, movies based on comic book series and graphic novels have been very popular. Since the 1990s there have been Spider-Man, X-Men, Superman, Hulk, Fantastic Four, and Batman movies, to name a few.

An important innovation in the comic strip, comic book, and related sequential art areas is the use of electronic or on-line formats. Computers and related technologies allow writers and artists storytelling and graphic art capabilities that have been previously unavailable.

CONTEMPORARY NEWSPAPERS AND MAGAZINES

According to "Media Power 50," published in the May 8, 2006, issue of *B2B*, newspaper circulations and newsstand sales have been dominated by super conglomerates such as *The Financial Times, Investor's Business Daily, The Wall Street Journal*, and *USA Today* ("flagship" of the Gannett Media Services). Classic Media Services (which includes the former Tribune Media Services) publishes major Chicago, New York, and Los Angeles newspapers. "Media Power 50" notes that *Investor's Business Daily* has a circulation of 237,407 papers. *The Financial Times* (which now competes with *The Wall Street Journal* for international business coverage) has a circulation of 137,845 papers and an advertising revenue of $270.9 million. *The New York Times* has a circulation of 1.1 million on weekdays and 1.7 million on Sundays, with an advertising revenue of $1.3 billion. *The Wall Street Journal* has a circulation of 1.8 million; *USA Today* has 2.3 million.

In an article for *Advertising Age* (August 23, 2004), Jon Fine provides a recent overview of paid circulations in consumer magazines. At the time of his article, Fine cited a six-month study of consumer magazine circulations that concluded June 30, 2004 (the Audit Bureau of Circulations Fas-Fax Report). According to the study, *AARP: The Magazine*, with a paid circulation of 22,720,073, was ranked number one. Following were *Reader's Digest* (10,228,531), *TV Guide* (9,016,188), *Better Homes and Gardens* (7,628,424), *National Geographic* (5,468,471), *Good Housekeeping* (4,623,113), *Family Circle* (4,372,813), *Ladies Home Journal* (4,108,619), *Woman's Day* (4,060,619), and *Time* (4,034,491). *People* ranked eleventh at 3,730,287; *Sports Illustrated* ranked sixteenth at 3,314,174; *Playboy* ranked seventeenth at 3,176,215. These were closely followed by *Newsweek, Cosmopolitan*, and *Guideposts*. Of course, these circulations and rankings are for paid subscriptions and do not account for newsstand sales. Certainly women's magazines such as *Better Homes and Gardens, Good Housekeeping, Family Circle, Ladies Home Journal*, and *Woman's Day* yield significant newsstand sales. Such is also the case with *TV Guide* and *Playboy*. Conversely, *Reader's Digest* and *National Geographic* are largely dependent on subscription sales and do not have the newsstand presence that the aforementioned magazines do. Celebrity magazines continued to maintain a significant market share. Magazines that target women in their twenties sold well. A general survey of the study Fine cites suggests that magazines that have grown most rapidly in paid subscriptions are news magazines and magazines that appeal to an aging "Baby Boomer" population.

Top circulating business magazines include *Barron's* (301,125), *Business 2.0* (600,000), *BusinessWeek* (988,068), *CFO Magazine* (450,000), *The Economist* (569,336), *Entrepreneur* (606,956), *Forbes* (900,000), *Fortune* (1,038,575 global), and *Inc.* (665,000). One page of advertising in *Fortune* costs $92,500, but this rate is not unique to *Fortune*. *Forbes* requires $96,150 per page of advertising, *BusinessWeek* $99,500. Top circulating trade magazines include *Aviation Week & Space Technology* (97,000), *Builder* (141,331), *Daily Variety* (60,300), *Hollywood Reporter* (29,090 daily), *Nation's Restaurant News* (78,000), and *Women's Wear Daily* (43,981).

Top circulating IT (information technology) magazines include *Baseline* (125,000), *CIO* (140,000), *Computerworld* (180,038), *EE Times* (150,000), *eWeek* (400,100), *Federal Computer Week* (102,467), *Information Week* (500,00), *Info World* (220,020), and *VARBusiness* (107,000).

POPULAR INTERNET/ELECTRONIC PERIODICALS

Circulations for Internet/electronic periodicals are measured in "unique monthly visitors." According to *The Daily*, top electronic periodicals and their respective monthly visitors include *Business.com* (4 million), *CNET Networks* (more than 6 million), *CNN.com* (21.2 million), *Forbes.com* (9.4 million), *Global Sources* (484,745), *GlobalSpec* (more than 2.5 million), *Google.com* (100.8 million use the search engine), *IndustryWeek.com* (100,000), *MSNBC.com* (27.2 million), *TechTarget.com* (4 million), *TechWeb* (more than 1.5 million), *ThomasNet* (2.5 million in March 2006), *WSJ.com* (761,000 paid subscribers), and *Yahoo!* (119.1 million use the search engine).

On August 22, 2006, Reuters reported that newsstand sales of magazines declined four percent in the first half of 2006 in comparison to similar magazines sales for the same period in 2005. This news service also reported that *Time* magazine reported that it lost 24 percent in newsstand sales. Several explanations for fewer newsstand sales are advanced in this report, including the increased popularity of Web-based news reporting. Interestingly, overall magazine circulation (including subscription circulation) increased 2 percent for the period.

The Internet also provides sports results more quickly than traditional magazines do. Because of this, sports magazines have had to alter their approaches to become more analytical. The end result is that electronic and print periodicals have complemented each other and in some ways have expanded their collective circulations (a phenomenon referred to as "the Web effect").

PERIODICAL PUBLISHING IN CANADA

Publishers of periodicals in Canada have seen a healthy increase in circulations and revenues in recent years. In an article from *The Daily* (published in June 2005) entitled "Periodical Publishing," new data from the *Periodical Publishing Survey* indicates that industry revenues hit nearly $1.6 billion in 2003, up 56.5 percent from 1993. In 1993, 1,256 publishers produced 1,678 titles with a total annual circulation of 575 million copies. In 2003, 1,633 publishers produced 2,383 periodicals and sold nearly 778 million copies. Advertising revenues hit $993.5 million in 2003. Business and trade magazines derived 84 percent of their revenues from advertising; general consumer magazines revenues earned 56 percent from advertising. As is the case throughout North America, publishers of paper-based periodicals have had increased competition for circulations and advertising dollars from Internet, television, and related media. English-language magazines are more dependent on advertising for revenues than French-language magazines are.

For many years, the most popular magazine in Canada has been *Reader's Digest*. The March 31, 2005, issue of *The Globe and Mail* reports that the circulation for *Reader's Digest* declined from 7.7 million in 2004 to 7.4 million in 2005. This same article states that nine of the top ten magazines in Canada experienced declines in readership from 2004 to 2005.

RESOURCE GUIDE

PRINT SOURCES

Ashley, Mike. *The Time Machines: The Story of the Science Fiction Magazines from the Beginning to 1950*. Liverpool: Liverpool University Press, 2000.

———. *Transformations: The Story of the Science Fiction Magazines from 1950 to 1970*. Liverpool: Liverpool University Press, 2005.

Blackbeard, Bill, and Dale Crain, eds. *The Comic Strip Century*. Englewood Cliffs, NJ: O.G. Publishing, 1995.

Blackbeard, Bill, and Martin Williams, eds. *The Smithsonian Collection of Newspaper Comics*. Washington, DC: Smithsonian Institution Press, and New York: Harry N. Abrams, 1977.

Bleiler, E. F. *Science-Fiction: The Early Years*. Kent, OH: Kent State University Press, 1990.

———. *Science-Fiction: The Gernsback Years*. Kent, OH: Kent State University Press, 1998.

———, ed. *Eight Dime Novels*. New York: Dover, 1974.

Carr, Nick. *Masters of the Pulps: The Collected Essays of Nick Carr*. Winchester, VA: Wildcat Books, 2006.

Ellis, Doug, John Locke, and John Gunnison. *The Adventure House Guide to the Pulps*. Silver Springs, MD: Adventure House, 2000.

Fine, Jon. "New Celeb Titles Rack Up Big Gains at the Newsstand." *Advertising Age* 75.34 (2004, August 23): 30.

Goodstone, Tony, ed. *The Pulps: Fifty Years of American Popular Culture*. New York: Chelsea House, 1970.

Goulart, Ron. *The Adventurous Decade: Comic Strips in the Thirties*. New Rochelle, NY: Arlington House, 1975. (Reprint, New Castle, PA: Hermes, 2005.)

———. *Cheap Thrills: The Amazing! Thrilling! Astonishing! History of Pulp Fiction*. New Rochelle, NY: Arlington House, 1972. (Reprint, New Castle, PA: Hermes, 2006.)

Hoppenstand, Gary. *The Dime Novel Detective*. Bowling Green, OH: Bowling Green State University Popular Press, 1982.

Hutchinson, Don, ed. *Scarlet Riders: Pulp Fiction Tales of the Mounties*. Oakville, Ontario: Mosaic Press, 1998.

Jones, Daryl. *The Dime Novel Western*. Bowling Green, OH: The Popular Press, 1978.

Jones, Robert Kenneth. *The Shudder Pulps*. West Linn, OR: FAX Collector's Editions, 1975.

Locke, John, and John Wooley, eds. *Thrilling Detective Heroes*. Silver Spring, MD: Adventure House, 2006.

Lowery, Lawrence F. *The Collector's Guide to Big Little Books and Similar Books*. Danville, CA: Education Research and Applications Corporation, 1981.

"Media Power 50." *B2B* 91.6 (2006, May 8), 36–44.

"Nine of Top 10 Magazines Lost Readers; Report on Business Magazine Sees Gain." *The Globe and Mail* (Canada) (2005, March 31): 82.

Nye, Russel B. *The Unembarrassed Muse: The Popular Arts in America*. New York: Dial Press, 1970.

Overstreet, Robert M. *The Comic Book Price Guide*, 37th edition. Cleveland, TN: Overstreet Publications, 2007.

Patrick, Mike. "The Web Effect—on Magazine Publishing Industry." *The Magazine for Magazine Management* (2000, November).

Powell, Chris. "Mag Readership Steady, Despite Online Growth." *Marketing Magazine* 111.15 (2006, April 17): 20.

Reuters. "Newsstand Magazine Sales Fell in the First Six Months of 2006." *The New York Times* (2006, August 22): Section C, Column 1; Business/Financial Desk, 5.

Roberts, Garyn G. *Dick Tracy and American Culture: Morality and Mythology, Text and Context*. Jefferson, NC: McFarland, 1993.

———. "Hugo Gernsback." Pp. 96–103 in Sam G. Riley (ed.), *Dictionary of Literary Biography 137: American Magazine Journalists, 1900–1960, Second Series*. Columbia, SC: Bruccoli Layman Clark, 1994.

————. "Joseph T. Shaw." Pp. 283–88 in Sam G. Riley (ed.), *Dictionary of Literary Biography 137: American Magazine Journalists, 1900–1960, Second Series*. Columbia, SC: Bruccoli Layman Clark, 1994.

————. "Understanding the Sequential Art of Comic Strips and Comic Books and Their Descendants in the Early Years of the New Millennium." *Journal of American Culture* 27. 2 (2004, June): 210–217.

————, ed. *The Prentice Hall Anthology of Science Fiction and Fantasy*. Upper Saddle River, NJ: Prentice Hall, 2001.

————, Gary Hoppenstand, and Ray B. Browne, eds. *Old Sleuth's Freaky Female Detectives (From the Dime Novels)*. Bowling Green, OH: Bowling Green State University Popular Press, 1990.

Robinson, Frank M., and Lawrence Davidson. *Pulp Culture: The Art of Fiction Magazines*. Portland, OR: Collector's Press, 1998.

Rouse, William Merriam, and Miriam DuBois Babcock. *The Pulps, The Adirondacks and Coon Mountain Bill*. Shelbourne, Ontario: Battered Silicon Dispatch Box, 2006.

Sampson, Robert. *Deadly Excitements, Shadows and Phantoms*. Bowling Green, OH: Bowling Green State University Press, 1989.

————. *The Night Master (The Shadow)*. Chicago: Pulp Press, 1982.

————. *Spider!* Bowling Green, OH: Bowling Green State University Press, 1987.

————. *Yesterday's Faces*. 5 vols. Bowling Green, OH: Bowling Green State University Popular Press, 1983–91.

Seelye, Katharine Q. "Newspaper Circulation Falls Sharply." *The New York Times* (2006, October 31): Section C; Column 6; Business/Financial Desk, 1.

Smith, Anthony. *The Newspaper: An International History*. London: Thames and Hudson, 1979.

Stepp, Carl Sessions. "Why Do People Read Newspapers?" *American Journalism Review* (2003, December/ 2004, January), 64–69.

Tebbel, John. *The Media in America*. New York: Signet Books (imprint of New American Library), 1976.

Weinberg, Robert. *The Weird Tales Story*. West Linn, OR: FAX, 1977. Rockville, MD: Wildside, 2001.

WEBSITES

California State University, Los Angeles. Asian Pacific Business Institute. *Popular Newspapers Listing*. http://www.calstatela.edu/centers/apbi/popularnews.htm. Includes links to the Websites of the most popular U.S. newspapers.

Magazine City, LLC. *[magazine]city*. http://www.magazinecity.com/. One of the largest magazine subscription sources on the web.

Magazines Canada. http://www.cmpa.ca/home.php. Website for Canada's leading professional magazine industry association.

onlinenewspapers.com. *Canada Newspapers Listing*. http://www.onlinenewspapers.com/canada.htm. Site includes links to hundreds of Canadian newspapers, as well as other news sites around the world.

"Periodical Publishing." *The Daily*. Updated Wednesday, June 8, 2005. http://www.statcan.ca/Daily/english/050608/do05608a.htm.

Queen's University Library. *Popular Magazines Listing*. http://library.queensu.ca/reference/magazines.htm. Includes links to the Websites of the most popular Canadian and U.S. magazines.

Tucows Inc. *News Directory*. http://www.ecola.com/. A guide to all online English-language media, including newspapers, magazines, and comics.

POPULAR MAGAZINES

Business and Technology

Business Week. McGraw-Hill,1929, http://www.BusinessWeek.com.

Forbes. Forbes, 1917, http://www.Forbes.com.

Wired. Conde Nast, 1993, http://www.Wired.com.

Children and Young Adult

Boys' Life. Boy Scouts of America, 1911, http://www.boyslife.org.
Children's Digest. Children's Better Health Institute, 1950, http://www.cbhi.org/magazines/childrensdigest.
Disney Adventures. Walt Disney, 1990, http://www.disney.go.com/DisneyAdventures.
Highlights for Children. Highlights Magazine, 1946, http://www.highlights.com.
Nickelodeon. Nickelodeon TV, 1990, http://www.nick.com.
Seventeen. Hearst Corporation, 1944, http://www.seventeen.com.
Sports Illustrated for Kids. Sports Illustrated, 1989, http://www.sikids.com.
Weekly Reader. Weekly Reader Publishing, 1928, http://www.weeklyreader.com.

Comics

Action Comics. DC Publications, 1938, http://www.dccomics.com.
Amazing Spider–Man. Marvel Comics, 1963, http://www.marvel.com.
Superman. DC Publications, 1939, http://www.dccomics.com.

Entertainment

Ebony. Johnson, 1945, http://www.ebonyjet.com.
Entertainment Weekly. Time, 1990, http://www.ew.com.
In Style. Time, 1995, http://InStyle.com.
Jet. Johnson, 1951, http://www.jetmag.com.
New Yorker, The. New Yorker, 1925, http://www.newyorker.com.
O, the Oprah Magazine. Hearst, 2000, http://www.oprah.com/omagazine.
People. Time, 1974, http://www.people.com.
Rolling Stone. Wenner, 1967, http://www.rollingstone.com
Soap Opera Digest. Soap Opera Digest, 1975, http://www.soapoperadigest.com.
TV Guide. Triangle Publications, 1953, http://www.TVGuide.com.
Vanity Fair. Conde Nast, 1913, http://www.vanityfair.com.

Fashion and Beauty

Cosmopolitan. Hearst, 1886, http://www.cosmopolitan.com.
Esquire. Hearst, 1933, http://www.esquire.com.
Glamour. Hearst, 1939, http://www.glamour.com.
GQ. Conde Nast, 1931, http://www.men.style.com/gq.
Modern Bride. http://ModernBride.com.
Vogue. 1916, Conde Nast, http://www.style.com/vogue.

Home and Cooking

Architectural Digest. Conde Nast, 1920, http://www.architecturaldigest.com.
Better Homes & Gardens. Meredith, 1922, http://www.bhg.com.
Bon Appetit. Conde Nast, http://www.epicurious.com/bonapettit.
Cooking Light. Southern Progress, 1987, http://www.cookinglight.com.
Country Living. Hearst, 1978, http://www.countryliving.com.
Good Housekeeping (Home & Garden). Hearst, 1888, http://www.goodhousekeeping.com.
Gourmet. Conde Nast, 1941, http://www.epicurious.com/gourmet.
Martha Stewart Living. Martha Stewart, 1993, http://www.marthastewart.com/living.

News and Current Events

American Spectator, The. The American Spectator, LLC. 1967, http://www.spectator.org.
Atlantic Monthly. National Journal Group, 1857, http://www.theatlantic.com
Economist, The. The Economist Newspaper Ltd., 1843, http://www.economist.com.
Harper's. Lapham and MacArthur, 1850, http://www.harpers.org.
Mother Jones. Foundation for National Progress, 1976, http://www.motherjones.com.
Nation, The. The Nation, 1865, http//:www.TheNation.com.
National Review. National Review, Inc., 1955, http://www.nationalreview.com.
Newsweek. Washington Post, 1933, http://www.newsweek.com.
National Geographic. National Geographic Society, 1888, http://www.ngm.com.
Reader's Digest. Reader's Digest, 1922, http://www.rd.com.
Smithsonian. Smithsonian Institute, 1970, http://www.smithsonianmagazine.si.edu.
Time. Time Warner, 1923, http://www.time.com.

Sports, Hobbies, and Leisure

Car & Driver. Hachette Filipacchi Media, 1955, http://www.caranddriver.com.
Cigar Aficionado. Shanken, 1992, http://www.cigaraficionado.com.
ESPN the Magazine. Walt Disney, 1998, http://www.insider.espn.go.com.
Field & Stream. Field and Stream, 1873, http://www.fieldandstream.com.
Golf Digest. Advance, 1985, http://www.golfdigest.com.
Muscle and Fitness. American Media, 1996, http://www.muscleandfitness.com.
Outside. Outside, 1978, http://www.outside.away.com.
Popular Mechanics. Hearst, 1902, http://www.popularmechanics.com.
Runners' World. Random House, 1996, http://www.runnersworld.com.
Sports Illustrated. Time Warner, 1954, http://www.sportsillustrated.cnn.com.

Popular Newspapers

Boston Globe. New York Times, 1872, http://www.boston.com/news/globe.
Chicago Tribune. Tribune Company, 1847, http://chicagotribune.com.
Financial Times. Pearson PLC, 1888, http://www.ft.com.
Los Angeles Times. Tribune Company, 1881, http://www.latimes.com.
New York Times. New York Times Company, 1851, http://www.nytimes.com.
San Francisco Chronicle. Hearst, 1865, http://www.sfgate.com.
USA Today. Gannett, 1982, http://www.usatoday.com.
Wall Street Journal. Dow Jones and Company, 1889, http://www.WSJ.com.
Washington Post. Washington Post Company, 1877, http://www.washingtonpost.com.

LITERATURE

LITERATURE: For many years, romance novelist Nora Roberts has awarded a creative writing scholarship (currently $20,000) to a promising senior at Boonsboro High School, near her rural Maryland home. She personally judges the entries. © AP Photo/Herald-Mail, Ric Dugan.

LITERATURE: Oprah Winfrey (right) talks with author Toni Morrison (left), whose book *Song of Solomon* became an Oprah's Book Club selection in 1996—some 19 years after its original publication. Publishers have printed hundreds of thousands of hardback and paperback copies of Morrison's 1977 novel. © Reuters/Corbis.

LOVE, SEX, AND MARRIAGE

LOVE, SEX, AND MARRIAGE: Young couple enjoying a nice day in the park in New York. © photographer: Lucian Coman; agency: Dreamstime.com.

LOVE, SEX, AND MARRIAGE: Stephanie Hoplens and Katt Mathias smile toward the crowd after their marriage ceremony under a gazebo on a float at the 26th annual gay pride parade in San Francisco, 1996. © AP Photo/Lacy Atkins.

MUSIC

MUSIC: Elvis Presley in Norman Taurog's film, *Speedway* (1968). Courtesy of Photofest.

MUSIC: Shown from left: Johnny Ramone, Joey Ramone, and Dee Dee Ramone in Jim Fields and Michael Gramaglia's film, *The End of the Century* (2004). Courtesy of Photofest.

PERIODICALS

PERIODICALS: Mary-Kate Olsen and Ashley Olsen autograph a *People* magazine at the premiere of their film *New York Minute* held at Grauman's Chinese Theatre in Los Angeles, 2004. © AP Photo/Chris Polk.

RADIO AND TELEVISION

RADIO AND TELEVISION: Johnny Carson interviews David Letterman on *The Tonight Show*, which aired on NBC from 1952–1992. Courtesy of Photofest.

RADIO AND TELEVISION: Shown from left, back: Garrett Morris, Jane Curtin, Bill Murray, Dan Aykroyd, (front) John Belushi, Laraine Newman, and Gilda Radner from *Saturday Night Live*, 1977. Courtesy of Photofest.

RADIO AND TELEVISION: Actor Lorne Greene is seen wearing his western costume from the TV series *Bonanza*, 1964. © AP Photo.

SPORTS AND RECREATION

SPORTS AND RECREATION: Lance Armstrong on the Alpe D'Huez time trial during the 2004 Tour de France. Courtesy of Shutterstock.

SPORTS AND RECREATION: Nascar racers Dale Earnhardt Jr. (# 8) and Jimmie Johnson (# 48) are neck and neck in a 2004 race in Florida. Courtesy of Shutterstock.

SPORTS AND RECREATION: Boxer Muhammad Ali lands a punch during a 1973 fight with Ken Norton. Courtesy of Photofest.

THEATER AND PERFORMANCE

THEATER AND PERFORMANCE: Mary Martin stars as Maria Rainer in Vincent J. Donehue's Broadway production of *The Sound of Music*. Courtesy of Photofest.

THEATER AND PERFORMANCE: A grand scene from Rouben Mamoulian's Broadway production of *Oklahoma*. Courtesy of Photofest.

TRANSPORTATION AND TRAVEL

TRANSPORTATION AND TRAVEL: Model T Ford touring car from 1920. Within a few years of its introduction in 1908, the Model T Ford was the world's most available, affordable, and practical car. © Kasiden / Dreamstime.com.

TRANSPORTATION AND TRAVEL: An aerial view of the interstate just outside Dallas, Texas. Courtesy of Shutterstock.

RADIO AND TELEVISION

JENNIFER DeFORE

The best way to understand what radio and television have become in the present day is by looking first at their pasts. The development of radio and television in North America, encompassing both the United States and Canada, was a journey involving many people and many diverse paths. Radio and television were brand-new media for dispersing information and entertainment and also proved to be the spiritual heirs of newspapers and of advertising through technology's ability to promote and sell. Radio was born first through changes in wireless telegraph technology, initially viewed as an improved way to communicate with ships at sea. It grew over time and through the ingenuity of many inventors and investors to become of monumental importance to both military and recreational needs. People were suddenly connected in ways they had never imagined, sharing knowledge and experience through radio dramas, commentators, and news programs. Commerce also changed in the face of radio, as advertisements were included in (and sponsored) radio broadcasts. The nature of radio content altered with the introduction of its greatest competitor, television, to provide more general entertainment, but its position as a major source of information was already well-established and it persevered.

Great advances in technology in modern times have also challenged radio to innovate and improve to remain vital. Radio has undergone a transformation of sorts, as it has evolved from a familiar portable device to more digital formats. Radio today can be had conveniently on the Internet, through such services as iTunes and other sources. iPods also pose a threat to radio and even television as many listeners customize their content with this handy device and listen far less to conventional radio—users are able to download and save songs as well as radio and television broadcasts. "Webisodes" of television shows now air on the Internet. Even cell phones offer the capability to download music and other content. Radio has also moved to the stars as satellite radio has swept the world in recent years, with familiar radio programs such as *The Howard Stern Show* and newly developed and more experimental programs, delivered commercial-free with the purchase of a specialized receiver. Some of the most popular satellite radio providers in America are XM Satellite Radio, Sirius, and Clear Channel, which also provide Internet radio; these companies also have Canadian subsidiaries to serve the north. Radio and television technology is looking up—literally.

With the creation of television, people witnessed the fruition of the advances radio had begun—the next big step in communication. For the first time, people were not only able to hear others across vast distances, but they could see them as well, albeit only in black-and-white at the beginning. It was a step that made many unsure, as technology had leapt ahead of the production of actual television programs, but one that forever altered the way people experienced life. Events such as the first landing on the Moon were broadcast to an astonished audience. Sitcoms and commercials were created with equal care and increasing cost, and beloved television characters were viewed as almost part of the family. The introduction of color, increased programming, and technological advances helped to make television watching one of the most popular leisure activities in North America, which it remains to this day.

Television has evolved in much the same way as radio, changing its format and content to meet new needs. The advent of cable television allowed for more experimental programming, as did subscription cable television services such as HBO. In current day, favorite television programs from yesterday and today, such as the classic comedy *Seinfeld*, are also being released onto DVD, promoting a growing nostalgia culture that is sweeping America as Baby Boomers and Generation X age. Obscure television shows that did not immediately catch on with the public are also gaining a new half-life in DVD form. In addition, television performance has raced forward, as high-definition flat-screen televisions and plasma televisions offer viewers spectacular image clarity to complement the highly populated and diverse television landscape.

America currently has numerous radio and television stations, far exceeding anything the early inventors could have imagined. As of 2006 the United States broadcasts 4,789 AM radio stations, 8,961 FM radio stations, and 19 shortwave stations, as well as 2,218 broadcast television stations.[1] The United States receives television stations from Canada (such as MuchMusic), Spanish language content (such as Telemundo), and Canadian and Mexican radio online and from broadcasters near the U.S. borders. Canada has far fewer stations currently, owing to its large land mass and smaller population focused in a smaller area (much of the population being within 100 miles of the American border). It broadcasts approximately 245 AM radio stations, 582 FM radio stations, and 6 shortwave stations (2004 statistics), in addition to 80 television broadcast stations and several repeater stations (1997 data).[2] Much of Canada's radio and television programming comes from America, though Canada balances this with a required amount of Canadian content that must be broadcast per day, often through local radio and television stations with local interests. By 2003, 99 million U.S. households had radio, and there were 260 million television sets in homes.[3] In Canada in 2000 there were 1,047 radios and about 708 television sets for every 1,000 people.[4]

With the growth of the two media came debate over how best to use them, for both profit and to promote the public interest. American law struggled to stay ahead of the rapid advances in technology, moving from a cautious but relatively open attitude in the early days of the media to a more stringent "cracking down" on obscenity, sexuality, and violence, whether in song lyrics or television programs and even commercials. Where once the two industries were opposed and battling for content, they now share similar difficulties in determining what content is acceptable and what topics are inappropriate. As attitudes toward such social issues change and the appetite for more extreme content increases, radio and television are poised at a crossroads in both subject matter and how to present it. Radio, television, and the world are moving ahead at great speed and we are all along for the ride.

COMPLETING A PUZZLE: THE EARLY DAYS OF RADIO

Radio as we know it today did not come into its own until the early twentieth century, but the concepts behind its development were fostered long before through the combined efforts of several visionaries and experimenters. Radio in its fully developed state can best be viewed as a large puzzle to which various thinkers added separate pieces, gradually forming a fascinating whole. The pieces in this case were technological advances and innovations. The telegraph had been in existence since the 1840s and the telephone since the 1870s. These were two important progenitors of the concepts that would be needed to produce radio. Various other forms of media and communication, such as the booming newspaper industry in the 1830s and the widespread use of the camera in the 1860s, also helped to pave the way for greater developments in later years and prepared people for the changes that television would also bring about.

Important discoveries appeared quickly in the late nineteenth century. In 1873 James Clerk Maxwell posited the existence of invisible wavelike electromagnetic energy, similar to light, that laid the groundwork for further exploration.[5] German scientist Heinrich Hertz followed up on this notion by conducting experiments in which he detected and created these waves, consequently known as "radio waves." Inspired thinkers across the globe sought to harness this newly discovered energy, whose major function then was facilitation of contact between ships at sea and ships and land in a wireless communication system. This improved Morse code was transmitted by telegraph and was commonly used at the time. What was developed in this time period was still little more than wireless telegraphing, but the technological and intellectual pieces were moving into place for larger innovation.

Most notable among experimenters at the time was the maverick inventor Guglielmo Marconi, credited with the first successful rudimentary radio transmissions. It was Marconi who helped most to reveal the completed puzzle that his forbearers had begun. In 1895, Marconi transmitted a message by radio waves one-and-a-half miles across his father's Italian estate.[6] Marconi was able to patent this discovery in England under the auspices of the English postal system, which controlled all forms of communications in the country, though he was later to start his own company to avoid British officials attempting to apply for licenses on his patent. The Marconi Company began its fruitful career by providing communication for the British military during the Boer War in South Africa, and by the dawn of the twentieth century Marconi had established the American arm of his company to great fanfare in the United States. Marconi's understanding of radio and its potential grew swiftly, and in 1901 he transmitted the first transatlantic radio signals. His success gained him joint ownership of the Nobel Prize in 1909, quite a feat for an amateur inventor.

Early Radio Development in the United States

Marconi's wealth by 1913 was such that he was able to acquire the bankrupted United Wireless Company, giving him unmitigated control over wireless communication in the United States. The technology he used was based on the original "point-to-point" method of telegraphic communication used for contact across the sea. The former owner of the defunct United Wireless Company, Lee De Forest, however, had created a device that would help lead to the creation of true broadband communication and radio—the Audion tube—which was essentially an updated vacuum tube. Bell Telephone purchased the rights to De Forest's invention in 1913. At the same time, other inventors such as Edwin H. Armstrong helped to create and patent the many devices and technological advances from which radio would soon emerge.

Another innovator who would come to have a defining effect on the development of radio (and later television) was a gifted youngster named David Sarnoff. As a teenager, Sarnoff joined American Marconi and quickly gained a certain reputation for daring and bold corporate maneuvering. As an inventor, Sarnoff envisioned how wireless communication could advance—from basic point-to-point contact with ships to large-scale communication—and provide greater profit to companies.

Conflict brewed at this time between competing holders of the wireless communication patents. American legislation had forced the companies to work together, but following World War I the United States saw that, if the Marconi Company retained control over the industry, Great Britain would be the most formidable power in communications. General Electric (GE) in the United States sought to buy American Marconi, while still managing the Marconi Company under the subsidiary Radio Corporation of America (RCA). RCA stock was held by many major communications companies—GE, Westinghouse, and American Telephone and Telegraph (AT&T). Sarnoff moved to RCA when the takeover occurred and helped to build his notion of "broadcasting" from a new base of operations.

In spite of Sarnoff's efforts, however, the broadcasting idea first flowered in the offices of Westinghouse, when an engineer, Frank Conrad, transmitted music to amateur operators listening to ship signals. Notice was taken of Conrad's ingenuity, and the purchase of amateur receiving sets was promoted. Westinghouse altered a radiotelegraph transmitter to handle "radiotelephony" and on November 2, 1920, brought this to the public in the form of radio station KDKA in Pittsburgh, Pennsylvania. WWJ in Detroit, Michigan, also broadcast at this time.[7] News and music were the first content to filter to the excited masses in the first official radio program. KDKA's success spawned several stations, and nearly 600 were licensed by 1922.[8] Sarnoff's clever marketing of the newborn radio programming through broadcast of the famous Jack Dempsey–George Carpentier boxing match in 1921 helped to boost sales of receiver sets. Through his efforts and the efforts of others, RCA moved to the forefront in sales and profit.

Sarnoff helped form the first radio broadcast network, the National Broadcasting Company (NBC), officially starting service in 1927 and gradually splitting into two stations, one of which was sold later to the American Broadcasting Company (ABC). Competition to NBC manifested in the fledging company Columbia Broadcasting Company (CBS), which was run by William S. Paley in 1928 and continued as a serious competitor to NBC. These stations opened the doors to the broadcasting that made radio a familiar part of American life at the time.

In the early days of American radio, several memorable programs stood out, most often providing music. Important radio programs were not produced exclusively in one specific area of the country, though currently radio stations in California often predominate in popularity, and the nation's largest radio station, Westwood One (managed by CBS Radio), is in New York City. Radio programs in the early days were produced in all corners of the nation and often transmitted cross-country if the popularity was sufficient. Many of these programs were transmitted across the border to Canada as well and aided its developing radio industry and fed an entertainment-hungry audience. Radio, as it was then and is now, was financed by sponsors and advertisements.

An early program of great importance was the *A&P Gypsies* in 1924. The show ran in later evening until 1936 and featured orchestra music suitable for the entire family. It was carried on six stations and beginning in 1926 was broadcast countrywide by NBC. *The Grand Ole Opry* proved to be the single most popular country-western radio program in history. Debuting in Nashville in 1925 on WSM, it remained on air through 1957, when it went into syndication, and continues to broadcast today. And in 1928, *Amos 'n' Andy* was first broadcast and remained on air an astounding 34 years. *Amos 'n' Andy* was significant in that it featured both white and African-American actors, though it presented a racist view of the African-American community in its portrayal of two down-and-out Harlem taxi drivers and their circle of friends. The program spawned a televisions series in 1951 that was canceled in spite of its popularity, at the behest of civil rights organizations.

Beyond the development of radio entertainment programs, radio news programs were also being produced, and with them came great changes in the nature of American radio. Early news commentators sought to put context on events in the confusing and fearful post-World War I period of the 1920s. In 1922 the first radio news commentary was heard, broadcast by Hans V. Kaltenborn from station WVP, which soon lead to a weekly news series. Kaltenborn was unique in that he was gifted with total recall and could repeat political speeches flawlessly and so react more naturally to them in his programs; additionally his German background led him to cover Adolf Hitler's rise to power and made him a figure of great admiration and a favorite of several presidents.[9] Commentators following Kaltenborn, often far from objective, spiced their reports with their opinions and attitudes and developed an entirely new genre of news reporting. However, where some were quite outspoken, others, such as Edward R. Murrow, took a more understated and analytic approach that brought them fame and respect. Evangelist Aimee Semple McPherson was a notable woman in the new field as well. This method of news reporting took on amazing popularity, and the number of commentators exploded by the 1940s.

Difficulties in defining the role of the commentator as opposed to newscasters and news analysts eventually demanded changes in policy. In 1933 an agreement was reached between networks and press associations that limited the daily number of newscasts that could be broadcast but placed no limits on the amount of commentaries that covered the news in a general way and allowed for commentaries to be sponsored like regular radio. Sponsorship lead naturally to greater amounts of advertisements being placed in news broadcasts. News broadcasts by commentators were encroaching on the territory of newspapers and threatening their livelihood. Commentators in later years were made to refrain from editorializing the news as well, particularly following the advent of World War II. The Federal Communications Commission (FCC) in 1941 issued the Mayflower Decision, which halted editorializing by broadcasters, and then reversed the decision with the Fairness Doctrine in 1949.[10] This was not the first debate over content that radio was to experience in the United States.

Radio commentators at this time also organized to protect their rights and in particular fight the "middle commercial" in broadcasts, which interrupted reports.[11] Some commentators, however, appeared to embrace advertising during broadcasting. Commercials in this time were often for household goods.

Advertising in the United States at this time was in something of a flux. Starting in the 1920s the radio industry provided a new medium for companies to promote their wares and proved to be increasingly effective. Advertisements were rather generic at the time, treating the audience as a homogenous group and pushing a "soft sell" approach.[12] Gradually economic hardships of the Great Depression and World War II changed the attitude of advertising to a "hard sell" approach, pushing consumers to buy rather than encouraging. Advertising generated great controversy at this time, as it was seen as manipulative and frivolous in the face of national uncertainty and poverty. The notion of "name brand" products, such as Campbell's soup and Gillette razors, was developing and companies sought to make consumers believe in the superiority of their brand names.[13] In the flurry to promote products and with the market flooded, falsified and fraudulent advertisements became an issue as well. In spite of conflict, advertisers did provide a boon to the listening public in that they sponsored radio shows that brought entertainment to an anxious populace. And following

QUIZ SHOWS

Quiz shows took America by storm beginning in the 1930s. Most often children participated in shows such as *The Quiz Kids*, running from 1940 to 1954, in which they answered brainteasing questions to win prizes, often money. Many of these children went on to fame from their radio appearances. Other notable radio quiz shows were *Quiz of Two Cities* (1944–46), in which contestants from two opposing cities competed to win fabulous prizes, and *Quick as a Flash* (1944–51), in which contestants were drawn from the audience to answer questions based on mystery drama sketches. Another massively popular radio program was *The $64 Question*, which, in the 1950s, transformed into the television show *The $64,000 Question*.

When television quiz shows took off in the 1950s, the genre was also rife with accusations of cheating and rigged shows, which denigrated the respectability of such programming. In particular the show *Twenty One* came under heavy fire and faced a lawsuit for its rigged competitions.

World War II, when the economy entered a sudden upswing, advertisers provided products for newly flush consumers to spend money on.

The radio became a political tool at this time as well, beyond the diatribes of commentators. President Franklin D. Roosevelt often used radio as a means to connect with the American public, explaining the turmoil of America's situation via radio in a series of "fireside chats." The radio became an early way for the government and the public to connect in a more personal fashion.

Along with other genres of radio entertainment, soap operas were established in this era and continue with great popularity on television (with some programs broadcasting on radio as well). These early soap operas set the tone for the radio soaps that would follow, as well as television soaps beginning in the 1940s. Aimed at women working at home, the shows typically told stories of a heroine's adventurous life and romantic entanglements. A classic of the genre was *The Romance of Helen Trent*, running from 1933 to 1960 on CBS in mid-afternoons. In the daytime, women were the target of much programming and advertising in general, with programs that offered housekeeping tips and cooking advice and that were often sponsored by companies that sold household goods relevant to women. Radio was learning to market to different audiences, and in other times of the day, when men and children returned home, programming typically changed to more family-oriented shows and children's programs. Viewer stereotypes would not change much over time.

Other genres of radio programs grew in this time and produced quite a few classics, particularly in adventure and sleuth programs. One of the most popular was *The Adventures of Dick Tracy*, running from 1935 to 1948 on NBC and ABC, based on the famous comic strip by Chester Gould. Broadcast primarily in the early evenings, it catered mostly to young boys. *The Adventures of Ellery Queen* ran approximately the same span of years on nearly all major stations, but considerably later in the evening as it was meant for an older and more discerning audience. This series lives on in a magazine, *Ellery Queen's Mystery Magazine*, the longest running mystery anthology magazine in American history.[14] Dark and brooding anti-heroes appeared in the form of characters such as *The Shadow*, a mystery program that ran in the evening and night from 1930 to the mid-1950s on CBS and NBC. Actor Frank Readick, Jr., made The Shadow a household name. People of all ages listened with anticipation of The Shadow's latest adventure and caught crook.

Children's programming also appeared more at this time, such as *Jack Armstrong, The All-American Boy*, which ran from 1933 until 1950 in the early evening on all major stations. Children and even teens thrilled to the daily adventure with the memorable theme song, portraying the derring-do of high schooler Jack Armstrong. The program, sponsored by Wheaties, helped to promote the product with an infectious jingle.

As a tie-in to the growing movie industry and a way to appeal to adults, *The Lux Radio Theater* sported an all-star cast featuring nearly every note-worthy movie star of that day, such as Lucille Ball and Alan Ladd. The show ran from 1934 to 1955 on NBC and CBS for an adult audience. An hour long, initially in mid-afternoon but moving to the evening hours, the show presented adaptations of movies often starring the original cast.

Comedy programs that were popular with all ages were also prevalent at the time and were a way to lift the nation's spirits. One of the most famous comedians of that

AMATEUR RADIO

In addition to the conventional radio most were beginning to enjoy, amateur radio was also a popular form of communication. Existing since the first hesitant days of radio, this form of communication, often called "ham radio," was and is a popular hobby and public service, with many people still using it in modern day. Making use of simple two-way contact, it is most often used for recreation but can be used to alert others in emergency situations. Amateur radio operators must be licensed and many continue to use Morse code.

era, Jack Benny, was introduced on a radio program hosted by Ed Sullivan (soon to make his own mark) in 1931. Benny quickly gained his own program, *The Jack Benny Show*, to broadcast his idiosyncratic comedy routines. A successful actor as well, Benny was a staple on the air on NBC and CBS until 1953, when his show moved to a more television format. A comedienne of equal stature was Fanny Brice, made famous in her work in Broadway in the *Ziegfeld Follies* and its radio counterpart, *The Ziegfeld Follies of the Air*, running from 1932 to 1936 in the weekend evenings on CBS. Brice's sketches made famous the mischievous character of "Baby Snooks." Brice moved to the *Maxwell House Coffee Hour* in the 1940s, playing Baby Snooks, and later earned *The Baby Snooks Show*, which lasted until 1951.

As radio evolved swiftly in this time period, legislation attempted to keep a step ahead of its development to make certain radio served the needs of the country, with varying degrees of success. Legislators and those in the newly emerged radio industry were both learning about what was possible in radio and what was permissible to American citizens. These laws would have lasting effects on radio's evolution over the years. The Radio Act of 1912 was seen as a solution in that it rigidly defined how and why radio was to be used on ships and controlled distress signal transmission.[15] This did not solve issues of broadcasting, however—government broadcasters had priority on the available airwaves, and the Department of Commerce could control airwaves and issue licenses, but they had no ability to deny licenses. One frequency was made available to nongovernmental stations, but it quickly reached maximum capacity with the onslaught of radio stations being formed. The government was forced to add extra frequencies to keep apace of the growth, but it was quickly apparent that new legislation would be needed. In the Radio Act of 1927 a licensing authority was created and political candidates gained equal opportunity provisions. The act also created the Federal Radio Commission (FRC) and established some basic notions about radio, such as that the public owned the airwaves, but that private entities may get licenses to air on these channels so long as it is in the "public interest, convenience or necessity."[16] The FRC gained power to choose station operators. The act also sought to spread broadcast equally across the United States and placed broadcast under the First Amendment as a free expression. These legislative powers could be appealed at this point and were reenacted in the later Communications Act of 1934. The Communications Act of 1934 also established the Federal Communications Commission (FCC), the ruling body on American and related international affairs in radio, television (including cable), wire, and satellite.

Early Radio in Canada

The development of radio in Canada in many ways paralleled that of the United States. The major technological developments that allowed for radio to spring forth—introduction of telegraph systems and the entry of the powerful Marconi Company (Canadian Marconi in this case) into the country's developing communication industry—happened at more or less the same time in both countries. Canada, however, faced unique challenges to the growth of its own radio (and later television) industry, as well as different goals for these industries.

Canada's initial experiences with radio were filtered through, and in part controlled by, the American developments in radio. Canada obtained much of its early radio programs from America. This was an issue of great debate, how much dissemination of American broadcasting to allow, as Canada feared losing control of much of its radio programming, and in some ways its very culture and identity, to the United States. Following the invention and spread of radio, Canadians generally felt dissatisfied with the nature of radio in their country for three main reasons: inadequate Canadian programs, an abundance of advertising (mostly American in nature), and the increased presence of American radio in general in Canada.[17] Canada was also privy to British radio programs (it did not gain sovereignty until 1930), which were equally unappealing. Canada had the standard American stations at the time and gradually developed some public and private national stations as well as local stations with local interests, a trend that continues today.

Many of Canada's first radio broadcasts, as in the United States, were simple news reports, regarding events from the doings of the British royal family to farming and fishing reports. As in the United States, Canada's radio production was not and is not centered specifically in one area as it is produced separately in French and English. Canada's first broadcasting license was issued in 1919 to XWA Montreal (a Marconi-owned station), and the first official national broadcast was July 1, 1927, for the Diamond Jubilee of Confederation.[18] By 1924 Canadian National radio was active, opening and leasing stations. In 1930 the Canadian Radio League was formed and Canadian television experimentation also began.

In terms of early attempts at regulation, Canada, in 1913 enacted the Canadian Radio Telegraph Act, which covered the newly fostered "radiotelephony" broadcasting. Beyond that, the Canadian Radio Broadcasting Commission (CRBC) was created in the First Parliamentary Committee on Broadcasting in 1932, but the CRBC was replaced by a Crown corporation, the Canadian Broadcasting Corporation (CBC), in 1936.[19] Much of Canada's communication industry was and still is government financed, in part due to Canada's regulations on content. CBC Television is currently the only public network in Canada. CBC radio stations run commercial-free, but the television stations sell advertising and do not collect license fees.

In the midst of World War II, which was announced by radio in Canada, the CBC News Service was initiated. The expansion of the radio industry and its contributors paved the way for institutions such as schools to have a voice in radio. French and English language networks were developing as well to meet the needs of Canada's diverse population.

In seeking to establish its own distinctly Canadian voice in its communications industry, Canada developed several radio programs that had lasting effects beyond the radio industry.

Radio dramas, very popular in the 1920s, also allowed for the struggling Canadian theater industry to express itself. As evidenced by its numerous theater festivals, Canada embraces drama and theater far more than many other countries. Canada sought as much as possible an authentic and original voice in its media to counterbalance the onslaught of popular American radio and television. Some cross-over occurred, however, between the industries of the two countries, as popular Canadian radio figures, such as Lorne Greene in the 1930s, became important in the United States (in the television show *Bonanza* beginning in the late 1950s).

Canada developed Radio Canada International (RCI), the international arm of the CBC, in 1945, as a way to keep the Canadian military in touch with Canada. Masterminded by Prime Minister Mackenzie King, it provided multilingual transmissions in Europe and later the world. In 1949 the station, called CBC International Service in its early years, witnessed the first episode of *Wednesday Night on CBC*, a popular program. The station continues today, but with less programming and languages offered. The language concern points to the multicultural nature of the country itself, with the largely Francophone province of Quebec. In spite of barriers French serial dramas proved successful. Under Andrew Allan, head of drama for the CBC, radio dramas reached their greatest fame in the 1940s. A pioneering program was *The Stage*, begun in 1944.

THE BEGINNING OF TELEVISION

Television was developed amidst the fanfare of radio's youth, beginning much the way its sibling did, by experimentation and much trial and error. The first attempts at television began in the early 1920s, with inventor Charles F. Jenkins experimenting with wireless television transmissions.[20] At the same time, Vladimir Zworkin, soon to be a major figure in the emerging television industry, patented his iconoscope cathode ray tube device. Jenkins soon promoted "radiovision," and by 1928 he began broadcasting from TV station W3XK. Another inventor, John Logie Baird, invented a device that made use of a spinning disk system, which was not a successful competitor to other designs. The first television transmissions of acceptable quality actually occurred in England in the mid-1930s.

Debates over patents for the television raged between inventor Philo T. Farnsworth, the actual owner of the rudimentary patent filed in 1927, and RCA, which cleverly marketed the television as their own invention in the 1939 World's Fair. Now an RCA employee, Vladimir Zworkin developed with RCA his cathode ray tube, and the company eventually came to an understanding with Farnsworth that same year regarding ownership of the patent. World War II halted activity in the new industry, but a boom in sales was soon to follow, and the FCC set regulations in the meantime. After the war, television sales took off, with over a million sets being sold in the 2 years following 1947.[21] Television swept ahead of the popularity of radio and retains a significant lead in current day. Like the silver screen, television in America moved to Hollywood for much of its production, but in its early days it was produced in other locations.

Sarnoff's RCA retained much of the control over television programming at this time, but Sarnoff's son brought about RCA's downfall soon after in a failed attempt at turning RCA into a conglomerate. Through a series of corporate purchases and sales among the major television companies, independent companies were gradually eliminated, leaving mainly the stations people know today (NBC, CBS, and ABC). As with its older sibling—and competitor—radio, television's profitability came from its advertisements.

Exciting advances came in 1954 with the introduction of color television. The first color broadcast was the 1954 Tournament of Roses parade in Pasadena, California, and audiences thrilled to see, at last, television in rich color. All the significant puzzle pieces for modern communications were now in place, and it was up to the broadcasters and producers to build content worthy of the changes in radio and television. Television at this time also did not run all day; that came in later years.

TELEVISION AND RADIO IN THE UNITED STATES

U.S. Television in the 1950s and 1960s

Television became common in the United States and Canada in the late 1940s and early 1950s. In America, the founding radio companies had ventured into television, providing a fairly large market for programming. American stations at the time were ABC, CBS, a small company called Dumont, which survived only a few years, and NBC. Currently there are countless American television stations, as the country shares national stations but each state has its own local and regional stations. The conventional formats created in radio—the drama, the soap opera, the western, the adventure, the mystery, and so on—all continued in altered form in television. Little in storytelling and narrative changed but for the visual element, and many radio programs simply crossed over into television shows. As in radio, daytime programming was typically more for women, assumed to be working predominantly in the home, and young children, while later programming was often more family-based and com-pelling for a wider demographic. The classic formats in programming were developed at this time, and shows in this era in many ways set the tone for future quality programming.

A typical genre, the western, was typified in *The Lone Ranger* series, moving from radio to television. It aired beginning in 1933 on WXYZ-AM radio in Detroit, Michigan, and later moved to television, where it continued through the 1950s. It has also been marketed into various other media, such as books, animated series, and a television movie in 2003, which met sour reviews. The show featured the masked hero, his horse Silver, and his companion, the Native American Tonto, righting wrong in the old west. It was very popular among chil-dren who longed to hear the famous "Heigh-ho, Silver, away!" A spin-off of the show was *The Green Hornet*, featuring The Lone Ranger's grand-nephew and his sidekick Kato.

Situation comedies flourished, especially with the immense and lasting popularity of *I Love Lucy*, starring comedienne Lucille Ball and her husband, Desi Arnaz. Though it only ran from 1951 to 1957 on CBS, it gained a huge fan following and continued on in syndica-tion on such channels as TV Land. The show introduced America to one of its most loved characters, Lucy, and pushed an already popular Ball to greater heights of fame. The show, produced by Desilu, the company owned by Ball and Arnaz, challenged some unusual boundaries at the time in that it featured a relatively independent female lead in an interra-cial marriage. Also unique about the show was that it was often filmed before a live audience, a technique that would become a standard on many sitcoms.

Beyond creating variants on established themes, television also introduced variety shows at this time. While radio had sported shows that featured various forms of entertainment, the visual nature of television allowed for a broader range of performances. *The Ed Sullivan Show* appeared in the late 1940s (as *The Toast of the Town* until 1955) and survived until the 1970s as a massively popular variety show. Sullivan, himself a Broadway fixture and radio host, helped to create a show that combined television and elements of vaudeville.[22] The show featured all manner of entertainment—dancers, musical acts, performers—everything that Sullivan hoped would entertain the largest amount of people. In its early days, the show aired later at night on CBS, catering to all ages as much as possible through its diverse content. On a related note, the hugely popular NBC talk show *The Tonight Show*, hosted by Johnny Carson, began in 1962 and continues to this day under Jay Leno. The show became a staple among American audiences and featured elements of the variety show format. The show was also important in that it moved its base of operations from New York to California in 1972 and continued to cement California as the home of America's visual culture.

Another development in television, game shows, also made an appearance in this time. While similar in style to quiz shows, game shows made the participants often engage in amusing activities or answer questions in order to win prizes. A staple of the genre was *The Price Is Right*, beginning in a rough form in 1956 and expanding to its current format in 1972 on CBS. The show has maintained a set design straight out of the 1970s and has also not replaced its host, the wise-cracking Bob Barker, since its inception. Both host and show are well-known to those who grew up in the time as well as, interestingly enough, college-age people who wish to win the often generous prizes the show offers. In its studied campiness the show has attracted viewers and through its prizes and contests (often involving guessing the cost of products) the show plugs its sponsors. *The Price Is Right* serves as an example of good marketing as well as crafty advertising and sponsorship techniques.

For children, the 1960s were an exciting time in America, as cartoons truly came to life then. The first animated series on a network station was *The Flintstones* (1960–66), playing on ABC in prime time hours. The show, while amusing and popular among children, also set the tone for family-type cartoons that would follow, such as *The Simpsons*. Cartoons would not make a large appearance in American media again for many years.

U.S. Radio in the 1950s and 1960s

In the 1950s radio helped music open up into several new genres. No longer were radio listeners offered only country-western or classical music. Rock and roll, jazz, rhythm and blues, and many others were now being played on the air. Airplay was beginning to determine record sales for many artists, and radio was a major factor in an artist's popularity. Elvis Presley and other popular singers became important figures in the early 1950s.

With the increase of radio's importance to promote acts, legal issues ensued in the form of "payola." Record companies often bribed influential disc jockeys to play certain songs, but it was not until the quiz show scandal that payola began to attract attention.[23] Popular disc jockey Alan Freed was prosecuted in 1960 for accepting payola, the first trial of its sort, and the consequence was serious—payola became illegal. Freed's career, and indeed his life, also met with tragic ends following this decree. Payola had been fairly commonplace in prior years.

Talk radio as a serious genre, while existing since radio's earliest days, also took off in the 1960s. KMOX in St. Louis, Missouri, and KABC in Los Angeles both took credit for becoming the first dedicated talk radio stations in 1960; talk radio focused on the AM channels especially. FM lured some listeners away in later years, but talk radio has maintained a presence as a staple, in particular in the programs provided by National Public Radio (NPR). At the same time radio disc jockeys were becoming increasingly important on their own, in particular the famous Dan Ingram of the Top 40 New York station WABC AM in the 1960s.

U.S. Television in the 1970s and 1980s

Television programming in the 1970s reached something of a peak, not merely in technical quality but in terms of more engaging programming. This era produced a great many programs of lasting quality, many of which remain in syndication. The horrors of the

Vietnam War, which America entered in earnest in the mid-1960s and left only in 1975, cast a pall over the country and altered programming content. The social consciousness of the 1960s coupled with fear and anger over America's involvement in the war encouraged radio (particularly music) and television programs to tackle new issues.

Programming opened up to explore new topics. Programs such as *The Jeffersons* on CBS, running from 1975 to 1985, and *Sanford and Son* on NBC, from 1972 to 1977, looked ahead and gave African-Americans a stronger voice in television, using humor and the often grave realities of their situations. *Happy Days* (1974–84) on ABC, conversely, looked back at a more innocent period in American history, the 1950s, as did its offshoot *Laverne and Shirley* (1976–83) on ABC, but with a more feminist slant. *The Mary Tyler Moore Show* (1970–77) on CBS also promoted an independent female character that had her own career and life. *All in the Family* (1971–79), a ground-breaking CBS program charged with issues of racism, sexuality, and politics, dealt with them both through the humorous rants of the main character, Archie Bunker, and in serious moments, such as the episode when his wife Edith is raped.

On the more lighthearted end of things, one comedy sketch show made a big impact in the 1970s, the long-lived *Saturday Night Live*, running continuously from 1975 to current day on NBC. In addition to sketches, the show features guest hosts and musical acts. The show, announced every Saturday as "live, from New York," gave many important actors and comedians their starts, such as the influential John Belushi, Dan Aykroyd, and Gilda Radner, and also helped to improve the flagging New York media scene. With programs like *The Tonight Show* leaving for Los Angeles in 1972, New York was anxious for quality programming and set about creating a competitive program. *Saturday Night Live* successfully kept New York in the spotlight. The cast has changed over the years, but the show remains a powerful proving ground for up-and-coming talent in comedy.

Television soap operas also blossomed in the 1970s with one of the longest running, *All My Children*, which continues today on ABC. Susan Lucci, a supporting actress in the early days of the show, now leads it as marriage-minded and sexy Erica Kane. *General Hospital* (1963–today) was at the time was a leader in ratings, but *All My Children* managed to surpass it in some seasons. Writer Agnes Nixon, creator of numerous soap operas, is considered the "queen" of daytime soap operas.

In the 1980s, competitors to the ruling powers of ABC, CBS, and NBC appeared in the form of cable networks. A ratings battle ensued, with all stations attempting to offer more challenging programming, which was not always successful and left programming somewhat stagnant in general. One of the most popular shows in the decade that did break some new ground was *Roseanne*, which ran from 1988 to 1997 on ABC, a situation comedy that starred comedienne Roseanne Barr and featured topical issues of the day, such as sexuality, drug use, and race in the lives of working class people, much as *All in the Family* had done years before. *The Cosby Show* (1984–92) on NBC, a comedy series starring comedian Bill Cosby, provided interesting opposition in that it posited African-American characters in an upper class setting and also sought to explore similar issues.

The soap programs of earlier days had developed in this era into epic drama series such as *Dynasty* (1981–89) and *Dallas* (1978–91) that drew viewers into the complicated, exotic lives of the rich and often corrupt. A fascination with indulgence and excess in the less socially conscious post-Vietnam decade of the 1980s peppered television programming with other shows such as *Lifestyles of the Rich and Famous* (1984–95), hosted by Robin Leach, offering viewers a look into the glamour of celebrity, as well as champagne wishes and caviar dreams. The show in part midwifed in modern day the cable Fine Living Channel, which offers much the same fare, and the MTV program *Cribs*.

Sensational programming also manifested in another form in the later 1980s, the infomercial, which appeared following regulation changes on commercial content. This paid programming proved to be a new sort of advertising in which the normal commercial is stretched often to as long as a half an hour, the length of a typical television episode. These infomercials, in spite of frequently low budgets and poor acting, have been successful in marketing many products through an innovative marketing technique that seeks to not only inform but engage the viewer by offering a great deal more information than can be had in a television spot. This advertising trend has carried over into current day. Infomercials can air at any time of day but are most frequently found late at night. Some products that have been successfully sold on infomercials are the Ronco Electric Food Dehydrator, Ginsu Knives, and the classic Chia Pet. This advertising format has also been used more seriously in promoting political candidates such as Ross Perot in 1996 and religious organizations. The format has also been lampooned in many comedy programs such as *Saturday Night Live.*

Cable television came into its own in the 1980s and new channels such as MTV, VH1, HBO, ESPN, and Showtime entered the fray. HBO (Home Box Office) and Showtime provided a new service to viewers, subscription television that escapes much regulation and provides unique content, often films and programs made especially for the channels. Premium channels like these continue with great popularity today and provide more daring fare than standard channels are often able to air. The news channel CNN also debuted at this time and offered news coverage all day. In spite of the increase in television programming and news, radio continued to hold strong, with FM stations distinguishing themselves by playing all genres of music, while AM focused on talk radio and news programs. Music had been televised in various forms for decades, often in the form of promotional clips, but the concept of the music video truly hit home to Americans in 1981 when MTV began its long career by playing The Buggles' "Video Killed the Radio Star." The station emphasized the importance of music video by playing videos all day long and giving artists an incentive to make videos—publicity and potential profit. It also began the era of artists having to create videos to compete and also present appealing images to the public, often sexualizing female artists as a result.

U.S. Radio in the 1970s and 1980s

Social awareness continued to be an issue with the creation of the highly regarded National Public Radio (NPR) organization as a nonprofit grouping of public radio stations. Formed in 1970 as a result of the Public Broadcasting Act of 1967, which also created the Public Broadcasting Service (PBS), the radio service continues to provide intelligent debate and reporting on current news events with such popular programs as *All Things Considered.* It competes for its listening audience with American Public Media and Public Radio International.

A major figure in radio in the 1970s was host Casey Kasem, host of the *American Top 40*, a weekly program that detailed the most popular songs on the Billboard Hot 100 Singles chart from the early 1970s to the late 1980s (and from then under different hosts, including Kasem, until it was taken over by new host Ryan Seacrest in 2004). Reruns continue to be broadcast on XM Satellite Radio. The program now uses a new format and new method of determining the top songs. Kasem hosted another influential radio program following his departure from the *American Top 40, Casey's Top 40*, from the late 1980s to the early 1990s.

In the following decade, rap took over the airwaves and radio waves, spreading controversy and censorship, which will be addressed later. Rap had technically begun in 1979 with the Sugarhill Gang's "Rapper's Delight" and continues to be one of the most popular forms

REALITY TELEVISION

Beginning in the 1990s, the concept of reality television took off with a vengeance and can probably be traced most clearly to the wild popularity of the first season of reality phenomenon *Survivor* in 2000. As a result, a score of sequels have followed, and reality television has overtaken much of American, and in some cases world, television programming. Channels that once focused on content like music, such as MTV and VH1, have experienced a shift in format in current years to promote more reality shows.

The reality programming of today is often seen as carefully constructed by producers and lacking the freshness of the heyday of reality television. The format of many television shows has moved in many cases to a reality format based on humiliation or deception of participants, such as FOX's *Joe Millionaire* (2003), which convinced a group of women that a handsome bachelor was indeed a millionaire to see if the woman he eventually chose, upon learning the truth, would give up a cash prize in favor of his love.

Reality television shows today are too numerous to count, but reality television is not a new concept; it has in fact existed in other formats in the past, particularly in the 1950s television program *Candid Camera*, starting as *Candid Microphone* in the 1940s on radio. In later times, one of the first true reality programs in its current sense was in 1973 with PBS's *An American Family*.

of music, but rap in its rawest and most challenging form emerged in this time. Artists like Ice-T and Easy-E fathered the "gangsta" rap movement in the time, taking the relatively innocent form begun by The Sugarhill Gang and pushing up the volume and the content. The debate over rap lyrics challenged many radio stations through increasing pressure not to play the heated rap songs.

U.S. Television from the 1990s to Today

The 1990s were dominated by changes in telecommunications regulations, in particular in the passing of the Telecommunications Act of 1996, which overhauled the Communications Act of 1934. The act deregulated the telecommunication industry and encouraged competition among companies.

Television began to focus more on a young demographic in the 1990s. The NBC hit series *Friends* (1994–2004) became a phenomenon and lives on through its fans and stars. And beginning in 1997 on ABC, soap operas took a turn for the strange with *Port Charles* (1997–2003), featuring vampires and the supernatural and focusing on a teenage female audience. The show proved fairly popular but fared poorly with critics and was soon cancelled. It also faced competition with NBC's *Passions* (1999–today), which targeted both the usual demographic, older women, as well as a surprisingly engaged audience of younger women and teens, the same demographic as *Port Charles*. The show's bizarre storylines, featuring witchcraft, demonic possession, and other supernatural elements, appealed to a curious audience with a sense of humor, though it is currently faring poorly against other more established soap operas such as *Days of Our Lives*.

Following in the footsteps of giants such as *The Tonight Show*, talk shows also experienced an explosion in the 1990s, particularly among women. A figure of immense importance and influence in daytime talk shows is Oprah Winfrey, whose show began in 1986 on ABC, leads the pack in terms of quality and power, and is the longest running show of its kind. *The Oprah Winfrey Show* impacts women in particular and deals most often with women's issues, relationship advice, health and spirituality, and even reading with Oprah's Book Club. Many women see Winfrey as a friend and guiding hand. Other talk shows often come and go rather quickly due to intense competition.

In particular in the twenty-first century, a growing attitude of nostalgia is overtaking much programming in both radio and television. Radio programs frequently replay old episodes of programs or countdowns and there are entire television programs dedicated to reminiscing about radio, television, and cultural events of the past few decades, such as in VH1's popular *I Love . . .* series, beginning with *I Love the 80's* in 2002. These programs have pushed nostalgia to the point of recapping events as little as a week gone by, in another VH1 series *Best Week Ever*, starting in 2004. The mode of such shows is often similar, featuring comedians who riff on the past, allowing people to remember the events while chuckling at themselves. Nostalgia has also changed content on the airwaves, as satellite radio has begun to incorporate replays of older programs in its content.

The syndication of a great many old television programs has also been an ongoing aspect of the increase in nostalgia in modern day. Beginning in the 1990s, a specialty cable channel dedicated to this, TV Land, was created, playing a wide assortment of older programs such as *Gunsmoke* and *The Andy Griffith Show*. The channel caters to an older viewing audience, while its subsidiary, Nick at Nite, often plays sitcoms from the 1980s and after to catch the younger demographic. Other specialty stations also provide content for the young. The Cartoon Network was created exclusively to air cartoons and other children's programming. A competitor, Nickelodeon, airs not only cartoons but also sitcoms and other shows for a teenage audience. College age adults have found a special niche with the Cartoon Network adjunct Adult Swim (recently split from the Cartoon Network to be treated as its own station), created in 2001. The channel speaks to a hip, humorous young adult audience by featuring bizarre and often mature cartoons and other programs. The channel's commercials are oriented directly to its young audience, often featuring comments from the channel's creators directly to its fans, or in response to fan letters, usually offering absurd advice.

FOX set a standard for its own programming when it began to show *The Simpsons*. Beginning in 1989, initially as a part of the sketch comedy *The Tracey Ullman Show*, it blossomed on FOX into a show of such massive popularity that it is still in production. The show appeals to adults and children in that it tackles, humorously, timely issues and social concerns. The show has been groundbreaking, and its creator, Matt Groening, has gone on to open the doors for similarly satirical programs such as *South Park* and the somewhat derivative *Family Guy*.

In general television in the current day has also gone flat—as in flat-screen. Technology in television has allowed viewers to purchase extremely high-definition televisions with plasma or LCD screens that offer vivid color and richer experiences. Gone are the days of a small fuzzy color television with rabbit ear antennas. Television advancements have been married in some ways to those in radio, as iPods can receive television content through podcasts. And television content can also be easily viewed on the Internet. In many ways, a typical television and radio are no longer needed. With the freedom offered by technological advances, the user has become the author, deciding what music he or she wants, creating his own video and broadcasting it on sites like YouTube and Google Video. The effects of passively receiving radio and television content have been widely debated, but radio and television carry on. Many older television programs have been released on DVD and help maintain the importance of television as a medium, and conventional radio is still a primary source for news and information.

U.S. Radio from the 1990s to Today

An eruption of talk radio, such a fixture for so long, caused some issues. The 1987 repeal of the "Fairness Doctrine" set up by the FCC allowed for more partisan and outrageous broadcasting and proved wildly popular, with about 16 percent of the population listening to talk radio in 2004.[24] A staunch conservative figure in talk radio in the 1990s was Rush Limbaugh, whose passionate commentaries led the way for other strongly conservative hosts such as G. Gordon Liddy and Laura Ingraham. Some of these radio programs are also broadcast on satellite radio. Liberal talk radio has met less success but perseveres in Air America Radio. The Pacifica network features more liberal commentary but is aired only in a limited area with a less dynamic marketing system. Clear Channel has also striven to add more liberal programming to its format, in an effort to attract a younger demographic.

A massive overhaul of both radio and television has occurred in recent years, to the glory of technophiles and the sorrow of enthusiasts of the classic format. Radio, in an attempt to remain vital and draw on emerging technology, has altered its format in many cases. Many people in current day get their music and other radio content online rather than through the familiar and bygone radio. Services such as iTunes, which provides not only access to numerous online radio services but also the ability to download music for low costs, have overtaken the market and are pushing conventional radio to the wayside. People no longer need to listen through hours of music in hopes of hearing their favorite song; they can now carry custom music in a pocket-sized device, the iPod or MP3 player, and even on their cell phones. Satellite radio may well prove the saving grace of radio as it combines conventional radio service—broadcast through a receiver—with higher quality audio and a plethora of content. Satellite radio, not locked by regulations that affect terrestrial radio stations, is free to explore many new forms of entertainment and is quickly spreading as a convenient way to get commercial-free entertainment.

CANADIAN TELEVISION AND RADIO

Canadian Television in the 1950s and 1960s

Canada began to build its own base of content for radio and television broadcasts more strenuously in the 1950s and 1960s as a vision for Canadian content became clearer in the minds of broadcasters. Canada had received most of the established radio and television genres at the time from America—the western, the drama, the comedy, among others—and it was time to make them its own. Most significant television programs were and are produced by the CBC. Mavor Moore, the first head of programming for CBC, set the tone of much of Canadian television broadcasting in his time. He desired to be more experimental with programming, and did so in productions such as Robert Allen's *Scope/Folio/Festival.*[25] The originality Moore promoted was not embraced by those who followed, and much programming became generic at the time in spite of his best efforts.

As is the case with much of Canadian content, the arts and drama came to the forefront and provided some interesting television options. Operas were produced, adaptations of Shakespeare were performed, and poetry was read, among many other delights. Shown in both French and English, *The Family Plouffe* (1953–59) was one of the early live family series, depicting the life of a down-trodden Quebecois family, developed by the French section of the CBC, la Société Radio-Canada. The French portion of the CBC, unlike its English counterpart, was not able to take American programs whole-cloth and rebroadcast them; with a smaller budget and language concerns, it relied on its own programming to satisfy its viewership and occasionally dubbed English programs. French Canadians developed a new genre of television programming called *téléromans,* a sort of social melodrama that appealed to French and English speakers alike, of which *The Family Plouffe* was one. In general this period of history is considered the "golden age" of Francophone programming. Important journalists at the time, Gerard Pelletier and Andre Laurendeau, thought of television as a way to introduce the world to Quebec and raise national pride, which it helped to do.[26]

A *téléromans* program that would shake the foundations of Canadian broadcasting was the hugely popular and influential *Wojeck*, a series about a coroner beginning in 1966 and running until 1968 at nights on CBC. The series competed successfully with American programming and was based on the real-life adventures of a Toronto coroner. The series failed to inspire continued successful Canadian dramas, but it was a landmark in indigenous programming.

Color television came to Canada in the late 1960s and with it came such programs as the popular children's show *Mister Dressup*, airing from 1967 to 1996 and featuring songs, stories, crafts, and more for children. Much educational programming was also set aside for children and adults as well. One such television program was the award-winning *Web of Life*, which ran in afternoons and evenings from the late 1950s to the early 1960s. The show was a serious look at animal life in Canada and the world and garnered great popularity and acclaim. Interview shows also found a niche in Canadian television programming in shows such as *Luncheon Date*, which ran from 1963 to 1975 and featured thousands of guests. Aired at noontime on CBC, it was geared more toward women at home. A more serious and enduring radio program was *Gilmour's Albums*, which ran from 1957 to about 1997, and was hosted by Clyde Gilmour and based on his enormous record collection.

Some of the most important figures in Canadian television at the time were comedians Johnny Wayne and Frank Shuster, stars of *The Wayne and Shuster Hour*. They came to prominence during World War II in radio shows such as *The Army Show* and a program they starred in that broadcast on the trans-Canada Network, which led to their television show. The two appeared numerous times on *The Ed Sullivan Show*, and their comedy style varied from the more conventional comedy routines in America, veering from intelligent and thoughtful humor often based on classic literature to basic screwball comedy. The show, beginning in the 1950s, continued in various iterations until the 1980s.

Radio quiz shows had already long been in existence in both America and Canada, famously featuring children, the "quiz kids." In Canada, popular quiz shows were often those that found fame in America, but their standing in the mind of the audience met the same fate as those in the American audience when news of the quiz show scandals leaked. Nevertheless, Canada had several television quiz shows of its own, such as *Who Knows?* in the late 1950s, in which contestants tried to identify museum artifacts, and *Whozit* in the mid-1950s, where contestants tried identifying well-known figures from caricatures. The credibility issues that befell American quiz shows seem to have been avoided in Canadian productions.

Canadian Radio in the 1950s and 1960s

As mentioned previously, Canada maintained and explored the radio genres established by American radio previously and crafted shows that followed those themes. Canada, however, had a strong bent toward sports that influenced much of its programming as well. Sports programs had been popular in Canada in radio since the 1930s, often featuring famous sportscaster Foster Hewitt. His *Hockey Night in Canada* was a beloved favorite until the 1990s, even as television had overtaken much of sports coverage. Sportscaster Don Cherry took the reins from Hewitt in later television sporting coverage. The Canadian love of sports also led to a masterpiece of drama first shown on CBC in 1955, *The Black Bonspiel of Wullie MacRimmon* by W. O. Mitchell, publicizing the sport of curling. The drama is still performed.

The formation of key Canadian radio groups happened at this time too. In 1953 the CBC French Radio Network was established, as was the CBC Bureau of Audience Research. In 1958 the Board of Broadcast Governors (BBG) was created to regulate Canadian broadcasting in the Broadcasting Act. The act also recognized private broadcasting in the country, and as a result the 1960s was an era of growth in which many radio stations burst onto the scene.

Canadian Television in the 1970s and 1980s

Canada continued to develop its own station and programming in this time, improving the quality of its radio and television in much the same way as America. Canada took measures to stem the tide of American media and to promote its own culture, with varying results.

Several major programs for radio and television emerged at this time. Canada, along with the United States, experienced greater choices in television channels in the 1970s and 1980s, but Canadian channels were controlled by the Canadian Radio and Television Commission (CRTC). In 1983 Canada also introduced pay cable channels, in the vein of HBO and Showtime. On regular cable programming, Canada began to distribute The Sports Network and MuchMusic in 1987. The Sports Network parallels ESPN, whereas MuchMusic was the young cousin of MTV and in current times proves to be good competition for the older channel.

A large portion of Canadian programming from the 1980s on has come in the form of news and documentaries, which are often more comprehensive and informed than American news reporting. Canadian news anchors, such as Knowlton Nash and Peter Mainsbridge in the 1980s, are often considered to have far more star power than actors in television or movies.

Francophone television increased somewhat in importance in this time as some of its programming made it into English television, with mixed results. Certain French programs dubbed into English did well in the larger English population, but others that were popular in French Canada, such as the hockey drama *Lance et Compte* in 1987, failed in English Canada. English Canada, much to the dismay of its French neighbors, has not made many attempts to appeal to the French audience or feature many French programs. In terms of other cultures, there have been some ventures made into representing the aboriginal population in Canada, often as an exotic "other" in a sort of western in the vein of American westerns.

Canadian Radio in the 1970s and 1980s

In Canada at the time, some of the changes in radio spilled over into television and other areas of culture. Stricter regimentation of content was brewing in Canada, for good or ill.

Comedy, a radio staple, again made an appearance in Canadian programming with the *Royal Canadian Air Farce*, which began in 1974 and continues today. The show began on CBC Radio but moved to television in 1981, where it lasted for a short time before disputes placed it back in radio. It returned to television in 1993 while maintaining a radio series and continues to be enormously popular.

Talk radio also entered the lives of Canadians in this period in much the same way as it did in America, though it began in earnest much earlier in Canadian history. Canadians favor well-produced news and found it in programs such as *Morningside* with Peter Gzowski. The show began in the late 1970s under another host but came to prominence under Gzowski, a household name in Canada through his retirement in 1997 and death in 2002. A veteran of morning and late night programming, Gzowski also published several books. In addition, *Gabereau* began airing in 1985 on CBC and switched to CBS in America, where it resides now. The show features charming host Vicki Gabereau of the CBC and her interviews of celebrities.

Canadian Television from the 1990s to Today

Although Canadian English radio and television received nearly every genre of programming devised in the United States, they did not receive soap operas on television until the 1990s. Attempts in the past to bring soap operas into radio had floundered, chiefly because the major station in the country, the CBC, simply did not produce soap operas. The CBC had made attempts in epic storylines in the past with programs but to little avail. One attempt at creating an engaging soap opera was *House of Pride*, which would pave the way for American programs such as *Dallas*.[28]

In current day, there has been something of a stronger aboriginal voice in the production of television programs, such as a series based on the works of aboriginal writer Thomas King, for example, but the loudest voice continues to be English-speaking Canada. The CBC affiliates in the less populated north do, however, tailor programming to the aboriginal populations there.

CANCON

Beginning in 1970, the notion of "Cancon" reflects the deep-seated fears Canadians had for their culture in the flood of American content coming their way. In radio, Cancon ("Canadian content") is referred to as the MAPL system, a way to identify Canadian content in a piece of music in order to increase the exposure of Canadian artists. Adopted in 1971 the current Cancon percentage required in music is 35 percent, though this can vary in musical genres where there is a limited Canadian presence. Satellite radio has slightly different standards and must meet Cancon rates in aggregate over a subscription package. Television Cancon requirements are even stricter given that it is cheaper and more convenient to rebroadcast American programs in lieu of creating new content.

Cancon has benefits in that it promotes indigenous content on radio and television, but it draws criticism by Canadians as it restricts their freedom to listen to or watch what they please. In addition, emerging Canadian music artists have a difficult time breaking through the Cancon rules to have their music played and must often gain support in other countries before being accepted and played in their native country. As a result, many Canadian artists oppose Cancon's limitations.

In spite of difficulties in gaining airplay in Canada due to Cancon, many Canadian artists are coming to prominence due in part to advertising. One such artist, the sexually charged Peaches, has experienced a boost in popularity due in part to her song "Do Ya" being featured in the fall 2006 The Gap advertising campaign. Where radio and the uncertainty of video airplay on music channels present issues, advertising has become a boon for Canadian artists as a way to be accepted in Canada and the world.

Canadian Radio from the 1990s to Today

In current times, many U.S. radio stations on the Canadian border have begun to parlay with Canadian advertisers and promote their radio in Canada. While American radio, like American television, is subject to restrictions, some Canadians think of these stations as essentially Canadian.

The government-controlled CBC, itself in control of nearly all television and radio in Canada, has recently made great strides in keeping abreast of the changing needs of its audience. The CBC now runs the digital audio service Galaxie and controls part of satellite radio broadcaster Sirius Canada, which airs additional CBC material.[29]

CENSORSHIP ISSUES IN RADIO AND TELEVISION

Censorship and serving the public interest have always been of concern to the radio industry, and it seeks to maintain standards of decency. Television is under the same sort of restrictions—even more so, perhaps, because of its visual aspect. Canada's federal restrictions have of late paled in comparison to American restrictions.

Some of the earliest American censorship was laid down by broadcasters themselves. In a notorious 1967 incident on *The Ed Sullivan Show*, The Doors refused to alter the lyrics to their hit "Light My Fire" to eliminate drug references and were never allowed back on the show.

Violence in music has become an issue in the American music of today. Drug references and sexual themes in music beginning in the early days of rock n' roll progressed to darker music in later years, such as heavy metal and death metal, which some parents worried encouraged their children to commit violent acts and even suicide. Rap and hip-hop music took a heavy blow in similar allegations that it promoted violent behavior, particularly toward women. In the 1980s and 1990s 2 Live Crew and NWA became symbols for the drug use and violence of the seductive gangsta lifestyle that had begun to emerge, with such songs as NWA's "Straight Outta Compton" (1989). Parents took charge and in 1985 The Parents Music Resource Center (PMRC) was formed to monitor musical content—its most lasting achievement has been the "explicit content" label on albums that feature profanity or sexual, drug, or violent content. C. DeLores Tucker of the National Political Congress of Black Women also targeted rap music in particular as a source of danger to young people. Violent content in the rap of current artists such as Eminem and DMX has continued to frustrate the public.

An artist who crystallized concern about unacceptable sexual content in music and television was Madonna, whose many sexually suggestive songs and explicit videos, such as "Justify My Love" (1990), drew critical fire from both parents and religious groups in the 1980s and 1990s. Representing the male end of concern over sexually explicit content was Trent Reznor, front man for the industrial rock band Nine Inch Nails, who stirred controversy and charges of misogyny for the explicit lyrics and drastically censored video for "Closer" (1994) and the over-the-top violence of the lyrics to "Big Man with a Gun" (1994). Like violence and drug use, sexual content continues to be an issue in music.

In current times, issues of content in radio and television came to a head during the 2004 Super Bowl, when Janet Jackson's breast was famously exposed. As a result, Viacom, the owner of CBS (before a 2006 split) and MTV, faced enormous fines from the FCC, and delays in live programs were put into effect in case a similar event should occur. Control over content in television and radio was greatly strengthened and radio and television stations were and are far more cautious in their programming choices. It remains to be seen what further changes in FCC regulations will occur.

In part to escape such censorship, radio has developed satellite radio, which evades typical decency laws and allows broadcasters such as Sirius to offer Howard Stern an uncensored radio program. By broadcasting via satellite and not airwaves, they cleverly dodge the restrictions the FCC applies to other land-based stations. Satellite providers may, however, censor their own content as they like.

RESOURCE GUIDE

PRINT SOURCES

Blumenthal, Howard J., and Oliver R. Goodenough. *This Business of Television*, 2nd edition. New York: Billboard Books, 1991.
Fortner, Robert S. *Radio, Morality, and Culture: Britain, Canada, and the United States, 1919–1945.* Carbondale: Southern Illinois University Press, 2005.
Jacobs, George, ed. *World Radio TV Handbook 2006.* Oxford: WRTH Publications, Ltd., 2006.
Lackmann, Ron. *The Encyclopedia of American Radio*, 2nd edition. New York: Checkmark Books, 2000.
McNeil, Alex. *Total Television*, 4th edition. New York: Penguin Books, 1996.

WEBSITES

The Museum of Broadcast Communications. The Museum of Broadcast Communications. August 18, 2006. http://www.museum.tv.

VIDEOS/FILM

Empire of the Air: The Men Who Made Radio (Public Broadcasting Service, 1991).
Good Night and Good Luck (Warner Independent Pictures, 2005).

EVENTS

Friends of Old Time Radio Convention, Holiday Inn-North, 160 Frontage Rd., Newark, NJ 07114. http://www.lofcom.com/nostalgia/fotr/. Held annually in Newark, New Jersey. An important event for radio enthusiasts.

ORGANIZATIONS

Friends of Old Time Radio, Hello Again (newsletter), Jay Hickerson, Box 4321, Hamden, CT 06514.
O.R.C.A., Old Time Radio Show Collector's Association of England, North American Branch, Tom Monroe, 2055 Elmwood Avenue, Lakewood, OH 44107.
Radio-Television News Directors Association of Canada, 2175 Sheppard Ave. E, Suite 310, Toronto, ON M2J 1W8. http://www.rtndacanada.com. RTNDA Canada is dedicated to fostering excellence in electronic journalism.

MUSEUMS

Museum of Television and Radio, 25 West 52nd Street, New York, NY 10019. http://www.mtr.org/.
National Broadcasters Hall of Fame, Anaheim Stadium Hall of Fame Office Complex
Anaheim, CA 92806. http://www.infoage.org/NBHF.htm.
National Museum of Communication, 6305 North O'Connor Road, Suite 123, Irving, TX 75039-3510.

NOTES

1. The World Factbook. https://www.cia.gov/cia/publications/factbook/geos/us.html.
2. Ibid.

3. U.S. Census Bureau, "Utilization of Selected Media: 1980 to 2003," in *Statistical Abstract of the United States: 2006*, 125th edition (Washington, DC: U.S. Census Bureau, 2005).
4. Encyclopedia of the Nations. http://www.nationsencyclopedia.com/Americas/Canada-MEDIA.html.
5. Russell O. Wright, *Chronology of Communication in the United States* (Jefferson: McFarland & Company, Inc., Publishers, 2004), p. 18.
6. Ibid.
7. Margaret A. Blanchard, ed., *History of the Mass Media in the United States: An Encyclopedia* (Chicago: Fitzroy Dearborn Publishers, 1998), p. 307.
8. Russell O. Wright, *Chronology of Communication in the United States* (Jefferson: McFarland & Company, Inc., Publishers, 2004), p. 21.
9. Ron Lackmann, *The Encyclopedia of American Radio* (New York: Checkmark Books, 2000), p. 154.
10. Blanchard, p. 560.
11. Ibid.
12. Ibid., p. 19.
13. Ibid.
14. Fantastic Fiction. "Ellery Queen." http://www.fantasticfiction.co.uk/q/ellery-queen/.
15. Blanchard, p. 559.
16. Ibid.
17. Fortner 2005 (in Resource Guide), p. 129.
18. CBC Radio-Canada, "CBC/ Radio-Canada Milestones." http://www.cbc.radio-canada.ca/history/1901-1939.shtml.
19. Ibid.
20. History of Television. http://history.acusd.edu/gen/recording/television1.html.
21. Wright, p. 23.
22. The Museum of Broadcast Communications, *The Ed Sullivan Show*. http://www.museum.tv/archives/etv/E/html/edsullivan/edsullivans.htm.
23. "Payola." http://www.history-of-rock.com/payola.htm.
24. State of the News Media 2006, "What Radio Formats People Listen To, 2004" chart. http://www.stateofthenewsmedia.org/2006/chartland.asp?id=501&ct=&dir=&sort=.
25. The Museum of Broadcast Communications, "Canadian Television Programming in English." http://www.museum.tv/archives/etv/C/htmlC/canadianproge/canadianproge.htm.
26. The Museum of Broadcast Communications, "Canadian Programming in French." http://www.museum.tv/archives/etv/C/htmlC/canadianprogf/canadianprogf.htm.
27. Canadian Radio-television and Telecommunications Commission, Canadian Content for Radio and Television fact sheet. http://www.crtc.gc.ca/eng/INFO_SHT.G11.htm.
28. The Museum of Broadcast Communications, "Canadian Television Programming in English." http://www.museum.tv/archives/etv/C/htmlC/canadianproe/canadianproge.htm.
29. Canadian Broadcasting Corporation. Radio Guide. http://www.cbc.ca/programguide/radio/.

SPORTS AND RECREATION

MICHAEL K. SCHOENECKE

Sport informs virtually every imaginable aspect of North American culture. Whereas the Puritans and other European early settlers of North America believed that exercise weakened religious devotion and corrupted the morals of the practitioners as well as all who supported or attended games, Americans in the 1820s began to embrace the ancient and the Enlightenment's philosophical, educational, and exercise reformers' beliefs that physical exercise unites body and mind. These visionary advocates, including physicians, educators, and health experts, contended that sport improved the athlete's physical well-being and character development and enhanced moral development. Although a few individuals still cling to the inaccurate Puritan ideas, most Americans, whether they actively participate in a sport or simply watch sports in person or on television, believe the latter.

Since the early 1900s, sport has influenced and permeated finance, communication, fashion, journalism, transportation, advertising, and the business world. Swimming pools, golf courses, baseball and softball diamonds, football and soccer fields, tennis and volleyball and basketball courts, bowling alleys, track and field facilities, gymnasiums, roller- and ice-skating rinks, horse and car race tracks, and so on, built by municipal communities and businesses dot the rural and urban landscape, and attract millions of people to the athletic facilities. Specialized and professional sports magazines catering to men, women, boys, and girls arrive daily at family dwellings; local newspapers, recognizing their readers' fascination with sport and local athletic accomplishments, include a Sports Section to attract subscribers and advertisers; high school, collegiate, and professional athletic events are broadcast on radio, television, and the Internet. Sport hats, shirts, slacks, swimsuits, jewelry, drinking mugs, and shoes are worn or used by millions of athletic devotees to identify them with their favorite teams and players. Businesses subsidize local youth and adult sports teams. Coaches, in an attempt to promote team unity and effort, employ films such as *Hoosiers*, *Remember the Titans*, and *Glory Road* to remind their players that "anything is possible, if we play as a team."

SPORTS ATTENDANCE

Attendance at live sporting events is flourishing. Major League Baseball's (MLB) 2005 New York Yankees drew 4,090,440 fans, which was 400,000 more than any other team; the lowly Tampa Bay Devil Rays, a team that seems intent on driving its fans from the ballpark, ended up in the cellar by hosting a few more than 1,124,000 to its inept version of the national pastime. The National Football League's (NFL) thirty-two teams drew better than 19,000,000 people during their 2005 season. The Washington Redskins' stadium swelled with better than 716,000, whereas the Arizona Cardinals, a perennial losing team, managed to coax a little over 297,000 for hometown support. The Montreal Canadians, National Hockey League's (NHL) 2005–6 season's attendance leader, skated before 872,000, whereas the New York Islanders' attracted a little more than 516,000. In total, better than 20,838,000 people attended NHL games. National Association for Stock Car Racing (NASCAR), a sport that plays out in larger arenas than other professional facilities, averaged over 127,000 people per event. For the 2005–06 National Basketball Association (NBA) season, more than 883,000 loud, adoring fans attended the Detroit Pistons' games, a team that many expected to win the championship; to no one's surprise the Portland Trail Blazers were lucky to attract a little over 617,000.[1] (The aforementioned attendances do not include playoff games.)

At the National Collegiate Athletic Association (NCAA) level, 2005 football's 117 Division I teams attracted 32,641,526, which includes home attendance, neutral-site attendance, and bowl game attendance. They averaged 46,039 at each game, with the University of Michigan averaging 110,915 at each of its seven home games. Although this attendance reflects the alumni and students' willingness to spend better than $35 per ticket, home attendance increased by 483 from 2004. Six hundred fifteen teams make up NCAA Men's Football. The total stadium attendance for all four divisions in 2005 was 43,486,574. However, 2003 remains the all-time attendance high with 46,114,539. Based on the way that the calendar fell that year, teams were permitted to play twelve games, one more than usual. NCAA men's 2006 basketball home attendance was 23,466,802; 670,254 people attended the Men's NCAA Championship Tournament. The University of Kentucky's men's team averaged 22,763 per game, whereas the University of Tennessee's and Texas Tech University's women's basketball teams averaged 15,356 and 11,934, respectively. Although no official figures for the Women's NCAA Championship are available, estimates are around 8,000,000.[2] (Note that home attendance records include doubleheaders with men; when this occurs, a separate attendance is taken by halftime of the women's game.)

SPORTS AND NORTH AMERICAN CULTURE

Aware that sport impacts popular culture, politicians and their pundits schedule photo opportunities for presidents to throw the first pitch at various baseball games, invite professional and collegiate championship teams to the White House, or wave starting flags at NASCAR events. Recognizing the importance that Major League Baseball plays in U.S. culture, on January 15, 1942, President Franklin D. Roosevelt personally, not officially, supported the playing of professional games during wartime because they provided recreation for the fans. Theodore Roosevelt encouraged soldiers to practice baseball, even on Sundays, because it was a form of exercise. Presidents Wilson, Eisenhower, Kennedy, Nixon, Ford, Clinton, and both Bushes played golf as a means of recreation and for political discussions away from the White House. During presidential campaigns, presidential contenders and their running mates are often photographed during hunting and fishing trips in an attempt to appeal to outdoorsmen. For the 2004 election, Bush, Cheney, and Kerry, dressed in appropriate hunting attire and carrying shotguns, were captured on film admiring their kills or, as with an unsteady Cheney, perched on a boat's helm fishing a river's rapids.

Early Sporting Events

Sport has grown into an institution that influences and captivates audiences and participants. The human inclination for athletic activity fulfills the desire for competition as well as creating gregarious individuals who enjoy life; sport provides outlets for human impulses and escape from what is often perceived as unexciting, uneventful lives. When North Americans think of indigenous sport and culture, they are often unaware that early settlers participated in athletic and entertainment events. The misconception that colonists avoided athletic activities springs from the notion that they worked all day, every day; actually, when they celebrated various holidays, they fished, hunted, or attended picnics. Plowing and spinning, extensions of daily work, functioned as a form of friendly play and competition.

European settlers encountered Native peoples who played various types of games with balls and hoops as well running events; the colonists and explorers brought their own sporting and leisure activities to relieve their daily tedium. These colonial Americans established the roots of sport in North America. For practical reasons and since survival dominated the settlers' thoughts and behavior, most of the sporting events were related to warfare and military training; males participated in most of these adventures. Outdoorsmen who hunted and fished employed techniques and strategies designed to catch or kill their prey, whereas riflemen and archers competed with one another by shooting at different types or sizes of targets; nevertheless, the most accurate shooter was determined by who could hit the center of the selected target. No matter what the distance, runners raced to see who was the fastest. For recreation and competition, they challenged frozen ponds with homemade skates and snow-laden hills with sleds and played an early form of soccer. A few, following Benjamin Franklin's lead, turned to swimming, although few probably swam for pleasure. Females, banned from strenuous activities, participated in fishing and hunting or short races to win a prize, such as an article of clothing, or they played more genteel, ladylike games such as "battledores" and "shuttlecocks," now called badminton. Children's athletic games included tag, jumping contests, a form of hide-and-seek, and other imaginative playground activities.

Because taming the menacing landscape and establishing thriving settlements required hard work, dedication, and determination, settlers focused their attention on survival. Religious doctrines and community ordinances discouraged leisure activities. In fact, travelers, military leaders, and others criticized the mere presence of sports and amusements on grounds of immorality, although some newspapers listed upcoming sporting events within the Commonwealth. Just as the English villagers who arrived on the *Mayflower* and the *Sarah Constant* brought their sports and pastimes with them, they also came with their religious biases against English forms of recreation. *Mayflower* governor William Bradford, one year after landing in the unsettled and untamed country, chided the boys and young men he found "in the streete at play, openly; some pitching ye barr, & some at stoole-ball, and shuch like sports." Denying them the opportunity to play while others worked, he continued: "If they made ye keeping of it mater of devotion, let them kepe their houses, but ther should be no gameing or reveling in ye streets."[3] Joining the Puritan railings against athletic activities and contests, including human and horse racing, the Philadelphia Quakers warned against racing, wagering, and "vain sports, for our time passeth swiftly away and our pleasure and delight ought to be in the law of the Lord."[4] Moralists insisted on strict adherence not only

BLOOD SPORTS

Because the early settlers lived on farms and raised farm animals, the animals served multiple purposes. Settlers—who did not have much sympathy for the animals, because they did not believe that they had souls, and who kept few animals as pets—considered animals vulnerable for human consumption and entertainment. Blood sports flourished. Because the animals were going to be butchered or die, settlers thought they could be tortured or trained to fight for human enjoyment and wagering. Dogfights, cockfights, bearbaitings, bullbaitings, and other forms of animal spectacle and sport took place in the colonies, north to south. An animal was declared victorious when it maimed or killed its opponent. Gander pulling, where a rider bore down on a live goose tied to a stake and attempted to pull its head off, was another blood sport. Turkey shoots, unlike the aforementioned practices, blended marksmanship with the game.

Cultural scholars maintain that blood sports functioned as allegorical battles. Blood sports mattered because they were ritualistic and because observers could solve conflicts between individuals and society. In other words, blood sports reminded observers of more significant combats involving human life and released tensions. Although blood sports are now illegal, interest in blood sports continues to exist, especially cockfighting. Although the early American settlers probably were not conscious of the impact that sport had on them, they did understand that they enjoyed watching and participating in these contests.

For further discussion of blood sports, readers should consult Gerald Carson, *Men, Beast and Gods: A History of Cruelty and Kindness to Animals* (New York: Scribner, 1992), and Richard E. Powell, Jr., "Sport, Social Relations and Animal Husbandry, Early Cockfighting in North America," *International Journal of the History of Sport* 10 (December 1993): 295–312.

to keeping the Sabbath holy, but also to preventing the innocent and impressionable from being lured into the evils that existed via loitering or the appearance of inappropriate and ungodly behavior.

Around 1820, major attitude changes regarding sport occurred; this new attitude connected the robust, thriving, and growing young country's intellectual conceptions to a maturing interest in and understanding of physical fitness and exercise. Of course, this new intellectual and historical evolution began slowly and did not receive general approval among the nation's population for a number of years, because religious and community leaders were not humanitarian democrats who created a haven for dissenters; nevertheless, the 1820s and 1830s provided a major transition in the changing attitude toward sport.

An Embrace of Sports Culture

By 1820 Americans gradually rejected the constrictive Puritan legacy. This new healthy attitude embraced ancient and the Enlightenment's philosophical, educational, and exercise reformers' beliefs that physical exertion united body and mind. The visionary advocates, including physicians, educators, and health experts, contended that sport not only improved a participant's well-being but also improved character development and enhanced moral development. Believing that education should free a person's soul and mind, these exercise educators praised athletics because sport served as a proving ground for manliness as well as a means to test the participants' mental and physical acuity.

Coaches, athletes, and sports enthusiasts adhere to the notion that participation in athletics teaches important life lessons in ethics, discipline, and teamwork. Without a doubt, sports contribute financially and as marketing venues to universities, high schools, and communities. Attendees connect with one another through their verbal and physical interaction. Bonds develop between teams and their fans;

shirts, hats, and other memorabilia advertise either where one attends school or where one might like to attend. Some high school athletes earn college scholarships, and a select few eventually make a living playing professionally. General Douglas MacArthur expressed the impact of athletics on life as follows:

> Sports is a vital character builder. It molds the youth of our country for their roles as custodians of the republic. It teaches them to be strong enough to know they are weak and brave enough to face themselves when they are afraid. It teaches them to be proud and unbending in honest defeat, but humble and gentle in victory. . . . It gives them a predominance of courage over timidity, of appetite for adventure over loss of ease.[5]

Sports change lives; sports can discipline participants and fans and mold them into successful, dedicated individuals for life.

Part of sports' appeal and praise comes from its practice and rituals. Like soldiers, athletes spend hours each week training for a game; they understand that mental and physical discipline enhances their self-confidence, self-image, self-control, and decision-making skills. For example, before a golf tournament, professional golfers literally hit thousands of golf balls. The purpose is to control drives, short irons, flop shots, sand shots, and putts; they hit shots from downhill, uphill, and sidehill lies, shots from divots, shots into and against the wind. They practice so they can hit draws, power fades, low shots, and high shots. Realizing that they must be prepared for every contingency within themselves, with a course (nature), and with their fellow competitors, they must know their game and exact yardages as well as the ever-changing conditions they might confront. Precision and control of the ball and life are needed. Baseball players also execute a choreographed pregame ritual that involves batting practice, warming up their arms, fielding grounders and fly balls, as well as the ceremonial singing of the national anthem. In a similar fashion, fans have their own rituals; after donning their team's jersey, they leave home or work at a prescribed time so that they can participate in the pregame meal or other activities in the parking lot or in the stadium. After, perhaps, drinking a favorite beverage and eating a hot dog or hamburger, they walk ceremoniously, perfunctorily to their designated seats. They, like the players, have prepared themselves not only for an evening of enjoyment but also for an evening of catharsis.

Superstars, Heroes, and Icons

Sports' superstars perform at the highest level and only to win: this is the essence of professionalism, not the fact of being paid. People unfamiliar with sport recognize the names of sports' iconic figures: Babe Ruth or Hank Aaron, Arnold Palmer or Tiger Woods, Billy Jean King or Pete Sampras, Brett Favre or Jim Brown, Michael Jordan or Larry Bird, Richard Petty or Dale Earnhardt, Seabiscuit or Secretariat, and the list goes on. Sports enthusiasts become fans for various reasons: based on a team's star player, such as Magic Johnson and LeBron James; winning teams, such as the New York Yankees and Green Bay Packers; or unforgettable moments in sports history, such as the Ryder Cup matches between U.S. and European golfers, or Bill Mazeroski's walk-off ninth-inning home run to defeat the Yankees in 1960. The players and their athletic prowess and achievements are held in awe. Fans identify with them, children pretend to be them, and the games are exciting.

America's fascination with sports heroes is fascinating, eclectic, and contradictory. Prior to *Patton*'s (1970) credits, General George Patton, via George C. Scott's cinematic reincarnation, provided the quintessential example of the nation's fascination with war and sports heroes; standing beneath a massive U.S. flag, he says: "When you were kids, you all admired the champion marble shooter, the fastest runner, the big-league ballplayers, the toughest boxers. Americans love a winner and will not tolerate a loser. Americans play to win all the time. I wouldn't give a hoot in hell for a man who lost and laughed."[6] Scott's reincarnation glorifies Americans' attraction to and appreciation of those who "play to win" rather than athletes or soldiers who try to merely hold their positions. Sacrifice, teamwork, and competitive desire embrace the martial spirit as well as sports.

Americans' attraction to power and violence is reflected in their heroes. During the 1920s, for example, Babe Ruth, Bobby Jones, and Red Grange infected and bolstered Americans' imaginations. The 1920s public celebrated and revered their athletic heroes because of their performances on the field of play. Babe Ruth's brute power produced towering home runs, set extraordinary records, and established him as baseball's most revered player. Red Grange's athleticism—quickness and ability to change directions—led to dramatic touchdowns that made the "Galloping Ghost of the Gridiron" one of football's most celebrated halfbacks. By defeating Jess Willard, the "Pottawatomie Giant," in three rounds in 1919, Jack Dempsey ignited the public's imagination; mauling characterized Dempsey's fighting style. These sports heroes achieved instant success and adulation; as a result, the American public enthusiastically identified with and embraced them. Sport offers human beings the chance to experience heroic action or to vicariously participate by witnessing heroic action. What people respond to is physical excellence, what they ideally are as bodies. Their reaction can be an aesthetic and/or euphoric appreciation.

Enjoyment of Sports: Connecting a Nation

For a few, life really would not be worth living if they did not have a sport to play or watch. Sport, like popular culture, is a serious business: it communicates individuals', communities', and a nation's deepest needs and beliefs. The local eventually becomes the national. George H. W. Bush's 1988 acceptance speech for the Republican presidential nomination hit upon the significance of small-town Texas football and culture: "Now we moved to West Texas forty years ago, forty years ago this year. . . . And in time, we had six children, moved from a duplex apartment to a house, and lived the dream—high school football on Friday nights."[7] In Texas as with many other states, Friday-night high school football is a constant: it is an integral part of the community; it strengthens teams, schools, and communities. Like an oak whose roots are deep and broad, football games anchor people to the land, the community, and their humanness.

Similarly, Iowa's high school girls' basketball not only provides a place for Iowans to meet and cheer but also serves as a rite of passage for players. Without a doubt, sport is the most powerful institution for the socialization of young people; sport activity brings generations together. Through basketball and other sports, young people are initiated into the joys and sorrows of adulthood. Games embrace ceremony and provide continuity and cohesiveness for players, schools, and community alike. Sports towns, to include those that house high school, college, and professional teams, often see themselves athletically as competing city-states, much as the ancient Greeks saw Athens and Sparta.

Since the early 1990s, the term *soccer mom* (*soccer dad* is the male equivalent) denotes the large group of generally politically conservative women who possess a hint of feminism who take their school-age children to athletic events. A woman in Denver, Colorado, who was seeking a seat on the city council, however, identified her occupation as "a soccer mom." The stereotype embraces women who drive SUVs and are considered to be poor drivers, carry cell phones, have school-age children, and are middle- or upper-middle-class, suburban, and generally white. The term generally implies, too, that the women lack individuality and practice poor parenting skills. Since the 1992 presidential election, they have been credited with electing Presidents William J. Clinton and George W. Bush. In Canada, *soccer mom* refers to women whose children participate in athletics. Therefore, variations include basketball moms, hockey moms, volleyball moms, tennis moms, golf moms, or whatever sport one wants to add.

Sport has been transformed from children's recreational games such as baseball into an industry of major proportions. Professional and collegiate basketball, baseball, golf, hockey, football, and NASCAR have depended on print and television to capture the public's attention and praise. This essay focuses on popular sport in America and how it is presented to the public.

PREVALENT SPORTS IN THE COUNTRY

Because so many professional sports teams exist—not even counting minor-league baseball, basketball, and hockey—listing them all would be a difficult task; however, some professional sports include MLB, NFL, NHL, Pro Bowlers Tour (PBT), Ladies' Professional Golf Association (LPGA), Professional Golfers' Association (PGA), Pro Beach Volleyball (PBV) (men's and women's), professional rodeo, professional poker, professional drag racers, Funny Car Drivers Association, professional softball teams, professional fishing tournaments, NASCAR, horse racing, lacrosse, professional basketball (men's and women's), professional soccer, pool, and numerous other professional associations. Each association has its own hall of fame.

Aquatics

Whereas only a few individuals pursued swimming as a means of recreation and exercise until the mid-1800s, North Americans, particularly those who settled near the Atlantic Ocean or lakes and rivers, pursued such water sports as rowing and yachting. Their initial involvement with water was utilitarian. Obviously, because yachts have always been expensive to purchase and maintain, the financially elite owned and raced the yachts. Rowing clubs, generally formed at universities such as Yale and Harvard or in cities with easy access to waterways, appealed to students and middle-income individuals. Around 1850 people began to swim for recreation; later, because amateur contests were being conducted and instructional schools opened, the first swimming meet was held in 1883, and swimming was included as an Olympic sport in 1896.

The Young Men's Christian Association (YMCA) offered swimming lessons to their attendees by 1910. Although popular magazines encouraged females to swim for exercise, muscle toning, and coordination, women hesitated until Annette Kellerman introduced the one-piece bathing suit. Esther Williams, an amateur swimming champion, and Johnny Weissmuller, a five-time Olympic gold medalist, appeared in films that popularized water sports. Williams appeared in *Bathing Beauty*, *Neptune's Daughter*, and *Million Dollar Mermaid*; Weissmuller portrayed Tarzan.

Swimming pools dot the U.S. and Canadian landscapes today. Although swimming remains an ever-popular form of recreation, therapy, and exercise, amateurs dominate the sport. During summer vacations, parents continue to take their children to swimming lessons in country hamlets and large cities; generally speaking, public and private swimming pools, ocean beaches, lakes, and individual house pools are used for tanning and visiting purposes among teenagers and adults, whereas children use the pools to cool off during hot weather or for recreational purposes.

Archery

The sport of archery developed from humans' use of the bow and arrow to hunt, in warfare, or in competition; it was generally regarded as a rural sport. However, in 1828 twenty-five men in Philadelphia created the United Bowmen Association. The early upper-class founders called their contest grounds "Sherwood Forest," drawing on the legend of Robin Hood, a noted bandit who employed the bow and arrow to "take from the rich and give to the poor." Competitions adhered to a strict etiquette to include uniforms and strict military marching formations when the competitors entered the contest grounds, and winners received a silver punch bowl.

Although archery was accepted as an Olympic event in 1900, it was suspended because the rules committee did not provide competitors with uniform guidelines. It was readmitted in 1972 when precise competitive guidelines were established. At the 1996 Atlanta Olympic Games, Justin Huish won the United States' first gold medals in individual and team competition, but his physical appearance—sunglasses, long hair, and earring—propelled him to celebrity status in a sport generally reserved for conservative attire and appearance.

Automobile Racing

The automobile (a French term), one of the last major inventions of the nineteenth century, appealed to people interested in contesting time and distance. One year after an 1894 French automobile race from Paris to Rouen, the *Chicago-Times Herald*, offering $5000 in prize money, sponsored the United States' first auto race on roads without railings; Americans preferred the term *motor-carriage* or *motorcycle* to describe their "horseless carriage." Like Henry Ford, bicycle makers turned their attention to manufacturing automobiles. To enhance sales and following a French precedent, American entrepreneurs realized that races promoted public interest. The speed merchants understood their clientele: driving machines at fast speeds on dangerous rough roads encapsulates a portion of automobile racing's appeal.

The Automobile Club of America, as well as racing clubs, was created for the Vanderbilt Cup and the Glidden Tour. Daytona Beach became a center for speed trials, and Savannah hosted the Grand Prize Race; other cities built racing tracks. In 1911, with the construction of the Indianapolis Speedway, America's fascination with automobile racing attracted mechanics and enthusiasts as well as those with a peripheral interest in the sport. Excepting 1942–45, America's attention turns each Memorial Day to "the greatest spectacle in racing," the Indianapolis 500, a race initially created by Carl G. Fisher to test automobile design and durability, and to promote the city as a potential center for the emerging automobile industry. Early critics deplored Memorial Day as race day because, they believed, racing detracted from honoring the war dead and from promoting patriotism. Proponents argued that the race celebrated the United States' innovativeness and bravery. Ray Harroun, the first winner, averaged 75 mph; because the crushed stone and asphalt track proved dangerous and inhibited speed in later races, the brick track was laid. Lewis Strang's demonstration, which averaged 91.81 mph over 5 miles and reached an unimaginable top speed of 111.86 mph, proved the new "brickyard track" as the better surface. Sam Hornish, the 2006 winner, averaged 157.085

mph to earn his $1.74 million victory check. In 1977, six years after women were admitted to the garage area, Janet Guthrie qualified to race at Indianapolis; since then, four other women have qualified, but flawless driver Danica Patrick's fourth-place finish in 2005 and her eighth-place finish in 2006 have been the best performances by a female. The Indianapolis 500, like all automotive events, continues to offer a tripartite attraction: people are fascinated by technological advancements, speed, and the potential for crashes. In 1986 American Broadcasting Corporation's (ABC) live broadcasts began, and Entertainment and Sports Programming Network (ESPN) provides race trial coverage.

NASCAR, whose early drivers included moonshine runners seeking new racing forms to test and hone their skills, offered its first sponsored race at Daytona in 1948. Racing's daredevils created an image of mavericks, rednecks, and outlaws that still embraces and attracts fans. Whereas the Indianapolis 500 hosts Formula One or Grand Prix races, NASCAR draws better than 127,000 fans at each event, making stock cars the premier racing attraction. Race days are spectacles complete with a sense of carnival and festival: fans arrive early wearing a T-shirt purchased from their favorite driver's concession stand, and often have an opportunity to speak with some drivers prior to the race. Although drivers speed down straightaways at better than 200 mph, they employ "drafting," which they use like a slingshot to pass a driver at race's end, as their primary driving strategy.

To enhance speed, danger, and visibility for drivers and fans alike, dirt tracks were replaced; drivers used their cars to advertise products, and reckless driving, prize money, and fan interest increased in the 1950s. NASCAR-sponsored events include the Winston Cup Series, the Bush Grand National, and regional events during the February to November racing calendar. Wendall Scott was the first African American to win a race. Legendary drivers such as Richard "King Richard" Petty (his 200-plus victories made him the sport's most celebrated driver), Glenn "Fireball" Roberts, Cale Yarborough, Dale Earnhardt, Rusty Wallace, Bill Elliott, Jeff Gordon, and others are revered for their courage and driving skills. In 1976 Janet Guthrie became the first woman to drive in a NASCAR-sponsored event. To enhance television viewers' experience, some drivers have allowed in-car cameras that capture crashes and "drafting" from the drivers' point of view; again, television viewers can vicariously experience the danger that the drivers experience. In recent years, politicians and the entertainment media have taken notice of the popularity of NASCAR, and political pundits have coined the term "NASCAR dads" to refer to generally conservative, blue-collar, white men.

Baseball

Baseball is the oldest and most documented sport in America, although where and when baseball first appeared in the United States remains a mystery. Historians have indicated that a baseball game was played in Canada as early as 1836. However, Abner Doubleday is falsely credited with creating the game in 1839 in Elihu Phinney's farm field in Cooperstown, New York. He may not have ever played or seen a similar game that was played in the 1840s, but bat-and-ball games, such as rounders, cricket, and o' cat, had been played since the English landed in America; these games also involved hitting a ball and running to a base before being tagged out with a ball. Early balls were made of rags and leather, and the bats were paddles or small tree branches. Like many later rural and urban homemade diamonds, participants used trees, stones, stakes, automobiles, or some other item to designate bases.

Baseball, uniquely American, is "the national pastime" and is the United States' most significant contribution to international sport. Some people are attracted to baseball for its romantic and pastoral tradition because it is played on a lawn and because a clock does not control the alternate rhythms and length of play. Although many individuals associate baseball as a country sport, it was popularized and created as an urban sport for tradesmen and laborers in New York City during the early 1800s.

Baseball has infiltrated and influenced American language and culture. Such phrases as "getting to first base" (or "getting to second base," etc.) suggest sexual accomplishments; "coming out of left field" refers to the occurrence of something unexpected. "Hardball" not only differentiates baseball from softball but also carries connotations associated with politics, the business world, and social lives. Players and their careers are associated with cultural or political achievements: Jackie Robinson represents the courage of the civil rights movement; Lou Gehrig symbolizes the emotional and psychological strength of one confronting death; Pete Rose, nicknamed "Charlie Hustle" because of his aggressive play before 1989, now suggests cheating, gambling, and lying; Barry Bonds and Rafael Palmeiro represent athletes who cheat by using steroids to enhance body image and performance.

Around 1880–90, significant rule changes regarding baseball occurred. By 1884 pitchers were permitted to throw overhand. By 1887 batters were no longer allowed to call for a high or low pitch. Prior to 1889 a walk was allowed if a pitcher did not throw as many as nine pitches over home plate. By the 1890s catchers wore masks and managers could make lineup substitutions. The distance between home plate and the pitcher's mound was standardized at 60 feet 6 inches. Foul balls were counted as strikes in 1901, and in 1895 the infield fly rule was adopted.

Bloomer girl teams provided turn-of-the-century women with an opportunity to play baseball, although Vassar and Smith colleges fielded women's teams. Although two men, called "toppers" because they wore wigs, could play on a team, women's success defied their critics who claimed that women were inferior athletes and should instead pursue domestic duties. Because the teams were connected to Amelia Jenks Bloomer, a suffragette, various cities fielded teams to play against amateur and semipro teams. Bloomer teams provided women an entrée into sports; by demonstrating that females can be athletic, these teams laid the foundation for the 1940s and 1950s All-American Girls Professional Baseball League. Penny Marshall's *A League of Their Own* (1992), perhaps the decade's most culturally significant sports film, celebrates the obscure league's cultural, feminist, and athletic accomplishments. Like *Field of Dreams* (1989), Marshall's cinematic work captures the nostalgia that permeates baseball as well as America's yearning for a simpler, less stressful time.

Major League Baseball comprises twenty-eight teams in the United States and two in Canada. Baseball stadiums are designed to attract and to reflect American culture. Although in previous years stadiums such as Tiger Stadium and Candlestick Park serviced baseball and football, today's owners distinguish and identify their team and their locale; as a result, these facilities, some privately owned and others financed via municipal monies, are unique because they function similarly to stages on which the players perform. In 1923 Governor Alfred E. Smith threw out the ceremonial first pitch in the $2,500,000 Yankee Stadium, "the House That Ruth Built," before a crowd of 74,200 adoring Yankee fans watched Babe Ruth hit a home run.

In 1919 the notorious "Black Sox" scandal broke out. Eight prominent Chicago White Sox players, including "Shoeless" Joe Jackson and Buck Weaver, who performed admirably, were banished for life from baseball for "throwing the World Series." No player was found guilty; nevertheless, baseball was in financial trouble, was perceived as being corrupt, and was losing its fan base. Two important men brought baseball back as the nation's national pastime. First, Commissioner Kenesaw Mountain Landis, who had previously served as a federal judge, restored public confidence by banishing the White Sox players. Landis's crusading vigilance and honesty reflected his personal values as well as those of baseball. Almost concurrently, for $125,000 the New York Yankees purchased a young pitcher from the Boston Red Sox in 1920. George Herman (Babe) Ruth, a character as boisterous and almost as humorous as Will Rogers, began a career of jettisoning baseballs out of ballparks. His long, lofty home runs and charismatic behavior not only attracted boys into stadiums but also appealed to everyone's childlike qualities. The Babe's home run power ignited imaginations, and his enthusiasm for the game and his desire for victory encouraged fans, even those in opposition parks, to admire his love for the game.

Because blacks were generally excluded from professional baseball and because black communities experienced an increased interest in baseball during the early twentieth century, Andrew "Rube" Foster, "the father of black baseball," who formed and coached the Chicago American Giants, his own team, is credited with being a major force in the founding of the Negro National League, which opened play in 1920. In doing so, he created the largest black-run business in the country. The league was popular during the 1940s and included such celebrated players as Leroy "Satchel" Paige, William "Judy" Johnson, Josh Gibson, and James "Cool Papa" Bell. Black communities were enthusiastic when their teams played white teams in exhibition games. Integration of the leagues occurred when Jackie Robinson joined the Los Angeles Dodgers; in 1959, after the Boston Red Sox added Pumpsie Green to their roster, every major-league team finally had at least one black player. Following the 1948 season the Negro National League disbanded because they could not field high-quality teams.

Since the 1930s, American cinema has celebrated baseball's innocence and addressed the deleterious effects of scandal on the game and society. The 1920s, sometimes called the Golden Age of American Sport because it produced legendary figures such as Babe Ruth, Jack Dempsey, Bill Tilden, Red Grange, and Robert T. Jones, Jr., celebrated the heroes' performances not only on the field but also in cinema; cinema has also allowed filmmakers to address scandals in baseball as well as the game's pastoral wholesomeness. Babe Ruth, whose nickname capitalized on his childlike behavior, is associated with American innocence and uncouthness as well as boyish awkwardness and brutishness. Hollywood created cinematic opportunities for Ruth such as *Headin' Home* (1920); in the film the Babe, playing a likable iceman who, during his spare time, employs a hatchet to form a baseball bat from a large piece of wood, is attracted to an attractive blonde, wins a World Series with his homemade bat, and then returns home to his sister and mother. *The Natural* (1984) captured the game and its hero, Roy Hobbs, as emblematic of the American dream and the American myth of success. The film suggests, like *Field of Dreams* (1989), that baseball can regenerate individuals, families, and communities by providing a focus on middle-American values and doing the right thing. In contrast, by focusing on the 1919 "Black Sox" scandal, *Eight Men Out* (1988) eschews the optimism of the other films by stating that the men are "out of baseball" because the evil owners are concerned solely with winning, no matter what the costs, and because the undisciplined, conspiratorial players do not respect the game.

In 1930 major-league attendance exceeded 10,000,000. Fans were attracted to the game and its heroes, particularly Babe Ruth, although Ruth has always had his detractors. Nevertheless, Babe Ruth still is the yardstick by which all baseball players are measured, particularly hitters. The era does not matter: Ty Cobb, Lou Gehrig, Joe DiMaggio, Ted Williams, Mickey Mantle, Hank Aaron, Willie Mays, Mark McGwire, Sammy Sosa, and Barry Bonds, who hit home run 715 on May 28, 2006, are always compared to the Babe. Even though Hank Aaron has hit 755 home runs, 41 more than Ruth, the Babe, or his ghost and aura, attract more attention and comparison than Aaron.

The Depression affected all aspects of American life, but Branch Rickey's St. Louis Cardinals developed a farm system that would train future big-league stars and financially help smaller cities. Following his lead were the Boston Red Sox and the Detroit Tigers, whose farm team experiments not only produced better ballplayers, and helped successful teams attract bigger audiences, but also enhanced the teams' financial status. The advent of night baseball provided another innovation that saved ball teams from possible financial ruin. Cincinnati was the first major-league team to play a night game, although some night-game experimentation had been conducted as early as the 1880s. Daylight saving time and reduced workdays enhanced the popularity of night games as well as twilight games for professionals and amateurs.

Other contributing factors to baseball's resurrection as the national pastime included the formation of semiprofessional baseball teams as well as the formation of American Legion Junior Baseball tournaments. Softball, indoor baseball, and the building of numerous playground fields enhanced children's participation in the game. In 1934 with George Sisler's guidance, the Amateur Softball Association was founded, and many of the games were played at night. Softball appealed to all ages of men and women, and several industrial leagues and state championships were staged.

During World War II all sports suffered; athletes either volunteered or were drafted in the military to assist with the war effort. The loss of players and financial support caused many teams, particularly minor-league clubs, to fold. Nevertheless, soldiers at home and in foreign countries either listened to the radio broadcast or received other reports via the *Stars and Stripes* or *Sporting News* of the Cardinals' 1942 World Series victory over the Yankees. In some ways, baseball, either through amateur games held at all times of the day because of workers' day shifts and night shifts or through pickup games played by military personnel, served as a means of relaxation and connection to American values and recreation.

Through the years baseball, like American society, has evolved and been forced to address cultural and social issues. As early as the 1880s players formed unions and forced actions from owners and athletes alike; the "reserve clause" contractually bound players indefinitely to a team. In 1969 St. Louis outfielder Curt Flood challenged the "reserve clause" by refusing to sign with the Cards, and the U.S. Supreme Court ruled that he could be a "free agent." Flood, who fought not only the system but also big business, became an icon of heroic proportions for working-class fans; other players, such as Catfish Hunter and Andy Messersmith, who sported long hair and mustaches and represented the rebellious spirit of the 1960s and 1970s, reminded fans of the late-nineteenth-century players who formed wildcat leagues. However, as in the 1994–95 strike, betrayed fans opposed the players' strike for more money and bargaining power because they believed that the players' requests were unjustified; fans viewed the players as rich, spoiled millionaires, given that baseball salaries averaged almost a million a year. When the 1994 World Series was canceled, owners swore that they would play the 1995 season with replacement players; however, by spring, the owners caved in to the players' demands.

During the twenty-first century, baseball remains popular among Americans, and when the Boston Red Sox and the Chicago White Sox won the World Series in 2004 and 2005, respectively, various jinxes were jettisoned. Perhaps more importantly, at the turn of the century and in 2006, individual accomplishments, such as Cal Ripken's successful quest to establish a new consecutive-game record, or Sammy Sosa's and Mark McGwire's 1998 home run race to surpass Roger Maris's single-season record, captured the public's imagination. In 2006 Barry Bonds caught and passed the Babe's home run mark of 714, but the public, with the exception of fans of the San Francisco Giants, his home team, were not enraptured; some were disappointed, because of his association with the use of steroids.

Like the 1919 "Black Sox" scandal, Bonds, although not yet proven guilty, had denigrated baseball's ethics.

Basketball

During the winter of 1891 Luther Gulick, a Massachusetts YMCA director, confronted a number of young athletes who were tired of studying gymnastics between football and baseball seasons. Gulick asked James Naismith, a Canadian who worked for Springfield College, to find a sport that would keep the boys' attention occupied and develop them physically. After trying and abandoning several different sports, he settled upon "Basket Ball," which utilized a soccer ball and peach baskets, nailed to walls, as goals. He provided thirteen rules. The first game was played in 1892, and in 1895 Minneapolis State School of Agriculture defeated Hamline University 9–3 in the first intercollegiate game; the first professional game was held in Trenton, New Jersey, in 1896.

Basketball became immensely popular among inner-city youth, men and women, and immigrants because it was inexpensive and did not require special equipment or much space. As a result churches, schoolyards, gymnasiums, particularly YMCAs, and even rural settlements could easily provide a court for the players. As early as 1898 the game was played professionally. The first amateur championship was held in 1897; the Buffalo Germans, the most successful early team, won the Pan American Games in 1901 and the national amateur championship and an Olympic gold medal in 1904. They then turned professional and were undefeated throughout 1909 and 1910; when they finally retired from professional basketball, they boasted a 792–85 record. Although the rules for professional basketball varied from league to league, many players wore padding and were allowed one dribble; courts were surrounded with a wire mesh cage to keep the balls on the court and to prevent players from fighting over the balls, and backboards were created to prevent fans from reaching through the nets and deflecting opponents' shots.

Although basketball was popular in college as a sport for males and females, games were low-scoring contests because the teams had a center jump after each basket, and because the games were extremely physical. Harvard University, for example, became so distraught by the physical play that it dropped basketball as an intercollegiate sport in 1909; perhaps it abandoned the sport, too, because of the team's losing records. Nevertheless, to eliminate rough play and to maintain the academy's support, the 1910 new rules added a second referee and lowered the maximum number of personal fouls to four rather than five. Female students, who already played field hockey and participated in track-and-field events, were particularly attracted to basketball; early uniforms generally included long stockings, bloomers, and blouses. Whereas some critics warned that athletics might psychologically and physically harm young women, others, particularly the participants, argued that athletics enhanced teamwork, school spirit, and good health; interestingly, some educators also noted that athletic participation would not only strengthen women physically and psychologically but also decrease their desire for premarital activity.

In the 1920s basketball was introduced to junior high schools, and rural communities built gymnasiums for their students. As a result, the game attracted more fans and athletes. As early as 1923 an invitational basketball tournament was held at the University of Chicago, and the state of Indiana became the nation's basketball hotbed; even today, scholars, sports broadcasters, and coaches refer to Indiana, Kentucky, and Ohio as the "heartland of American basketball," although West Coast and East Coast teams have won the NCAA Men's and Women's championships. The Depression and World War II disrupted basketball because people either had little money or had little time to attend athletic events, and basketball was relegated to a second-tier sport. However, in 1938 the Intercollegiate Athletic Association (IAA) announced that they would change their name to NCAA and would host a "one and out" March tournament to determine a national champion: thus, March Madness was born.

In 1949 the National Basketball Association (NBA) was formed when the National Basketball League (NBL) and the Basketball Association of America (BAA) banded together to create a seventeen-team league. Caucasians dominated early basketball, particularly from the 1930s to the 1960s, but race was an issue then as now. For example, in 1918 Eddie Gottlieb formed the South Philadelphia Hebrew Association (SPHA), and the teams were successful on the court and attendees shelled out $2 per ticket; however, in the 1930s, anti-Semitism, caused in part because some people believed that Jewish bankers had caused the economic depression, and harassing crowds followed the SPHAs. In fact, the American Nazi Party threatened to sue the teams. Chuck Cooper broke basketball's color barrier when he signed with the Boston Celtics in 1950. From the 1950s to the present, some American fans harass African-American players; in the 1980s when Larry Bird, the "Great White Hope," battled Ervin "Magic" Johnson's Lakers, people, predominantly white audiences, cheered for the Celtics because they thought that basketball had become a black sport. Some black athletes, such as the Pistons' Isaiah Thomas and Dennis Rodman, claimed that Bird's stardom was the result of race rather than play. Over the past ten years, American NBA players have complained that too many foreign-born players have taken roster positions away from American players.

For collegiate basketball, the 1950s got off to a good start, or so it seemed; between 1947 and 1950 players were involved with point shaving, including three CCNY members, the National Invitation Tournament champion, three Bradley University players, and two Kentucky All-Americans. Collegiate basketball's purity and image were stained, as was the image of New York City, basketball's mecca.

In an attempt to attract more fans to professional and collegiate basketball, the game needed to change. The game was too slow: because fifty to sixty fouls were called per game, audiences were bored; they were also tired of two-handed set shots and the ban on dunking. In the late 1940s Joe "Jumpin' Joe" Fulks popularized the jump shot and averaged over 20 points per game, and Bob Pettit, who ranks seventeenth in NBA scoring, honed the jump shot in the 1950s. In 1954 the NBA instituted the 24-second clock. In college as well as the NBA, Bill Russell's teams changed basketball strategy. Coached by Red Auerbach, the Celtics' Russell anchored the defense, Frank Ramsey was the original sixth man, K. C. Jones, the tenacious defensive artist, shut down the opponent's top scoring guard, and Bob Cousy, who led the NBA in assists for eight straight years, was the playmaker. Sam Jones opened up the floor with his accurate long-range shooting; the Celtics' other great role players included Tommy Heinsohn, Don Nelson, Sam Jones, John Havlicek, and Bill Sharman. The list goes on, but the Celtics, with sixteen NBA championships, won eleven from 1957 to 1969. The success of their dynasty will likely never be equaled in the NBA; however, at the collegiate level, the teams of Coach John Wooden, the "Wizard of Westwood," won nine championships from 1964 to 1973. In 1966 Texas Western, the first collegiate team to start five black players, defeated Kentucky, which started five white players, 72–65. Coach Don Haskins's book *Glory Road*, which examines Texas Western's championship season, was filmed and released with the same title in January 2006.

College and professional basketball has flourished through the 1980s to the present, although the usual roadblocks have emerged; for example, players continue to be arrested for drugs, murder, sex scandals, and gambling. High school graduates including Kevin Garnett and Kobe Bryant did not attend college. NBA Commissioner David Stern has cleaned up the professional game, negotiated contracts that financially helped more franchises, and required players to present a positive image to children. In 2006 Stern instituted a dress code that stated that players must wear business casual attire whenever they are engaged with team or league business.

Women's basketball has experienced tremendous growth at the collegiate and high school levels; although the Women's National Basketball Association (WNBA) provides a professional venue, attendance and coaching salaries do not rival those at the collegiate level. In 2006 the University of Tennessee's Pat Summitt's contract was extended, and she will receive an average of $1.3 million for the next six years; Summitt's teams have 913 victories. Women players such as Nancy "Lady Magic" Lieberman, the first woman to play in a men's professional league, Sheryl Swoopes, hired by Nike as its first spokeswoman, and other players have transformed women's basketball from a tedious, slow-paced, ladylike game to an exciting athletic competition with deft three-point shooting and aggressive defense.

Bowling

The earliest mention of bowling in American literature is by Washington Irving, when Rip Van Winkle awakens to the sound of "crashing ninepins." By the late 1800s bowling had become popular in America; people with money bowled in country-club-like alleys while the working class bowled in "saloons," a word used to describe early skating rinks and ice cream parlors. Early Dutch settlers initially used ninepins and played on lawns. In 1895 the American Bowling Congress, which standardized the rules, was founded, and leagues held their tournaments in New York City. By 1916 women bowlers organized the Women's National Bowling Association, later called the Women's International Bowling Congress.

By adding proper lighting and clean facilities, 1930s bowling alleys, which enhanced camaraderie, popularized and attracted more women and industrial workers to their sport. Professional bowling, which did not initially exclude amateurs from participating or accepting money, emerged with the 1939 ABC Cleveland tournament. Because bowling is not as physically strenuous or as expensive as several other sports, it appeals to all ages, sexes, and classes: participants can bowl at any time of the day or night, and weather does not affect play. Millions of people participate in organized leagues for youth, adults, senior citizens, amateurs, collegiate athletes, professionals, and the physically challenged. Teams generally consist of three to five participants and can include gender-exclusive or gender-mixed teams. In 1950, under pressure by the National Association for the Advancement of Colored People (NAACP) for ten years, the National American Bowling Congress finally lifted its ban on African Americans from membership.

Boxing

Boxing has been ever-present in North America. The British aristocracy boxed during the colonial period as a pastime and as an opportunity to hone combat skills. The sport did not achieve popularity until the 1880s, because religious, state, and local authorities believed that the sport epitomized immorality not only because of its brutality but also because gamblers, thieves, and social outcasts frequented the matches. To avoid conflicts with the law, early boxing contests were often held in isolated locations. Without a doubt, however, boxing has been a means for impoverished urban and rural Americans to gain social status and wealth; to achieve these goals, they are often felled physically and neurologically by the accumulation of blows to the body and head.

The sport gained popularity in the United States and Canada during the Civil War because cramped soldiers used boxing to settle grudges as well as to test their skills,

Joseph Louis Barrow (Joe Louis) is regarded as one of the best boxers of all time and for accomplishing as much for blacks in the sport of boxing as Jackie Robinson did in baseball. Although he lost his first amateur fight in 1932, he won forty-three of his next fifty by knockout while losing four; he turned professional on July 4, 1934. In the ring, he set up his opponents with wicked jabs from either hand and then punished them with jackhammer-like punches. For many boxing aficionados, Louis symbolizes the classic, quintessential boxing style that has been emulated by thousands of young fighters. He won the championship by defeating James J. Braddock in 1937; although Braddock floored Louis early in the fight, Louis knocked out the champion in the eighth round and became the hero for many black youths.

Just as Jessie Owens's triumphs at the 1936 Olympics elevated him to national attention and favor, Louis became a hero for all America by defeating Max Schmeling, who represented Hitler's Nazism and "master race," in 2:04 minutes of the first round. White Americans accepted Louis because he maintained a discretionary private life. His reputation and fame soared during World War II because, unlike Dempsey's and Jess Willard's evasion of military service in World War I, Louis declined a military deferment, donated his two title defenses' winnings to the Army and Navy Relief Funds, and gave exhibition matches at military camps and hospitals. Nonetheless, when Jackie Robinson faced a court-martial because he refused to ride in the back of a bus, Louis supported him; Louis also threatened to abandon his exhibition matches unless the army allowed all members of the armed forces in England to use the same theater entrances. Louis symbolized patriotism and sacrifice, but he also epitomized honesty, personal restraint, and modesty.

For further discussion of Joe Louis and America, readers should consult Gerald Astor, *And a Credit to His Race: The Hard Life and Times of Joe Louis Barrow, a.k.a. Joe Louis* (New York: Dutton, 1974) and Chris Mead, *Champion: Joe Louis, Black Hero in White America* (New York: Scribner, 1985).

courage, toughness, and intelligence; boxing also relieved tedium. With the 1882 crowning of John L. Sullivan, "the Boston Strongboy," as the heavyweight champion because he had defeated all challengers from the United States and England, the world had its first "world champion." Sullivan captivated the public's imagination; he gave hundreds of exhibitions throughout the United States as he toured with a theatrical troupe; Sullivan is the United States' first legendary sports hero. During this time, fights were bare-knuckle and no time limits were set.

On September 7, 1892, at New Orleans's Olympic Club, James J. ("Gentleman Jim") Colbert fought and defeated the aging Sullivan; for the first time, the press covered the match not only before the fight but also after the fight. The modern era of pugilism had dawned. John L.'s boxing success and legendary status influenced Theodore Roosevelt, who celebrated the strenuous life, and ranks him among the most popular and respected all-time boxers. Like Colbert and those who followed him, working-class Americans and Canadians pursue boxing because it is a version of the American dream: one can earn upward mobility in an acceptable manner. Prize money reflects the winner's prosperity, his hard work and determination, and success in a hard world; winning the heavyweight championship fulfills the American desire for machismo and social status. If a few of the champion's private sins become public, they are generally forgiven, particularly if the champion is Caucasian. For example, Sullivan drank a lot and bragged about his accomplishments both in and out of the ring; Jack Dempsey managed to avoid World War I: both were revered.

Blacks, on the other hand, have historically remained a peripheral group within the United States. African-American Jack Johnson's status as heavyweight champion challenged white culture because he was not modest, did not seem to be grateful, and, above all, was not white. Instead, Johnson, who won the heavyweight championship in 1908 and held it until 1915, was perceived by white society as being too socially aggressive outside the ring and as flaunting his success: he openly dated white women, wore brash, "tasteless" clothes, and drove expensive cars. In other words, he was the stereotypical example of black male virility. When Johnson brutally demolished Jim Jeffries, a retired former white champion, numerous race riots, fueled by black celebrations and white rage, erupted throughout the United States. Some white boxing executives prohibited the film of the fight from crossing state lines. Although no fighter could stop Johnson, Congress did. Because interracial marriages were banned and because Johnson's marriages to two white women received national publicity, he was convicted of transporting his wife across state lines prior to their marriage. Johnson and his boxing career symbolized the defiant black champion who refused to adhere to white society's prescribed roles.

During the early days of boxing, blacks were allowed to contend for championships in the lighter weights, but no black heavyweight crossed the color line until Joe Louis ("The Brown Bomber") won the title in 1937. Whereas Johnson ignited white ire and reflected the stormy racial problems of the Progressive Period, Louis gained white respect and personified the New Deal and World War II. Later, Muhammad Ali, born Cassius Marcellus Clay, champion from 1964 to 1967 and again from 1974 to 1978, symbolized the rebellious, defiant 1960s and early 1970s.

Ali, like Johnson and Louis, emerged when boxing needed to recover from a recession. After Rocky Marciano retired in 1956, the heavyweight division was riddled with three unpopular champions: Floyd Patterson, noted for avoiding tough competition; Ingemar Johansson, truly an inept fighter; and Sonny Liston, who served two prison terms and was reputed to be contractually connected to gangsters. Ali, a former Olympic champion, rescued professional boxing and established himself as both a revered and hated man. By hurling racial epithets at future competitors, calling himself "The Greatest," and joining the Nation of Islam, a militant Black Muslim group, and changing his name, Ali was hated by many people from all races. In the ring, Ali used adept footwork and boxing skill, which he described with the phrase "float like a butterfly, sting like a bee." When he refused military induction in April 1967, he was found guilty of violating the Selective Service Act, stripped of his championship, and barred from professional boxing. The Supreme Court unanimously reversed the conviction in June 1971.

Ali's public image depended on the ever-changing sentiment regarding the Vietnam War and the racial friction that existed in the United States. His was able to transform his image by 1974, when he defeated George Foreman: *Sports Illustrated* designated him as "Sportsman of the Year," and Philadelphia created and celebrated "Muhammad Ali Day." Howard Cosell, ABC's innovative sportscaster and vocal spokesman against racism, defended Ali for his antiwar stance, and his interviews with Ali prior to championship fights increased their mutual celebrity status. Like Johnson and Louis, Ali is a mythical figure that transcends sport. Unwilling to be a humble, patriotic black athlete, Ali threatened society because he forced society to confront a volatile and contradictory champion and proponent of racial equality. No matter what one thinks of Ali, he represents the United States' contradictions and conflicts during a turbulent, anxious, and repressive time.

LANCE ARMSTRONG

Lance Armstrong (1971–) is the United States' most celebrated and accomplished cyclist. Although he was accused of using steroids, he was cleared of the charge in 2006. Because of his acclaimed achievements, he is known as "the greatest" cyclist of all time. Seven consecutive victories (1999–2005) in the Tour de France, cycling's most prestigious and grueling test of human endurance, testify to his skill and determination. In 1996, after battling tremendous stomach pain, he was examined and told that he had testicular cancer, which had invaded his stomach, lungs, and brain; his physical hardships and his steadfast focus to overcome cancer epitomizes the individual who must confront all obstacles aggressively. Because of his Tour de France victories, combined with his cancer survival and with his regimented work ethic, Armstrong symbolizes the battles and victories that all people confront. During Armstrong's cancer treatment, while working diligently with physicians, dieticians, therapists, and other medical consultants, he learned the importance of teamwork, which he later used to revolutionize tour cycling competitions.

For further discussion of Lance Armstrong, readers should consult Lance Armstrong with Sally Jenkins, *It's Not about the Bike: My Journey Back to Life* (New York: Berkley Books, 2000), and Bill Gutman, *Lance Armstrong: A Biography* (New York: Simon Spotlight Entertainment, 2003).

Since Ali, the heavyweight division has been searching for a champion who can and will transcend their times and athletic achievements. Excepting Evander Holyfield, the champions have been personal and financial failures. For example, Mike Tyson burst on the 1990s boxing scene with headlines that focused more on his personal behavior than his boxing skill. Noted as a "bad boy," he destroyed opponents with vicious rights; he seemed unstoppable, until James "Buster" Douglas, a 42–1 underdog, KO'd him in ten rounds. Tyson's self-destructive, erratic behavior—such as sexually assaulting Desiree Washington in 1992 and serving three years in an Indianapolis prison, and being fined $3 million and having his boxing license revoked for biting off part of Holyfield's ear in 1997—left him outside public understanding. Rather than fighting racial or social demons, Tyson could not control his personal battles and temperament.

Cycling

Initially exciting, but dangerous because mid-1800s cycling enthusiasts contended with dirt roads and their ruts, the "velocipede," as the first two-wheeled machines were called, became an obsession among children and adults; following the rough start, a renewed interest in bicycling emerged in 1877 when Cunningham and Company, a New England manufacturing firm, began selling English imports and when the Boston Bicycle Club was founded in 1878. Whereas most cyclists still tend to ride for recreational purposes, competitive interest appeared in many New England towns. In 1880 the League of American Wheelmen, convening in Rhode Island, was formed to promote cycling as a means of liberation, travel, sport, and amusement. To meet the growing interest in cycling, several magazines—*Wheelman* (later called *Outing* in 1883), *Bicycling World*, and *Cycling Gazette*—chronicled the sport's growing popularity. Women enhanced the cycling craze by pedaling their way through city parks and roads as well as trekking through beautiful countrysides, whereas others pursued cycling competitively; women's participation also altered fashion with the creation of "bloomers." Bicycles are still employed by many police crews to patrol towns, parks, and universities. Marshall (Major) Taylor, a black cyclist, held three world records, fought discrimination in his sport in the 1890s, and contributed to the entrance of minorities in cycling.

Extreme Sports

Youth have always sought means to differentiate and express themselves, whether it is through fashion, language, or sport. Extreme sports, which have been defined as "action sport" or "alternative sports," generally describes individual sports that encourage speed, height, danger, and spectacular stunts. The term gained popularity in 1995 with ESPN's broadcast of "Extreme Games"; the name was changed to "X Games" because the participants were Generation Xers. Such sports as aggressive in-line skating, BASE jumping, bodyboarding, climbing, extreme skiing, skiboarding, skydiving, skateboarding, downhill bike racing, snowboarding, and others are often classified as "extreme sports." Individuals who participate in these sports seek a rush or unique experience that cannot be achieved without the severity of a course or the dangerousness of the activity; these sports rely on actual levels of danger. For example, football, though dangerous and certainly adrenaline-producing, is too traditional, whereas skiing down steep inclines and jumping off mountain ledges produce challenges not confronted via traditional downhill skiing. The activity, combined with the generation's attire and music, allows for individual expression and new physical boundaries to be tested. Danger and the possibility of death in inhospitable environments allow the "adrenaline junkie" to employ risk-taking as a rite of passage.

The term "extreme sport" gained popularity at the end of the twentieth century with young adults who were looking to escape life's daily rigors; on the snow slope, in the water, or racing down a city street on a board one inch removed from the pavement, participants challenge their physical and mental stamina as well as the environment. Some sports enthusiasts, who refuse to concede that "extreme sports" are truly sports, condemn the activities and refer to the participants as stupid, reckless, and suicidal; they also maintain that because "extreme sports" do not have established rules, uniforms, and teams, they are not sports. Parodies of extreme sports have emerged, such as extreme ironing, urban housework, extreme croquet, and extreme wheelbarrow racing.

Football

Writing at the beginning of the twentieth century, James Bryce recognized the growing American fascination and passion for watching sport:

> It occupies the minds not only of the youth at the universities, but also of their parents and of the general public. Baseball matches and football matches excite an interest greater than any other public events except the Presidential election, and that comes every four years . . . (and) the interest in one of the great contests, such as those which draw forty thousand spectators to the great "Stadium" recently erected at Cambridge, Massachusetts, appears to pervade nearly all classes more than does any "sporting event" in Great Britain. The American love of excitement and love of competition has seized upon these games.[8]

In less than one hundred years, a passion for athletic events enveloped North America. Americans had become more conscious of sports, the Puritan discipline and exclusion of athletic activities was gone, and a growing concern for the nation's health and well-being had influenced the public.

As an offshoot of the Industrial Revolution's soccer and rugby, early U.S. and Canadian participants played football primarily as a kicking game, although teams could kick or carry a ball across the opposition's goal line. The sport's primitive nature resulted in arguments over rules as well as the game's violence. In fact, Harvard's faculty, after what was called "Bloody Monday," voted 25–4 to abolish the game because of violence and the participants' excessive drinking in 1885. Spontaneous university games were used by upperclassmen to initiate the underclassmen. The first intercollegiate football game pitted Rutgers against Princeton in 1869, which Rutgers won 6–4. An 1874 match between Harvard and McGill marks the first time that a football game emphasized running with the ball rather than kicking it. The Intercollegiate Football Association was created at the Massasoit House at Springfield, Massachusetts, in 1876. Canadian football prospered in Montreal and Toronto, but supporters, who could not decide whether to emphasize rugby or soccer, eventually adopted the U.S. brand of football; however, their game blended U.S. and British influences. In the 1890s football soared into prominence as a collegiate and sandlot game.

College coaches such as Amos Alonzo Stagg, Pop Warner, Bob Zuppke, and Knute Rockne are credited with developing and adapting football's fundamental offensive formations and strategies; ironically, some of the coaches, because they produced winning teams, received significantly more pay than the universities' professors and almost as much as the universities' presidents. Because colleges began to emphasize winning, because commercialism, professionalism, and brutality dominated the collegiate game, and because investigative newspapermen attacked the recruiting scandals, the financial costs, and the win-at-all-costs ethic, football developed the Intercollegiate Athletic Association (IAA) in 1906; it was renamed the National Collegiate Athletic Association (NCAA) in 1910. This association continues to investigate violations in the collegiate game as well as provide guidelines for play.

While the collegiate game dominated fans' interest, professional football had difficulty because few players were paid to play. Two Pennsylvania teams, one from Latrobe and one from Jeannette, played the first professional football game in 1895 in Latrobe. Whereas the Pittsburgh Professionals are recognized as the first pro team, the Pittsburgh Duquesnes, financed by two steel executives, William C. Temple and A. C. Dinkey, was the first full-salaried team. The players were generally steelworkers who were rescued from work during the season so that they could practice for games; these workers also received financial bonuses to play. Later teams employed coal miners, boilermakers, and longshoremen as well as steelworkers; team names such as the Packers, the Steelers, the Steamers, and the Tanks reflect the teams' composition.

In 1922 the National Football League (NFL) was established. Red Grange, who played at the University of Illinois, ignited the league when he played for the Chicago Bears in 1925. His dashing touchdown runs excited and attracted large crowds. As a result of his success, professional football began to recruit more college players to the pro game, although professional and collegiate football were virtually indistinguishable. Professionals worked salaried jobs during most of the year because their professional pay was lean.

Outstanding teams such as the Chicago Bears, the Chicago Cardinals, the Detroit Lions, and the New York Giants dominated early professional football, and players such as Sammy Baugh, Don Huston, Cliff Battles, and others filled stadiums. When the Browns, 49ers, and Colts joined the NFL and when players such as Norm Van Brocklin, Y. A. Tittle, Johnny Unitas, Jim Brown, Ray Nitschke, and Frank Gifford became professionals in the 1960s, professional football became financially prosperous and popular. Vince Lombardi's Green Bay Packers epitomized hard work, determination, and precision. In 1956 the Columbia Broadcasting System (CBS) broadcast selected games. Television, trading cards, Wheaties, and other forms of popular culture created and promoted the country's football icons. Although the television screens were small, the public could see their football heroes, those individuals who personified their values and ideals, each week in competition. Television's multiple cameras, which captured players and coaches with close-ups and high angles that allowed viewers to watch the action unfold, brought excitement to the viewing audience. Also, more sensitive microphones helped viewers hear the hits and experience the game's violence. Later, video-taped replays shown between plays and at halftimes captured the game's ferocity.

Lamar Hunt created the American Football League (AFL) in 1960 to rival the NFL. The Houston Oilers, the Kansas City Chiefs, and the New York Jets battled financially for players and media attention. Although it took several years for the AFL to create equal teams, players such as Joe Namath, Lance Alworth, and Jack Kemp established the AFL's credibility. As a result, on January 15, 1967, the leagues' two champions, the Kansas City Chiefs and the Green Bay Packers, played the first AFL-NFL Championship Game, later renamed Super Bowl I. Approximately 62,000 cheering fans attended the game. In 1970 the rival leagues merged into two thirteen-team conferences under the NFL name.

Since Super Bowl I, media coverage has changed dramatically to meet the United States' fascination and hunger for football. For example, Super Bowl XL featured the Seattle Sea-hawks and the Pittsburgh Steelers, which had won four previous Super Bowls. The NFL Net-work's 60-plus hours (up to 11 hours a day) of coverage included live press conferences, head coach conferences, Commissioner Tagliabue's Super Bowl press conference, and spon-sor award conferences, as well as halftime and pregame entertainment and the Man of the Year award. On Super Bowl Sunday, January 31, 2006, fans were treated to 5½ hours of pregame and hours of post–Super Bowl coverage live from Ford Field. They could also watch a 30-minute special on the ads to be shown during the game.

According to CBS News, better than 90.7 million people (which represents the game's average audience at any given minute) watched Super Bowl XL, which was the largest Super Bowl audience since the Dallas Cowboys defeated the Steelers, when 94.1 million people watched the game. The 2006 Super Bowl was 5 percent bigger than the previous year's con-test between the Patriots and the Eagles. Viewers also focused on the Rolling Stones to see if Mick Jagger might include sexually explicit lyrics to rival Janet Jackson's wardrobe malfunc-tion in 2004. Nielsen reported that a total of 141.4 million people watched at least part of the game. It should be noted that approximately 98 percent of the viewing public comes from North America; time differences certainly curtail foreign viewership.

Super Bowls are obviously big business and extremely popular with the American and international public—football aficionados as well as individuals simply interested in the commercials—and businesses. Although teams, the league, and corporations of various types make a significant amount of money selling T-shirts, mugs, hats, DVDs and video-tapes, books, and various other memorabilia, the host city's tourism and economy reach record levels: hotel rooms that normally rent for $125 a night balloon to over $500; parking costs skyrocket as well as other expenses. Parking, food, airline tickets, and local transporta-tion fees for attendees prevent many fans from attending a Super Bowl. According to Mar-keting Information Masters, Inc., Super Bowl XXXVII generated a total economic impact on San Diego County of $367 million.[9]

Golf

American golf was born on February 22, 1888, when a transplanted Scot, John Reid, who is regarded as the father of American golf, invited four friends to play three improvised holes in a cow pasture in Yonkers, New York. Although golf had been played in several states prior to this time, Reid's and his friends' enthusiasm for the game led to the founding of St. Andrews Golf Club of Yonkers, America's first permanent club, on November 14, 1888. This excitement encouraged Bob Lockhart, Reid's friend, to bring back more clubs and gutta-percha balls from Tom Morris's shop at St. Andrews, Scotland.

By 1895 golf flourished in the United States. There were seventy-five golf clubs in operation, and they wanted to organize so that the United States could create its own national championship, particularly after there had been two unofficial national championships in 1894. Henry O. Tallmadge, secretary of Yonkers' St. Andrews, and others created the United States Golf Association (USGA) on December 12, 1894. The USGA has provided American golf with a central authority, which establishes and enforces uniformity in the rules of play, a handicap system, and an executive committee as a court of reference and final authority; most importantly, the USGA decides on what courses the national championships will be played. The U.S. Men's Open was created for professionals, who were generally foreigners and who were regarded as being in a low social stratum. The U.S. Men's and the U.S. Women's Amateur Championships were designed for Americans who golfed primarily for fun.

All three championships were held in 1895. The men's championships were held at Newport Golf Club, Newport, Rhode Island. Thirty-two men participated in the amateur tournament, which was won by Charles B. McDonald; Horace Rawlings, a 21-year-old assistant pro, won the U.S. Open. In November Mrs. Charles Brown captured the women's amateur title at Meadow Brook Club, Hempstead, New York, with an eighteen-hole victory over Nellie Sargent. Beatrix Hoyt dominated the women's amateur tournament with victories in 1896, 1897, and 1898. She remains the youngest champion at age 16; she retired from competitive golf at 21.

By 1900 a thousand golf clubs existed in the United States. In order to learn golfing skills and to build golf courses, Americans imported UK golfers. Harry Vardon, the greatest player of the era, gave exhibitions to promote golf and introduced A. G. Spalding & Bros.' new gutta-percha golf ball. Foreigners dominated the U.S. Open as Willie Anderson, a Scotsman, won four tournaments, three consecutively.

Johnny McDermott was the first native-born American to win the Open, in 1911 and 1912. However, in 1913 Francis Ouimet, a 22-year-old caddie, defeated the "invincible" Harry Vardon and Ted Ray in a playoff to become the first amateur to win a U.S. Open. Later, Charles "Chick" Evans won the Open and the Amateur in 1916, the first amateur to accomplish this feat. Ouimet and Evans stimulated amateur interest in golf, which reached its peak in the 1920s. Alexa Stirling captured three U.S. Women's Amateurs in 1916, 1919, and 1920.

Because professional golfers were lowly regarded, received low pay, and remained relatively obscure, Rodman Wanamaker in January 1916 suggested that the professionals develop a national championship. By July they had established the championship of the Professional Golfers' Association (PGA), and they held their tournament at Siwanoy Country Club, Bronxville, New York; "Long" Jim Barnes won and received $500. The PGA Championship includes touring players, club pros, and foreign invitees.

No U.S. championships were held in 1917 and 1918; however, U.S. golf improved dramatically, and by 1923 Americans were among the best golfers in the world. Walter "The Haig" Hagen, golf's most revered match player, gained worldwide attention with his flamboyance and drive. Hagen is credited with bringing the professional golfer out of the caddie shack and into the clubhouse. "The Haig," the first professional golfer to win and spend $1 million, won five PGAs, eleven majors, and better than sixty tournaments. Tommy Armour, Gene Sarazen, MacDonald Smith, Bobby Cruickshank, and Leo Diegel ignited Americans' golfing dominance and imagination.

From 1923 to 1930, Robert "Bobby" Tyre Jones, Jr., America's greatest amateur, ruled both the amateur and the professional ranks. He won thirteen national championships: four U.S. Opens, three British Opens, five U.S. Amateurs, and one British Amateur. At age 28, he retired from competitive golf. Glenna Collett Vare, the greatest women's amateur, won her first of six amateur titles in 1922. During the 1920s, the golden age of golf course architecture began in the United States, dentist William Lowell invented the golf tee, and the USGA approved the use of steel shafts. American teams won the inaugural Walker Cup in 1922 and Ryder Cup matches in 1927.

In 1920, 477 golf clubs joined the USGA. By 1930, 1154 courses of the 5700-plus courses in the United States joined the USGA. Nonetheless, golf course development nearly stopped because of the Great Depression and World War II. However, one of the greatest accomplishments in golf course design emerged when Augusta National Golf Club, the quintessential example of strategic design, opened in 1932. Golfing equipment was improved and standardized during the 1930s. Gene Sarazen perfected the sand wedge, and the USGA approved a new ball measuring 1.68 inches in diameter and weighing 1.62 ounces; Phil Young, owner of Acushnet, used x-rays to check every ball produced. The USGA limited the number of clubs that a golfer could carry in a competitive round to fourteen.

Golf's modern era began after World War II; the pros played a new game because steel shafts, matched clubs, and improved golf course maintenance introduced lower scores. In 1953 the World Championship was broadcast on television, and purses topped $500,000. The hard-swinging Ben Hogan epitomized the new golfer with his Open wins in 1948, 1950, 1951, and 1953. Babe Zaharias won her third and last U.S. Open in 1954, which was added to the USGA's roster of national championships in 1953. Arnold Palmer's emergence as "The King" began with his Amateur victory in 1954 and his win at his first professional tournament in 1955; however, "Arnie's Army" fell in love with his hitch of the pants, his lunging swing, and his attacking approach to courses, particularly during the final rounds. Palmer's exuberant personality and charismatic appeal revolutionized golf. Only Tiger Woods and, perhaps, John Daly are able to ignite the uncontrolled yelling and screaming of adoring fans. In 1946 Hope

BEN HOGAN

Since the 1950s, Ben Hogan has been one of the world's most revered golfers. During his long and frustrating apprenticeship on the PGA Tour, Hogan, who could not control his game, decided to spend more time, isolated from his peers, on the practice range. He hit golf balls for 8 hours or more each day, honing and digging his future success out of the dirt. As a result, Hogan's mystique is grounded in his work ethic. By 1946 Hogan ruled the tour. Following a near fatal automobile accident in 1949, which shattered both legs, a limping Hogan returned to the PGA Tour in 1950 but lost the Los Angeles Open in a playoff to Sam Sneed. (*Follow the Sun* [1949], starring Glenn Ford, depicted Hogan's life.) Nevertheless, his determination, stoicism, and icy stare appealed to fans; the Scots called him "Wee Ice Mon," while many simply referred to Hogan as "The Hawk." Both nicknames capture Hogan's intensity and the respect that others had for him.

Shot-making precision, focus, and an impeccable, repeatable golf swing characterized Hogan the golfer. In 1957 Hogan published *Ben Hogan's Five Lessons: The Modern Fundamentals*, which many golfers such as Jack Nicklaus, Lee Trevino, and David Ledbetter refer to as "the bible." As a competitor, Hogan won four U.S. Opens (1948, 1950, 1951, 1952), one British Open (1953), two Masters (1951, 1953), and two PGA Championships (1946, 1948); in total, he had sixty-three wins, although World War II and the automobile accident interrupted his career. He was also undefeated in Ryder Cup competition as a player and team captain. For further discussion of Ben Hogan, readers should consult Curt Sampson, *Hogan* (Nashville, TN: Rutledge Hill Press, 1996), and Robert Sommers, *The U.S. Open* (New York: Atheneum, 1987).

Seignious, a young golf pioneer, created the Women's Professional Golfers' Association (WPGA). The fledgling association needed better leadership, promotion, tournaments, and exposure; because Seignious refused to relinquish control, a rival body, which called itself the

Ladies' Professional Golf Association (LPGA), was formed, and it remains the ruling body for women's professional golf. By 1950 the LPGA offered an annual purse of $45,000 over nine events and attracted such superstars as Mickey Wright, Carol Mann, Sandra Haynie, Judy Rankin, Jane Blalock, and Donna Caponi.

The year 1960 is significant in U.S. golf because Arnold Palmer shot a 65 at Cherry Hills in Denver to defeat the aging Ben Hogan and the young Jack Nicklaus, golf's next superstar. "The Golden Bear" is known for his unmatched twenty-two majors (U.S. Open, U.S. Amateur, Masters, British Open, and PGA), which reflects quality of victories rather than quantity; Tiger Woods, although still young and a dominant force, has won eleven majors. In 1965 Sam Snead won his eighty-fourth tour victory. The decade also introduced technological developments: Ram Golf made a ball with a Surlyn cover, and Spalding's Top-Flite introduced the first two-piece ball. Resorts started offering "golf packages"—rooms, meals, and green fees—at attractive prices designed to lure the public to "golfing getaways."

Title IX legislation enacted by Congress in 1972 provided equal opportunities for women athletes. The Colgate–Dinah Shore, the first big money event for women professionals, debuted that same year. By 1973 the LPGA, under the leadership of Bud Erickson, offered an annual purse of $1,471,000 and conducted its first qualifying school. Kathy Whitworth, who has more tournament wins than anyone, man or woman, with eighty-eight, and Mickey Wright, with eighty-two victories, dominated the early part of the 1970s. The latter portion belonged to 1978 Rookie of the Year Nancy Lopez, whose remarkable skill and effervescent personality created "Nancy's Navy," because she won nine tournaments, five consecutively, and $189,813. Winning five tournaments in a row literally wowed the golfing community and created tremendous media excitement. Like Palmer, Lopez was approachable, had an unorthodox swing, and was a marvelous putter. For some people, Lopez was a one-lady promotion for the LPGA, and the association began to attract larger crowds and receive better television promotion.

Through the 1980s and 1990s golf interest boomed. New courses were constructed in California's deserts, the USGA added the U.S. Senior Open, and the public was bombarded with a video explosion as professionals, such as Jack Nicklaus and Johnny Miller, and noted teachers marketed golf instruction tapes. By 1990 approximately 14,500 courses existed. However, a sense of gloom dominated U.S. men's golf because of the "foreign invasion" led by Spain's Seve Ballesteros and England's Nick Faldo; foreign golfers assumed dominance not only with the PGA Tour but also with the majors, Masters, U.S. Open, British Open, and PGA Tournament. On the other hand, Beth Daniel, Betsy King, Julie Inkster, and others controlled the LPGA. During the late 1990s and into the twenty-first century, the image of American golf changed.

Excepting Ben Hogan and Jack Nicklaus, no player has intimidated the competition and dominated courses like Tiger Woods. After an extraordinary amateur career in which he won two U.S. Junior Amateurs and three straight U.S. Amateur Championships, he turned pro in 1995. In 1996 he won thirty-seven tournaments including eleven majors. When Woods turned professional, Nike offered him $40 million over 5 years to endorse their shoes and clothing; Titleist initially offered him $3 million to wear their gloves and play their balls, but they later sweetened that offer to $20 million if he played Titleist clubs. Whereas American male golfers led by accomplished players, particularly Woods and Phil Mickelson, have reestablished American dominance of the PGA, a "foreign invasion," led particularly by Annika Sorenstam, has maintained a stranglehold on the LPGA. Nevertheless, young American players such as Cristie Kerr, Natalie Gulbis, and Paula Creamer, as well as established players such as Julie Inkster and Pat Hurst, have worked to gain a foothold in their tour. In October 2005 Michelle Wie, a 16-year-old golfing phenom from Hawaii, who has not won a professional tournament or significant amateur tournament, signed an endorsement deal with Nike and Sony for $10 million. At present, she can only be invited to play LPGA events.

Gymnastics

Following the Civil War, gymnastics was recognized as a derivative of physical education in the United States and Canada. Friedrich Ludwig Jahn's principles were integrated into the Round Rock School by Charles Follen and others (Jahn was a German innovator who established the Turnverein movement in Prussia); concurrently, the first public gymnasium was established in Boston. Harvard University is credited with building the first college gymnasium in 1826. Physical education and gymnastics were stressed because young people, decried for neglecting their exercises, needed to improve their body control, endurance, and minds. Physical education teachers conducted fitness tests, although students preferred such outdoor sports as tennis, football, lacrosse, fishing, and others. Similar to the fitness test, gymnastics requires strength, flexibility, and kinesthetic awareness, yet blends circus-like acrobatic skills to illustrate fitness and beauty of movement.

The YMCA and the Young Women's Christian Association (YWCA), credited with promoting "muscular Christianity," encouraged youths to visit their gymnasiums, swimming pools, bowling alleys, and baths. Attendees climbed ropes, lifted weights, used parallel bars, swung on suspended rings, and engaged in other athletic activities such as high-jumping and pole-vaulting, now associated with track-and-field. Gymnastics, regarded as a minor sport in the early twentieth century, attracted several athletically talented performers. During the 1904 St. Louis Olympic Games, which did not include many foreign competitors, America's men failed to win only the all-around and the combined competitions, while taking the horizontal bars, parallel bars, long horse vault, pommel horse, rings, rope climb, and team combined competitions.

Women's Olympic competition began in 1928. Women's events generally include the vault, uneven bars, balance beam, and floor exercise; competitors must demonstrate flexibility, strength, endurance, and attention to time and space limitations. In 1982 the NCAA held its inaugural Team Championship, and the University of Utah has won nine National Championships. Although Marcia Frederick was the first American woman to win the World Gymnastics Championships, Olga Korbut's and Nadia Comaneci's performances in the 1972 and 1976 Olympics inspired thousands of North American girls to pursue gymnastics. Eight years later West Virginia's Mary Lou Retton won Olympic Gold via her performance on the vault, and her victory encouraged girls to continue their exercise programs. Since Retton's performance, Shannon Miller, the most revered and decorated American gymnast, Kerry Strug, Dominique Dawes, and Carly Patterson, a 16-year-old Texas phenom, have continued popularizing female gymnastics. Rhythmic gymnastics, which emphasizes the aesthetic more than the acrobatic, includes routines with a ball, ribbon, hoop, clubs, and ropes. Men's gymnastic events include floor exercises, pommel horse, rings, vault, parallel bars, and high bar. Men's exercises emphasize strength and flexibility, and they are generally considered more dangerous because they are performed above the floor. The inaugural Men's NCAA Team Championship was held in 1938.

Racket Sports

Sports using rackets (racquets) were a pastime favorite with wealthy, genteel individuals in the United States and Canada, an original member of the 1934 International Badminton Federation, during the 1850s. Racket sports include badminton, squash, table tennis, and tennis. Badminton evolved from an English children's sport called *battledore* (paddle) and *shuttlecock* (also called a bird or birdie). Because it required a limited court, it was suited to rural and urban participants of both sexes; badminton can be played indoors or outdoors.

In 1935 the American Badminton Association (ABA) was founded, and it conducted its first national championship in 1937. By 1972 the Olympics accepted badminton as a demonstration sport and in 1992 included it for singles and doubles competition for men and women; mixed doubles was accepted in 1996. Although badminton was originally played by noncompetitive, genteel participants, the powerful swings of today's successful amateurs and professionals send the bird flying over the net at 200 mph or more, making badminton the world's fastest racket sport; at the same time, competitors must be able to execute deft flicks with hands and wrist. Although many American players experienced international acclaim prior the 1970s, Judy Devlin Hashwin, originally from Manitoba, won fifty major championships, which includes her twelve U.S. national and ten All-England titles. The Ladies' Montreal Tennis and Badminton Club, the oldest club in Canada, was founded in 1907, seven years after the game was introduced in Ottawa. By the 1930s Jack Purcell and Dorothy Walton dominated the Canadian game; in 1937 Walton became the only Canadian woman to win the All-England championship. Other players of note include Jamie Paulson and Denyse Julien.

The first recordings of lawn tennis (later called tennis) occur in Ottawa and Montreal. Miss Mary Ewing Outerbridge is credited with introducing the game in the United States; she also founded a Ladies' Club in 1877. However, James Dwight is generally referred to as "the father of American lawn tennis" because he established the United Lawn Tennis Association in 1881. In 1900 Americans returned from England with the Davis Cup, and in 1905 May Sutton won Wimbledon.

Although the elite steadfastly worked to keep tennis as their own, the game spread rapidly to the Pacific states, which formed its association in 1890. Maurice "California Comet" McLaughlin revolutionized the game with his powerful serves, foot speed, and precise ground stokes. Bill Tilden's performances in the 1920s tennis world symbolized American ideals of hard work, excellence, and determination; he rebuilt his weak and inaccurate backhand stroke and was proclaimed as the sport's golden boy. Tennis remained a minor sport from the 1930s through the 1950s. Althea Gibson broke tennis's color barrier, won Wimbledon (1957–58) and the U.S. Open (1957–58), and overpowered her opponents with thunderous serves and aggressive, attacking play.

During the 1970s tennis's "whiteness" was broken with the arrival of yellow tennis balls, pastel outfits, and the first African-American male to earn greatness on the tennis court, Arthur Ashe. Ashe won the U.S. interscholastic club championship in 1961, won the intercollegiate singles championship in 1965, and achieved a number one world ranking in 1968 with victories in the U.S. Amateur and U.S. Open. What differentiated Ashe, other than his outstanding play and sportsmanship, was his poise and leadership. Concurrently, Billie Jean King became so prominent that she helped create the Virginia Slims tour, for women only, and gained equal winnings for U.S. Open winners in 1974. After breaking the $100,000 on-court barrier, she thrashed Bobby Riggs in the Astrodome before 30,000-plus fans and better than 50,000 television viewers.

Although stars such as Ashe and Chris Evert have attempted to introduce tennis to lower-income children, the sport continues to attract participants from higher-income families. However, the Williams sisters, Venus and Serena, flamed brightly for a while by winning major titles, but injuries have hampered their performances over the past few years.

Work Sports

Sports that combined work and amusement began with the Puritans and have continued to be practiced in various forms. For example, prior to the Civil War, local fire stations competed against one another; because the firemen often belonged to rival political or ethnic groups, competition ignited battles not only to extinguish the fire but also with one another. Other early forms of work sport competition included steamboat races, logging, and rodeos.

Today, via ESPN, ESPN2, and the Outdoor Life Network (OLN), rodeo roundups and competitions are broadcast to millions of interested viewers nationwide. Whereas cowboys in the 1800s tested their roping, bull-riding, and bronc-riding skills as a pastime or to determine who was the best drover on a cattle drive, today's professional cowboys can earn millions of dollars on their rodeo circuit. In 1936 the Professional Rodeo Cowboys Association (PRCA) began in Boston. Years later they formed the Cowboys' Turtle Association. "Turtle" was adopted because the new organization was slow to organize and because they stuck their heads out for what they believed; however, in 1975 they changed their name once again to the Rodeo Cowboys Association, which represents the PRCA. Early rodeo contests were anchored to stock horse use and included bareback riding, steer wrestling, team roping, saddle bronc riding, calf roping, and bull riding as well as barrel racing by female equestrians; today's rodeo emphasizes reining and horse and cow cutting.

Rodeo shows reflect, too, the individual competitions' roots in Wild West shows, which combined theater and competition with the intent to make money and to glamorize and prevent the disappearance of the American frontier. Some of the most successful venues included those operated by Buffalo Bill Cody, Pawnee Bill's Wild West Show, or the 101 Ranch Wild West Show. Country-western music often celebrates the cowboy lifestyle and legacy, even though the open range era lasted for only a few years. Both the rodeos and much of the music celebrate western America: its rugged individualism and the people who tamed the land and the animals. Rodeo stampedes include children or "little britches," high school, and college competition; likewise, rodeo organizations, which exist at the national, state, county, and local levels, host their events in rural North America. Major competitions include Canada's 2006 Calgary Stampede, which offered $1.6 million in total prize money, or Oregon's Pendleton Roundup.

CANADA

Although sports in Canada are generally the same as in the United States, including professional teams in, for example, Major League Baseball and of course the National Hockey League, there are a number of teams that are especially popular with or unique to Canadians.

Curling

Like hockey, skiing, and figure skating, curling originated as a winter sport because of climatic factors. Scottish immigrants brought curling to Canada, and the sport is more firmly associated with Canada than with the United States. The name evolved from the Scottish word *curr*, which captures the sound that the rocks or stones made as they traveled over the ice. The Royal Montreal Curling Club, the oldest athletic club in North America, was established in 1807, whereas the United States did not open a club until 25 years later. Youth, high school, junior, college and university, wheelchair, Special Olympic, and high-performance leagues and teams curl in Canada. Because the sport does not emphasize strength, speed, or stamina, curling's precise execution and strategy led to the "chess on ice" label. Although Canadian tournaments offer cash prizes, no professional curlers exist. As a result, housewives can not only claim curling as their profession but also earn significant financial winnings.

Curling is most popular in Canada, and the Canadian Curling Association (CCA) conducts the country's championships and policy decisions. In June 2006 The Sports Network (TSN) and

CCA announced a 6-year broadcast deal that made TSN the sole home of television curling coverage. TSN plans to broadcast Canada's major championships as well as 2010 Olympic coverage via radio, broadband, mobile, video-on-demand, interactive television, and podcasts. Approximately 872,000 play curling in Canada, and 3,573,000 Canadians watch curling on television.

Five-Pin Bowling

As early as 1909 Thomas F. Ryan was officially recognized for developing five-pin bowling, a sport that is played in every Canadian territory and province but is not played in the United States. The sport is uniquely, solely Canadian. Ten-pin bowling served as a recreational activity, but some people wanted to speed up the game whereas others complained about the ball's weight. As a result, Ryan, owner of the private Toronto Bowling Club, which catered to the wealthy, asked his father to whittle down five pins to approximately three-fourths of their original size; to satisfy those who sought a less strenuous game, the bowling ball's weight was reduced to approximately 3.5 pounds and its diameter was reduced to 5 inches. Ryan's experiment successfully attracted a luncheon crowd; to enhance pin action in the game, Ryan placed a rubber band around the pins' throats. Junior, high school, youth, men's, and women's leagues are conducted annually in Canada. A perfect score is 450 points.

Hockey

Many Canadians argue that they created hockey, that the best players come from their country, and that they "owned" international competitions. The first claim is true; the others were true until the mid-1990s. A fissure in their confidence and control occurred when the Canadian-dominated NHL allowed franchises to relocate in the United States. As of 2006 the NHL consists of thirty teams, and five are Canadian. However, when the Edmonton Oilers agreed to send Wayne Gretzky, "The Great One," to the Los Angeles Kings in 1988, many Canadians were emotionally distraught and felt betrayed by the NHL. Violence via hard checking and fighting characterize hockey and appeal to the game's fans.

Women's ice hockey, one of the world's fastest-growing sports, originated around 1890. Although fewer hockey venues are available for females, organized leagues include the National Women's Hockey League and the Western Women's Hockey League, as well as international and collegiate leagues, Olympic teams, and some recreational leagues. Whereas men's games permit bodychecking, it is penalized in the women's game; as a result, the women's game depends on accurate passing and shot selection and less on physical play. At the 1998 Winter Olympics, women's hockey was offered as a medal sport.

Collegiate America has six NCAA Division I conferences and one independent team. They also have a national championship.

Lacrosse

Canadian lacrosse is a blend of games practiced by the Cherokees, Creeks, Choctaws, and several other Native American tribes. Although the sport was initially called *baggatawa*, Canadians called the game *lacrosse*, a French word that describes the stick that is employed during play. As early as 1850 lacrosse had become a favorite pastime. Native Americans followed elaborate rituals prior to a contest; for example, players adhered to strict dietary

WAYNE GRETZKY

Although Wayne Gretzky is only 6 feet tall, weighs only 180 pounds, and was not drafted by an NHL team, he became hockey's greatest player, and in 1998 the *Hockey News* named him the best all-time player in league history. As a rookie who could not bench-press 140 pounds, he became hockey's most dominant offensive player, often compared to basketball's Michael Jordan or soccer's Pele; actually, Gretzky's statistics surpass theirs. By 1998 he held sixty-two NHL scoring records and retired with all-time career marks for goals, assists, and points. In fact, he was the first player in league history to record more assists than any other player had points. For example, by 1997 Gretzky had 1,851 assists, giving him more assists than Gordie Howe—the league's number two scorer, who played twenty-six years with the Detroit Red Wings and the Hartford Whalers—had goals and assists combined. Records such as his 163-assist season, his 215-point season, and his fifty-one-game scoring streak are equal to Joe DiMaggio's fifty-six-game hitting streak and Byron Nelson's eleven consecutive victories on the PGA Tour.

By vaporizing existing records, Gretzky mesmerized hockey aficionados and players alike. Misdirection characterized his game; his deft passing, particularly his accurate backhand passes, and inspired shot selection exposed defensive weaknesses and provided teammates with easy scoring opportunities. Perhaps his greatest trademark, however, was his innate, burning desire to win; during the closing minutes and seconds of a hockey match, he turned losses and ties into ties and victories.

Currently Wayne Gretzky is head coach of an NHL team, the Phoenix Coyotes, a post he has held since 2005. Gretzky is also a part owner of the team.

For further discussion of Wayne Gretzky, readers should consult Andrew Podnieks's *The Great One: The Life and Times of Wayne Gretzky* (Chicago: Triumph Books, 1999) or visit the NHL's Hall of Fame interactive Website at http://www.nhl.com/hockeyu/halloffame/index.html.

regulations and abstained from sex. Prior to contests, they were segregated in sacred places and spent the evening designing costumes for play, painting their bodies, and dancing ritualistically.

Early forms of lacrosse, like many sports, lacked specific rules and regulations regarding play, although the object was simply to score more goals than the opponent; a winner, according to the Cherokee version, was the first team to score twelve goals.

Early fields, which ranged from several hundred feet to several miles in length, contained two sets of goalposts; because games did not have a time limit, they could last for as long as several days. During play, women would encourage their teams and were noted for whipping their legs. Historically, George Beers, the "father of lacrosse," wrote the first rulebook and promoted the sport among young, enthusiastic English athletes in the 1860s. These early sportsmen sought to create Canada's "national pastime."

Following the Civil War, lacrosse's popularity spread to the United States; collegiate play began with the 1877 contest between New York University and Manhattan College. By 1879 an amateur association was formed, and by 1882 an intercollegiate association was founded. Women, wanting to demonstrate their athletic skills, created a national governing association in 1931. In 1971 and 1981 (men's and women's, respectively) the NCAA recognized lacrosse, which serves as a statement to the game's widespread appeal among young people. Today many Canadian and U.S. universities field women's and men's teams that compete in intercollegiate contests as well as for a national championship.

RESOURCE GUIDE

PRINT SOURCES

Alexander, Charles. *Our Game: An American Baseball History*. New York: Henry Holt, 1991.

Andersonn, Christopher, and Barbara Andersonn. *Will You Still Love Me If I Don't Win? A Guide for Parents of Young Children*. Dallas, TX: Taylor Publishing, 2000.

Andre, Judith, and David W. James, eds. *Rethinking College Athletics*. Philadelphia: Temple University Press, 1991.

Asinof, Eliot. *Eight Men Out: The Black Sox and the 1919 World Series*. New York: Henry Holt, 1963.

Bailer, Darice. *Extreme Sports: Dive!* Washington, DC: National Geographic, 2002.

Berlage, Gai. *Women in Baseball*. Westport, CT: Praeger, 1994.

Browne, Ray B., and Pat Browne, eds. *The Guide to United States Popular Culture*. Bowling Green, OH: Bowling Green State University Popular Press, 2001.

Carnegie, Tom. *Indy 500: More Than a Race*. New York: McGraw-Hill, 1989.

Cozens, Frederick W., and Florence Scovil Stumpf. *Sports in American Life*. Chicago: University of Chicago Press, 1953.

Cusic, Don. *Baseball and Country Music*. Madison: University of Wisconsin Press/The Popular Press, 2003.

Duncan, Joyce, ed. *Sport in American Culture: From Ali to X-Games*. Santa Barbara, CA: ABC-CLIO, 2004.

Gerdy, John R. *Sports: The All-American Addiction*. Jackson: University Press of Mississippi, 2002.

Guttmann, Allen. *From Ritual to Record: The Nature of Modern Sports*. New York: Columbia University Press, 1978.

———. *Sports Spectators*. New York: Columbia University Press, 1986.

Halberstam, David. *The Breaks of the Game*. New York: Alfred Knopf, 1981.

Harris, Reed. *King Football: The Vulgarization of the American College*. New York: Vanguard Press, 1932.

Leifer, Eric M. *Making the Majors: The Transformation of Team Sports in America*. Cambridge, MA: Harvard University Press, 1995.

Lewis, Guy, and Gerald Redmond. *Sporting Heritage: A Guide to Halls of Fame, Special Collections and Museums in the United States and Canada*. New York: A. S. Barnes & Co., 1974.

Novak, Michael. "American Sports, American Virtues." Pp. 34–49 in Wiley L. Umphlett (ed.), *American Sport Culture*. Cranbury, NJ: Associated University Presses, 1985.

Oriard, Michael. *Reading Football: How the Popular Press Created an American Spectacle*. Chapel Hill: University of North Carolina Press, 1993.

Pope, S. W., ed. *The New American Sport History: Recent Approaches and Perspectives*. Urbana, IL: University of Illinois Press, 1997.

Raabe, Tom. *Sports in the 20th Century*. Golden, CO: Fulcrum Publishing, 1995.

Rooney, John F. *The Recruiting Game: Towards a New System of Intercollegiate Sports*. Lincoln, NE: University of Nebraska Press, 1980.

Spivey, Donald, ed. *Sport in America: New Historical Perspectives*. Westport, CT: Greenwood Press, 1985.

Wells, Jeff. *Boxing Day: The Fight That Changed the World*. Pymble: HarperCollins (Australia), 1999.

Zimblast, Andrew W. *Unpaid Professionals: Commercialism and Conflict in Big-Time College Sports*. Princeton: Princeton University Press, 1999.

WEBSITES

ESPN: Entertainment and Sports Programming Network. Last updated on October 17, 2006. http://www.espn.com.

NCAA. NCAA: The Online Resource for the National Collegiate Athletic Association. Last updated on October 17, 2006. http://www.ncaa.org.

ORGANIZATIONS

College Football Hall of Fame, 111 South St. Joseph Street, South Bend, IN 46601. http://www.college football.org.

Hockey Hall of Fame, BCE Place, 30 Yonge Street, Toronto, Ontario, Canada M5E 1X8. http://www.hhof.com.

International Boxing Hall of Fame, 1 Hall of Fame Drive, Canastota, NY 13032. http://www.ibhof.com.

International Tennis Hall of Fame, 194 Bellevue Avenue, Newport RI 02840. http://www.tennisfame.org.

Naismith Memorial Basketball Hall of Fame, 1000 West Coluue, Springfield, MA 01105. http://www.hoophall.com.

National Baseball Hall of Fame and Museum, 25 Main Street, Cooperstown, NY 13326, 1-888-HALL-OF-FAME. http://www.baseballhalloffame.org.

Pro Football Hall of Fame, 2121 George Halas Drive NW, Canton, OH 44708. http://www.profootball hof.com.

World Golf Hall of Fame, 1 World Golf Place, St. Augustine FL 32092. http://www.wgv.com/.

NOTES

1. Statistics are culled from a number of sources; see http://www.sports.espn.gocom/mlb/attendance, http://www.football.about.com/od/histo2/a/Sbattendance/htm, http://www.sports.espn. gocom/ nhl/attendance, http://www.nbafinals/attendance.030916.html, http://www.msnbc.msn.com/id.

2. Statistics are culled from a number of sources; see http://www.scac-online.org/football/fattendance. htm, http://ncaasport.com.

3. William Bradford, *Bradford's History "Of Plimoth Plantation"* (Boston, 1898), p. 135.

4. Archives of Maryland, XLIV, "Proceedings and Acts of the General Assembly of Maryland, 1745–1747," edited by Bernard Steiner (Baltimore, 1925), p. 647.

5. Donald Chu, *The Character of American Higher Education and Intercollegiate Sport* (Albany, NY: State University of New York Press, 1989), p. 65.

6. *Patton* (20th Century Fox, 1970), directed by Franklin J. Schaffer.

7. George Bush, Presidential Acceptance Speech, Republican National Convention, 1988.

8. James Bryce, "America Revisited: The Changes of a Quarter-Century. *Outlook* 79 (1905): 738–739.

9. See http://www.superbowl.com/features.generalinfo.

THEATER AND PERFORMANCE

THOMAS A. GREENFIELD AND MONICA MOSCHETTA

Live theater is a singularly inefficient, labor-intensive endeavor. The staggering amount of time and effort required to mount a single evening's performance—especially when weighed against the relatively miniscule number of people who will see that performance—perpetually begs the question as to why anyone in his or her right mind would choose to work in professional theater. (The question commonly elicits the facetious rejoinder from theater artists that no one in their right mind actually does.) Unlike popular music, television, or film, live theater as an art form or "medium" has neither been invented nor fundamentally transformed by modern technology and mass culture. An intimate, immediate artist-audience connection has been essential to the mystique of live theater since before the discovery of electricity. The fact that it remains so is both the charm and the burden that live theater has carried into the twenty-first century and the era of mass-market popular culture.

In the United States and Canada, the economics and logistics of maintaining that artist-audience connection account for the vastly different ways that modern professional theater evolved in these closest of neighboring countries on either side of the longest unsecured border in the world. Even more so than the much vaunted contrast between Canada's English-French bilingualism and America's predominant monolingual culture, the fact that theater tends to nest in densely populated urban centers meant that modern American theater and modern Canadian theater were fated for two very different destinies. With 25 percent less land mass and almost ten times the population of Canada, the continental United States established the foundations of professional theater in North America. By 1850 the United States could lay claim to a fledgling but functioning indigenous theater industry. Barely half a century thereafter, the United States had developed the most dynamic theater district in the world—not coincidentally in its densest population center, New York City. Each year the best New York plays and musicals become major events in the English-speaking theater world. By contrast, prior to the twentieth century, Canada relied heavily on imported professional productions and touring companies from Europe for its theatrical entertainment. Modern Canadian theater artists and producers made a virtue of necessity and elevated the importation of plays to the level of cultural phenomena. Although a strong Canadian-centered theater movement has emerged since the 1970s, Canada has also perfected the art of the international theater festival and has become the world's beloved second home to Shakespeare, English satirist George Bernard Shaw, and French neoclassicist Molière. Furthermore, in the 1980s Toronto, Canada's largest city, effectively positioned itself as a reasonably priced, family-friendly alternative to New York, annually mounting an impressive Canadian "Broadway season" of major musicals and plays.

CANADA

Background: Before the Twentieth Century

Since its beginnings, Canadian live theater has had to contend with formidable obstacles to its creation. Unlike England, which had a well-established professional theatrical tradition prior to the twentieth century, or the United States, which had more than the rudiments of one, Canadian theater prior to 1900 was largely made up of fiercely determined but hopelessly underfunded amateur and semiprofessional theatrical groups as well as professional touring companies from abroad. In the late 1700s Canadians began constructing theatrical halls across the country for touring companies, musical concerts, and whatever suitable productions might be mounted locally by amateur or semiprofessional theater societies. The expansion of Canadian rail travel and the opening of a transcontinental rail line in the 1880s actually created a functioning theater circuit for the convenience of performers and audiences eager to see them. Opportunities for Canadian artists to practice, develop, and earn a living in professional theater began in earnest in the 1920s with the evolution of Canadian radio broadcasting. From the outset, Canadian radio broadcast pioneers relied heavily on original radio plays and dramatic series for programming content. In so doing, they succeeded in cultivating a national interest and popular audience for live Canadian drama. While radio drama is viewed as a tangential curiosity in the history of American theater, it was an essential element and the true starting point for professional popular theater in modern-day Canada.

Canadian Radio Drama

In 1925 the Canadian National Railways Radio Department, a pioneering predecessor of the Canadian Broadcasting Company (CBC), began broadcasting plays. Two years thereafter, a Vancouver producer, Jack Gilmore, launched Canada's first regular radio drama series, the *CNRV Players*, named after the Canadian National Railroad of Vancouver, which produced original scripts and radio adaptations of classical plays and fictional works. Throughout the 1930s and beyond, Canadian playwrights as well as Canadian actors, directors, and producers made significant contributions to the expanding influence of Canadian radio. Many of Canada's leading post–World War II stage artists got their start in radio drama and figured prominently in its early development. Lorne Green (1915–87), although best known as the star of the U.S. television series *Bonanza*, was a major radio personality in Canada in the 1930s and 1940s. In addition to acting in many CBC radio drama productions, he founded one of Canada's first professional schools of broadcasting and was a highly regarded radio news announcer during World War II. Merrill Dennison (1893–1975), Canada's first major modern-era stage playwright, wrote a groundbreaking series of radio plays on Canadian history in the 1930s. Actor and producer Mavor Moore (1919–), a founding governor of the Stratford and Charlottetown theater festivals and first chairman of the Guild of Canadian Playwrights, was a teenage radio actor and an employee of the CBC in the

1930s. Lister Sinclair (1921–), stage playwright, radio playwright, and on-air personality, was a seminal figure in advancing both radio and stage drama in the 1940s.

French-language radio drama also began in earnest in the 1930s and provided a critical training ground for the emerging theater talent of the next generation. Radio serial programs were more popular with French radio drama audiences than were formally produced plays, although both were part of the early history of French-language radio. Edouard Baudry's (1905–43) *Rue Principale* premiered on a Montreal station in 1937 and ran continuously until 1959. Marcel Dube (1930–), one of Canada's most prolific playwrights, has written for radio, television, and stage. Award-winning playwright Marie-Clair Blais (1939–) contributed to French-language radio toward the beginning of her prodigious career.

Radio drama reached its apex in the 1940s under the guidance and vision of Andrew Allan (1907–74), head of drama for the CBC. Allan significantly expanded the number of programs and broadcast hours that the CBC devoted to drama. He not only mounted numerous individual dramatic productions but also developed successful weekly drama series programs. Allan was committed to using his influence to establish the foundations of a Canadian national theater. In so doing, he gave many Canadian playwrights their first national exposure. Moreover, by generating a heretofore unknown number of work opportunities for actors, directors, and theater artisans (and paid opportunities at that), he is often credited as the person most responsible for developing a critical mass of trained professional Canadian theater performers who could populate the nation's stages. After World War II, they did.

By the 1950s the cohort of accomplished theater artists who had cut their teeth in radio (as well as in the emerging regional theaters throughout the provinces) began to advocate for the development of indigenous national productions featuring Canadian performers and plays. The issue of Canadian playwriting became, and to some extent remains, an issue of particular importance because of Canada's historical reliance on imported theatrical works. To be sure, stage production and playwriting were ongoing during the 1940s radio boom. Robert Davies (1913–95), one of Canada's most important twentieth-century playwrights, did his most enduring work during this period without becoming heavily involved in radio drama. Nevertheless, the task of transporting Andrew Allan's vision of a strong, national Canadian theater from the radio to the country's stages would prove to be a challenge in the following decades.

Canadian Theater Festivals

The nationalistic push for indigenous theater scarcely chafed against Canada's deeply ingrained love for imported plays from both classic and modern repertoires. The period after World War II saw significant growth and milestone accomplishments in both domestic and imported stage drama. Theater festivals were a force in all provinces throughout the twentieth century; many new ones came into being and flourished after World War II. Currently, Canada boasts an impressive diversity of theater festivals that effectively maintain professional Canadian theater as a part of national culture rather than as a one- or two-town industry. Two of the most enduring and successful of the Canadian theater festivals are the internationally renowned Stratford Festival of Canada and the Shaw Festival, both located in Ontario.

The Stratford and the Shaw

The larger of the two, the Stratford Festival of Canada (more commonly known as the Stratford Festival or the Stratford), is, in fact, the largest permanent professional repertory theater company in North America. The brainchild of Stratford native son Thomas Patterson, a journalist and civic activist, the Stratford Festival was originally conceived in the early 1950s as a festival devoted exclusively to the plays of Shakespeare. No doubt mindful of successful, lucrative American summer festivals, such as Jacobs Pillow and Chautauqua, which had become financial boons to isolated areas, Patterson put together a coalition of local business, civic, and artistic leaders who promptly brought his vision to reality. The Stratford Festival opened in the summer of 1953 with British stage legend Alec Guinness playing *Richard III*. The Stratford Festival flourishes to this day. Its repertoire has expanded to include modern masterworks, musicals, and the occasional new play, but its world-renowned Shakespeare productions remain its signature accomplishment. Most of the major figures in Canadian theater in the latter half of the twentieth century were associated with the Stratford Festival at one time or another. Most prominent among them was Tyrone Guthrie (1900–71), the Stratford Festival's first artistic director, who is generally credited with bringing the festival the extraordinary prestige and success it has enjoyed for decades. Toronto-born actor Christopher Plummer (ca. 1928–), an international theater and film star, has performed at the Stratford Festival throughout his storied career, despite having been ignominiously rejected in an audition for the Stratford's opening season. Hume Cronyn (1911–2003), born in nearby London, Ontario, periodically acted and directed at Stratford. He also served on the board of directors. Actress Zoe Caldwell (1933–), whose credits include four Tony Awards for Broadway performances, is also a veteran of Stratford performances. Today, the Stratford Festival is one of, if not the most, important professional training ground for young stage actors and other theater artists.

Although smaller than the Stratford Festival in scope, budget, and total audience, the Shaw Festival (popularly Shawfest or The Shaw) is the second largest repertory theater company in North America after the Stratford. The Shawfest accomplished this remarkable achievement through a combination of ambitious artistic vision and deft niche marketing. Founded in 1962, the Shawfest devotes itself to the plays of George Bernard Shaw and his contemporaries (Shaw's writing career spanned an astounding seven decades, giving him contemporary status with virtually everyone who might reasonably be considered a "modern" author; the Shawfest is notorious for taking a broadly inclusive view of which playwrights might reasonably be called Shaw's contemporaries). Each season two or three of Shaw's plays, both major works and less-well-known pieces, share the bill with another half-dozen musicals and plays by modern masters from O'Neill to Wilde to Brecht. The Shawfest benefited at the outset from the success of the Stratford Festival, many of whose established actors and directors lent their talents to the fledgling, semiprofessional company in its formative years. The Shawfest's first three artistic directors, former CBC dynamo Andrew Allan, Barry Morse, and Paxton Whitehead, were already well-established figures in professional theater circles when each assumed leadership of the festival. Using their considerable influence and connections to persuade top-flight talent to work at the Shaw, the three directors established the festival's reputation for artistic quality, innovation, variety, and low-key commercial savvy—a reputation it still enjoys. The Shawfest continues its long-standing record of success under the guidance of its first woman artistic director, Irish native Jackie Maxwell, who took over the festival in 2002. Situated between the popular tourist havens of Toronto and Niagara Falls, the Shaw's three stage venues (one major theater and two intimate play houses) attract nearly 400,000 playgoers a year, almost all arriving by cars and tour buses that rather awkwardly navigate the narrow, shop-lined streets of the festival's picturesque country village, Niagara-on-the-Lake.

Other venerable Canadian festivals include the Drama Festival of Newfoundland and Labrador, founded in 1950 by the province's drama society. The festival's activities combine professional productions with education and outreach programming targeted to the communities of the region. Ottawa's relatively new Magnetic North Theatre Festival, initiated in 2003, is a weeklong summer gathering dedicated entirely to original English-language Canadian drama. Montreal's Festival de Théâtre des Amériques was founded in 1985 and has established itself as one of Canada's leading showcases for international theatrical productions. Countries from all over the world send theater companies and productions to the Théâtre des Amériques festival. Toronto's younger du Maurier World Stage Festival, founded in 1996, also mounts an eclectic, broad program of plays, usually with an eye for cutting-edge or avant-garde productions. One of Canada's first and arguably most important feminist theater collectives is the Company in Montreal. Established in 1979 by playwrights Pol Pelletier, Nicole Lecavalier, and Louise Laprade, the Company sponsors productions, festivals, and workshops on women's theater and feminism. Although no longer in existence, the Bilingual Institution in Montreal holds a special place in the history of Canadian theater festivals. The Bilingual Institution (also known as the Montreal Theatre Guild and the Montreal Repertory Theatre, 1930–61) is described in *The Canadian Theatre Encyclopedia* as one of the key institutions "at the source of a (Canadian) national theatre." Focusing primarily on a traditional repertoire of classics and modern standards, the Bilingual Institution served as a training ground and launching platform for many of Canada's professional theater artists for over 30 years.

Even as the Stratford and Shaw festivals, both English-language drama companies, grew to international stature, French-speaking theater maintained a strong presence through the last half of the twentieth century and into the present. The most venerated of the many active Canadian French-speaking theater companies is the Théâtre du Nouveau Monde Company in Montreal, founded in 1951. Building its reputation and niche on Canada's centuries-old love affair with the plays of Molière, the Nouveau Monde has been closely associated since its inception with the seventeenth-century satirist's works. Founding Artistic Director Jean Gascon (1921–88) led a committed group of artists in establishing the Nouveau Monde as a major force in Canadian theater, aided in considerable measure by a triumphant tour of France with Molière productions.

French-speaking theater also produced Canada's first modern avant-garde theater artist, Gratien Gélinas (1909–99). Like many other Canadian stage stars, Gélinas started out in radio comedy in the 1930s, developing a popular, recurring character named Fridolin. Fridolin carried Gélinas, and vice versa, for six decades through musical revues and stage shows, as well as a return to radio and television based on the satiric character and the quirky irreverent humor that became his trademark. In the 1950s, Gélinas formed an independent theater group, Comédie-Canadienne, which developed a reputation for cultivating the careers and aspirations of young, innovative Canadian theater artists.

Broadway North

Since the 1980s one of the most important developments in all of North American professional theater has been the emergence of Toronto as a world-class popular theater district—not the equal of London's West End or New York's Broadway, but a cut above any other city in the English-speaking world. By the end of the 1970s, Toronto was well poised to develop a sophisticated downtown theater district: the city had received outstanding press notices as a safe, visitor-friendly town, and a new 300-store downtown mall was bringing in many first-time visitors with money to spend. The driving forces behind the subsequent transformation of Toronto from a "good theater town" to a major professional

GARTH DRABINSKY

One of the most colorful and controversial figures in contemporary Canadian theater is Toronto-born impresario Garth Drabinsky (1948–). Through his production company, Livent, Drabinsky found great success on Broadway in the 1980s and 1990s with a string of award-winning hits that included *Fosse, Parade, Ragtime, Kiss of the Spider Woman,* and the 1995 revival of *Showboat.* At the same time Drabinsky used his Broadway connections and savvy to help advance the development of the downtown Toronto theater district as "Broadway North." Along with rival producers Mirvish Productions, Drabinsky purchased and renovated theater property and mounted top-flight productions of current or recent Broadway shows. A pivotal turning point in Drabinsky's and Toronto's efforts to create an upscale popular theater scene was Drabinsky's 1989 Toronto production of *Phantom of the Opera,* opening one year after the Broadway premier. The production ran for 10 years and became a North American theater phenomenon. Critics and audiences raved about the show, often praising it as equal or superior to its sister productions in Broadway and London. Toronto's *Phantom* became the centerpiece of Toronto's tourist industry for a decade and catalyzed further investment in Toronto theater.

By the time Drabinsky's *Phantom* closed in 1999, downtown Toronto had established itself as the third-largest theater district in the English-speaking world and a bustling center for first-rate musical theater. At what appeared to be the height of his success, Drabinsky found himself embroiled in a spectacular legal controversy with some of his business partners at Livent, including American entertainment titan Michael Ovitz. In 1998 Drabinsky was suspended from Livent over allegations of mismanagement. The following year he was indicted by U.S. courts on charges of fraud. Similar charges followed in Canada shortly thereafter. By 2000, Drabinsky and Livent were effectively out of the theater production business.

theatrical center were two rival production companies, Mirvish Productions and Livent. Although both companies were involved in virtually all facets of theater production—from mounting individual shows, to promoting investment in theater, to purchasing and renovating Toronto theater venues—the styles and public personae of the corporations and their leaders could not have contrasted more starkly. Prior to the 1986 establishment of their theater company, Mirvish Productions, the Mirvish family (principally Ed Mirvish and his son, David) were well known and highly regarded in the Toronto business community as a result of successful ventures in retail sales, commercial property development, and restaurants. When Mirvish Productions took the family into large-scale theater production in Toronto, their solid reputation bolstered the confidence of the city government and business leaders that the venture could work. The faith of the citizenry was born out in the years that followed as the Mirvishes produced and hosted in their theaters such Toronto successes as *Les Miserables*, the North American premier of the British hit *Mamma Mia, Miss Saigon,* and *The Lion King.*

While the Mirvishes brought credibility and stability to the development of Toronto's theater district, rival Garth Drabinsky and his company, Livent, brought Broadway panache, edginess, and flare. Drabinsky (1948–) was a Toronto-born attorney who had found enormous success in New York as a producer of hit Broadway musicals. Although the Mirvishes controlled more Toronto theatrical venues, Drabinsky's ownership of the magnificent Canon (formerly Pantages) Theatre in the heart of downtown and his rights to the Toronto production of Andrew Lloyd Webber's *Phantom of the Opera* (1989–99) gave him Toronto's biggest theatrical success of the last quarter of the twentieth century. (To his credit, Drabinsky's marketing of Toronto's *Phantom* in the 1990s was a masterpiece of international promotion that reaped enormous returns for virtually all tourist-based Toronto businesses.) Toronto benefited incalculably from the efforts of both companies and by 2000 held legitimate claim to the title of "Broadway North." Beset by legal problems, Drabinsky and Livent are now out of the theater production business. Mirvish Productions continues to flourish as the principal producer of Toronto's mainstream Broadway shows. In their 2006–07 season, the Mirvishes doubtless took some level of competitive satisfaction against their former rival when they staged a new Toronto production of *Phantom of the Opera* in one of their own theaters.

New Canadian Playwrights

The last quarter of the twentieth century saw a long-awaited emergence of new Canadian playwrights. Michael Tremblay (1942–) is credited with giving contemporary Canadian playwriting a powerful sense of national identity, imbuing his plays with characters, language, themes, and settings that are distinctly Canadian. He is also generally believed to be the person most responsible for introducing meaningful gay and lesbian

---

THE SIMINOVITCH PRIZE

The single most generous theater prize in all of North America is Canada's Elinore and Lou Siminovitch Prize in Theatre. The Siminovitch is a single prize awarded annually since 2001 to the person who has done the most to advance Canadian theater as determined by a peer review of recent work. The award carries a $100,000 cash prize along with the stipulation that the awardee designate $25,000 of the prize to a theater protégé of his or her choice. The Siminovitch Prize is awarded for direction, playwriting, and design in 3-year cycles, although it is common for Canadian theater artists to be accomplished in multiple theatrical fields.

2001	Daniel Brooks, Directing
2002	Carole Fréchette, Playwriting
2003	Louise Campeau, Design
2004	Jillian Keiley, Directing
2005	John Mighton, Playwriting
2006	Dany Lyne, Design

---

themes into Canadian drama. Robert Lepage (1957–), an astonishingly versatile playwright, actor, filmmaker, director, and arts administrator, is one of Canada's leading avant-garde theatrical figures. He received international acclaim for his multimedia/performance art play *Aiguilles et Opium* (1992). He is also a former director of French-language theater for Ottawa's National Arts Centre. Daniel MacIvor (1962–) is a nationally known "alternative" playwright, combining conventional theatrical playwriting with elements of performance art and cabaret. His plays are performed extensively in Canada. His 1999 play *Never Swim Alone* won an award at the New York Fringe Festival and was produced off Broadway the following year. Montreal native Carole Fréchette (1949–), a novelist and playwright, is most closely associated with Québec theater circles. Her plays have won numerous awards and have been performed regularly since the 1970s. Her play *Les Quatre Morts de Marie* (1995) won the Governor General's Award (widely considered to be Canada's most prestigious literary award) for best French-language play. Berni Stapleton, an actress and comic as well as a playwright, has written extensively for stage as well as radio and television. In addition to having her work produced throughout Canada, she has mounted productions of her plays in New York and Ireland. Her plays reflect a fondness for social satire that also characterizes her work as a radio and stage humorist. Her stage play *A Tidy Package* (2003) was adapted for broadcast on CBC radio and television. John Mighton is a university lecturer in mathematics, whose play *Possible Worlds* (1997) has been made into a feature film by Robert Lepage. His play *Half Life* (2005) earned him one of his two Governor General's Awards for best English-language play. Judith Thompson (1954–), who is associated with Toronto's vibrant theater community, often writes in expressionistic and other experimental dramatic modes. She, too, is a two-time winner of the Governor General's Award. Thompson has also directed for the Shaw Festival. Daniel Danis (1962–) is one of Canada's leading experimental French-language playwrights and a multiple Governor General's Award winner. He often works in association with the Montreal-based Théâtre d'Aujourd'hui, one of the premier French-language theaters in Canada.

THE UNITED STATES

In the middle of the nineteenth century, the most popular commercial stage productions in America consisted of sentimental melodramas (both home-grown and European), operettas, farces, and comedies, as well as classical plays. However, by the beginning of the twentieth century, the realistic and naturalistic movements in modern European literature had exerted their influence on popular American theater and had spawned the beginnings of modern American playwriting. James Herne's (1839–1901) *Margaret Fleming* (1890) is widely considered to be America's first modern popular play. Herne's writing reflected the style of Norway's pioneering realist playwright Henrik Ibsen through naturalistic dialog, domestic settings, and rejection of happy resolutions. In the realm of social realism, a youthful Edward Sheldon (1886–1946) offered dramas on race relations (*The Nigger*, 1909) and labor conditions (*The Boss*, 1911), ushering in the American theater's enduring interest in socially and politically oriented plays.

Complementing the late nineteenth-century audiences' growing interest in socially relevant drama was an ever-expanding taste for comedy and light entertainment. British and French touring burlesque variety shows, popular in America throughout the eighteenth and nineteenth centuries, inspired American-born variations in the years just before 1900. These entertainments, which featured slapstick humor, rudimentary comedy "sketches," mild (by today's standards) sex comedy, and novelty acts (including child singers, animal acts, and jugglers) evolved into American vaudeville. Vaudeville's growth as an indigenous American entertainment was enhanced in the late nineteenth century by the expansion of the railroad, which could take performing companies on tours from town to town, north to south, 12 months a year. Peaking in popularity between the 1890s and the 1930s, American vaudeville and burlesque were the progenitors of many forms of American popular culture: the pop music concert, night club and sketch comedy, the stage revue, radio and television variety shows, early "talking" motion pictures, and musical theater.

The Birth of Modern American Theater, 1900–29

The history of twentieth century American theater is inextricably linked to the history of New York City. Throughout the era of immigration, beginning with the German and Irish waves of the mid-nineteenth century and ending with the border-tightening Federal Immigration Act of 1924, New York City was the major point of entry for close to 35 million immigrants, primarily from Europe but also from Asia, Latin America, and Puerto Rico. An additional 2 million African Americans from the South migrated to the North in the same period of time, with New York ultimately claiming many of them as permanent residents. The city responded to the population surge with an expansive commitment to public education at all levels. Expanding educational opportunities fueled New York City's ascendance as the center for many of America's new mass-market enterprises: finance, broadcasting, tourism, fashion, shopping, and perhaps most distinctively, arts and entertainment.

By 1900 New York City had already evolved into the cultural center of the nation. In turn, Midtown Manhattan evolved into the cultural center of New York City, with professional theater leading the way. In 1900, as much as now, America's theatrical shows and stars were made, broken, anointed, and dethroned in Midtown Manhattan. The first important Broadway theaters were located south of (properly "downtown from") the now famous Times Square theater district, whose epicenter is located where Broadway crosses: 42nd Street and 7th Avenue. Today relatively few "Broadway theaters" actually have Broadway street addresses. Since the 1920s, the theatrical term "Broadway" has referred to a cluster of high-profile, prestige theater houses located in a twenty-four-square-block area around Times Square. However, the first modern theater district of New York City was more linear than square and actually followed Broadway's diagonal jut across Manhattan's grid of streets and avenues between 13th and 34th streets, roughly one to two miles downtown from today's New York theater district. Among the early twentieth-century major Broadway show palaces were the Star Theater, the Academy of Music, and the Union Square Theater, all demolished before World War II but, in their glory days, all located on Broadway. The pre–World War I era's major vaudeville venue, Koster and Bial's (later named more famously Bryant's Opera House and thereafter the Trocadero), was also located downtown on Broadway. Until the end of World War I, when Times Square became the city's and the world's undisputed premier theater district, performers who said they were appearing "on Broadway" could be taken at their word.

The vision of Times Square as a concentrated theater district was formulated in the early 1900s by Oscar Hammerstein (1846–1919), grandfather of the famous musical composer, Oscar Hammerstein II. A manufacturer and theater builder, the elder Hammerstein envisioned Times Square (until 1907 called Longacre Square) as a smaller version of what it became—a dazzling entertainment village within the center of the city where theaters, hotels, and upscale eateries would draw theatergoers from far and near to its attractions. Hammerstein's foray into urban landscaping succeeded immediately. Other investors took notice, and new development followed through World War I. Since the main business of the theater and its related industries takes place after dark, the city and Times Square's entrepreneurs developed large-scale outdoor lighting, a new concept at the time. Times Square's lights emanating across the darkened city could be seen for miles, and a walk through the gaudy lights of the "Great White Way" became what it has been for a century: an integral part of the Broadway theater experience.

As early as the 1890s, East Coast theater owners such as Hammerstein, with few antimonopoly regulations to stop them, formed syndicates for multitheater ownership and management. By the 1910s the granddaddy of all syndicates, appropriately named the Syndicate, controlled over 700 performance venues along the East Coast. The Syndicate's competitors, the Schubert family, served as worthy rivals, and the epical competition between the Syndicate and the Schuberts created modern theater business practices as we know them: per-show financing and profit projection; written contracts; penalties for artist cancellations and no-shows; and guidelines for artist-producer disputes, among others. Audiences and artists in Syndicate- and Schubert-run theaters, for better or worse, knew in advance what they were getting and generally got it. Moreover, a successful performance in a prestigious Schubert or Syndicate theater could be a financial boon to an artist and, ultimately, a significant factor in determining an actor's or playwright's standing in American theater history. This was certainly true of American actress Maude Adams, the original *Peter Pan* (1906) in the Syndicate-produced American staging of J. M. Barrie's novel. In the years just after World

War I, Lionel Barrymore's successful turns in Schubert stage productions helped launch his film career.

The Modern American Musical

With influences from nineteenth-century burlesque, vaudeville, and operetta, the modern American musical emerged after the turn of the twentieth century. Musicals eventually became a distinctive stage genre and the most popular, commercially successful form of twentieth-century American theater. Maintaining the story, song, and dance format of operetta, American musicals moved away from operetta's lavishly exotic settings and romantically overwrought plots, emphasizing instead everyday, "common person" situations that mirrored vaudeville humor and turn-of-the century drama. Musical comedy songwriters and composers abandoned the linear structure of operetta, which avoided musical repetition within a single musical score. Instead, they substituted readily "singable" riffs, catchy songs, and recurring musical themes that were more accessible to a mass audience. From the late 1800s to the 1930s, plot and character development tended to be subservient to songs and to dance numbers. Showcasing the show's star performers' singing or dancing talents was the main business of musicals.

The stage musical achieved its true dominance of American theater in the 1920s. As many as fifty Broadway musicals could open in a single season, thanks to the increasing wealth and population growth in New York and the urban Northeast. (Today a typical Broadway season might open fewer than a dozen musicals, including revivals). These early musicals established lasting trademarks of the genre: sentimental boy-meets-girl formulaic plots, comic relief (often in the form of "low comic" minor characters modeled after vaudeville comedy), dance and chorus spectacles, and "show-stopping" star vehicle songs and dance routines.

Major productions from this period include the legendary musical *Showboat* (1927) by Jerome Kern (1885–1945) and Oscar Hammerstein II (1895–1960), *Strike Up the Band* by Gershwin brothers George (1898–1937) and Ira (1896–1983), and *No No Nanette* (1925) by Irving Caesar (1895–1996), Otto Harbach (1873–1963), and Vincent Youman (1898–1946). *Showboat* was particularly significant both for launching a string of major hit songs, including "Old Man River" and "'Can't Help Loving That Man of Mine," and for introducing social and racial themes into what was essentially escapist entertainment. With the advent of the hit musical came the ascendance of the musical star. Popular performers such as Adele (1897–1981) and Fred Astaire (1899–1987), Marilyn Miller (1898–1936), William Gaxton (1890–1963), and Al Jolson (1886–1950) rose to stardom. Fred Astaire and Jolson, among others, used their stage stardom as an entrée into films, which, like musicals, were coming into their own in the 1920s and 1930s.

During the Depression, the New York theater industry enjoyed a relatively prosperous decade with Broadway musicals providing the principal drawing power. New stars emerged during the Depression, their audience appeal enhanced by the success of another Midtown Manhattan homegrown industry—network radio. Radio's daily programming demands created an abundance of opportunities for skilled stage singers, musicians, and comedians. Among the first generation of performers to grow from "star of stage" to "star of stage, screen, and radio" were Ethel Merman (1908–84), Jimmy Durante (1893–1980), and Bob Hope (1903–2003). Frugal Depression-era producers tended to invest in relatively low-cost revues, most notably Flo Ziegfeld's (1867–1932) *Follies* and other starless spectacles. Ticket prices soared as high as $3.00 (almost 1 percent of the price of a new car, or roughly equivalent

OKLAHOMA! THE FIRST THOROUGHLY MODERN MUSICAL

Oklahoma! was Rodgers and Hammerstein's 1943 inaugural collaboration. It not only set new artistic standards for musicals, but it also rewrote the rules for marketing them. The show presented the most unified approach to plot, character, song, and choreography to date, introducing the Broadway musical to a new level of literacy. *Oklahoma!*'s 5-year, 2,200-performance run was unheard of at the time and inaugurated the modern concept of the long-running musical blockbuster. Essential to the show's success was its string of hit songs: "Oh, What a Beautiful Mornin'," "People Will Say We're in Love," "Surrey with the Fringe on Top," "Kansas City," and the finale—and eventual Oklahoma state song—"Oklahoma!" Decca Records producer Joe Kapp took notice, and only months after the show opened, he devised a plan to have the cast and an orchestra record the songs as they were heard in performance. The record album sold more than 1 million copies, a rare achievement in the 1940s. With Kapp's *Oklahoma!* the original Broadway cast album was born. The popularity of the album sustained audience interest in *Oklahoma!* long after it closed in 1948. A 1955 film adaptation brought the musical to an even larger audience. The film was a hit, won an Academy Award for music, and catalyzed Hollywood's interest in stage-to-screen movie musicals. In the ensuing years *Oklahoma!* became the first true Broadway musical franchise, generating a sound track album from the film; another cast recording from a 1979 Broadway revival; three more cast recordings from separate London productions (1947, 1980, and 1998); the DVD release of the 1955 movie; the 1999 DVD release of London's 1998 Royal National Theatre performance; the 1999 Broadway staging of the London show; performance fees from countless school and community productions; and royalties from commercial performances of the show's eternally popular hit songs.

to $150 in an updated comparison), but Broadway musicals still drew audiences even in the hardest of economic times.

The musical's economic and artistic growth during the Depression brought the genre to a new, more mature level of theatrical achievement after 1940. Sophisticated writers, composers, and producers collaborated to give musicals more complex plots and characters, thematically unified musical scores, and upgraded stage and production values. In 1943 Richard Rodgers (1902–79) and Hammerstein's *Oklahoma!* broke ground for the new American musical and expanded the entire concept of what the stage musical could accomplish both artistically and commercially. *Oklahoma!* was the first major American musical that was fully story driven, with songs, dancing, and dramatic pacing all enlisted to advance the central dramatic conflicts. Its artistic achievement was exceeded only by its commercial success. *Oklahoma!* ran on Broadway for a then unprecedented 2,200 performances over 5 years, in the process expanding Broadway's tour-bus appeal into the Midwest and South. With *Oklahoma!*'s success, the American musical became "musical theater."

Oklahoma! ushered in the "Golden Age" of Broadway musicals, which was characterized by ever-increasing sophistication of plot and character, song and score, theatrical craft, production values, and marketing. Production costs soared, forcing producers to cut back on the number of musicals they could mount in a season. The practice in the 1930s of a single producer sending up several shows each season in the hope of making a whole year's profit on one success was gone forever. As the number of musicals decreased, their quality increased exponentially, and the period between 1950 and the middle 1960s produced what is now considered to be the canon of great American musical theater.

What *Oklahoma!* accomplished for Broadway in the 1940s was nearly matched by what *My Fair Lady* (1956) did for the 1950s. Alan J. Lerner (1918–86) and Frederic Loewe's (1904–88) adaptation of George Bernard Shaw's play *Pygmalion* excised Shaw's socialist carping but maintained much of his sparkling English parlor wit and comedy-of-manners satire. *My Fair Lady* boasted an urbane, intelligent May-to-December love story with "absobloominlutely" "loverly" performances by 48-year-old London stage veteran Rex Harrison (1908–90) and 22-year-old ingénue Julie Andrews (1935–). *My Fair Lady* ran for a then stupefying 7 years and 2700 performances. A hit motion picture based on the musical sustained its legend throughout the 1960s and beyond. The same period also spawned the Broadway classics *Peter Pan* (1950), *The King and I* (1956), *The Music Man* (1957), *South Pacific* (1958), *Gypsy* (1959), *Bye Bye Birdie* (1960), *Camelot* (1960), and *Fiddler on the Roof* (1964), as well as *West Side Story* (1957), Leonard Bernstein (1918–90) and Steven Sondheim's (1930–) modern mean-streets retelling of Shakespeare's *Romeo and Juliet*. Directed by choreographer Jerome Robbins (1918–98), *West Side Story* brought Broadway choreography to previously unknown levels of sensuality, bravado, and complexity. *West Side Story* permanently elevated the importance of choreography on Broadway and conferred upon the Broadway choreographer star status comparable to that of the director or lead performer. (Noting the havoc that conceptual choreography can wreak on plot and character development, critics have viewed this turn of events as either a welcome rebirth of the original musical form or a catastrophic degeneration back to plotless illiteracy.)

By the mid-1960s, the postwar baby boom generation had entered young adulthood. Weaned since childhood on radio-based, youth-centered rock and roll music, which to that point had virtually no connection with the world of musical theater, young adults were by and large uninterested in musicals. The Broadway musical audience became older and smaller, and press attention to the musical—even in New York—waned as "serious" journalism emerged out of rock music culture. However, theater producers are nothing if not resourceful. Broadway could not "beat 'em," so they "joined 'em." Beginning in the late 1960s, some Broadway producers took the bold step of infusing rock music and culture into new Broadway shows in a transparent effort to reach the youth market that considered Golden Age musicals to be establishment, or worse, irrelevant. The move proved fortuitous and yielded immediate rewards. *Hair* (1968), *Grease* (1972), Andrew Lloyd Webber and Tim Rice's London import *Jesus Christ Superstar* (1973), and *Godspell* (1976) gave rock music a permanent place in the Broadway musical and brought a new generation of heretofore reluctant ticket buyers (often in the form of out-of-town school tour groups) into Broadway theaters.

From the late 1970s to the present, the Broadway musical has been open to a wide variety of artistic approaches. Consequently, the last several decades have produced some very surprising successes as well as unexpected failures. Andrew Lloyd Webber's *Cats* (1982), a pageant of human love and folly portrayed through the elaborate costumes and hair-ball choreography of cats clashing in an alley, ran for 18 years and 7,000-plus performances. Traditional, sentimental, yet stylish productions scored with audiences, including *Annie* (1977), which ran for 6 years, and the show-dance-heavy *My One and Only* (1983). So-called Euro-pop musicals contributed major hits to Broadway, including *Les Miserables* (1987) and *Phantom of the Opera* (1988) by Webber, who by this time was rivaling Rodgers and Hammerstein for status as the most successful purveyor of original musicals. The appearance of gay and lesbian themes in major Broadway plays during this period, such as

Matthew Crowley's *The Boys in the Band* (1968), combined with the theater industry's history of support for gay and lesbian communities, opened the door for uncompromising portrayals of gay and lesbian themes in musicals. Many of these productions were received enthusiastically by Broadway audiences. Harvey Fierstein and Jerry Herman's *La Cage aux Folles* (1983) and Kander and Ebb's *Kiss of the Spider Woman* (1993) are two of the most important and successful musicals associated with the gay and lesbian theater movement of the last 40 years.

The gift that *West Side Story* gave to Broadway choreography in the 1960s kept on giving through this period. Choreographer Michael Bennett's (1943–87) concept musical *A Chorus Line* (1975), which inverted the roles that choreography typically plays in advancing character development and dramatic action, became the longest-running American musical, closing in 1990 after 15 years and over 6,000 performances. Bob Fosse (1927–87) created stylish, sexy choreography for *Chicago* (1975) and *Dancin'* (1978). He was posthumously immortalized in a Tony Award–winning musical based on his own work (*Fosse*, 1999). Susan Stroman (1954–) has proven to be an outstanding choreographer for both revivals (*Oklahoma!* 1998; *The Music Man*, 2000) and original conceptual shows (*Contact*, 2000). Rock radio music maintained its presence in hits such as *Mamma Mia* (1993), *Movin' Out* (2002), *Jersey Boys* (2005), and *Lennon* (2005), based on the songs of pop-rock music crossover artists ABBA, Billy Joel, the Four Seasons, and John Lennon, respectively. The rock-influenced *Rent* (1996) was one of the most successful shows of the decade, with a 10-year run and over 4,000 performances, although its most famous song, "Seasons of Love" (525,600 minutes) was a soft love ballad.

The 1990s saw a new phenomenon in the financing of musicals by corporate conglomerates that assumed the role of show producer. The conglomerates rivaled and, in some cases, replaced the "independent" producer, who historically had focused his or her business activity primarily on theater production. The most important and influential of the new corporate producers is Walt Disney Productions, which used its own animated movies to create the highly successful musicals *Beauty and the Beast* (1994) and *The Lion King* (1999). Both shows became entire subfranchises that included the musical production itself; the sound track CD; touring companies; the original animated film in multimedia releases; and countless souvenirs, toys, and other merchandise. Disney rival Warner Brothers branched into musical production in the 2006 Broadway season with an ultimately unsuccessful musical *Lestat*, based on Anne Rice's best-selling novels about a neurotic vampire. The Nederlander Corporation and the Schubert Foundation (created by the Schubert family) have expanded their interests since the 1990s from theater operation and development to musical show production, increasing their already formidable influence over the musical theater industry. Broadway critics, many of whom indict the enlarged corporate presence for homogenizing the contemporary musical, begrudgingly concede the benefit of having new money and strong structural support for a business that, even in good years, is fraught with economic peril.

The diversity of contemporary Broadway is such that, even with the strong presence of corporate management, independent productions still achieve success. *Urinetown* (2001) was created by Broadway novices. Similarly, *Avenue Q* (2004), an altogether improbable muppet/puppet musical with sexual and drug-related content worthy of "mature" entertainment, endeared itself to Broadway audiences and won a Tony for Best Musical. The ultimate proof that the independent musical producer can still succeed on Broadway came in the form of an independently produced musical about independent musical producers: film comic Mel Brooks's (1926–) *The Producers* (2001) has won more Tony Awards than any other musical in history.

The Birth of Modern American Drama

Before the first decade of the twentieth century, the writing and production of serious contemporary literary plays was largely the province of European "masters," often associated with the highly regarded national theaters of Europe: the Moscow Art Theater, the Comédie-Française or Théâtre Français of France, or the newly founded Abbey Theatre in Ireland. Among the American intelligentsia and the general public, playwriting was not yet considered to be America's forte, a belief reflected in the American theater-going public's burgeoning interest in music hall, vaudeville, comedy, and variety theatrical performance. Dissatisfied with the paucity of opportunities to develop serious new plays, a group of young, restless New York–based artists formed a summer collective in Provincetown, Massachusetts, in 1915 for the purpose of writing and producing original, artistically adventurous drama. They called themselves the Provincetown Players. Although some members of the group were already established artists in one field or another, the Provincetown Players became the creative incubator for the then unknown Eugene O'Neill (1888–1953), whose rueful, soul-searching early works, such as *Bound East for Cardiff* (1916), gave the group the impetus to establish itself in New York City and carve out a niche for serious original playwriting in the flourishing cultural scene.

By the time of its demise in 1929, the Provincetown Players had launched the careers of Eugene O'Neill and Susan Glaspell (1882–1948), respectively America's first internationally known modern playwright and America's first major woman playwright. In addition, the group helped established America's independent "little theater" movement, which for the next 20 years shaped the artistic and intellectual direction of American drama. Other experimental New York–based theater groups sprang up throughout the 1920s and 1930s, most notably the Group Theater and the Theater Guild, which laid the foundation for mainstream American theater's permanent acceptance of serious literary dramatic works by American writers and theater artists.

The Emergence of the Major American Playwright: O'Neill, Miller, Williams, and Albee

Notwithstanding the accomplishments of many members of the Provincetown Players, Eugene O'Neill was their star from the outset. At first with the Players and soon thereafter quite on his own, O'Neill was the first American playwright whose body of work received significant recognition in the United States and, notably, in Europe. In the years between the two world wars, O'Neill's powerfully emotive and enigmatic tomes of loss and sacrifice demanded the attention of an increasingly sophisticated American public and impressed the heretofore disdainful Europeans. O'Neill experimented successfully with avant-garde European theatrical techniques in the Expressionistic works *The Emperor Jones* (1920) and *The Hairy Ape* (1922), and he worked skillfully within the realm of Greek myth in *Mourning Becomes Electra* (1931). Two of his plays are ranked among the masterpieces of all modern Western drama: *The Iceman Cometh* (which premiered in 1946 but was written several years earlier) and his searing autobiographical play about his family, *Long Day's Journey into Night* (which opened posthumously in 1957 but was written in 1941). O'Neill's prolific output of stirring, difficult, yet effecting dramas helped make the American public more receptive to the plays of some of his excellent, serious-minded contemporaries, including Thornton Wilder, Edna St. Vincent Millay, Clifford Odets, and Elmer Rice. O'Neill is largely responsible for the advent of this first generation of modern American playwrights, even though his reputation eventually overshadowed the others. Apart from his status as America's first major playwright, O'Neill is widely acclaimed as the best American playwright that ever lived.

O'Neill has a few formidable rivals for his place of primacy among American playwrights. Arthur Miller (1915–2005) shared O'Neill's strong sense of theatrical craftsmanship and, like O'Neill, was a student of both modern and classical drama. Miller's political and class-conscious themes, on one level, appear to be more obvious than O'Neill's enigmatic portraits of tortured souls. But Miller skillfully wedded contemporary social issues to the art form of the well-made play and, in so doing, forged the most successful American playwriting career of the post–World War II era. He created his two most highly regarded works toward the beginning of his career. *Death of a Salesman* (1949), the most widely read and best known of all American plays, produced what one writer has called the "American Hamlet" (Hulin 2002) with *Salesman* hero Willy Loman serving as "exhibit A" in the recurring theatrical debate over whether a common, undistinguished character can be a true tragic figure. In *The Crucible* (1953), a parable about zealotry and the repression of human rights in times of intense political conflict, Miller presents the Salem witch trials of the seventeenth century as an allegory for the 1950s Red Scare, Congress's infamous drive to rid the country, and the entertainment industry in particular, of Communists and their sympathizers. A target of these investigations himself, Miller became a hero to artists and political progressives both for his refusal to "name names" when interrogated by the House Un-American Activities Committee (HUAC) and for protesting so forcefully against HUAC in his play, *The Crucible*. Although Miller wrote steadily until his death in 2005, he never regained the critical acclaim or public acceptance he received for his earlier dramas.

Miller's reputation is often closely linked to that of Tennessee Williams (1911–83), notwithstanding the fact that the two men had strikingly contrasting approaches to playwriting, were not close friends, had very different backgrounds, and did not engage in professional collaborations within the course of their lives. The frequent pairing of the two can be accounted for by the fact that they both had their first Broadway successes in the 1940s, and both are best remembered for plays written in the late 1940s and 1950s. More significantly, during the 1950s, the works of both became fixtures in high school and college English classes and drama clubs, with *Death of a Salesman* and *The Glass Menagerie* (1945), respectively, and many Americans were first introduced to these authors' plays at about the same time. However, their styles and dramatic interests were quite different. Williams explored personal relationships more intimately than did Miller. In plays such as *A Streetcar Named Desire* (1947) and *Cat on a Hot Tin Roof* (1955), Williams introduced a level of mature sexuality in his characters that had heretofore been all but unknown in mainstream Broadway theater. He is largely credited with (or condemned for) bringing mainstream American theater audiences to a new level of understanding and acceptance of how adult characters can be presented on stage. A Southerner and Midwesterner for most of his life, Williams also brought new locales and sensibilities to the Eastern-centric Broadway scene, and he is considered by advocates of Southern literature to rank with novelists William Faulkner and Eudora Welty as one of America's great Southern writers. Like Miller, Williams came along in time to ensure that, with O'Neill's retirement from playwriting in the late 1940s, the newly established legacy of world-class American playwriting would sustain itself for at least another generation.

Although Miller's and Williams's story-driven, largely naturalistic plays were the dominant forces in American drama in the late 1940s and 1950s, many European dramatists were experimenting with new antiliterary plays and antitheatrical productions. Falling somewhat uncomfortably under the term "the theater of the absurd," playwrights Eugene Ionesco

(Romania), Samuel Beckett (Ireland and France), and Jean-Paul Sartre (France) wrote plays that were openly hostile to the concept of theater as middle-class entertainment and disdainful of the realistic, semitragic, or sentimental stories of love and domestic strife that dominated modern drama on both continents. Until the late 1950s, the American theater community met this new European movement with indifference and condescending curiosity, more or less assuming that absurdism was strictly a European phenomenon. That remained the case until the American Edward Albee (1928–) began writing plays in the manner of the European avant-garde. The adopted son of one of America's legendary vaudeville producers, Albee premiered his first work, *The Zoo Story* (1959), appropriately enough, in Europe. Within 2 years, critically acclaimed yet controversial American productions of his short plays, *The Zoo Story, The Sandbox* (1960), and *The American Dream* (1960), gave absurdism and other new forms of theatrical experimentation a permanent place in American theater. Albee became a truly major playwright in 1962 with *Who's Afraid of Virginia Woolf.* While containing familiar character types, plot, and setting, *Virginia Woolf* is also infused with experiments in language and story-within-a-story digressions that characterized Albee's earlier, more radical works. Albee is credited with giving voice and direction to later theatrical American iconoclasts, including Amiri Baraka, Arthur Kopit, David Mamet, and Sam Shepard.

Major American Stage Actors and Actresses

With challenging, complex, and exciting roles emerging from the writing of O'Neill, Miller, Williams, and Albee, new actors found fame and adulation for bringing these new characters to life. Jason Robards, Jr. (1922–2000) became closely identified with Eugene O'Neill's plays, starring in *The Iceman Cometh* and *Long Day's Journey into Night.* He also played the starring role in Arthur Miller's play *After the Fall,* (1964), an extended semifictionalized examination of Miller's courtship and marriage to film legend Marilyn Monroe. Lee J. Cobb (1911–76) immortalized the character of Willy Loman in Miller's *Death of a Salesman.* The character of Loman and the persona of the big, lumbering Cobb became fused in the public's mind until the smaller, athletic Dustin Hoffman (1937–) revived the character in 1984 and gave Willy Loman a nervous, tragicomic edge. Prior to becoming the most important American film star in the 1950s, Marlon Brando performed in a half-dozen Broadway productions in the late 1940s, culminating with a now legendary performance as Stanley Kowalski in Tennessee Williams's *A Streetcar Named Desire.* No single actor or elite group of actors dominated the New York scene after the Robards-Brando-Cobb era. However, Frank Langella (1940–) has been a perennial favorite on Broadway since the late 1960s. The only male actor to have won two Tony Awards for Best Actor in a Play (winning them 29 years apart), Langella's longevity and versatility are legendary in contemporary theater. During the Golden Age of the Broadway musical from the 1940s to the 1980s, Robert Preston (1918–87), Alfred Drake (1914–92), and John Raitt (1917–2005) emerged as major romantic leading men, while Zero Mostel (1915–77) became one of Broadway's most "bankable" comedic actors.

Arguably the most revered American stage actress in the twentieth century was Helen Hayes (1900–93). The winner of numerous awards including three Tonys, Hayes's professional stage career lasted an astonishing 60 years. Hayes moved easily from Shakespeare and classical theater to light comedy, musicals, and serious modern drama. Hayes originated the role of Coquette in George Abbott's play of the same name (1927) and starred in the American premier of J. M. Barrie's *Dear Brutus* (1918). If Hayes has a competitor, it is Julie Harris

(1925–). The winner of six Tony Awards for acting, including a Lifetime Achievement Award, Harris's role as Emily Dickinson in the one-woman play *The Belle of Amherst* (1976) revitalized the one-character drama as a potent theatrical genre. Harris's Dickinson stands as one of the standout performances in the history of modern American theater. English-born Jessica Tandy (1909–94) became a fixture on the Broadway stage from the 1940s into the 1990s, frequently performing opposite her Canadian-born husband, Hume Cronyn (1911–2003). Tandy originated the role of Blanche DuBois opposite Brando in the original Broadway production of *A Streetcar Named Desire*. The first and most important female modern musical star was Ethel Merman (1908–84). In her 40-year career, she originated some of musical comedy's most important characters, including Annie Oakley in *Annie Get Your Gun* (1946), Rose in *Gypsy* (1959), and Dolly Gallagher-Levi in *Hello Dolly* (1964). Between 1949 and 1959, Mary Martin (1913–1990) scored three historic triumphs as the original Nellie Forbush (*South Pacific*, 1949), Peter Pan (*Peter Pan*, 1954), and Maria (*The Sound of Music*, 1959). British-born actress Julie Andrews (1935–) performed in only four original Broadway productions, but two of those performances—Eliza Doolittle in *My Fair Lady* (1956), and Guinevere in *Camelot* (1960)—are among the most popular and enduring female roles of the musical's Golden Age. A stunning dancer from age twenty to age seventy, Chita Rivera (1933–) has been one of Broadway's most beloved and versatile performers for decades.

African Americans in American Theater

Not surprisingly, the first commercial plays with African-American characters and themes were written by whites. Dion Boucicault's *The Octoroon* (1859), a melodrama about race mixing, probably did as much to perpetuate prejudice as it did to examine it, but it remains one of American theater's earliest forays into racial themes. Ridgely Torrence's *Three Plays for a Negro Theater* appeared on Broadway in 1917. Eugene O'Neill's *The Emperor Jones* (1920) is credited with creating Broadway's first major starring role for an African-American actor. Charles Gilpin (1878–1930), who was a pioneering figure in early twentieth century "Negro theater" movement, originated the title role on Broadway. A 1925 Broadway revival of *Emperor Jones* became a star vehicle for Paul Robeson (1898–1976), American theater's preeminent African-American stage singer at the time. His stellar performance in the expressionistic *Emperor Jones* secured his position as the lead of the 1933 film based on the play and made Robeson the first internationally famous African-American film star. In 1926 Paul Green won a Pulitzer Prize for *In Abraham's Bosom*, a play about the persecution of an African-American teacher (the play was produced in New York by the Provincetown Players).

Harlem Renaissance and the Federal Theater Project

Certainly prior to World War II, and some would argue even now, an African-American presence on Broadway and in "legitimate theater" has been sporadic at best. However, African-American professional theater sustained itself in the years before World War II principally through the Harlem Renaissance and the Federal Theater Project. The Harlem Renaissance, a 20-year flourish of artistic activity in a predominantly African-American (formerly Dutch) neighborhood in Upper Manhattan, generated an abundance of professional and community-based theater by and for African Americans and made a lasting impact on twentieth-century American art and culture. Langston Hughes (1902–67) emerged as the leading playwright and poet of the Harlem Renaissance. African-American women playwrights such as Thelma Myrtle Duncan (1902–?), Georgia Douglas Johnson (ca. 1878–1966), and most notably Zora Neale Hurston (1891–1960) received their first professional recognition and acclaim during the Harlem Renaissance period. Actors Robeson and Gilpin were active professionally in both "uptown" Harlem-based and "downtown" commercial Broadway theater. The Harlem theater and music scene also produced actresses Florence Mills (1895–1927) and Pearl Bailey (1918–90). After World War II, Bailey became a highly successful singer and comic, headlining in Las Vegas and making frequent network television appearances at a time when only a handful of African-American entertainers appeared on television.

The Federal Theater Project, an initiative of Franklin Roosevelt's New Deal, had two major objectives: to sustain commercial theater (which Roosevelt, a former governor of New York, understood as a national resource) and foster noncommercial, experimental theater. Unapologetic in its controversial racial equality philosophy, the Federal Theater Project commissioned and funded numerous racially integrated productions and African-American plays throughout the country. Among the historically noteworthy African-American theatrical ventures undertaken by the Federal Theater Project were an African-American cast production of Shakespeare's *Macbeth* and the African-American "Living Newspapers," short but direct productions based on current events.

African-American Playwrights after World War II

Although a handful of African-American performers had appeared in Broadway productions prior to World War II, African-American playwrights were excluded from Broadway theater until 1959. The first genuine Broadway hit play written by an African-American was Lorraine Hansberry's (1930–1965) *A Raisin in the Sun* (1959), which traces a Chicago working-class family's struggles with poverty, racism, and the African-American community's internal debates over politics and self-definition. Hansberry's sharply written dialog and masterfully drawn characterizations place *A Raisin in the Sun* among America's most important social dramas. The prophetic play introduced white audiences to issues that previously had received little attention in mainstream America, including Pan-Africanist philosophy, tensions between the African-American middle and working classes, and the political symbolism of African-American hair and dress styles. Hansberry's death from cancer at age thirty-five cut off a very promising career, but the success of *A Raisin in the Sun* generated new interest in African-American playwrights and energized African-American theater artists around the country.

With the advent of the black power movement in the early 1960s, other playwrights took up Hansberry's racial themes but intensified the theatrical presentation to match the heated political rhetoric of the times. Leroi Jones (1934–) renamed himself Imamu Amiri Baraka, subsequently shortening it to Amiri Baraka, and ushered in a new wave of African-American theater with his plays *The Dutchman* and *Slave* (1964). The uncompromising anger and dramatic tension of Baraka's works attracted national attention despite premiering in small, off-off Broadway and community theaters. Lonne Elder III (1927–96) and Ed Bullins (1935–) also wrote important plays in the 1960s, which, although less strident in rhetoric than Baraka's works, placed a higher priority on exploring racial themes and racial anger than they did on giving theatergoers a pleasant evening out on the town. August Wilson (1945–2005), whose body of work is increasingly regarded as a singular contribution to American theater, became the most important African-American playwright of the post–civil rights era and, along with Hansberry, one of the most important African-American playwrights in history. The bulk of Wilson's writings comprise a ten-play cycle of plays about African Americans in each decade of the twentieth century. Two of the plays, *The Piano Lesson* (1986) and *Fences* (1985), each earned Wilson a Pulitzer Prize, and two others, *Ma Rainey's Black Bottom* (1982) and *Joe Turner's Done Come and Gone* (1984) still enjoy repeated performances in universities and regional professional theaters more than 20 years after their premieres. Notwithstanding his death at sixty-one, Wilson's reputation as one of the twentieth century's best and most important American playwrights is secure. Adrienne Kennedy (1931–) is simultaneously associated with the advance of politically oriented African-American and feminist theater movements (see also Women Playwrights and Feminist Theater below). An award-winning novelist and playwright, Kennedy's most famous dramatic works include *Funny House of a Negro* (1962) and *A Rat's Mass* (1969). Lori Suzan Parks (1964–), who won the Pulitzer Prize in 2002 for her play *Top Dog/Underdog*, is a significant upcoming force in American theater.

The Jewish Stage Comedy Tradition

Although eighteenth- and nineteenth-century American satirical comedy was often modeled after the English lampoons of mannered aristocratic society, modern American stage comedy owes its greatest historical debt to the comedians of vaudeville. Imported English parlor wit and ironic epigrams gave way to rapid-fire put downs, percussive one-liners, American comic stage stereotypes, and half-shouted set-up-and-punch-line jokes. When combined with a healthy dose of stage slapstick, this new comic style evolved as an indigenous urban American aesthetic for stage comedy previously unknown in the English-speaking theater. Italian and Irish Americans may have been the predominant balladeers on the vaudeville circuit, but theater historians note that Jews dominated the comic scene throughout the vaudeville era. Before becoming stage, television, and film stars, Jewish comics such as the Marx Brothers, Jack Benny, George Burns, Milton Berle, Eddie Cantor, Sid Caesar, Fanny Brice, and Danny Kaye were all vaudevillians. Not surprisingly, this tradition produced some of the first important writers of Broadway stage comedy and plays, who emerged in the wake of vaudeville's demise. Frequent collaborators George S. Kaufman (1889–1961) and Moss Hart (1904–61) were among the first successful Broadway comic playwrights, winning a Pulitzer Prize for *You Can't Take It with You* (1936) and penning a number of other commercial successes that still enjoy an occasional amateur or semiprofessional revival (most notably *The Man Who Came to Dinner*, 1939). On his own, Kaufman won another Pulitzer Prize for the political satire/musical *Of Thee I Sing* (1932); toward the end of his career, he won a Tony Award for writing the script for the musical *Guys and Dolls* (1951). These and other Kaufman plays, such as *My Sister Eileen* (1940) and *Dinner at Eight* (1932), represent the development of sophisticated, well-crafted American stage comedies that retained the snappy dialog and pace of their "vaudeville routine" ancestry.

Comedy playwright Neil Simon (1927–) is the most commercially successful playwright of comedy or drama in the history of American theater. Simon has had twenty-seven original Broadway successes since his Broadway debut with *Come Blow Your Horn* (1961). He is the only playwright ever to have four shows running simultaneously on Broadway. No Neil Simon Broadway opening has failed to make a profit. Although dismissed early on by serious-minded drama critics as a formulaic television gag writer, which he was in the 1950s, Simon's maturity as a playwright, combined with the long-overdue open-mindedness on the part of American intellectuals, allowed his stature as a major author to catch up to his unparalleled standing with American audiences. Like Simon, to whom she was compared throughout her career, satirist Wendy Wasserstein (1950–2006) fashioned the nuances of Jewish-American life into wit-spun mainstream humor. She was the most successful American woman playwright of the latter part of the twentieth century.

Women Playwrights and Feminist Theater

The first woman playwright to have a major impact upon the development of American theater was Susan Glaspell (1882–1948). Notwithstanding her professional beginnings as a journalist and novelist, Glaspell is generally acknowledged as the first American feminist playwright. A founding member of the Provincetown Players, Glaspell wrote in the naturalistic and realistic mode of the time. She won a Pulitzer Prize for her play *Alison's House* (1931). Her best-known play, *Trifles* (1916), a murder mystery with a clever feminist "twist," is a canonical work in twentieth-century American feminist literature. Zora Neale Hurston, an African-American playwright, was a major figure within the Harlem Renaissance movement of the 1920s. A highly versatile writer, Hurston wrote ten plays (including a collaboration with Langston Hughes) that ranged from sentimental comedy (*Spunk*, 1935) to satire (*Meet the Mama*, 1925) to multiscene club revues. In the years between the world wars, Edna St. Vincent Millay (1892–1950) was primarily known for her poetry but acted in and wrote plays for the Provincetown Players. Lillian Hellman (1905–84) gained fame in the 1930s for hard-edged, controversial plays, including *The Children's Hour* (1934), concerning two teachers whose lives are destroyed by a rumor that they are lesbians, and the labor-strike drama *Days to Come* (1936). Her best-known play, *Little Foxes* (1939), veered from specific social issues and explored family tensions in the South at the turn of the twentieth century.

After World War II, and especially after the 1960s, the opportunities for women playwrights and women's theater in general expanded significantly. Lorraine Hansberry's *A Raisin in the Sun* (see African-American Playwrights after World War II, above) proved to be a breakthrough production for both women and African Americans in theater. A posthumous adaptation of her writings, *To Be Young, Gifted, and Black* (1969), directed and compiled by her husband Robert Nemiroff, became successful as a Broadway musical and is frequently revived in professional and amateur theaters. From the1980s until her death in 2006, Wendy Wasserstein became the most successful American woman playwright of the post–World War II era (see The Jewish Stage Comedy Tradition, above). Her best-known plays, *The Heidi Chronicles* (1989) and *The Sisters Rosenzweig* (1993), both won Tony Awards for Best Play. Wasserstein also earned a Pulitzer Prize for *The Heidi Chronicles*. At the same time, many new women writers benefited from the efforts of regional theaters to discover new plays from young, unheralded playwrights. Marsha Norman (1947–) premiered most of her earlier plays at the Actors Theater of Louisville, including her most famous play *'night Mother,* which won the Pulitzer Prize in 1983. Beth Henley (1952–) wrote prolifically for stage and film throughout the 1980s and 1990. She won acclaim and a Pulitzer Prize for her first play *Crimes of the Heart* (1981) and found success with some of her later works, including *The Miss Firecracker Contest* (1984) and *Impossible Marriage* (1998).

The American feminist theater movement evolved in conjunction with the women's movement of the 1970s and 1980s. The formal beginnings of feminist theater in the United States are generally ascribed to the 1972 establishment of the Women's Theater Council, a collective of New York–based women playwrights. The council's founders included Megan Terry (1932–), whose innovative plays earned acclaim both in and out of feminist theater circles. Her play *Viet Rock* (1966) was the first professional staging of an American play about the Vietnam conflict and is a major work in the history of American protest drama and literature. Adrienne Kennedy (see African-American Playwrights after World War II, above) was also one of the founders of the Women's Theater Council. An enduring legacy of the feminist theater movement has been Eve Ensler's *The Vagina Monologues* (1996), which has become a political and theatrical phenomenon unique in American theater history. Based on over 200 interviews with women of varying ages and cultural backgrounds *The Vagina Monologues*, a series of vignettes, soliloquies, and sketches, careens back and forth between sexual satire and political outrage over violence against women and repressive social attitudes about sexuality. Ensler periodically updates the play, and theater groups producing the show select from her growing inventory of material for the ever-evolving piece. Many social action theater troops and university women's organizations produce the show annually to raise funds and promote awareness of women's rights issues.

Bye-Bye Broadway: Off Broadway, Off-Off Broadway, and Regional Theaters

Prior to World War II, American commercial theater was more accommodating to unknown playwrights and new plays than it became after 1950. The economics of the 1920s and 1930s and the low production costs of the pre- and post-Depression era allowed producers to mount several different shows in a single season, hoping that one or two would turn a solid profit and cover the cost of the flops. However, after World War II, the combination of escalating production costs and the "flight" of a large portion of the white middle-class theater-going public to the suburbs turned a social evening on Broadway from a spur-of-the-moment outing to a major excursion, for which family finances, schedules, transportation, and babysitters had to be carefully marshaled. As a result, producers were forced to take fewer risks, both commercially and artistically. A typical Broadway season, which in the 1930s might mount over 200 different productions, had cut back that number by as much as 75 percent or more in 1960. From 1960 to 2000, most major Broadway productions fell into one of three categories: musical comedies (both new productions and revivals), revivals of major dramatic works, and a Neil Simon (or a Simon-like) new comedy. The young, serious playwright and, by extension, the rising dramatic actor and director, were almost extinct in the New York theater district, all the more so if he or she could not sing, dance, or compose music.

In addition to prohibitive play production costs, the tightening Broadway market also had to contend with lucrative opportunities for writers and actors in television and film. Money and the chance for massive exposure made Hollywood increasingly attractive to theatrical talents after 1960, especially since American filmmaking was starting to garner international prestige as a serious art form. Depression-era stage actors such as Jason Robards, Lee J. Cobb, or Helen Hayes had established their reputations on the stage first, and then had begun to develop their identities as film actors later in their careers. However, after the 1960s, young actors such as Dustin Hoffman, Robert Duvall, and Meryl Streep, all trained and apprenticed as New York–based stage actors, were firmly established film stars by the time they were in their twenties or early thirties. Nevertheless, the lure of stagecraft was irresistible to serious artists, even if the finances were singularly unpalatable. From the 1960s on, a strident theatrical rebellion against Broadway commercialism had been taking place right under its nose.

The social rebelliousness of the American theater community in the 1960s matched that of the American political left, with which it had strongly come to identify since the founding of the Provincetown Players and Washington Square players in the first decade of the twentieth century. Reflecting the angry energy of the 1960s peace movement, civil rights movement, and women's movement, as well as the artistic anarchy of the European absurdists, U.S. off-Broadway and off-off Broadway theater developed a radical, anticommercial disposition. From the 1960s through 1980, numerous radical theater groups emerged in New York and elsewhere, often housed in church basements, old movie theaters, colleges and universities, coffee houses and clubs, and, occasionally, on the streets. Several of these groups made their mark and helped define the American radical theater movement of the time.

First among equals was Julian Beck's Living Theater, which operated out of New York but also maintained a presence in Europe during that time. German-born Beck (1925–85) began performing experimental, European-influenced avant-garde theater in New York in the early 1950s but found his voice and eventual notoriety in the radical climate of the 1960s. The Living Theater featured improvisations, happenings ("productions" staged on unsuspecting audiences in streets, business offices, and bus terminals), audience interaction, and intimidation. Beck and the Living Theater's most famous productions were *The Brig* (1963), a fictional exposé of military prison life, and *Paradise Now* (1968), a series of street theater improvisations that evolved into a biting satirical revue of American social hypocrisy. Nudity and profanity in performance led to more than a few production shutdowns and arrests—especially when the Living Theater toured outside New York City. Beck and the Living Theater are largely credited with broadening the boundaries of what constituted American theatrical performance.

The other major, lasting New York–based experimental theater company from the 1960s was La MaMa. Less directly political than the Living Theater, La MaMa productions, although highly unconventional and innovative, were generally more seriously crafted than were those of the Living Theater. La MaMa was also somewhat more receptive to genuine playwriting than was the Living Theater. With a permanent theater building in Manhattan and an annual production season, La MaMa remains a major showcase for new playwrights, actors, directors, and other theater artists.

On the West Coast, the San Francisco Mime Troup (SFMT) shared the Living Theater's love of street performance and irreverence but leaned toward a more widely accessible, current-events focus on social and political satire. Founded in 1959, the SFMT, which does not perform pantomime, is still in operation. It enjoys success with national and international tours, youth theater, and community outreach projects. The SFMT has received a Tony Award for excellence in regional theater and is considered a vital element in both the current and historical American radical theater movements.

Performance Artists

The radical theater movement of the1960s shared an artistic kinship with avant-garde visual arts movements and poetry-as-performance movements of the same period. From this kinetic if occasionally haphazard amalgam of genres came the performance artist, who emerged in the 1970s and 1980s as a new kind of theatrical entertainer, notwithstanding some historical indebtedness to 1960s radical theater and to sixteenth-century Italian commedia dell'arte. Usually working solo, performance artists place their bodies in the center of a ménage of sound, image, movement, music, and spoken word. America's premier performance artist is Chicago-born Laurie Anderson (1947–), who relies heavily on her early training as a violinist to make string music a powerful force in her performances. Anderson's venues range from street corners to "coat and tie" evenings at New York's Town Hall. Eric Bogosian

(1953–), in addition to being an award-winning playwright, film director, and actor, also develops and acts in performance art productions. Spalding Gray (1942–2004), like Bogosian, was a monologist, whose one-man theatrical productions received wide critical acclaim. John Leguizamo (1964-), a New York theater performance artist and stand-up club comic, achieved mainstream fame and notoriety shortly after 2000 when he began appearing regularly on network television series and talk shows.

Regional Theaters

Even though New York retained its position as the nation's theater capital for virtually all of the twentieth century, regional professional theater companies became well established throughout the country—particularly after 1960. Developing primarily in urban communities, high-quality regional professional theater companies were usually established through three-way partnerships among local government, business community, and artistic leadership. The artistic leadership generally took the form of a highly visible artistic director, who was sometimes "home grown" but more often aggressively recruited from New York, London, or other established regional theaters. The formula worked well in many medium and large population centers. In 1976, recognizing the importance of regional theater to the health of the American stage, the American Theater Wing (purveyors of theater's coveted Tony Awards) began presenting an annual award honoring an outstanding regional theater. Minneapolis's Guthrie Theater, the Seattle Repertory Theater, the Denver Center Theater, and Actors Theater of Louisville—all past winners of this award—are among the most well established and venerated of this type of theater company. Regional theaters have become excellent training grounds for actors, directors, and technicians hoping to go on to Broadway or Hollywood. Some of contemporary America's most venerated film, television, and Broadway actors "paid their dues" in regional theater companies, including John Malkovich, Denzel Washington, and Meryl Streep.

From the 1960s to the mid 1970s, regional theaters tended to specialize in revivals of well-established, popular, and proven hit shows, striving annually for a season of perhaps four to eight major productions that would please hometown audiences yet engage the company's professional theater artists. However, by the mid-1970s, many regional theaters had established such strong reputations and community support that they could safely offer previously unproduced plays by fledgling playwrights while still holding their key audience, the all-important season subscriber. Young playwrights, ever desperate to get their plays produced professionally, responded enthusiastically. In addition to the expansion of opportunities to showcase new work, playwrights rejoiced in the enhanced visibility, press coverage, and audience response that a regional opening could offer, in comparison to what they would likely contend with in a New York opening. By the 1980s new play production and playwright discovery had become so popular in many regional theater communities that the regionals often found themselves competing for the talents of unknown writers rather than elbowing each other out for performance rights to old standbys from Miller, Williams, Simon, or Rodgers and Hammerstein. Since 1975 most of the plays that have won the Pulitzer Prize premiered in regional theaters, including Sam Shepard's *Buried Child* (1979, Magic Theater in San Francisco), Beth Henley's *Crimes of the Heart* (1981, Actor's Theater of Louisville), and August Wilson's *Fences* (1987, Pittsburgh Public Theater). Regional theater remains an increasingly powerful force in American theater as both a proving ground for new talent and as professional theater's emissary to the American public.

Producers and Directors

Among the numerous producers and directors who have contributed to the strength of American theater, a few have earned "star status" through their landmark achievements. Elia Kazan (1909–2003) was the most honored and most controversial of American stage directors. In a career that spanned 70 years, Kazan directed or staged many of the most important dramatic premiers in the history of American theater: Clifford Odets's *Waiting for Lefty* and *Paradise Lost* (both in 1935 with co-Group Theater director Harold Clurman); Arthur Miller's *All My Sons* (1947), *Death of a Salesman* (1949), and *After the Fall* (1964); Tennessee Williams's *A Streetcar Named Desire* (1947) and *Cat on a Hot Tin Roof* (1955); and Thornton Wilder's *The Skin of Our Teeth* (1942). In 1952 Kazan became a scourge to the left wing of the theater and film communities when he gave HUAC names of Communist sympathizers he had known at the beginning of his career. The controversy followed Kazan for the rest of his life.

Lee Strasberg (1901–82) possessed a rare combination of relentless creative fire and superb administrative instincts. His directing career covered 40 years and included Odets's *Paradise Lost* (1935), *Golden Boy* (1937) and *Awake and Sing* (1939), and a major revival of Eugene O'Neill's *Strange Interlude* (1963; revival of the 1928 original). He was a founder and/or principal administrator of two of the most important theater organizations in American history: the Group Theater and the Actors Studio. In the 1930s the Group Theater discovered and nurtured Clifford Odets who, with Elmer Rice, first brought issue-driven social drama to a commercial theater audience. Strasberg became artistic director of the Actors Studio in 1951 and held the position until his death. Strasberg developed the Actors Studio into the single most prestigious training ground for American stage and film actors, directors, and writers. Artists who studied at the Actors Studio include Edward Albee, Marlon Brando, Jane Fonda, Marilyn Monroe, Paul Newman, Robert De Niro, Al Pacino, Sidney Poitier, Julia Roberts, and Tennessee Williams.

Joseph Papp (1921–91) brought back to the high-cost world of 1970 and 1980s theater a pre–World War II sensibility by showcasing unknown actors and writers while, at the same time, making professional theater accessible to a wide audience. Papp took a large portion of his considerable earnings as the producer of commercial successes (including *A Chorus Line*) and invested in public theater enterprises, most notably New York's fabled Shakespeare in the Park and numerous other civic-oriented theater companies and productions.

RESOURCE GUIDE

PRINT SOURCES

Benson, Eugene, and L. W. Conolly, eds. *The Oxford Companion to Canadian Theatre*. Oxford: Oxford University Press, 1989.

Bigsby, C. W. E. *A Critical Introduction to Twentieth-Century American Drama: Volume 1, 1900–1940*. Cambridge: Cambridge University Press, 1982

———. *A Critical Introduction to Twentieth-Century American Drama: Volume II, Williams, Miller, Albee*. Cambridge: Cambridge University Press, 1984.

———. *A Critical Introduction to Twentieth-Century American Drama: Volume III, Beyond Broadway*. Cambridge: Cambridge University Press, 1985.

Brown, John Russell, ed. *The Oxford Illustrated History of the Theatre*. Oxford: Oxford University Press, 1993.

Chapman, Vernon. *Who's in the Goose Tonight?: An Anecdotal History of Canadian Theatre*. Toronto: ECW Press, 2001.

Gavin, Christy. *African American Women Playwrights: A Research Guide.* New York: Garland, 1999.

Grant, Mark N. *The Rise and Fall of the Broadway Musical.* Boston: Northeastern University Press, 2004.

Hulin, Charles. "Lessons from Industrial and Organizational Psychology." Pp. 3–22 in Jeanne M. Brett and Fritz Drasgow (eds.), *The Psychology of Work: Theoretically Based Empirical Research.* Mahwah, NJ: Lawrence Erlbaum Associates, 2002.

Jones, John B. *Our Musicals, Ourselves: A Social History of the American Musical Theatre.* Lebanon, NH: University Press of New England, 2003.

Kennedy, Brian. *The Baron Bold and the Beauteous Maid: A Compact History of Canadian Theatre.* Toronto: Playwrights Canada Press, 2004.

Lindsay, John C. *Palaces of the Night: Canada's Grand Theatres.* Toronto: Lynx Images, 1999.

Mulcahy, Lisa. *Theater Festivals: Best Worldwide Venues for New Works.* New York: Allworth, 2006.

Murphy, Brenda, ed. *The Cambridge Companion to American Women Playwrights.* Cambridge: Cambridge University Press, 1999.

Nash, Knowlton. *Cue the Elephant: Backstage Tales at the CBC.* Toronto: McClelland & Stewart, 1996.

Roudane, Matthew. *American Drama since 1960: A Critical History.* Woodbridge, CT: Twayne, 1996.

Rubin, Don, ed. *Canadian Theatre History: Selected Readings.* Toronto: Playwrights Canada Press, 1996.

Van Bridge, Tony. *Also in the Cast.* Oakville, Ontario: Mosaic Press, 1995.

Wilmeth, Don B., and Tice L. Miller, eds. *The Cambridge Guide to American Theatre.* Cambridge: Cambridge University Press, 1993.

WEBSITES

American Vaudeville Museum. May 28, 2006. http://vaudeville.org/. An archive of historical vaudeville information. AVM also publishes a journal.

Association for Canadian Theatre Research. http://www.actr-artc.ca/. This Website of a professional and academic organization devoted to Canadian theater research contains conference and events information as well as a members-only archive bibliography of recent research in Canadian theater.

eONeill.com. http://eoneill.com/. An online archive of information on Eugene O'Neill.

International Broadway Data Base. http://www.ibdb.com/default.asp. A comprehensive almanac of Broadway productions, searchable by show, actor, director, producer, composer, choreographer, and other topics.

Kenrick, John. *Musicals 101.com: The Cyber Encyclopedia of Musical Theatre, TV and Film.* http://www.musicals101.com/.

Nothof, Anne, ed. *The Canadian Theatre Encyclopedia.* http://www.canadiantheatre.com/. A fully searchable, comprehensive online encyclopedia with 100- to 300-word entry articles, many with photographs.

Playwrights Guild of Canada. http://www.playwrightsguild.com/pgc/main.asp. The site provides biographical information on active Canadian playwrights as well as information on festivals and other events focusing on Canadian plays.

Theatre Historical Society of America. http://www2.hawaii.edu/~angell/thsa/welcome2.html. The society focuses on the preservation of historic theater buildings.

EVENTS

Adirondack Theatre Festival, PO Box 3203, Glens Falls, NY 12801, 1–518–798–7479. http://www.atfestival.org/whoswho.htm. Held for 6 weeks in June and July each year, the ATF focuses on new work by young, emerging actors, directors, playwrights, and designers.

Carrefour International de Théâtre de Quebec, 369, rue de la Couronne, 4e étage, Québec, CQ G1K 6E9, 1–418–692–3131. http://www.carrefourtheatre.qc.ca. Carrefour is an international, multilingual festival; it serves as a key connection between French-Canadian theater artists and the international theater community.

Charlottetown Festival, Confederation Centre of the Arts, 145 Richmond Street, Charlottetown, PE, C1A 1J1, 1–800–565–0278. http://www.confederationcentre.com/festival.asp. An annual festival of Canadian theater with an emphasis on musicals.

Festival de Théâtre des Amériques, 300 De Maisonneuve East, Montreal, Berri-UQÀM metro station, 1–514–987–6919. http://www.fta.qc.ca/. The festival, held annually in May, presents new and often experimental works from around the world.

The Humana Festival of New American Plays, Actors Theater of Louisville, 316 West Main Street, Louisville, KY 40202–4218, 1–502–584–1265. http://www.actorstheatre.org/humana.htm. The Humana Festival is one of the most prestigious venues for American new plays. It is held annually in March and April.

Los Angeles Women's Theatre Festival, 11411 Cumpston Avenue, Suite 204, North Hollywood, CA 91601, 1–818–760–0408. http://www.lawtf.com/. Founded in 1992, the LAWTF provides a vehicle for the development of women solo performance and other theater artists.

The Orlando International Fringe Theatre Festival, Loch Haven Park, Orlando, FL, 1–866–599–9984. http://www.2camels.com/festival244.php3. Held annually in May, the festival is a ten-day celebration featuring performance art and experimental theater.

PlayRites Festival, Alberta Theatre Projects Administration, 220–9 Avenue SE, Calgary, AB, T2G 5C4, 1–403–294–7475. http://www.atplive.com/index.html. Annual winter festival in Calgary, Alberta, founded in 1987. It features main stage productions and premieres of Canadian works.

Provincial Drama Festival (Newfoundland and Labrador), 27 Nungesser Avenue, Gander, NF A1V 1M2. http://www3.nf.sympatico.ca/rsgoulding/drama2003/index.htm. The Provincial Drama Festival is held annually in the spring and features a variety of performances from area drama groups.

Redlands Theater Festival, Highland Ave & Cajon St., Redlands, CA 92373, 1–909–792–0562. http://www.rtfseason.org/. The Redlands Festival, founded in 1972, annually presents four to five plays in repertory: a major Broadway musical, an off-Broadway musical, a contemporary drama, a recent Broadway release, and a period piece.

Shakespeare Festivals (Canada). http://shakespeare.about.com/cs/festivalscanada/index.htm?terms= shakespeare+festivals+canada. About.com currently lists seven Canadian Shakespeare festivals, including the Stratford Festival of Canada listed below.

Shakespeare Festivals (United States). http://www.google.com/Top/Arts/Performing_Arts/Theatre/ Shakespeare/Festivals/United_States/. Google currently lists Websites for an astonishing seventy-seven American festivals located throughout the country and devoted largely or entirely to the works of Shakespeare.

Shaw Festival, Box 774, 10 Queen's Parade, Niagara-on-the-Lake, ON, Canada 10 LOS 1JO, 1–800–657–1106. Annual festival of productions by George Bernard Shaw and his contemporaries. The season runs from April through November.

Spoleto Festival USA, P.O. Box 157, Charleston, SC 29402, 1–843–722–2764, Fax 1–843–723–6383. http://www.spoletousa.org/index.php. Spoleto USA is world-renowned festival of the arts, including theater, held for seventeen days each spring in Charleston, South Carolina.

Stratford Festival of Canada, P.O Box 520, Stratford, ON N5A 4M9, administration 1–519–271–4040. http://www.stratford-festival.on.ca/. The largest theater festival in North America, the Stratford runs annually from May to October. It produces classical and contemporary works with special emphasis on Shakespeare.

Teatro de la Luna, Gunston Arts Center, 2700 S. Lang Street, Arlington, VA, 1–202–882–6227 or 1–703–548–3092. http://teatrodelaluna.org/homes/festival_i.htm. Teatro de la Luna holds an annual staging of three to ten plays from Spain, the Caribbean, and the Americas.

RESEARCH COLLECTIONS

Chicago Theater Collection, Chicago Public Library, Harold Washington Library Center, 400 South State Street, Chicago, IL 60605, 1–312–747–4400. http://www.chipublib.org/001hwlc/spetheater.html. An extensive and varied collection of theater material developed continuously since 1896.

Curtis Theatre Collection, University of Pittsburgh Library, University of Pittsburgh, Pittsburgh, PA 15260, 1–412–244–7067. http://www.library.pitt.edu/libraries/special/curtis2.html. A "non-book" collection of ephemera with emphasis on theater in New York and Pittsburgh from the nineteenth century to the present.

Harvard Theater Collection, Houghton Library, Harvard University, Cambridge, MA 02138, 1–617–495–1376. An extensive book, periodical, and archive holding of the history of theatrical performance in America.

Museum of the City of New York Theatre Collection, 1220 Fifth Avenue, New York, NY 10029, 1–212–534–1672. http://www.mcny.org/collections/103.html. The collection documents the relationship between New York City and its theater industry from the eighteenth century to the present.

Ransom Theater Collection, Harry Ransom Center, University of Texas, 21st and Guadalupe, P.O. Box 7219, Austin, TX 78713–7219, 1–512–471–8944. http://www.hrc.utexas.edu/about/visitor/ (this site is for the center, not the collection itself).

The Billy Rose Theater Collection, New York Public Library for the Performing Arts, 40 Lincoln Center Plaza, New York, NY 10023–7498, 1–212–870–1639. http://www.nypl.org/research/lpa/the/the.html. A vast archive of both traditional research material and ephemera from New York's theater history.

Organizations

Actors Equity, 165 West 46th Street, New York, NY 10036, 1–212–869–8530. http://www.actorsequity.org/home.asp. The labor union for American stage actors.

Alberta Playwrights Network, 2633 Hochwald Avenue SW, Calgary, AB T3E 7K2, 1–403–269–8564 or 1–800–268–8564. http://www.albertaplaywrights.com/.

The American Society for Theatre Research (ASTR), P.O. Box 1798, Boulder, CO 80306–1798, 1–888–530–1838 or 1–303–530–1838. http://www.astr.org/index.html. ASTR provides an organization and public voice for theater scholars and promotes the cause of theater as a field for serious scholarly study and research.

American Theater Wing, 570 Seventh Avenue, New York, NY 10018, 1–212–765–0606. http://www.americantheaterwing.org/index.php. A professional theater advocacy organization best known for its Tony Awards.

Associated Designers of Canada, 145 Queen Street South, Box 111, Streetsville, ON L5M 2B7, 1–416–410–4209. www.designers.ca. A nonprofit organization dedicated to improving the status of set, lighting, and costume designers in Canada.

Canadian Actors Equity Association, 4 Victoria Street, 12th Floor, Toronto, ON M5C 3C4, 1–416–867–9165. http://www.caea.com/EquityWeb/Default.aspx. Canada's national actors' union.

The Drama League, 520 8th Avenue, Suite 320, New York, NY 10018, 1–212–244–9494. http://www.dramaleague.org/league_info/staff.htm. A theater advocacy group with a special emphasis on developing theater directors.

League of Historic American Theatres, 616 Water Street, Suite 320, Baltimore, MD 21202, 1–410–659–9533. http://www.lhat.org/. A theater building preservation society.

League of Professional Theatre Women, 226 West 47th Street, 6th floor, New York, NY 10036, 1–212–268–5846. http://www.theatrewomen.org/index.php.

Playwrights Guild of Canada, 54 Wolseley Street, 2nd Floor, Toronto, ON M5T 1A5, 1–416–703–0201. http://www.playwrightsguild.com/pgc/main.asp. Promoters of the production and dissemination of contemporary Canadian plays.

Prairie Theatre Exchange, Unit Y300, 393 Portage Avenue, 3rd Floor, Portage Place, Winnipeg, MB R3B 3H6, 1–204–942–7291. http://www.pte.mb.ca/. The organization is dedicated to theater education, play production, and outreach for citizens of Manitoba.

Professional Association of Canadian Theatres/PACT, 215 Spadina Ave. Suite 210, Toronto, ON M5T 2C7, 1–416–595–6450. http://www.pact.ca/. Promotes and gains recognition for professional English-language theater in Canada.

The Rodgers and Hammerstein Organization, 1065 Avenue of the Americas, Suite 2400, New York, NY 10018, 1–212–541–6600. http://www.rnh.com/org/.

The Siminovitch Prize in Theatre, c/o BMO Financial Group, 55 Bloor St. West, 4th Floor, Toronto, ON M4W 3N5, 1–416–867–4914. http://www.siminovitchprize.com/. The Siminovitch is the largest single cash prize for theater arts in North America.

Theatre Library Association, c/o New York Public Library for the Performing Arts, 40 Lincoln Center Plaza, New York, NY 10023, http://tla.library.unt.edu/. Professional association for theater historians, librarians, and archivists.

TRANSPORTATION AND TRAVEL

Travel and transportation became significant focal points of North American popular culture during the nineteenth and twentieth centuries as individuals found themselves with more efficient and realistic options for getting from place to place. The ease, reliability, and availability with which people traveled became much more commonplace during the Industrial Revolution, the period from which evolved such transportation technologies as steamships, railroads, streetcars, automobiles, and the airplane. It was the growing dependability, practicality, and efficiency of such modes of transportation that enabled people to leave the confines of their households and experience the world that lay beyond the boundaries of their local communities.

Given the sheer geographical size and scope of North America, it makes sense that efficient and effective transportation of people and goods would become an essential element in the evolution of the region. This is also a region of steady, rapid population growth. The United States had a population of 281,421,906 people in 2000, with over 80 percent of all residents living in what are considered metropolitan areas. Las Vegas, Nevada, experienced the most rapid population growth: an 80 percent increase between 1990 and 2000.[1] Canada had a total population of 30,007,094 in 2001, a 4 percent increase over the previous census in 1996. Of Canada's current population, about 62 percent reside in the two provinces of Quebec and Ontario. Like the United States, about 80 percent of Canada's entire population lives in urban/metropolitan areas.[2]

Currently, North America is dominated by private motor vehicle use, although air travel is the second most used method of national transportation. By the late 1990s in the United States, for example, private motor vehicles (such as automobiles) accounted for the majority of all annual passenger traffic. While 89 percent of Americans traveled by car, another 10 percent traveled by air. Only about 1 percent of Americans, by the end of the twentieth century, traveled by railroad and/or public transit.[3]

By the end of the 1990s the United States contained over 215 million registered motor vehicles, a total that included motorcycles. Of this number, over 61 percent were cars, with another 33 percent being sport utility vehicles (SUVs), small/light trucks, and other kinds of vehicles with two axles and four wheels. Of all fifty United States, the most registered motor vehicles were located in California, followed by Texas, Florida, and New York. As these statistics demonstrate, the majority of registered private vehicles are located in areas possessing large populations of people needing to traverse great expanses of land.

The United States, during this time, contained about 3.95 million miles (6.36 million km) of roads, highways, and streets, with about 60 percent of that amount being paved. Of the approximately 40 percent of unpaved roads, almost 90 percent were located in rural areas. America's national highway system measured 161,188 miles (259,407 km), with 46,677 of those miles (75,119 km) being interstate highway. The remaining 114,511 miles (184,288 km) comprised American expressways and freeways. Of all fifty United States, Texas had the most miles of roads, with California, Illinois, and Kansas also containing many miles of streets and highways.[4]

The same was true in Canada. In 1998 Canada had 4,241,000 registered motor vehicles (a number that includes motorcycles and mopeds). The country also registered 3,694,000 commercial vehicles. All of these registered vehicles had 901,930 kilometers (546,515 mi) of national road on which to travel that same year, about 32 percent of which was paved. The Trans-Canada Highway, a federal-provincial project constructed between 1949 and 1962, can carry vehicle traffic all the way from Vancouver, British Columbia, to St. John's, Newfoundland. Rail travel in Canada, like in the United States, is not as widely used. Canadian railroads, like those in America, carry far more by way of freight and goods than passengers. VIA Rail Canada provides national rail service for passengers, even though the availability of services was cut by more than half by the Canadian government in 1989. Passenger rail service in Canada, like that provided for rail passengers in the United States by Amtrak, is subsidized by the federal government.[5]

Almost all intercity passenger railroad service in the United States of America is overseen by Amtrak. This line has undergone drastic reductions in recent years, going from over 11,000 passenger cars in use in 1970 to fewer than 1,900 cars in the year 2000. In 2000 Amtrak carried a total of about 22.5 million passengers for the year. Much of the decline in American passenger rail travel is because of government deregulation of the airline industry during the early 1980s. Once American air carriers were deregulated, price competition and mergers intensified the growth of passenger air service. As such, over 640 million people fly on airlines in the United States every year. The United States currently contains about 5,100 public and more than 13,000 private airports.[6] Despite fears that acts of terrorism could ultimately endanger passenger air service—the direct result of the September 11, 2001, attacks on the World Trade Center in New York City and the Pentagon in Washington, D.C., by hijacked American-based airliners—travelers are once again taking to the skies with confidence. Airline travel is popular in Canada as well, with two major national carriers (Air Canada and Canadian Airlines International) serving Canada with a broad network of both domestic and international routes from over 1,200 airports governed by Transport Canada.[7] Use of the Internet to research, schedule, and pay for airline reservations without the assistance of a professional travel agent has also helped increase the popularity of North American air travel. The busiest airports in the United States include Hartsfield International Airport (near Atlanta, Georgia), Chicago-O'Hare International Airport, and John F. Kennedy Airport in New York. Widely used Canadian airports include Pearson International Airport in Toronto, Vancouver International Airport, and Calgary International Airport.

Before automobiles and airlines, however, transportation options were much more limited. The first useful resource for transporting people was water. North America had many natural waterways that enabled early travelers to move about the wilderness via boat, either the paddled variety (like a canoe), by wind-powered sail, or by horse-drawn canal. Some of these earliest canal-type systems, such as the Erie Canal in the American East, which provided access to the Great Lakes during the nineteenth century, have grown into larger, more sophisticated pathways for ships that carry both freight as well as passengers. The St. Lawrence-Great Lakes navigation system, for example, allows ships to travel almost 2,300 miles (3,800 km) inland into Canada.[8]

During the nineteenth century, another early form of mass transportation was the steamboat, most often recognized in the style of the paddle-wheeled riverboat, like those popularized in the stories and novels by the American writer Mark Twain. A central and essential waterway, such as the Mississippi River, made travel by steamboat possible. The limitations to this mode of travel were many, however, because these boats required large rivers, canals, or bays through which to navigate and their boilers had the potential to explode when under an excessive amount of pressure. Steamships, larger steam-powered water vessels, were also used, most often for ocean-going voyages. Steamships carried many immigrants to North America during the later years of the nineteenth century and the early years of the twentieth. Overall steamboats and steamships were neither efficient nor accessible to the majority of North Americans looking to travel domestically.

RAILROADS

The first true mode of domestic mass transit to develop during the early years of the Industrial Revolution was the railroad. Railroads using steam power had been a viable part of transporting goods since the 1850s in the United States. The first train to attempt carrying passengers, however, was the "Best Friend of Charleston," which transported 141 people over a 6-mile route in 1830. Eastern cities such as Charleston, Baltimore, and Boston were some of the first to develop railroad lines so as to attract commerce through modes of travel not restricted to water navigation; there were areas in the East that were not connected via waterways, so rail lines made business and travel possible. By 1840 over 2,800 miles of track had been laid down in America, and, by the time of the Civil War (1860–65), about 30,000 miles of railroad had been laid throughout the nation.[9]

The Railroad Act of 1862 brought the federal government directly into the era of rapid, national railroad growth. Federal loans enabled companies to make use of free land grants, and this arrangement allowed railroads to branch out and grow across the American West. The driving of the ceremonial golden spike near Promontory Point, Utah, on May 10, 1869, marked the moment at which the United States of America was officially traversed from coast to coast with railroad tracks. The Union Pacific Railroad was officially joined by track with the Central Pacific Railroad, and the United States was now able to use rail travel from the Atlantic to the Pacific.[10]

Canada's first public railroad, the Champlain and St. Lawrence, began service during the summer of 1836. This system would eventually become part of the Grand Trunk Railway. The Grand Trunk brought service into the United States when it leased the Atlantic and St. Lawrence Railway, which was able to provide rail access to Portland, Maine, by 1853. In 1880, the Grand Trunk Railway extended into Chicago, Illinois, giving the railroad route coverage from the American Midwest to Montreal and Quebec through to the Atlantic coast at Portland.

The first transcontinental railroad in Canada was completed on November 7, 1885, when a ceremonial final spike was driven at Craigellachie, British Columbia. On the following day, a Canadian Pacific train—the first train to cross Canada from sea to sea—arrived in Port Moody at Pacific Tidewater.[11] North America, by the end of 1885, had complete transcontinental railroad coverage, setting the stage for migration, settlement of the west, and the growth of industry.

Rail travel took shape as regions of the United States, such as the Western "frontier," were made accessible via more efficient, affordable, and safe means of crossing the plains. Migration westward was now made more realistically possible without the physical demands once placed on settlers by the hardships of traveling by either covered wagon or stagecoach. The time needed to traverse North America was dramatically cut by railroad use, and climate was no longer an issue, since enclosed railcars kept travelers out of the elements. Despite rain, heat, wind, or snow, railroads allowed people to travel without the inconveniences of poor weather conditions. As railroads became a common part of North American society, long-distance travel became more commonplace, helping populate the American West: people from the East Coast and the Midwest could easily migrate to such regions as Southern California to capitalize on its temperate climate, fertile landscape, and agricultural potential. Similar migration west also took place in Canada.

Expansion of railroad lines throughout North America gave way to the creation of the vacation industry. Passenger railroads were better able to transport travelers to tourist destinations since they allowed people the opportunity to travel more quickly over longer distances for less money. Vacation locales, such as the New Jersey Shore or hotel resorts in the Catskill Mountains of Upstate New York, were suddenly easier to access from places such as New York City or Philadelphia. Whereas a trip from New York City to the Catskills used to take a day and a half by steamer and horse-drawn coach, by railroad it took only six and a half hours.[12] Vacation destinations once considered too far from home were, by the later decades of the nineteenth century, being enjoyed by middle-class families who were able to climb aboard a passenger train for a summer getaway. By 1917 there were about 253,000 miles (407,165 km) of railroad track being used all across the United States, even though rail travel was to become —over the next few decades—a relic of the past.[13]

A more domesticated form of rail-based travel was the streetcar, which carried its passengers in horse-drawn carriages that followed steel rails embedded in the avenues of American cities such as New York (in 1832) and New Orleans (in 1835). Using rails meant a reduction in friction under the wheels, so fewer horses could pull larger car loads of people. One horse, for example, could pull 30 to 40 passengers in a carriage that had more room, a larger exit, a smoother ride, and better brakes.[14] The streetcar was an improvement of an existing mode of urban mass transit called the omnibus. Omnibuses, using a system originally developed in Nantes, France, before coming to America in 1829, were horse-drawn, stagecoach-like carriages that followed a specific route, albeit not on permanent rails. Passengers would pay a modest fare, ride to their destination, and then signal for the driver to stop by pulling on a leather strap attached to the driver's ankle.[15] Omnibuses were anything but practical, however, as their pace was slow; the carriages only carried twelve people, and most streets at that time were paved with rough cobblestones. Despite these drawbacks, omnibuses operated in American cities between 1829 and about 1905.[16]

Modern technology entered urban mass transit near the end of the nineteenth century, when steam and electric power made horse-drawn streetcars obsolete. The first of these innovations was the creation of the cable car in 1873. Streetcar rails were modified to house a long cable that ran the entire length of the streetcar's route. The cable, running in an enormous loop, was put into motion by a massive steam engine contained within a powerhouse. Cable cars could connect to the buried cable in order to move, or they could release from the cable if the car needed to stop. A system of wheels and pulleys along the buried cable helped the car negotiate turns and changes in grade.[17] Although the city of San Francisco, California, is best known for its cable cars, the largest network of cable cars was located in Chicago, Illinois. By 1890 most major American cities had at least one cable car line in operation. At that time the United States, for example, contained 500 miles of cable car track in twenty-three cities. Cable car lines nationwide served about 373 million passengers each year.[18]

Steam and cables were used to facilitate the use of electricity near the end of the nineteenth century. Richmond, Virginia, had a streetcar system powered by electricity by 1888.

Frank Sprague, an 1878 graduate of the United States Naval Academy, developed an idea for clean and efficient mass transit while working for Thomas Edison. Sprague's system worked on the notion that streetcars could be attached to electric cables through the use of a long pole that sat on top of the carriage. The pole would touch a power line strung along the streetcar rails that ran along city avenues. Steam engines would power large generators, and the generators would create the electricity needed to operate the streetcars by sending current through the lines over the rails.[19] The electric streetcars became known as trolleys, and they helped to revolutionize mass transit in cities into the early years of the twentieth century. By 1904 the United States contained about 30,000 miles of streetcar-type track, and 98 percent of it was electrified to facilitate trolley service.[20]

Perhaps the most recognized form of urban mass transit today is the subway. As the right-of-way for public transportation became an issue in cities, it was apparent that street congestion would have to be addressed by relocating mass transit systems. The first attempt at this was development of the elevated train, which began operating for the first time in New York City in 1870. Elevated railway lines, unfortunately, were not the most suitable solution because they were dirty, noisy, and very expensive to build.[21] What proved to be the best option was development of the underground subway, which allowed cities to enjoy rapid mass transit without interrupting the traffic flow on streets, as the "el" tracks did. Boston, Massachusetts, had the first American subway line as of 1897. It was the New York City subway system in 1904, however, that revolutionized the idea of mass transit. By 1937 New York City had over 300 miles of subway routes, serving over 4 million passengers every day (separate from existing bus and streetcar lines). The city's subway system was the first in the world to offer both express and local routes, and its "cut-and-cover" method of construction (developed by Chief Engineer William Barclay Parsons) was copied by subway systems across North America.[22] In Canada, Toronto had the country's first subway system, which opened for service in 1954. By the end of 1959 Montreal had ceased its local streetcar/trolley service. The city then developed a subway system, which opened to passengers in October of 1966.[23]

THE AUTOMOBILE

Development of the automobile during the later years of the nineteenth century changed the notion of transportation and tourism in North America forever. No technology has had a more enduring influence on American culture than the gasoline-powered, internal combustion engine, and no other transportation power source has so dramatically altered the composition of our environment. Despite the effect of the automobile on the North American landscape, no other vehicle has done so much to shape the ways in which we travel and the reasons we do so. With the introduction of the automobile during the late nineteenth century, people in North America found themselves rethinking their motives for where they lived, where they worked, and where they traveled. As such, the advent of the automobile forever changed the travel attitudes and destinations of North Americans.

At first the automobile was more likely to be seen as a machine for only the very wealthy or the very mechanically inclined. By the time Henry Ford (1863–1947) began using more modern assembly methods to build Model T Fords in 1908, automobiles were just beginning to be considered accessible to the general American public (Ford did not institute the moving assembly line until 1913). Within a few years, the Model T Ford was the world's most available, affordable, and practical car, and the Ford Motor Company was selling them by the millions.[24]

Henry Ford, a native of Dearborn, Michigan, realized that by making automobiles afford-able and more reliable than earlier models built by other manufacturers, Americans would be able to escape the confines of their surroundings. People living in rural regions would be able to travel for both commerce and pleasure, and they would be able to do so at their own leisure. No longer would people's travel be limited to train schedules, streetcar routes, or the endurance of their trusted horses; families could now travel together and set their own pace, following their own schedule. As a result, North Americans found the freedom provided by the automobile, and the Model T Ford in particular, to be exactly what they needed after years of being almost stranded on farms or in small towns.

Henry Ford saw the benefit in creating a mechanically sound automobile that was afford-able for a mass market. His first attempt at such a vehicle, the 4-cylinder Model N (built from 1906 to 1907), sold for a list price of about $600. The Model N's commercial success prompted Ford to design an entirely new automobile, one with more horsepower and more public appeal. When the first Model T rolled out of Ford's Dearborn assembly plant in 1908, anyone could buy the brand new car for less than $850. Improvements in manufacturing enabled Ford to lower retail prices for his vehicles. By 1912, a Model T cost about $500; by 1927, with the advent of the moving assembly line, a new Model T coupe could be pur-chased for $290.[25] With millions of automobiles on the road (most of them Model T Fords), the notion of personal mobility had changed forever.

It's All about Image

As American society began to shift from horse-drawn personal transportation to every-day use of the automobile, it was only a matter of time before formal research into the socioeconomic impact of the automobile got underway. In 1929 sociologists Robert and Helen Lynd published *Middletown*, a book based on the results of fieldwork the pair con-ducted in Muncie, Indiana, during 1924 and 1925. Their studies and observations of this typical, midwestern American community discovered that the Model T Ford was the auto-mobile of choice and that few residents could see themselves being without the use of an automobile. According to one respondent, their car was more important than their bathtub. Perhaps the most interesting discovery made by the Lynds was an apparent shift in cultural values among the citizens of Muncie: the modest community that, at one time, was highly civic-minded had become—because of its dependence on the automobile and the freedom it provided—much more materialistic and consumer-based.[26]

Middletown, as a piece of scholarship, marked one of the first true analyses of an emerg-ing automobile-based culture and its possible implications for the future course of Western civilization. A follow-up study published by the Lynds in 1937, *Middletown in Transition,* found that the citizens of Muncie, Indiana—considered an example of most "American" communities—were in the grip of consumerism, a population being preyed on by a grow-ing, elitist business class.[27] The autonomy once enjoyed by the citizens of Muncie, the Lynds discovered, had given way to an emerging dependence on America's new, consumer-based economy. An emphasis on the freedom that came from owning an automobile and the consequences of individual choices allowed by having such freedom demonstrated an inher-ent change taking place within Western culture.

Part of this change came from the idea that owning an automobile enabled consumers to become part of a more sophisticated, yet personally free and individualistic society. The automobile allowed people freedom from restrictive railroad schedules, limitations from poor weather conditions, and the speed limitations of using horse-drawn transportation. As such, the mass media emphasized the automobile's ability to turn average, middle-class

WHAT "MIDDLE" AMERICANS DROVE

Part of Robert and Helen Lynd's fieldwork involved gathering statistical data regarding the kinds of automobiles owned by the citizens of "Middletown." According to the Lynds' research, over 15,500,000 automobiles were registered in America by 1924, and the people living in Muncie, Indiana, owned 11,660 of them. Those cars, ranked by manufacturer, were documented by the Lynds as follows:

1. Ford: 2,578
2. Chevrolet: 590
3. Overland: 459
4. Dodge: 343
5. Maxwell: 309
6. Buick: 295
7. Studebaker: 264
8. Oakland: 88
9. Willys-Knight: 74
10. Nash: 73
11. Interstate: 73
12. Durant: 65
13. Star: 62
14. Oldsmobile: 59
15. Saxon: 53
16. Reo: 50
17. Chalmers: 47
18. Franklin: 45
19. Essex: 45
20. Cadillac: 36
21. Chandler: 32

The United States has been home to about 2,200 different automobile manufacturers since the nineteenth century. Most companies were small and failed quickly, some after making only one or two vehicles. Some companies, such as Studebaker, switched from building horse-drawn wagons to automobiles. Other makers, such as Chalmers, tried manufacturing cars after starting with farming implements, such as plows and tractors, because they already had a retail organization in place.[28]

The "Big Three" in the mass media today (DaimlerChrysler, the Ford Motor Company, and General Motors) are the only American manufacturers to "survive" what might be called "Industrial Darwinism." Those three companies managed to evolve and adapt to changing technologies and markets, and that strategy can be seen in the previous list of automobiles. The makes of Chevrolet, Buick, and Cadillac are part of today's General Motors (and Oldsmobile was also part of GM until the make was phased out in 2004). Changing trends in automobile purchasing, however, eventually had a severe effect on the fortunes of the "Big Three." As North American consumers began buying more mechanically reliable and fuel-efficient kinds of cars, such as those built by foreign manufacturers such as Toyota and Honda, the "Big Three" automakers made dramatic reductions in their labor forces and factory operations. These changing trends, combined with ever-increasing benefits and pension costs for retired employees of the "Big Three," required companies such as Ford and General Motors to lay off tens of thousands of workers during the summer of 2006.

The Lynds' data clearly reflect that Ford was the model of choice in Muncie, Indiana, in 1924. The popularity of Ford was driven, for the most part, by its rugged reliability and affordable price, the perfect combination for working midwestern families.[29]

North Americans into modern-era motorists. Initially automobile advertisements were created within the company by the manufacturers themselves. By the early 1920s, however, automakers began employing professional advertising agencies to market their products through an emphasis on social status, personal image, and cultural attitudes. At this point the automobile becomes less of a machine and more of a symbol of a social aesthetic.

Print advertisements, such as the one created by Edward S. "Ned" Jordan in 1923 for the Jordan Motor Car Company of Cleveland, Ohio, associated the automobile with personal freedom, adventure, and the romance of the rugged American landscape. The Jordan Car Company, started by Ned Jordan in 1918, took full advantage of the benefits provided by print advertising by running its advertisements in color and by specifically marketing automobiles to young people and women. In a now-legendary advertisement for the Jordan *Playboy,* the automaker took readers "Somewhere West of Laramie" with "a broncho-busting, steer-roping girl" who crossed the plains behind the wheel of "eleven hundred pounds of steel and action." The young woman—"whose face is brown with the sun when the day is done of revel and romp and race . . . rides, lean and rangy, into the red horizon of a Wyoming twilight"—was inspired by a woman riding on horseback whom Ned Jordan spotted while traveling across Wyoming on a train. As the lore behind this advertisement goes, Jordan asked a fellow passenger where they happened to be at that time, and the passenger replied, "Oh, somewhere west of Laramie." Jordan immediately wrote the copy for the advertisement, which was then illustrated by Fred Cole and soon thereafter published in *The Saturday Evening Post.* At that point this automobile advertisement entered the realm of marketing genius and is still regarded today as perhaps the greatest automobile advertisement of all time.[30] "Somewhere West of Laramie" is the first national print advertisement to promote a product not for what it did, but rather for what it meant, projecting an image of what the product could represent socially to potential consumers.

What made this national advertisement for the Jordan *Playboy* so successful was how it depicted a young woman as being in total control of the automobile and how this "lass . . . loves the cross of the wild and the tame." The advertisement's copy speaks of the woman's free and spirited past, one of unattached, romantic (and even, dare we say it, sexual?) adventure, explaining a "savor of links about that car—of laughter and lilt and light—a hint of old loves—and saddle and quirt." The advertisement projects a culturally mythic, idealized perception of the American frontier, celebrating a popular relationship between civilized humanity and its ability to conquer uncivilized nature. Above all else, the Jordan *Playboy* is depicted as a hybrid of sorts: an athletic and rugged "Everycar," "a brawny . . . yet a graceful thing for the sweep o' the Avenue," an automobile designed for "when the hour grows dull with things gone dead and stale."[31]

Another means of marketing to a mass audience through use of the media was to present the automobile as a machine of utmost quiet, quality, and accomplishment. The Cadillac Motor Car Company ran an advertisement in *The Saturday Evening Post* on January 2, 1915, that highlighted their automobile's place as a "leader," telling readers, "If the leader truly leads, he remains—the leader." This advertisement, entitled "The Penalty of Leadership," outlined, in prose that bordered on the philosophical, Cadillac's intent to be regarded as the best in the industry. As the copy of the advertisement states:

> Whether the leadership be vested in a man or in a manufactured product, emulation and envy are ever at work. In art, in literature, in music, in industry, the reward and the punishment are always the same. The reward is widespread recognition; the punishment, fierce denial, and detraction. When a man's work becomes a standard for the whole world, it also becomes a target for the shafts of the envious few.[32]

The intent of such an advertisement is obvious, and the reputation of the Cadillac Motor Car Company (today part of General Motors) was established over the past 90 years, in part, because of the effectiveness of such socially driven rhetoric. The owner of a Cadillac, like the automaker, was a sophisticated and intelligent participant in the modern technological era, a thoughtful consumer who recognized and respected quality in design and construction when he or she saw it (and could afford to buy it). Such social and cultural change was fostered by automobile advertising, and the popular mass media was the means through which this sociocultural evolution occurred.

Much of the social and cultural change in automobile buying habits during the late twentieth and early twenty-first centuries has been driven by advertisements that reflect basic attitudes and values present within North American civilization. Consider, for example, the popularity of sport utility vehicles (SUVs); these automobiles are built for rugged conditions, designed with high ground clearance, four-wheel drive, and large engines that are less than fuel efficient but capable of carrying large loads of people and their cargo through rough terrain over almost impassable roads. The everyday driving demands of the average motorist do not require travel through such rigorous conditions, yet there are hundreds of thousands of SUVs occupying North American roadways. It is not unusual to see SUVs rolling along the crowded streets of North American cities in regions where annual snowfall amounts to less than six inches each winter. Despite this, SUVs remain popular with motorists, even as fuel prices have climbed with changing political and economic tensions in the Middle East and sales of the vehicles have decreased somewhat over the past few years.[33] Much of the SUVs' popularity stems from the inherent North American attitude that connects people in that part of the world with an almost mythic heritage/tradition tied to the notion of self-reliance, "rugged individualism," and the fact that much of North America began with migration into (and settlement of) the vast wilderness of the continent. In this regard, the meaning implied by the SUV outweighs the necessity of the machine itself. These motorists may never traverse an isolated prairie through snow and mud, but they believe the romanticized idea that they could if they wanted to. What they decide to buy and drive is loaded with essential social and cultural meaning that helps define Americans as both individuals and consumers.

Not only did mass purchase of automobiles by the general public create a sense of newfound personal mobility and freedom, but it also changed the basic infrastructure of North America. The first mode of personal transportation to affect the layout and construction of the North American overland trails directly was the bicycle. Cycling was a highly popular pastime during the 1880s, and active organizations such as the League of American Wheelmen (founded in 1880) lobbied very successfully—under the development of their "Good Roads Movement"—for smoother and more consistent roadways. This marked the advent of paving some public roads to reduce bicycle tire failure. In 1891 the state of New Jersey assumed both financial and design control over the development and improvement of all local roads. New Jersey also created the first official state highway department, an idea that was duplicated by the state of Massachusetts in 1892. Cars also required better roads and bridges, and it did not take long for local, state, provincial, and federal governments to improve conditions. At the dawn of the automobile age, roads were made mostly of dirt. Thawing snow or hard rain quickly turned these dirt trails into vast mud pits. Early automobiles lacked the horsepower and agility needed to avoid or escape such trouble, which often led stuck motorists to rely on another, more traditional form of "horsepower," the four-legged kind. The 1916 Federal Aid Road Act allowed for the construction of roadways better suited for increased automobile travel. This was soon followed by passage of the 1921 Federal Highway Act.[34]

Traveling by Car

With better roads came better traveling conditions for North American motorists. As with the development of efficient national railroad service, the creation of national highways and improved secondary roads enabled people to pack up and get away for much needed holidays far from home. Automobile ownership among the emerging North American middle class made vacations, once limited to the very wealthy, available to a larger number of people. The relative ease with which people could travel by automobile enabled families to explore the North American landscape. Historic sites, such as Civil War battlefields and the homesteads of famous people, suddenly became spots at which to stop. National landmarks and natural areas also attracted tourists' attention. As the price of automobiles plummeted during the 1920s, North American motorists found they could enjoy a simplistic means by which to "get away from it all"—that being the pastime of what was known, by the early years of the twentieth century, as autocamping.

Autocamping allowed people to enjoy the splendor of the great outdoors while not taxing their often limited vacation budgets. Early autocamping was sometimes called, by motorists around 1910, "gypsying" or "vagabonding." All "vagabonding" required was for traveling motorists to find a nice place along the road (or at least near it) where they could stop and pitch a tent for the night. Motorists would sometimes sleep in their cars, and they always made sure to bring sufficient foodstuffs for cooking over a fire or having a picnic. Autocamping was an aspect of automobile ownership that celebrated the rights of the individual, an offshoot of what President Theodore Roosevelt called the need to live a "strenuous life."[35] Autocamping was a response to the Victorian sensibilities of the late nineteenth and early twentieth centuries, an era when social institutions stifled individualism, attitudes of gentility prevailed, and North Americans felt restricted by what were thought of as "proper" behavior. Since autocamping often meant acting spontaneously and living off the land, it was a welcome respite from the confines of socially acceptable existence.

Eventually, as early as the 1920s, autocamping gave way to the creation of more formal, commercial roadside services such as diners and campgrounds. Gypsying meant an outdoor experience, which included sleeping and eating in meadows, in pastures, or along the roadside. As a result, autocampers were often very careless about dealing with trash and other people's property. Much of this behavior stemmed from the fact that autocamping was seen as an escape from expected social behaviors. Escaping social institutions led to stolen fruit, vegetables, and flowers and widespread littering of campsites established in a farmer's open pasture. Sanitation concerns arose, as well; tourists were susceptible to drinking unclean water from roadside sources. The era of autocamping began to wane as business people discovered that they could provide many of the needed services required by travelers "gypsying" their way around North America.[36]

Many municipalities opened free campgrounds in order to entice families on the road to stop, visit, and (most of all) spend money in their communities. Free campsites were put in public parks near the business districts of towns, partly to reduce the damage done by motorists "vagabonding" along highways and on people's property, but also to generate positive word-of-mouth publicity that could be spread from traveler to traveler as they crossed paths and swapped stories at filling stations and other roadside businesses such as rural produce stands. Towns found themselves trying to attract motorists because the travelers were often middle-class families looking for a hot meal or a quiet place to sleep, people with money to spend and needing basic necessities while away from home.

Free camps established in towns along highways actually caused tourism to grow as a North American industry because the municipal campsites attracted people who were neither ready nor willing to fend for themselves in the great outdoors. If a family or a couple did not feel as though they were able to camp and cook sufficiently along the highway in unknown territory, stopping at a free camp with clean water and bathroom facilities might make the trip easier. Being with fellow travelers seeking the same comforts and staying near an established town with stores and other businesses tended to make some motorists feel more confident and willing to see the country by automobile. As such, campgrounds intended to serve the motoring public did a brisk business during the 1920s. Automobile historian Warren Belasco has written that, by the middle of the 1920s, perhaps as many as 10 million Americans had attempted autocamping at least once. Some of these motorists were no doubt inspired by media accounts of highly publicized auto-camping trips taken by such famous public figures as Thomas Edison, Henry Ford, and President Warren G. Harding.[37]

As both road conditions and automobiles improved, the leisure of autocamping or free camping gave way to a need for speed and efficiency. Drivers on vacation wanted to make good time and maximize their holidays, so the era of the free camps gave way to a more per-manent, more established, and more recognizable form of automobile touring: the age of the pay camp, the tourist cabin, and the motor lodge/motel. These new forms of tourist con-venience, evolving from self-serving to full service (complete with national chains providing standardized, uniform accommodations), offered motorists the advantage of enjoying more premium facilities. Part of this stemmed from the issue that free camps allowed anyone and everyone to camp while traveling, an egalitarian ideal that meant travelers were likely to encounter tourists who were otherwise unable to pay for lodging. Migrant workers and ped-dlers were camping alongside middle- and upper-class families, and this closeness to "the other" made some people feel uncomfortable. Therefore, by the mid-1920s, some campsites began charging fees, money that would keep "undesirables" out while allowing the camp-ground to pay for necessary upkeep that would (hopefully) draw in more middle- and upper-class families.[38]

Tourist cabins followed the same progression of commercial evolution as the free camps. At first, inexpensive and less elaborate facilities could be easily established along any piece of roadside property. Eventually, however, operators strived to expand these simple cabins into more competitive and more sophisticated businesses. Owners of filling stations, hot dog stands, and even farmers began opening tourist cabins, and most towns would have several establishments from which motorists could choose along incoming roadways. As a result, cabin owners tried to make their businesses appealing to more middle- and upper-class tourists. Like the campgrounds before them, tourist cabins tried to attract a "better" clientele and, in order to do so, they opted to combine rustic qualities with the conveniences not eas-ily associated with autocamping, such as hot and cold running water, bathtubs and showers, and flush toilets. Tourist cabins were not as sophisticated, or as costly to rent, as hotel rooms, but they provided inexpensive accommodations for those who wanted to maintain an affordable travel budget. This was especially helpful during the Great Depression (1929–41), when even the upper class opted to save money.[39]

By World War II (1941–45 for North American involvement), the quaint, nostalgic atmosphere of tourist cabins gave way to the era of motor courts. These replaced the home-spun qualities of the tourist cabin with the controls and regulations of national chains. As the 1940s began, better constructed cabins (some with brick walls and steam heat) matched the improvements in automobiles and roads. The national motel chains did not gain promi-nence until after World War II, when limited access highways criss-crossed North America. This new type of highway bypassed many of the locally owned and operated "mom and pop" tourist cabins and campgrounds, giving way to the familiar standardized, efficient, and conformist style of the present hotel and motel chains. Interstate highways made property near interchanges much too expensive for the local cabin operators; as such, only the national chains were able to purchase these premium parcels of easily accessible land.[40] As automobiles and roads allowed for greater speeds, motorists opted once again to exchange "making good time" for "getting off the beaten path." Since the motel chains were located near interstate interchanges, these were the first businesses to get regular lodging traffic. The local tourist trade (not only in lodging, but also in food and gasoline service) received what customers were left, if there were any customers left at all.

Tourist destinations of all sorts became reachable by automobile as roads, bridges, and the cars themselves improved over time. Not only did nature-based destinations, such as national parks and lakeshores, become popular, but so did museums, historic landmarks, and the homesteads of famous people. Historic landmarks in geographic proximity to each other, such as the Civil War battlefield at Gettysburg and the farm/weekend retreat of former President Dwight and First Lady Mamie Eisenhower (both in southern Pennsylvania), benefited greatly from automobiling because tourists could arrive and depart via the Pennsylvania Turnpike (America's first, opened for use in 1940) and see both destinations as part of one trip. Another popular destination that still attracts tourists is directly tied to the advent of the automobile within working- and middle-class American society: the Henry Ford Museum and Greenfield Village in Dearborn, Michigan, grants visitors a trip back in time, thanks to Henry Ford's vast interest in all things valuable to maintaining a sense of a national culture. Tourists can see artifacts connected to all forms of transportation, domestic life, and a collection of structures considered by Ford as examples of what life in small town, rural America was meant to represent. A village inn, the workshop where Henry Ford built his first gasoline-powered, four-wheeled vehicle (the 1896 Quadricycle), and even Ford's childhood home are all gathered on the premises of Greenfield Village as reminders of America during what Ford thought of as a more simple era. It is ironic that such physical reminders of "the good old days" are part of a collection assembled by the man who, over a century ago, forever changed how people traveled.

Popular historic tourist destinations in Canada include some 2,100 museums and sites. Many may be found in the National Capital Region, such as the Canadian Museum of Civilization in Hull, Quebec, and the Canadian Museum of Nature (once known as the National Museum of Natural Sciences) in Ottawa. Other Canadian historical attractions include Upper Canada Village, a collection of eighteenth- and nineteenth-century buildings in Ontario, and the Royal Canadian Mounted Police Centennial Museum in Regina, Saskatchewan.[41]

Given the popularity of so many well-known North American tourist destinations, it is interesting to note that variables such as rising gasoline prices often do little to affect the number of visitors who frequent such attractions each year. Even though fuel prices increased sharply during 2006, partly because of heightened sociopolitical tensions throughout the Middle East and partly because of oil refinery damage suffered along the United States' Gulf Coast in the wake of Hurricane Katrina in 2005, travelers did little to curb their desire to see all that North America had to offer. Travel industry studies calculated that increased gasoline costs would add only $30 to $50 to the total cost of a six-night, 800-mile trip taken during the summer of 2006, an added expense that the average tourist would consider manageable and worth the trouble. Some travelers even suggested that they would reduce their dining and lodging expenses in order to make their vacations possible.[42]

Concern over rising fuel prices did, however, cause some North Americans to think differently about their driving habits. Whereas SUVs were generally still popular with motorists, a growing number of North American automobile purchases, following sudden and dramatic increases in gasoline prices during the spring and summer of 2006, demonstrated that consumers were beginning to lean toward more fuel-efficient modes of transportation. Many of these purchases were of automobiles that used new developments in alternative fuel options such as hybrid technology (cars and SUVs that run on a combination of gasoline and electrical power) and ethanol blend (a clean-burning fuel derived by blending unleaded gasoline with an additive distilled from corn, soybeans, or some other renewable source).[43] As fuel prices continued to rise during the summer of 2006, many motorists throughout North America explored additional options for powering their automobiles, such as incorporating biodiesel technology. This form of alternative energy enabled automobiles and SUVs to run on highly efficient fuels derived either entirely from vegetable oils or animal fats (such as those used in deep fryers), or from a mixture of these oils or fats combined with standard diesel fuel to make a clean-burning and renewable biodiesel blend.[44]

AVIATION

Another mode of transportation that emerged during the early years of the twentieth century would also go on to forever change travel patterns and habits in North America. The airplane, first successfully flown by Orville Wright at Kitty Hawk, North Carolina, on December 17, 1903, eventually evolved—over the next 50 years or so—into a practical means by which passengers could traverse long distances in great comfort at great speed. By 1905 Orville and Wilbur Wright, brothers who operated a bicycle shop in Dayton, Ohio, could keep their heavier-than-air creation aloft for 38 minutes to cover a distance of 24 miles. This 1905 flight (done aboard Flyer III), marked the first true test of the airplane's practicality; the flight involved controlling the machine over a prolonged distance for a prolonged period. Based on the success of that flight, the Wrights sought to find a commercial market for their winged vehicle.[45]

Aviation became fairly commonplace over the next 30 years, with airplanes used for aerial combat during World War I, for global exploration, for carrying the mail, and for mass entertainment (the 1920s and 1930s being the era of "barnstorming" thrill shows). During this time the airplane was also first used for carrying commercial passengers. Mailbags were given higher priority than people in those early days of aviation because bags of letters and packages were lighter and less schedule-driven, and they represented less responsibility for the pilot in the case of a mechanical problem or accident. It was not until after World War I that passengers, namely government officials taking part in peacekeeping negotiations, began being transported by airplane. The Royal Air Force in England operated the first regular air service in 1919, making flights to both France and Germany.[46]

During the years immediately following World War I, most air service was limited to postal delivery. Large, national air mail contracts allowed the aviation industry to create a modern convenience for most North Americans: faster and more consistent mail service. Passengers were still stranded on the ground because most air carriers saw people as less lucrative cargo than mailbags. Most manufacturers opted to build airplanes that were designed to maximize their hauling capacity, not the creature comforts required to facilitate carrying paying passengers. As a means of being able to capitalize on transcontinental postal contracts, airplane companies began building larger, multi-engined aircraft able to cover longer distances more quickly. It was not until the late 1920s and early 1930s that the transportation of people became an important aspect of the aviation industry.[47]

The true potential of the airplane was demonstrated in May of 1927, when Charles Lindbergh flew nonstop from New York to Paris in 33 hours. Lindbergh's achievement had been deemed nothing short of impossible (especially since several other aviators had attempted to fly across the Atlantic, never to be heard from again). Charles Lindbergh's flight was, according to historian William Welling, "a feat that electrified the world and galvanized public acceptance of the airplane and commercial aviation."[48]

The first air service to North America began during the late 1930s. A flying boat, the *Dornier* Do 26, was meant to fly nonstop from Europe to North America, carrying passengers and mail, but the planned route had to be scrapped once World War II began. The

THE TEN LEADING UNITED STATES PASSENGER AIRLINES IN 2004

1. American
2. Delta
3. Southwest
4. United
5. Northwest
6. US Airways
7. Continental
8. America West
9. Alaska
10. American Eagle[49]

aircraft made only 18 mail runs before being grounded. The first airline to fly with a regular schedule in the United States was Ryan Airlines, which entered into business in 1925, rather late given the history of air service in Europe. The United States Congress passed important legislation aimed at creating an active commercial aviation market in America during 1925 and 1926. Part of this legislation involved the creation of "lighted" airways, where every airport was equipped with a bright flashing beacon. More lights were placed at 3-mile intervals along the flight paths between each airfield, with the entire transcontinental route being marked by 1930. This system of lighted airways became perhaps the most significant navigational aid in aviation, a system still used today nearly a century later.[50]

The Boeing company, in an effort to capture a large share of the transcontinental postal business, designed and constructed a specialized aircraft called the Mailplane, one that was efficient, powerful, and able to transport the mail effectively. Boeing also built passenger seats in its Mailplane, which enabled one carrier, Stout Air Lines, to profit from its discovery that passengers were willing to pay more for air service than the mail contracts did. Stout Air Lines had already been flying the Ford Tri-Motor, a popular aircraft known for its reliability and comfort. By 1929 United Airlines began offering passenger service as well, acquiring about 75 percent of the New York-San Francisco route. The remaining 25 percent was handled by National Air Transport, which began carrying its passengers in a twin-engined, very luxurious, Curtiss Condor biplane. By May of 1930 United was able to buy out National Air Transport and control the important east-west air route. Other airlines scrambled to develop a southern route across the United States but, even with the lighted airway navigation system in place, such service proved difficult. Transcontinental Air Transport, which flew the rugged and dependable Ford Tri-Motors, was forced to use surface transport to carry passengers along rougher sections of the airline's southern, cross-country route.[51]

Despite the logistical and geographical pitfalls of transcontinental air travel, the airlines did not stop promoting their mode of transportation as the best way to get from place to place. Like other early twentieth-century advertisers, airlines presented the luxury of flying as just that—a luxury affordable to most everyone and a sure way to express your level of social standing. Airlines marketed flying as an egalitarian method of travel in much the same way the Ford Motor Company presented the Model T. The idea was to convince travelers that they deserved the very best that modern technology could offer and that the new technology was well within their budgets. As the Model T was depicted as an automobile for the masses, a car that both families and farmers could afford, so too did early airlines market themselves as being the means by which anyone could enjoy the comforts of clean, efficient, scenic, and state-of-the-art transportation.

Unfortunately, airline marketing campaigns and North American economic realities were different. Whereas traveling by rail cost about 1.3 cents per passenger mile during the 1930s, traveling by air cost almost four times that amount. The benefits of airline travel ultimately appealed to "average" passengers such as businessmen, the class of North Americans who associated saving time with making money. Since businessmen were often able to pay for airline tickets with company expense accounts, they were more likely to embrace this modern mode of transportation.[52]

By the middle of the twentieth century, airlines were able to service ever increasing numbers of both business and leisure passengers. Advances in airplane design, and developments such as heated and pressurized cabins, made flying more comfortable since the airliners could now reach higher altitudes and avoid previously bothersome obstacles such as bad weather and mountain peaks. In 1940, in the United States alone, about 3 million passengers took to the skies. By 1956, once postwar design changes had become standard equipment on commercial aircraft, the number had grown to 55 million. While the automobile allowed North Americans the freedom of personal transportation, airlines gave passengers, in the words of James C. Kruggel, "a growing sense of mastery over the world and control of one's destiny."[53]

Trans World Airlines (TWA) capitalized on the historic exploits of Charles Lindbergh and called itself "The Lindbergh Line" in an attempt to attract passengers who sought to emulate the accomplishments of "The Lone Eagle" and fly above the North American landscape. Lindbergh's connection to TWA was in an advisory capacity, but this did not stop the airline from promoting itself as Colonel Lindbergh's personal mode of passenger airline travel. As aviation became more commonplace in the 70 years that followed,

THE TOP TWENTY-FIVE AMUSEMENT/THEME PARKS IN NORTH AMERICA: 2004

1. Magic Kingdom at Walt Disney World (FL)
2. Disneyland (CA)
3. Epcot at Walt Disney World (FL)
4. Disney-MGM Studios at Walt Disney World (FL)
5. Disney's Animal Kingdom at Walt Disney World (FL)
6. Universal Studios at Universal Orlando (FL)
7. Islands of Adventure at Universal Orlando (FL)
8. Disney's California Adventure (CA)
9. SeaWorld/Orlando (FL)
10. Universal Studios Hollywood (CA)
11. Adventuredome at Circus Circus (NV)
12. Busch Gardens (FL)
13. SeaWorld/San Diego (CA)
14. Knott's Berry Farm (CA)
15. Paramount's Kings Island (OH)
16. Paramount Canada's Wonderland (Ontario)
17. Cedar Point (OH)
18. Morey's Piers (NJ)
19. Santa Cruz Beach Boardwalk (CA)
20. Six Flags Great Adventure (NJ)
21. Hersheypark (PA)
22. Six Flags Magic Mountain (CA)
23. Camp Snoopy at Mall of America (MN)
24. Busch Gardens (VA)
25. Six Flags Great America (IL)[54]

more and more North Americans took to the skies to reach their destinations quickly, with less of the bother that sometimes accompanies lengthy automobile trips, such as traffic, road construction, and the need to pay for meals and lodging. Despite a decrease in air travel following the terrorist attacks on New York and Washington on September 11, 2001, tourists have once again selected the ease and relative comfort of airline travel as their means by which to see the world.

TOURISM

Tourism has yet to diminish as popular recreation for North Americans. During the late 1990s Americans spent over $425 billion on transportation, food, lodging, and assorted kinds of amusement (such as admission to theme parks, like Disney World in Florida, or national parks, such as Yellowstone in Idaho, Montana, and Wyoming). An economic "trickle down" effect is created through the desire to travel: businesses connected to travel demands also benefit greatly from Americans' need to "get away from it all." Gasoline and service stations, restaurants, motel chains, and car rental agencies have all profited from a working relationship with the tourist industry. Retail stores that carry cameras, film, casual clothing, and assorted souvenirs have also profited greatly from the residual business generated by families on the road.[55] In 2004 the United States was the number one country in tourism earnings, generating $74.5 billion for the year, an increase of 15.7 percent over 2003.[56]

Tourism is also one of the leading industries in Canada. During 2000 close to 19.6 million tourists visited and spent about $10.8 billion while exploring the country's many natural landmarks, exciting cities, and outdoor recreational areas. In springtime, numerous blossom festivals occur, especially in the regions near Nova Scotia and British Columbia. Each May, visitors gather to enjoy the Ottawa Festival of Spring; in July, tens of thousands of tourists attend the Calgary Exhibition and Stampede in Alberta. The livestock show and the rodeo are legendary, attracting visitors from all parts of the world. Another highly popular summer attraction in Canada is the annual Stratford Shakespeare Festival in Ontario. Central Ontario draws thousands more tourists to its Shaw Festival at Niagara-on-the-Lake, its annual color tours each fall, and its Niagara Grape and Wine Festival. Canada has preserved close to 375,000 square kilometers (about 144,790 sq. mi) of natural regions for use as national and provincial park areas.[57] As such, Canada provides tourists with numerous opportunities for outdoor recreation. Skiing during the winter months is popular in Canada, much as in regions of the American Northeast, Northern Midwest, and Western states. There is no shortage of recreation to be had when traveling throughout the Canadian provinces, no matter what season of the year it is, no matter what your interests may be.

North America has enjoyed a rich and complex history of tourism and travel. There are no limitations regarding where people will go, how they will get there, or what they will do once they arrive at their final holiday destination. From rivers and overland trails, to railways, highways, and skyways, North America offers something for everyone, shaping Americans' attitudes and behaviors about transportation and recreation with each passing generation. Whether travelers are visiting a theme park, marveling at the wonders of a national landmark, seeing a museum, or simply "getting away from it all" for a needed break from the rigors of everyday life, North American transportation, travel, and tourism are economically important and socially significant aspects of America's global popular culture.

RESOURCE GUIDE

PRINT SOURCES

Blake, John, with illustrations by John Young. *Aviation: The First Seventy Years*. London: Triune Books, 1973.

Foner, Eric S., and John A. Garraty, *The Reader's Companion to American History*. Boston: Houghton Mifflin, 1991.

Foster, Mark S. *A Nation on Wheels: The Automobile Culture in America since 1945*. Belmont, CA: Wadsworth/Thompson Learning, 2003.

Jakle, John A., with Keith A. Sculle and Jefferson S. Rogers. *The Motel in America*. Baltimore: The Johns Hopkins University Press, 1996.

Lewis, David L., and Laurence Goldstein, eds. *The Automobile and American Culture*. Ann Arbor: University of Michigan Press, 1983.

Lynd, Robert S. and Helen Merrell. *Middletown: A Study in Modern American Culture.* New York: Harcourt Brace, 1959 reprint of the 1929 first edition.

———. *Middletown in Transition: A Study in Cultural Conflicts.* New York: Harcourt Brace, 1982 reprint.

Murray, Tom. *Canadian Railroad History* (MBI Railroad Color History). St. Paul, MN: MBI Publishing Company, 2004.

Solomon, Brian. *Amtrak* (MBI Railroad Color History). St. Paul, MN: MBI Publishing Company, 2004.

Witzel, Michael Karl. *The American Motel.* Osceola, WI: MBI Publishing Company, 2000.

WEBSITES AND ORGANIZATIONS

Colin Churcher's Railway Pages. http://www. railways.incanada.net. A railroad historian located in Ottawa, Ontario.

The Electric Railway Historical Association of Southern California. http://www.erha.org/index.html.

Motel Americana: History of the Motel. http://www.sjsu.edu/faculty/wooda/motel/history/index.html.

The Pennsylvania Turnpike (Official Website). http://paturnpike.com.

The Railroad History Archive at the University of Connecticut. http://railroads.uconn.edu.

The Railways of Canada Archives. http://www.trainweb.org/canadianrailways/index.html.

An Unofficial Pennsylvania Turnpike Website. http://pahighways.com/toll/PATurnpike.html. A well-done and accurate resource for a general historical overview and photographs.

U.S. Department of Transportation/Federal Highway Administration: History Resources. http://www.fhwa.dot.gov/infrastructure/history.htm.

NOTES

1. "United States of America," World Almanac/OCLC FirstSearch. Accession Number: fw00un0106000a (http://firstsearch.oclc.org.proxy.nmc.edu).
2. "Canada," World Almanac/OCLC FirstSearch. Accession Number: fw00ca0240000a (http://firstsearch.oclc.org.proxy.nmc.edu).
3. "United States of America," World Almanac/OCLC FirstSearch. Accession Number: fw00un0106000a (http://firstsearch.oclc.org.proxy.nmc.edu).
4. "United States of America," World Almanac/OCLC FirstSearch. Accession Number: fw00un0106000a (http://firstsearch.oclc.org.proxy.nmc.edu).
5. "Canada," World Almanac/OCLC FirstSearch. Accession Number: fw00ca0240000a (http://firstsearch.oclc.org.proxy.nmc.edu).
6. "United States of America," World Almanac/OCLC FirstSearch. Accession Number: fw00un0106000a (http://firstsearch.oclc.org.proxy.nmc.edu).
7. "Canada," World Almanac/OCLC FirstSearch. Accession Number: fw00ca0240000a (http://firstsearch.oclc.org.proxy.nmc.edu).
8. "Canada," World Almanac/OCLC FirstSearch. Accession Number: fw00ca0240000a (http://firstsearch.oclc.org.proxy.nmc.edu.
9. John F. Stover, "Railroads," in Foner and Garraty 1991 (in Resource Guide), 906–907.
10. See "History of Railroads and Maps," http://memory.loc.gov/ammem/gmdhtml/rrhtml/rrintro.html#NT.
11. From Colin Churcher's Railway Pages at http://www.railways.incanada.net/candate/candate.htm.
12. Cindy Sondik Aron, "Vacations and Resorts," in Foner and Garraty 1991 (in Resource Guide), 1108.
13. "United States of America," World Almanac/OCLC FirstSearch. Accession Number: fw00un0106000a (http://firstsearch.oclc.org.proxy.nmc.edu).
14. Kenneth T. Jackson, "Public Transportation," in Foner and Garraty 1991 (in Resource Guide), 884.
15. Extracted from the Federal Transit Administration (www.fta.dot.gov): Brian J. Cudahy, "Mass Transportation in the Cities of America—A Short History and a Current Perspective."

16. Kenneth T. Jackson, "Public Transportation," in Foner and Garraty 1991 (in Resource Guide), 882.

17. Extracted from the Federal Transit Administration (www.fta.dot.gov): Brian J. Cudahy, "Mass Transportation in the Cities of America—A Short History and a Current Perspective."

18. Kenneth T. Jackson, "Public Transportation," in Foner and Garraty 1991 (in Resource Guide), 883.

19. Extracted from the Federal Transit Administration (www.fta.dot.gov): Brian J. Cudahy, "Mass Transportation in the Cities of America – A Short History and a Current Perspective."

20. Kenneth T. Jackson in Foner and Garraty 1991 (in Resource Guide), 884.

21. Ibid., 884.

22. Ibid., 884–885.

23. From "Colin Churcher's Railway Pages."

24. James J. Flink, "Automobiles," in Foner and Garraty 1991 (in Resource Guide), 65.

25. Ibid., 65.

26. Foner and Garraty 1991 (in Resource Guide), s.v., "Middletown."

27. Ibid., 382–383.

28. Floyd Clymer, *Treasury of Early American Automobiles: 1877–1925* (New York: Bonanza Books, 1950), 107.

29. "The Power of the Ad," http://xroads.virginia.edu/~UG00/cavanaugh/project/ads.html (accessed 1/31/07).

30. Phil Roberts, "Somewhere West of Laramie: An Advertising Legend" for the Wyoming Department of State Parks and Cultural Resources. Found online at http://sweetwatertimes.com/buffalobones. 0606.htm and also http://www.charleswelty.com/authors/jordan.htm

31. Floyd Clymer, 165.

32. Ibid., 164.

33. Dee-Ann Durbin, "Big Three, CAW Launch Contract Talks" found online at http://www. theglobeandmail.com/servlet/ArticleNews/TPStory/LAC/20050718.

34. Flink, "Automobiles," in Foner and Garraty 1991 (in Resource Guide), 65.

35. Warren Belasco. "Commercialized Nostalgia: The Origins of the Roadside Strip," in *The Automobile and American Culture* (in Resource Guide), 107.

36. Ibid., 113.

37. Ibid., 114.

38. Ibid., 116–117.

39. Ibid., 117–118.

40. Ibid., 120–121.

41. "Canada," World Almanac/OCLC FirstSearch. Accession Number: fw00ca0240000a (http://firstsearch. oclc.org.proxy.nmc.edu).

42. See Jayne Clark, "Don't Let High Gas Prices Get Your Goat This Summer." *USA Today. Academic Search Elite, EBSCO host* (accessed October 18, 2006).

43. See http://www.ethanol.org (accessed October, 19, 2006).

44. See http://www.biodiesel.org (accessed October 19, 2006).

45. Blake 1973 (in Resource Guide), 6.

46. Ibid., 30.

47. Ibid., 36.

48. William Welling, "Lindbergh, Charles A." in Foner and Garraty 1991 (in Resource Guide), 665.

49. "United States of America," World Almanac/OCLC FirstSearch. Accession Number: fw00un0106000a (http://firstsearch.oclc.org.proxy.nmc.edu).

50. Blake 1973 (in Resource Guide), 36.

51. Ibid., 36–40.

52. James C. Kruggel, found online at http://www.centennialofflight.gov (accessed October 16, 2006).

53. Ibid.

54. "United States of America," World Almanac/OCLC FirstSearch. Accession Number: fw00un0106000a (http://firstsearch.oclc.org.proxy.nmc.edu).

55. "United States of America," World Almanac/OCLC FirstSearch. Accession Number: fw00un0106000a (http://firstsearch.oclc.org.proxy.nmc.edu).

56. "Top 10 Countries in Tourism Earnings, 2004," World Almanac/OCLC FirstSearch. Accession Number: fw00un0106000a (http://firstsearch.oclc.org.proxy.nmc.edu).
57. "Canada," World Almanac/OCLC FirstSearch. Accession Number: fw00ca0240000a (http://firstsearch.oclc.org.proxy.nmc.edu).

GENERAL BIBLIOGRAPHY

Arnheim, Rudolf. *Visual Thinking.* Berkeley: University of California Press, 1969.

Barbas, Samantha. *Movie Crazy: Fans, Stars, and the Cult of Celebrity.* New York: Palgrave, 2001.

Benjamin, David, ed. *The Home: Words, Interpretations, Meanings, and Environments.* Brookfield, VT: Avery, 1995.

Berger, Arthur Asa. *The Comic-Stripped American: What Dick Tracy, Blondie, Daddy Warbucks, and Charlie Brown Tell Us about Ourselves.* New York: Walker, 1973.

Bigsby, C. W. E., ed. *Approaches to Popular Culture.* London: Edward Arnold, 1976.

Bordo, Susan. *Twilight Zones: The Hidden Life of Cultural Images from Plato to O.J.* Berkeley: University of California Press, 1998.

Browne, Ray B., and Marshall Fishwick, eds. *Icons of America.* Bowling Green, OH: Popular Press, 1978.

Carney, George O. *Fast Food, Stock Cars & Rock-n-Roll: Place and Space in American Pop Culture.* Maryland: Rowman & Littlefield, 1995.

Cawelti, John. *Adventure, Mystery, and Romance: Formula Stories as Art and Popular Culture.* Chicago: University of Chicago Press, 1976.

Egendorf, Laura. *Urban America: Opposing View Points.* Farmington Hills, MI: Greenhaven Press, 2005.

Fishwick, Marshall, ed. *An American Mosaic: Rethinking American Culture Studies.* New York: American Heritage, 1996.

———. *Popular Culture in a New Age.* New York: The Haworth Press, Inc., 2002.

Gottdiener, Mark. *The Theming of America: American Dreams, Media Fantasies, and Themed Environments.* Boulder, CO: Westview, 2001.

Hall, Dennis, and Susan Hall, eds. *American Icons: An Encyclopedia of the People, Places, and Things That Have Shaped Our Culture.* 3 vols. Westport, CT: Greenwood, 2006.

Holliss, Robert, and Brian Sibley. *Walt Disney's Mickey Mouse: His Life and Times.* New York: Harper & Row, 1986.

Inge, Thomas M., and Dennis Hall. *The Greenwood Guide to American Popular Culture.* 4 vols. Westport, CT: Greenwood, 2002.

Kingsbury, Paul, and Alan Axelrod, eds. *Country: The Music and the Musicians.* New York: CMF/Abbeville Press, 1988.

Kottak, Conrad Phillip. *Researching American Culture.* Ann Arbor: University of Michigan Press, 1982.

Lewis, David L., and Laurence Goldstein, eds. *The Automobile and American Culture.* Ann Arbor: University of Michigan Press, 1983.

McMann, Jean. *Altars and Icons: Sacred Spaces in Everyday Life.* San Francisco: Chronicle Books, 1998.

Moran, Joe. *Star Authors: Literary Celebrity in America.* London: Pluto Press, 2000.

Santino, Jack. *All Around the Year: Holidays and Celebrations in American Life.* Urbana: University of Illinois Press, 1994.

Smith, Henry Nash. *Virgin Land: The American West as Symbol and Myth.* Cambridge, MA: Harvard University Press, 1950.

Sturken, Marita, and Lisa Cartwright. *Practices of Looking: An Introduction to Visual Culture.* New York: Oxford University Press, 2001.

Turner, Graeme. *Understanding Celebrity.* Thousand Oaks, CA: Sage, 2004.

ABOUT THE EDITORS AND CONTRIBUTORS

THE VOLUME EDITOR

MICHAEL K. SCHOENECKE teaches Film and Media Studies at Texas Tech University and is Executive Director of the Popular Culture Association and the American Culture Association. He has been involved with popular culture studies since 1975 and has published articles on sports, cinema, literature, music, and architecture. He serves on the editorial boards of *The Journal of Popular Culture* and *Film and History*. His recent publications include *Sport Films* and an article in *Film and History*, and his teaching interests include the classical Hollywood style and cinematic sports narratives.

THE GENERAL EDITOR

GARY HOPPENSTAND is Professor of American Studies at Michigan State University and the author of numerous books and articles in the field of popular culture studies. He is the former president of the national Popular Culture Association and the current editor-in-chief of *The Journal of Popular Culture.*

THE CONTRIBUTORS

SCOTT L. BAUGH is Assistant Professor of Film & Media Studies at Texas Tech University. His research and teaching focus on multicultural American cinema with special attention to Chicana/o and Latin American media arts, and his work has appeared or is forthcoming in *Journal of Film & Video, Quarterly Review of Film & Video, Film & History,* and *The Columbia Companion to American History on Film.*

PATRICIA KENNEDY BOSTIAN is an instructor in English and Humanities at Central Piedmont Community College, Charlotte, North Carolina. The editor of *The Wild Goose Poetry Review* and *Teaching American Literature: A Journal of Theory and Practice,* she has written extensively on American literature.

MARY CAROTHERS is Associate Professor of Fine Arts at the University of Louisville. Her photographically based installations investigate issues of semiotics and perception and have been exhibited at venues including CEPA (Center for Exploratory and Perceptual Art) Buffalo, Atlanta College of Art, and Pittsburgh Filmmakers. She has received grants from The Warhol Foundation, the Mid Atlantic Arts Council, the Johnson Foundation, and The Kentucky Foundation for Women.

PATRICIA A. CUNNINGHAM is Associate Professor and Dress Historian at Ohio State University. She is currently working on a book titled *Fashioning America*. She is author of *Reforming Women's Fashion, 1850–1920: Politics, Health and Art* (2003), and coeditor of *Twentieth-Century American Fashion* (2005), *Dress and American Culture* (1993), and *Dress and Popular Culture* (1991). In 1998 she was named Fellow of the Costume Society of America.

DON CUSIC is the Music City Professor of Music Industry History at Belmont University in Nashville and is the author of sixteen books, most of which are about or related to country music.

JENNIFER DEFORE is a master's student in telecommunication, information studies, and media at Michigan State University. Her area of study is digital media art and technology, focusing on the creation of art for digital games.

VICTOR C. DE MUNCK is Associate Professor of Anthropology at SUNY–New Paltz. He received his Ph.D. in Anthropology from the University of California at Riverside in 1985. Most recently Dr. de Munck received a National Science Foundation grant to study cultural models of romantic love and gender in Russia and the United States. In 2002 he received a one-year Fulbright award to work and conduct research in Lithuania. Dr. de Munck has edited a volume titled *Romantic Love and Sexual Practices* and has written numerous cross-cultural and ethnographic articles on sex, romantic love, and marriage in Europe, South Asia, and North America.

THOMAS A. GREENFIELD is on the faculty of SUNY–Geneseo, where he is Professor of English and American Studies as well as Instructor of Music in the School of the Arts. He is the author of *Work and the Work Ethic in American Drama 1920–1970* and *Radio: A Reference Guide* (Greenwood Press). He has published numerous articles, essays, and reviews on drama, mass media, and American culture among other subjects. His play, *Entertaining Charlene*, was a finalist in the National Ten-Minute Play Contest (1989). He has also written the lyrics and music to an original musical, *A Dean's Day*, which has been performed in community theaters in upstate New York. He is the former Chair of the Kentucky Humanities Council and former Vice Chair of the Federation of State Humanities Councils in Washington, D.C.

MARK D. HOWELL is Professor of Communications at Northwestern Michigan College in Traverse City, where he teaches classes in writing, film, popular culture, and public speaking. He is an automobile historian who has published extensively about the subject of motor sports, with special emphasis on NASCAR and American society.

MONICA MOSCHETTA is a 2006 graduate of SUNY–Geneseo with a BA in English Literature. After attending the University of Denver's Summer Publishing Institute, Monica will pursue a career in book publishing.

EDMUND REISS has published extensively on medieval literature and thought, as well as on American literature. Since retiring from Duke University, he has become an avid tree farmer and organic gardener, and researches widely on food and travel.

GARYN G. ROBERTS is an award-winning author and editor of a range of books, articles, essays, and literary dictionary entries on American culture and popular culture topics. His book *Dick Tracy and American Culture: Morality and Mythology, Text and Context* was a Mystery Writers of America Edgar Award finalist in 1995, and his *Prentice Hall Anthology of Science Fiction and Fantasy* won the Ray and Pat Browne National Popular Culture Book Award in 2001. He is a faculty member of the Communications/English academic area at Northwestern Michigan College (Traverse City, Michigan).

SHARON SCOTT is an international scholar and visual artist. Her most popular work investigates Zapatista doll-making in Chiapas, Mexico. A graduate of Vanderbilt University's English Department, Scott is pursuing her Ph.D. at the University of Louisville. She recently presented her research on the American Art Fair at Monash University, Italy, and the University of Carthage, Tunisia.

LIBBY SMIGEL serves as Area Chair for Dance and Culture for the Popular Culture Association and American Culture Association and is an associate editor of the *Journal of American Culture*. She currently teaches in the Theatre and Dance Department of the George Washington University.

JOY SPERLING is Associate Professor of Art at Denison University. She holds graduate degrees from Edinburgh University and the University of California–Santa Barbara. Her special interests are art history, modern art, and the history of photography. She has written on the nineteenth century as well as on modern and postmodern art.

BEVERLY TAYLOR, Professor of English at the University of North Carolina–Chapel Hill, is Area Chair for the national Popular Culture Association's panels on food. She has published numerous essays on nineteenth-century British literature, coedited two essay collections, and written books on British and American Arthurian literature since 1800 and on the poet Francis Thompson.

CARROLL VAN WEST is the Director of the Center for Historic Preservation at Middle Tennessee State University and the Senior Editor of the *Tennessee Historical Quarterly*. He has written on American history and architecture, and his books include *The New Deal Landscape of Tennessee* (2001).

INDEX